INTE

UNION OF SOVIET
SOCIALIST REPUBLICS

CHINA

INDIA

AUSTRALIA

MEMBERSHIP IN WESTERN EUROPEAN ORGANIZATIONS

	1 Austria	2 Belgium	3 Denmark	4 France	5 Germany F.R.	6 Greece	7 Iceland	8 Ireland	9 Italy	10 Luxembourg	11 Netherlands	12 Norway	13 Portugal	14 Sweden	15 Switzerland	16 Turkey	17 U.K.
Organization for European Economic Cooperation	✓	✓	✓	✓	✓	✓	✓	✓	✓	✓	✓	✓	✓	✓	✓	✓	✓
European Payments Union	✓	✓	✓	✓	✓	✓	✓	✓	✓	✓	✓	✓	✓	✓	✓	✓	✓
Council of Europe		✓	✓	✓	✓	✓	✓	✓	✓	✓	✓	✓		✓		✓	✓
North Atlantic Treaty Organization (includes Canada and U.S.A.)		✓	✓	✓	✓	✓	✓		✓	✓	✓	✓	✓			✓	✓

KOTSCHAR

THEORY

PRACTICE

POLICY

International Economics

Other Rinehart Books in

American Foreign Policy

EDGAR S. FURNISS

American Military Policy: Strategic Aspects of
  World Political Geography

EDGAR S. FURNISS AND RICHARD C. SNYDER

An Introduction to American Foreign Policy

HARRY C. HAWKINS

Commercial Treaties and Agreements: Principles
  and Practice

RICHARD C. SNYDER AND EDGAR S. FURNISS

American Foreign Policy: Formulation, Principles,
  and Programs

► THEORY

► PRACTICE

► POLICY

International Economics

Jack N. Behrman

Washington and Lee University

Wilson E. Schmidt

The George Washington University

Rinehart & Company, Inc., New York

To

L. ^gS. ^dB.

and

E. S.³

1113962

Preface

International economics like all economics is useful, we believe, to the extent that it assists in solving the problems men and nations face in making a living and in obtaining wealth. We believe that economic analysis should be relevant; we therefore have stressed the public policy issues in international economic relations. This orientation has enabled us to meet one of the more difficult problems facing teachers of international economics—that of the heterogeniety of their students; our students enter with varied backgrounds and have a variety of interests. The policy approach demonstrates to the foreign affairs student, for example, the importance of economic considerations in international relations; the economics student primarily interested in domestically-oriented subjects is shown the importance to domestic policy of opening an economy to influences from abroad.

The policy orientation makes it imperative that political considerations be included in the analysis of important issues, for international economic policies are significantly affected by both domestic and international political factors. We have, therefore, taken pains to present the political setting and/or the political overtones of economic policies and problems. Yet we have attempted to keep economic costs and objectives to the fore. We have covered the topics usually included in the course in international economics, but they (especially the theory) are examined with the purpose of illuminating prominent policy problems.

We have avoided making policy prescriptions, despite the strong temptation at times. We have, rather, attempted to present the major views on both sides of the issues discussed. Even the theoretical discussions are aimed at showing the consequences of one type of action as compared to another. By the same token, we have tried to avoid giving the impression that any of the problems faced in international economic relations are subject to ready solutions. The student may become annoyed at the absence of pat answers, but, as we see it, there are none. Still, with a sufficient understanding of the principles developed herein and of the important aspects of the problems examined, a student should be able to use his knowledge effectively to come to his own conclusions within the scheme of his own value judgments.

The study of international economic policy must include a full measure of history—or at least of historical examples—for policy is made in a particular context, under particular forces. Historical discussion of policy problems provides to students, in our experience, a meaningful way of viewing various policy objectives and techniques.

Following the above approach, we first summarize the scope of foreign economic policies, noting the purposes, problems, and conflicts of national programs. Part I sets out the theory of trade and then proceeds to outline the major views supporting policies of greater or less freedom in international economic activities. An examination of selected historical situations and accompanying international economic policies to the end of the 19th century is given in Part II: mercantilism, the rise and fall of free trade policy in Europe, American protectionism, and a survey of the character and consequences of factor movements.

We delay until Part III a detailed discussion of the monetary and short-run aspects of international economic activity. This delay is founded upon our experience that mixing the long-run problems of the allocation of resources with the short-run problems of monetary and balance-of-payments disturbances obfuscates the long-run principles. Once these principles are mastered, a better understanding can be gained of the significance of policy responses to short-run disequilibria. This organization is, of course, a pedagogical device, for obviously all elements crowd into the formulation of public policy at any given moment of time.

Part III presents two major problems faced by an open economy: internal instability caused by variations in its international economic transactions and balance-of-payments difficulties. While giving full consideration to the automatic processes of adjustment, a major portion of Part III discusses and compares the policy instruments used by governments to ameliorate these two problems. The course of history is picked up again with examples from monetary and financial experience since World War I; primary emphasis is placed on post-World War II problems and policies. In order to preserve the continuity of policy development from World War I to the present, we discuss in this Part the major post-World War II intergovernmental financial institutions and techniques of international financial cooperation.

Part IV encompasses U.S. foreign economic policy after World War II concerning aid, trade, and investment. Extraordinary foreign aid, assistance to economic development, the expansion of private foreign investment, and the economic and strategic aspects of trade and trade barriers have dominated U.S. international economic policies. The U.S. Government has, of course, been concerned with the balance-of-payments problems of other nations; but these are discussed in Part III and provide a necessary background for the comprehension and analysis of U.S. policies on aid, trade, and investment.

The instructor who prefers a different organization will find that Parts I, II, and III can be re-ordered. The historical discussions in the chapters of Part II might be used prior to Part I if one wished to defer the theoretical analysis. Or it is feasible to present Chapters 9-11 on financial procedures and balance-of-payments adjustment before trade theory is discussed. The organization within the Parts is not rigid. For example, the chapters on postwar commercial policy may be re-ordered and/or may be taken up after Part II. Furthermore, individual chapters, such as 5 or 9, may be given earlier attention.

Realizing that we could not include in an introductory text all the relevant material and that we have had to slight many of the refinements of theory and policy, we have provided an annotated selection of readings at the end of each chapter. These selections are a partial bibliography; they provide a more extensive examination of the topics that we discuss, and readings are suggested for certain topics that we were unable to include because of space limitations.

Among the many acknowledgements we owe, the first should go to our families: the children endured disruptions of normal routines; Louise Behrman bore the responsibilities of parenthood alone during the summers; and Eleanor Schmidt was a gracious hostess to the co-author over many months and, in addition, diligently proofread the entire manuscript. Second, we wish to note for others who may make a similar attempt that our joint labor has produced an intellectual Jonathan-and-David friendship which has been most rewarding. Though we originally set strict limits to the responsibility of each, during the flow of drafts throughout the academic years and after three "over-the-shoulder" summer sessions, the product has become joint in the fullest sense of the word—to the point where it would be inaccurate to identify chapters with either author.

We would also like to acknowledge the encouragement given us by the administrations of our respective universities, which have assisted us financially and reduced our teaching assignments. Our students also gave us encouragement and advice and withstood the onslaught of several different organizations of ideas with which we experimented. A debt is owed to numerous persons who read parts of the manuscript in its various stages: President Howard Bowen of Grinnell College, Dean L. W. Adams of Washington and Lee University, Professors William R. Allen, Walter D. Fackler, Robert Gemmill, Edward Marcus, John Perry Miller, Marvin Perry, William Storer, Robert Willson, and Dr. William H. White of the International Monetary Fund. Our gratitude and debt are especially great to Professor Frank W. Fetter of Northwestern University who read, re-read, and criticized the entire manuscript, helping us to reduce its length and to select topics for emphasis. Neither he nor the others, of course, bears any responsibility for the inadequacies remaining.

We wish also to record a debt to the Princeton University International Finance Section, with which Professor Behrman was formerly associated, and to the Princeton University Press for permission to draw extensively, both directly and indirectly, from materials published in the various *Survey(s) of United States International Finance* covering the years 1949 through 1953. And we are grateful to Andreas and Lois Grotewold, of the University of Missouri, for permission to reproduce in Chapter 1 the trade-distortion map from the journal, *Economic Geography*.

Finally, we wish to express our gratitude to a corps of typists who labored through numerous drafts: Mrs. Gladys Varner, Mrs. Marion Smith, Miss Leonne Fleury, Mrs. Carmel Cassidy, and especially Mrs. Vivian Loe, who typed the final manuscript under the pressure of several deadlines.

J. N. B.   W. E. S.
Lexington, Virginia   Alexandria, Virginia

January, 1957

Contents

PART II DEVELOPMENT OF THEORY AND POLICY THROUGH THE NINETEENTH CENTURY

12 Monetary and Fiscal Policies   217

13 Exchange-Rate Policies: I   244

14 Exchange-Rate Policies: II   272

Figures

Maps

Tables

THEORY

PRACTICE

POLICY

International Economics

1 Problems of Foreign Economic Policy

Since the rise of the nation-state system, all countries—democratic, totalitarian, rich, and poor—have been struggling to formulate desirable foreign economic programs. They have not always adopted similar policies, for what is desirable for one country is not necessarily so for another. Some persons argue that the objective of foreign economic policies should be the most efficient use of resources over the world; others, the maximum profit for individual traders; and still others, the greatest wealth for the nation. Each of these objectives is at some point tied to the "national interest": those who argue for the most efficient use of the world's resources believe that world prosperity leads to national prosperity and to world peace; those who argue for maximum profits believe that "What is good for my business is good for the country"; and those who seek the greatest national wealth compared to other nations argue that only national prosperity and power in the hands of the right people can preserve peace and progress. Although governments are concerned with the prosperity of *other* nations and of individual domestic firms, they are much more concerned with the relative power and wealth of their own nations.

All governments establish and change their policies in the light of the national interest. The national interest is difficult to describe specifically. In broad terms, the primary interest of any nation is its preservation as an independent body; from this stem the goals of national power and wealth through which independence is maintained. These goals in turn may be broken down into objectives of economic growth, higher standards of living, improved distribution of incomes between the rich and the poor, economic stability, internal political stability, national security, and so on.

A swift reading of these objectives suggests that they are complementary aims in the national interest. But this is not always so. It is the purpose of this book to show the clash or harmony of these objectives and

1

the policies to effectuate them. In practice, nations change specific goals; or, while espousing the same goals, they shift tactics as circumstances change or new data come to light. Whether they mesh or conflict depends on what internal and external methods are employed to attain them. One of the most important means of adding to national wealth and power is through the gains from international trade.

A. THE GAIN FROM TRADE

Trade of any kind is based on the idea that the parties will benefit by the exchange. Each is able to improve his lot because the exchange of goods and services enables him to specialize in one or a few pursuits in which he is most capable; he then obtains goods from others with the least effort to himself. This phenomenon holds both within and among nations; the result is an increase in the efficiency of production and in the over-all living standards.

The division of labor and the process of specialization are aspects of the broader problem of the allocation of resources and the location of economic activity. They raise the question of interdependence of (national) economic units. Interdependence is desirable from an economic standpoint because no two nations are blessed (or cursed) with precisely the same resource agglomerations; for example, Canada produces almost all the world's nickel, and Malaya and Bolivia the world's tin. Differences in social, political, and economic institutions, in national wealth, climate, location, and individual and social propensities exist. These differences allow each nation to produce some items more efficiently than others.

Some of these differences are also found within nations and between regions. What distinguishes international from interregional trade is that it must overcome certain man-made obstacles. First, there are different currency systems—pounds, koruna, pesos, rupees—which require that domestic accounts be translated into foreign currencies through rates of exchange. When the purchasing powers of currencies change within the domestic economies, it is only logical that they should change among countries, introducing additional elements of uncertainty. Second, customs of business practice and consumption habits differ widely among nations, more widely than is found within most nations, adding to the knowledge that must be gathered concerning the market and increasing the risks. Third, national boundaries provide artificial demarcations by which "domestic" and "foreign" relations are designated. This boundary provides an opportunity to the national government to act as individuals do within a nation—to discriminate. Given the sovereign authority of a government over an area, it can choose to expand or contract economic relations with other nations. Finally, the differences in customs and the existence of boundaries tend to restrict the mobility of men and capital among nations more than within them; thus, international trade is founded upon wider disparities in resource supplies than is domestic trade.

To expand trade and encourage freer movement of factors of production usually leads to greater wealth, through a more efficient use of resources, and perhaps even to peace, through strengthening allies and making the economy of a potential enemy dependent on others. But under certain conditions a contraction of trade may lead to greater wealth either *absolutely* or *relatively* to other countries. And trade restrictions are sometimes a means of gaining political and economic stability and national security. A major problem, then, is to decide whether or not to depend upon trade: i.e., whether or not trade will gain the objectives of national economic policy.

B. OBJECTIVES OF NATIONAL ECONOMIC POLICY

The economic objectives are approximately the same for all countries: economic growth and stability. But these are modified by or reconciled with noneconomic objectives of political and military security.

ECONOMIC GROWTH

Economic growth—that is, a rise in over-all output, an increase in the living standards of the people, and/or an improved distribution of income between the rich and the poor—is sought by each country, though not in the same ways. For example, Russia places more emphasis on over-all production than on increased living standards (except for a select few) or on improved distribution. Many backward areas of the world are placing more emphasis on production capacity. Contrarily, such advanced countries as Britain and France, though greatly concerned with their capacity to produce, are apparently more interested in an equitable distribution of existing income and wealth.

The different emphases placed on these objectives are reflected in international economic policy. One country, seeking maximum production potential, may decide that international trade would interfere with its optimum development and may seek to protect its growing industries and manufactures, yet it may attempt to attract foreign capital and technicians. Others may see trade as a means of gaining goods needed for rapid expansion and may view international finance as a means of gaining necessary long-term loans to permit it to live beyond its means for a while. A nation which finds a large portion of its poor producing goods in competition with foreign products or with immigrants may exclude both; but if these same poor find foreign goods essential to their diet, the government will seek to import large quantities of these goods cheaply. The over-all objective of economic growth does not, therefore, dictate any particular international policy or technique.

FULL EMPLOYMENT

The desire for economic stability is reflected most clearly in policies aiming at domestic full employment. The term full employment usually means a fairly steadily increasing level of income coupled with the absence of all but seasonal and frictional unemployment. Since any fluctuation in incomes and employment in foreign countries is transmitted to other countries through variation in the volumes of exports and imports, the failure of any nation to maintain full employment will tend to reduce incomes of others. Such a failure is all the more important for countries in which international trade is a substantial portion of the national income: for example, over 50 per cent of Holland's national income is derived from foreign trade, and some agricultural countries earn large portions of their national incomes from the export of only one or a few commodities.

Because international (like domestic) demand is not characteristically stable and because governments can more readily regulate the demand for imports than for domestic goods, some countries have decided that it would be better to minimize their international trade than to suffer wide swings in income. They choose lower (but steadier) levels of income with an assurance of steadier (but less efficient) work for all. Some unemployment and instability is the price of high levels of trade with its concomitant fluctuations—*unless* a flexible internal economy is erected to adjust to the swings of international supply and demand, *or* unless a sufficiently large supply of gold or acceptable currencies can be held to pay for excessive imports during a time of depression abroad. Not all countries have such supplies of foreign currencies (or gold), called "international reserves," and not all are willing to let individual firms or industries become subject to the winds of international trade, for reasons of national security and political stability.

NATIONAL SECURITY

An overriding objective in the pursuit of national interest is that of national security. Historically, national security has been thought of in terms of the power of an individual nation as compared with that of an enemy or a coalition of enemies. Or, it has been seen as the sum of individual powers of nations allied against a common enemy. The former concept led to an emphasis on national economic self-sufficiency so that dependence on other nations would not prevent successful war. Military preparedness meant a high degree of economic isolation in those commodities deemed strategic.

In former centuries, even the necessity of allying one's national forces with another's did not necessarily lead to economic interdependence, since the allies chosen were not always the same and military coalitions did not require joint supply. The idea that a nation can "go it alone" economically and militarily still persists, and some of those who would agree that *joint military* action is now required still argue that *economic isolation* is desirable. Contrary to these views is one that the national security objectives of a nation require an expansion of international trade and greater economic interdependence.

The importance of the national security objective in the determination of international economic policy can be seen in the conflict between the United States (plus the Western world) and Russia (plus countries of Eastern Europe and the Far East). The East-West conflict may be resolved (in the absence of actual war) in favor of that side which proves itself politically and economically stronger. Strength can be gained only through the most efficient mechanical, scientific, and other techniques of production and distribution—one such technique is international specialization and exchange.

The view that international trade is a weapon in the struggle between the East and the West should not minimize the other aspects of the East-West conflict, which are cultural, social, and ideological. The complexity of the conflict emphasizes that international economic policies cannot be decided without reference to the over-all political and strategic situation. For example, in order to diversify sources of supply and not to concentrate lines of transportation and communication which might be severed easily in wartime, it may be necessary to redirect trade and to subsidize the production of some strategic items in areas which would normally not be considered the most efficient. This argument has been employed to justify, for example, protection of optical instruments, watches, and a host of other industries in the United States; clock-making in England; and iron and steel in Italy. But the decision to maintain certain domestic production has to be made with reference to *given* strategies and currently calculated risks concerning the danger of particular threats to sources of supply. In the present world situation, there can be no general condemnation of all trade as weakening the strategic position of a country or of trade with the potential enemy as strengthening him; some trade will and some will not; generalization is dangerous. Excessive restriction of trade would impoverish the domestic economy by causing an uneconomic use of resources and a too rapid depletion of domestic minerals and raw materials. A neat balance must be achieved between dependence on foreign sources and reliance on domestic resources and manufacturing.

POLITICAL STABILITY AND SPECIAL INTERESTS

Political stability in most countries, despite the claim that governments represent *all* the people, entails that those individuals and groups having the economic and political power be satisfied as to the division of favors and privileges available within the economy and extended by the government. This means that, regardless of possible inconsistency with pronounced national or international policy, the favoring of special interests may have to be carried out first. Pressure groups continually present their cases before the government.

In the realm of international economic policy, the domestic producers competing with imports from abroad have been able to persuade most governments of the desirability of protecting many of their businesses from foreign competition. The American duties on many items range between 50 and 150 per cent; for example, pistols and revolvers valued under $4 carry a duty of 150 per cent, knives enter under duties of 64 to 92 per cent, and women's fur felt hats around 70 per cent. Protection reduces the volume of trade and is opposed by other special-interest groups in the United States, only recently urging the benefits of freer trade: those in the business of exporting and importing. The U.S. government's policy must now strike a balance between these opposing forces in the formation of an appropriate foreign economic policy.

Nations have an interest also in the stability of *foreign* political systems. The existence of a weak government in one nation can be a threat to the security of another nation. It is in the latter's interest to help strengthen the hands of foreign officials *or* to encourage a turnover of the government to stronger hands. These measures may be accomplished partially by diplomacy, but where the weakness of a government stems in part from economic ills, the extension of financial assistance—as with aid to Europe after World War II—will provide the recipient government time to make adjustments and reforms necessary to regain stability. Also, a government may aid another in accelerating its economic development in an effort to gain the latter's political allegiance or, if the government is already an ally, to remove domestic threats to its stability. Similarly, commercial policies may change trade from the most efficient economic channels in order to assist another country in its economic development or in achieving economic stability, so as to gain an economically and politically stronger ally.

In sum, international economic policy is not formulated with sole reference to the desirability of using trade to increase economic growth. Other objectives influence this decision and tend to expand or depress the volume of foreign trade. Out of the aggregate forces pressing on foreign trade policy must come a governmental determination of the degree of economic interdependence which is deemed desirable. Once this has been done, the decisions with regard to international economic relations are less than half over.

C.   DISTURBANCES TO TRADE AND THEIR ADJUSTMENT

Except in those countries where the government runs everything, importing, exporting, and foreign lending and borrowing are carried on largely by individuals. Because the decisions of individuals are independent of one another, their combined foreign expenditures do not always equal their combined receipts from abroad. Any equality in expenditures and receipts is likely to be temporary because the ceaseless change in domestic demand and supply and foreign business conditions will upset the equilibrium. What is called "balance of payments disequilibrium" virtually always exists or is threatened. Things frequently thought of as internal problems—such as crop failures, changes in interest rates, changes in savings and investment, taxes, and government expenditures—all affect international transactions and thus alter the equation of international payments. The disturbances caused by World War II kept the countries of Europe under pressure to import more than they exported for several years after the end of the war.

An imbalance in international payments is not always worthy of high-level official consideration. If it is temporary, a country can finance its excessive expenditures abroad by drawing down its international reserves, i.e., paying out its holdings of gold and foreign currencies acceptable to other countries. Sometimes a slight rise in interest rates in the country losing reserves will induce foreign nations to lend their currencies, thus providing the money to meet the excessive expenditures.

It is only when the disequilibrium is not temporary and/or cannot be met out of international reserves or by a shift of lending that there is cause for worry and even new policies. A nation cannot indefinitely spend more than it receives from abroad; it eventually exhausts its international reserves. When a disequilibrium persists for a long time, it must be adjusted by changing some international transactions; more receipts must be earned by expanding exports or less must be spent on imports.

To balance the international accounts the government has three alternatives. It may, as has Britain, employ *direct controls*. These affect the decisions of particular private individuals and firms by requiring specific actions under penalty of law. To reduce the volume of imports, the government may, for example, grant licenses to individual firms for the importation of only particular products and make other imports illegal. To expand exports, it may grant subsidies to certain exporters, or it may restrict domestic consumption of exportable goods.

The government may, like the United States, rely mainly on *indirect controls*. These operate through the market by changing the general level of internal prices and/or incomes, by altering interest rates, and by adjusting prices at which foreign currencies are bought and sold. Indirect controls are distinguished from direct controls in that the latter specify the particular individuals or commodities to make the desired adjustments while the former alter general market conditions and permit individuals to decide how to react specifically.

Finally, the government may employ *state trading*. The business of international trade and lending is operated by the government itself. State trading may encompass only one or a few commodities, as in France, or may involve the establishment of a complete foreign trade monopoly, such as that of Russia. In both state trading and direct controls, the foreign earnings and expenditures are forcibly balanced by administrative action.

Whether indirect or direct controls or foreign trade monopolies are used depends in part on the nation's attitude toward governmental controls. Those nations which are steeped in the doctrines of socialism and believe in the efficacy of general national planning will see indirect controls as being imprecise in their effects and unfair in distributing the burden of adjustment among particular groups, e.g., too little burden on the rich. Such countries prefer to juggle the rights to import so that essential goods (wheat, rather than imported liquor) are restricted little and imports for favored investment and production projects receive special encouragement. Nations adhering to the philosophy of individualism prefer the freedom of choice which accompanies indirect controls; no particular individual is told what to do.

When the pains of adjusting items in the balance of payments appear too great, the government may obtain funds from foreign governments to cover the imbalance. Financial aid from the United States in the decade after World War II has permitted the rest of the Free World to live beyond its means to the tune of over $50 billion. But various problems arise with its extension. Should the funds be extended as gifts or as loans? If loans, can they be repaid? When accepted do they make the recipient nation a political lackey of the lender? Does the grant of such funds carry with it the right of the lender to intervene in the economy of the borrower so that the funds are used for the "right" purpose? The problems of the use of extraordinary assistance cross over into the realm of politics and demonstrate the close relation of foreign economic policy with the broad national interest.

D.   CONFLICTS OF NATIONAL INTERESTS

International economic relations are complicated by the fact that the means one government employs to attain its national interest do not always coincide with or support those used by others. Although all nations assert that they are seeking progress and power, they do not employ coordinated techniques, and are unwilling to give up sovereignty for the interdependence necessary for concerted action.

International trade is a means to economic progress and power. And, each nation wants the benefits of increased trade *but* under conditions designed for its own national benefit. For example, both the Soviet bloc and Western Europe assert that they desire an expansion of trade between the two areas. But each is willing to do so only on its own terms. The

Soviet bloc's terms have been that it receive capital equipment and manu-factured goods and that it be the sole judge as to the correctness of the shipment and any damage in transit. The terms of Western Europe are that no strategic goods shall be shipped to the Soviet bloc and that prompt delivery of desired raw materials and other goods be made at reasonable prices. Inability of the two sides to come to terms has resulted in a virtual severance of prewar patterns of trade which were to the economic ad-vantage of each.

A further conflict arises out of the discrimination by other countries of the Free World against United States exports. Other nations, not having sufficient gold or dollars to buy all the U.S. goods their citizens want, have placed special restrictions on imports from the United States. Some countries which impose these restrictions on trade and payments do so for the purposes of maintaining domestic programs of social welfare and full employment and of supporting rearmament and mobilization which would otherwise place unbearable pressure on their international payments. The U.S. government opposes this discrimination in principle (though it has countenanced the practice) because it diverts trade from the most economically efficient channels and reduces American exports. A large part of its postwar foreign aid was directed to helping to remove this dis-crimination. The conflict is not only between the restricting countries and the United States; differences in the degree of discrimination among the restricting countries give rise to difficulties in settling accounts among themselves.

Problems of discrimination and foreign aid are shared by the under-developed countries of the world. Nations which have low per capita standards of living desire to achieve their place in the sun through economic development. Reading the lessons of history provided by the development of the United States and most of the countries of Europe, including the recent rapid rise of Russia, they see their progress tied closely to policies of protection of their domestic industries and restriction of international trade and lending. Their policies have come into conflict with those of the Western European countries and of the United States. The more developed countries would like freer trade with the underdeveloped areas in order to gain markets and find ready sources of supply of raw materials and foodstuffs.

In the field of international lending, the United States sees its national interest in an expansion of private capital exports; foreign investment would, among other things, reduce the pressure to increase its imports or reduce its exports in order to balance its accounts. The United States would also like to substitute loans for gifts. But the developing countries wish to receive such loans only if they coincide with their over-all economic development programs and do not lead to exploitation or intervention by the lenders.

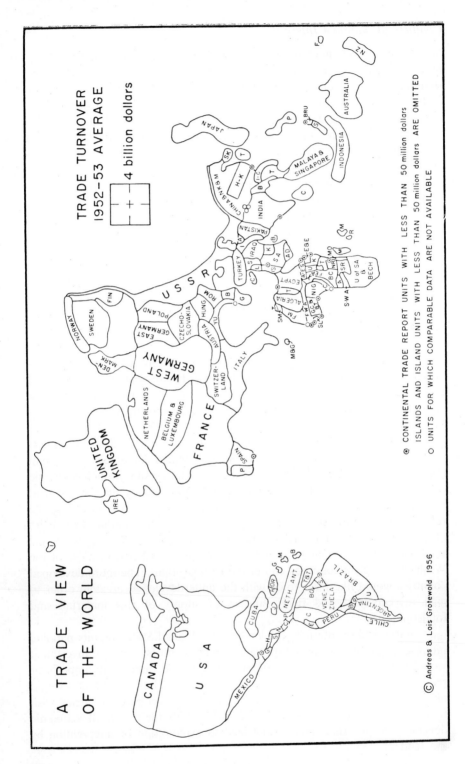

A TRADE VIEW OF THE WORLD

TRADE TURNOVER
1952–53 AVERAGE

4 billion dollars

⊙ CONTINENTAL TRADE REPORT UNITS WITH LESS THAN 50 million dollars
ISLANDS AND ISLAND UNITS WITH LESS THAN 50 million dollars ARE OMITTED

○ UNITS FOR WHICH COMPARABLE DATA ARE NOT AVAILABLE

© Andreas & Lois Grotewold 1956

Most of the underdeveloped areas have a recent or current history of direct political dependence on a European nation; they fear its re-introduction or desire its cessation. They see their national interest in "self-determination" and independence. The metropolitan countries, being or having been dependent on these areas for sources of supply and markets, are reluctant to withdraw completely from their positions of economic and political dominance over the areas.

Russia has identified her interest with that of greater independence for these areas in the hope that she will gain both economically and politi-cally. United States policy has shifted between encouragement of the movements for independence and support for the mother country, since it has at different times felt more strongly the need for economic and political allies in one area and then the other. The problems of international lending and of trade with colonial areas display again the close tie between foreign economic and political policies.

Just prior to World War II, nations followed their national interest through trade and financial policies now referred to as "economic warfare." After World War II, the United States and its allied nations sought inter-national agreement on commercial and financial principles and policies and on cooperative means to carry them out in order to forestall a repetition of economic conflict. Over 50 nations established several organizations under which they agreed on procedures relating to international financial and commercial arrangements. Some of these have been singularly success-ful; others are still having growing pains. The postwar developments in U.S. foreign economic policy shed light on whether or not the conflicts of national interest can be resolved through international institutional co-operation or have to be approached on a day-to-day and country-by-country basis through the channels of economic and political diplomacy.

Not all nations are equally interested in or affected by movements in world trade. Also the policies of others toward world trade do not affect all nations equally. The accompanying map is a distortion of the world according to each nation's volume of exports and imports. As can be readily seen, the United States, the United Kingdom, and Western Euro-pean countries are the predominant traders. Not only is their foreign economic policy important to their own growth but it also is important to other nations. After a discussion in Part I of the principles of trade applicable to all nations, we will examine their international economic policies, especially those of the United States and Britain.

PART I THEORY OF TRADE AND THEORY OF POLICY

2 The Theory of Trade

The purpose of Part I, consisting of this and the two succeeding chapters, is to present broad theoretical bases for judging the desirability of government intervention in the movement of goods, services, and factors of production among nations. In order to compare the effects of free trade and unhampered factor movements with the effects of restricted trade and factor movements, it is necessary to show first the causes and consequences of trade; this is done in the present chapter. Chapter 3 presents the cases for and against free trade, and Chapter 4 examines the pros and cons of free factor movements.

A. THE CAUSE OF TRADE

Common sense suggests that the cause of trade is a difference between countries in the money prices of products: foreign goods are bought if they are cheaper than home-produced goods of equivalent quality.

But, to compare the *dollar* price of a product in the United States with the *peso* price of the same product in Mexico requires the introduction of a third price, namely the price of a dollar in terms of pesos. The price of one currency in terms of another is called the exchange rate because it arises in the exchange of currencies. For example, Mexicans who export goods to the United States for dollars receive a currency which they cannot spend in Mexico. But these Mexican exporters can sell their dollar receipts to other Mexicans (through financial intermediaries) who wish to buy American goods with dollars. The Mexican importers who buy the dollars pay pesos for them, and the number of pesos they pay for each dollar is the exchange rate.

MONEY PRICES

The role of money prices in international trade can be readily shown by a hypothetical example. Suppose that Mexico and the United States

15

are the only nations in the world, that there are no costs of transporting goods, and that the following prices would prevail if each were isolated from the other economically.

PRICES BEFORE TRADE

	Baby buggies	Leather belts
Mexico	100 pesos	5 pesos
U.S.	$10	$1

Assuming that the exchange rate is 4 pesos per dollar and that trade is permitted between the two nations, Mexicans will wish to buy American belts and buggies because they are cheaper. The $10 which a Mexican importer must pay for an American buggy cost him only 40 pesos as compared to 100 pesos for a Mexican buggy. Similarly, an American belt costs 4 pesos as compared to 5 pesos for a Mexican belt.

Because American buggies and belts are cheaper than the Mexican products at these prices and exchange rate, Americans have no incentive to buy them from Mexico. Supposing that these are the only products which either nation produces, Mexico will export nothing. The absence of Mexican exports will frustrate the desire of Mexicans to buy American goods if potential Mexican importers can buy the dollars they require only from Mexican exporters. With the demand for dollars in excess of the supply, Mexican importers will offer *more* than 4 pesos for a dollar. And, when the price of a dollar is bid above 5 pesos, Mexican belts become cheaper than American belts, inducing Americans to buy Mexican belts. These American purchases of Mexican belts provide dollars to Mexican exporters, who, having no use for the dollars, will sell them to Mexican importers.

The rate of exchange will settle at a level where the supply of dollars coming into Mexico through belt exports just equals the demand for dollars in Mexico to be used to buy American buggies. It must ultimately rest somewhere between 5 pesos and 10 pesos per dollar. Since American buggies are cheaper than Mexican buggies only if the rate is below 10 pesos per dollar, Mexicans will demand dollars only if the rate is below 10 pesos; and, as we just saw, there will be a supply of dollars only if the rate is above 5 pesos.

The shift in the exchange rate from 4 pesos per dollar to somewhere within this range can be avoided if the Mexican government is willing to sell a dollar's worth of gold to Mexican importers for 4 pesos. Mexican importers, instead of offering more than 4 pesos to obtain each dollar they require, can ship the gold to the United States Treasury where it can be exchanged for American currency with which to pay for imports. But this movement of gold contains the seeds of its own destruction. As long as the Mexican government does not spend the pesos it receives from the sale of its gold, prices fall in Mexico under the force of smaller circulation of pesos and because of the heavy purchases in America instead of Mexico.

Simultaneously, the increase in dollar circulation in the United States as the Treasury pays out dollars for the gold and the heavy purchases of American goods by Mexicans drive up prices in the United States. Eventually, Mexican belts become cheaper than American belts, giving rise to Mexican belt exports. When the dollar value of Mexican belt exports equals the dollar value of Mexican buggy imports, importers will no longer need to ship gold to finance their purchases and, with the cessation of gold movement, prices will cease to shift in both countries.

In sum, no matter whether the exchange rate changes or money prices within each country shift, an equilibrium is obtained in which Mexico exports belts and imports buggies. Because of the passive responses of money prices and/or the exchange rate, the differences in money prices which existed at the opening of trade are inadequate guides to the pattern of trade which finally develops.

RELATIVE PRICES

A more fundamental explanation for the export of buggies from America and belts from Mexico is found in differences in relative prices, i.e., differences among nations in the value of a product measured in terms of other products instead of in terms of money. In Mexico, before trade opens, a buggy sells for as much as 20 belts since a buggy is priced at 100 pesos and a belt at 5 pesos. In America, before trade, a buggy sells for as much as 10 belts. Therefore, measured in terms of each nation's own belts, America's buggies are cheaper than Mexico's buggies; the United States has a *comparative* advantage over Mexico in buggies. Contrarily, a belt costs as much as $\frac{1}{20}$ of a buggy in Mexico and $\frac{1}{10}$ of a buggy in America so that Mexico has a comparative advantage over the United States in belts. As long as money prices or the exchange rate adjust passively to balance the exports and imports of each country, differences in relative prices will eventually determine the pattern of trade, and each country will, following the law of comparative advantage, export that product in which it has a comparative advantage and import that product in which it has a comparative disadvantage.

The overpowering role of relative prices in international trade is attested by the following example in which relative prices are the same before trade in both nations.

EQUAL RELATIVE PRICES

	Buggies	*Belts*
Mexico	100 pesos	10 pesos
U.S.	$10	$1

We see that, no matter what the prices and exchange rate may be, no trade is possible in the long run. At any rate of exchange *below* 10 pesos per dollar, Mexicans will want to import American belts and buggies because they are cheaper. But there will be no Mexican exports to provide the dollars to finance the imports, and the shortage of dollars will push the rate toward 10 pesos per dollar. At any rate *above* 10 pesos per dollar, Mexico will export belts and buggies because Americans will prefer them to the more expensive American counterparts. But, Mexicans will not wish to import American belts and buggies, so that there will be no demand for the dollars which Mexico's exports earn, and the surplus of dollars will force the rate toward 10 pesos per dollar. The rate therefore ultimately settles at 10 pesos, and, when this happens, the incentive for trade is removed because neither product is cheaper in either country.

In summary, differences among nations in their relative prices are the essential condition for trade, and money prices or the exchange rate, no matter what their levels as trade opens, will adjust so that a country exports that product in which it has a comparative advantage and imports that product in which it has a comparative disadvantage. In the long run, money is neutral and the pattern of trade depends upon relative prices or, supposing that competition wipes out abnormal profits so that prices and costs are the same, upon relative costs in each country.

B. WHY RELATIVE PRICES DIFFER

The reasons for the differences in relative prices among nations lie in differences in their relative factor endowments, in their relative demands for products, and in the ways in which commodities are produced.

Prices are determined by supply and demand so the reason that the price of belts is lower, relative to the price of buggies, in Mexico than in the United States must stem from supply and demand conditions. With the same conditions of supply in both countries, Mexican belts would be relatively cheap if the Mexican demand for Mexican belts were lower than the Mexican demand for buggies in comparison to the relative American demand for American belts and buggies. With the same demand conditions, Mexican belts would be relatively cheap if Mexico, in comparison to the United States, were more capable of producing belts than buggies; the relatively greater supply would depress their price.

The prices people are willing to pay for various quantities of a product are determined by their preferences among goods and by their incomes; that is apparent enough. The costs of production (and under competition, the prices) of various quantities of a product are determined by the supplies of the factors of production and the various combinations of quantities of those factors required to produce the product. This requires some explanation.

RELATIVE FACTOR ENDOWMENTS

Like brains and good looks among people, the factors of production are not spread evenly among countries or regions. Some nations, such as the United States, have a relative abundance of capital and land and a relative scarcity of labor. Others, like Argentina and Australia, have a relative abundance of land and a relative scarcity of labor. Still others, such as India, have a relative abundance of labor while land and capital are relatively scarce. Mexico has a relative abundance of labor and land but a relative scarcity of capital in comparison with the United States.

The word "relative" has special significance. The statement that the United States has a relative abundance of capital and a relative scarcity of labor while the reverse holds true in Mexico implies a comparison of the ratios of labor and capital in both nations. It does *not* imply a comparison of the absolute amount of labor in the United States and the absolute amount of labor in Mexico. It does *not* say that Mexico has a greater amount of labor than the United States, which is false. Nor does it say that Mexico has a smaller supply of capital than the United States, which is true but irrelevant for our purposes. Rather the statement says that the United States has a greater quantity of capital compared to the size of its labor force than Mexico has of capital compared to its labor force, i.e., the amount of capital per worker is greater in the United States than in Mexico.

FACTOR ENDOWMENTS AND FACTOR PAYMENTS

The reward paid to any factor of production for its contribution to the total output is determined, like the price of a commodity, by supply and demand. Because factors of production are a means to an end, namely, the production of goods and services, the demand for each factor is derived from the demand for the goods it produces and from its productivity.

The productivity of any particular factor depends upon the proportions of factors used in production. According to the law of diminishing returns, beyond a certain volume of production each successive addition of a unit of one factor, while the quantities of other factors are kept constant, raises total physical output of a product by smaller and smaller amounts. The change in total output consequent to a one-unit change in the employment of the variable factor is the marginal physical product of the variable factor. Therefore, the law of diminishing returns means that the marginal physical product of a factor declines as more of it is used in conjunction with a fixed amount of other factors. Since, according to this law, it is the ratio between the quantities of the variable and fixed factors which is important, we may conclude that the greater the ratio of labor to capital, the lower the marginal physical product of labor. And, since the law is reversible and applies to all factors, we may conclude that the smaller the ratio of capital to labor, the higher the marginal physical product of capital. Putting these together, we can summarize that the greater the ratio of labor to capital, the smaller the ratio of the marginal physical product of labor to the marginal physical product of capital.

In Mexico the ratio of the marginal physical product of labor over the marginal physical product of capital is lower than in the United States because the ratio of labor to capital is higher in Mexico than in America, that is, because labor is relatively abundant and capital is relatively scarce in Mexico while the converse holds true in the United States.

The implications of this for the ratio of the payments to the factors in the two countries can be seen from the following. When competition prevails among businessmen in the sale of goods and the hiring of factors and when it also prevails among all units of each factor in the sale of their services, each factor tends to receive a payment equal to the value of its marginal physical product. For example, suppose each businessman in the buggy industry has hired labor and capital in such proportions that the marginal physical product of an additional laborer would be 10 buggies in each firm. If the additional laborer can be hired for a money wage which is less than the money value in the market place of 10 buggies, the employment of an additional worker will add to the profits of each firm. This is because the extra buggies can be sold for more than must be paid to the extra worker who will produce them. With this incentive for hiring more men, businessmen will bid up the money wage rate as they demand more labor. And, as more workers are employed relative to other factors, the marginal physical product of labor will decline. And, finally, as the output of buggies rises consequent to the employment of more workers, the price of buggies will fall under the force of additional supply. These changes cease only when there is no further profit in hiring more labor, and this happens only when the money wage rate is just equal to the value of labor's marginal physical product.

Therefore, in equilibrium, the worker receives a money reward equivalent to the market value of what he produces. This implies that he could buy just as many buggies as he produces if he wishes. That is, his real reward, measured in terms of the product he produces, equals his marginal physical product. The lower his marginal physical product, the lower his reward. Having already shown that the ratio of the marginal physical product of labor to the marginal physical product of capital is lower in Mexico than in the United States, it follows that the reward to labor (wages) will be lower relative to the return on capital (interest) in Mexico than in the United States. As compared to the ratio of factor payments in the United States, labor will be relatively cheap and capital will be relatively expensive in Mexico.

FACTOR INTENSITY OF PRODUCTS

Products may be characterized by the relative amounts of the several factors of production which they utilize. Steel production requires a higher ratio of capital to labor than the production of leather gloves, or lace, or shirts simply because of the technological requirements of these products. Because steel production requires larger amounts of capital per worker than these other products, steel is considered to be capital intensive. Conversely, leather gloves, lace, or clothing are labor intensive.

Technological requirements do not alone determine the proportions in which factors are combined in the production of a product. There are usually several different combinations of the factors which can be used to produce a given amount of a product, and businessmen will select that mixture which minimizes costs. Thus, if the price of labor rises relative to capital in a nation, businessmen will substitute capital for labor where possible; more capital will be used relative to labor than before. But even though more capital will be used per worker in all products, differences in the technology of products will dictate that, at the new factor prices, more capital will still be used per worker in some products than in others, thereby preserving the distinction between capital-intensive and labor-intensive commodities.

Suppose that belts are labor intensive and buggies capital intensive in order to show why relative prices differ between Mexico and the United States. We have already seen that, because of differences in their relative factor endowments, the ratio of wages to interest is lower in Mexico than in the United States. It therefore follows that belts are cheaper relative to buggies in Mexico than in the United States. That is true because belts use relatively more of the factor which is relatively cheap in Mexico while buggies use relatively more of the factor which is relatively expensive in Mexico.

The table on page 22 depicts this conclusion. Given the rates of payments to the factors of production in columns 1 and 2, businessmen combine certain quantities of the factors shown in columns 3 and 5 to produce the product most cheaply. The resulting costs of production and prices of the products, as shown in columns 7 and 8, are determined by multiplying the prices of the factors times the quantities of each that are employed. Note that 10 belts sell for as much as 1 buggy in the United States while 20 belts sell for as much as 1 buggy in Mexico, i.e., belts are cheaper relative to buggies in Mexico than in the United States.

Table 1 reflects the previous discussion: (a) Capital is cheaper relative to labor in the United States than in Mexico, i.e., wages are ten times the return to capital in the United States but half the return to capital in Mexico. (b) The ratio of capital to labor in both countries is higher in buggy production than in belt production; this reflects the fact that buggies are capital intensive while belts are labor intensive. (c) The ratios of capital to labor in both products are higher in the United States than in Mexico; capital is relatively cheap in the United States and therefore American businessmen substitute capital for the relatively expensive American labor; the converse situation holds in Mexico, and, therefore, Mexican businessmen substitute the relatively cheap Mexican labor for the relatively expensive Mexican capital.

Table 1. Factor Rewards, Factor Ratios, and Relative Prices

1	2	3	4	5	6	7	8
Wage per hour	*Return per unit of capital*	*Quantities of factors needed to produce one buggy*	*Factor ratio in buggies*	*Quantities of factors needed to produce one belt*	*Factor ratio in belts*	*Price of one buggy*	*Price of one belt*
U.S.							
$1	10¢	50 units of capital plus 5 labor hours	10 units of capital per labor hour	2½ units of capital plus ¾ labor hour	3⅓ units of capital per labor hour	$10	$1
Mexico							
1 peso	2 pesos	30 units of capital and 40 labor hours	¾ unit of capital per labor hour	1 unit of capital plus 3 labor hours	⅓ unit of capital per labor hour	100 pesos	5 pesos

From the foregoing analysis we may conclude that differences among nations in their relative factor endowments lead to differences in their relative factor payments which, because of differences in the relative factor intensity of products, lead to differences among nations in the relative prices of products.

But this conclusion must be qualified for differences in relative demand. Suppose, as above, that wage rates are lower relative to interest rates in Mexico than in the United States. Then suppose that Mexicans shift their demand toward Mexican belts and away from Mexican buggies. The consequent expansion of the belt industry will require additional labor and capital while the contraction of the buggy industry will release them for employment. The belt industry, being labor intensive, will want, say, 4 laborers per unit of capital while the buggy industry, being capital intensive, will release only, say, 2 workers per unit of capital. As the result of the consequent shortage of labor, money wage rates will rise relative to interest rates, and businessmen in both industries will substitute capital for labor in so far as possible.[1] Therefore, following the law of diminishing returns, the marginal physical product of capital will fall relative to the marginal physical product of labor in both Mexican industries. Hence, in final equilibrium, the ratio of wages to interest will rise in Mexico as a result of the stronger Mexican demand for the product using labor intensively and the weaker Mexican demand for the product using capital intensively.

Applying this to international differences in relative prices, even though Mexico has a relative abundance of labor and America a relative abundance of capital, the ratio of wages to interest could be the same in both countries. This might occur if Mexicans have a relatively greater demand for the product produced primarily by labor and Americans have a relatively greater demand for the product produced primarily by capital. If opposite relative demand conditions do offset different factor endowments to the point of equating relative factor payments in both countries, relative commodity prices will also be the same. In that event, trade would not be possible.

Summarizing, relative prices in each nation are determined by supply and demand. And differences among countries in their relative prices in the absence of trade arise from differences in their relative demands and relative supplies, though only if disparities in their relative supplies are not offset by differences in their relative demands and vice versa. Differences among nations in relative factor endowments (if not offset by differences in their relative demands for products) imply differences in relative factor payments which, coupled with differences in the relative factor intensity of products, imply differences in relative commodity prices. Because a nation tends to export that product in which it has a comparative advantage or, in other words, the one which it can produce relatively cheaply, each nation will export that product which uses its relatively abundant factor of production more intensively. Similarly, a country tends to import that product which uses its relatively scarce factor more intensively.

THE QUESTION OF EFFICIENCY

Nowhere in this analysis has the efficiency of Mexican laborers been compared with the efficiency of American workers; nowhere has the relative quality of the two countries' capital been compared. Economy-wide differ-

---

[1] That this is possible even though the total quantities of the factors are unchanged in Mexico is seen from the following. Suppose that, before the change in demand, the total quantities of labor over capital are 4,000/1,000 in belt production and 2,000/1,000 in buggy production; this agrees with the assumed differences in factor intensity. By shifting 300 workers and 100 units of capital from buggy to belt production we obtain the ratios of 4,300/1,100 in belt production and 1,700/900 in buggy production; thus, there is less labor per unit of capital in both industries than before.

ences in the efficiency of production between the two countries are irrelevant to the existence of trade.

For example, suppose that the production of one buggy required 4,000 Mexican laborers and 3,000 units of capital instead of 40 and 30 respectively, as assumed in the Table 1. The price of a buggy would then be 10,000 pesos instead of 100 pesos at the factor payment rates previously assumed. And if the production of one belt required 300 laborers and 100 units of capital instead of 3 and 1 respectively, the price of a belt would be 500 pesos instead of 5 pesos. The relative price of one buggy would, however, still be 20 belts since the 10,000 pesos which would have to be spent to buy a buggy would be sufficient to buy 20 belts at 500 pesos each. The relative price of belts would still be lower in Mexico than in the United States (where it is 10 belts per buggy), and trade would still be possible, despite the fact that, in this example, Mexican labor and capital is 100 times less efficient than it was before.

C. TRADE EQUILIBRIUM

So far the analysis has been concerned chiefly with the conditions which must exist in the absence of trade if trade is to arise. Once trade opens, what is its effect on prices, production, consumption, and the allocation of resources?

EQUILIBRIUM FOR ONE PRODUCT

Part of the answer to this question can be found in the following graphs which depict the demand and supply schedules of buggies by residents of each country. To permit the comparison of prices, assume that Mexican peso prices are converted into dollar prices through a fixed exchange rate and assume that equal heights on both graphs measure equal

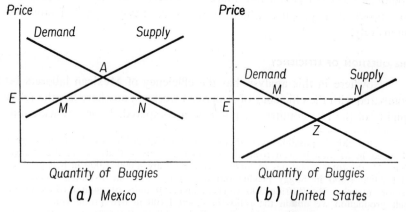

Fig. 1 Prices before and after Trade

prices. Suppose further that there are no costs of transporting buggies and no other obstacles to trade. If the two nations are isolated economically, the price in each settles where supply and demand are equal—at A in Mexico and at Z in the United States, as shown in Figure 1. Because the price of buggies is lower in America than in Mexico, the moment that trade is permitted, Mexicans buy buggies in the United States rather than in Mexico. This depresses the Mexican price and raises the American price. As can be seen from Figure 1(a), when the price drops in Mexico below A, Mexicans demand a greater quantity of buggies while the supply of Mexican-produced buggies declines. Conversely, as the price rises in the United States above Z, the quantity which Americans demand declines and the quantity supplied rises. At any given price above Z, the difference between the American supply and the American demand (the excess supply) is the amount that the United States has available for export. The excess supply of the United States is plotted on Figure 2 as the American export supply schedule. It begins at price Z where the American demand and supply schedules in Figure 1(b) show there is no excess supply available for export, and it continues through all prices above Z, including the price E, at which American supply exceeds American demand by the amount MN, as seen in Figure 1(b). The Mexican import demand schedule in Figure 2 is derived by plotting from Figure 1(a) the excess of Mexican demand over Mexican supply at each price. It starts at price A where Figure 1(a) indicates there is no excess demand, and it continues through all prices below A, including the price E, at which Mexican demand exceeds Mexican supply by the amount MN, according to Figure 1(a).

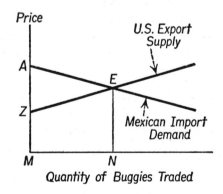

Fig. 2 Equilibrium Price with Trade

Starting from A in Mexico and Z in America before trade, the prices settle at E in equilibrium with a volume of trade equal to MN. No other price and no other volume of trade could long exist under the assumed demand and supply schedules. At the price E, American supply exceeds American demand by MN, and that amount must be exported if the price is to remain at E; otherwise, the excess supply would drive down the price in America. And, at the price E, Mexican demand exceeds Mexican supply by MN, and that amount must be imported if the price is to remain at E in Mexico; otherwise, the unsatisfied excess demand would drive up the price in Mexico. At price E, the quantity the United States must export just matches the quantity which Mexico must import. Mexico's excess demand is satisfied and America's excess supply is removed simultaneously through trade in MN buggies; consequently, there is no tendency for prices to change in either country. Furthermore, because prices are the same in both nations, Mexicans have no incentive to increase the rate of their buggy purchases from America above MN, and Americans have no incentive to sell a greater volume of buggies to Mexico than MN. If these conditions had not been met, the price and volume would not have settled where they did.

Summarizing, the effects of unhampered trade are as follows: (1) prices in both nations are equalized, (2) the rise in the price in the exporting country induces a fall in its consumption and an increase in its production of the exportable product, and (3) the fall in the price in the importing nation induces a rise in its consumption of the type of product which is imported and a fall in import-competing production. While these conclusions are derived from a discussion of trade in buggies, exactly the same conclusions apply to trade in belts, though the position of the two countries would be reversed because Mexico exports belts to the United States.

EQUILIBRIUM FOR TWO PRODUCTS

Let us now broaden the analysis by taking account of the simultaneous adjustments with respect to both belts and buggies within a single economy. This is required because a change in the price of one product is likely to induce changes in the demand and supply of another product.

Resource reallocation

Suppose that, before and after trade opens, the United States has a fixed supply of fully employed factors of production and that there are no technological improvements in methods of production. This means that an increase in the output of one product requires a shift of resources (factors of production) from the production of some other item. The amount by which the production of other items must decline in order to permit one more unit of a given product to be produced is the alternative cost of that particular product.

Assume that the alternative cost of producing one more buggy in the United States prior to trade is 10 belts, and suppose that the minimum dollar cost of producing that buggy or the 10 belts is the same. Under competition, price and cost are the same, and therefore the dollar value of one buggy must equal the dollar value of 10 belts, i.e., the relative price of one buggy must be 10 belts.

As trade opens, relative prices change in each nation. American purchases of Mexican belts depress the price of belts within the United States, and Mexican purchases of American buggies raise the price of buggies in the United States. Thus, the relative price within America shifts from 10 belts per buggy to more than 10 belts. In Mexico, because the import of buggies and the export of belts make buggies cheaper and belts more expensive, the relative price changes from 20 belts per buggy, prior to trade, to less than 20 belts.

In equilibrium the relative price will be the same in both nations, for, as just seen, the equilibrium price of each product must be the same in both. Suppose that the relative price shifts to 15 belts per buggy within each nation with the opening of trade. These are the terms of trade, i.e., the terms on which the products are exchanged. For example, suppose that in the United States the price of a buggy settles at $12 while the price of a belt shifts to 80¢. At 80¢ apiece, the export of 15 belts by Mexico to the United States provides Mexico with $12, and this is sufficient to pay for the import of one buggy from the United States.

When the relative price shifts from 10 to 15 belts per buggy in America with the opening of trade, American businessmen can profit by moving resources from belt to buggy production. The relative price of buggies exceeds their alternative cost. If one additional buggy is produced, it can be sold for the dollar equivalent of 15 belts. The dollar cost of producing that buggy is equivalent to the dollar cost of producing only 10 belts. Thus, the businessman makes a profit in dollars equivalent to the value of 5 belts.

Assuming that the relative price remains at 15 belts, the extent of the change in belt and buggy production in America depends upon cost conditions. If the alternative cost of a buggy remains constant at 10 belts no matter what the level of production in either industry, businessmen will move factors out of the belt industry until none are left to be moved. Only then will businessmen have exhausted the opportunity for profit through the shift of resources.

But if costs increase as buggy production expands, the complete desertion of the American belt industry is less likely. Under increasing costs, each one-unit rise in buggy production requires more and more factors of production. Therefore, the rate at which belts must be given up increases as buggy production expands. Starting from 10 belts per buggy, the alternative cost rises to 11, 12, and so on until enough extra buggies are produced to take the profit out of further reallocation of factors. Assuming that the relative price remains at 15 belts per buggy, the profit from *further* reallocation of resources disappears only when buggy production rises enough to raise the alternative cost to 15 belts per buggy. Depending

upon how fast costs rise, this equality may be obtained before resources
are shifted entirely out of belt production.

Gains from trade

From this analysis we perceive the gain from trade. With an alternative
cost of 10 belts per buggy in the United States prior to trade, the production of one more buggy requires America to forego the production and
thus the consumption of 10 belts. With the opening of trade, an additional
buggy can be sold to Mexico for 15 belts—or for money sufficient to
pay for 15 Mexican belts when imported into the United States. The
American resources which are shifted to produce one more buggy in fact
"produce" more belts through trade than they can if they are left in the
American belt industry. *Thus, more goods are available to a nation under
trade than in the absence of trade.* Under constant alternative costs, every
additional buggy produced has this effect. But, under increasing alternative
costs, this holds true only for those additional buggies whose alternative
cost is less than 15 belts, i.e., for all but the last buggy which can be
produced when the relative price is 15 belts per buggy.

While resources are shifting from belt to buggy production in America
because the relative price of belts falls in the United States, Mexican
factors shift from buggy to belt production because the relative price of
buggies falls in Mexico. These resource shifts are interdependent. Belts
for export to the United States by Mexico are provided through an increase
in Mexican belt production along with a possible fall in Mexican belt
demand consequent to the rise in the relative price of belts. Without these
belts from Mexico, the fall in the relative price of belts in the United
States could not be sustained; the fall in price reduces U.S. belt production and may raise U.S. belt demand. Without the belt imports, there
would be an unsatisfied demand for belts in the United States, forcing
the price back up. Without a fall in the relative price of belts in the United
States, American resources would not shift to buggy production. And
without an increase in American buggy production to provide exports to
Mexico, the relative price of buggies in Mexico would not fall. This in
turn would mean that resources would not shift into belt production in
Mexico.

Determination of the terms of trade

The terms of trade were simply assumed to be 15 belts per buggy
above. They are in fact determined by reciprocal demand and supply.

The equilibrium terms of trade equate the import demand and export
supply of each product. Furthermore, in conjunction with the physical
volumes of commodities exchanged, they equate the value of each nation's
exports and imports. That is, if the terms of trade are 15 belts per buggy,

then 15 belts sell for just enough dollars to pay for one buggy, and Mexico must export 15 times as many belts as she imports of buggies in order to pay for her total buggy imports.

Equality in the values of each nation's exports and imports is obtained through exchange rate adjustments or internal price changes as described in Section A. For example, if the dollar value of Mexico's buggy import demand exceeds the dollar value of her belt exports, the shortage of dollars with which to pay for American buggies causes the peso price of each dollar to rise. This raises the cost of American buggies to Mexicans, and it induces them to restrict their purchases from the United States, which helps to remove the excess of Mexican import demand. The change in the exchange rate also normally increases the dollar value of Mexico's belt exports. Mexican belt producers obtain more pesos for each dollar's worth of belts they sell in America when they sell the dollars they receive to Mexican importers. This induces Mexican belt producers to shift some of their sales from the Mexican market to the American market.

Lifting the veil of money, suppose the terms of trade are 15 belts per buggy. If Mexico wants to import 100 buggies at these terms, she must export 1,500 belts to pay for them. If America wants to export only 80 buggies and import only 1,200 belts, the terms of trade must change. Mexico offers too many belts and wants too many buggies relative to the amounts which the United States demands and supplies, and the volume of belts which the United States will accept is not sufficient to finance the volume of buggies that Mexico wishes to buy. Since Mexico offers more belts than are demanded by the United States, the price of belts will fall. Since Mexico wants more buggies than the United States supplies, the price of buggies will rise.

Suppose then that the terms of trade shift from 15 to 16 belts per buggy. Because of this rise in the relative price of buggies, Mexicans reduce their demand for buggies and Americans increase their supply of buggies. And, because of the fall in the relative price of belts, Mexicans reduce their supply of belts and Americans increase their demand for belts. If, at these new terms of trade, the demands and supplies of Americans and Mexicans agree and each nation's exports just pay for its imports, the terms of trade change no further. But if both nations' import demand and export supply respond so meagerly to the shift in the terms of trade and Mexico continues to offer too much and demand too much, the terms of trade continue to change. From this example we may conclude that the stronger the Mexican import demand and the greater the Mexican export supply relative to the American export supply and import demand, the less favorable for Mexico are the equilibrium terms of trade, i.e., the more belts she must export to pay for a buggy.

In the final analysis, trade equilibrium is the product of the interaction of a number of economic variables. Export supply and import demand affect the terms of trade, and the terms of trade, through their effect on resource reallocation and demand shifts within each country, affect the import demand and export supply. As an example of this interaction, suppose that constant alternative costs prevail in both nations and that the cost is 20 belts per buggy in Mexico and 10 belts per buggy in the United States. American buggy producers can always undersell Mexican buggy producers because it costs less to produce a buggy in the United States than in Mexico. Similarly, Mexican belt producers can always undersell American belt producers. This suggests by itself that each country will tend to specialize entirely in the production of its export product, producing nothing of the commodity which it imports. But this is true only so long as the demand of each country for the other's products and the supply available for export produce equilibrium terms of trade of *less* than 20 belts and *more* than 10 belts per buggy. Only at such terms are American belt production and Mexican buggy production unprofitable. But Mexico, even though completely specialized in belt production, may not be able to satisfy the American demand for belts when the United States produces no belts, if the American demand for belts is strong and if Mexico's total resources are few in number. In that event, some belt production must persist in the United States, and the terms of trade and the relative price in the United States must settle at 10 belts per buggy in order to induce it to supply belts also. At 11 belts per buggy, for example, American resources would not remain in belt production.

MULTICOUNTRY, MULTICOMMODITY EQUILIBRIUM

The introduction of more commodities and countries only complicates the foregoing analysis; it does not affect the conclusions. Suppose there is a third nation, France, with a relative price and alternative cost of 15 belts per buggy. With respect to Mexico, France has a comparative advantage in *buggies* because buggies cost 20 belts each in Mexico. But, with respect to the United States, France has a comparative advantage in *belts* since the cost of a buggy in America is only 10 belts. Hence, France could export either product. Suppose, in order to keep the presentation manageable, that constant alternative costs prevail in all nations. If the equilibrium terms of trade lie above 15 belts per buggy, France will specialize completely in buggy production. If they lie below 15, she will specialize in belts.

It is quite possible that France might not specialize in either product because of demand and supply conditions in all three nations. Given the cost conditions which we have assumed, the United States will specialize in buggy production and Mexico in belt production. If in addition France specialized completely in the production of either product, she might add so much to the total world supply of the product in which she specialized that the relative price (terms of trade) would fall below the alternative cost of producing it in France. In that event, some French resources would shift into the production of the other product, reducing the supply of the product in which she had previously specialized and therefore raising its price. If supply and demand conditions are such that France cannot specialize entirely in the production of either product, the terms of trade must ultimately rest at 15 belts per buggy so as to cover the cost of producing both belts and buggies in France.

In a multicountry world, the value of a nation's exports to and imports from another nation need not be the same in equilibrium. Rather, the value of a nation's exports to *all* other countries and imports from *all* other countries must be the same. Suppose, to take an extreme pattern of trade, that France exports $100 worth of goods to Mexico, Mexico exports $100 worth to America, and the United States exports $100 worth of goods to France. Suppose further that French sales to Mexico are paid in pesos, Mexican sales to the United States are for dollars, and French purchases from the United States must be paid for in dollars. France can obtain dollars with which to pay for her imports from America by exchanging, with Mexico, the pesos France earns for the dollars that Mexico earns on sales to the United States. Multilateral trade, distinct from bilateral trade in which each nation's exports and imports with each other nation are balanced, depends upon convertibility of currencies; that is, in this example, upon the willingness of Mexico to convert the pesos that France earns on sales to Mexico into dollars.

Returning to a two-country situation, suppose now a third commodity, boats, which has a relative price and alternative cost of 1½ buggies and 30 belts in Mexico, and 2 buggies and 20 belts in the United States. In terms of *buggies,* boats are relatively cheaper in Mexico than in the United States; in terms of *belts,* they are relatively cheaper in the United States. Hence, either nation could export boats, with the final result depending upon the terms of trade. If Mexico produces boats as well as belts, the terms of trade must be 30 belts per boat in order to cover the cost of producing both products in Mexico. If America produces boats as well as buggies, the terms of trade must be 2 buggies per boat for the same reason. Should the juxtaposition of demand and supply in both nations be such that both nations produce boats—perhaps Mexico exporting them and the United States making up a deficiency in the American market through home production—the ultimate terms of trade would be 30 belts = 1 boat = 2 buggies, i.e., a combination of the costs of producing belts and boats in Mexico and buggies and boats in the United States.

The number of commodities and countries could be multiplied further. But the principles drawn from the above would be the same. Export supply and import demand affect the terms of trade, and the terms of trade, through their effect on the allocation of resources and on demand within each nation, affect the import demand and export supply. Equilibrium is obtained only when the import demand and export supply of each product are equated and when the value of each nation's exports to all other countries equals the value of its imports from all other nations.

Selected Readings are found after the summary of Part I.

3 Cases for and against Free Trade

Arguments over the relative merits of free trade and restricted trade may proceed from at least three points of view. The advantages and disadvantages of either government policy may be set forth in terms of the effects on particular individuals or groups within a nation. They may be analyzed in terms of the effects on the nation as a whole, without regard to the benefit or hurt to particular people or groups. And they may be considered in terms of the effects on the world as a whole, without regard for the advantages and disadvantages to particular individuals, groups, or nations.

This chapter will consider the question of free trade versus restricted trade from all three points of view. The first task is to show how free trade equilibrium differs from restricted trade equilibrium, and, in doing so, we will see how particular individuals and groups within a nation are affected by greater or smaller volumes of international trade.

A. RESTRICTED AND FREE TRADE EQUILIBRIUMS COMPARED

Today sovereign nations use a multiplicity of devices to affect the composition and volume of their trade. The principle effects of the instruments available for restricting trade may be readily seen through an analysis of the effects of taxes on trade.

EFFECTS OF IMPORT DUTIES

Effects on one product

In Figure 3 the curve marked S is the export supply schedule of buggies from the United States, as determined by the underlying demand and supply schedules for buggies within the United States. This schedule shows the various prices which Americans must receive for different volumes of buggy exports if they are to undertake to supply them. In the absence of any obstacles to trade, Mexicans need not pay more for any given quantity of U.S. exports than the various amounts indicated by S. But if the Mexican government imposes a duty on buggy imports, Mexicans must pay the prices indicated by the American export supply schedule *plus* the duty, as shown by S_t. The vertical distance between S and S_t measures the duty per imported buggy.

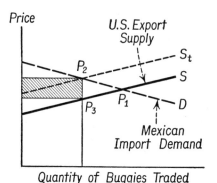

Fig. 3   Effects of an Import Duty

Prior to the imposition of the duty, the free trade equilibrium price of buggies is P_1 in both nations because, at that price, the Mexican import demand and American export supply are equal. After the duty is imposed, the Mexican import demand at P_2 equals the American export supply at P_3. Therefore these are the new equilibrium prices in Mexico and the United States respectively. The price in Mexico exceeds the price in America by the amount of the duty. The total revenue collected by the Mexican government equals the duty per buggy, or P_2P_3, times the new quantity of buggies imported, i.e., the shaded rectangle.

Supposing that there are no qualitative differences between Mexican and American buggies, the price of buggies within Mexico rises from P_1 to P_2. This will force some contraction of Mexican consumer demand for buggies, and it will induce some expansion of Mexican buggy production. The volume of trade declines, and Mexican buggy producers enjoy greater sales. The price received by American buggy producers falls from P_1 to P_3. This induces some increase in American buggy consumption which partly compensates for the loss of sales to Mexico, but the fall in the price received by American producers dictates a decline in U.S. buggy output.

These conclusions must be modified if Mexico takes a negligible portion of American total buggy production prior to the imposition of the duty. In that event American producers can sell in other markets, at home or abroad, the negligible quantities sold to Mexico prior to the tariff, without causing the price in these other markets to fall. Therefore there would be no reason for American producers to accept a lower price from Mexico. United States producers would supply no buggies to Mexico at a price below that ruling elsewhere; the American supply schedule of exports *to Mexico* would be perfectly elastic at a level equivalent to the price in other markets. These circumstances are shown in Figure 4. No change in the American price of buggies ensues from a Mexican tariff, for P_1 is the same as P_3; but the volume of Mexican imports falls and the price in Mexico rises by exactly the amount of the tariff, or from P_1 to P_2.

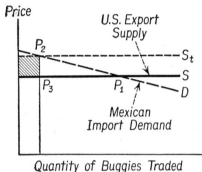

Fig. 4   Effects of an Import Duty

1113962

Effects on two products

With the imposition of the duty, the dollar value of Mexican buggy imports declines because the physical volume drops and the dollar price falls or remains the same. Assuming that Mexican exports and imports were equal before the duty, after the duty the demand for dollars by Mexicans desiring American buggies falls short of the supply of dollars arising from Mexican belt exports. In consequence, the peso price of a dollar falls. This shift in the exchange rate restrains the rise in the peso price of buggies within Mexico after the imposition of the tariff because each dollar required to pay for buggies is cheaper in terms of pesos. It also reduces the number of pesos which Mexican belt producers receive for each dollar they earn through belt exports. Finding that they receive fewer pesos per exported belt, Mexican belt producers shift some of their sales to the Mexican market, depressing the price of belts within Mexico. If Mexico should supply more than a negligible portion of America's total belt demand, the reduction of Mexican exports would lead to a rise in the price which Americans pay for belts.

In summary, normally the imposition of a duty on the buggy imports by Mexico raises the price of buggies and lowers the price of belts within Mexico. That is, the relative price of buggies in Mexico rises. In consequence, resources shift from belt to buggy production, reducing Mexican belt production and increasing Mexican buggy output. If Mexico supplies more than a negligible part of America's total belt demand and if Mexico takes more than a negligible portion of America's total buggy production, Mexico's import duty on buggies causes the U.S. price of buggies to fall and the U.S. price of belts to rise. That is, the relative price of buggies in America falls, and, in consequence, resources shift from buggy to belt production. This brings a change in the composition of American output contrary to that which occurs in Mexico. On the same assumptions, Mexico's terms of trade improve and those of the United States worsen. The price received by American buggy exporters falls, and the price paid by American belt importers rises. Instead of exchanging 16 belts for each buggy, perhaps the two nations exchange 15 belts per buggy. As a result of the tariff, Mexico gives up fewer belts to obtain each buggy she continues to import.

Under free trade, the equilibrium price of each product is the same in both nations. Therefore, under free trade, relative prices are equal among nations. With a duty on Mexican buggy imports, the equilibrium price of buggies is higher in Mexico than in the United States by the amount of the duty, while the equilibrium price of belts, which are not taxed, is the same in both nations. Therefore the equilibrium relative price of buggies in Mexico exceeds that in the United States by the amount of the tariff. Under increasing costs, resources shift in each country until alternative costs equal relative prices, and therefore the alternative cost of a buggy in Mexico in equilibrium also exceeds that in the United States. Finally, the volume of trade in buggies and belts is smaller with a duty than under free trade.

EFFECTS OF EXPORT TAXES

Results similar to those of a Mexican buggy import duty can be obtained through a tax on Mexican belt exports. The Mexican belt export supply schedule marked S in Figure 5 indicates the prices which Mexican belt producers must receive to supply various quantities of belts to

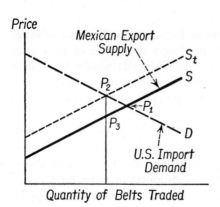

Fig. 5 Effects of an Export Tax

foreigners. Add to this the amount of the export tax which Mexican producers must pay as their belts leave Mexico, and we find the sum which Mexican exporters must charge American importers, as indicated by S_t.

Before the tax is imposed, P_1 is the free trade equilibrium price in both nations. After the tax, the American import demand at P_2 equals the Mexican export supply at P_3, and these are the new equilibrium prices in America and Mexico respectively. The Mexican export producer receives less and the American importer pays more; the Mexican government receives P_2P_3 as revenue from each unit traded.

If Mexico supplies a negligible part of the total number of belts bought by the United States prior to the tax, then the United States could replace all the belts it buys from Mexico with belts from other sources without raising the price it must pay for them. In that event, Americans would demand no Mexican belts at a price above that ruling in other markets, and the American import demand for Mexican belts would be perfectly elastic at the prevailing price. As shown in Figure 6 the effect of the export tax would then be to reduce the price received by Mexican belt producers by the full amount of the tax, and the price paid by American importers would not change.

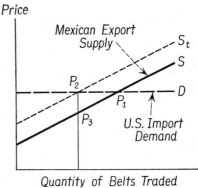

Fig. 6 Effects of an Export Tax

Price

Mexican Export Supply

S_t

S

P_2

D

P_1

P_3

U.S. Import Demand

Quantity of Belts Traded

Suppose that the export tax leads to a reduction in the total number of dollars which Americans pay for Mexican belts. The supply of dollars to Mexico thus falls short of the demand for dollars by Mexicans desiring to buy American buggies. Consequently the peso price of a dollar rises, and this raises the peso price of imported buggies, thereby raising the price of buggies in Mexico. If Mexico takes more than a negligible share of America's total buggy output, the lower Mexican demand for American buggies caused by the higher peso price will also lower the price of buggies in the United States.

In sum, as with the duty on buggy imports, the tax on belt exports raises the relative price of buggies in Mexico. If Mexico is more than a negligible buyer and supplier in trade with America, the export tax also lowers the relative price of buggies in the United States and improves Mexico's terms of trade.

DISTRIBUTION OF THE TAX BURDEN

Part of the burden of trade restriction is put upon foreigners if a nation's terms of trade improve with the application of trade taxes for then foreigners are obliged to give up more of their own product for each unit of the taxing nation's exports. In addition, part of the burden is borne by particular groups within each nation, as follows.

In Mexico, the trade taxes discussed caused the price and production of buggies to increase and the price and production of belts to fall. This suggests that those consumers who mainly purchase import-type products suffer from trade restriction while those who mainly purchase export products gain from trade restriction. It also suggests the generalization that trade restrictions benefit import-competing industries and hurt export industries. Little wonder, therefore, that these classes of industries clash before legislative committees on the relative merits of freer and less free trade—their pocketbooks are involved. In the United States and elsewhere, labor unions in the import-competing industries often take a stand opposite to those in export industries. And businessmen of the same general political and ideological affiliations oppose each other on tariff matters. Even the farmers are split. The tariff debate pits labor and capital in one industry against labor and capital in another.

Yet, in the long run, the adversaries should not divide this way. Though rarely recognized by the participants in the debate, the long-run interest of all units of the same factor is the same in a mobile and fluid society. An expansion of trade involves a decline in import-competing industries and an expansion of export industries. If Mexico removes her trade taxes, the belt industry expands at the expense of the buggy industry. The growing belt industry, being labor intensive, requires much more labor and only a little more capital while the declining buggy industry, being capital intensive, releases much capital and only a little labor. Hence, the demand for labor for belt production rises by more than the amount of labor released from buggy production; therefore, money wages tend to rise. Conversely, the amount of additional capital demanded by the belt industry is less than the amount released from the buggy industry; therefore the money reward to capital tends to fall.

As wage rates rise relative to interest rates in Mexico, businessmen in both industries substitute capital for labor. With the ratio of capital to labor consequently greater than before in both industries, the marginal physical product of capital falls in terms of both products, and the marginal physical product of labor rises in terms of both products. Therefore, in Mexico, the real income of capital falls and the real income of labor rises,

From this we may generalize that the expansion of trade, by changing the composition of output and the demand for factors, tends to raise the real income of the relatively abundant factor and to lower that of the relatively scarce factor. This follows because the growth of trade induces an expansion of export production and a contraction of import-competing output, and because the exported product uses the relatively abundant factor more intensively and the import-competing product uses the relatively scarce factor more intensively.

With only two countries and two factors, the relatively abundant and cheap factor in one nation is the relatively scarce and expensive factor in the other nation. Thus, prior to the opening of trade, the ratio of wages to interest was lower in Mexico than in the United States. The growth of trade tends to equalize the ratio of factor rewards in both nations. The shift from buggy to belt production raises the ratio of wages to interest in Mexico; the opposite shift of production in America reduces the ratio of wages to interest in the United States.

Hence, given sufficient time for the movement of resources among industries, all Mexican laborers and all American capitalists should favor free trade, for it provides the utmost expansion of trade. But in fact they give more attention to the short run. Unless the total economy is growing so that additional demand is created for imported goods, a fall in prices consequent to the inflow of foreign products wrecks profits, forces layoffs, and leads to bankruptcy in import-competing industries. In fact, this is the way in which the expansion of trade sets in motion a shift of resources out of import-competing industries. In the real world, there is always some uncertainty about obtaining new employment once the present job folds. A shift of jobs may require a person to learn new skills, and, if the shift involves geographical relocation, old friendships and patterns of life are broken and the cost of moving must be borne. For these and other reasons we normally find labor and capital on the same side of the free trade versus restricted trade argument, the particular side depending upon the industry they are in.

B. THE CASE FOR WORLD-WIDE FREE TRADE

The case made here for free trade is a cosmopolitan one. It looks to the effect of an unhampered volume of trade on the world as a whole, and it assumes that no government intervenes in international trade.

MAXIMIZATION OF OUTPUT

From a fixed and fully employed supply of the factors of production in the world, world-wide free trade brings a maximum current output of whatever goods and services are demanded when competition prevails. Maximum output is defined to exist when it is impossible to increase the output of one product without reducing the production of some other product.

Suppose that there are no costs of transportation, that relative prices equal alternative costs in each country, that prior to the opening of trade the relative price of a buggy is 10 belts in America and 20 belts in Mexico, and that the two countries produce the following total amounts prior to trade.

TOTAL PRODUCTION BEFORE TRADE

	Buggies	Belts
Mexico	1,000	30,000
U.S.	5,000	70,000
Total	6,000	100,000

Since buggies are relatively cheaper in America and belts are relatively cheaper in Mexico, the law of comparative advantage tells us that Mexico will export belts and America will export buggies. With the opening of trade, resources will shift from import-competing to export production in both nations. Suppose that a small volume of trade causes buggy production to rise by one unit in America and to fall by one unit in Mexico. With the assumed alternative costs, the concomitant shift of resources forces U.S. belt production down by 10 and permits Mexican belt production to rise by 20, resulting in the following total production.

TOTAL PRODUCTION AFTER TRADE

	Buggies	Belts
Mexico	999	30,020
U.S.	5,001	69,990
Total	6,000	100,010

Though the same total number of buggies are produced, there are more belts available to the world as a whole than before, i.e., than prior to trade. The reason lies in the fact that buggies can be produced more cheaply in terms of belts in the United States than in Mexico, as evidenced by the disparity in their alternative costs. If still another buggy were produced in America, compensated by an additional one-unit decline in Mexican buggy production, the combined output of belts would rise to an even higher level, though only if the alternative cost of a buggy in Mexico still exceeds that in the United States.

Under constant alternative costs, every shift of resources as trade expands increases total output because of the constant disparity in the alternative costs of the two nations. As seen on page 27, the shifting of resources can continue until one of the nations becomes completely specialized. When one country becomes specialized maximum world output is attained. The only way to increase global output of belts, if Mexico were completely specialized in belt production, would be to shift American resources from buggy to belt production, that is, by decreasing the world output of buggies. Thus, the possibility of increasing the output of one product without reducing that of another is exhausted.

Under increasing costs of production in both nations, every shift of resources with expanding trade raises alternative costs in export production. Starting from 10 belts per buggy in America, the expansion of U.S. buggy production raises the cost of buggies above 10 belts, and the cost rises with every increase in output. And, starting from 20 belts per buggy, the contraction of Mexican buggy production is accompanied by a fall in the alternative cost of buggies below 20 belts, and the cost falls with every decline in buggy output. Even so, as long as the alternative cost of buggies in Mexico exceeds that in America, further expansion of trade and shifting of resources raises total output. Only when resources in both countries have shifted enough to equalize the alternative costs will the possibility of increasing total output be exhausted. This happens when free trade equilibrium is attained.

Previous analysis (page 26) showed that in the absence of obstacles to trade the price of each product would be the same in both countries in equilibrium. Therefore, in equilibrium, the relative price of each product must be the same in both countries. And, since relative prices equal alternative costs in each nation, alternative costs must also be the same in both countries. Thus, when free trade equilibrium exists, total output is maximized. As we saw in the discussion in the previous section, equilibrium with trade taxes involves an inequality in the relative prices of trading nations. It therefore also involves an inequality in alternative costs. Any volume of trade short of free trade means that resources have not shifted enough to equalize alternative costs. Under restricted trade, some units of the world output of a product are produced at a higher cost in terms of other products than they need be. The production of one of the products can be increased without reducing the output of the other. The possibility of increasing global output is not exhausted unless free trade prevails.

In sum, on the assumptions of competition and full employment, more goods and services are available to the United States and Mexico together under free trade than in its absence.

CONSUMER SATISFACTION

Free trade also insures that the total world output, no matter what the products, is distributed among consumers so that no one person's satisfaction from goods and services can be increased without reducing someone else's satisfaction.

In attempting to maximize the satisfaction or utility which they obtain from the goods they buy with their incomes, consumers adjust the distribution of their expenditures among commodities with an eye to relative prices. Imagine some Mexican who has a fixed income which he spends on X and Y. Suppose that, given the present distribution of his purchases between those two commodities, his total satisfaction would not change if he lost 3Y and found 1X or vice versa, i.e., suppose he is indifferent as between 3Y or 1X. Further assume that, in the market place, the money value of 1X is the same as that of 2Y, i.e., the relative price of 1X is 2Y; if he were to buy one more X he would be obliged, because his income is fixed, to forego the purchase of 2Y.

Because his total satisfaction would remain unchanged if he gave up 3Y to gain 1X, his total satisfaction must rise if he gives up only 2Y to obtain 1X. Therefore he will buy at least one more X and two less Y. Having more X and less Y after changing his expenditure pattern, additional units of X are likely to be less useful to him while he will regard his remaining units of Y more favorably. Thus, for still another unit of X, he might become indifferent between 1X and only 2.9Y instead of 3Y. Nonetheless, he will continue to substitute X for Y until he has so much more X and so much less Y that one more X just compensates for the loss of satisfaction in giving up 2Y. Only then, with the relative price of X being 2Y, would the consumption of more X and less Y fail to increase his total satisfaction. Thus, in equilibrium, the relative prices of X and Y just equal the quantities of X and Y between which he is indifferent.

To apply this reasoning to international trade, assume that the relative price of X is 1Y in the United States and 2Y in Mexico in isolation. Therefore, in pretrade equilibrium, consumers in each country will have adjusted their expenditure patterns so that they are indifferent as between the following quantities of the two products.

INDIFFERENCE RATIOS

Mexican Consumers	*American Consumers*
Indifferent between	Indifferent between
IX and 2Y	IX and IY

Since X is relatively cheaper in the United States, Americans will export X to Mexico, according to the law of comparative advantage, while Mexicans will export Y to the United States when trade opens. Should an American export 1X and import 1Y, his total satisfaction would be unchanged because he is indifferent as between 1X and 1Y. The loss of satisfaction in giving up 1X would be exactly compensated by the gain in satisfaction through having one more Y. But a Mexican would gain through the exchange because the 1X he imports gives him just as much satisfaction as 2Y and he is required to give up only 1Y to get it. Only when consumers in both countries are indifferent as between the same quantities of X and Y will additional exchange fail to add to the satisfaction of at least one consumer without subtracting from another's. Since consumers adjust their expenditure patterns with regard to relative prices, this condition is met only when relative prices are the same in both countries. Since free trade equates relative prices among countries, the condition is met only when free trade prevails.

The arguments set forth above apply to trade within nations as well as between nations. Leaving aside transportation costs, if the prices faced by each consumer within a single country, or in a city, or even in a city block are not the same, it is possible to increase the satisfaction of one consumer without reducing that of another. The principle involved is not different if two boys trade marbles or if Brazilians and Americans exchange cars and coffee. In both situations, differences in their respective valuations of the commodities which are exchanged explain why at least one of the parties to the trade may benefit without hurting the other. Similarly, inequalities in the relative prices ruling in different parts of a nation indicate that the nation has not maximized its output of goods and services. Differences in the relative factor endowments of cities and rural areas within a single nation provide exactly the same basis, in principle, for maximizing output through specialization as do differences in the relative factor endowments of Argentina and England. Political borders are not essential to the theory of the effects of free trade.

C. FREE TRADE FOR ONE NATION: THE TERMS OF TRADE

Free trade does not necessarily maximize the output of a particular nation, nor does it necessarily insure that some consumer within a nation cannot be made better off without hurting another consumer in the same nation.

THE GAIN TO ONE NATION

To show the validity of these statements suppose that, in free trade, the terms of trade are 16 belts per buggy. Assume also that, with Mexico producing some of both products under free trade, the relative price and alternative cost of a buggy are also 16 belts within Mexico. In equilibrium, with this relative price, each Mexican consumer would find his total satisfaction unchanged if he lost one buggy and found 16 belts.

Suppose now that Mexico imposes an import duty which reduces her demand for U.S. buggies so that her imports fall by one unit. Suppose also that, as the analysis on page 36 suggested might occur, the terms of trade shift to 15.9 belts per buggy, allowing Mexico to export 1/10 belt less for each buggy she continues to import. Had Mexico been importing 100 buggies before, she would have been exporting 1,600 belts to pay for them, since the terms of trade under free trade are assumed to be 16 to 1. If she imports 99 buggies now, she need export only 15.9 x 99, or about

1,574 belts, to pay for them. Thus, by giving up one buggy, Mexico gains 26 belts (1,600–1,574) for home use because her exports fall by that much. Or, if Mexican consumers do not want any additional belts, resources capable of producing 26 belts can be shifted into the production of other products, increasing the amount of other domestically produced goods available for Mexican use.

The gain to Mexico from this trade restriction can be seen in several ways. (a) With respect to consumer satisfaction, the particular Mexican who is obliged to give up an American buggy would not be hurt if he got 16 belts in return. Since Mexico gains 26 belts when she imports one less buggy, there are more than enough additional belts in Mexico to compensate that Mexican. The extra belts above the number required to compensate that Mexican could be enjoyed by him or by any other Mexican. Therefore the total satisfaction of at least one Mexican consumer can be increased without hurting any other Mexican consumer. (b) With respect to production, the alternative cost of one buggy is 16 belts. That is, the production of one more buggy within Mexico requires a shift of an amount of resources from belt production which is capable of producing exactly 16 belts. When Mexican exports fall by 26 belts, no more resources than those capable of producing 16 belts need be shifted into the Mexican buggy industry to replace the American buggy no longer imported. The remainder of the factors can be put to work making even more buggies for Mexicans or they may be left in the belt industry to produce more belts for Mexicans. Thus, through trade restriction, Mexico can have more of either product without having less of the other.

If the terms of trade had not changed when Mexico imposed the tax which reduced her buggy imports by one, Mexico's exports would have fallen by exactly 16 belts. The 16 belts no longer exported would be just sufficient to compensate the Mexican who was obliged to give up an American buggy, or they would provide just enough resources to replace the American buggy with a Mexican-produced buggy; Mexico obtains no gain by restricting buggy imports by one. A higher tax, by further restricting trade, would do positive harm. If another American buggy were no longer imported, with the terms of trade remaining at 16 to 1, Mexico's exports would fall by another 16 belts. With rising alternative costs within Mexico, a second additional buggy could be produced in Mexico only at a cost *in excess* of 16 belts; Mexican belt production would have to decline by more than 16 if enough resources were shifted to the buggy industry to replace the American buggy. Therefore the additional 16-unit fall in belt exports would not be sufficient to replace the second American buggy. Similarly, this change in exports would not be sufficient to compensate a Mexican who gave up a second American buggy. He would want more than 16 belts to compensate him for the loss because, having already lost one buggy and gained 16 belts, the loss of still another buggy would be more painful to him while he would regard additional belts less favorably.

In the event that Mexico's tax does improve her terms of trade, a higher tax rate would improve her terms of trade even more. By further restricting Mexican demand for American buggies, a higher tariff would depress even more the price received by U.S. exporters. Mexican exports would ultimately decline even further, and the reduced supply of belts available to Americans would raise the price paid by American importers to a higher level.

Does Mexico gain with every increase in the trade tax? A monopolistic businessman would not attempt to maximize the difference between the price he charges for his product and his cost of production per unit of output because that would not maximize his total profits—only his profit per unit of output; the drastic curtailment of sales which would accompany a very high price would also curtail total profits. The same applies to Mexico. While an improvement in the terms of trade may increase Mexico's gain from trade *per unit* of trade by causing her to give up fewer belts for each buggy imported, the consequent decline in trade volumes might be so great as to reduce her total gain from trade. When the terms of trade can be affected, there is always some particular tax which maximizes the goods and services available to the taxing nation, and a tax which is higher than this optimum one restricts trade too much. The determination of the optimum tax is a difficult task, involving, for example, an estimate of how the terms of trade and volume of trade will respond to various levels of taxation.

In summary, the arguments used to support free trade on a world-wide basis support free trade for individual nations only if each nation demands and supplies such a negligible portion of the world's goods and services that it cannot affect its terms of trade.

CONFLICTS OF INTEREST AMONG NATIONS

The conflict of interest among nations stands out when any one nation can affect its terms of trade. Assuming only two countries, Mexican restriction of trade results in a smaller combined output for Mexico and the United States than would be produced under free trade, because alternative costs no longer are equal in both nations. If Mexico obtains a greater amount of goods and services through the improvement in her terms of trade while the combined output falls, the United States must have less than under free trade.

Should the United States retaliate by imposing a tariff on Mexican belts in an effort to return the terms of trade to their former level, *each* country might lose as compared with its situation under free trade. With each country restricting imports from the other, the volume of trade will decline and much of the gain from specialization, i.e., the greater total output, will be thrown away in a battle over the *division* of the gain. The possibility of retaliation may, however, deter Mexico from initiating or increasing trade restriction.

D. REMOVAL OF FREE TRADE ASSUMPTIONS

The arguments set forth above for free trade assume that relative prices reflect alternative costs in each country. We showed that equilibrium under restricted trade implied an inequality of Mexican and American relative prices. This in turn, we said, implies an inequality of their alternative costs. Thus, a tax on Mexican buggy imports causes part of the world supply of buggies to be produced at a higher cost than need be, and the world fails to maximize its total output. Also, in the event that Mexico cannot affect its terms of trade, the alternative cost of replacing the buggies no longer imported would exceed the number of belts which were retained as a result of the restriction of trade. When alternative costs do not equal relative prices, what happens to these arguments?

UNEMPLOYMENT

Relative prices do not equal alternative costs when unemployment exists. The alternative cost of a product is zero because an increase in the production of one commodity through the use of previously unemployed resources does not require a reduction in the output of some other product.

Suppose, for example, that when buggies become somewhat cheaper in Mexico with the opening of trade, resources in the Mexican buggy industry refuse to move into other employments and are also unwilling to accept a cut in their remuneration. With no flexibility in their rewards, the money cost of producing buggies in Mexico does not change. The resources become unemployed because the lower money price of buggies will not cover the unchanged money costs of production. Despite the fact that the money price of a buggy, and therefore the relative price of a buggy, in Mexico is positive, the alternative cost of a buggy is zero. In terms of the belts that must be given up, it is cheaper to produce buggies in Mexico than in the United States, and, in the interest of maximizing world output, buggy production should be increased in Mexico and contracted in the United States—the opposite of the effects of expanded trade. Trade restriction finds justification also if the purpose is to maximize the goods and services available to Mexico. Mexico must export belts to pay for the buggies she imports, but she need give up no belts if she produces buggies at home with previously unemployed resources.

An alternative to trade restriction would be to find means of increasing the mobility of resources and of inducing resources to accept cuts in their remuneration. The former might be attempted through the provision of greater information on alternative employment opportunities and even through government financial assistance with respect to the costs of moving. The latter might be attempted by reducing the power of groups to determine their own remuneration. If satisfactory solutions can be found, both full employment and the gain from trade can be obtained.

Suppose that after free trade equilibrium has been reached general unemployment occurs in Mexico as a result of a fall in the level of business activity. Again the alternative cost of buggies would be zero, and Mexico might wish to stem the unemployment by preventing imports of buggies. Her effort will fail if her exports drop off, for that would tend to reduce employment in the Mexican belt industry. In the short run it is possible for Mexico to export more than she imports if the United States will ship gold to pay for the difference. But even in the short run Mexican exports may fall if the United States, now suffering unemployment because of the fall in buggy exports, should retaliate with a tariff on belt imports. An alternative which would preserve both full employment and the gain from trade would be for Mexico to solve its unemployment problem through greater public works expenditures, lower taxes, and/or lower rates of interest, which would expand investment and consumption expenditures so as to increase employment.

MONOPOLY

Monopolistic business practices, such as restrictions on the entry of firms into the production of one of the two products, restrain the shift of resources which, as seen in the previous chapter, tends to wipe out the surplus profit available when relative prices exceed alternative costs. They keep the relative price of a product above its alternative cost; therefore, though free trade equalizes relative prices, it cannot equalize alternative costs under monopoly conditions. Consequently, world output is not maximized.

Yet, the existence of monopoly may constitute an argument for free trade. Free trade may make what was a monopolistic firm in a country into a competitive one by subjecting it to competition from firms in the rest of the world. Free trade does not always create competitive conditions, however. Competition exists when each firm believes that it has no power to affect the price of its product through its own action. This happens when each firm produces a negligible part of the total supply. When free trade prevails, there may not be enough firms in the whole world to create this condition if entry into an industry is barred in other countries as well.

Free traders used to say that "the tariff is the mother of monopoly." But it need not be. If the imposition of a tariff on a particular product should cause the setting up of one firm in a country where previously there had been none, that would not automatically make the firm a monopolist. For, as long as there are many firms in the world, each acting competitively, the protected firm cannot raise its prices above what the foreign firms charge plus the tariff. That is, the firm has no power to affect the price of its product through its own action.

SPECIAL COST SITUATIONS

The arguments for free trade proceeded on the assumptions of constant or increasing costs as output rose. But costs may fall with time or with an increase in output. What does this imply for the arguments for free trade?

Infant industries

Even ardent free traders have in the past admitted that it is legitimate to extend tariff protection to an industry under certain conditions to offset the "comparative advantage" of an early start held by foreign producers.

Starting a new industry in a country is replete with dangers and pitfalls that come with trying something new. Mistakes are made; people have to be trained; old processes need to be adjusted to different surroundings. But when all the initial problems are overcome, the new industry sometimes does become more efficient, i.e., has lower alternative costs, than the older industry overseas, because the nation in which the new industry grows is better fitted for the production of the item. But because the older and more developed nations got there first, made the mistakes, corrected them, and then obtained the markets, they hamper the growth of infant industries in the newer or less developed countries.

Protection to encourage such industries would constitute a current deviation from free trade. Yet the future output, for both the nation giving protection and others, may be greater if the industry becomes *more* efficient than its foreign competitors *and if the foreign competitors shift into different lines.* If the objective of free trade is the maximization of output, protection in these instances can be justified on the same grounds as free trade; the ultimate effect of protection may be much greater output for the world later. Here, the sacrifice of some of the gain from free trade *now* may mean more output for all later.

A serious problem, however, arises in determining whether a nation has a potentially successful infant industry within its borders. The successful prediction of economic events is notoriously difficult. One cannot know for sure that an industry will fail until it is born and grows a little. And mere uncertainty of success or failure is neither an argument for or against protection. If protection is given and the infant fails to achieve efficiency, the nation has wasted resources. But failure does not prove that the effort should not have been made, for it may have resulted from unforeseeable changes in demand or production conditions. The waste may be multiplied, however, by the persistence of protection long after the industry has shown itself to be incapable of maturing to efficiency; the industry may be politically powerful enough to induce the government to maintain its protection, or the government may feel sorry for the owners and workers who were mistakenly drawn into the industry and who must find employment elsewhere if the tariff is removed.

Even success of the infant industry does not prove that it should be protected. First, another industry might have grown up had not the protected industry raised its costs by bidding factors of production away from it. Second, the protected industry itself might grow up rather promptly *without* protection and at considerably less cost in loss of trade. The question sometimes resolves itself into whether the nation wants the industry *sooner* or *later*. If the answer is "sooner," and a tariff is imposed, some of the gains from free trade are sacrificed; hence it is necessary to compare the advantage in having the industry sooner against the advantage derived from the gain from free trade.

If the decision favors having the industry sooner, there remains still another doubt. Will protection stifle the infant industry by making the businessmen wasteful and indolent as they hide behind the tariff in a protected market? Or will the reduction of business uncertainty provided by the protection enhance their incentives to invest, to innovate, and to take the necessary risks in developing the industry?

Internal and external economies

Suppose that costs of production fall as output expands in an industry subject to import competition. Suppose further that the inflow of foreign goods prevents the industry from expanding output and thus from obtaining lower costs. If the cost level which could be obtained with greater output were lower than costs abroad, a shift of production from abroad to the potentially lower-cost nation would increase total world output and would increase the total amount of goods and services available to that particular nation. Thus, protection of the industry with potentially lower costs would seem desirable in order to permit it to expand production.

Costs fall with the expansion of output, though only up to a certain point, when internal or external economies exist. External economies occur when the costs of production of a firm decline consequent to a rise in the output of any industry including the one of which it is a member. Internal economies arise when the cost of production in a firm drops solely because of the expansion of that firm's output.

Internal economies are frequent in large-scale manufacturing or agriculture where high levels of output and sales permit individual firms to use costly machinery which would not be economically feasible at lower levels of output. This kind of internal economy reflects the indivisibility of factors: a steel firm cannot use half of a small rolling mill to produce half as much output.

External economies may arise for several reasons. The size of the market for a product often determines the degree of specialization in an industry, and the degree of specialization sometimes affects the cost of producing the product. The growth of an auto industry, for example, permits the development of a large number of producers of small parts for new cars; each supplier may specialize, reducing the costs of producing an auto.

Similarly, the protection of some industry which requires transport facilities may lead to the building of railroads or other transportation facilities which reduce costs for other industries. While the cost of production may rise in the protected industry (which alone would make the tariff undesirable), the fall in costs elsewhere would tend to offset that rise in so far as the effect on world output or the protecting nation's output is concerned.

The protection of a particular industry may lead to the growth of an industrial community, and the consequent urbanization may increase the opportunities for transferring ideas and skills among people, providing benefits to the protected industry and to other industries. The rise of a mechanized industry requiring extensive skills may create general benefits for the economy by interesting people in complicated processes, thereby increasing the supply of skilled people and increasing the chances of new inventions. Some industries act as teachers, permitting the later expansion of other industries:

> The textile and shoe industries have served as skill educators and inculcators of work discipline in many underdeveloped areas within the United States, as well as abroad. A typical sequence of development begins with these industries as the first step. . . .
> In the United States, for example, the textile industry started in New England with simple techniques. As skill levels rose, industries requiring higher level skills began bidding labor away from textile mills using lower skills. Metal working industries and machine makers, for example, bid for such labor. Even within the textile industry, the mills producing finer materials and using more advanced methods bid this sort of labor away from less advanced mills and those producing coarser materials.[1]

Some contend that manufacturing industries are more likely to provide external economies than agriculture or mining. It is argued that the most important contribution of manufacturing is not the immediate expansion of total output, but its effect on the general level of education, skill, inventiveness, technological growth, and the way in which it moves people off the bedrock of traditionalism. The deduction for trade policy is that countries that would be obliged to specialize in agricultural or mining pursuits under free trade should impose tariffs to facilitate the growth of domestic manufacturing, thereby obtaining greater economic progress.

It is true that a number of countries which are extremely poor today

---

[1] Yale, Brozen, "Entrepreneurship and Technological Change," in H. F. Williams and J. A. Buttrick, eds., *Economic Development, Principles and Patterns* (New York: Prentice-Hall, 1954), pp. 234–235.

are agricultural or mineral producers. But the wealth of Iowa, New Zealand, Nevada, and Canada clearly indicates that specialization in agricultural or mineral production does not doom an economy to poverty.

In any event, several problems may prevent favorable results from protection when internal and external economies exist. First, firms operating under internal economies have a tendency toward monopoly because the larger firms, by virtue of having lower costs, drive other firms out of the industry. The beneficial effects of the tariff may thus be wiped out by monopolistic pricing, unless means are found to make the monopolist act like a competitor. Second, even if the tariff preserves the entire home market to domestic firms, the level of income in the country may be so low that the demand for their products may be insufficient to sustain the level of output at which economies (internal or external) are obtained; this condition would certainly be true of steel plants in a number of under-developed countries today. Third, if a nation has such an unfavorable factor endowment for a particular industry that the lowest costs that can be reached through economies still exceed the cost of imported products, there is no gain in providing protection. Even if bananas could be produced with falling costs in Alaska, neither Alaska nor the world as a whole would be benefited by shifting Alaska's resources out of export industries into banana production.

Finally, there is always a danger that protection to take advantage external and internal economies may increase costs abroad. If steel production is protected in Mexico, exports of steel from the United States decline. And if steel production enjoys economies in Mexico, it probably also enjoys them in America. Therefore the cost reduction in Mexico may be offset by a cost increase in the United States as American steel exports and production contract.

E.   TRADE POLICY AND THE THREAT OF WAR

In a world threatened by war, sovereign nations may forego the benefits of trade for reasons of national security.

TRADING WITH POTENTIAL ENEMIES

Free trade may improve the economic position of *each* country over what it was without free trade. If it does, the ability of each to wage war is also increased, since war potential depends significantly on economic strength. But if they are potential enemies, though both gain in an absolute sense, the one which gains less than the other may think trade undesirable because the *relative* strength of the other grows through trade. Since wars are won by the nation with greater *relative* strength, trade would hurt the chances of victory of that country which obtains the smaller share of the gain from trade.

But this presumes a conflict of interests between the two countries.

Some people believe that international trade, by bringing together the international traders of nations, spreads international goodwill, induces harmony, and reduces the conflicts leading to war. If personal contact does induce mutual understanding, free trade may be an instrument of peace.

A supporting view is that the dependence of nations on each other, caused by increased trade, makes war between them less feasible because essential imports will be cut off in time of strife. This view would promise some hope of peace in the world if nations would practice free trade. But historically they have been more inclined to fear this very interdependence because of the vulnerability it creates in time of conflict.

NATIONAL DEFENSE INDUSTRIES

In modern war, a nation may lose some or all of its foreign sources of supply. Prior to the outbreak of war, adequate alternative sources might be developed at home if domestic producers are given encouragement. The problem of whether to do so with tariffs or other means becomes important for those industries and products essential to the national defense. United States dependence on German dyes plagued its war effort in World War I as did its dependence on Far Eastern quinine and natural rubber during World War II. The American merchant marine and watch and optical instrument industries are currently deemed essential for national defense. Tariffs and subsidies help to maintain them in operation so that their goods and services and their workers' skills will be available in time of national peril.

Adam Smith wrote that defense was more important than opulence, and few Americans would trade their national freedom for freedom of trade. But even admitting this preference, complications develop, for, as Bentham replied, opulence is necessary for defense. In the age of total war, virtually everything is essential. If one industry is protected rather than another, factors are shifted to the protected industry from the others and the latter are hurt. If all save export industries are protected from imports, resources shift out of export industries to the protected ones. The export industries may also be essential to defense, e.g., the American auto industry. And if all products are equally protected or aided (exports and import-competing products alike) no resources will shift, and no one product has an advantage over another.

Furthermore, in the selection of the industries to receive protection, the policy makers are subjected to specious claims for protection on the grounds of national defense needs. The American Jeweled Watch Association, which claims its industry should be protected in the interest of national defense, asserts that, with respect to pleas for continued protection from imports on national defense grounds, the tendency among federal officials "has been to discount the security question . . . on the ground that industries involved were merely using the issue to avoid tariff modifications (*which was often the case*) . . ."[2] Is the statement by representatives of the Schiffli Lace and Embroidery Manufacturing Association such a case? Speaking of their industry, they said:

> . . . It is important to remember, however, that in time of national insecurity and peril, it was the one and only industry the United States military forces could turn to for the manufacture of all the shoulder patches and insignia . . . considered vitally necessary for the morale of our soldiers and sailors . . . no industry capable of producing such a valuable military commodity necessary for morale, should be allowed . . . to wither and become extinct because of the lowering of tariff rates. . . .[3]

The problem is further complicated by the fact that allies may be essential too. Barriers against the exports of allies may annoy them, making their governments less willing or, because of internal politics, less able to cooperate with the United States in defense efforts prior to the outbreak of war. More generally, free trade for the Free World will increase its economic strength and thus increase its military strength. Why should we impose tariffs on organic chemical imports when Western Germany can produce them more cheaply? But what about the proximity of Western Germany to Russian forces? Is Western Germany too easy prey for the potential enemy to entrust important production to them? And who precisely are allies of the United States? today? tomorrow?

Finally, the relevance of the national defense argument for protection comes into question if the next war is to be an unlimited nuclear one. Some people contend that such a war will probably not be won by the amounts of strategic items the United States is capable of producing after the war begins; the war would be over before industry could be mobilized.

F. THE PROBLEM OF DISCRIMINATION

A final qualification to the cases for free trade is that they do not necessarily constitute justifications for the removal of just any trade restriction or the reduction of obstacles to trade in particular commodities. The favorable effect on output and consumer satisfaction from an increase in the volume of trade resulting from a smaller duty on a particular product may be offset by a reduction in trade in commodities not subject to tariff reduction.

Discrimination among countries presents such a possibility. Suppose that while trade is prohibited between France and the United States, both supply buggies to Mexico; and suppose that Mexican buggy imports suffer

---

[2] Statement of the American Jeweled Watch Association to the Commission on Foreign Economic Policy. Italics supplied.

[3] *Trade Agreements Extension Act of 1953.* Hearings before the House Ways and Means Committee, 83d Cong. 2d Sess. (Washington: U.S. Government Printing Office, 1953), p. 406.

a duty equal to 100 per cent of the amount paid by the Mexican importer to the French or American buggy exporter. Assuming that buggies produced in Mexico, France, and the United States are exactly the same, they must have the same price within Mexico. The equilibrium relative price within Mexico of a buggy, no matter where it is produced, must exceed the price outside of Mexico by 100 per cent because of the duty, as in the following data:

RELATIVE PRICES BEFORE DISCRIMINATION

	Relative Price
Mexico	40 belts per buggy
France	20 belts per buggy
U.S.	20 belts per buggy

Suppose now that Mexico discriminates against French buggy exporters by reducing slightly the duty on American buggies without giving a similar reduction on French buggies. American buggies become cheaper to Mexicans than both Mexican and French-produced buggies; Mexicans are therefore induced to buy more American buggies and fewer Mexican and French buggies. Thus, the tariff reduction creates trade between Mexico and the United States, but it destroys trade between Mexico and France while reducing Mexican buggy production.

Assume that, as a result, U.S. buggy production rises by two units while French and Mexican production fall by one unit each. In consequence, supposing that relative prices equal alternative costs, the combined output of belts in the three countries rises by 20 while total buggy production remains constant: the output of buggies is unchanged because the two-unit rise in American production is offset by a fall in French and Mexican production by one unit each; the production of two more buggies in America requires a contraction of U.S. belt output by 40, the production of one less buggy in Mexico permits an increase in Mexican belt output by 40, and the production of one less buggy in France permits a rise in French belt output of 20 for a total change in belt production of 20. The effect on total output through the destruction of trade between France and Mexico is more than offset by the effect on total output through the creation of trade between America and Mexico.

With the foregoing tariff and trade changes accomplished, suppose that Mexico further reduces her duty on U.S. buggies to a level of 20 per cent while the duty on French buggies remains at 100 per cent. On the assumption of increasing alternative costs, the consequent additional shift in Mexican purchases away from French and Mexican buggies to American buggies causes a further rise in U.S. production, and it raises the alternative cost and relative price of American-produced buggies. It also reduces French and Mexican production, and lowers their alternative costs and relative prices for buggies. In equilibrium, though the price of buggies within Mexico is lower than before, it must exceed the price in France by 100 per cent and in America by 20 per cent, as in the following:

RELATIVE PRICES AFTER DISCRIMINATION

	Relative Price
Mexico	30 belts per buggy
France	15 belts per buggy
U.S.	25 belts per buggy

Given this situation, suppose a further slight reduction in the Mexican tariff on American buggies which, as a consequence of the shift in trade, raises U.S. output by two and lowers French and Mexican output by one unit each. In the Mexican market place, one of the additional American buggies displaces a French buggy and the other displaces a Mexican buggy. Note in the table above that the relative price and hence the alternative cost is still lower in America than in Mexico but now lower in France than in the United States. The substitution of an American buggy for a higher-cost Mexican buggy suggests that the effect of the shift in trade is to increase total output; but the displacement by one of the American buggies of a lower-cost French buggy suggests a fall in total output. In this example, the net result is a fall in combined belt output by 5: +30 in Mexico, +15 in France, and −50 in America where two more buggies are produced. Whereas the first slight tariff reduction raised total output, this slight reduction has reduced total output. Thus, at some point, discriminatory tariff reduction may not achieve favorable results. The net effect depends upon whether or not the rise in output attributable to the creation of trade exceeds the fall in output consequent to the destruction of trade.

Selected Readings are found after the summary of Part I.

4 Freedom of Factor Movements

Factors of production may move among nations. A case for freedom of factor movements can be made on the same grounds as the case for free trade, namely the maximization of total output. If either free trade or free factor movements can maximize output, the question arises whether or not free trade and free factor movements are perfect substitutes for each other. Even if they were, not all countries would permit free factor movements, for, as with free trade, not all persons or nations would improve their economic position. Hence, conflicts of interest arise between nations and among groups over the desirability of free factor movements.

A. THE NATURE OF FACTOR MOVEMENTS

The movement of labor between countries involves complex problems of tearing up old roots, getting passports, finding new jobs, and adjusting to new social and economic environments. Still, the nature of an international transfer of labor is comparatively simple to comprehend. The physical movement of capital is not so readily understood. Capital movements are not merely transfers of money; money is just a veil. Consider what basically takes place when one person lends another a nickel to buy a Coke. The borrower does not want the nickel; he wants the Coke. In fact, a borrower has not really borrowed anything worthwhile until he has spent the lender's money on goods or services; generally, money is no good unless it is used. The same holds true for loans between nations. If Mexico borrows dollars from the United States but does not spend them, Mexico has not borrowed goods, i.e., it has not borrowed anything worthwhile.[1]

---

[1] Because money is a store of value, money not spent now may still be useful if spent later. Also, a store of unspent foreign money held by one nation gives confidence to its citizens and to foreigners; this is discussed in Chapter 10.

The only way in which Mexico can borrow *goods* is for Mexico to import more goods and services than she exports. Lending a nickel to a friend permits him to buy more goods than his income presently allows. Lending money to Mexico allows Mexico to import more goods and services than her exports will pay for. And the transfer of capital can be made either through a rise in American exports to Mexico and/or a fall in Mexican exports to the United States. Either increases the amount of goods available for Mexican use.

If the money borrowed by Mexicans from the United States is used for financing the erection of a building in Mexico City, that does not mean, for example, that America must export more wood, cement, and other building materials as Mexico borrows goods from the United States. If American consumer goods, perhaps foodstuffs and textiles, are purchased instead, some Mexicans can leave their vegetable gardens and knitting mills to work in cement factories and lumber mills within Mexico to produce at least some of the materials necessary for building.

B.   THE EQUALIZATION OF FACTOR PAYMENTS

One incentive for the movement of factors is the greater real income that may be obtained in one nation than another. The migration of factors from areas of lower real income to those of higher real income raises total output, as we see from the following analysis.

In the example in Chapter 2 which illustrated the economic situation in both countries before trade occurred, each unit of capital earns 10¢ in the United States and 2 pesos in Mexico. Because a buggy sells for $10 and a belt for $1 in the United States, the real income of the owners of capital must be 1 per cent of a buggy or 10 per cent of a belt for each unit of capital owned, since those are the quantities which may be bought for 10¢. In Mexico, by similar calculation, the real income of capitalists is 2 per cent of a buggy or 40 per cent of a belt. Since the real reward to capital is higher in Mexico than in the United States, in terms of both buggies and belts, capital has an incentive to move to Mexico.

The effects of such a movement on the total output of both countries can be discerned from the marginal productivity of capital in both countries. Earlier (page 20), it was shown that the marginal physical productivity of a factor is equal to its real income.

Imagine that production in the two countries before trade and before any factor movements is the following:

	Buggies	*Belts*
Mexico	1,000	30,000
U.S.	5,000	70,000
Total	6,000	100,000

If one unit of capital moves from the United States to Mexico, production in the United States declines by 1 per cent of a buggy *or* 10 per cent of a belt, depending upon the industry from which capital is withdrawn. But when that capital is put to work in Mexico, it increases buggy production by 2 per cent of a buggy *or* increases belt production by 40 per cent of a belt. Production declines less in the United States than it rises in Mexico; the combined output of either buggies or belts of the two countries is increased, as shown by the following new production figures:

	Buggies		*Belts*
Mexico	1,000.02	*or*	30,000.40
U.S.	4,999.99	*or*	69,999.90
Total	6,000.01	*or*	100,000.30

As more and more capital moves from the United States to Mexico, the law of diminishing returns dictates that the marginal product of capital in Mexico declines while it rises in the United States. This follows because there is less capital per unit of labor in the United States and more capital per unit of labor in Mexico. Because of these changes, the real reward to capital falls in Mexico and rises in the United States.

When the marginal products of capital in the two countries are equalized, no further increase in combined output of the two countries can occur simply by moving capital. And, as long as there is freedom for capital movements and no costs of transportation, capital will continue to move to Mexico until the marginal products are equalized: only when the marginal products are the same in both countries is the real reward to capital the same, and only then is the incentive for capital movements removed.

Exactly the same reasoning applies to the migration of labor. However, labor will emigrate from Mexico because the real income of labor is higher in the United States than in Mexico. The results will be a fall in labor's real income and marginal product in the United States and a rise in them in Mexico until equality is reached.

The movement of one factor substitutes for the movement of the other in the foregoing respects, because in part it is the ratio between labor and capital which governs the real income and marginal product of each. For example, either the inflow of Mexican workers or the outflow of American capital reduces the amount of capital per worker in America, and either movement raises the real income and marginal product of capital remaining in the United States and lowers that of American labor.

The freedom for movement of capital and labor tends to maximize *total* output as does free trade. It would seem plausible therefore that freedom of either trade *or* factor movements would be sufficient to gain the highest aggregate output for the nations concerned.

C. FACTOR MOVEMENTS AS A SUBSTITUTE FOR TRADE

If the factors are free to move, the abundant factor becomes less plentiful in each country while the scarce factor becomes less scarce; in the above example, labor becomes less abundant in Mexico and less scarce in the United States while the reverse holds for capital. As labor leaves Mexico and capital moves away from the United States, the relative endowments of the factors of production in the two countries tend to become similar. Because international trade is founded on differences in the relative factor endowments of countries, it follows that these factor movements may decrease the volume of trade. Thus under certain conditions, factor movements *are* a substitute for trade. For example, in Mexico, where wages are rising as capital flows in and labor moves out, labor-intensive products become more expensive to produce while they become less expensive to produce in the United States where wages are falling. Some Mexican belt export producers will be unable to compete with American producers, and the volume of trade in belts will decline.

But factor movements are not a complete substitute for trade and will not always reduce the volume of trade. Some commodities are producible either mainly or exclusively in certain areas, and trade is the only way to distribute them. Movements of factors into the production of these products increases the volume of trade in them by increasing their supply.

D. TRADE AS A SUBSTITUTE FOR FACTOR MOVEMENTS

Earlier analysis showed that a nation tends to export that product which uses its relatively abundant factor most intensively and to import that product which uses its relatively scarce factor most intensively. And we saw that the expansion of trade leads to an increase in export production and a decline in import-competing production. From this we reasoned (pages 38–39) that, as trade expands, the real income and marginal product of the relatively abundant factor rise in each nation while the real income and marginal product of the relatively scarce factor fall because of differences in the factor-intensity of products. With the relative factor endowments we have supposed, this means that in Mexico the real income and marginal product of labor rise while the real income and marginal product of capital fall. And in the United States converse changes occur.

If free trade, like free factor movements, should equalize the marginal products of the same factor in both nations, the incentive for factor movements would be removed because real income would be equalized and world output would be maximized. But free trade is not likely to produce this result.

The previous analysis has assumed that the ratio of the factors of production in a country, along with the composition of output, determines the relative marginal productivity (and thus the relative real income) of each factor within a nation. Thus, the ratio of the marginal product of labor to the marginal product of capital was lower in Mexico than in the United States before trade occurred because there was more labor relative to capital in Mexico than in the United States. But the *absolute* level of any factor's productivity depends upon more than the ratio of the factors and the composition of output. Climatic elements or social and psychological forces also affect it. Differences in the "atmosphere" of production between the two nations may induce (or allow) greater output by the factors of production in America than in Mexico—differences which perhaps give Americans superior vigor and induce them to harder work and greater enterprise.

In that event, even after free trade has raised the ratio of the marginal product of labor to the marginal product of capital in Mexico and lowered it in the United States, the absolute productivity of both labor and capital would be higher in America than in Mexico. In the interest of increasing total output, factors should be permitted to move from Mexico to the United States. As long as freedom of factor movements exists, such factor movements will occur because the higher productivity in America implies higher real income, which acts as an inducement for the shift of factors. Hence, we may conclude that, while free trade will maximize the two countries' combined output *given the geographical distribution of the factors of production,* movements of the factors of production may increase total output additionally, even if free trade exists.

E. THE DISTRIBUTION OF GAINS FROM FREE FACTOR MOVEMENTS

As under free trade, a particular nation does not always gain and not every group always benefits from free factor movements.

CONFLICTS WITHIN NATIONS

The migration of labor or of capital tends to change the real income of factors within both the sending and receiving countries by changing the proportion of factors in each nation. The flow of capital out of the United States or the flow of labor into America tends to raise the real reward of capital remaining in the United States and to depress the real income of American laborers. As one professor pointed out, "The real cause of both low salaries and low tuition [in American universities] is, I am inclined to believe, that universities have not been faced with any manifest shortage of teachers. . . . Contributing to the supply [of professors] has been the impressive immigration since 1935 of scholars from other lands. . . . No liberal minded persons would deplore this inflow—it has enriched our scholarship, if not our scholars—but in accounting for the weakening of the American professor's position, it cannot be entirely put aside."[2]

Although the American public is not particularly conscious of the adverse effects which American capital exports may have on the level of real wages, partly because the level of such exports is so low, certain segments are concerned with the inflow of labor, particularly when it consists of directly competitive labor. The migration of Mexican laborers to California in 1954 and 1955 caused some anguish in California, and a number of American labor unions have consistently opposed the relaxation of United States bars to immigration.

CONFLICTS AMONG NATIONS

Gains to receiving nations

Though not every citizen of a country which receives factors of production derives benefits, the nation as a whole usually does.

An expansion of population through immigration raises output per head if the optimum population level has not been reached. A sparsely settled nation tends to have a low *total* real income, even though each person may have a high income, because of the fewness of people. Within limits, a rise in population increases total real income, and therefore creates a larger market. As argued earlier, the degree of specialization is often determined by the extent of the market. An expanding market permits cost reductions, up to a point, through internal and external economies connected with large-scale production. Such cost reductions raise real income (or output) per head. Eventually output per head declines with additional population growth because the disadvantage of each person working with less capital, land, and natural resources begins to outweigh the advantages obtained through economies of large-scale production.

But even after diminishing returns set in, the country receiving factors benefits. The addition of one laborer to a nation increases that nation's total output by the laborer's marginal product. The immigrant laborer's real income equals his marginal product so that he receives no more than he produces. Therefore the total real income of persons residing within the nation before the immigrant arrives (or the total output available to them) does not change. The arrival of a second immigrant worker, who also produces and earns his marginal product, depresses real wages and increases the real income of other factors of production. This latter redistribution of income consists partly of a redistribution of income between persons already in the country before the first and second immigrants arrived and partly of a redistribution of income from the first immigrant

[2] Clarence D. Long, "Professors' Salaries and the Inflation," *Bulletin of the American Association of University Professors,* XXXVIII (Winter, 1952–1953), 583–584

laborer to persons already in the country. That is, the second laborer gets no more than he produces (so he can not benefit through redistribution) while the first immigrant suffers a decline in his real income. The real income, and hence the goods and services, lost by the first immigrant become available to persons who were in the country before he got there. As a group, those persons have more, though laborers are worse off while capitalists are better off. The same analysis applies to the importation of capital.

Another way of looking at the gain from importing capital is to consider the consequences of capital formation without foreign borrowing. If a nation wishes to increase its stock of capital (factories, machines, roads, and the like) in hopes of raising output per man in the future, it must reduce consumption in the present, assuming full employment. To raise the capital stock, resources must be diverted from the production of consumer goods to the production of capital goods, which contribute to total output only after they are put in use. The reduction of current consumption which capital formation requires can be avoided through foreign borrowing. It was argued earlier that a nation which borrows capital must import more than it exports in order to have borrowed something worthwhile. The extra imports could themselves be capital items, in which case resources would not have to be diverted from current consumer goods to capital goods production. But the additional imports need not consist of capital goods. They may as well consist of consumer goods which, when imported by Mexico, permit Mexican resources producing similar goods to shift to the production of capital items.

Effects on sending nations

Countries from which labor or capital tend to emigrate may lose if complete freedom of factor movements exists. For example, extensive emigration of people may reduce the population below the optimum level discussed above. Complete freedom of capital movements may reduce a nation's investment income. But first let us see the gain in exporting capital. The real income which can be obtained abroad must be higher than the income that can be obtained at home if there is to be an incentive for a nation to export capital. Under competition, these real-income levels reflect the marginal productivity of capital in the sending and receiving nations. Thus, when the capitalists having investments abroad sell the foreign currency which they obtain through the earnings of their capital to fellow citizens who wish to import goods, the goods which are imported as an indirect result of the productivity of the capital abroad exceed the goods that the capital could have produced at home. Hence, as long as the real income on capital abroad is higher than at home, foreign investment benefits the nation as a whole. But this must be qualified.

Assume that the first unit of capital sent abroad receives a reward equivalent to its marginal product. A second unit depresses the marginal product of capital abroad and therefore reduces the income received by the first unit. The same is true of the third, fourth, and so on. Eventually a point may be reached where the marginal product of capital abroad is only slightly higher than its marginal product at home. The owner of the millionth unit of capital would be benefited by exporting it because it earns more abroad than at home. But his gain would be slight because the marginal productivities differ little, while the total decline in income received on all capital already invested abroad may be great (a small decline on each unit to be sure, but there are so many units abroad). If the decline in total income on the capital already invested abroad would exceed the gain to be obtained by the owner of the millionth unit, total income of residents in the capital-exporting nation drops with the export of the millionth unit.

The terms of trade

The terms of trade play a role in determining the distribution of gains from factor movements.

In the discussion of the nature of capital movements, it was emphasized that for the export of capital from the United States to Mexico to occur, American exports of goods and services would have to rise relative to her imports. And in Chapter 3 we saw that changes in the volume of trade may affect the terms of trade.

If Mexicans, having borrowed dollars in the United States, immediately spend *all* of them for American commodities, the required upward adjustment in American exports will occur smoothly. But the result is different if certain Mexicans borrow dollars in the United States and spend only *part* of them on American goods. The Mexican borrowers no doubt hope to sell their remaining dollars to other Mexicans to obtain the pesos with which to pay, for example, the Mexican workers who assist in the project for which funds were borrowed. (It may sound unreasonable for certain Mexicans to borrow dollars they do not plan to use in the United States, but if the interest rate is lower in the United States than in Mexico, it will be advantageous to do so.) If the amount of the borrowed, but unspent, dollars is large, the Mexican borrowers may have some difficulty selling the dollars to other Mexicans; in fact the Mexican borrowers may be able to sell them only by charging other Mexicans a lower peso price for each dollar than previously existed. If the Mexican borrowers get only six pesos for every dollar they sell rather than, say, the seven-peso price ruling before, the terms of trade go against the United States because everyone else will also trade dollars for pesos at this new price. At this new price, every dollar's worth of U.S. exports to Mexico will buy Americans only six pesos' worth of Mexican goods rather than seven. Only after this change in the terms of trade may U.S. exports expand by the full amount of the borrowed money, but Americans get fewer imports per export.[3] Capital movements, while in process, may therefore affect each country's gain from trade by affecting the terms of trade.

The terms of trade may also be affected by changes in the supply of commodities consequent to factor movements. If Mexico and the United States were completely specialized, the movement of capital to Mexico would reduce the total output of the American product (because fewer resources are available to produce it) and raise the total output of the Mexican product. The change in relative supplies would, unless offset by changes in demand, reduce the price of the Mexican product relative to that of the American. Mexico's terms of trade would worsen and America's improve. On the other hand, if Mexico exported belts and also produced some buggies while the United States exported buggies and also produced some belts, the terms of trade would tend to go against the United States and in favor of Mexico. A shift of capital from America to Mexico induces a contraction of America's capital-intensive industry and an expansion of Mexico's capital-intensive industry, i.e., the buggy industry in both nations. Since the marginal productivity of capital is higher in Mexico than in the United States, the rise in Mexican buggy production exceeds the fall in American buggy production, and the total world supply of buggies rises relative to the supply of belts. The relative price of buggies drops, and America's terms of trade worsen.

Thus, in sum, free factor movements, as with free trade, increase total output but do not assure that every person and every nation gains.

Selected Readings are found after the summary of Part I.

SUMMARY OF PART I

The essential condition for the development of trade is that relative prices differ among nations in the absence of trade. The over-all efficiency of a country does not affect the possibility of trade, and money prices adjust to make two-way trade profitable.

Differences in the relative factor endowments of countries, unless offset by differences in the relative demands for products, imply differences in their relative factor rewards. These differences, coupled with differences in the relative factor-intensity of products, lead to differences in relative prices.

Each nation tends to export those products which it produces relatively cheaply, i.e., the products in which it has a comparative advantage. Those

---

[3] This is a more complicated matter than suggested above. Actually the terms of trade might move in favor of the United States, depending on the various elasticities of demand and supply; these factors are discussed in pp. 250–251 infra.

products are the ones which use the relatively abundant (cheap) factor intensively. Conversely, each nation tends to import goods for which its production costs are relatively high, i.e., products in which it has a comparative disadvantage. These products are the ones which use the relatively scarce (expensive) factor intensively.

Within each nation, the opening of trade leads to a rise in the relative price of the export product and a fall in the relative price of the import product. This induces an expansion of export production and a contraction of import-competing output, accompanied by a shift of resources from import-competing to export industries.

In equilibrium, trade may be free or it may be restricted. In either event, the equilibrium terms of trade and volume of trade are attained only when each nation's exports—leaving aside capital movements—are just sufficient to pay for its imports and when the import demand and export supply of each product are equal. Also, within each nation under full employment and competition, equilibrium exists only if the relative price of each product which is produced at least covers the alternative cost of producing it; otherwise, resources shift to other employments. Depending upon the interplay of supply and demand, equilibrium may find a nation specializing entirely in the production of one product or producing some quantity of all products.

In equilibrium under free trade, aside from transportation costs, relative prices are the same in all trading nations. Alternative costs are also equal among nations because, under full employment and competition, alternative costs equal relative prices. In equilibrium under restricted trade, however, the equalization of relative prices is prevented; this prevents the equalization of alternative costs, and it restrains the shift of resources from import-competing to export production in each nation. The restriction of trade also restrains the rise in real income of the abundant factor and the fall in the real income of the scarce factor which accompanies the expansion of trade. The terms of trade of the restricting nation improve if that nation supplies and demands more than a negligible amount of goods.

In free trade equilibrium, with full employment and competition, the combined output of the trading nations is maximized, i.e., it is impossible to increase the output of one product without reducing that of another. The resource shifts accompanying the expansion of trade increase total output because of disparities in alternative costs among nations. These resource shifts continue until at least one nation becomes completely specialized or until alternative costs are equalized.

Free trade equilibrium also assures that output is distributed among consumers so as to make it impossible to increase the satisfaction of one consumer without reducing that of another. Inequalities in the relative prices of nations imply that consumers in different nations are not indifferent in their choice between the same quantities of products; one consumer can increase his satisfaction without hurting another through an exchange of commodities. When relative prices are the same, that possibility is exhausted.

Considering the economic welfare of residents of only one nation, the above arguments support a policy of trade restriction if a nation can improve its terms of trade. In that event, the terms of trade in free trade equilibrium understate the amounts of the export product which a nation can retain if its imports are reduced. Either the quantity of imports which is foregone can be more than replaced through domestic production or consumers who are obliged to forego the imports can be more than compensated for their loss with the export goods retained. However, when a nation cannot affect its terms of trade, these results cannot be obtained; the above arguments therefore support a policy of free trade for a single nation as well as for the world as a whole. Even when a nation can affect its terms of trade, a free trade policy may be desirable; there is a danger that retaliation to the imposition of a tariff will reduce the volume of world trade so much that the gain of each trading nation falls as compared to the gain under free trade.

The foregoing arguments for free trade assume that relative prices accurately reflect alternative costs. When unemployment exists within a nation, the alternative cost of producing a product is zero even though its relative price is positive. Trade restriction may induce production of that product, and, since its alternative cost is zero, world output and the output available to the restricting nation increases. But there may be better ways of removing the unemployment without losing the gain from trade.

Monopolistic practices prevent the equalization of alternative costs and relative prices. However, free trade can make monopolistic firms into competitive ones by opening markets to foreign competition, though it will not necessarily do so.

Trade restriction may be justified when alternative costs fall with the expansion of infant industries or with those subject to internal or external economies. Because goods are produced at a lower cost, world output and the output available to the restricting nation may be increased. But there are a number of problems in this policy. For example, the selection of the industries which will enjoy lower costs is an uncertain task, and, even though costs may fall, they may not fall by enough to justify trade restriction.

Nations may forego the benefits of trade for reasons of national security. A country, even though obtaining an absolute gain, may suffer a relative loss in trade with a potential enemy. However, trade may increase the chances of peace between potential enemies, either by increasing contacts or by creating such interdependence that war is impossible. A nation may desire to protect industries whose products or skills are essential in time of war. But the accurate selection of national defense industries is difficult. And, in the modern world, there may be no justification for national defense protection, either because free trade among allied nations will increase their economic strength and thus their military strength or, because of the possibility of a short, nuclear war, there is no need for a mobilization base.

The arguments for free trade do not justify the reduction of just any tariff; secondary consequences may adversely affect global output. For example, discriminatory tariff reductions create trade as well as divert trade; it is possible that the unfavorable effects on world output of trade diversion may exceed the favorable effects of trade creation.

With freedom for the movement of factors of production, factors shift their location until real incomes are equalized. This implies an equality of marginal products, which in turn means that world output is maximized.

Factor movements may reduce the volume of international trade by tending to equalize relative factor endowments, though some products can be produced only in certain areas, and movements of factors into their production increase world trade. Free trade substitutes for free factor movements in maximizing world output if free trade equalizes the absolute marginal products of factors in different countries, but this is unlikely because of social, psychological, and climatic differences among nations. Therefore both free trade and free factor movements are necessary for the maximization of global output.

Factor movements change the distribution of real income among factors within both the sending and receiving nations. Disregarding these internal shifts of income, the receiving nation benefits from factor movements on the following counts: per capita real income rises when immigration moves the total population toward the optimum level; per capita real income of people within a nation before immigration rises as the real income of each immigrant is reduced by subsequent immigrants; consumption need not fall in a nation undertaking capital formation if it imports capital. The sending nation may lose if its population falls below the optimum level, and it may lose as additional capital exports reduce the real income received on capital previously invested abroad. Finally, the terms of trade may shift during the transfer of capital and after the transfer has taken place, and the sending or the receiving nation may lose thereby.

SELECTED READINGS FOR PART I

GENERAL

Haberler, Gottfried. "A Survey of International Trade Theory," *Special Papers in International Economics, No. 1.* Princeton: International Finance

Section, Princeton University, 1955. A brief survey of the development of trade theory and the theory of policy; it also contains an excellent bibliography.

Viner, Jacob. *Studies in the Theory of International Trade.* New York: Harper, 1937. Chapters 8 and 9 survey the history of trade theory; the former chapter considers comparative advantage and the latter concerns the gain from trade.

THEORY OF TRADE

Graham, Frank D. *The Theory of International Values.* Princeton, N.J.: Princeton University Press, 1948. This study stands alone in the analysis of multicountry, multicommodity trade. A brief treatment of the ideas appears in his "The Theory of International Values Re-examined," reprinted in *Readings in the Theory of International Trade.* Homewood, Ill.: Irwin, 1949, pp. 301–330. A review article by L. A. Metzler. "Graham's Theory of International Values," *American Economic Review,* XL (June, 1950), 300–322, gives a short summary and evaluation.

Hansson, K. E. "A Theory of the System of Multilateral Trade," *American Economic Review,* XLII (March, 1952), 59–68. A discussion of world trade patterns in terms of relative factor endowments. For a criticism see Charles Wolf, Jr. "A Comment," *American Economic Review,* XLII (December, 1952), 891–892.

Kravis, Irving B. " 'Availability' and Other Influences on the Commodity Composition of Trade," *Journal of Political Economy,* LXIV (April, 1956), 143–155. An empirical discussion of a number of influences upon the composition of trade which have not been considered here.

Leontief, Wassily. "Domestic Production and Foreign Trade: The American Capital Position Re-examined," *Proceedings of the American Philosophical Society,* XCVII (September, 1953), 332–349, reprinted in *Economia Internazionale,* VII (February, 1954), 9–38. An empirical analysis of the factor intensity of American exports and imports, the conclusions of which vary from what is normally expected. For one of the critical responses see Paul Ellsworth. "The Structure of American Foreign Trade," *Review of Economics and Statistics,* XXXVI (August, 1954), 279–285. See also Haberler, above, pp. 22–25.

Meade, James. *A Geometry of International Trade.* London: G. Allen, 1952. The theory of trade in 51 graphs, with explanations.

Ohlin, Bertil. *Interregional and International Trade.* Cambridge, Mass.: Harvard University Press, 1933. Part II presents the core of his arguments on the role of relative factor endowments in international trade.

Robinson, Romney. "Factor Proportions and Comparative Advantage," *Quarterly Journal of Economics,* LXX (May, August, 1956), 169–192 and 346–363. An extensive examination of factor proportions and factor intensity, the distinction between resources and factors, the importance of heterogeneous factors, and the relation of factor proportions to trade policy.

THE CASES FOR AND AGAINST FREE TRADE

Haberler, Gottfried. "Some Problems in the Pure Theory of International Trade," *Economic Journal*, LX (June, 1950), 223–240. A diagrammatic discussion of the assumptions underlying the case for free trade with special emphasis on matters of unemployment and mobility.

Meade, James. *Trade and Welfare*. London: Oxford, 1955. Chapters 4 and 9 provide the basic arguments for free trade. Chapter 17 concerns the terms of trade. Chapter 28 analyzes the distribution of income within each nation in response to changes in trade. Chapter 14 considers the significance of monopoly. Chapter 26 presents the infant-industry and economies-of-scale arguments. Chapter 32 concerns discriminatory tariff reductions.

Vernon, Raymond. "Foreign Trade and National Defense," *Foreign Affairs*, XXXIV (October, 1955), 77–88.

Viner, Jacob. *International Economics*. Glencoe, Ill.: The Free Press, 1951. See the Introduction; also his "International Trade Theory and Its Present Day Relevance," *Economics and Public Policy*. Washington: Brookings, 1955, pp. 100–130. These are two essays on the relevance of trade theory to policy formulation. The first-mentioned contains a critical discussion of the terms-of-trade argument.

FREEDOM FOR FACTOR MOVEMENTS

Meade, James. See above. Chapter 27 concerns factor movements, the terms of trade, and the distribution of income within nations. Chapters 20–23 analyze six reasons why free trade is not likely to substitute for factor movements in the maximization of output. A brief account of these reasons appears in Meade's *Problems of Economic Union*. Chicago: University of Chicago Press, 1953, pp. 61–72.

Economics Library Selections, Series II, No. 1. Baltimore: Department of Political Economy, Johns Hopkins University, December, 1954. A useful annotated bibliography of books covering the many aspects of international economics.

PART II DEVELOPMENT OF THEORY AND POLICY THROUGH THE NINETEENTH CENTURY

5 Mercantilism

Modern foreign economic policies have their beginning in the mercantilist period, extending from about 1400 to 1800. The nation-state system was being born. The Commercial Revolution released economic activity from its traditional mold. The Industrial Revolution hastened the economic independence of individual merchants and capitalists. These events opened the way for rapid economic growth and extension of markets at home and abroad. National governments became obliged to adopt some policies toward the international trade of their citizens.

Mercantilism covered much more than foreign economic policies; it included policies on domestic agriculture and industry, on domestic prices and interest rates, on population, on poor laws and relief, on labor conditions and wages, on the fisheries and the merchant marine, on colonies, on taxation, on war, and on governmental structure. This chapter is concerned with the proposals of mercantilist writers and governmental policies regarding foreign economic relations.

A. OBJECTIVES OF MERCANTILISM

Foreign trade was a primary means of obtaining the objectives of mercantilist policy. These objectives were to increase national *power* and *wealth* so as to protect and nurture newborn states. In the words of one mercantilist: "Foreign trade produces riches, riches power, power preserves our trade and religion."[1] In this succinct statement are bound up several of the most important features of mercantilism: the emphasis on foreign trade, the desire for wealth, the search for power, and a circuitous relation shown in the need of power to protect trade and other desirable characteristics of national life, such as religion.

[1] Josiah Child, as quoted in Jacob Viner, *Studies in the Theory of International Trade* (New York: Harper, 1937), p. 112.

73

NATIONAL POWER

The mercantilist period was one in which the Commercial and Industrial Revolutions were overturning the traditional ways of doing things. The manorial system was being overthrown in favor of centralization of power in the hands of the king. And nations dissected by river tolls and road charges were being unified.

The process of cementing national economies and polities was accompanied by an increasing jealousy among newborn nations, resulting in international anarchy. Each nation sought to increase its own power as compared to others. The concept of *relative* power was recognized early; policies were frequently urged which, though they would possibly injure the user, would harm the foreign nations even more. Nations even saw in disaster abroad a help to themselves.

International anarchy was fostered by the belief that the world was in a more or less static condition. There was a given amount of wealth. Wealth and power were identified with gold and precious metals, which could be obtained only by exports if the country had no mines. The pressure to export led to conflict, for the volume of trade in the world was thought to be fairly constant. Since trade was the only way of getting wealth or power, it behooved every nation to get the largest share for itself. While one nation might be able to grow and prosper, it could do so only through the decline or impoverishment of others. Mercantilists did not generally recognize that both parties to trade may gain.

NATIONAL WEALTH

Although power was an end in itself to the mercantilist, it was not the only objective sought. National wealth was desired both as a means to power and for its own sake. Most mercantilists would have subscribed to the following relationships between wealth and power: (a) both wealth and power are appropriate final goals of national policy; (b) wealth is a necessary means to power; (c) power is a necessary means to the accumulation and protection of wealth; and (d) wealth and power are harmonious in the long run, though it may be necessary to make short-run economic sacrifices to obtain power in order to gain long-run economic growth and prosperity.[2] But proposals for attaining "power and plenty" for the nation often involved measures which also helped accomplish some individual's personal objectives.

PRIVATE PROFIT

Most of the mercantilist pamphleteers in England had a personal interest in the application and results of their proposals. Professor Viner

---

[2] Jacob Viner, "Power versus Plenty as Objectives of Foreign Policy in the Seventeenth and Eighteenth Centuries," *World Politics,* I (October, 1948), 10.

concluded, after an extensive search of the literature, that "Pleas for special interests, whether open or disguised, constituted the bulk of the [English] mercantilist literature. The disinterested patriot or philosopher played a minor part in the development of mercantilist doctrine."[3] Trading, agricultural, and industrial interests each pleaded for regulations on the others and on their competitors and for special favors for themselves—*all* urged in the national interest.

Men have changed little of their basic nature during the past five hundred years in their willingness to see their own individual fortunes as special cases of the national welfare. This is not to argue that the interests of private groups are not at times identical with that of the nation; nations relying on private enterprise generally believe that private profit is in harmony with the pursuit of national goals.

One of the distinctions between mercantilist and later foreign economic policies is the way in which private profit was seen as supporting national wealth and power. Although Adam Smith, writing at the end of the mercantilist period, asserted that "the great object of the political economy of every country, is to increase the riches and power of that country,"[4] he argued that the relatively free pursuit of profit by individuals would more or less automatically achieve that goal. The mercantilists, on the other hand, believed that the interests of private persons were often contrary to those of the state in that poor products were passed off as being of better quality; profit-seeking businessmen raised prices of some products which (in the national interest) should be sold cheaply to increase exports; and competition lowered prices of products which ought to be sold abroad under monopoly conditions (to increase the gold inflow). To the mercantilist, the private interests of certain groups had to be checked if the interests of the state were to be advanced; the interests to be checked were, of course, almost always those of "the other fellow."

B. ROLE OF GOLD

Among the mercantilist roads to wealth and power, the accumulation of gold and other precious metals was considered the best. The precious metals were identified with both wealth and power: gold was wealth and

---

[3] Viner, *Studies* . . ., p. 115. Viner quotes Davenant as follows: ". . . most of the laws that have been made relating to trade, since the Act of Navigation [1651], may be presumed were calculated rather for particular interests than public good; more to advance some tradesmen than the trade of the nation." (*Ibid.,* p. 95.) Elsewhere he quotes Sir Francis Bacon's record of a parliamentary discussion in the fifth year of James I's reign in which one speaker states that, though there is a sympathetic relation between the wealth and welfare of the merchant and that of a nation, "it was a thing too familiar with the merchant, to make the case of his particular profit the public case of the kingdom." ("Power versus Plenty . . .," p. 20.)

[4] *An Inquiry into the Nature and Causes of the Wealth of Nations,* Edwin Cannan, ed., Modern Library edition, p. 352.

gold was power. In many mercantilist writings, the terms "riches," "wealth," "treasure," "gains," "prosperity" are used interchangeably. And, though it sounds absurd today, their strong emphasis on the continued amassing of gold and other precious metals reflected the view that money was more valuable than other goods.[5] The identification of wealth with gold was not the only reason for its accumulation; almost all mercantilists argued either that it provided a national treasure in time of war or that it performed various desirable functions—as a store of private wealth, as money capital, and as a circulating medium.

STATE TREASURE

A major reason for the state's hoarding gold was to even out its expenditures during times when tax receipts might fall off; this was especially true when taxation had not yet become a normal means of financing governments.

Of somewhat more importance was the hoarding of gold as an emergency reserve. Wars were frequently fought abroad, usually with mercenaries; funds were needed to finance such ventures; gold was "the sinews of war." But neither the need for funds for the state treasury nor for war would have required an indefinitely large and increasing accumulation of gold, as was usually proposed by the mercantilists. Thus gold for a state treasure was not an adequate justification for mercantilist proposals to secure large volumes of precious metals.

STORE OF WEALTH AND CAPITAL

Hoarding of gold

Some writers argued that saving or wealth accumulation was the *primary* objective of economic activity. The storing of gold seemed the only or the most practicable method of saving. These writers criticized all consumption of luxury goods and urged various types of sumptuary legislation in order to force individuals to save their income. Since gold and precious metals were durable, took less space, and were standard in value, they were the ideal form of saving. Since saving was identified with wealth and since gold was the means of saving, the wealth of a country could increase only through the accumulation of gold. The identification of national wealth with personal saving derived from an analogy with personal finances; all men recognized that if they spent less (and therefore saved) they would become rich—so would a nation if it hoarded gold.

---

[5] As with most other generalizations, it is necessary to qualify the statement that gold was considered the most valuable item in a nation's wealth by the admission that *a few* mercantilists recognized that other commodities (such as land and houses, ships, and goods in storehouses) also constituted the wealth of the nation. See, Viner, *Studies* . . . , pp. 15–22.

Circulation of money

The proposal to hoard gold or save it in the form of plate was strongly opposed by those mercantilists who wished to increase the circulation of money. These mercantilists regarded money not only as a medium of exchange but also as an active force in expanding trade. The mercantilists who emphasized the volume of money as a stimulus to trade implicitly assumed the velocity of circulation of money constant. They then argued that if men had more money, the volume of trade and therefore of production would have to increase. Therefore the wealth and power of the nation would rise. However, some of the more ardent proponents of the circulation of money idea pursued the argument to its logical end and advocated the printing of paper money, and abandoned the idea that an increase in gold was necessary or desirable.

Capital funds

Some mercantilists asserted that, whether or not a gold inflow increased the circulating media, it would, by increasing the supply of capital funds, lower the interest rate and thus expand business activity. They regarded money and loanable capital as identical. They argued that, since interest was the price paid for money, the rate of interest depended upon the quantity of money and that a high interest rate was evidence of a scarcity of money.

Whatever the immediate purpose of obtaining gold, the direct means of increasing the quantity of money were to prohibit the export of gold and the precious metals and to force or encourage the sale of goods abroad for gold rather than for other commodities. Traders were required to return a certain percentage of the value of their exports in precious metals and were permitted only a certain proportion of gold exports.

It was very difficult to enforce prohibitions on the movement of gold, however. In Spain, which was a net importer of large amounts of gold from the Americas, penalties of loss of limbs or death did not prevent smuggling of gold to other countries. Partly because of the impossibility of enforcement, the restrictions on export of bullion and foreign coin were removed by England during the mid-seventeenth century and restrictions were relaxed by other countries. By the middle of the 1700's, little control existed over the shipment of gold. The heaviest reliance was placed on a continued surplus of exports over imports to bring in the gold and to keep it within the nation.

C. THE BALANCE OF TRADE AND TRADE REGULATIONS

For a country that had no mines of gold or silver, the only way in which it could obtain more money or treasure was through exporting more than it imported. It was considered almost self-evident that a nation should have an export surplus, that is, a "favorable balance of trade." This "balance-of-trade doctrine" was expounded quite clearly late in the fourteenth century and possibly earlier; it was current throughout the sixteenth century and employed by writers on foreign trade policy into the nineteenth century; the concept was used by American congressmen to support protective tariff arguments during the 1890's, and one still sees it today on occasion. Mercantilist regulations over external trade were directed primarily at causing an import of bullion or foreign coin so as to increase the quantity of gold and the wealth of the nation.[6] The modern techniques of tariffs and prohibitions, controls over trade and international payments, and subsidies to exports were employed throughout the mercantilist period.

TARIFFS AND PROHIBITIONS

Duties on imports were advocated by almost all mercantilists. The purpose was largely to reduce foreign purchases, though some emphasized that much-needed state revenues could be raised by the duties. Others proposed the imposition of duties so high as to prohibit imports, but prohibitive duties had some undesirable features.[7] They supplied no revenue, and they induced smuggling. Direct prohibitions were more effective in preventing smuggling of some goods. But, as practiced, prohibitions were usually accompanied by import licenses extended to favored individuals or trading companies, giving them a monopoly in trade. The extensive smuggling reduced the effectiveness of all trade restrictions.

Another check on the stringency of restrictions was the possibility of retaliation by other countries, though mercantilists disagreed as to its importance. Some argued that it would be impossible for other nations to retaliate, since all "wise" nations would have already imposed all the restrictions that it was profitable for them to apply.

---

[6] An increase in the supply of gold and precious metals was not the sole objective of the regulations Government officials imposed restrictions and the Parliaments passed laws in order to grant favors, to repay past favors to the king, and to reduce internal opposition both political and economic.

[7] One of the specific arguments employed for tariffs and prohibitions was that for the protection of infant industry. The purpose was to provide a buffer against risks and uncertainties arising from entering a new field, and the protection was to be removed as soon as the industries might be able to stand on their feet. One writer recommended a duty on the imports of all sorts of linen products for seven years, arguing that "by virtue of this tax or imposition, there will be such an advantage given to the linen manufacture in its infancy, that thereby it will take deep rooting and get a good foundation on a sudden, . . ." The idea of *temporary* encouragement of manufactures was supported by other writers; one states that "if after their improvement they can't push their own way, by being wrought so cheap as to sell at par with others of the same kind, it is in vain to force it." The practice of infant-industry protection was so widespread that another writer asserted that "all wise nations" impose restrictions on foreign manufacture for the purpose of "encouraging manufactures in their infancy." (For citations, see Viner, *Studies* . . . , pp. 71–72.)

Mercantilists advocated the restriction of low-valued exports also, to increase the favorable balance. They assumed that foreign countries would have to take a higher valued (manufactured) product if raw materials were under export prohibition. Rather than export a raw material, its use in manufacturing would increase economic activity in the nation and raise the value of traded items. Also, the prohibition of its export would lower the domestic price of the material by increasing the domestic supply and the price of the manufactured product would be lower, encouraging larger exports. The question as to the degree of manufacture desirable for exports led one mercantilist to recommend taxes on exports varying inversely with their degree of manufacture up to prohibitions on raw materials exports; he also proposed duties on imports varying directly with degree of manufacture.[8]

The prohibitions on export of raw materials were supplemented by prohibitions on capital goods and by restrictions on the emigration of technicians. The combined set of prohibitions was aimed largely at preventing the development of competitive industry abroad. The drive for colonies to develop raw-material production controlled by the metropolitan country was a reflection of the impact of these prohibitions and restrictions. Each nation tried to outdo the others in imposing its own restrictions and circumventing those of others.

COLONIAL POLICIES

The acquisition of a colony placed under the control of the metropolitan country an area which otherwise would itself have developed eventually into a nation or else fallen into the hands of another country. A competitor would have arisen or another country been strengthened. By making a colony of a foreign land, the mother country gained a larger productive territory and a place for an expanding population. It also gained a source of raw materials for its domestic manufacturing for which it did not have to pay in gold; instead, it paid by exporting manufactures. In order to prevent these advantages from being shared by others, the areas had to be shut off from all but the mother country. This was done through trade regulations. And in order for the colony to supplement and not compete with metropolitan economic development, its own development had to be controlled. This was done through both encouragements to primary production and discouragements to industrial growth.

Trade regulations over the colonies followed the pattern of those used at home. But because of an inability to administer many of them effectively, requirements were imposed over all aspects of shipping to and from the colonies. For example, the Navigation Acts required that trade with the American colonies be routed through England. There the tolls were taken and the goods shipped on to the colonies. These taxes were considered

---

[8] Viner, *Studies* . . . , p. 64.

only just, since Britain supplied protection on the seas and financed the Indian wars. Likewise, many goods shipped from the colonies had to be carried in British ships, which were routed through England. The colonies were partly compensated for these burdens by the virtual monopoly their exports enjoyed in the mother country. The burdens of the trade regulations seemed onerous but were mitigated by the ease of smuggling and the laxity of administration. The main adverse result was the higher prices which had to be paid for imports and the inability to export to other markets, which turned the terms of trade against the colonies.

Given the fact that the purpose of obtaining colonies was to enhance the wealth and power of the mother country, mercantilist doctrine led to the location of higher-valued production and exports in the latter. To prevent the growth of industry in the colonies, manufacturing was prohibited or restricted. For example, Britain prohibited colonial production of any fine woolens and the export of any wool, yarn, or woolen cloth; it prohibited colonial manufacturing of any iron products save pig and bar iron; and the manufacture of hats from fur was prohibited. The restrictions were either redundant or ineffectual, or both. The metropolitan producers were efficient enough to undersell colonial exports, or the interest of the colony in domestic manufactures was so strong that they grew up despite prohibitions. As substitutes for manufacturing, metropolitan countries encouraged the production of naval stores and raw materials through subsidies and bounties. But the larger production of raw materials only made manufacturing more attractive in the colonial areas.

The balance sheet on colonies is difficult to draw up. The metropolitan area received returns in greater trade and political control but at high administrative and military costs; the balance in their favor cannot be proved to have been positive. The colonial areas themselves benefited from the influx of capital and manpower and from protected markets in the mother country; contrarily, their progress was retarded by the lack of free markets abroad and by the prohibitions against their domestic development of industry.

SUBSIDIES AND SHIPPING PREFERENCES

Governments during the mercantilist period helped to expand exports through extending preferences to trading companies and shippers, by paying bounties to exports and by offering drawbacks (refunds) of duties on goods re-exported, i.e., goods that were imported and then exported.

Trading monopolies

Preferences were extended to imports of crown trading companies to help them over the first rigors of competition and through the first uncertainties of doing business in expanding and unknown markets abroad. But the monopoly privileges were not withdrawn once the trade was firmly established. Monopoly profits were made both in the selling of home goods in the foreign country and in buying the products of the foreign country. These profits brought in gold and provided the company a means of persuading officials to continue its privileges. Government officials could see a national advantage in the monopoly not only in its ability to push out foreign competitors but also in the larger return of gold through the higher monopoly profits.

Drawbacks

The fact that the trading companies brought goods home, as well as precious metals, raised the problem of how to get rid of the increased quantity of goods and obtain more gold. In order to foster transshipment of goods and to obtain the shipping and port business, governments extended the privilege of a drawback of duties on imported items when they were re-exported. Yet, so as to avoid injuring the export of domestic manufactures, this privilege was usually restricted in some degree to commodities which could not be produced at home.

The re-export trade was so important to England that several mercantilists proposed that all import and export duties be abolished in favor of domestic excises on consumption of foreign goods. Export duties were imposed not only to restrict trade but also to obtain revenue. But, as we can see from the analysis in Chapter 3, they fell at least partly upon domestic producers of exports. In the early 1700's, Walpole removed export duties on all commodities except those such as lead, tin, and leather, which were in such strong demand abroad that the foreigner was supposed to bear the tax. Though the arguments of Chapter 3 were not then recognized, England considered that she could move the terms of trade in her favor on these items and increase its earnings of gold. But political opposition prevented Walpole from making any extensive substitution of internal excises for import duties; the opposition arose from the traditional fear that excises would become an arbitrary power in the hands of the government against the people.

Bounties

In order to expand the export of domestic manufactures and production, most mercantilist countries paid bounties for larger export volumes. Bounties permit a seller to charge lower prices and still maintain his profits. Their purpose was to improve the trade balance by permitting manufactures to compete more easily in other countries and by preventing the growth of competitive industry abroad, particularly in the colonies.

Shipping preferences

Strong support was given the merchant marine in order to obtain the carrying trade and to build up a fighting fleet. This support was mostly in the form of indirect subsidy through preferences to the domestic shipping and shipbuilding industries and through prohibitions or taxes on foreign ship operators. Restrictions by European nations varied from none in the case of Holland to stringent ones imposed by England.

Holland had, without restrictions, attained a position during the late seventeenth century in which she was carrying perhaps half of Europe's foreign trade, and she was the builder of most European ships. She achieved this dominance through competition. Instead of requiring Dutch crews, she hired seamen of any nation and thereby paid the lowest wages. She developed a highly efficient flyboat which was light, easily handled, and fast; it required a crew of only about half that needed to handle the heavy and heavily armed "tub" used by other countries. With faster voyages, smaller crews, and lower wages, her costs were far below those of other nations. In the production of ships, she early employed the techniques of mass production, using standard designs and parts, labor-saving machines, and assembly-line methods.

In the face of such competition and in fear of imminent war with the Dutch, the British imposed regulations aimed at accelerating their own merchant marine development. The Navigation Acts of 1651 and 1660 required that British ships had to be built in England or the colonies, be commanded by a British captain, and be manned by a crew which was at least three-fourths British. Imports of certain important goods could be made only in British (or colonial) vessels, with the exception that imports from Europe might be in ships of the exporting country, also manned by a crew which was three-fourths native to that country; this regulation effectively excluded Dutch ships. Any goods imported in European ships had to pay double duties. Also, all exports to British colonies (including any from other countries) had to be shipped in British vessels. All the coastwise trade of England was reserved to British vessels. British exports to other areas were left free to be carried in any foreign ships. The purpose of this exception was to expand exports and encourage foreign ships bringing goods to England to take a return cargo. To encourage Englishmen to become seamen and to build ships, the privilege of marketing fish was restricted to Englishmen, and additional "fish days" were proclaimed to raise consumption.

Whether or not England required the restrictions to gain a strong fleet and whether the struggle with Holland for control of the seas was necessary at that time is still an open question. Adam Smith asserted over a century later that England no doubt lost economically from the restrictions but concluded that they had been most successful in gaining their purpose. He said: "The act of navigation is not favourable to foreign commerce, or to the growth of that opulence which can arise from it . . . . foreigners are hindered from coming to sell. . . . By diminishing the number of sellers, we necessarily diminish that of buyers, and are thus likely not only to buy foreign goods dearer, but to sell our own cheaper, than if there was a more perfect freedom of trade. As defence, however, is of much more importance than opulence, the act of navigation is, perhaps, the wisest of all the commercial regulations of England."[9] Besides defense, an objective of the acts was to cause Dutch shipping to decline, as it did!

The Dutch themselves attributed their decline in foreign commerce and shipping not to the regulations of the British, which many thought cost the British more than they hurt others, but to the fall in profits occasioned by high domestic taxation in Holland and to a shift in world trade patterns.[10] It is conceivable that, given the large and growing volume of England's foreign commerce, her fleet would have increased rapidly without support. Certainly, the continued large volumes of trade were of greater support to the fleet, once established, than were the regulations. And, to the extent that the shipping regulations reduced total trade, part of the natural support of her merchant marine was removed.

Other nations, such as Spain and France, were not so successful in using similar techniques to support their fleets, which suggests that factors other than regulations contributed to England's rise to undisputed mastery of the seas. The preferences were a burden on England, borne for power purposes in an age of international anarchy. In fact, all of the commercial policies of mercantilist nations were aggressive in their nature, since they saw foreign trade as a technique in the war for power and plenty—a war which had to be fought in order to gain a greater share of the fixed amount of world wealth.

D. MERCANTILISM DESERTED AND TRANSFORMED

Toward the latter part of the eighteenth century, England's foreign trade policy was closely scrutinized and began a gradual change under the impact of new ideas. Several of the basic ideas of mercantilism were discarded under the pressure of the growing sentiment for noninterference by the government and of the demonstrations by various writers of the desirability of freer trade and unrestricted gold movements. In England, the move to freer trade got a boost from the peaceful relations after the Napoleonic wars and gathered momentum during the last half of the nineteenth century. The free trade movement was not nearly so strong in other nations as it was in England. Though several other countries followed Britain's lead, the policies of mercantilism were not completely discarded. Its broad purposes of power and wealth for the nation were retained even by England but were pursued in different ways. And a variety of mercantilist practices were employed by many countries, America included,

---

[9] *Wealth of Nations, op. cit.,* p. 431.
[10] J. B. Condliffe, *The Commerce of Nations* (New York: Norton, 1950), pp. 99–100.

throughout the nineteenth century. The more recent expansion of state controls during the 1920's and 1930's caused some historians to characterize the interwar period as one of neomercantilism.

DISCARDED IDEAS AND THEIR SUBSTITUTES

What distinguishes the mercantilism of the 1400's to 1800's from foreign economic policies of succeeding periods is not, as is sometimes asserted, the change in objectives from power *to* plenty, but the different approaches and methods used to implement the continuing goals of both power *and* plenty. The major elements of the mercantilist program which were discarded were those relating to the role of gold, government regulation, and economic self-sufficiency.

Gold inflows versus "specie flow"

The idea that a continuous increase in the quantity of gold in a country was necessary to its wealth and power was attacked through the "specie-flow" concept of the way in which gold was distributed among countries.

The mercantilist writers considered that each country's balance of trade was the activating force in distributing gold among them. In the 1750's, David Hume advanced the idea that gold (specie) flowed among countries according to the general level of prices, which in turn dictated the trade balance.[11] If a nation had an export surplus, gold would flow in and raise prices within the nation. Higher prices would make it less desirable to buy in the gold-receiving country and more desirable to buy in the gold-exporting country. Thus the export surplus would be eliminated and gold would cease to flow in.

If prices were higher in one country than in another, that nation's export trade would fall off, causing an outflow of gold and increasing its domestic supply of goods; domestic deflation would result. Each country would retain that supply of gold necessary to keep its prices in line with those in other countries and would lose or gain gold as its prices rose above or fell below those abroad. It was therefore useless to restrict trade in an effort to gain more gold.

In the same period thrift was attacked as slowing trade. It was attacked also on the ground that the purpose of economic activity was not to accumulate money but to consume goods so as to satisfy wants. Consumption was promoted as encouraging further economic activity by providing an incentive to work and to take risks, thereby expanding production and the nation's wealth. The argument for de-emphasizing saving was supported by the reduced need for gold as a state treasure and for use in war.

A final blow to the importance attached to gold was delivered by those who argued that the value of money lay in its functions—especially

---

[11] David Hume, "Of the Balance of Trade," *Political Discourses,* 1752.

in providing a circulating medium. The mercantilist idea that there was a continuing scarcity of money—as evidenced by high interest rates, low prices, slack trade, or general poverty—had led to an emphasis on the need for an increased quantity of gold. But when it was shown that either bank credit or paper money would perform the same function and that a nation need not rely on the foreign trade balance to increase its money supply, these props for the mercantilist policy toward gold also fell.

With the role of gold greatly reduced in importance, the management of the balance of trade became less important, and so did any management of trade at all or any regulation of internal activity for the purpose of gaining a favorable balance of trade. But the new policies of noninterference in trade were supported in a positive fashion as well.

Government regulation versus laissez faire and free trade

The mercantilist proposals for regulation of internal and external commerce were based in part on the idea that the national interest was not always best served by permitting men to do what they thought was in their own best interest. There was no doubt in the minds of pamphleteers that the private-profit motive was the single, or at least controlling, factor in determining man's work and actions—each man trying to sell dearly and buy cheaply and each seeking the maximum private fortune. But the pamphleteers did not necessarily approve of this motive and they insisted that it be closely regulated in support of the national interest. Any economic activity contrary to the national interest had to be restricted or prohibited by the government, for if it were profitable, private individuals would pursue it.

One basis for contesting this view and proposing *laissez faire* arose from political and moral philosophy. The social philosophy of the classical school in economics included the belief that each man's search for private profit would serve other men. The checks and balances of the free market system made private efforts favorable to the welfare of the whole, much more than the regulations of a government could.

Another approach was used by pamphleteers who doubted the desirability of regulations. They queried, "Who is to govern the government?", pointing up the interests and biases of the officials who made and carried out the regulations. Those who opposed regulations asserted that most of the government's interference was in favor of special interests and that many of the restrictions were to help those who were inefficient and could not withstand competition: "Most of the statutes . . . for regulating, directing, or restraining of trade have, we think, been either political blunders, or jobs obtained by artful men, for private advantage, under pretense of public good."[12] Such statements tended to weaken the confidence of men

---

[12] Pollexfen, *A discourse of trade, coyn, and paper credit*, 1697, p. 149; as quoted in Viner, *Studies* . . . , p. 95.

in their government and made it easier to accept ideas of *laissez faire* which others were urging. The basis of much of the complaint against regulation was the inefficiency, corruption, and profiteering of the monopolies both at home and abroad; public indignation was aroused. A growing laxity in administering regulations led to freer economic activity and freer trade.

Economic nationalism versus the international division of labor

Given the conditions of international political and economic anarchy of the mercantilist period, it was not surprising to see the mercantilists proposing economic self-sufficiency or autarchy. But even in the seventeenth century some argued that the advantages of domestic trade, in which there was obviously a gain by both parties, should be sought in international trade. They argued that labor displaced by imported goods could be shifted into other production; they came quite close to formulating the benefits of specialization in terms of *comparative* advantage. The advantage of foreign trade was counted in the ability to import goods through less expenditure of labor than would be required to produce them at home.

These ideas show a fairly sophisticated grasp of the essential elements of the advantages of trade. But the recognition of the advantages of free trade in fostering a division of labor among nations was not incorporated into a program of economic action until Smith's *Wealth of Nations,* which itself relied more on the philosophical arguments for freedom than on the "practical" views of the pamphleteers. The retreat from mercantilism towards greater economic freedom was never complete, however.

NEOMERCANTILISM

The continuing manifestations of mercantilism are the protectionist policies of most all nations and the pervasiveness of state control over both internal and external economic relations.

Protectionism

Protectionist policies during the nineteenth and twentieth centuries have employed all the techniques of mercantilism, though there have been some differences in emphasis. The arguments used by mercantilists who were not attached wholly to the balance-of-trade concept were the same as those used today and during the past century. Mercantilist nations restricted imports of manufactured goods so as to increase employment at home; this action has its counterpart in the policies of the 1930's aimed at increasing domestic employment. Also, many of the pleas for regulation during the mercantilist period were forerunners of the special pleading of individual interests for protection during the nineteenth and twentieth centuries. Thus the modern protectionist, following the mercantilist, calls for restrictions on imports for the purposes of increasing production of particular items, of raising employment at home, and of supporting individual interests—all in the national interest.

State controls

Like the mercantilist, the modern state planner argues that the pursuit of private interest cannot be left unwatched by the government; the commonweal is not sought or guarded by competition of individuals. Like some of the mercantilists, modern state planners of the socialist variety argue that man should not be so selfishly motivated, but others take this selfishness for granted and wish to set up systems to check it and turn it out of pursuits harmful to the national interest. State planning of, and interference with, trade has not stopped with a channeling of the exports and imports of a nation, nor with the flow of money across its borders. It has also extended, as under mercantilism, into the control of domestic production for export and into the regulation of the monetary system so as to supplement internal and external trade controls. The extent to which state controls have remained part of every nation's economic policies and practices indicates that there are strong reasons why nations are unwilling to accept the gains possible from a freer allocation of the world's resources and from freer trade.

SELECTED READINGS

A. OBJECTIVES OF MERCANTILISM

Viner, Jacob. "Power and Plenty as Objectives of Foreign Policy in the Seventeenth and Eighteenth Centuries," *World Politics*, I (October, 1948), 1–29. This is a closely documented study showing that mercantilists gave as much weight to the objective of wealth as they did to national power.

B. ROLE OF GOLD

Heckscher, Eli. *Mercantilism*, 2 vols. London: Macmillan, 1935. This is the standard work on mercantilist policies both internal and external.

Viner, Jacob. *Studies in the Theory of International Trade*, New York: Harper, 1937. Chapters 1 and 2 present the reasons for the mercantilist emphasis on gold and discuss mercantilist trade regulations.

C. BALANCE OF TRADE AND TRADE REGULATIONS

Buck, P. W. *The Politics of Mercantilism*. New York: Holt, 1942. Chapter 2 has some supplementary materials on the impact of mercantilist internal regulations.

Ellsworth, P. T. *The International Economy*. New York: Macmillan, 1950. Chapter 3 presents mercantilist trade regulations in detail.

Monroe, A. E. *Early Economic Thought*. Cambridge, Mass.: Harvard University Press, 1946. This contains several interesting reprints of mercantilist writings.

D. MERCANTILISM DESERTED AND TRANSFORMED

Buck, P. W. *The Politics of Mercantilism*. New York: Holt, 1942. Chapter 5 examines the relation of mercantilism and modern state controls.
Ellsworth, P. T. *The International Economy*. New York: Macmillan, 1950. Chapter 4 discusses several facets of the transition to economic liberalism.

6 The Free Trade Movement in the Nineteenth Century

The period of mercantilist restriction of trade was followed by a swing toward free trade and factor movements which reached its height in the latter part of the nineteenth century. The shift of attitudes and policies was a slow and grueling struggle involving economic principles, international relations, and bitter domestic politics. The many forces impinging on trade policy are pointed up by the movement toward free trade in the nineteenth century.

At the close of the Napoleonic Wars, Latin America was undeveloped economically and held a colonial status. Africa was largely an unknown continent. Australia was primarily a penal colony. New Zealand was uninhabited by whites. Japan was isolated, and China was hardly touched by Westerners. The Atlantic Coast of the United States was settled only in spots. India was governed by a British trading company from a few coastal forts. Neither Germany nor Italy existed as nations. By 1914 this was radically changed. Between 1830 and 1878, world trade increased approximately eightfold, and, from 1820 to 1860, the physical volume of British exports of manufactures rose at the annual rate of 5½ per cent. Capital swept from economy to economy seeking the highest return. Emigration from Europe filled up relatively empty spaces elsewhere, relieving areas whose resources were less plentiful.

A. TOWARD AN INTERNATIONAL ECONOMY

The nineteenth century was an age of immense economic growth and change. Progress resulted from break-throughs in science and technology and the application of new and old inventions, acceleration of capital formation, and new forms of economic organization. Internal change was matched and supplemented by reduced government intervention in foreign trade, resulting in the closest approximation to an international economy, as opposed to isolated national economies, that the world has known.

The prime force in the expansion of world trade and economic welfare was the industrialization of Britain. The mechanization of textile production followed technical discoveries in both the eighteenth and nineteenth centuries; England provided cheap cloth to the world. Technical advances in iron and steel production in the same period reduced costs and permitted British exports of hardware, rails, cutlery, machines, and other products. British coal was exported to provide fuel for the steam engine, itself a product of British ingenuity, and for other industrial uses. Products from the textile, iron and steel, and coal industries comprised about three-quarters of Britain's exports in the 1880's. England had become the industrial workshop of and for the world.

The industrialization of Britain brought urbanization. At the start of the nineteenth century, less than a third of her population lived in towns of 2,000 or more people; by 1871, the figure was close to two-thirds. Industrialization and urbanization along with population growth required additional imports of raw materials and foodstuffs for Britain. Whereas England had been roughly self-sufficient in foods at the end of the Napoleonic Wars, by 1875 about half of her wheat and flour consumption was imported. Timber imports increased to provide materials for construction and supports for coal shafts. Cotton imports expanded with the growth of cotton textile production for both home and overseas markets. Large amounts of wool were imported in the early 1880's, half of which was re-exported.

The revolution of world trade, besides being a product of technical changes and industrialization in Britain, was also the consequence of a revolution in transport. Railroads and steamships helped to shape the international economy by reducing transportation costs among countries and by making transportation available where it previously had not been. The cost of transportation had been a serious obstacle to the expansion of trade in all but highly valued products which could easily bear the cost. For example, there was little trade in Europe in grains before 1850 except when famine prevailed; at other times the price would not cover transportation costs. The construction of railroads led to the economic penetration of hinterlands and opened up vast productive areas, such as the American prairies, making their products available to the world. Substitution of iron and steel for wood and the screw propeller for sails gave speed and efficiency to shipping, and the Suez Canal was opened in 1869, shortening routes.

The growth of mutual interdependence was assisted by the development of specialized markets. The rising volume of British raw material and foodstuffs imports nurtured the growth of dealers and brokers specializing in the purchase and sale of individual staples. Britain became the focal point of the international price system as orders and supplies came in from all over the world. The price of Minnesota wheat was determined by supply and demand in Liverpool, and fluctuations in Liverpool prices affected world-wide plantings and demand. This tendency toward the equalization, apart from transportation costs, of prices throughout the world was aided by improved communications. The laying of transoceanic cable connections and overland telegraph facilities increased the speed with which changes in demand and supply conditions anywhere could be reflected in the British markets and then passed on to producers and buyers everywhere.

Necessary to the growth of world trade was the development of international financial services. In London, a complex and efficient galaxy of financial institutions evolved to provide short-term credit to finance shipments to and from England and also between other countries. British banks cleared international receipts and payments on their books, paying sterling to exporters and receiving sterling from importers all over the world.

The foregoing changes which did so much to increase world trade and output were assisted by a retreat from mercantilist restrictions. Prior to the nineteenth century, British internal economic regulations were wiped out or lay unenforced in increasing degree; regulations on external trade were eased. During the nineteenth century, Britain accepted a virtually free trade policy, and other countries moved toward it also. By the end of that century, the British tariff consisted of duties on 15 items; these duties were low; they produced great revenues required by the government and gave little protection. The slight protective effect of the low duties was minimized by the imposition of excise taxes on domestic products similar to those imported.

Why Britain attained this virtual free trade position and how she carried, for a while, some of the rest of the world with her is a story of domestic and international politics, of scientific, technological, and economic growth, and of theoretical economic arguments stressing the gains from freer trade.

B. THE ECONOMIC ARGUMENTS

Underpinning virtually every reform movement are the arguments of scholarly men who buttress with theoretical justifications the statements and pleas of those who stand in the battle line of politics. These theories rarely receive widespread public recognition, much less understanding, but they often do affect the thinking of public officials in their formulation of policy.

ADAM SMITH'S DOCTRINES

In 1776, Adam Smith published *The Wealth of Nations,* an economic philosophy of natural liberty and individualism which provided a foundation for the growing public aversion to governmental control. Smith's view basically was that *laissez faire* was the best policy because the individual's and the national interest were the same or were at least consistent. The objective was to increase the wealth (goods, not precious metals) of nations. And this could be done by giving maximum opportunity to the individual enterpriser because, in his own self-interest, he would direct his capital to those endeavors in which it would produce the greatest value of output. While he intends only his own gain (and could not know the interest of the nation), the enterpriser is led by an "invisible hand to promote an end which was no part of his intention."[1] Smith argued that the individual is in a better position, because he knows the circumstances better, to judge where his capital will produce the greatest value than any statesman or lawgiver. Hence, the other side of the invisible-hand argument was that

The statesman, who should attempt to direct private people in what manner they ought to employ their capitals, would not only load himself with a most unnecessary attention, but assume an authority which could safely be trusted, not only to no single person, but no council or senate whatever, and which would nowhere be so dangerous as in the hands of a man who had folly and presumption enough to fancy himself fit to exercise it.[2]

The obvious implications of these views for government regulation of trade were supported by Smith's doctrine of international specialization:

It is the maxim of every prudent master of a family, never to attempt to make at home what it will cost him more to make than to buy. The taylor does not attempt to make his own shoes, but buys them of the shoemaker. The shoemaker does not attempt to make his own clothes, but employs a taylor. . . . All of them find it for their interest to employ their whole industry in a way in which they have some advantage over their neighbors, and to purchase with a part of its produce, or what is the same thing, with the price of a part of it, whatever else they have occasion for.

What is prudence in the conduct of every private family, can scarce be folly in that of a great kingdom. If a foreign country can supply us with a commodity cheaper than we ourselves can make it, better buy it of them with some part of the produce of our own industry, employed in a way in which we have some advantage. . . .

The natural advantages which one country has over another in producing particular commodities are sometimes so great, that it is acknowledged by all the world to be in vain to struggle with them. By means of glasses, hotbeds, and hot walls, very good grapes can be raised in Scotland, and very good wine too can be made of them at about thirty times the expense for which at least equally good can be bought from foreign countries. Would it be a reasonable law to prohibit the importation of all foreign wines, merely to encourage the making of claret and burgundy in Scotland? But if there would be a manifest absurdity in turning towards any employment, thirty times more

---

[1] *An Inquiry into the Nature and Causes of the Wealth of Nations,* Edwin Cannan, ed., Modern Library edition, p. 423.
[2] *Loc. cit.*

of capital and industry of the country, than would be necessary to purchase from foreign countries an equal quantity of the commodities wanted, there must be an absurdity, though not altogether so glaring, yet exactly of the same kind, in turning towards any such employment a thirtieth, or even a three hundreth part more of either. . . .[3]

Smith believed that the value of a product was determined by the quantity of labor embodied in it. So, when he suggests that a nation should import those products which can be produced more cheaply abroad, it might seem that a nation should import only those goods whose production required less labor abroad than at home. In 1817, David Ricardo, a highly successful stock exchange speculator and a member of Parliament, showed, however, that a nation might advantageously import a product which required more labor to produce abroad than was required to produce it at home.

DAVID RICARDO'S DOCTRINE OF COMPARATIVE ADVANTAGE

To demonstrate his theory of *comparative* advantage, Ricardo supposed that Portugal could produce wine with the labor of 80 men and cloth with that of 90 men, while England could do the same with 120 and 100 men respectively. Even though England was less efficient than Portugal in the production of both products because it required absolutely more men to produce the commodities in England than in Portugal, Portugal would gain by trading wine for cloth with England.

Ricardo assumed that one unit of cloth exchanged for one unit of wine in international trade. He saw that Portugal, by shifting labor from cloth to wine production and exporting the wine, could import cloth, which would require the labor of 90 men if produced at home, through the labor of 80 in the wine industry—a saving of 10 men. Conversely, England, by shifting labor from wine to cloth production and exporting the cloth, could import wine, which would require the labor of 120 men if produced within England, with the labor of 100 men in cloth production—a saving of 20 men. In terms of the analysis in Chapter 2, supposing that the quantities of labor reflect the cost of production, Portugal had a comparative advantage in wine because the ratio of the cost of producing wine to the cost of producing cloth was lower in Portugal than in England; for the same reason, England had a comparative advantage in cloth.

Only in international trade could a unit of a product requiring the labor of 80 men (Portuguese wine) exchange for a unit of a product requiring the labor of 100 men (English cloth). Ricardo held that in purely domestic trade the value of each product would correspond to its labor content. Thus, if the quantities of labor required to produce both products were lower in one English town than another, the cheapness of production in the one would attract and force resources to migrate from

---

[3] *Ibid.*, pp. 424–425.

the more expensive town, wiping out production in the latter and forcing the values of the products down to the lower town's costs of production through competition. But the same result would not obtain internationally because, in Ricardo's view, resources were rather immobile internationally. Factor immobility was a result of a "natural disinclination which every man has to quit the country of his birth and connections, and intrust himself, with all his habits fixed, to a strange government and new laws . . ." and partly the result of a "fancied or real insecurity of capital, when not under the immediate control of its owner. . . ." Thus the immobility of resources among nations constituted a distinguishing feature of international and domestic trade and values.

Ricardo considered that his doctrine of comparative advantage supported a policy of free trade:

> Under a system of perfectly free commerce, each country naturally devotes its capital and labour to such employments as are most beneficial to each. This pursuit of individual advantage is admirably connected with the universal good of the whole. By stimulating industry, by rewarding ingenuity, and by using most efficaciously the peculiar powers bestowed by nature, it distributes labor most effectively and most economically: while, by increasing the general mass of commodities, it diffuses general benefit, and binds together, by one common tie of interest and intercourse, the universal society of nations through the civilized world.[4]

JOHN STUART MILL AND THE TERMS OF TRADE

Ricardo simply assumed the terms on which cloth and wine were exchanged. The task of showing how they were determined fell to John Stuart Mill, a man who is probably as famous for his extraordinary education—for example, he began to learn Greek at the age of three—as for his contributions to trade theory. To illustrate the determination of the terms of trade, he supposed that 10 yards of cloth cost as much, measured in terms of labor, as 15 yards of linen in England, and in Germany as much as 20 yards of linen. Ten yards of cloth could sell for no more than 20 yards of linen because of the force of competition in Germany, nor could they sell for less than 15 yards of linen for otherwise British costs would not be covered and no supply would be forthcoming at all. Thus the terms of trade would settle somewhere between 15 and 20 linen for 10 cloth, the precise level being determined by the inclinations of consumers in both nations—he gave little emphasis to supply conditions —and by the requirement that the quantity of exports be just sufficient to pay for the imports of a nation, as explained in Chapter 2.

Mill emphasized that the direct advantage of foreign commerce lies in the imports a nation obtains and not, as often held then and now, in the

---

[4] *The Principles of Political Economy and Taxation,* Everyman's Library edition, p. 81.

exports of which a nation purges itself. He criticized Adam Smith, who seemed to argue that the benefit of foreign trade was that it afforded an outlet for the surplus produce of a nation.

The expression surplus produce seems to imply that a country is under some kind of necessity of producing . . . [that] which it exports; so that the portion which it does not itself consume, if not wanted and consumed elsewhere, would either be produced in sheer waste, or, if it were not produced, the corresponding . . . [resources] would remain idle. Either of these suppositions would be entirely erroneous. The country produces an exportable article in excess of its own wants from no inherent necessity, but as the cheapest mode of supplying itself with things. If prevented from exporting this surplus, it would cease to produce it, and would no longer import anything, being unable to . . . [export]; but the labour and capital which had been employed in producing with a view to exportation, would find employment in producing those desirable objects which were previously brought from abroad. . . . These articles would of course be produced at a greater cost than that of things which they had previously been purchasing from foreign countries.[5]

Thus, by exporting, a nation gains imports which it either could not produce at all or would produce at greater expense of labor and capital than the cost of the things which are exported to pay for the imports.

Mill believed that trade was valuable for a nation in the early stages of industrial advancement with a quiescent and indolent people who fail to put forth the whole of their productive energies for lack of any sufficient material inducements. He argued that the opening of trade would acquaint them with new products or would tempt them by making things cheaper, working a sort of industrial revolution in a nation whose resources were previously undeveloped for want of energy and ambition among the people. He also contended that trade is a civilizing agent, bringing together peoples of different modes of thought and action, and that commerce is "rapidly rendering war obsolete, by strengthening and multiplying the personal interests which are in natural opposition to it." Expanding world trade is "the principal guarantee of the peace of the world."[6]

C. THE EDEN-RAYNEVAL TREATY OF 1786

William Pitt, who became the British Prime Minister at the age of 24, was a disciple of Adam Smith. Pitt set out on a number of financial reforms because Britain's internal government finances were in disreputable shape as a consequence of the expenditures required to fight the American colonies. Among these reforms was a reduction of duties on imports; the high duties of the time brought little revenue because they either severely reduced imports by raising their cost or were circumvented by smuggling.

---

[5] J. S. Mill, *Principles of Political Economy,* Ashley edition, 1923, pp. 579 f.
[6] *Ibid.,* pp. 581 f.

England also needed markets to replace those lost when the monopoly over the American colonies was broken. An increase in both imports and exports could be obtained through a treaty with other nations to reduce trade restrictions reciprocally. This was the setting for a treaty with France.

The French interest in such a treaty stemmed partly from physiocratic doctrine. The first person to suggest the treaty was a physiocrat, Dupont de Nemours; the French Minister of Foreign Affairs, Vergennes, and the person who negotiated the treaty, Rayneval, were also physiocrats. The physiocrats, a compact school of French economists, had no theory of the gain from trade; in fact, they thought trade was sterile because it involved the exchange of things of equal value, i.e., it did not produce any surplus value. Their favorable attitude toward free trade arose in part from a philosophical system of liberty: the individual, motivated by self-interest, is more likely to act in accordance with the natural law than a government. Also, a treaty in which England reduced her duties on French agricultural products would be appealing to the physiocrats because agricultural production was identified with the national interest since agriculture, through the bounty of nature, produced the only surplus value in the economy; in all other pursuits, the price just covered the cost of the labor and capital used in production.

The French were also interested in the treaty as a matter of international politics for they saw it as a means of keeping the peace. The French were afraid that England would attempt to renew their war. The French Foreign Minister felt that a treaty of commerce would produce a relaxation of tension which would lead to an era of peace and friendship.

After a peace treaty was signed in 1783 in which England and France had agreed to negotiate a commercial treaty, the English were rather reluctant to enter into negotiations. Britain's internal political and economic conditions were unsettled, and the young Prime Minister was insecure. The French tired of waiting for England to enter into negotiations, and, in 1785, they raised the duties on several manufactured products from Britain or forbade their importation. (This was not the last time that duties have been raised in order to induce another nation to reduce its duties.) The French increased the pressure by negotiating a treaty with Holland, for England feared a French-Dutch alliance threatening their interests in the Lowlands. Thereafter Pitt took steps to initiate the negotiations which France desired.

In France there was no parliament to endorse or oppose the treaty after it was finally negotiated. But in England the opposition was vocal. In this early step toward free trade, the industrialists of England were split. The large-scale, progressive industries producing cotton, iron, and pottery had much to gain by entering French markets; the older industries, such as those manufacturing silk, ribbons, paper, leather, and glass, which had not enjoyed great progress in production techniques and were therefore not in condition to meet foreign competition, opposed the treaty. It was not, however, the principle of free trade, as pronounced by Adam Smith, that garnered the interest of the more progressive industries to freer trade. These very same manufacturers had, only a few years earlier, opposed freer trade with Ireland for fear of its cheaper labor, lower taxes, and the bounties given to Irish manufacturers. They did not favor commercial freedom for England; rather, they favored reciprocal tariff reductions. And the reciprocity they favored was only that with countries where industrial conditions gave the English manufacturer a favorable chance of establishing his superiority.

Opposition in England to the treaty swelled for political reasons. In the parliamentary debates, the dangers of ties with France (England's persistent enemy) were stressed, amplified by suspicion of French motives in urging the treaty.

But the treaty was approved after vigorous debate. It might have marked the beginning of an uninterrupted trend toward free trade in Europe had not the French Revolution and the Napoleonic Wars intervened. The exigencies of these two national efforts were too strong for the incipient liberal trade policy of France to withstand. Revenue needs induced higher duties and export taxes. French policy was subordinated to the aim of ruining England, the major and key antagonist in the European coalition against France, by ruining her trade. Prohibitions were placed against the importation of British goods into France in 1793. Later Napoleon instigated the Continental System under which all commercial relations between Europe and England were prohibited; a blockade of England was announced, and any ship which had called at a British port was subject to seizure.

When the Napoleonic Wars ended in 1815, French industry had expanded under protection from British competition and through governmental assistance. With peace, the French industrialists were loath to give up their monopolies of domestic markets, and they were able to obtain extensive protection from foreign manufactured goods. The French legislature, dominated by the landed interests, extended protection to agricultural items also. Thus the protection provided by war led to demands for protection in peace, and, by 1826, schemes for protection seemed to aim at making France self-sufficient.

D. POSTWAR ENGLISH REFORMS

The burden (or benefit) of carrying on the collapsed free trade movement fell to England. England first had to make up some lost ground, for her duties were higher after the Napoleonic Wars than before. Wartime fiscal requirements had obliged the government to raise them. Furthermore, the protective effect of certain of the duties automatically rose with the postwar deflation. Ad valorem duties were calculated as a given percentage of the value of the imported product. Specific duties were levied as a fixed sum of money per physical unit imported—shillings or pence per dozen, yard, quart, etc. (If the ad valorem rate of duty or the specific duty differs for various values of a product, it is called a sliding-scale duty. And a combination of an ad valorem duty and a specific duty on a given product is a compound duty.) With the postwar deflation driving down the prices of British imports, England's specific duties became a greater percentage of the value of the imports on which they were imposed; thus the relative tax burden on British imports rose.

The analysis in Chapter 3 showed that tariffs hurt the export interests of the nation imposing them. The expanding industrial sector of Britain became increasingly restless as the higher burden of English duties raised the cost of raw material imports and reduced imports which, in turn, reduced the ability of foreign nations to buy England's manufactured products. In 1820 a group of London merchants petitioned the Parliament with the following rather astute economic arguments:

> That foreign commerce is eminently conducive to the wealth and prosperity of a country, by enabling it to import the commodities for the production of which the soil, climate, capital, and industry of other countries are best calculated, and to export in payment those articles for which its own situation is best adapted.
>
> That freedom from restraint is calculated to give the utmost extension to foreign trade, and the best direction to the capital and industry of the country.
>
> That the maxim of buying in the cheapest market, and selling in the dearest, which regulates every merchant in his individual dealings, is strictly applicable as the best rule for the trade of the whole nation.
>
> That a policy founded in these principles would render the commerce of the world an interchange of mutual advantage, and diffuse an increase of wealth and enjoyment among the inhabitants of each state. . . .
>
> That the prevailing prejudice in favor of the protection or restriction system may be traced to the erroneous supposition that every importation of foreign commodities occasions a diminution or discouragement of our own productions to the same extent, whereas it may be clearly shown that although the particular description of production which could not stand against unrestrained foreign competition would be discouraged, yet, as no importation could be continued for any length of time without a corresponding exportation, . . . there would be an encouragement, for the purpose of that exportation, of some other production to which our situation might be better suited, thus affording . . . a more beneficial employment to our capital and labour.[7]

Such arguments supported William Huskisson, President of the Board of Trade, in making a number of trade reforms. During the 1820's, he simplified customs regulations and reduced from 1,500 to 11 the number of acts regulating trade. He removed a large number of duties on raw

---

[7] Quoted in F. W. Hirst, *Free Trade and Other Fundamental Doctrines of the Manchester School* (London: Hager, 1903), pp. 118–119.

material imports and relaxed restrictions on others. Yet his reforms were limited, for the protectionist cult still remained strong in England.

In his pleas before Parliament for tariff reduction or for the removal of prohibitions on imports, Huskisson gave special emphasis to the favorable effects of competition. According to him, but contrary to the analysis in Chapter 3, lower trade barriers would hurt no one. The consumer would benefit through lower prices. The producer would be stimulated, by increased foreign competition, to employ new production techniques and reduce costs. Contrarily, protection created mediocrity and, in eliminating competition, destroyed the best incentive for excellence. Finally, he believed that a reduction of trade restrictions by Britain would set an example to be followed by other states and, by lessening tariff competition, would go far to bring international harmony.

Through a series of treaties with other countries Huskisson removed some of the discrimination under the Navigation Acts against foreign shipping. These treaties were necessitated by the fact that the United States and some European nations had retaliated by discriminating against British shipping. As one economist of the time put it, "Navigation laws and restrictive regulations are weapons we can no longer wield with success. We have taught others to use them with equal dexterity and more effect."[8] Adam Smith had excepted the Navigation Acts from his attacks on mercantilist restrictions because of their importance to the development of England's naval power and defense. But it is doubtful that they were needed after 1815, because Nelson's victory at Trafalgar had made the English fleet supreme and peace reigned.

One scholar summed up the British policy after the Napoleonic Wars as follows:

> Liberty from the many restraints of parliamentary acts was the central strand of the new policy. It was accepted by Great Britain out of the necessity to breakdown protection in Europe, in order to have a readier market for the accumulating output of her industries. It was the lusty call of self-interest that directed her to open the doors of her home markets. Her commercial and industrial power no longer rested on national protection. Her industries had grown to vigorous manhood. They no longer feared rivals, for they were robust enough to be confident of victory in competition. Their imperative need was wider markets attained through freedom of exchange with other states. Without this, Britain's early industrialization was valueless, because her industries could not grow.[9]

Bismarck, in justifying protection for Germany much later in the century, charged that Britain had moved toward free trade only when her competitive superiority was assured. In his view, this superiority had been

---

[8] McCulloch, quoted in Alexander Brady, *William Huskisson and Liberal Reform* (London: Oxford, 1928), p. 93.

[9] *Ibid.*, p. 111.

nurtured under protection. There is truth in this, but another interpretation, at least of the postwar reforms, is that England was shaking off the greater burden of protection which had arisen during and after the Napoleonic Wars.

E. THE GERMAN ZOLLVEREIN

While the free trade movement on the European continent failed to find rebirth in France after the Napoleonic Wars, the liberal spirit caught hold in Prussia and advanced under her tutelage through the other German states. Previously, each of the 39 separate German states had maintained tariffs against each others' products, and within Prussia provinces had imposed duties against each others' products.

In 1818, the Prussian monarch, whose advisers were greatly influenced by the doctrines of Adam Smith, wiped out the internal customs barriers and set a low tariff against imports from outside of Prussia. Public support for this policy came from a significant portion of Prussia's agricultural population, which was directly interested in increasing its exports of agricultural products. The coastal towns on the Baltic also desired an expanded trade because of their shipping interests. The Prussian government soon began to exert pressure on those independent states which were completely surrounded by Prussian territory to form a customs union with her, i.e., to remove all tariffs on trade with Prussia, to adopt the Prussian tariff for all imports from elsewhere, and to receive a proportion of the joint customs revenue to be collected by Prussia on imports into the combined areas. One method of gaining the cooperation of these surrounded states was the imposition of transit duties by Prussia on their shipments through her territory. Power politics was strongly mixed with this free trade movement as Prussia was contending for the leadership of the German states. This leadership had fallen to Austria when the Congress of Vienna (1815) had set up a very loose confederation of states under the presidency of Austria.

Suspicion of Prussia developed among the German states as Prussia's economic borders expanded. But a conciliatory policy paved the way for the extension of the customs union which ultimately led, through a series of treaties, to the Zollverein (Customs Union) of 17 states in 1834. It was renewed and expanded on several occasions thereafter, but it was always subject to the danger of pressure from Austria. Largely oblivious of what was going on in her own back yard until 1833, Austria soon thereafter attempted to negotiate a larger union of both Austria and the Zollverein, which Prussia opposed for political reasons. A strong weapon which Prussia had for keeping Austria out of the Zollverein was the latter's low tariff, which Austria would not stomach. Austria also attempted to induce the withdrawal of some of the more protectionist-minded southern German states which might be attracted by the high-tariff policies of Austria. Austria's efforts failed, and the Zollverein persisted as a free trade area with a low common tariff against the rest of the world until the 1870's.

The community of interests, though by no means complete, which was created among German states through the Zollverein prepared the way for their political unification under Bismarck. Prussia had qualified herself for the political leadership of Germany and accustomed the German states to cooperate without Austria.

F.   THE CORN LAWS OF ENGLAND

The scene of dramatic progress toward free trade shifted to England in the 1840's. The most entrenched element of British protection, the Corn Laws or the tariff on grain imports, was repealed in 1846 after a political debate which, in its particulars, was little more than a class conflict. Chapter 3 showed that the expansion of trade, e.g., through the reduction of tariffs, would raise the real income of the relatively abundant factor and lower that of the relatively scarce factor; in this debate, the protection minded landowners were placed against the rising manufacturing capitalists.

In 1840, a parliamentary committee noted that 10 of the 1,150 items in the British tariff produced 90 per cent of the tariff revenue. After re-instituting the income tax as a substitute source of revenue, Prime Minister Peel was able to clear away some of the complex, detailed, and confusing duties; 750 duties were reduced in 1842, and another 500 in 1845. But Peel retained the tariff on grain imports which was desired by the agricultural interests so that England would not have to rely on foreign sources for such an essential product. He also considered that the Corn Laws were compensation to the landowners, who were subject to special governmental burdens.

Agitation for the reduction of the tariff on grain imports had been developing since the time of Huskisson's reforms when its reduction was considered by some as an equitable *quid pro quo* for the reduction of protection of British manufacturers. Manufacturers were instrumental in the formation of the Anti-Corn-Law League in 1839; under the leadership of Richard Cobden and John Bright, it became the energizing force of a popular movement against the Corn Laws and eventually against all tariffs. English manufacturers believed that free trade would increase their exports by increasing English imports and by inducing other countries to follow England's example of reducing tariffs. Some also believed that free trade in corn would reduce the cost of food for the workers, permit a reduction in money wages, and thereby improve the manufacturers' competitive position in foreign markets. (A theoretical justification of this latter line appeared in Ricardo's discussion of land rent and related matters; he argued that land rents and profits on capital moved inversely since higher prices of food, which increased land rents, would cause higher money wages and thus cause lower profits.) Contributions rolled into the Anti-Corn-Law League, and, with a staff of some 800 people, it distributed nine million free trade tracts in 1843 alone and provided numerous speakers.

The conflict extended beyond that between the landed interests and the exporting manufacturers. The Chartists, a working-class movement, opposed free trade in grain for fear that agricultural laborers would be thrown out of work and would be driven to the cities to compete with the factory workers. They debated against the League propagandists and even resorted to riots to break up League meetings.

The landlords attempted to counter the Anti-Corn-Law League's propaganda with a league of their own. But they were incapable, in spite of their financial strength, of mounting an offensive equal to that of the League. An inborn conservatism prevented them from appealing to the populace: such action would enhance the political prestige of the individual voter; it would lend support to ideas of democracy, which had not fully arrived in England, as evidenced by the fact that the franchise was not yet extended to all males; and it suggested mass action which the landed aristocracy opposed, for they still remembered the bloody riots of the French Revolution. These restraints plus a faith in Peel's government made the landed gentry singularly incapable of using the techniques of the Anti-Corn-Law League.

The debates on the Corn Laws in and out of Parliament were fervid, and there was great tension throughout England. The landlords, who perpetuated the Corn Laws through their control of Parliament, were charged with raising the price of food to the workingman and were called everything from power-proud plunderers to bread stealers. Robert Peel was hanged in effigy. The landed interests responded by challenging the motives of the manufacturers, arguing that they desired lower wages through cheaper bread for their own benefit. To show that the manufacturers were not pleading for a lower grain tariff because they were interested in the workers' welfare, the landowners publicized the unhappy working conditions of factory laborers.

A combination of events was the immediate cause of the repeal of the Corn Laws in 1846. Peel was converted to free trade in grain by the force of Cobden's arguments in Parliament and by his own investigations. He found, after studying costs and prices in Europe, that the volume of likely imports would not be sufficient to hurt the British farmer, particularly if the landlord made use of the scientific advances available to agriculture. He also recognized that the Corn Laws were an exception to an extremely successful policy of tariff reduction, a policy in which he had played so important a part and which had brought prosperity to England after the depressed years immediately prior to 1842. In addition, the Corn Laws were a certain cause of bitter and dangerous animosity in the body politic, so strongly had the Anti-Corn-Law League's activities gripped parts of public opinion. When England had a bad harvest of grain and when there was a failure of the Irish potato crop in 1845, Peel decided that the only effective means of easing the food shortage would be the removal of the barriers to the importation of grain.

What is surprising is that the House of Commons and the House of Lords agreed with him, though reluctantly, despite the fact that they were dominated by the landed gentry which the Corn Laws protected. Part of the explanation lies in party loyalty, for the British governmental system had developed great reliance on the leadership of the office of the Prime Minister. But the landed gentry had also recognized that this was the time for retreat in the interest of self-preservation. A failure to repeal the Corn Laws might have led to public indignation strong enough to attack the foundations of the British government. This was not the first time that the unrepresentative oligarchy which governed England had retreated in the face of pressure to change that which they held dear. The Catholic Emancipation and the Reform Bill of 1832 were both reluctantly approved.

The corn-law issue could not be separated from the many other conflicts in this age of reform. Cobden must have recognized this when he set about to get 700 Manchester ministers to declare the Corn Laws as "opposed to the law of God, anti-scriptural, and anti-religious." By infusing a religious tone, Cobden exploited the division between the landed aristocracy and the middle class over the Church of England versus the Protestant Dissent.

When the repeal was complete, the Parliament eased the burden of agricultural adjustment by providing governmental loans to farmers. And, in spite of dire predictions, British agriculture did not suffer significantly at the hands of foreign competition until a quarter of a century later.

Following this most important victory for free trade, Britain required her colonies to have low tariffs. The free trade policy was adopted by other nations, particularly Belgium, Denmark, and Holland, as free traders had predicted would happen when England set the right example.

G. THE COBDEN-CHEVALIER TREATY OF 1860

After further tariff reductions in 1853, the free trade movement in England paused for the Crimean War. But, in 1860, renewed efforts brought England almost to free trade and started France toward free trade again. The instrument was the Cobden-Chevalier Treaty of 1860 in which the two nations reciprocally reduced trade restrictions.

Just prior to this treaty, relations between France and England were far from cordial. Louis Napoleon was attempting to annex two Italian states, much to the displeasure of the British queen because it would weaken the Austro-Hungarian monarchy. The English resented the fact

that the French had, in the Crimean War, signed a peace treaty with
Russia before the Russian army could be defeated in a predominantly
British victory. A plot by a deposed French royal family to assassinate
Emperor Napoleon which was hatched on British soil raised French ire.
Many Englishmen thought that Napoleon III was planning to invade
England, and a corps of volunteers was organized in England. On both
sides of the Channel, the parties initiating the treaty considered it a means
of reducing tension as well as a move in the right direction economically
—toward free trade.

The initiator of the treaty idea was Michel Chevalier, the French
counterpart of Richard Cobden. Paradoxically, for all his free trade con-
victions, Chevalier believed in extensive governmental control of economic
activity, being a Saint-Simon socialist. Even more surprising is the fact
that Chevalier had to convince Cobden that the reciprocal reduction of
duties by treaty was desirable. Cobden, as with a number of doctrinaire
free traders in England, believed that tariff reductions were so beneficial
that any country should reduce its tariffs without demanding reciprocal
action by other countries. To retain tariffs in order to be able to give tariff
reductions in future treaty negotiations with other countries makes, as
Sir James Graham put it earlier, "the folly of others the limit of our own
wisdom." (Note that this argument does not allow for the more favorable
effects of reciprocal reduction on England's terms of trade than if England
were to reduce her tariffs alone.)

But Cobden was won over to Chevalier's cause. The need to reduce
tension between the two countries was one element in his conversion, and
another was that Chevalier convinced him that there was no other way
by which France could proceed to lower her tariffs. The French legislature
was strongly protectionist, and the bulk of the Frenchmen favored protection. France was a peasant democracy; there was no landed aristocracy
as in England which could be charged with stealing bread from the workers'
mouths. The numerous small manufacturers of France did not have the
ambitions of English manufacturers for export markets. If free trade was
to come to France, its proponents had to detour around the legislature and
avoid publicity. Under the French constitution, the emperor, who was then
rather liberal and probably a free trader, could effectuate duty reductions
without legislative approval if they were part of a treaty with a foreign
state. The situation showed the desirability of having an administrative
tariff rather than a legislative one when the objective was free trade.

To reduce the opportunity for the protectionists to organize public
opinion against the treaty, the negotiations were carried out in the greatest
secrecy. Even some of the ministers of the French government had to be
kept ignorant of the negotiations. "The Treaty of 1860 was signed for
France through an act of autocratic power in violation of public opinion
and in defiance of the well-known views of the majorities in both houses

of the French parliament."[10] To reduce the difficulties of adjustment to lower duties, the government made loans available to industry, just as England had done for agriculture after the repeal of the Corn Laws.

The unconditional most-favored-nation clause was a significant part of this treaty. It had appeared in treaties before 1700 and was standard in treaties beginning in the second half of the eighteenth century. The clause required each party to the treaty to apply to the other's products as low duties as were given to imports from any other country. Hence, as among foreign nations, there would be no specially favored nation. For example, given the most-favored-nation clause in the English-French treaty, if France reduced duties on certain imports from the Zollverein, then the lower duties would also be applied to the same British goods. In this way, the Zollverein would not be favored over England with regard to specific commodities, i.e., nondiscrimination prevailed.

One of the reasons why free traders had opposed treaties involving reciprocal reductions of duties was that they had sometimes been used as instruments of economic warfare; they discriminated against nations not party to a treaty because the negotiated tariff reductions were not generalized to outsiders. The Cobden-Chevalier Treaty, with its most-favored-nation clause, showed that bilateral negotiations could be used successfully to obtain free trade without discrimination. England immediately generalized to other nations the tariff concessions which she gave to France under the treaty. But France did not. Other nations, desiring to enter their goods in the rich French market and concerned over the discrimination by France against their products, negotiated treaties with France which lowered duties and provided for most-favored-nation treatment. These other nations also negotiated among themselves to the same effect. Thus France led Europe toward free trade and into a network of treaties which governed duties and prevented discrimination.

H.   THE DRIFT TO PROTECTION

Starting in the late 1870's, there was a gradual tendency toward protection in Europe. A number of forces explain the reversal of the free trade movement. The fiscal requirements of governments, though perhaps of minor importance, led to increased duties in a number of cases. The great depression from 1873 to 1896 increased demands for protection. This was a period of relative economic stagnation that started with the depression of 1873–1879—the longest and severest depression yet seen in the nineteenth century. Protection was claimed anew by European agriculture which suffered intense competition from Russian and American

---

[10] Arthur Dunham, *The Anglo-French Treaty of Commerce of 1860 and the Progress of the Industrial Revolution in France* (Ann Arbor: University of Michigan, 1930), p. 59.

grain consequent to the improvement of transportation facilities. Germany, France, and Italy responded to the flood of foreign grain by raising tariffs, partly for national defense reasons such as a fear of dependence on foreign grain. Denmark, however, shifted to animal husbandry. England shifted further out of agriculture, for food taxes were unpopular after the repeal of the Corn Laws and the soldiers which farm life could produce were not needed.

The fact that the Industrial Revolution arrived on the European continent after it had occurred in England also played an important role in the return to protection. Whereas England had no competitors to interfere with her industrial growth and whereas free trade would help her industrial progress by increasing export markets and providing raw materials, the same could not always be said for those countries, such as Germany, that were latecomers in industrial progress. In a number of instances, in Europe and in America, as described in the next chapter, tariffs were raised to further industrial progress.

Bargaining between nations on tariffs continued during the drift toward protection. Treaties, often a decade in duration, provided stability of duties during their terms, giving businessmen assurance that their activities would not be hindered by tariff upheavals. Nondiscrimination continued in force, partly through the threat of discrimination; nations set high priority on obtaining equal treatment for their exports, and the tariff systems in use permitted a nation to discriminate against the products of any other nation which discriminated against its exports. The system finding greatest use was the general-and-conventional tariff, which resulted in a double-column schedule of duties. The legislature would establish duties. But the executive branch of the government would negotiate treaties (conventions) which granted lower duties to other countries and provided for most-favored-nation treatment; a nation would usually generalize these lower duties only to those countries which did not discriminate against its exports.

With an attitude of obtaining as great duty reductions *from* other nations as possible, governments often padded their tariff schedules just prior to tariff negotiations by legislating rates well above what they actually needed for domestic protection and revenue. They hoped that by offering greater concessions in their own tariffs, they could obtain greater concessions for their exports from other countries. When practiced by both sides, such procedures led to tariff wars, causing severe dislocation of trade and much animosity. Sometimes the failure of negotiations left a nation with a padded tariff which endured and which was badly adjusted to the requirements of the country. Tariff bargaining, once nations begin to pad their tariffs, is a kind of poker in which all the players can lose, and once tariff padding begins there is a strong incentive for all nations to pad their tariffs in order to protect their bargaining strength.

International politics continued to affect tariff policy. Unlike the previous period of English dominance, its role tended to favor increased protection. While peace is not a sufficient condition for free trade, it helps by removing fears of dependence. The unification of Germany under Bismarck broke the particular balance of power in Europe which England had worked so hard to maintain. As political animosities developed among nations, tariff wars increased. To be sure, trade treaty negotiations were sometimes used as instruments of peace, as in the two English-French treaties discussed, but even then a competitive power element was involved. For example, the French dangled a treaty before Italy as an inducement for her withdrawal from the Triple Alliance; when the negotiations failed, one of the bitterest economic wars of the period ensued.

The political frictions were reflected in minute aspects of national prestige; for example, French-Italian negotiations were long delayed over the question of whether Rome or Paris should be the site of the negotiations. The growing nationalism of the late nineteenth and early twentieth centuries produced an environment unfavorable to free trade. The emphasis on patriotism and on national prestige reduced the sensation of participation in a world economy and enhanced the citizen-state relationship. Political borders became economic boundaries, and after World War I, nations found a variety of reasons for and means of restricting their international economic relations, which we will examine in Parts III and IV.

SELECTED READINGS

A. TOWARD AN INTERNATIONAL ECONOMY

Ashworth, William. *A Short History of the International Economy*. London: Longmans, 1952. Chapter 6 provides a broad sweep of the development of the international economy after 1850.

Clapham, John H. *An Economic History of Modern Britain*, 2 vols. Cambridge: Cambridge University Press, 1926, 1932. Chapter 12 of Book II and Chapters 6 and 7 of Book III present details which are useful because the growth of the international economy was centered on Britain.

Condliffe, J. B. *The Commerce of Nations*. New York: Norton, 1950. Chapter 10 describes the evolution of trade during the nineteenth century; it is particularly good on the marketing process.

Ellsworth, Paul T. *The International Economy*, New York: Macmillan, 1950. Chapter 9 presents the role of Britain in the development of the international economy.

B. THE ECONOMIC ARGUMENTS

Mill, John Stuart. *The Principles of Political Economy*. Chapters 17 and 18 of Book III concern the theory of trade and its implications for trade policy.

Ricardo, David. *The Principles of Political Economy and Taxation*. Chapter 7 includes his discussion of comparative advantage.

Smith, Adam. *An Inquiry into the Nature and Causes of the Wealth of Nations.* Book IV, which is primarily an attack on mercantilism, presents Smith's views on trade and trade policy.

C. EDEN-RAYNEVAL TREATY

Bloomfield, Arthur. "The Foreign Trade Doctrines of the Physiocrats," *American Economic Review,* XXVIII (December, 1938), 716–735. Though not specifically related to the treaty, the importance of physiocratic ideas in initiation of the treaty makes this article useful.

Bowden, Witt. "The English Manufacturers and the Commercial Treaty of 1786 with France," *American Historical Review,* XXV (October, 1919), 18–35. Particularly useful on the attitudes of British manufacturers toward the treaty.

Rabb, Reginald. *The Role of William Eden, First Baron Auckland, in William Pitt's Liberal Trade Policy.* New York: Columbia University Press, 1942. Chapter 4 reports the events leading up to and the reactions to the treaty.

Rose, J. H. "The Franco-British Commercial Treaty of 1786," *English Historical Review,* XXIII (October, 1908), 709–724. Includes material on how the French finally induced England to negotiate the treaty.

D. POSTWAR ENGLISH REFORMS

Brady, Alexander. *William Huskisson and Liberal Reform.* London: Oxford 1928. Chapters 4 and 5 provide a discussion and interpretation of the trade reforms in Britain after the Napoleonic Wars.

Imlah, Albert. "The Fall of Protection in Britain," *Essays in History and International Relations in Honor of George Hubbard Blakeslee,* ed. by D. C. Lee and G. E. McReynolds. Worcester, Mass.: Clark University Press, 1949, pp. 306–320. See this essay for the argument concerning the burden of tariffs after the Napoleonic Wars.

Redford, Arthur. *Manchester Merchants and Foreign Trade.* Manchester: Manchester University Press, 1934. This study concerns mainly the attitudes and policies of members of the Manchester Chamber of Commerce in the struggle for free trade. Chapter 10 covers the period from 1785 to 1828 and Chapter 11 continues through the repeal of the Corn Laws.

E. THE ZOLLVEREIN

Henderson, W. O. *The Zollverein.* Cambridge: Cambridge University Press, 1939. A comprehensive study.

Viner, Jacob. *The Customs Union Issue.* New York: Carnegie Endowment for International Peace, 1950. Pages 97–105 present a brief history and analysis of the Zollverein.

F. THE CORN LAWS

Barnes, D. G. *A History of the English Corn Laws.* London: Routledge, 1930. This is more comprehensive and detailed than the analysis by Fay. Chapter 11 provides a useful report of the activities of the Anti-Corn Law League and of the debates leading up to the repeal of the Corn Laws.

Clark, G. Kitson. "The Repeal of the Corn Laws and the Politics of the Forties," *Economic History Review,* second series, IV (1951), 1–13. Also, "The Electorate and the Repeal of the Corn Laws," *Transactions of the Royal Historical Society,* fifth series, I (1951), 109–126. These essays cast light on the relationship between the political setting and the repeal of the Corn Laws.

Fay, C. R. *The Corn Laws and Social England.* Cambridge: Cambridge University Press, 1932. A series of analyses of the Corn Laws starting from 1660, including a chapter on the effects of the law on corn prices.

Morley, John. *The Life of Richard Cobden,* 2 vols. London: Macmillan, 1908. Chapters 6 through 16 of this brilliant biography deal chiefly with the corn-law struggle and the motives, hopes, disappointments, and techniques of the major protagonist.

Mossé, George. "The Anti-League: 1844–1846," *Economic History Review,* XVII (1947), 134–142. A discussion of the activities of and the reasons for the failure of the landlords' organization favoring the Corn Laws.

G. THE COBDEN-CHEVALIER TREATY

Dunham, Arthur. *The Anglo-French Treaty of Commerce of 1860 and the Progress of the Industrial Revolution in France.* Ann Arbor: University of Michigan, 1930. The best and most comprehensive source on the treaty.

Haight, F. A. *A History of French Commercial Policies.* New York: Macmillan, 1941. Chapter 2 provides a brief discussion of the treaty.

H. THE DRIFT TO PROTECTION

Harvey, Walter B. *Tariffs and International Relations in Europe.* Chicago: University of Chicago, 1938. A description and analysis of a number of instances in which international politics and tariff policy were mixed from 1860 to 1914.

Kindleberger, Charles P. "Group Behavior and International Trade," *Journal of Political Economy,* LIX (February, 1951), 30–46. An analysis of the differences among countries in their responses to the fall in the price of grain.

Page, T. W. *Memorandum on European Bargaining Tariffs.* Geneva: League of Nations, 1927. A brief discussion of the tariff systems used in Europe prior to and after World War I, with special reference to their bargaining features, including tariff padding.

United States Tariff Commission. *Reciprocity and Commercial Treaties.* Washington: Government Printing Office, 1919. Part III discusses in detail the commercial policies and tariff systems of Continental Europe from 1860 until World War I.

Useful summaries of trade policy in the nineteenth century are found in the following:

Ashley, Percy. *Modern Tariff History,* 2nd ed. London: Murray, 1910. Part I concerns Germany from the formation of the Zollverein and Pt. III concerns France from the Revolution.

Bastable, C. F. *The Commerce of Nations,* 10th ed. London: Methuen, 1927. Chapter 6.

Bowden, W., M. Karpovich, and A. P. Usher. *An Economic History of Europe since 1750.* New York: American Book, 1937. Chapters 16–18 and 30.

Isaacs, Asher. *International Trade: Tariff and Commercial Policies.* Homewood, Ill.: Irwin, 1948. Chapter 17 concerns European nations.

Rees, J. F. *A Short Fiscal and Financial History of England, 1815–1918.* London: Methuen, 1921. Chapters 2–5.

United States Tariff Commission. *The Tariff and Its History.* Washington: Government Printing Office, 1934. Pages 15–61 give concise histories of the tariff policies of a large number of countries.

7 American Protectionism, 1789-1913

The United States rose during the nineteenth century from colonial status to that of a great power. The means by which it did so have been carefully examined by other, especially new, nations, for they have desired to make similar progress. One of the major techniques used was the restriction of trade relations with other countries. This was sometimes done purposely through commercial policy; at other times it was the incidental result of war. The wars, in turn, tended to induce restrictive commercial policies in the postwar periods.

The history of U.S. commercial policy prior to World War I is that of the tariff. The U.S. government early limited itself to the use of the tariff both in obtaining revenue and carrying out its trade policy. Import duties were imposed or removed, raised or lowered, when governmental finances and changes in protectionist sentiment dictated. This mixture of revenue and protective duties led to some highly complex and inappropriate measures. The most protective of duties would preclude the entry of goods, thus reducing revenue; a duty low enough to allow large imports and bring high revenue was not likely to be very protective.

The movements in the U.S. tariff reflect also a host of purely political conflicts. Some of these issues were fabricated for campaign purposes, but others arose from basic conflicts of interest. The tariff was generally raised for protection both in peacetime and as an aftermath of war.

From an economic standpoint, the U.S. tariff was modified in the light of changing conditions of production and trade during the various stages of economic development. It displays decided shifts in policy and justification during four periods: 1789–1816, 1816–1833, 1833–1861, and 1861–1913. The first three periods encompass the growth and maturing of the industrial system. During the last period, the tariff reflected the disturbances of the Civil War and of industrial crises and the power of

111

vested interests to continue protection despite the industrial maturity of the nation.[1] The tariff issue was given an exaggerated role in American political and economic debates because it was at times closely related to more controversial issues: slavery and states' rights before the war and business monopoly and trusts around the turn of the century.

A. TOWARD FREE TRADE THROUGH PROTECTION, 1789–1860

The first tariff act (1789) was passed mainly to supply the new federal government with badly needed revenue. It imposed duties on only a few commodities; ad valorem rates ranged from 5 to 15 per cent, and specific rates were equivalent on the average to about 8½ per cent ad valorem. The rates were set low so as to bring in revenue; also, higher rates would have encouraged smuggling, which had reached large proportions under the British colonial regulations. The rates were also a compromise among those which the various states had imposed immediately after their severance from Britain. The tariff act of 1789 replaced these divergent duties and made the states into a large free trade area.

There was some sentiment at the time for protective duties, particularly to retaliate against the British, but neither retaliation nor protection was a major purpose of the 1789 tariff. During the latter part of the year, Secretary of the Treasury Hamilton was requested to make a report on how to foster manufactures in America. His report set the pattern of thinking for half a century despite the fact that many of its more important recommendations were not followed.

HAMILTON'S REPORT ON MANUFACTURES

Hamilton's report, delivered to Congress in 1791, examined the status of manufactures at that time, analyzed the advantages of industry and trade, and proposed ways of promoting manufactures in the United States. The economy was almost wholly agrarian at the time, and the majority of people believed in free trade. Farmers felt that free trade increased the size of their market by expanding foreign sales and cheapened the cost of manufactures they imported. Without the chance to trade abroad, the farmer would have turned toward producing for subsistence, and America's growth would have been stifled. With freer trade, it was argued, the standard of living of the American farmer would be raised considerably.

It was Hamilton's task to show the inapplicability of free trade to the situation of the United States and to present favorably certain of the mercantilist programs for regulating trade without accepting others already

---

[1] The names of the specific arguments employed are printed in boldface type. Our discussion of an argument within one period of history does not mean that it was not used, or that it was not important, in others; the selection of arguments with each period is done largely on the grounds of initiation and/or significance for tariff policy at that time.

discredited. He succeeded so well in presenting a reasoned case for protection that proponents drew on his work for over a century, embellishing his ideas but seldom introducing a new one.

Desirability of manufactures

Hamilton believed, as did most of the other political leaders of the time, that international specialization was desirable since it brought gains from the division of labor. The benefits of free trade were widely accepted as evident, with the exceptions stated by Smith of protection for **defense** and for **retaliation;** retaliation was justified by Smith, however, only to obtain lower duties abroad by bargaining in commercial treaties. Protection of a commodity or of shipping for purposes of national security was widely accepted in Hamilton's day as necessary and desirable.

Hamilton wished to use tariffs and other techniques for **retaliation** against the exclusion of U.S. products by other countries. His view was that free trade is advantageous only if *all* nations practiced it. Restrictions abroad must be retaliated against as a matter of fairness, in his view, *even if the duties could not be used to persuade others to relax their restrictions.* But, as shown in Chapter 3, the case for free trade does not depend upon all nations practicing it. While there is a case for protection when a nation can improve its terms of trade at the expense of others, the mere fact that others restrict imports does not mean that a nation *can* improve its terms of trade by protection. No matter how high the rest of the world's tariffs, if a nation cannot affect its terms of trade by protection and if the other arguments for tariffs in Chapter 3 do not apply, free trade is its best policy.

Hamilton's advocacy of retaliation against Europe was closely related to his views on American agriculture: The predominance of agriculture in America required that other nations also accept free trade if America was to practice and benefit from it. But European nations placed a host of restrictions on imports from America in order to protect their own raw material and agricultural production. American agriculture was placed in a highly unstable and undesirable position, since the United States was the first to receive a cut in foreign demand and the last to feel an increase as other nations gave preference to their own farmers.

In order, therefore, to provide a **home market** for agricultural products—one which would be more stable and nearer and thus would not involve the costs of transportation—America must build up her own manufactures using American raw materials. Why, asked Hamilton, should Americans be taxed to provide and promote the means of economic growth and then have the benefits turned over to the foreigner? Reservation of the home market for the farmer would give him first place in a growing market rather than the last place in a foreign one.

Whether or not the protected domestic market would be a better one depended on whether employment was higher and economic stability greater at home than abroad and whether the domestic market was large enough to absorb most domestic agricultural production. The evaluation of the home-market argument rests, therefore, on whether protection is an appropriate means of remedying economic instability; the argument for protection to reduce instability and unemployment was discussed in Chapter 3.

Hamilton went still further in his support of protection. He argued that protection was right for America at that time because it was necessary to develop the economy to a level at which it could afford the benefits of freer trade. Protection was to help **infant industries** overcome the early start of other nations and to permit America to build up its natural advantage in cheap materials. The infant-industry argument has been presented in Chapter 3. A complementary argument is that broader development would provide a "balanced" economy of both agriculture and industry.

Hamilton argued that the facts showed that balanced economies were the most prosperous and that their economic **diversification** attracted foreign trade. Wealth and power, the two objectives of commercial policy, were directly correlated in his mind with the prosperity of manufacturing, for it was through manufactures that basic means of subsistence (shelter, clothing) and national existence (weapons) were provided. All of these were needed in developing the most stable political situation and in gaining the requisite national safety and welfare. The growth of manufactures would be given a continuing stimulus by diversified development throughout the entire economy and vice versa. Not only would industrial growth induce a search for more and different minerals and materials but also a variety of opportunities would provide greater satisfaction to the people, for they could choose among many occupations and develop a variety of skills.

Opposition and obstacles

Southerners, being large exporters, had opposed U.S. restrictions on trade on the grounds that they would suffer retaliation and that tariffs would increase domestic monopoly and raise the prices of things they had to buy. Hamilton admitted in his report that protection might lead to a temporary increase in prices. But he contended that prices would eventually fall as the techniques of manufacturing were improved—recall the discussion of tariffs under special cost conditions in Chapter 3. And, rather than monopolies forming, wide industrial development would increase competition and lower the prices to farmers. Thus the South, having a stable and growing market, would share in the increasing prosperity and eventually would obtain its manufactures from the North at lower cost than from abroad. Hamilton's prediction was correct for some protected commodities but not all.

Besides replying to the opposition of the agricultural states, Hamilton had to contend with those arguing that America faced insurmountable obstacles to manufacturing at that time. These obstacles consisted of cheap land, which was an attraction to labor to move out of urban areas; a resultant scarcity of labor, making wages high; and a lack of capital. Land was plentiful and productive; it yielded readily to small amounts of labor and could be easily obtained. So long as this was the case, men would move out onto the land rather than settle in crowded places to take jobs in industry. To overcome this obstacle, Hamilton urged that industry locate where labor already existed—in the larger settlements. This action would offset the relative scarcity of labor; the scarcity could be reduced also by hiring women and children. The scarcity of capital would just have to be overcome with time, and he argued it *would* be, as evidenced by the industry which had already arisen. The process of American development showed that it did take over fifteen years to break these bottlenecks and another thirty to establish the factory system firmly in the economic life of the country.

Governmental aids

Hamilton believed that industry in time would overcome the obstacles to its growth. But he was not willing to let time pass unassisted. Being convinced that America required and would have industry, he concluded that it would be to her advantage to encourage domestic manufactures. He therefore proposed a variety of governmental aids to industry. They were aimed at helping to break the existing patterns of commerce, production, and consumption and to overcome the lack of enterprise resulting from a fear of failure. The risks of new enterprise were admittedly great because of untried markets and processes of production. Market risks were increased because of the competition faced from established enterprises abroad, which were sometimes supported by bounties and premiums given by foreign governments to exporters.

He proposed that America adopt most of the measures employed by others: protective duties, prohibitions, bounties, premiums, drawbacks, and encouragements to invention and innovation.

The best technique of all was a direct subsidy ("pecuniary bounty," in Hamilton's phrasing). It would be paid to the domestic producer according to his output, thus permitting him to reduce his price on the market. Subsidies were more positive in their operation than duties on imports. They would not cause a scarcity and therefore would not lead to any increase in price. A protective duty, on the contrary, induces a scarcity and leads to a price rise. A duty is paid by the domestic consumer using the taxed product, despite the fact that the protection is ostensibly for the benefit of all citizens, while a subsidy would be paid by all out of general tax funds. But Hamilton qualified this; subsidies must not be continued long, else it would be evident that "there were natural and inherent impediments to success" of the enterprise and that the support was inefficient and wasteful in promoting superior lines of industry.

He recognized, however, that the public might object to subsidies on the grounds that it was "giving away" their money without an immediate benefit—whereas duties would bring in some revenue—and that they would enrich particular groups at the expense of others. He replied to the latter objection that *all* means of encouragement involved a benefit to a few at the expense of others. Yet, he asserted, there was no greater benefit to all than the development of a new and useful industry. To the argument that subsidies did not bring in revenue, he replied that the growth of the country would eventually increase trade (internal and external) and thereby raise the revenue from the tariff as well as from internal excises.

Hamilton's recommendations for a *variety* of government restrictions on trade and of aid to manufactures were disregarded throughout the nineteenth century, and it was not until 1820 that the tariff was used mainly for protection. But his general arguments were readily and widely repeated.

WAR-INDUCED PROTECTION

Tariff legislation from 1792 through 1807 regularly increased duties but hardly to protectionist levels. Despite duties averaging three times those in 1789, imports in 1807 were four and a half times those of 1791, while exports were over five times the 1791 value. The total tonnage of U.S. trade in 1807 was greater than that of any nation other than Britain; on a per capita basis it outranked even that country. After 1807, these high levels of trade were reduced by war in Europe and were not reached again until 1837; by then, the surge of U.S. protectionism had passed and freer trade had been re-instituted.

Although no policy decision was taken in favor of protection, American duties rose during 1807–1816 under the requirements of federal finances and pressures of wars both foreign and American. During the Napoleonic Wars, England and France attempted to stop the other's trade with America by blockading or capturing American ships bound for the other's ports. In an effort to force them to cease their interference, President Jefferson in December, 1807, imposed an embargo which forbade American ships to take cargo to foreign countries. He hoped that the loss of American goods would be so costly that England and France each would permit U.S. trade with the other in order to obtain its own imports. But neither relented, and American trade declined rapidly to levels approximating those of 1791. American retaliation was intensified by the Non-intercourse Act of 1809 which prohibited any and every commercial relation with England and France. This action added to the existing friction between America and Britain and was a factor in the outbreak of the War of 1812.

The fiscal requirements of this war with England forced duties to twice the previous levels. These rates brought the desired higher revenue in 1813 despite a drop in trade; their protective nature was reflected in further declines in trade and revenue in 1814.

The decline in U.S. foreign trade prior to and during the War of 1812 gave a strong push to domestic industry. Manufacturers of pottery, glass, woolen textiles, iron, etc. sprang up over the country; carding and spinning of cotton quadrupled. The obstacles to manufacturing previously enumerated by Hamilton were gradually overcome, though capital within the United States remained timid because of the competitive risks involved and the unsettled political situation.

The risks faced by new American enterprises were increased with the cessation of war. English producers drove hard to recover their former markets by dumping their goods in the United States, i.e., exporting at prices below those in England. American voices were raised in support of **anti-dumping** duties. Many American firms failed. The pressure for protection of the war-born American industries grew intense. The situation was so grave that even as ardent a free trader as William Graham Sumner wrote that "Embargo and war had created a false and artificial state of things . . . . The return of peace, if it reopened trade and let things return to their normal condition, would [have been] a calamity."[2] French firms suffered competition, as noted in Chapter 6, and the growth of protection there supported the American movement.

President Madison lent his prestige to protectionist sentiment by asserting that, as an exception to the general rule, industries providing for defense, or supplying everyday necessities of citizens, or using domestic raw materials should be given support. Rates were raised to prevent failure of many American businesses. The tariff of 1816 was avowedly protectionist, raising duties to preserve capital invested in manufactures.

These duties had a legitimate justification, for when dumping is intermittent or sporadic and is used to drive out domestic competitors, it becomes pernicious. Were such a tactic permitted to succeed, a monopoly from abroad could be created. The cost to the consumer would be raised and a less economic use of resources would result. Such was the nature of most of the dumping by England in America after the War of 1812. Anti-dumping duties are undesirable, however, when the dumping is to be permanent. Under this condition, the country importing the commodities would benefit by the lower costs of its imports.

"THE AMERICAN SYSTEM"

Protectionism was given a further boost by the postwar depression which lasted into the 1820's. Strong pressure was placed on Congress to

---

[2] William Graham Sumner, *Lectures on The History of Protection in the United States* (New York: Putnam, 1895), p. 36. Sumner did not conclude that protection even after war was good, for it still saddled the consumer with the same scarcities of embargo and war; but it did save capital investment.

reserve the home market for domestic products, especially agricultural. Most of the New England states and even some central agricultural states advocated higher duties; they were opposed by those New England states dependent on shipping and by the Southern states. These divergencies of interests illustrate the difficulty of trying to form a commercial policy on the identification of the national interest with the desires of various regional or special-interest groups.

The South opposed protection because it recognized that (a) cheap unskilled labor (slavery) made manufacturing unprofitable as compared with agriculture; (b) its prosperity depended on its sales of cotton abroad, which required a low cost of production and therefore cheap manufactures were desired to reduce the costs of maintaining the labor supply; and (c) it was vulnerable to retaliation against U.S. tariffs by a foreign country. In terms of the analysis in Chapter 2, the South had a comparative advantage in cotton production, stemming from the relative abundance of labor and from the labor- and land-intensiveness of cotton production compared to manufacturing.

A general increase of the tariff was accomplished in 1824 under the guidance of Henry Clay, who had advocated an "American System" of protective tariffs and internal improvements as a temporary means of accelerating growth. The act raised duties to average rates which were equivalent to about 40 per cent ad valorem. The clamor for protection was so great and the process of imposing duties so haphazard that *protective* rates were imposed on items not then produced in the United States. By this act, Congress firmly upheld the principle of protection. The justification was that of facilitating the growth of industry and thereby increasing the prosperity of the country, which some considered still to be depressed. It was generally recognized, however, that the duties should be only temporary.

But the level of duties was raised even higher in 1828. The increase was not the result of a careful examination of the economic desirability of higher duties or the necessity of higher rates to make them protective. Rather, the act was a political misjudgment on the part of its proponents, who fully expected it to be voted down and hoped it would be. The tariff issue became a political football for the purpose of gaining support in crucial sectors of the country for the Presidential hopefuls: Adams and Jackson. The framers of the bill included duties on raw materials to gain votes in the Midwest but which they were certain would be thought "too high" by New England's manufacturing states; other duties were imposed to curry favor in New England which they were certain would be thought "too high" by the Western and Midwestern states. While this opposition did arise, each side thought that rates in its favor were not too high, and the bill was passed. It raised the average ad valorem equivalent to around 50 per cent. The protectionists were satisfied for the first time.

But the act, called the "tariff of abominations," backfired. South

Carolina passed the Nullification Act, stating that the rates did not apply to her trade, and even threatened secession. To the force of this threat was added the fact that federal revenue was running far ahead of expenditures; there was an embarrassing surplus in the Treasury. President Jackson called for a reduction of duties, and the tariff of 1832 cut the rates, especially on items of wide consumption. Revenue was reduced but not protection, since the duties on basic consumer items which had been cut were not previously at protective levels. But the South still objected. The growing tension between the North and South forced a compromise bill in 1833 which began a drift toward freer trade.

EVALUATION OF PROTECTION FOR DEVELOPMENT

The period of infant-industry protection came to an end in 1832. By that time American industry was considered able to stand on its own feet. The evidence gathered by Professor Taussig suggests, however, that most of the industries protected were able to stand upon their own feet even before the "American System" was inaugurated.[3] He argues that protection of cotton textiles would have been useful after 1808 if it had not already been provided by the embargo and the war. Protection was useful in easing the crises of 1816 through 1819; but after 1820, if the tariff had any effect on production at all, it was harmful because the textile industry was already fully established.

The woolen manufactures, he concluded, were also well established by the 1820's—before the higher tariffs were imposed. Producers could compete effectively with foreign firms and needed only to be able to obtain their raw materials equally as cheap. Since the raw materials were subject to duty, there might have been some justice in protecting the manufacturers and enabling them to sell at home at higher prices. But apart from this, the protection offered, which in 1828 reached over 100 per cent ad valorem equivalent on some products, was no longer needed.

Taussig drew similar conclusions for glass, pottery, paper, cloth, cordage, and other products. Of special significance was the impact of tariffs on the development of the iron industry. The major reasons for its advance were the improved means of transportation of materials and improvements in technology. Taussig asserted that the tariff itself was an impediment to growth, holding back technological improvements which would have been forced had foreign competition been felt more keenly. The tariff permitted them to make satisfactory profits using old processes, while foreign manufacturers were still able to invade the expanding U.S. market because of mass-production operations and new processes. Once the U.S. industry adopted the new processes in the 1830's, advance was rapid and the protection was no longer needed.

Taussig modified this conclusion in a study some twenty years later:

---

[3] F. W. Taussig, *The Tariff History of the United States* (New York: Putnam, 1914), Part I, Chapter 1.

. . . the unbiased inquirer must hesitate before committing himself to such an unqualified statement of what would have been. Rich natural resources, business skill, improvements in transportation, widespread training in applied science, abundant and manageable labor supply—these perhaps suffice to account for the phenomena. But would these forces have turned to the protected industry so strongly and unerringly but for the shelter from foreign competition? Beyond question the protective system caused high profits to be reaped in the iron and steel establishments of the central district; and the stimulus from great gains promoted the unhesitating investment of capital on a large scale. . . . The mounting output was the unmistakable evidence of profitable investment. . . .The same sort of growth would doubtless have taken place eventually, tariff or no tariff; but not so soon or on so great a scale. With a lower scale of iron prices, profits would have been lower; and possibly the progress of investment, the exploitation of the natural resources, even the advance of the technical arts, would have been less keen and unremitting.

No one can say with certainty what would have been, and the bias of the individual observer will have an effect on his estimate of probabilities.[4]

Encouragements to industry will no doubt accelerate its advance, but not without costs in a loss of trade.[5] Related to the costs of protection are the problems of administering the policy so as to aid economic growth. The correct industries must be supported in order to minimize the cost involved in reducing international trade. It is difficult to determine which industries will be able to stand on their own feet after a short period of protection. It is even more difficult to determine what level of protection should be provided. And if the history of the U.S. tariff is indicative, the argument will be used successfully to continue protection long after industries have matured or shown themselves to be uneconomic.[6] It is almost impossible to remove the duty once it has been imposed and the industry becomes accustomed to it.

It seems to have taken about thirty years for the American economy to overcome, with some government assistance, the obstacles to develop-

---

[4] F. W. Taussig, *Some Aspects of the Tariff Question* (Cambridge, Mass.: Harvard University Press, 1931), pp. 150–151. Another student of American commercial policy did not dare to undertake the task of making a "scientific determination" of the practical consequences of protection because "this matter is so difficult and unsafe, the complication of facts so enormous, the isolation of them so unmanageable, the clear distinction between cause and effect so perplexing. . . ." Ugo Rabbeno, *The American Commercial Policy* (London: Macmillan, 1895), p. 112.

[5] For example, during a later period of intense protection, it has been estimated that the proportion of total production exported by the United States dropped from 2.4 per cent in 1860 to 1.5 per cent in 1880; the percentage of imports in total consumption dropped from 12.4 per cent in 1860 to 7.4 per cent in 1880, despite a tripling of both production and consumption in the U.S. economy. (Rabbeno, *op. cit.,* p. 226.)

[6] "The true reason, therefore, of the rise of protectionism in a new country is to be found in the formation of a class of industrial capitalists, who, as soon as it is in their power to do, devise means for safeguarding their own interests." (Rabbeno, *op. cit.,* p. 170.)

ment of manufacturing cited by Hamilton: high wages, profitable land, and lack of capital. There had to be some encouragement to people to stay off the land, but the encouragement had to be covert. It would not have been politic to give bounties and premiums to manufacturers because the payments would have been borne by agriculture. Protective duties concealed the fact that resources were being diverted and that economic power was being shifted to the capitalists.

In any event, the protection provided fortuitously by the Napoleonic Wars and the War of 1812 and their aftereffects was far more effective than the legislated protection of the 1820's, for it came at a more appropriate time. The later protection, on balance, was probably not very harmful but was also probably unnecessary. It was easy, therefore, to argue in 1832 and 1833 that the goals of protection had been reached: stimulation of American industry, independence of foreign supplies, accumulation of capital and increased efficiency of labor, safeguarding of investments in new enterprises, and preparation of defense materials and manufactures. Any protection in the future, it was accepted, should definitely be transitory and would be used solely to guard "the general welfare of the country and not special interests."[7] Special interests were never far away during tariff legislation, however, and they quickly developed other arguments to retain their benefits, even succeeding in causing a temporary reversal during 1842–1846 of the trend toward freer trade.

DRIFT TOWARD FREE TRADE

Though there has never been a "free trade movement" in the United States, the period 1833–1860 displayed a drift toward the use of the tariff principally for revenue. Responding to the pressure from the South and recognizing that protection was no longer vitally needed by American industry, Congress passed the Compromise Tariff of 1833. It declared that duties would be cut very gradually over a decade until none was greater than 20 per cent ad valorem. The debate was hardly one in which the economic advantages of free trade were clearly stated and were victorious over the arguments for protection. Rather, a shifting public opinion, which made other issues more important, and political pressures within the government itself were the primary determinants.

An argument used during the debates on the Compromise Tariff of 1833 and which has come to the fore again in recent discussions of tariff policy is that concerning the support of **vested interests** erected behind the tariff. When capital has been induced to enter business protected by tariffs, some argued, removal of the duty would work an undesirable and inequitable hardship on the capitalists and laborers. These capitalists had invested funds and laborers had learned skills in the belief that the price

---

[7] Statement attributed to the Secretary of the Treasury by Rabbeno, *op. cit.*, p. 163.

and market would be protected; an unexpected removal of the protection would be unjust. Partly because of this argument, the duties after 1833 were reduced only gradually.

The trend toward freer trade was reversed temporarily in 1842 in a hasty attempt by the Whig party to gain campaign strength by support of tariffs for special interests. Certain manufacturing interests were powerful enough to gain protection; their claim was that the crises of 1837 and 1839 resulted from the reduced duties. This can hardly be proved, however, for duties were only minutely decreased during the period 1832–1840 and then rapidly in 1840–1842. The higher rates imposed in 1842 were opposed by the general public, and the Democratic party made political capital out of its intent to repeal them. The 1846 act imposed duties lower than any except those in the 1816 tariff and those just prior to the act of 1842. The act was based on a careful inquiry by Secretary of the Treasury Walker, whose conclusions constituted a firm defense of free trade. He argued that duties should be no higher than the lowest rate which would yield the largest revenue.

By 1857, when duties were cut still further, manufacturers were more interested in duty-free raw materials than in protection for their own products, and the general public was much more concerned with other issues. The country seemed adjusted to a level of duties relatively low compared with its nineteenth century experience; they averaged about 20 per cent ad valorem equivalent on all dutiable items. It appeared that the tariff issue had died, having been resolved in favor of freer trade and of duties mainly for revenue.

THE AMERICAN EXPERIENCE AND LIST'S "NATIONAL SYSTEM"

Frederick List was a close observer of American economic development to 1850, having spent several years of his exile from Germany in the United States. His interpretation of that growth and his analysis of the progress of nations has been widely accepted by countries hoping to follow in the path of U.S. development.

List's initial purpose in writing his *National System of Political Economy* (1856) was to refute some of the ideas of the classical school —namely, those of Smith. He argued that Smith's system did not show how the wealth of an individual nation was to be gained; rather it related either to the wealth of an individual or to the prosperity of the whole of humanity. Yet, in List's view, it was necessary to consider the wealth of *a* nation before that of *all* nations could be fostered. He assumed that nationalism was an intermediate stage in the development of higher governments which would eventually evolve into one unifying all peoples. But the world of his day, he asserted, was not yet ready for the "international economy" of a single world community. Before this stage could be reached, all nations would have to attain similar cultural and power positions, involving vast industrialization of each.

In the interim stage, before the creation of an international polity and economy, each nation must seek economic wealth and political power in order to preserve its position. Each must advance to the point at which all will find it possible and desirable to give up national sovereignty. In order to gain prosperity and security, a nation must be relatively independent of foreign resources. This independence is attained by building a balance among the agricultural, manufacturing, and commercial sectors of the economy. It is only through manufacturing that the relative poverty of a nation can be removed; in List's view, an agricultural state would always remain poor and without power. Even if it were argued, as some of his critics did, that an agricultural state could prosper through trade (such as is true currently of Denmark and New Zealand) and in fact could prosper *only* through extensive trade, he replied that the aim of the *national* economy was not just to gain material goods. Its aim included also increasing *productive power* and *political power* so as to continue the national growth and reduce dependence on others. (Just how such a process of increasing independence would blossom forth into a world community of interdependent and harmonized nations, List did not analyze; he assumed that this was the inevitable result and that nationalism was a requisite stage.)

Tariff protection was a most appropriate means of hastening industrial development, in List's view, but it was appropriate only for a certain time —during the time necessary to educate workers to the factory system and to overcome the obstacles to a shift to manufacturing which exist in an agrarian state. When the education to industrialism is complete, protection should cease. Protection is harmful in the very early stages of development, when population is inadequate to permit movement off the land and when labor skills are low and land is still relatively plentiful; what is needed in the early stages is free trade and improved communication. But when capital becomes available and the competition from foreign industry prevents expansion of domestic manufactures, then protection is desirable.

List admitted that free trade is the best policy in the long run, after nations have developed their domestic economies. But temporary losses of the gains from trade are desirable when they permit even greater gains in the future from the rapid growth of production. Further, free trade is desirable only when other nations are also practicing it. List advocated protection for Germany because other nations had closed their doors to her exports (reminiscent of Hamilton's argument); yet he insisted on free trade within the Zollverein. His arguments in favor of a German Zollverein, based on observations in America, provided a theoretical and historical foundation for its establishment.

In line with his objective of promoting national power and independence, List advocated the protection of only those goods which were not luxuries; luxuries could be left in the control of others without harming growth. The highest protection would be extended those industries using the most machinery and consuming the largest amounts of domestic raw materials; these industries would promote rapid internal growth and would encourage lending by savers who were reluctant to invest without the protection. This type of protection would also secure the home market for domestic manufacturers and farmers, improve the competitive position of domestic industry in foreign markets, provide secure sources of manufactured consumer goods, and diversify the domestic economy, giving it "ballast."

List's ideas fit closely with those of Hamilton. Both admitted that their policies were appropriate only for a given stage of development. The American experience before 1860 does not prove their analysis faulty in entirety or their advice inappropriate. But the experience after 1860 shows that a nation, once on the protectionist road, finds it difficult if not impossible to get off or turn around, thus losing some of the gain from trade for longer periods than envisaged by Hamilton or List.

B. PROTECTION FOR SPECIAL INTERESTS, 1861–1913

TARIFF ACTS AND ARGUMENTS

The pattern of U.S. commercial policy during the latter part of the nineteenth century was set by the wartime tariffs of 1861–1864. Much of the rapid increase in duties during these years was a result of the pressure of war finances. But the Republicans had been elected in 1860 on a protectionist platform, and the act of 1861 raised the duties to the 1842 levels. Increases of tariffs were frequent during the Civil War. By 1864 the average duties had been raised to about 47 per cent with individual rates ranging from 5 to 200 per cent (ad valorem equivalents). Except for temporary reversals, U.S. tariffs remained high to World War I. Protection was advocated and, by 1890, had seemed to become a permanent policy reflecting an antipathy to foreign trade in principle. This policy was a far cry from

---

[8] Contrary to some protectionists today who do not oppose all trade, some of the early opponents of trade were 100 per centers. For example, during consideration of the McKinley Tariff of 1890, when one senator opposing protection observed "that he did not understand on what principle its supporters voted the expenses for the maintenance of lighthouses, Senator Hiscock abruptly replied that were it not for the coasting-trade he would willingly see every beacon extinguished on the shore of the United States." (See Rabbeno, *op. cit.,* p. 207.) Pressure for protection arose also from those who were against the interdependence caused by trade. For example, Senator Henry Cabot Lodge (R., Mass.) stated: "Free trade . . . makes trade of the first importance as a condition of natural wealth and prosperity. . . . The true and lasting source of wealth is production, and trade, even though it

the temporary protection of Hamilton, Clay, and List, advocated for the early stages of economic growth.

This period exemplifies the extent to which special interests may succeed in identifying, in the minds of Congress and the public, their welfare with that of the country as a whole. Professor Taussig notes that, while there were great demands for tariff revenue in 1864 and Congress was led by protectionists, their mixing of revenue legislation with protective tariffs "resulted in a most unexpected and extravagant application of protection, and moreover, made possible a subservience of the public needs to the private gains of individuals. . . . The line between public duties and private interests was often lost sight of by legislators."[9]

The tariff issue was used by both parties to sharpen campaign differences, particularly in the elections of 1888, 1892, and 1896. As a result, duties were imposed to reward financial supporters or to please constituents who pleaded for special benefits. Duties on beet sugar and some mining products imposed in 1897 were of this nature, and those on wool, hides, and flax were set to woo the farm vote for the next election. To the "justifications" for protection claimed by special interests was added the pressure on industry and finance of the various depressions during the post-Civil War period. The advocates of protection were able to convince the public that depressions resulted from lowered duties. For example, the public became convinced that, because the panic of 1893 was followed by duty reductions in 1894 and a continued depression, higher duties would regain prosperity. The pressure for tariffs was intensified by the lobbying activities of the large business combinations and financial trusts, which seemed to be fostered by both higher tariffs and depressions. These pressures were reflected in uncoordinated and economically inappropriate rates and in confused and complex tariff measures.

Pauper-labor argument

A tariff argument developed earlier, but used extensively in the 1870's and 1880's and made the keynote of the campaign of 1888, was the **pauper-labor** argument. This rationalization holds that wages in the United States are relatively high as compared with the rest of the world. For the

---

enhances the value of the product, is at the same time a tax upon production, on account of the cost of transportation. A nation without trade may be permanently rich and prosperous, but a nation without production and dependent solely on trade holds riches and prosperity by a frail tenure." (*Congressional Record*, April 10, 1894, p. 3620; as quoted by W. R. Allen, "Issues in Congressional Tariff Debates, 1890–1930," *Southern Economic Journal* (April, 1954), p. 343 n.)

[9] Taussig, *Tariff History*, p. 166. Referring to the period after the Civil War, Ugo Rabbeno asserts that "Every increase of import duties demanded by native producers was granted; the general welfare was entirely lost sight of, and laws were made to favor special interests; and on the foundations laid by the war and by political corruption was erected the edifice of absolute protection, fostered by the sentiment of national exclusiveness and isolation." (*Op. cit.*, p. 202).

American laborer to continue to enjoy such wages, U.S. prices have to be relatively high also; to keep them high, protection is needed. Thus protection is required to give the American laborer a "fair" standard of living, or to maintain the high levels to which he has become accustomed. Without the protection, labor would be unemployed or have to take the wage paid abroad. Manufacturers argued that they would gladly forego the protection if they could pay foreign wages.

This argument overlooks the fact that wages are based on productivity of labor and its complementary factors. American labor could not be paid the wages it gets unless it were relatively more efficient, which it is in many instances. (It is *not* more efficient in some products and is *comparatively less* efficient in still others; this relative inefficiency prevents their production in the United States.) This higher productivity results partly from a high capital-labor ratio, partly from superior skills, from superior management techniques in organizing labor's efforts, and from climatic and socio-political conditions. Free trade will not remove these differences and bring money or real wages to equality; (the argument of Chapter 4 on equalization of factor prices showed that each of these causes, save the existing factor ratios, would prevent a complete equalization of returns even under free trade). Regardless of the particular cause, the low wages abroad are a result of low productivity. Such countries, in their turn, complain of the "unfair" competition they have to face from mass-produced and low-priced American products which flood their markets. They attempt to shut out competition from American "high-wage," large-scale industries, while some elements in the United States want to shut out low-wage goods from abroad.

Equalization argument

The Republican platform of 1908 presented a new version of the "true" and "long-established" Republican doctrine concerning tariff protection: "In all protective legislation, the true principle of protection is best maintained by the imposition of such duties as will equal the difference between the cost of production at home and abroad, together with a reasonable profit to American industries."[10] This "scientific principle" had been discussed before, but it was now hailed as the definitive solution to the entire tariff problem. It provided for **equalization of costs of production.** This criterion of duty levels was embraced by both political parties after World War I, but with slightly different interpretations.

On the face of it, the principle seems only fair: producers would compete on an equal basis. But when it is recognized that if costs were equal there would be no basis for trade, the prohibitive aspects of this argument are clearly seen. As shown in Chapter 2, were *all* items to have

---

[10] Quoted in Taussig, *Tariff History,* p. 363.

protection sufficient to equalize their costs with those abroad, each country would produce all its own goods, however expensive they might be. The principle of cost equalization, if carried out strictly, would mean a cessation of all trade.

Apart from this devastating criticism, it is all but impossible to calculate the difference between costs at home and abroad and, therefore, the tariff necessary to equalize them. A major obstacle is the determination of *which* costs to equalize: foreign or landed? costs on individual or bulk sales?, etc. Once this is decided, cost figures are themselves difficult to obtain from manufacturers, especially on a basis which makes comparisons possible. Finally, since many firms make a given product, *whose* shall be selected?—the high- or low-cost firm's?

In practice, whatever duty was considered desirable was said to be the "equalizing" rate. The sponsors of the Payne-Aldrich tariff of 1908 asserted that no duty remained which was higher than the "equalization" point. But the fear of Germany's competitive strength made it desirable and the difficulty of determining costs abroad made it easy to keep many duties quite high. Some duties were raised despite pledges of the parties that reductions were the objective.[11]

These increases reflected the facts that the Senate was more under the control of the protection-minded corporations and monied interests and that its equal representation gave the interests of smaller constituencies an equal hearing and thus encouraged logrolling. The process of logrolling was described by Representative Payne in reporting to Congress the events leading up to the 1897 duty on hides:

> When the Dingley bill came before the House, reported by the Committee, it was reported with free hides, and I saw a number of gentlemen on this [the Republican] side of the House, and a number of gentlemen on the other side of the House, led by Jerry Simpson of Kansas, voting for a duty on hides. He was a little more frank than some of these modern-day tariff-for-revenue people. He said he wanted to get his share. He did not believe in a duty on hides, but he wanted to get his share. . . . It went over into the Senate. We did not have a Republican majority in the Senate in those days, but we did

[11] The way in which increases were made and the passage of the bill through Congress are instructive in showing some of the political irresponsibility of the period and in displaying the haphazard results of setting individual duties through legislation. While Rep. Payne was a firm believer in the "equalization" principle as a means of squeezing the excess protection out of tariff, Sen. Aldrich was a staunch protectionist. He helped make over 400 substantial amendments in the Senate, almost all upward over the House bill. When committees of the two houses met in conference to iron out the differences between the bills, the Democratic members were excluded from private sessions at which rates were determined. The Republicans traded item for item among themselves without relation to their protective effects or their impact on the general economy. A conference committee is supposed to reconcile the differences in the Senate and House bills, but in this case it exceeded its terms of reference by imposing rates *higher* than either bill provided.

have a majority of those who claimed to be protectionists, and one of these protectionists of populistic tendencies would not vote for the bill unless it carried a duty on hides, and the Senate accommodated him. *That is one of the courtesies of the Senate when any member wants something done.*[12]

The general reaction against free trade was reflected also in the unwillingness of the U.S. government to use reciprocal commercial treaties to reduce barriers multilaterally.

COMMERCIAL TREATIES

Commercial treaties usually relate to consular matters, problems of transport, rights of foreigners, and trade and tariff questions. The tariff provisions of American commercial treaties were intended to reduce duties on selected commodities and to certain countries. By 1860, most European nations were extending the benefits of tariff reductions under commercial treaties to all countries so entitled through the unconditional most-favored-nation clause. But the U.S. government used a conditional most-favored-nation clause in its treaties from its first treaty (with France in 1778) until 1922. The conditional phrasing is the same as the unconditional but with a qualification: each party agrees "not to grant any particular favor to other nations which shall not become common immediately to the other party, who shall enjoy the same favor, freely, if the concession was freely made, or on allowing the same compensation, if the concession was conditional." The qualification "if the concession was conditional" meant that if the United States had a conditional most-favored-nation treaty with Germany and if the United States gave a reduced duty to France on wines conditional upon a French reduction of duties on American products, Germany could not claim the same low wine duty without giving the United States a duty reduction. Thus the conditional form was little more than an invitation for further bargaining. One justification for the conditional form was that it would be unfair to give concessions freely to one nation when another had obtained them only by giving compensation.

Those nations using the *un*conditional form considered that adequate compensation existed in the fact that each country received freely the concessions given by others to third countries. They obtained equality of treatment, which was highly prized, as we saw in Chapter 6. Though the avoidance of discrimination may have lessened political friction somewhat, the fact that concessions were extended multilaterally may have hampered the reduction of duties; a nation might wish to reduce a duty to one nation but not to all, particularly because of the loss in bargaining power with those nations gaining tariff reductions freely. To avoid this, Germany negotiated her treaties simultaneously; she thus displayed to each the

---

[12] Taussig, *Tariff History*, p. 378 n. Italics added by Taussig.

benefits they would receive through the unconditional clause from the other treaties.

The U.S. practice gave rise to diplomatic disputes between the United States and its treaty partners over the precise privileges each held under the clause. One of the more difficult problems to resolve was whether a concession offered by a third country was equal to that obtained by the United States from the treaty partner. For example, if Germany gave the United States a concession on American exports of cotton for a reduction of the American duty on rugs, Egypt might claim the same reduced duty on rugs by offering an identical reduction of her duty on cotton. But since Egypt is a cotton producer and hardly likely to buy American cotton in any event, can the concession be said to be equivalent to that given by Germany? In making this type of decision, American officials held that they should be the sole judge of whether an offer was equivalent to the concession received in the original bargain; this arbitrary action did not satisfy third countries at all times.

Disputes arose also over whether the United States had a right, without giving compensation, to a concession granted by a treaty partner to third countries. Since a European country had treaties containing the unconditional clause with other European countries and the conditional clause with the United States, it would freely extend some reductions to third countries under the unconditional form. Since this concession would have been extended freely to a third country, the U.S. government claimed that, under the conditional form, it was privileged to receive the same concession freely. Most European nations readily conceded this claim to the United States until about 1890, extending reductions freely even while they were prohibited from receiving like treatment from the United States.

But this "best of all worlds" of getting all concessions freely and extending them only for compensation could not last. Because of the ill treatment received at the hand of the United States, most European governments began to discriminate systematically against American goods. After 1890, the U.S. government could not obtain, through its new treaties, the same treatment which European countries enjoyed among themselves freely as a result of the use of the unconditional form of the clause. It could obtain only a partial removal of the discriminations aimed at its products. The discrimination was intensified as the nature of U.S. exports shifted from agricultural products to industrial goods and came more into competition with European production. Some European nations even denounced their most-favored-nation treaties with the United States.

After World War I, the U.S. government accepted President Wilson's recommendation, made as one of his Fourteen Points, that all nations treat all others equally in commercial matters. Nondiscrimination was to be the rule and the unconditional interpretation was to be employed for all most-favored-nation treaties. Since 1923, the U.S. government has been as insistent on the unconditional form as it was previously on the conditional interpretation.

PRE-WORLD WAR I PICTURE

Despite the high duties imposed through 1908, public sentiment seemed to be shifting. By 1910, protectionists were on the defensive, and once again the high-water mark of tariffs seemed to have been reached just prior to another drift toward freer trade. That is, *toward* tariffs for revenue. The general picture and public sentiment before World War I has been painted as follows:

. . . the partially closed economy encouraged formation of monopolies and trusts, which, undeterred by foreign competition, could manipulate price and supply to the detriment of the community's welfare. Promotion of selected economic interests fostered uneven income concentration. By curtailing imports and relying on domestic production to meet almost all consumer needs, depletion of our natural resources was hastened. The farmer, with exportable surpluses, had to sell on the world market, but he was forced to buy in a protected market. Protection encouraged sloth and inefficiency; indeed, the degree of protection for an industry generally was determined by the needs of the weakest firm. Uncertain reliance upon artificial and immoral protection was one side of the coin of which the other was the decadence of government to a position of dispenser of special privilege. Erection of unreasonable trade barriers had inspired foreign retaliation. Nevertheless, on the basis of 'the favoritism . . . ingrafted in these bills,' vast investments had been made and thousands of laborers were employed in the protected industries, so tariff reform should proceed gradually.[13]

When reform did come in 1913, the reduced rates were prevented from going into effect by the war. And the proposal of Wilson to employ the unconditional most-favored-nation clause was not implemented until 1923. Once again, war severed the economic dependence of nations and gave a new impetus to U.S. economic growth. The impact of war and its aftermath threw the United States, and other countries, into fits of protection and isolationism during which the mercantilist, nineteenth century, and some new protectionist arguments were brought forth.

Nationalism was already a strong factor in influencing the nature of commercial policies and national attitudes toward factor movements among countries. War intensified its influence; it became of overriding importance in setting the pattern of international relations during the period between the world wars. Today it remains a predominant factor which must be reckoned with by those who advocate a more cosmopolitan allocation of the world's resources and a freeing of trade.

---

[13] Allen, *op. cit.*, pp. 348–349.

SELECTED READINGS

GENERAL

Isaacs, Asher. *International Trade: Tariff and Commercial Policies.* Homewood, Ill.: Irwin, 1948. Chapters 11 and 12 provide a convenient survey of the tariff policies of the United States during 1789–1914.

Rabbeno, Ugo. *The American Commercial Policy.* London: Macmillan, 1895. This study by an Italian provides an interesting and instructive analysis of the early stages of American development and the use of protection as well as of U.S. tariff policy in the latter part of the nineteenth century.

Stanwood, E. *American Tariff Controversies in the Nineteenth Century,* 2 vols. Boston: Houghton Mifflin, 1903. This is a vast chronological record of debates in and out of Congress; it is especially good in Chapter 4 on the influence of Hamilton.

Sumner, William G. *Lectures on the History of Protection in the United States.* New York: Putnam, 1895. These lectures were given in 1876 on the controversy over protection and its practice to that time. Sumner was a staunch free trader.

Taussig, F. W. *Some Aspects of the Tariff Question.* Cambridge, Mass.: Harvard University Press, 1931; and *The Tariff History of the United States.* New York: Putnam, 1914. These two works are the standard references on the issues surrounding U.S. tariff policy; they also provide case studies of the effects of protection on various industries.

U.S. Tariff Commission. *The Tariff and Its History.* Washington: Government Printing Office, 1934. This pamphlet provides a brief record of each U.S. tariff act, concisely relates tariff policies of other countries over past centuries, and gives an explanation of types of customs duties.

A. 1789–1860

Haberler, G. *The Theory of International Trade.* London: Macmillan, 1936. Chapters 16 and 17 are still the best source for analyses of the varied arguments for protection.

Hamilton, Alexander. *Report on Manufactures* (1791), reprinted in *State Papers and Speeches on the Tariff,* F. W. Taussig, ed. Cambridge: Harvard University Press, 1893.

List, F. *The National System of Political Economy.* Philadelphia: Lippincott, 1856. These arguments provide the foremost historical apology for protection as a means to accelerate economic development.

Nurkse, R. *Problems of Capital Formation in Underdeveloped Countries.* New York: Oxford, 1953. Chapter 5 analyzes the importance of capital in the early stages of development—a primary concern of both Hamilton and List.

Taylor, G. R., ed. *The Great Tariff Debate, 1820–1830.* Boston: Heath, 1953. The debate between Clay and Webster is presented as well as other congressional speeches, editorial and other opinions, and memorials by various conventions.

B.   1861–1913

Allen, W. R. "Issues in Congressional Tariff Debates, 1890–1930," *Southern Economic Journal,* XX (April, 1954), 340–355. This article contains a rich selection of views of congressmen responsible for tariff legislation.

Bolen, G. L. *The Plain Facts as to the Trusts and the Tariff.* New York: Macmillan, 1902; and Pierce, F. *The Tariff and the Trusts.* New York: Macmillan, 1907. These two books provide a flavor of the controversy over the impact of tariffs on the growth of business combinations and vice versa.

Viner, J. "The Most-Favored-Nation Clause in American Commercial Treaties," reprinted in *International Economics.* Glencoe, Ill.: Free Press, 1951, pp. 17–40. This article, first published in the *Journal of Political Economy* (1924), evaluates the use and impact of the conditional interpretation and the reasons for the U.S. policy shift.

8 Factor Movements in the Nineteenth Century

The century between the Napoleonic Wars and World War I was the golden era of factor movements among nations. What were the causes of these movements? What determined their direction? What were the benefits? the losses? In this chapter we go beyond the theoretical models of Chapter 4 to cite fact and figure and to take account of the political aspects of factor movements and their impact on economic growth.

The economic achievements of the nineteenth century resulted partly from extensive movements of people and capital as well as from an expansion of international trade. The migration of people, of capital, and the growth of trade were interrelated and generally complementary. The massive factor movements were toward the underpopulated and underdeveloped countries, rich in natural resources and land. These areas consequently became important markets as well as sources of supply for the countries from which people and capital emigrated.

Three countries, Britain, France, and Germany, were the major sources of international capital in the nineteenth century. Large-scale international investment by Germany and France did not occur until after 1870; Britain's contribution started after the Napoleonic Wars and assumed enormous proportions after 1870. The immense contribution which these lending countries made to the capital-receiving nations is suggested by the fact that Western Europe, in the forty or fifty years before World War I, invested abroad almost as much as the entire national wealth of Great Britain. Just prior to World War I, Britain's annual overseas investment was at a rate equal to half of her annual savings, and France invested abroad one-third to one-half of her savings between 1880 and 1913. American private foreign investment in the middle of the twentieth century would have had to be some thirty times greater than it was to match the proportion of national income which Britain invested abroad in 1913.

The importance of foreign capital to the economic growth of capital-receiving countries is suggested by the ratio of foreign to domestic capital invested. Between 1908 and 1913, Canadian borrowing from abroad equaled more than half the increase in Canada's stock of capital; the same was true for Sweden between 1860 and 1890. In 1850, foreigners contributed to the United States an amount equal to about 7 per cent of its reproduceable tangible wealth. In the 1870's capital imports equaled 11 per cent of U.S. domestic capital formation. Almost half of the U.S. federal debt, over half of the states' debts, and a quarter of the railroad bonds were owned by foreigners in the middle of the nineteenth century. Foreign capital in the United States financed, in addition, land speculation, cattle raising, brewing, liquor distilling, oil development, mining, banking, insurance, and a variety of manufacturing enterprises.

A. CAPITAL EXPORTS: CAUSES, CHARACTER, AND BENEFITS

CAUSES AND CHARACTER OF FOREIGN INVESTMENT

British capital exports

A number of forces operated to move Britain from the status of a probable net debtor to foreign nations in 1800 to the rank of chief international creditor of the nineteenth century. Essential to England's achievement was the growth of real income which provided the savings for investment abroad. Underlying this were Britain's industrial progress and the gains accruing from her freer trade policy. In the first part of the century, the growth of savings was probably also assisted by a rather unequal distribution of income, for it was the wealthy who made the foreign investments. Later, general economic progress and the rise of business proprietorships created a large number of small savers whose funds were also tapped.

Opportunity for greater income was the major force pushing British capital abroad. For example, during the period of 1870–1880, the average yield on all foreign bonds was 5.5 per cent, and it was nearly 7 per cent on other foreign securities. For the same interval, the yield on British government bonds was less than 4 per cent. The income earned on foreign investment was both an incentive and a source of supply for capital exports. Instead of using all her foreign earnings to buy goods from foreign nations, Britain reinvested abroad approximately three-quarters of her net investment income between 1870 and 1913, a period which saw British overseas investment rise by 300 per cent. The reinvestment of earnings was an essential part of the system because borrowers, particularly governments, repaid old loans out of the proceeds of new ones, and the possibility of continued borrowing from England was the best incentive for a debtor to keep up payments on principal and interest.

Assistance in pushing British capital abroad came from internal business practice. England's internal industrial expansion was financed mainly by ploughing back profits into the firm that earned them or by direct arrangements with wealthy individuals. The savings of the general investor —particularly of one who had no personal knowledge of promising domestic ventures—were not required for industrial expansion within Britain; they therefore became available for foreign investment.

To gather the public's savings for export, a complex network of financial institutions developed. Chief among these were the powerful private banks with such famous names as Rothschild and Baring. On behalf of foreign borrowers, they issued securities to brokers for later sale to the public, and they appended their good reputations to the securities, giving confidence to the potential investor. On the whole these large issuing houses handled only the big government and railroad bonds transactions. Smaller private banks and some brokers handled the lesser issues. In addition, numerous land and investment companies were engaged in promoting and underwriting foreign investment, particularly in the provision of capital for pioneer, risky ventures abroad.

The major portion of British investment took place through the purchase of securities yielding a fixed rate of return. However, ventures such as mines in Africa, rubber plantations in Malaya, and coffee and tea operations in India, Africa, and Latin America were financed in large part through "direct" investment (involving ownership and control by the investor, and varying dividends) rather than portfolio investment (involving fixed-interest payments and no ownership or control). The lack of specific requirements for repayment of the capital or of payment of earnings on equity capital made direct investment superior to portfolio investment in agricultural and mineral production, because such ventures often do not bear fruit for long periods and are subject to extreme variability of earnings.

There were few branches of profit-making activity which British private capital and enterprise did not enter, from jute mills in India to department stores in Argentina. In the beginning, however, loans to foreign governments held first place, starting with loans to France after the Napoleonic Wars, to make it possible for France to pay reparations to England. (To double the paradox, one of the reasons why the French securities found acceptance in England was that huge wartime borrowing by the British government to finance expenditures for the defeat of France had accustomed British investors to the purchase of government bonds.) Just before World War I, only about 30 per cent of Britain's overseas investment was in the form of loans to foreign governments. The remainder went into private economic ventures. About 40 per cent of her investments were in railroads (four-fifths of the investment in the United States being such), and the remainder went into raw-materials production, financial institutions, commerce and industry, and public utilities.

An equally radical shift occurred in the geographical pattern of her foreign investments. In the early nineteenth century, the main British investment had been in Europe, financing governments, railroads, and industrial enterprises, thereby accelerating Europe's economic growth. But in the latter half of the century, as industry and savings grew in Europe, British capital shifted elsewhere until, just before World War I, a meager 6 per cent of her overseas investments remained in Europe. After 1880, British capital and enterprise turned increasingly to developing agricultural and raw-material-producing areas; the profitability of such investments stemmed, in no small degree, from the food and raw-material requirements of Europe's growing population and industrial machine. By 1913, nearly four-fifths of England's investments were in countries that relied chiefly on the exportation of primary products; nearly half of her investments were in the British Empire, 20 per cent in the United States, and 20 per cent in Latin America.

Throughout the nineteenth century, in keeping with its laissez-faire attitude, the British government kept formal intervention in foreign investment to a minimum. However, in 1900, investment in the Empire received a governmental boost when the securities issued by British dominions and colonies were given trustee status; this permitted the purchase of such securities by trusts and other institutions whose choice of investments was otherwise closely restricted. The effect was to give these securities a position in the London market with which the bonds of other countries could not compete; dominion and colonial governments were able to borrow more cheaply in London than many first-class private domestic English businesses could.

When political interests would be ill-served by foreign investment the British government asserted itself. On a number of occasions it induced British banking firms which would handle the sale of securities to the British public to break off loan negotiations with foreign borrowers. For example, it acted in 1910 to prevent loans to Persia while the Russian and British governments, which had divided Persia into spheres of influence, were attempting to gain Persian acceptance of certain conditions on loans to that country. Had not the British government stopped the proffered loans, its bargaining position with the destitute Persian government would have been weakened. On another occasion British banks were persuaded to abandon a proposal for the joint financing with German banks of the Baghdad Railway in Turkey; the British government feared that the project would start the expansion of alien interests in the Persian Gulf region. British investors were also asked to withdraw from certain negotiations in Latin America which conflicted with American interests; Britain had no desire to be drawn into difficulties with the United States government.

The British government sometimes entered into the arena of investment to protect the interests of British investors. For example, the visit of a British battleship to Guatemala induced the latter to restore payments of principal and interest on loans held by British investors. Yet on many other occasions when the British investor desired assistance, the British government stood aloof.

Those who directed the foreign affairs of Great Britain between 1870 and 1914 desired uninterrupted friendly relations with outside powers. Thus they were inclined to eschew fields of action which multiplied disputes with other countries without bringing great benefit. The vicissitudes of British capital and enterprise in search of opportunity abroad often fell . . . in that class. The underlying wish of the government—to be detected in phrases, gestures, unexplained actions of omission or commission, not in formal utterances—was that this hunt for opportunity should engage the Foreign Office as infrequently as possible. The importance of the operations of British capital abroad was not underestimated, once the philosophy and calculus of empire were generally accepted. But a place achieved solely through private effort and arrangement was doubly valued, for it involved the government in no rivalries, no difficult and uncomfortable negotiations.[1]

Pattern of French investment

France, the second largest creditor nation prior to World War I, had quite different experiences. She emerged as a major international creditor only late in the nineteenth century, though sizable overseas investments were made beginning in the 1850's. France was a nation of small savers—small farmers, traders, and artisans. One estimate suggests that out of a population of 40 million in 1914 some 10 million people were savers. French industry did not require all of their savings. Many of the capital extensions and improvements in French industry were financed without an appeal to the public for funds. There was a paucity of domestic investment opportunities because the general growth of manufacturing techniques was less rapid than in other countries, the unexplored natural resources of France were few, and a virtually stationary population gave little impetus to urban construction. Thus the public's savings were available for export. The organization of the French banking system helped to push public funds abroad. The Paris banks which handled foreign loans had numerous branches throughout the country that acted as selling agents for foreign securities, giving advice and encouragement to their depositors to invest in foreign securities. These branches were allotted quotas of securities to sell, and their profits stemmed primarily from these sales.

Under these pressures, the Frenchman's savings went abroad, mostly into government bonds because the small saver desired liquidity and safety.

---

[1] Herbert Feis, *Europe: The World's Banker* (New Haven: Yale University Press, 1930), p. 95.

But French savings did not travel far. Sixty per cent of French investment in 1914 was in Europe, and 40 per cent of that in Europe went to Russia. Only a tenth of France's investment was in her colonies as compared to the nearly 50 per cent of England's overseas investment which went to the British Empire.

The geographical distribution of French investment was significantly determined by political, rather than economic, considerations. Nearly 60 per cent of her investment went to areas in which it might be expected to produce political benefits. The French government could forbid the negotiations of any foreign securities on the Paris stock exchange; this control allowed France to use her capital as a bargaining weapon. For example, Belgium was obliged to make territorial concessions to France in the Congo as the price of government approval of a French loan. A loan to Serbia in 1913 was conditional on her evacuation of Albania. The flotation of railway securities in Paris by Russia, in 1913, with whom France had long nurtured a political alliance, was made conditional on an increase in Russia's military strength and on the construction of a strategic railroad planned in advance with the aid of the French general staff.

The development of French-Russian financial entanglements occurred side-by-side with the development of a political alliance. When the English lost interest in Russian bonds, partly because of a shift of interest away from Europe and partly because of a political estrangement, and when the German capital market was closed to Russia in 1887, France filled the financial gap. France was desirous of building an alliance with Russia against Germany after losing the Franco-Prussian War of 1871. In the years before World War I, each sale of new Russian securities in Paris was preceded by discussions between the two governments covering both the use of the borrowed funds and various aspects of their foreign political policies. Important loan transactions were handled directly by the finance *and* foreign affairs ministers and sometimes even by the czar. The Russian government went so far as to bribe the French press into laudatory statements to encourage acceptance of its securities by the French investor. (The antipathy of the Soviet Union and of Lenin toward foreign borrowing may be explained partly in terms of French lending to czarist Russia. The unsuccessful Russian revolution of 1905 was thwarted partly because of the availability of French funds to the czar.)

On numerous occasions, the French government initiated loan negotiations with foreign countries and brought the French banks which would handle the loans into the discussion at a later stage. This was the procedure in several loans to Balkan countries where France was desirous of preventing German lending and penetration. If the banks were reluctant to accept the risks, as was sometimes the case, the French government urged their cooperation on grounds of national welfare.

The French government controlled international investment in order also to obtain economic advantages. Denmark was refused a loan because she intended to raise her duties on French wine. Loans to foreign industries which would compete with French producers were sometimes refused; for example, permission to buy or sell in Paris the common stock of the U. S. Steel Corporation was denied in 1909. In a number of instances, a loan was made conditional upon the borrower spending the borrowed funds for French products, i.e., the loans were "tied." Because French industrial products were often higher priced than those of Germany or England, such tied loans were sometimes rejected by the potential borrowers who turned to other capital markets.

German experience

Germany's contribution to international investment was made against heavy demands for capital at home by a nation whose economy was industrializing and expanding rapidly and whose government required funds for a vast military establishment. With rates of interest generally higher than In addition, German banks and industries actively stimulated foreign foreigners to obtain funds. Nonetheless, Germany was the world's third largest creditor nation in 1914. In part, the lending was possible because Germany augmented her domestic supply of loanable funds by borrowing short-term capital from England and France, lending it on long term. in London or Paris, the Berlin market was a less desirable place for investment. The German banks themselves, and not individual private investors, owned a large proportion of the investment.

Overseas banks, plantations, and trading companies were established, and so were branches of German industrial plants such as those in Austria-Hungary, Russia, Italy, and Spain to install and make electrical equipment. But lending for such purposes was still not the predominant type. As with France and England, foreign government and railroad securities headed the list of German foreign investments, and the majority of the investments were in securities yielding a fixed return.

There was relatively little formal government intervention in the course of German foreign investment. But the government did have potent powers to prevent loans, and on occasion it used those powers. Czarist Russia was driven into the financial arms of France in 1887 by Bismarck when he closed the Berlin capital market to Russia in retaliation for higher Russian tariffs and a decree forbidding alien—mainly German—acquisition of land on Russia's western frontier. The German government took the initiative on several loans, inducing bankers to handle them in the national interest, and helped to obtain concessions for German enterprise abroad from foreign governments. In addition to formal government action, it was customary for the banks handling foreign investment to consult the German foreign office as to its position on any projected flotation.

For all three of the lending nations, the record shows that economic considerations, as reflected in the market place, were not the sole determinant of the allocation of capital. To the guiding hand of profits and the price system was added the sometimes gentle and sometimes not-so-gentle fist of the foreign office. Politics was added to productivity.

BENEFITS TO THE CAPITAL-EXPORTING NATIONS

What did the capital-exporting nations gain in return for their overseas investment? Foreign investment is not a costless act. Recalling the analysis in Chapter 4, the exports of the lending nation must rise, or its imports must fall, if a loan is to be transferred to the foreign borrower in the form of real goods and services; hence, foreign investment reduces the supply of goods and services available for use within the lending country when full employment prevails.

Returns on investments

One offset to the sacrifice of goods is the income (interest, dividends, and profits) received on investments abroad. In 1880, these receipts formed 4 per cent of the British national income, and in 1913 they equaled 9 per cent. For approximately the same dates, the figures for France were 2½ per cent and 5 per cent. But these data overstate the true gain, because allowance must be made for what the capital invested abroad would have earned if it had been used at home instead. Data presented earlier for Britain suggested that the return on foreign investment exceeded the yield on home securities. However, assuming diminishing returns, had the capital which was invested abroad been employed at home, the return of home investment would have been even smaller.

The French experience does not show foreign investment as favorably. At the turn of the century, the yield on foreign securities seems to have differed little from that on domestic securities. This may be explained by the tendency of French investors—small savers with cautious ways—to put their funds in foreign government bonds, which carry the lowest interest rewards.

It may be doubted that the French citizen-saver was in a good position to judge the risk element. New security issues were misrepresented to the public, and investors relied to a great extent on the advice of bankers who distributed foreign securities—bankers who were not averse to favoring those securities on which their commissions were greatest. Investing in Russian bonds was the patriotic thing for Frenchmen to do, and Russian bribery of French newspapers made their financial advice a poor basis for investment decisions.

Defaults

For Frenchmen much international investment was a failure through losses of principal. France lost a sum equivalent to two-thirds of her net foreign investment as a result of World War I. Russia, Turkey, Greece,

Austria-Hungary, the Balkans, and some South American countries repudiated or suspended payments on their debts. The Communist Revolution led to the repudiation of the heavy French investment in Russia. Had the French investor known that the czarist government was on the verge of bankruptcy even before the turn of the century and that a war or revolution would bring certain default, perhaps he would not have helped to cement the French-Russian alliance with his francs. But on a broader criterion, perhaps the French investments in Russia were profitable; czarist troops did keep a few divisions of the kaiser's military forces busy on the Eastern front for three years during World War I.

The British investor also suffered losses. For example, the early loans to foreign governments, especially those in South America, were in default on their interest payments a decade after Waterloo. Several American states repudiated their debts during the depression which followed the panic of 1837. Heavy defaults occurred in the 1870's. But the proportion of such losses was much less than that suffered by France, partly because British capital went largely to politically stable areas, e.g., the Empire.

Indirect gains

Britain gained indirectly from her foreign investments through the cheapening of her imports. (Recall the analysis in Chapter 4 regarding the effects of factor movements on the terms of trade.) The decline in the prices of imported foodstuffs between 1880 and 1900 was partly due to railroad construction and agricultural development abroad, aided by British capital. British capital opened up productive areas in the United States, Argentina, India, Canada, and Australasia, increasing the supply of primary products and increasing world trade through greater marketings of them. (An experience similar to that of Britain is suggested for the United States by the fact that currently about 20 per cent of American imports are produced by American-owned companies abroad; the degree of dependence on United States investment abroad is greatest for raw-material imports.) [2]

The decline in real wages in the lending country, which the analysis in Chapter 4 suggested would result from capital exports, finds a powerful offset in the cheapening of foodstuffs in the instance of Britain. The expansion of overseas agricultural production was highly desirable because the rising population which accompanied Britain's economic growth increased the demand for foodstuffs by Britain. Britain's dependence upon trade was increased by her foreign investment, for the inflow of cheap primary products made British agriculture increasingly unprofitable, and agricultural acreage fell greatly after 1875—a result assisted by England's free trade policy.

Britain shared the benefits of cheap food and raw materials with other industrial countries, but few other countries benefited from their own investments in the way that England did. France was not in much

---

[2] *Survey of Current Business* (December, 1953), p. 14.

need of the products of Russia, Turkey, or the Balkans, which were the areas of heavy French investment.

Britain may have gained through economies of large-scale production made possible by a higher level of exports consequent to foreign investment. British loans were intimately correlated with increased exports of railroad rails and other manufactured equipment. Manufacturing often provides opportunities for economies of large-scale production. The higher level of demand for such British products may have brought a decline in costs of production which, while it benefited the foreigner through lower prices, also reduced prices for home consumption.

Britain may have also benefited through the effect of her foreign investment on her employment levels. Since foreign lending involves a rise in exports and/or a contraction of imports by the capital-exporting nation, it reduces the supply of goods and services available for use within the lending nation. But if the additional exports or substitutes for the imports are produced with resources which would otherwise be unemployed, foreign investment does not reduce the home supply of goods and services; the unemployed resources would not be producing them for the home market even if there were no foreign investment. The British economy was marred by eleven business and financial crises in the nineteenth century, and the period from 1873 to 1896 was particularly difficult. The evidence suggests that capital exports and rising internal business activity were closely correlated in Britain and that it was foreign investment that pulled Britain out of most of the depressions before 1914.

Finally, in judging the benefits to lending countries of foreign investment, we must allow for the effects of foreign investment on home investment and economic growth. Taking periods longer than those covered by a single business cycle, British home and foreign investment tended to move in opposite directions. Thus in the long run, foreign investment was made at the expense of domestic investment and vice versa, which suggests that investment abroad restrained capital formation at home over the long pull. To judge from the complaints, French internal economic growth was adversely affected. Relative to Germany and England, France did not enjoy the great industrial expansion of the forty years prior to World War I. The sluggish development of French industry was blamed on the lack of sufficient capital for domestic industry and the financial segment of France was excoriated for its bias toward foreign investment. One Frenchman said that France "leaves her powers of production partially unfertile and idle . . . improving neither machinery nor methods. She employs capital to make fertile the labor of other nations. . . . She desires only to continue her lazy role of banker to the world."[3]

---

[3] R. Masse, *La production des richesses* as quoted in H. D. White, *The French International Accounts, 1880–1913* (Cambridge, Mass.: Harvard University Press, 1933), p. 298.

B. CAPITAL IMPORTS: SOME ISSUES

With the advent of self-conscious economic growth in the relatively poor nations since World War II and with the development of nationalism in those countries since the 1930's, the legacy of nineteenth (and twentieth) century foreign investment in capital-receiving countries has come under increasingly critical questioning.

In Chapter 4 we showed that an advantage in receiving capital from abroad is that it permits capital formation without contracting domestic consumption. But there are some alleged shortcomings, and the importation of capital is not without cost.

PAYMENTS FOR CAPITAL

Borrowers sometimes assert that the price paid for foreign capital in the form of interest, dividends, or profits withdrawn by foreign-owned enterprises is unfairly high. This attitude was clearly expressed by the appellation "The Drain" used to describe payments from colonial India to Britain before World War I, the majority of which were related to foreign investment.

The "proper" price for capital involves ideas of fairness and therefore it cannot be determined purely from economic criteria. But three economic questions should be part of the analysis: (1) Would the foreign capital have been supplied at a lower price? (2) Could the capital have been obtained within the capital-receiving country more cheaply? (3) Was the productivity of the capital greater than the cost?

It is difficult to generalize whether foreign capital would have been available at a return lower than actually charged. The railroads of India were probably financed on terms excessively favourable to the lender.[4] And unsavory practices among British financial firms transacting loans added to the cost, e.g., San Domingo issued securities for which she got only 5 per cent of their face value. But such instances cannot stand as an indictment of all nineteenth century foreign investment. Borrowers had a choice between borrowing in London, Paris, and Berlin in the latter part of the century, and, on the whole, the British investment houses which handled the issuance of securities competed with respect to new borrowers. However, borrowers did not frequently transfer their business among investment houses, because a long-standing relationship with one house was an advantage in obtaining acceptance by the investing public of securities to be issued.

Even if the borrowers did pay higher returns than lenders would have required to supply the funds, the capital recipients still gained if they

---

[4] Daniel Thorner, *Investment in Empire* (Philadelphia: University of Pennsylvania Press, 1950), Chapter 7.

could borrow more cheaply abroad than at home. In the nineteenth century very few countries had a capital market for large loans, so this alternative was not usually present; capital in the borrowing countries was scarce and interest rates were generally higher there.

The answer to the problem of the appropriate rates of return on borrowed capital depends partly on its productivity. To obtain the foreign currency with which to service its debt, a nation must increase its exports or reduce its imports. If the flow of goods and services resulting from the use of the borrowed capital, i.e., its productivity, leads either directly or indirectly to an increase in exports or a fall in imports equal to the charges for the capital, the service of the debt will not require a reduction in the total goods and services available to the debtor nation; that is, despite the export surplus, the amounts available afterward will be greater than those prior to borrowing. Thus it is desirable that the product of the capital be great enough and its composition be such that it generates an export surplus at least equal to the cost of the borrowed funds.

When a nation receives capital through the issuance of common stock or through the growth of foreign-owned enterprises, an automatic check is provided to insure that the capital-receiving country does not pay more for the capital than its productivity. Dividends on common stock and profits in foreign-owned enterprises cannot be paid unless they are earned, i.e., unless the capital is sufficiently productive to permit them. No such automatic check, except the possibility of default by the borrower, exists for interest payments on bonds. Failures in borrowing through bonds were often a result of unproductive expenditures by governments, such as the maintenance of large military establishments or erection of magnificent state buildings for reasons of prestige.

FOREIGN CAPITAL AND ECONOMIC GROWTH

A major criticism of foreign investment is that it has not adequately promoted the economic development of borrowing countries. Among the charges levied against foreign enterprises, past and present, are (1) that they are never fully integrated into the host country, the interests of the foreign stockholders being placed above those of native workers as, for example, when market conditions require a cutback in production; (2) that they remove irreplaceable natural resources which could be the basis for future economic growth, leaving only wages and taxes behind; (3) and that they favor foreign labor for technical jobs, leaving natives untrained, and that foreign employees receive much higher pay, live in isolated colonies, and regard themselves as temporary residents.

The dual economy

The foreign financing of mines, plantations, and other "colonial" forms of investment, it is charged, has resulted in a dual economy: a domestic sector, living at the subsistence level with low productivity because it has little capital, and a foreign-financed sector with high output per man, using capital-intensive methods of production. The foreign-financed sector of the capital-receiving country is little more than an outpost of the lending nation to whose needs it caters by providing raw materials and foodstuffs. Observation of any underdeveloped country today shows that there is truth in this description.

An explanation for the "outpost" or dual-economy phenomenon is that the economy of the capital-receiving nation is often so poor that the domestic market will not support large-scale production. A shoe factory is of little use if the people are too poor to buy shoes. During the nineteenth century, the growing markets were largely in Western Europe, and it should not be surprising that capital abroad would primarily serve that market. Despite the pull of market forces, little of the nineteenth century foreign investment went directly into the production of primary products. Though 80 per cent of Britain's overseas investment went to countries producing primary products, more than two-thirds went into government and railroad bonds. In addition there were extensive loans for public utilities. This leaves few investments of the so-called "colonial" type. The dual-economy complaint can be exaggerated.

Just because the "colonial" investments serve foreign markets and do not produce goods primarily for the host country does not mean that such investments make no contribution to the host country's economic growth. The wages paid by a foreign-owned firm to native workers over what they would obtain in native employment plus its tax payments to the host government constitute an increase in the real income of the native economy. The services of the native workers to the foreign enterprise and the "services" of the government, as measured by the taxes, are the host country's "exports" to foreigners; if the enterprise buying these services sells none of its product in the host country, it must exchange foreign currency, which it obtains by selling its product elsewhere, for that of the native government in order to pay local wages and taxes. The increase in real income is reflected in the increased power of the host country to buy foreign goods and services with the foreign currency obtained.

Social overhead capital

The contribution which the non-"colonial" type of investment can make to capital-receiving country's economic development is also important. Industrial growth under conditions of private enterprise requires what is now called public or social overhead capital. Such things as railroads, waterworks, gas works, roads, canals, and power plants were (and are) preconditions of individual business investment. The foundation for future economic growth was laid in the provision of overhead capital by foreigners, for example, as with the railroads in the United States, Canada, and Europe. Sometimes, of course, the railroads were built primarily to bring goods from the interior for export; but this did not preclude their use for hauling other goods and also facilitating the growth of internal markets.

The provision of overhead capital may, at best, lay the foundation for economic growth; it will not necessarily cause it. In India, the construction of railroads plus a low-tariff policy imposed by Britain facilitated the decline of some indigenous industry by introducing cheap foreign goods such as textiles. It is a matter of speculation, but perhaps India's industrialization would have come earlier if international specialization had not been thrust upon her through the expansion of foreign trade, and if foreign investment in railroads and in primary production, such as jute, had not created alternative opportunities for employment. India's primary-producer status in the world economy was and still is a sore point among many Indian nationalists; the grievance toward what foreign trade and British capital did to India is heightened by the fact that ancient India was once a major manufacturing area.[5]

Technical assistance

Foreign capital also made and still makes a contribution to the economic development of the receiving nation through the provision of technical assistance; that is, techniques are brought to areas where they are unknown. After the Napoleonic Wars, British investors founded important industrial enterprises in Europe, such as railway companies, river navigation companies, gas works, water works, cotton and other textile mills, and engineering establishments. In a number of instances, foreign technical knowledge left a permanent imprint on the receiving economy. Brassey, one of England's foremost international railroad builders, showed foreigners how the complex business of constructing a railroad could be efficiently organized. Not only was the construction of railroads done with British engineers and labor but even the locomotives were sometimes run by Englishmen. British capital and an Irishman named Mulvaney did much to improve the efficiency of coal mining in the Ruhr. With their capital and skill, Lister and Holden assisted in the introduction of mechanical wool combing into France and, despite many difficulties, successfully trained a number of French workers in the various operations required.

Clearly foreign investment can make an important contribution to the economic growth of the capital-receiving country, but the net benefit depends on several additional factors. For example, a rise in per capita real income can be wiped out by the rise in population that it makes possible. If population grows as fast as aggregate real income rises, per capita real income is unchanged. In a number of presently underdeveloped

---

[5] See Bruce McCully, *English Education and the Origin of Indian Nationalism* (New York: Columbia University Press, 1940), pp. 272–277.

countries which received capital in the past, population pressure was probably strong enough to seriously reduce the benefits of foreign investment. Sometimes the population pressure increased in direct response to foreign investment; for example, the building of railroads in India reduced the problem of famines by improving the transportation of foodstuffs within India.

THE TERMS OF TRADE AND TECHNOLOGICAL GROWTH

Another argument in the case against "colonial" investment concerns the terms of trade and the distribution between borrowing and lending countries of the fruits of technological progress.

Certain data suggest that since 1870 there has been a secular decline in the prices of primary products relative to manufactured goods, and that therefore the terms of trade have moved against countries exporting primary products and in favor of those exporting manufactures.[6] This would not imply a reduction in the gain from trade of primary producers if it were attributable to greater technological progress in primary production than in manufacturing. Technological progress permits a fall in prices by reducing costs, i.e., by reducing the quantities of factors required to produce a unit of output. While the fall in the price of exported goods consequent to technological progress reduces the quantities of imports which may be bought per physical unit of export, the quantities of factors used per physical unit of export also fall so that the nation "gives up" in its exports no more resources for its imports than before. That is, the nation is obliged to divert no more resources from production for the domestic market to export production in order to obtain a given quantity of imports.

However, according to the opponents of "colonial" investment, technological progress has been greater in manufacturing than in primary production. Therefore the terms of trade should have improved for primary producers since 1870.[7] But this allegedly was not the case. Rather, the industrialized countries have "appropriated" to themselves the benefits of technical progress. These benefits were denied to those countries doomed to primary production through the law of comparative advantage and colonial foreign investment.

The data underlying this argument are questionable, but even if they

---

[6] United Nations, *Relative Prices of Exports and Imports of Underdeveloped Countries* (New York: Columbia University Press, 1949), pp. 21 ff.

[7] Several explanations have been offered for the failure of the terms of trade of primary producers to improve. One is that the demand for primary products rises less, when real income increases, than the demand for manufactured goods. Another is that wages tend to rise in industrial countries during booms and do not fall during depressions, so that the gains of technical progress are absorbed through a secular rise in the incomes of the factors of production; the same downward inflexibility of wages during depressions does not exist in primary producing countries.

did accurately reflect the course of the terms of trade their significance for the direction of the gain from trade may be doubted. The quality of rubber, tin, and other primary products has not changed much since 1870 while the quality of manufactured goods has improved vastly. Thus, what the primary producers failed to gain through lower prices on manufactured goods, they may have picked up through product improvement.[8]

NATIONAL INDEPENDENCE

An important noneconomic objection to foreign investment is that there is an implicit loss of independence and sovereignty by the capital-receiving country. This aspect of foreign investment is intimately related to the growth of nationalism since the 1930's in present-day under-developed countries.

The governments of all three major creditor countries did from time to time assist their foreign investors in obtaining concessions—special dispensations—from foreign governments, often involving monopoly privileges. In part the need for these reflected the undeveloped legal and governmental systems of the countries in which investors wished to set up foreign enterprises; the concessions provided security for the enterpriser in lands which sometimes had little Western justice and little order. Sometimes the purpose of government pressure for concessions from foreign countries for investors was to prevent investors from other countries from setting up enterprises. Nineteenth century "imperialism" rode into China and part of Africa on the back of concession agreements. Perhaps the most humiliating aspect of some of these was the extraterritoriality rights given to Europeans by a number of undeveloped countries, which freed Europeans of native court jurisdiction and sometimes made the native government responsible for all damages to foreigners' property caused by a failure to maintain order. Claims were inflated, and the local government was blamed for all sorts of unlikely events. "Please shut that window," Ismail Pasha, ruler of Egypt, was reported to have said to one of his attendants during an interview with some European concessionaire, "for if this gentleman catches cold it will cost me £10,000."[9]

The major accusation is that some foreign-owned enterprises tend to constitute a state within a state and even attempt to manipulate governmental policy. "There is a well-founded distrust of the motives, powers, and actions of all large capitalistic foreign enterprises. The record is replete with cases of their dominating governments, corrupting legislators, and ruling entire states with selfish disregard of national interest. . . . Many are the charges against foreign corporations [in Latin America] of buying

---

[8] See Paul Ellsworth, "The Terms of Trade between Primary Producing and Industrial Countries," *Inter-American Economic Affairs*, X (Summer, 1956), 47–65.

[9] Eugene Staley, *War and the Private Investor* (New York: Garden City, Doubleday, 1935), p. 161.

out governments and fomenting revolt, and, I suspect, there is a great deal of truth in these accusations."[10] An official of the United Fruit Company, which has heavy interests in Central America, responded that such a charge "is the biggest sham that ever existed. There is absolutely nothing to it. There is no chance to exercise a large measure of political influence. . . . Besides, the political history of all these countries closely indicates that the ins of today are the outs of tomorrow. . . . A corporation that goes down there with a heavy direct investment must do so with the idea that it is to be there a long time, and that it cannot play favorites with people in politics."[11]

The fears of a loss of independence have not been limited to investments which involve foreign ownership of plants and firms. A member of the Chinese (pre-Communist) Ministry of Economic Affairs summarized China's loss of "integrity" as a result of foreign railway loans as follows: "(1) The lender shared the administration and management of the railway, which infringed the Chinese government's unified railway administration." (Some of the loans required that foreigners should be chief engineers or accountants until the loans were paid.) "Further, the safety of China was endangered, (2) the lender controlled the railway's finances, which directly affected the raising of new capital for the extension of the railway. This railway's finance constituted an important part of national finance. Therefore, indirectly the lender infringed upon the financial sovereignty of China."[12]

The political role which foreign capital can now play in a debtor country has altered greatly from what it was, but resentment against past experience remains high. As we shall see in Chapter 22, the fears of borrowing countries concerning a loss of political and economic sovereignty have had a serious effect on modern foreign investment.

C. HUMAN MIGRATION

CAUSES AND CHARACTER

Like the movement of capital, the transfer of people among nations reached a peak in the nineteenth century. The overseas migration of people from Europe (some 60 million during four centuries) began in the sixteenth century following the famed voyages of discovery and conquest. But prior to the nineteenth century, the volume of emigration from Europe was relatively small. Many who emigrated were military or commercial ad-

---

[10] J. Lloyd Mecham, "Latin America's Reaction to Foreign Investments," *Economic Relations with Latin America* (Ann Arbor: University of Michigan, 1940), pp. 37–38.

[11] *Ibid.*, p. 41.

[12] Kao Ping-Shu, *Foreign Loans to China* (New York: Sino-International Research Center, 1946), p. 46.

venturers, deported criminals, and/or political or religious refugees. Governments restricted emigration severely, partly because they feared special skills would be lost, partly because mercantilist doctrine emphasized the desirability of much cheap labor, and partly because they wished to retain a greater potential supply of soldiers. On occasion, when it served the national interest, governments assisted emigration. For example, emigrants were recruited by governments or by government-sponsored trading companies for the organized colonization of the New World.

The mass movement of the nineteenth century stands in contrast with the preceding centuries. It was primarily a spontaneous movement of individuals; it was relatively free of legal restrictions (democratic ideals had taken hold), and the dominant motive was individual economic improvement. Until 1880, the major source of emigration was the British Isles. After that time, there was a rapid rise in emigration from eastern and southern Europe. The countries receiving almost all the immigrants from Europe were, in descending order, the United States (with much the largest share), Argentina, Canada, Brazil, Australia, New Zealand, and South Africa. These countries were also major recipients of capital, so there was a complementarity in the movement of people and capital, particularly to countries with great natural resources and abundant land.

A number of economic forces operated to move people out of Europe in the nineteenth century. Population pressure was one. The number of people in Europe grew from 187 million to 400 million between 1800 and 1900. The crowding on agricultural lands induced emigration. The practice of dividing lands among all the heirs reduced the size of individual landholdings to uneconomic levels. The absorption in England of small farms into larger ones in order to expand grain production, and the conversion of cropland into pasture forced small farmers and agricultural workers to migrate. Famines were an important cause of migration before the middle of the century, as the number of Irish in America testifies.

The decline of handicraft industries consequent to industrialization induced migration of craftsmen, though industrialization, as evidenced by the decline in Germany's importance as a source of emigrants later in the century, probably deterred the emigration of others by raising real incomes. It is generally argued that the mobility of factors between nations is less than their mobility within a nation, for people dislike breaking their cultural and social ties. But the decline in handloom weaving in England after the introduction of new techniques induced emigration of artisans who often preferred to sail overseas rather than "trudge two hundred miles to the new Yorkshire factories."[13] Sometimes international mobility is greater than internal mobility.

The availability of cheap land in the New World was an attraction to people in Europe, railway building and the efforts of native pioneers

---

[13] Rowland T. Berthoff, *British Immigrants in Industrial America* (Cambridge, Mass.: Harvard University Press, 1953), p. 37.

having made large areas of land available and profitable. The growing markets in industrializing Europe opened the way for large-scale agricultural and raw-material production in overseas countries. However, toward the end of the century, the industrialization of the United States created employment opportunities for emigrants, and, as early as 1890, over 60 per cent of the foreign-born white population lived in urban areas.

Although not of great importance in the total picture, specific U.S. tariff policies induced migration. For example, in 1890, the United States bought about 70 per cent of Welsh tin output, but the McKinley tariff set such high duties that half the mills closed; both capital and labor force then migrated to the United States. The same occurred in the silk and lace industries. Such movements of factors in substitution for trade offset some of the adverse effects of tariffs on world output.[14]

Improvements in transportation facilities which gave rise to expanded trade also made it possible for many to improve their economic position through emigration. In the seventeenth century, a trip from France to Canada took two months and the mortality rate was as high as 50 per cent. By 1873 about 95 per cent of all the emigrants were carried in steamships, greatly reducing the time, cost, and the danger.

GAINS TO COUNTRIES OF IMMIGRATION

What did countries gain from immigration? It appears that the major portion of immigrants to the United States were young and male. This increased the percentage of the total population which was economically active and reduced the relative number of unproductive persons who were dependent upon others. This rise in the American labor force occurred at some saving to Americans because the immigrants had obtained some of their training, both formal and technical, abroad.

The savings of immigrants out of the greater income earned in their new countries permitted additional capital formation in the receiving countries. The Chinese immigrant in Far East areas has probably made an important contribution to the growth of his host country in this way. The receiving countries also gained through the capital that the immigrants brought with them. British emigrants to all countries took with them £125 million in the nineteenth century. But these advantages were somewhat offset by the remittances of immigrants to people in the homeland.

Immigrants also brought technical assistance of the kind discussed in regard to capital movements. In the eighteenth and nineteenth centuries, English skilled workers in Europe installed new machinery and instructed workers how to use it. British textile workers taught Frenchmen how to use the fly shuttle, the water frame, and the mule-jenny, and English

---

[14] Not all migration in response to tariff changes has this effect. The emigration of silk workers to America's protected industry following the reduction in the English duty on French silk in the Cobden-Chevalier Treaty probably reduced the favorable effect of tariff reductions on world output.

puddlers moved about Europe showing foreigners their craft. In the United States in the nineteenth century, "To start a gingham mill, a carpet factory, a tinplate works, or a pottery, or to open a coal, ore, or stone field, employers liked to have a leavening of foreign—usually British—workingmen, foremen, and superintendents."[15] Obviously some of their skill was passed on to the native Americans working beside them or under their direction. There are more dramatic examples of technical assistance such as the familiar escape of Samuel Slater to America with the secret of manufacturing cotton textiles.

Even where technical assistance was not involved because unskilled workers dominated the flow of immigrants, some see a gain to the receiving country. For example, the increased availability of unskilled labor in the United States, when emigration shifted from northern to eastern and southern Europe, is alleged to have induced the invention of skill-saving machinery. Others find this immigration of unskilled workers a boon to America's industrial expansion because it increased the supply of labor.

EFFECTS ON THE COUNTRY OF EMIGRATION

How did the countries losing people fare? They lost men of skill in some cases, though the skills were not always still required. The countries of emigration lost young men who could have been extremely productive, and they lost men who had been raised to manhood and trained at their expense. In some cases emigration did not relieve the population pressure in the country of emigration. The poverty of Italy, for example, was not eased significantly; the birth and death rates responded to replace the emigrants. But Britain gained cheaper imports of food and raw materials with the help of her emigrants. And Italy, like other countries, received some benefit for the money that emigrants sent back to the home folks, increasing the ability of Italy to purchase goods abroad. Probably a significant portion of these remittances was used, however, to bring over the families and friends the immigrants left behind; at the end of the century, 70 per cent of the total number of immigrants had their passages paid by persons who had emigrated earlier.[16] Furthermore, the gain to England through remittances from emigrants was more than offset by the capital taken out by them.

D. DECLINE OF MIGRATION AND CAPITAL MOVEMENTS

The advent of World War I disrupted the flow of capital over the world and gave rise to restrictions on migration. In 1920, many of the countries of immigration began to impose bars against people entering the country or to intensify quota systems already in existence. The main

---

[15] Berthoff, *op. cit.,* p. 85.

[16] H. A. Citroen, *European Emigration Overseas Past and Future* (The Hague: Martinus Nijhoff, 1951), p. 11.

objective was to prevent the populations uprooted by war from creating problems of resettlement in the new lands. Even nations which could readily have absorbed large immigration decided to control the flow and make it more selective, accepting only persons with skills or knowledge wanted by the economy. The restrictions were partly a protection of existing wage levels but also a means of preventing an increase in social welfare problems. The result was a gradual decline in migration among nations; after World War II, migration into the developing countries was usually sponsored by the receiving government and/or an intergovernmental agency.

Capital movements did not decline because of governmental restrictions so much as because of the general economic depression of the 1930's and the uneconomic lending which preceded it. During World War I, the United States turned from a net debtor of about $4 billion to a net creditor of over $12 billion. The shift was a result of sales by European countries in the American market of securities of U.S. firms they owned, of new borrowing by Europeans to pay for munitions, and of borrowing from the U.S. government under the Liberty Loan acts. The debt to the U.S. government was funded into long-term obligations, as was the inter-Allied debt which arose during the war. Some of the debts among the other Allies were canceled, but the U.S. government declined to do so.

Lending after World War I was mostly on private account, but with encouragement from the U.S. government to lend to Germany and other European countries to ease their reconstruction problems. The dollars extended permitted Germany to meet its reparations payments just as the English loans to France after the Napoleonic Wars had, and they also permitted France and England to meet their payments on their U.S. war debts. Britain only slowly re-entered the capital market as a lender and France and Germany even more slowly. The United States had become the principal supplier of capital for the world. It was not experienced in the field, however, and many loans were extended during the 1920's without regard to their economic justification or the ability of the recipient to repay.

The boom of the U.S. stock market tended to dry up the source of U.S. funds and even caused foreign capital to flow into the United States. The volume of long-term lending over the world declined in favor of short-term flows. The ensuing depression in 1930 brought flights of short-term capital and defaults on the long-term loans. The flow of capital was reduced to a trickle, with almost all U.S. capital going to Canada during the middle and late 1930's. The instability and unprofitability of lending throughout the 1920's and 1930's was an experience which private lenders, particularly in the United States, have found difficult to forget. The flow of capital over the world has, since World War II, become predominantly governmental or governmentally directed or controlled. The period of massive capital movements seen during the nineteenth century came to an end during the 1930's. Large movements have not occurred since World War II despite the efforts of the U.S. government which is impressed with the assistance that private foreign investment can give to the growth of under-developed countries.

SELECTED READINGS

A. CAPITAL EXPORTS: CAUSES, CHARACTER, AND BENEFITS

Cairncross, A. K. *Home and Foreign Investment, 1870–1913.* Cambridge: Cambridge University Press, 1953. Chapter 9 provides much of the material on the benefits to capital-exporting nations used in this chapter. Part 2 of Chapter 5 presents a brief discussion of the London foreign capital market, with an outline of the techniques used (including the shenanigans) in issuing securities.

Feis, Herbert. *Europe: The World's Banker, 1870–1914.* New Haven, Conn.: Yale University Press, 1930. Part I provides a general survey of the causes, direction, type, and mechanisms of foreign investment by the three major lenders. Part II describes governmental intervention in foreign investment, and Part III consists of case studies, many of them laden with international politics.

Jenks, Leland H. *The Migration of British Capital to 1875.* New York: Knopf, 1927. This presents the details, including the techniques and institutions involved, of particular capital movements.

Kuznets, Simon. "International Differences in Capital Formation," *Capital Formation and Economic Growth,* ed. by M. Abramovitz for the National Bureau of Economic Research. Princeton: Princeton University Press, 1955, pp. 19–106. Part 2 of this essay concerns the relation between foreign investment and total capital formation. An appendix provides a convenient compilation of data.

Nurkse, Ragnar. "International Investment Today in the Light of Nineteenth Century Experience," *Economic Journal,* LXIV (December, 1954), 744–758. A good summary of the subject of this chapter as it relates to current foreign investment questions.

Royal Institute of International Affairs. *The Problem of International Investment.* London: Oxford, 1937. Chapter 9 presents the statistical record on nineteenth century investment with some discussion of the reasons underlying the course of investment.

Salter, Arthur. *Foreign Investment.* Essays in International Finance, No. 12. Princeton: Princeton University Press, 1951. Part II of this brief essay surveys British capital exports in the late nineteenth century for use in considering American capital export conditions today.

Viner, Jacob. *International Economics.* Glencoe, Ill.: The Free Press, 1951. Chapter 3 concerns international finance and balance of power diplomacy from 1880 to 1914.

B. CAPITAL IMPORTS: SOME ISSUES

Baldwin, Robert. "Secular Movements in the Terms of Trade," *Papers and Proceedings, American Economic Association,* XLV (May, 1955), 259–

269 and the discussions on pp. 288–293. These papers discuss the significance and the measurement of long-term movements in the terms of trade. Desirable preparation for this material is found in Viner, Jacob. *Studies in the Theory of International Trade.* New York: Harper, 1937, pp. 555–564.

Henderson, W. O. *Britain and Industrial Europe, 1750–1870.* Liverpool: University Press, 1954. This brief book provides a number of examples of technical assistance.

Kindleberger, Charles P. *The Terms of Trade, A European Case Study.* New York: Wiley, 1956. Chapters 10 and 11 discuss the course of the terms of trade with respect to underdeveloped countries and primary-producing nations. A number of hypotheses attempting to explain their course are presented in the former chapter.

Kuznets, Simon. See above.

Lewis, Cleona. *America's Stake in International Investments.* Washington: Brookings, 1938. Chapters 1–5 present a detailed account of American capital imports up to 1914.

Nearing, Scott, and Joseph Freeman. *Dollar Diplomacy.* New York: Huebsch, 1925. See Chapter 4 for examples of imperialism relating to foreign investment.

Nurkse, Ragnar. *Problems of Capital Formation in Underdeveloped Countries.* New York: Oxford, 1953. Chapter 1 provides an explanation of the dual-economy phenomenon.

Singer, H. W. "The Distribution of Gains between Investing and Borrowing Countries," *Papers and Proceedings, American Economic Association,* XL (May, 1950), 473–485. This paper attacks "colonial" investment. For a critical response see A. N. McLeod, "Trade and Investment in Underdeveloped Areas: A Comment," *American Economic Review,* XLI (1951), 411–419.

Staley, Eugene. *War and the Private Investor.* New York: Garden City, Doubleday, 1935. Part I provides examples relating to imperialism and foreign investment.

C. HUMAN MIGRATION

Berthoff, Rowland T. *British Immigrants in Industrial America.* Cambridge, Mass.: Harvard University Press, 1953. Part I provides numerous examples of technical assistance to the United States through immigration and also discusses some of the motives for immigration.

Handlin, Oscar. "International Migration and the Acquisition of New Skills," *The Progress of Underdeveloped Areas,* ed. by B. F. Hoselitz. Chicago: University of Chicago Press, 1952. A discussion of the technical assistance provided to the United States by immigrants.

United Nations. *The Determinants and Consequences of Population Trends.* New York: Columbia University Press, 1953. Chapters 6 and 16 summarize the course of human migration and present many of the views on the causes and effects. An excellent bibliography is provided.

PART III EXTERNAL AND INTERNAL DISTURBANCES AND THEIR ADJUSTMENT

9 Techniques of Payment and the Balance of Payments

Money has received little attention in the previous discussions. In fact we argued in Chapter 2 that, under certain conditions, money prices had no role in the determination of international economic patterns; the important determinants were relative prices and rewards. In Part III, we reintroduce money. The discussion of events deals primarily with the decades after World War I, for in that period money became independently important with a vengeance.

In the present chapter we first show how international payments for individual transactions are made; we then aggregate them into what is known as the international balance of payments. The next two chapters outline the pathology of international payments, both internal and external. The remaining chapters of Part III consider various policies used to relieve or cure the diseases we have discovered.

A. TECHNIQUES OF INTERNATIONAL PAYMENT

THE PROCESS OF PAYMENT

Since dollars are not the coin of the British realm nor are pounds sterling the currency of America, it is unlikely that Americans will have pound sterling notes with which to pay Englishmen whom they owe or that Englishmen can use in Britain dollar bills that Americans could pay. No matter how payment is made, Americans who pay Englishmen must eventually finish with fewer dollars and the Englishmen must eventually obtain pounds sterling.

Suppose that an American importer wishes to pay a British exporter for goods. The fundamental elements of the process would be as follows: (1) The American importer pays dollars to his bank, say, in New York;

(2) his New York bank pays the London Bank of the British exporter *either dollars or pounds sterling;* (3) the London bank pays pounds to the British exporter. The methods involved depend upon the instruments used.

The British exporter may draw a draft on the importer or, if the American importer is unknown and/or untrusted, on a bank at which the importer has made advance arrangements. This draft is an order addressed to the American importer, or to his bank, to pay a certain sum of money, either dollars or pounds. The British exporter gives the draft, along with certain documents which give title to the goods he has shipped, to his London bank; in return the British exporter receives sterling from the London bank.

The major banks of each nation keep accounts with each other to facilitate international payments; such banks are "correspondents" to each other. Several British banks and some American banks, such as the National City Bank of New York, have branches all over the world which perform the same service. Thus, to obtain payment from the United States, the London bank sends the draft and documents to its correspondent bank in New York which presents the draft to the importer or his bank. If it is a "sight" draft it must be paid when presented; the importer does not receive the documents which permit him to pick up the goods at the wharf until he has paid the required sum. If it is a "time" draft, which grants the importer credit by delaying payment for usually thirty, sixty, or ninety days, the importer is required to "accept" the draft before receiving the documents. By writing "accepted" across the face of the draft, signing and dating it, the importer (or his bank if the draft were drawn on it) agrees to pay the stated sum in the specified number of days.

If the sight draft calls for payment in dollars, the correspondent bank in New York, upon receiving the dollars from the importer or his bank, advises the London bank that the London bank has more dollars in its deposit at the New York correspondent bank. In this way, the London bank is compensated for the sterling it pays to the British exporter. If the importer's bank rather than the importer pays the dollars to the correspondent bank, the importer's bank recoups its funds from the importer. Not a single pound note or dollar bill or ounce of gold has crossed the seas, yet the British exporter has more pounds, the American importer has fewer dollars, and the London bank has more dollars in New York. The disposition of the London bank's dollar deposit in New York is discussed below.

If a time draft—or an acceptance, as it is called after the draft has been accepted—is used, the British exporter may provide credit to the importer by holding it until maturity. By prearrangement with the importer, the time draft includes an interest cost for the credit as well as the cost of the goods shipped. But if the exporter desires his money earlier than the maturity of the acceptance, he may discount (sell) the acceptance with someone who wishes to make a short-term investment. In this event, the purchaser of the acceptance actually provides the credit to the American importer. The British exporter receives a sum slightly smaller than the face value of the acceptance. The difference between the face value, which is the sum the American importer eventually pays, and the amount received by the British exporter accrues to the purchaser of the acceptance as interest income. Upon maturity, the acceptance is presented to the American importer or his bank for payment; the funds are remitted to the last holder of the acceptance in the manner used for the sight draft.

If the sight or time draft drawn on the American importer had required him to pay pounds sterling, he might do so by buying a cable or a bank draft from his New York bank. Through the cable and the bank draft, the New York bank orders its correspondent bank in London to pay sterling to the British exporter. Both are similar to personal checks, except that a bank, rather than an individual, orders another bank to make payment. The correspondent bank in London, upon receiving the cable or bank draft, pays the British exporter sterling and recoups its funds by reducing the sterling deposit of the New York bank on its books. The New York bank's loss of pounds abroad is offset by the gain of dollars from the American importer who bought the cable or bank draft.

THE CLEARING OF PAYMENTS

Suppose that the London bank receives dollar deposits in its New York correspondent bank, and that it pays sterling to the British exporter. The London bank may sell these dollar deposits to Englishmen who wish to make payments to the United States. That is, an Englishman may buy a dollar draft or cable from the London bank; the draft or cable orders the London bank's correspondent in New York to pay an American a certain amount of dollars. When all the payments are completed, the American receives dollars from the correspondent bank in New York, and the London bank loses dollars in New York while gaining sterling from the Englishman who buys the cable or draft. This transaction is the reverse of the transaction supposed above in which the London bank obtained dollars and paid out sterling; we see how, in this simplified example, international payments and receipts by each country are cleared on the books of banks.

The clearing process may involve more than two countries. Peruvian banks accumulate sterling deposits in London banks as a result of Peruvian exports to Britain. If the Peruvian banks need additional dollars to permit Peruvians to pay for imports from the United States, the Peruvian banks might then exchange with London banks some of the sterling balances they have in London for the dollars that the London banks have in New York. This is the payments side of multilateral trade.

Still another posssibility is that, when London banks gain dollars in New York, they may request their correspondent banks to invest those dollars in American securities, usually of the federal government; in this way the London banks earn some interest. Whether or not this happens depends partly on the interest rates in New York and London, because if the rate is higher in London the London banks would prefer to sell the dollars to Englishmen and invest in London the sterling they receive.

Another possibility when London banks gain dollars is that they will simply leave them on deposit with their New York correspondents. Banks dealing in foreign exchange, i.e., drafts and cables giving claim to foreign currency, must have inventories of products in which they deal just as druggists have stocks of tooth paste in order to meet the requirements of their customers. If the London banks find that their working balances of dollars are low, they will accumulate some dollars in their deposits abroad.

Over any given period of time—a day, a month, a year—British banks will receive dollars in American bank accounts through payments to England. Over the same period of time, there will be a demand for those dollars to make payments. What happens if the supply of dollars forthcoming in any period falls short of the demand? The British banks may meet the excess demand by drawing down their dollar deposits abroad which they have accumulated from previous periods. Or, if they own some gold, they may sell it to the United States for dollars, and the dollars will then be sold to persons wishing to make payments. Or the Bank of England, Britain's central bank, may sell some of its gold to the United States to be sold for dollars; the Bank of England then sells the dollars to the British commercial banks, who in turn sell the dollars to Englishmen who wish to make payments abroad. Or the British commercial banks or the Bank of England might borrow dollars from American banks. Or, if the excess demand seems to be persistent, the British government might borrow dollars from the American government or perhaps even ask for a gift.

B.   THE BALANCE OF PAYMENTS

A fairly comprehensive picture of international transactions is provided by the balance of payments. The balance of payments is a statistical tabulation of the economic transactions between the residents of one country and the residents of all (or sometimes only a part) of the rest of the world for a given period of time.

AN INTRODUCTORY VIEW

The general nature of the balance of payments is most easily perceived by imagining that all transactions between the United States and the rest of the world require payment in dollars. In the following hypothetical balance of payments for 195X "Receipts" refer to payments by foreigners to the United States, while "Payments" refer to payments by the United States to foreigners.

U.S. BALANCE OF PAYMENTS, 195X
(billions of dollars)

Receipts		*Payments*	
Exports of goods and services	$15	Imports of goods and services	$7
		Donations, net	3
		Capital outflow, net	4
		Gold imports, net	1
	$15		$15

In the year under consideration, foreigners bought $15 billion of American goods and services. How did they obtain the dollars with which to pay for these goods and services? Americans bought $7 billion of foreign goods and services, and therefore provided that many dollars to foreigners. In addition, the United States gave foreigners $3 billion more gifts than foreigners gave the United States; these *net* donations made additional dollars available to foreigners to finance their purchases of American goods and services. Another $4 billion was provided by a net loan from the United States to foreigners; the net loan is a result of a combined outflow of American capital to foreigners and a withdrawal of capital from the United States which foreigners had previously loaned to America and a smaller combined flow of foreign capital to the United States plus repayments by foreigners of American capital previously loaned to them. Finally, an additional $1 billion was provided to finance foreigners' purchases of American goods and services through U.S. imports of gold from foreign nations, which gold imports were paid for with dollars.

ACCOUNTING PRINCIPLES

International transactions are divided between two columns: debits and credits. Those transactions which, when considered individually, give rise to a claim for payment against residents during the period under consideration are entered in the debit column; those which lead to receipts from foreigners are entered in the credit column.

For example, suppose that, on a given day, an American exports $100 of merchandise. Imagine that the accompanying draft or cable is cleared immediately so that either an American bank receives additional deposits in a foreign bank or a foreign bank undergoes a decline in its dollar deposits in an American bank. To understand balance-of-payments accounting most easily, the shipment of the goods and the change in bank deposits should be considered separately.

Commodity exports appear as a credit item; credit items in the U.S. balance of payments are those which give rise to payments to the United States, and American exports must be paid for by foreigners.

The change in bank deposits is a movement of capital between nations, if capital is considered as a financial asset. For example, an increase in American-owned deposits abroad means an increase in American assets abroad or a movement of capital from the United States to foreign nations, i.e., a capital export from the United States. A reduction of foreign-owned dollar deposits in the United States is a fall in foreigners' assets in America or a movement of foreign capital out of the United States, i.e., a capital export from America.

Recalling that debit items are those which require payments to foreigners, the position of capital exports in the balance of payments is best remembered by concentrating on the idea that, if the United States is to export capital, the United States must pay foreigners a sum equivalent to the value of the capital. Therefore capital exports appear in the balance of payments as debit entries. Hence the balance of payments entries of the United States on the particular day of the export transaction appear as follows:

Credits		*Debits*	
Exports of goods	$100	Capital exports	$100

Suppose that, on the next day, the United States buys goods from foreigners, and that there is an immediate fall in American-owned deposits abroad *or* a rise in foreign-owned dollar deposits in America as a result of the payment for these goods. The United States balance-of-payments entries on this next day are as follows:

Credits		*Debits*	
Capital imports	$100	Imports of goods	$100

The import of goods appears under debits because Americans must pay foreigners for the commodities. The increase in foreign-owned deposits in the United States is an import of foreign capital from abroad into the United States; alternatively, the decline in American-owned deposits abroad is an import of American capital into the United States from abroad. In either case, the United States imports capital. Since capital imports, if considered separately, require foreigners to pay the United States, the capital imports are entered under credits.

If we put together the two days' transactions, we have a balance of payments for a two-day period as follows:

Credits		*Debits*	
Exports of goods	$100	Imports of goods	$100
Capital Imports	$100	Capital exports	$100

By canceling the capital imports and capital exports, we see that American exports of $100 finance American imports of $100 over that two-day period.

If United States exports had been $100, as above, while American imports were only $90, then the capital movements connected with those transactions could not completely offset one another. Rather, there would have been a net capital export of $10 which would reflect a net decline in foreign bank deposits in the United States or a net increase in American-owned bank deposits abroad as follows:

Credits		Debits	
Exports of goods	$100	Imports of goods	$90
		Net capital exports	$10

Some transactions involve no payment at all. For example, suppose the United States government gives goods to foreign governments free of charge. The goods would be entered as a credit in the U.S. balance of payments. A second entry would be made in the debit column with a title suggesting the character of the transaction, i.e., donation, gift. Thus, the balance-of-payments entries would appear as follows:

Credits		Debits	
Exports of goods	$100	Donations	$100

In this instance, American gifts have financed American exports. Since there is an offsetting debit entry for every credit, and vice versa, the balance of payments always balances in an accounting sense.

TYPES OF TRANSACTIONS

The balance of payments summarizes the flow of transactions over a period of time. Similar types of transactions are aggregated in the balance of payments. Each of the various types may be found on both sides of the balance payments. For simplicity of exposition, we shall only provide examples of debit entries in the U.S. balance of payments, i.e., transactions which give rise to claims for payment against the United States. The credit entries for the same type of transaction can be determined simply by reversing the direction of the flow.

One broad grouping of transactions is found on the *current account*. It embraces all goods and services. *Merchandise* imports, which consist solely of commodities, is one aggregation within the current account. The current account also contains several types of imported services called "invisible" items. *Income on investment,* comprising payments of interest and dividends to foreigners, and the profits of foreign-owned firms in the United States, is the payment which is entered in the balance of payments to reflect the use of foreigners' capital made available to Americans. The expenditures of American tourists abroad for lodging, food, amusement, etc., involve the purchase of services by Americans from foreigners; these expenditures are entered in the balance of payments as *travel*. Americans purchase the services of foreign-operated ships, airlines, etc., to carry passengers and goods; the expenditures for this purpose are entered in the balance of payments as *transportation*. (It should be noted that the payments by Americans to American ship operators, for example, are not international transactions, and therefore they do not appear in the balance of payments.) In addition, Americans make payments for the use of foreign-owned patents, for the rental of foreign films, for insurance written by foreign companies, and for a host of other items classified under *miscellaneous services*.

Another broad group of transactions is called *unilateral transfers*. These are gifts. To qualify as a debit entry in the U.S. balance of payments, the gifts must be from the United States to foreigners. When the gifts take the form of goods, a debit entry in unilateral transfers offsets the credit entry under merchandise which reflects the exportation of goods. Unilateral transfers are usually divided into *private remittances* and *government grants*.

The *capital* account constitutes another broad class of transactions. We have already seen that an increase in American-owned bank deposits abroad or a fall in foreign-owned deposits in the United States constitutes an export of capital from the United States (a debit entry). Export of capital from the United States occurs also when Americans (a) purchase foreign stocks and bonds or erect American-owned plants abroad, (b) repay capital which they had previously borrowed or received from foreigners, and/or (c) provide short-term credit to foreigners such as when American exporters draw thirty-day drafts in conjunction with the sale of goods. Capital movements are divided into short-term and long-term movements; the dividing line between the two is determined by whether or not the maturity of the investment or loan is in excess of one year. Thus the purchase of a newly issued foreign bond having a maturity of twenty years would constitute a long-term capital export from the United States. The accumulation of foreign bank deposits by American banks is considered a short-term capital export, as is the thirty-day credit referred to above. Long-term capital movements are divided into *direct* investment and *portfolio* investments. Direct investments are those capital movements to firms abroad in which Americans have an important voice in management; portfolio investments consist primarily of stocks, bonds, and loans not included in direct investments. Capital movements may also be designated according to the owners: *private* and *government* capital movements are sometimes distinguished in the balance of payments; sometimes the movements of *foreign*-owned and *United States*-owned capital are set forth separately.

Finally, *gold* movements may be distinguished from the foregoing

Table 2. United States Balance of Payments, 1946
(millions of dollars)

Credits		Debits	
		CURRENT ACCOUNT	
Exports of Goods and Services:		*Imports of Goods and Services:*	
Military transfers under aid programs	$ 69	Military expenditures abroad	$ 493
Merchandise, other than military	11,707	Merchandise, other than military	5,073
Transportation	1,384	Transportation	459
Travel	257	Travel	457
Income on investments	772	Income on investments	212
Misc. services	596	Misc. services	256
		UNILATERAL TRANSFERS	
		Private remittanccs, net	679
		Government grants:	
		Military, net	69
		Other grants and transfers, net	2,249
		CAPITAL ACCOUNT	
		United States Capital	
		A. Private	
Repayments, long-term	$308	Direct investments, net	$230
		New issues	85
		Other long-term, net	96
		Short-term, net	310
		B. Government	
Repayments, long-term	86	Long-term	3,348
Short-term, net	238		
		Foreign Capital	
		Long-term, net	$347
		Short-term, net	633
		GOLD	
		Net Gold Imports	623
Total Recorded Credits	$15,416		
Net Errors and Omissions	204		
Total Credits	$15,620	Total Debits	$15,620

SOURCE: *Survey of Current Business,* July, 1954, Table 1, pp. 14–15. This table provides data on the U.S. balance of payments from 1850 through 1953.

transactions because of their special importance in international finance. Gold imports to the United States would be entered as a debit, for, recalling that debits require payments to foreigners, the imported gold must be paid for with dollars or with foreign currency.

All of the foregoing transactions could be reversed to show the kinds of credit entries which appear in the U.S. balance of payments.

U.S. BALANCE OF PAYMENTS IN 1946

To provide an integrated illustration of credit and debit entries, the preceding table presents the American balance of payments for 1946. The reader must be cautioned that entries in published balance-of-payments statements are, for the most part, estimates of the actual transactions and flows. The balance of payments is not kept on a day-to-day basis, and the governments which publish balances of payments do not obtain information on every transaction that occurs. The result is that the total debits and credits which are recorded do not equal each other. Previous analysis showed, however, that for each debit entry there is an offsetting credit entry and vice versa. Therefore the government agencies which collect and present balances of payments enter a figure called "Errors and Omissions" to make the balance of payments balance. This is a net figure showing the difference between the errors in the debit and credit columns.

The extensive blank space in the credit column of the 1946 U.S. balance of payments under unilateral transfers and in the capital and gold accounts does not mean that foreigners gave the United States no gifts, or sent no capital, or bought no American gold. Most of these items are netted, and, because the balance of debits and credits favored the debits, the figure for each item was entered only on the debit side.

The first entry on the credit side of the current account, "Military Transfers under Aid Programs," consists of military items provided by the American government to foreign governments free of charge; the offsetting item is found on the debit side under unilateral transfers, "Military, net." The first entry on the debit side, "Military Expenditures," includes purchases from foreigners by American military personnel overseas, who are regarded as residents of the United States for balance-of-payments purposes, and purchases by the U.S. military establishment from foreign countries.

APPENDIX: A NOTE ON FINANCIAL PROCEDURES

There are numerous instruments for effecting payments among countries and a variety of terms under which payments may be made. Some of them extend credit to the importer for varying lengths of time; others require immediate payment, and all involve a variety of channels.

For some transactions "cash in advance" is required; this method is favorable to the exporter since he gets his money before shipment. Such onerous terms may have to be accepted by the buyer when a strong seller's market prevails or when the seller dominates the market so completely as to be able to dictate the terms. In the absence of these conditions, partial payment in advance may be required for expensive goods produced to the specifications of the buyer. In machine tool production, which involves the use of expensive special dies, partial payment in advance is not uncommon.

Provision of credit may be on "open account" or through a time document. The former is similar to a charge account one might have at a department store; the goods are shipped to the foreign buyer and a bill (invoice) is rendered which is paid at some future date by cable, bank draft, or other means of final settlement. Payments may be made every month, as with a charge account, or after the goods are resold by the foreign buyer. In the latter case the exporter sells "on consignment." Such credit terms reflect the exporter's confidence in the integrity and resources of the foreign buyer; they are often used in sales to foreign branches or subsidiaries of the supplier.

Drafts drawn by the exporter on the foreign buyer may call for payment when they are presented to the importer (at sight), a certain number of days after presentation to the importer (time draft), or on a specified day (date draft). These drafts may be accompanied by documents which permit the importer to take possession of the goods. (Not all drafts are accompanied by documents; if not, they are called "clean" drafts.) The documents may be obtained only upon payment of the draft or upon its acceptance by the importer. In the former situation, the draft is called a D/P draft (documents on payment), and in the latter, a D/A draft (documents on acceptance).

A D/P draft is in effect a C.O.D. shipment because the importer must pay before obtaining the goods. In fact, a D/P draft which must be paid on sight can become a cash-in-advance sale if the documents and draft, which must be presented to the importer by the correspondent bank upon their arrival, arrive by airmail or fast passenger steamer in advance of the goods. To avoid this burden on the importer, exporters may instruct the correspondent bank to hold the documents until the goods arrive. A D/A draft provides the buyer with credit for the period of the draft; he may obtain the goods in advance of payment. A time draft (D/P), even though it delays payment for a certain number of days, does not provide the buyer with credit, because he may not obtain the goods without first paying for them. Such a procedure may be satisfactory to a broker-importer; upon arrival of the goods he may obtain permission from the correspondent bank which holds the documents to draw samples of the goods to show prospective purchasers. When the broker makes the sale, he obtains the money from the purchaser with which to pay the draft, receives the documents, and turns the documents over to the purchaser to enable him to obtain the goods.

If the importer desires to take possession of the goods before payment under a time draft (D/P), he may arrange with the correspondent bank holding the documents to "borrow" the goods. The importer receives the documents upon signing a trust receipt and takes the goods in trust. If the importer does not pay the draft when it is due, the entrusting bank must make payment. The exporter who drew the draft may never know of the transaction between the importer and the correspondent bank. In fact if he had known that the bank would provide the importer with credit, the exporter might have been willing to draw a D/A instead of D/P time draft; inadequate information of the credit standing of the importer leads the exporter to draw the draft on a D/P basis to insure payment.

An exporter having a draft which he has drawn has three procedures through which he may obtain his money even if the draft is not yet accepted or immediately due. If the draft calls for payment in his own currency, he may discount it at a bank, receiving the face value less collection charges and the interest on the money between the time the draft is due and the time the exporter is paid. If the draft calls for payment in foreign currency, he may sell it to his bank, receiving in return an amount of local currency smaller by the amount of the collection and interest charges. Finally, he may ask his bank to collect the proceeds for him when due; unless he can borrow against pending collection he must wait for his money until the importer has paid. In the instance of a collection, the bank does not take ownership of the draft.

In the use of the commercial draft, the exporter stands a risk that the importer may not accept the goods and may attempt to void the sales contract. Or he stands a risk that the importer may take the goods after accepting the draft but not make payment when called upon to do so. Such risks can be minimized through a letter of credit. This instrument substitutes the known credit standing of a bank for the unknown status of the importer. The importer obtains a letter of credit from a bank, the details of which are sent to a correspondent bank in the exporter's country. The letter extends permission to the exporter to draw a draft on the bank opening the letter of credit, or on the correspondent opening the letter of credit, rather than on the importer. The letter of credit specifies the goods to be shipped and the terms on which they are sold. Should the letter of credit be an irrevocable one, the exporter may disregard the credit standing of the importer since, as long as the exporter meets the specifications in the letter, he may draw on the bank without regard to the importer. Added assurance is provided to the exporter if the correspondent bank in his country confirms the letter of credit; the correspondent thereby guarantees payment also.

If the draft drawn by the exporter on the bank opening the letter of credit is a time draft, the draft is sent to the opening bank for acceptance rather than for immediate payment. Upon acceptance, the draft is called a bank acceptance to distinguish it from a trade acceptance in which the importer accepts the draft. The bank acceptance is readily salable if the exporter wishes his money in advance of the due date of the draft, because it has the name of a well-known bank upon it from which any prospective purchaser of the acceptance is most certain to obtain payment. The letter of credit is a surety given to the exporter by the importer, and the importer is charged for it by the bank which opens the letter of credit; sometimes the opening bank reduces the bank account of the importer upon opening of the letter of credit, which tends to impair the cash position of the importer. The importer, however, gains in that the exporter must ship the goods within the time limit of the letter and must meet all the specifications to obtain payment; this reduces the dangers of having careless suppliers abroad.

American banks accept drafts drawn upon them in behalf of both American and foreign importers, though in the latter case arrangements are usually first made through the foreign correspondent bank of the American bank. In some instances American transactions are financed on an acceptance basis without directly involving the foreigner. An American exporter may draw a time draft, after shipping goods, upon an American bank. The time draft is then discounted by the bank, and the exporter receives funds; the exporter repays the American bank out of his later receipts from the foreigner. American imports are similarly financed. Thus, when a sight draft is drawn upon an American importer, the importer draws a time draft on an American bank which then discounts it, providing the funds with which to pay the sight draft. When the time draft is due, the importer pays the American bank.

Individual American banks often discount drafts drawn against themselves, in which case they earn the interest on the acceptance. The American banks may not wish to hold their own acceptances, however, but may swap the discounted acceptances among themselves through the services of acceptance dealers. These dealers do not normally hold the acceptances, but sell them at a slightly higher price to persons, firms, or institutions desiring to make short-term investments. This swapping results in there being two bank names on the acceptance, because the purchasing bank also endorses the acceptance. Such acceptances are in strong demand by foreign central and commercial banks which wish to invest their idle dollar balances. Bank acceptances are regarded as traditional investments by foreign banks and frequently have a higher yield than Treasury bills, particularly because income on acceptances is exempt from the U.S. withholding tax on foreign-interest earnings.

SELECTED READINGS

A. TECHNIQUES OF INTERNATIONAL PAYMENT AND A NOTE ON FINANCIAL PROCEDURES

"Bankers' Acceptance Financing in the United States," *Federal Reserve Bulletin,* XLI (May, 1955), 482–494.

Crump, Norman. *The ABC of the Foreign Exchanges.* London: Macmillan, 1951. Chapters 1–10 (all short) provide a relatively simplified discussion of the international payments mechanism.

Rosenthal, Morris S. *Techniques of International Trade.* New York: McGraw-Hill, 1950. A comprehensive discussion of the business aspects of international trade.

Shaterian, William S. *Export-Import Banking.* New York: Ronald, 1947. A detailed source on foreign-exchange operations from the standpoint of the foreign department of a bank and on the related instruments of international trade.

Southard, Frank A., Jr. *Foreign Exchange Practice and Policy.* New York: McGraw-Hill, 1940. Chapters 2 and 4 are especially valuable.

"United States Banks and Foreign Trade Financing," *Federal Reserve Bulletin,* XLI (April, 1955), 357–367. Especially noteworthy for data and for its comparison of foreign banking facilities.

von Klemperer, Alfred H. "Present Foreign Payments Practices in the United States," *International Monetary Fund Staff Papers,* II (April, 1952), 199–212. A description of the U.S. foreign-exchange market, including nontraditional practices.

B. THE BALANCE OF PAYMENTS

Allen, R. G. D., and J. Edward Ely, eds. *International Trade Statistics.* New York: Wiley, 1953. Essays by 25 experts on the collection, presentation, and interpretation of trade data, including a bibliography of trade-data sources from many nations.

Badger, Donald G. "The Balance of Payments: A Tool of Economic Analysis," *International Monetary Fund Staff Papers,* II (September, 1951), 86–197. A discussion of many knotty problems in balance-of-payments accounting methodology.

International Monetary Fund. *Balance of Payments Yearbook.* Washington: annually. Presents balance-of-payments data for a large number of countries with interpretations of the forces at work in some instances. Data for countries are also made available in a loose-leaf form in advance of publication of the full yearbook. A detailed explanation of the individual accounts may be found in the Fund's *Balance of Payments Manual.*

U.S. Department of Commerce. *Balance of Payments of the United States, 1949–1951.* Washington: Government Printing Office, 1952. Chapter 2 discusses the methodology of balance-of-payments accounting, the techniques of collecting data, the sources of data, along with the components of the various classes of entries in the balance of payments.

————. *Survey of Current Business.* Various issues each year present quarterly and annual balance-of-payments data for the United States, including a regional breakdown.

10 International Reserves and Balance-of-Payments Difficulties

In the remainder of Part III we shall consider two problems faced by an open economy, i.e., by a nation that has international economic relations. The manner in which these problems are solved determines in an important degree the extent to which a nation will participate in the international economy and partake of the gains from international trade. The first of these problems, to be discussed in the present chapter, is that of disparities in international payments and receipts, i.e., the problem of external instability. We postpone to the next chapter a discussion of the problems of internal instability peculiar to an open economy.

A. NATURE AND FUNCTION OF INTERNATIONAL RESERVES

THE NEED FOR RESERVES

The magnitudes and direction of economic transactions among nations shift ceaselessly—daily, seasonally, cyclically, and secularly. Yet, over any period of time, the total debit transactions of a nation cannot differ from its total credit transactions, for the balance of payments always balances. From this it follows that a change in the size of one type of debit or credit entry must involve an equivalent change in the size of some other type of debit or credit entry.

The need for compensating changes in balance-of-payments entries can be readily seen by supposing that all transactions among nations require payment in dollars. France, for example, cannot pay out more dollars for imports of goods and services, exports of capital, gifts to foreigners, and purchases of gold than the number of dollars it obtains through exports of goods and services, imports of capital, gifts from foreigners, and sales of gold. If France wishes to increase her payments to foreigners for, say, imports of goods, she must reduce her payments of other types or must obtain more dollars.

A large number of individual international transactions are undertaken independently of one another. It is unlikely that, just when some Frenchman finds himself obliged to remit alimony to his former American wife, some French exporter will knowingly and purposefully increase his sales to the United States in order to provide the required dollars. A French corporation which plans to remit dividends to an American stockholder will hardly cancel its plans just to free dollars for payment to the American divorcée.

But some transactions in the balance of payments occur because of others. One class of these transactions consists of movements of international reserves. As a first approximation, international reserves may be said to consist of gold, bank deposits of foreign currency, and short-term foreign investments held by the central bank and/or treasury of the nation concerned. In order to see how movements of gold and of these types of short-term capital are induced by other transactions, suppose that no unilateral transfers occur and no long-term and other short-term capital movements take place. All that is left in the balance of payments then, besides movements of reserves, are movements of goods and services.

Suppose that at a given moment of time, Frenchmen wish to buy more imports of goods and services than they wish to export. When Frenchmen demand dollars to make payment for their imports, they offer francs in exchange. When the supply of dollars provided by exports falls short of the demand for dollars, Frenchmen will offer more francs to obtain the scarce dollars, i.e., the franc price of the dollar will rise. When the franc price of a dollar rises American goods become more expensive for Frenchmen, obliging them to reduce their purchases. But suppose that the French government does not wish to see Frenchmen cut their imports. That is, suppose that the government is committed to stabilizing the exchange rate while meeting all demands for dollars. The monetary authorities (the central bank and/or the treasury) can provide the excess dollars required by the Frenchmen by (1) selling some of their dollar deposits in the United States to Frenchmen; (2) selling some of their short-term investments for dollars in the United States and selling the dollars to Frenchmen; and/or (3) shipping gold to the United States to be sold for dollars and selling the dollars to Frenchmen. In the absence of any of these, the excess French demand for dollars would force up the franc price of dollars; French payments of dollars would have to fall to the level of French dollar receipts. But so long as the government is committed to stabilizing the exchange rate and meeting all demands for dollars, movements of international reserves will have to occur in response to changes in other international transactions, and these movements will meet the excess demand for foreign currency.

When a nation loses reserves, we say that it has a balance-of-payments deficit; conversely, when a nation gains reserves, it has a balance-of-payments surplus. These terms reflect respectively a net debit and a net credit of the nonreserve items in the balance of payments, i.e., of goods, services, unilateral transfers, and other capital movements. Thus, a movement of reserves finances a deficit (or surplus) in the other items in the balance of payments.

The definition and the measurement of a balance-of-payments deficit is made difficult by the fact that other items in the balance of payments may substitute for movements of reserves. That is, there are other items in the balance of payments, besides those included in reserves above, which arise because of still other items in the balance of payments. For example, the French government may borrow or receive dollars from the U.S. government for the same purpose as the French monetary authorities would pay out reserves. When the reason for such loans or gifts is the same as that which would motivate a movement of reserves, the loans or gifts are also evidence of a French balance-of-payments deficit. In addition, certain other capital movements may qualify as means of covering balance-of-payments deficits. Commercial banks and other private owners of short-term capital may sell their holdings of foreign currency assets, thereby making them available for international payments, in times of strain on the balance of payments. This is quite likely if the monetary authorities make it profitable for them to do so by raising the rate of interest at home. The higher rate of interest will induce them to sell their foreign currency for home currency to be used for investment in securities at home. To the degree that private short-term capital movements occur in ready response to the requirements of the monetary authorities for foreign exchange, they substitute for movements of officially owned reserves and they should be regarded as movements of international reserves.

THE LEVEL OF RESERVES

The function of reserves is the settlement of balance-of-payments deficits, but reserves can settle only temporary differences between other receipts and payments—not persistent ones. A nation with a continuing balance-of-payments deficit eventually runs out of reserves. A nation without gold mines cannot export gold forever; no nation has an infinitely large supply of foreign balances (bank deposits of foreign currency and short-term investments abroad). Hence, a nation undergoing a balance-of-payments deficit must sooner or later find ways of increasing its foreign receipts or cutting its foreign expenditures. These disparities between receipts and payments must be removed.

A nation dare not allow its international reserves to fall to zero or even close to zero. In the event that a nation had no reserves at all, payments and receipts would have to be matched at all times. A fall in receipts would require a simultaneous fall in payments with an abrupt dislocation of the people denied imported goods and of creditors denied payment. Reserves are essential as a buffer against changes in international receipts and payments; they ease the impact on the domestic economy of shifts in international economic relations.

Whether or not a current loss of reserves is a pressing problem varies among nations, partly with the size of their reserves. The United States has about $22 billion of gold which would allow her a fairly long period of reserve losses; it is hardly conceivable that an American deficit in any single year would be anywhere near that figure. But other nations are not so fortunate; their reserves are low, and their deficits tend to run high at times. They cannot readily build up their reserves because reserves are obtained by giving up real goods and services. Their receipts from exports, from net long-term borrowing, and from net unilateral transfers which they use to buy gold or set aside as foreign balances are not available to purchase imports of goods and services. Many nations are too poor not to import all the goods and services their foreign receipts permit, and, like a person with a low income, they cannot afford to keep much money (international reserves) on hand.

The likelihood of a reserve loss reversing itself is an additional factor determining the significance of a current loss of reserves. Some nations' exports and imports change rapidly and independently; consequently their international reserves fluctuate severely. This is particularly true of the "one-crop" countries whose major export earnings occur just after the seasonal harvest but whose imports arrive rather steadily through the year. Just before Colombia harvests coffee, her international reserves are very low, although they are very high immediately thereafter. Between harvests, Colombia's imports of goods and services pare down her international reserves. But this loss of reserves should not be considered serious, because the next harvest will replenish them. It is for this same reason that a person does not worry about the decline in his bank balance between pay checks; he is reasonably certain that another pay check will replenish his balance. Even the United States undergoes a fairly clear seasonal pattern of receipts and payments. From the third to the fourth quarter of each year there is often a decline in foreigners' holdings of gold and dollar balances in the United States. This reflects the facts that American interest and dividend receipts rise (heavy end-of-the-year dividends cause this), American tourist expenditures abroad decline (summer travel is over), and the amortization of many of the U.S. government's loans abroad occurs at the end of the year. Seasonal variations in reserves perform the useful function of allowing goods to be bought when desired rather than only when export and other earnings occur; such variations are not a cause for alarm.

COMPOSITION AND LEVEL OF RESERVES: SOME QUALIFICATIONS

If a person spends more than he earns, he can meet the difference in a number of ways. He may draw upon his bank balance; he may sell some securities; he may sell some physical assets such as jewelry, his car, or his house; he may borrow, or ask his relatives for a gift. Some of these are better forms in which to hold reserves against rainy days than others. The more readily available an asset to meet deficits, the more acceptable an asset to his creditors, and the more easily a loan or gift can be obtained, the greater is his ability to meet deficits in his own personal finances. The same is true of nations.

The *entire* amount of monetary gold that a nation has does not necessarily constitute part of its international reserves. Some of the gold may have to be kept in the country as backing for its currency according to law; it is not readily available for settling balance-of-payments deficits. Nor may all the demand deposits and short-term investments which a nation has abroad always be counted as international reserves. For example, many nations had large short-term investments in London which were "blocked" by the British government after World War II. This action prevented them from being used for settling international transactions.

Some foreign balances are readily available for certain kinds of international settlements but not for others. For example, during most of the post-World War II period, pound sterling balances obtained by Norwegians could not be used for settling debts of Norwegians to the United States, though they could be used for settling debts to many other countries. The international reserve status of these particular sterling balances was impaired because they were not fully convertible into dollars.

In calculating the size of the international reserves of a nation, it is sometimes wise to subtract the nation's short-term liabilities to foreigners from its gold, demand deposits, and short-term investments abroad. The reason for this is that foreigners can in some instances withdraw (use up) their deposits and short-term investments in the nation by demanding gold in exchange for their deposits or investments at a moment's notice. If such a threat does exist, it means that the ability of the nation to settle its international transactions is not as great as it appears; in effect its gold and foreign balances are not necessarily available for its own use.

In addition to the previously discussed types of reserves, holdings of long-term securities of stable foreign governments may be included. For example, some of the long-term foreign capital inflows into the United States must be counted as increases in foreigners' international reserves. Foreign monetary authorities have invested dollar receipts in long-term U.S. government bond issues. They would normally hold these dollars in U.S. banks or invest them in short-term securities, but the greater return presumably attracts them. Long-term investments are a less satisfactory form of international reserves than short-term investments because the extent to which a nation may meet its deficits by selling long-term investments is less certain than in the case of short-term investments. The monetary authorities of a nation with a balance-of-payments deficit can hold short-term securities until their maturity without great inconvenience and thereby obtain their face value—a specific amount. But to wait for the maturity of a long-term security would be impossible; therefore, a nation must accept the market prices of long-term securities if they are sold to meet the deficit, and these market prices are less certain because, unlike the short-term security, the option of owners to hold to maturity does not restrict as much the extent to which their prices may fall. This analysis also shows why gold and foreign-currency balances are better than short-term securities; there is no uncertainty about the debt-paying power of gold or of the creditor countries' currencies which a debtor nation holds.

The long-term investments abroad of the *citizens* of a nation may sometimes be considered as near reserves. For example, if a nation is in payments difficulties, the government may, as Britain did during World War II, require that citizens turn over their foreign stocks and bonds and other long-term assets to the government. These then are sold for foreign currency to be used to settle international transactions. But this is clearly an extreme action (except in totalitarian states), and such long-term investments are not normally available for use in settling deficits.

Getting even further away from money and liquid assets, any calculation of a nation's international reserves must consider its inventories of imported goods. Several times since World War II, Britain obtained additional, but illusory, gold and dollar balances. A major reason for the improvement in her international reserves was that, in a significant degree, British residents were using up their inventories of imported goods instead of importing goods for current consumption. Eventually the additions to Britain's gold and dollar balances had to be paid out to replenish the inventories.

B.   CAUSES OF A LOSS OF RESERVES

The forces causing a loss of international reserves are found in the ceaseless change that occurs in the modern world economy. Some changes are small but recurrent, so that the accumulated pressure is great; others are instantaneous and large, causing a severe drain of reserves. Some balance-of-payments deficits result from changes in internal economic activity and general price levels, while others result from shifts in basic patterns of real demand and supply. The latter are called structural changes to distinguish them from the former, which involve changes in monetary activity and in the general level of employment and incomes. While these forces may be distinguished for analytical purposes, they frequently occur together and they interact.

STRUCTURAL CHANGES

Technological innovation is one type of structural disturbance. The development after World War I of synthetic nitrogen, used in fertilizers and explosives, severely reduced the price and volume of Chile's natural nitrate exports. The switch from silk to rayon and nylon, made possible by technological progress, impaired Japan's export earnings; between 1937 and 1949 the use of silk in the United States dropped 93 per cent. The substitution of synthetic detergents for soap tended to reduce American imports of copra from which coconut oil is derived. Had it not been for the general growth of American activity requiring more tin, the displacement of the process of dipping steel cans to produce tin cans by an electrolytic process would have reduced American tin imports. Technological change, however, does not always reduce international trade; the introduction of the automobile increased U.S. natural rubber imports (though later development of synthetic rubber has reduced the volume and value of United States natural rubber imports.) Technological changes leading to greater use of alloys have increased American imports of certain minerals such as tungsten.

A disturbance of a broader nature is the disparate rates of growth of output per man among countries. Some economists emphasize that the high rates of U.S. capital formation, the cost-consciousness of U.S. businessmen, and the propensity of U.S. businessmen to innovate threaten the markets of foreign nations. New products produced with American ingenuity are in constant demand by foreigners. Cost reductions accompanying economic growth give the United States an advantage in the sale of export goods over other countries in which productivity grows more slowly. United States business competes more easily for export markets, and exports to the United States become increasingly difficult.

Overseas economic growth has played havoc with Western Europe's balance of payments during the recent postwar period. Prices of primary products generally rose more than the prices of manufactured goods, with a consequent adverse shift in the terms of trade for the industrialized countries of Europe. This shift meant that Europe received fewer physical units of imported goods for each physical unit of exports. The importance of this shift is indicated by the fact that Europe, to obtain through exports the same volume of imports during the postwar period that she did in 1938, had to export 44 per cent more than her 1938 volume of exports.

The reason for the adverse change in Europe's terms of trade is found, partly, in the industrialization programs of the primary producing countries; resources which might have produced goods to meet the rising postwar demand for raw materials were diverted to the creation of manufacturing establishments. Population growth and inflation in the developing countries also increased their demand for domestically produced raw materials and foodstuffs. The political division of Europe facilitated the adverse turn of the terms of trade, especially as the Soviet satellites proceeded with their own industrialization programs. Like her imports, some of Europe's exports suffered from the industrialization process abroad. One of the first industries to be developed in an underdeveloped country is the textile industry, partly because it fits its factor endowment, i.e., the textile industry requires comparatively little capital equipment and much labor. As a result, British textile exports suffered.

The consequences of war provide additional examples of structural changes leading to balance-of-payments difficulties. The sale of Europe's overseas investments to finance the costs of the war, wartime damage to investments not sold, plus inflation which cut the real value of investment income from what remained, reduced the portion of Europe's imports covered by investment income; to make up for this loss, there was required a 23 per cent increase in Europe's export volume over 1938. Although the European maritime powers were able to restore their sunken fleets rather quickly, other nations, such as the United States, emerged from the war with enlarged merchant fleets, which prevented income from shipping service from returning to its prewar importance in Europe's balance of payments. The same occurred with the financial, insurance, and commercial services provided by Europe to foreign nations because of the growth of these services in other countries. The residual wars in Burma, Indonesia, and Indo-China and the costs of occupying the territory of former enemies and maintaining troops abroad burdened England, the Netherlands, and France; government expenditures for overseas forces during the postwar period required an increase in exports of approximately 6 per cent over the 1938 volume. All these structural changes, including the adverse shift in the terms of trade mentioned earlier, required an 80 per cent increase in Western Europe's exports over the 1938 level if she were to import during the postwar period the same volume as she did in 1938. And that volume of imports was insufficient to regain the 1938 per capita level because of population growth.

In 1947, Europe had a current account deficit equivalent to $7.6 billion. The major part of this deficit was with the United States, amounting to $5.7 billion; the shortage of dollars required to pay for goods from the United States was the major balance-of-payments problem of the postwar period. Before the war, Europe had paid for a smaller deficit with the United States through earnings from elsewhere in the world. But Europe found it difficult to obtain dollars from others during the postwar period. Europe's export position with those nations which gained greater dollars after the war through sales to the United States had been historically weak and continued to be so, and those nations preferred to spend their dollars for American products rather than spend them elsewhere. In addition, Europe's dependence on North America was increased; under the pressure of industrialization, inflation, and population growth, the exportable surpluses of basic foodstuffs and raw materials elsewhere in the world shrank. To satisfy these needs and to fulfill requirements for heavy equipment for reconstruction of its war-torn economy, Europe turned to the northern Western Hemisphere. Europe's imports from the United States and Canada were nearly double their 1938 level in 1947, while imports from other overseas nations fell to three-quarters of their 1938 level. This change in trade patterns connected with the war provides another example of structural forces at work in creating balance-of-payments difficulties.

CHANGES IN LEVELS OF ECONOMIC ACTIVITY AND PRICES

To an important degree, changes in a nation's exports and imports, and hence in international reserves, are determined by changes in domestic economic activity and prices.

Deflationary pressures

Suppose that a nation undergoes a serious fall in employment and production in connection with a decline in its domestic spending such as occurred in the early 1930's in the United States. With lower production, there is less demand for imports; almost half of American imports are industrial raw materials and semimanufactures. With lower employment, there are lower incomes which mean a lower demand for foreign-produced goods and less interest in foreign travel. Profits fall and bankruptcies occur; therefore interest and dividend payments decline. The fall in incomes reduces the portion of exportable goods which are consumed domestically, thereby making an expansion of exports possible, and the fall in general employment makes resources available for export production. The general decline in prices and costs of production which accompanies a business depression makes some home-produced goods cheaper than foreign products with a consequent reduction in the imports of the depressed country. At the same time the fall in prices and costs makes the depressed nation's exports more attractive to foreigners, which results in an increase in the physical volume of exports sold abroad. The changes in prices and the changes in the aggregates of production, employment, and income operate to reduce the imports and raise the exports of the nation suffering a depression caused from within its own economy; these changes put pressure on the balances of payments of other nations and drain their reserves.

The relation between changes in the physical volume of American imports and in the U.S. Gross National Product (total output of goods and services) is seen from Figure 7 which uses a scale designed to permit comparisons of rates of change. In all but the war years, when imports were naturally restricted, there is a close relationship. The most spectacular of the changes occurred in the crash of the American economy in the early 1930's. The United States GNP, in constant dollars, fell by about 30 per cent; the physical volume of U.S. imports dropped by 40 per cent, and total U.S. current-account payments fell by 60 per cent. Today, the United States is the world's largest trader, importing about 15 per cent of the world's merchandise trade; variations in its imports have an important impact on the rest of the world's exports and thus on the rest of the world's international reserves.

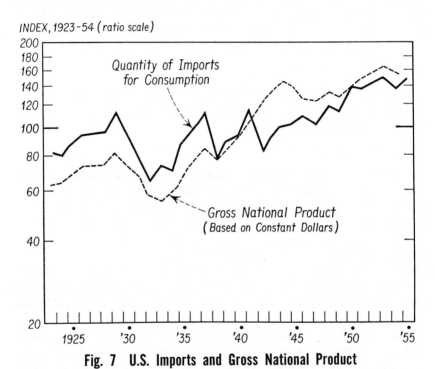

INDEX, 1923–54 (ratio scale)

Fig. 7   U.S. Imports and Gross National Product

SOURCE: *Survey of Current Business,* November 1955.

Inflationary pressures

An upward movement in a nation's internal activity and prices caused by a rise in its domestic spending induces a loss of reserves by that nation. The rising level of activity requires more imported raw materials, and rising incomes induce citizens to buy more from abroad. The accompanying rise in the general price level of the expanding country makes foreign goods relatively cheaper; imports are purchased instead of the more expensive domestically produced products. The higher level of domestic aggregate demand, which accompanies rising output, diverts exportable products into domestic consumption and investment. The higher price and cost level makes the nation's exports less attractive to foreigners; export producers' profit margins are squeezed by the higher costs, and export production is made difficult as buoyant home demand takes more raw materials and a greater share of the labor force. By raising imports and reducing exports, internal inflation and/or rising internal economic activity cause a loss of international reserves.

These effects of inflation were reflected in the payments of Peru between 1940 and 1946. Peru is an exporter of newly mined gold and had paid for about 15 per cent of her imports in this way before World War II. Peru's wartime internal inflation raised the cost of producing gold, but the price of gold, as set by the U.S. government, remained fixed. It became so unprofitable to mine and export gold that her exports fell by about 50 per cent between 1940 and 1946; the percentage of imports paid for by newly mined gold declined to about 4 per cent. Peru consequently lost a normal export and suffered a reduction in reserves.

World-wide inflation

A general inflation of commodity prices over the entire trading world creates a different kind of problem. Any trade deficit is immediately increased and, without any change in the physical volume, composition, or direction of trade, the drain on international reserves in increased. For example, if Brazil has a deficit of $100 million resulting from exports of $100 million and imports of $200 million, a 100 per cent rise in the prices of traded goods would make exports and imports $200 million and $400 million respectively; the trade deficit would rise from $100 million to $200 million. Thus the foreign purchasing power of Brazil's reserves falls and the former level of reserves is less adequate. Barring a general deflation, the solution lies partly in raising the price of gold in terms of all currencies so that each ounce of gold exported would cover a larger deficit. One of the major elements in the postwar European dollar shortage was the fall in the real value of the gold produced in South Africa, Australia, and the African territories which, before the war, had been acquired by Western Europe to cover its dollar deficit. With the prices of American exports nearly doubled by 1950 and the price of gold fixed at $35 per ounce, gold could buy only half as many goods as in 1938.

Capital movements

Changes in economic activity also affect the level of international reserves through changes in long-term capital movements. Between 1919 and 1929, U.S. capital exports and her internal economic activity varied inversely. For Britain, between 1880 and 1913, capital exports and economic activity varied together; in France for the same period no definite pattern developed. The inconsistency of these patterns results from pulls of opposing forces. The rise in loanable funds and savings which accompanies a boom in a capital-exporting nation's internal economic activity makes greater capital exports possible. The rise in imports which accompanies the same boom also makes foreign economies more profitable places for investment, because their exports rise and because the boom in the capital-exporting country enhances its need for raw materials from abroad, which induces greater investment in supply facilities abroad. On the other hand, the boom in the activity of the capital exporter makes home use of loanable funds more profitable, and this tends to reduce capital exports. Whether capital exports rise or fall, and therefore whether reserves tend to fall or rise, depends upon which of these forces dominates.

The relation of capital movements to international reserves is made more complex by the fact that structural changes may also alter the flow of lending. The general decline in American private foreign investment abroad over the last twenty-five years is partly attributable to a shift in the basic attitudes of borrowing nations toward foreign capital and its owners, as well as to the relatively better opportunities in the United States for investment since World War II. Believing themselves to have been exploited by previous foreign investors, and stricken with national pride, numerous countries have placed legal, tax, and other obstacles in the way of private capital imports.

Capital movements may also occur for monetary or political reasons directly related to changes in economic activity and prices and/or structural shifts. Speculative capital movements frequently result if an exchange rate change is expected. For example, if Englishmen expect the pound, worth, let us say, $4 today in the foreign exchange market, to be worth only $2 soon, a transfer of sterling assets into dollars would be advantageous; that is, a pound spent today to buy $4 would return the smart operator £2 later if his expectations are correct. Such transactions tend to occur when monetary instability exists. Capital flight has also occurred when fear for life or property resulted from political changes such as the persecution of the Jews in Germany in the 1930's. Threat of war, as in the late 1930's, provides the same inducement if there is danger of invasion. In these cases, the nation undergoing a loss of capital suffers a loss of reserves; gold must be exported to obtain the foreign currencies which citizens wish to own, or the holdings of foreign balances by commercial banks and the monetary authorities are sold to private citizens.

The international financial crisis of 1931 was significantly a matter of capital flights. An Austrian bank was found to be insolvent upon revaluing its assets; it had made loans to industries and held securities whose value had fallen precipitously because of the depression. This frightened foreigners who had made short-term loans to Austria, and it called attention to the doubtful position of a number of other countries' financial structures, particularly Germany's, which had a net short-term debt of 5 billion marks to foreigners. With the failure of an important German bank, the rush to withdraw capital spread to Germany, and in the space of a few weeks a quarter of Germany's total short-term loans from foreigners was withdrawn by the creditors. Rather than see her gold and foreign-exchange reserves exhausted in meeting the demands of foreigners for their own currencies, Germany stopped payment on her external short-term debts. Fear spread then to London. England was rumored to have lost heavily in the Austro-German crises, and she had extensive short-term liabilities to foreigners of her own which could be withdrawn on short notice. An international run on England ensued as foreigners feared for the safety of their assets and as they required funds to replace those blocked in Germany, Austria, and elsewhere. Britain's loss of gold and foreign-exchange reserves forced her to drop the fixed tie between sterling and gold, and to allow the sterling price of gold and dollars to rise. Then the rumor spread that the United States would be next, and in the six weeks following England's action the United States lost $730,000,000 of her gold reserves.

In summary, the open economy is subject to numerous types and sources of strains, centered on its balance of payments and stemming from the ceaseless change which pervades all economic and financial activity.

SELECTED READINGS

A. NATURE AND FUNCTION OF INTERNATIONAL RESERVES

Lederer, Walther. "Foreign Aid and the United States Balance of Payments," *Social Science,* XXIX (October, 1954), 231–236. Relevant to the problems involved in using the volume of foreign aid as a measure of a balance-of-payments deficit.

Machlup, Fritz. "Three Concepts of the Balance of Payments and the So-called Dollar Shortage," *Economic Journal,* LX (March, 1950), 46–68. An analysis of a "market" imbalance, a "programmed" deficit, and an "accounting" disequilibrium in the balance of payments and the differing policies required to adjust each.

"The Adequacy of Monetary Reserves," *International Monetary Fund Staff Papers,* III (October, 1953), 181–227. The best single source on the need for, the desirable level of, and the composition of international reserves.

B. CAUSES OF A LOSS OF RESERVES

Bradshaw, Marie, Daniel Roxon, and Max Lechter. "Imports and Domestic Business," *Survey of Current Business,* XXXV (November, 1955), 16–23. An empirical discussion of cyclical and structural factors in the U.S. balance of payments.

Economic Commission for Europe. *Economic Survey of Europe Since the War.* Geneva: United Nations, 1953. Chapter 2 provides extensive information on Europe's postwar structural balance-of-payments problem.

Kindleberger, Charles P. *International Economics.* Homewood, Ill.: Irwin, 1953. Chapters 21–24 provide a useful discussion of the meaning of balance-of-payments disequilibrium and of cyclical, secular, and structural disequilibrating forces.

Lary, Hal B. *The United States in the World Economy.* Washington: Government Printing Office, 1943. A discussion of the U.S. balance of payments from 1919 through 1939; the discussion of the 1930's is particularly relevant to this chapter.

Lederer, Walther. "Major Developments Affecting the United States Balance of International Payments," *Review of Economics and Statistics,* XXXVIII (May, 1956), 177–192. A discussion of structural and cyclical factors in the U.S. balance of payments. See pp. 178–181 in connection with A, above.

Zassenhaus, Herbert K. "Direct Effects of a United States Recession on Imports: Expectations and Events," *Review of Economics and Statistics,* XXXVII (August, 1955), 231–255. The impact of the U.S. recession of 1953-54 on U.S. imports.

11 Trade, Capital Movements, Economic Activity, and Balance-of-Payments Adjustment

In the previous chapter we developed the first of the two problems faced by an open economy, namely that of a balance-of-payments deficit. In the present chapter we show how that problem, under certain circumstances, tends to be relieved automatically. We shall find that the relief of the first problem requires variations in output, employment, and prices; it thus gives rise to the second problem, namely, internal economic instability.

A. THE BASIC EQUATIONS

A major portion of the analysis in this chapter turns on how variations in the current account of the balance of payments—exports and imports of goods and services—affect the internal economic activity of the nation undergoing the changes. The basic interrelationships between the current account and economic activity are best perceived through the following equations:

Gross National Product + Imports = Exports + Domestic Expenditure

Gross National Product = National income + Indirect business taxes + Depreciation

In the first equation, the total of the left side (GNP plus imports) is the amount of goods and services obtained by a nation over a given period, and the components indicate the sources of those goods and services. The total of the right side (exports plus domestic expenditure) is the total expenditure on those goods and services, and the components indicate the sources of that expenditure. The second equation shows, on the right side, the total "cost of producing" the GNP and the elements of that "cost."

GROSS NATIONAL PRODUCT

The Gross National Product is the total output of final goods and services, valued at their selling prices, produced by a nation during a given period of time by its own factors of production. The GNP includes only final goods and services in order to minimize double-counting. It does not include the intermediate products and transactions which are part of the final output. For example, the GNP includes the value of all the loaves of bread produced, but it does not count separately the value of the grain or flour produced; these are already counted in the loaves of bread. If, in determining the GNP, we added the value of the flour to the value of the loaves of bread, we would count the value of the flour twice—as flour and also as bread.

"COST OF PRODUCING" THE GNP

The cost of the GNP may be broken into factor costs and other charges. Payments to the factors of production to induce them to produce the final output of goods and services are, in aggregate, the national income. The other charges that buyers of the GNP must cover in their purchases are the depreciation and obsolescence charges for capital and the excise taxes which are imposed. In a breakdown of the cost of producing the GNP, no entry is required for the raw materials used in the final output of goods and services; the payments to the factors of production to produce the raw materials and the depreciation and excise taxes related to those raw materials are already included in the above.

EXPENDITURES

The production of goods and services is contingent upon the demand for them. The actual expenditures for the goods and services which a nation produces domestically or imports may be classified into several types. Total spending of residents of a nation is called "domestic expenditure," and it may be divided into private consumption expenditures, government purchases, and investment expenditures. The last comprises not the purchase of stocks and bonds but expenditures for the construction of buildings, machines, and the accumulation of inventories. Foreigners' expenditures, leading to exports of goods and services, constitute the remaining type of expenditure on the goods and services obtained by a nation. Foreigners' expenditures (exports) plus domestic expenditures constitute the total demand for the goods and services obtained by a nation, whether domestically produced or imported.

A given amount of consumption expenditures does not constitute a demand solely for domestic production (GNP), nor does it give employment solely to domestic business and labor. Many of the consumer goods which Americans buy contain imported materials, such as the copper in automobile wiring systems, the lead in antiknock gasoline, the aluminum (or bauxite) in pots and pans, etc. United States government expenditures also include expenditures on imported goods such as generators from Britain for federal hydroelectric projects. United States investment expenditures have an import content, such as the Italian marble on the fronts of American buildings or British knitting machines in American textile plants. Only when the import content of each of these types of expenditures is subtracted from the total expenditures does the demand for U.S.-produced goods and services appear, i.e., the demand for the United States GNP or the demand for goods and services produced solely by American factors of production.

Foreigners' expenditures have an import content which also must be removed before the foreigners' demand for American output can be isolated. When a Mexican buys an American automobile, he may actually buy some lead from his own country, for the lead in the battery of the car may come from Mexico. Only that portion of foreigners' expenditures for American-produced goods and services can be counted as a demand for and an expenditure on the United States GNP. The average import content of British exports in selected years during the past three decades has been estimated to be as high as 37 per cent and as low as 14 per cent.

B. CHANGES IN THE CURRENT ACCOUNT

A balance-of-payments deficit caused by changes in exports and/or imports of goods and services tends to be relieved automatically by internal economic changes induced by the causes of the deficit. The process involves changes in the general level of employment, output, and prices.

DIRECT IMPACT OF A RISE IN EXPORTS

Suppose that foreigners' purchases of American exports rise by $110. If we assume that, prior to this change, no country suffered a balance-of-payments deficit, the rise in American exports creates one. Some other country or countries must now be importing more in value than they previously had; therefore they must be losing international reserves to the United States.

The value of American exports may rise through an increase in their prices and/or a rise in their physical volume. Because changes in prices have an independent role to play in adjusting the balance of payments, we shall isolate the other forces at work by assuming that the increase in export value results solely from a rise in the physical volume of exports without any change in prices.

The assumption of constant prices rests upon an assumption of unemployment. When extensive unemployment exists in the United States, additional foreign demand for American goods can be readily met by employing unutilized workers, raw materials, and plant capacity. But under full employment an expansion of export production would involve a shift of resources from alternative employments, and this can be done only by raising the prices of export products to attract the required factors of production. When unemployment prevails, higher prices are not necessary to induce the factors to work in export industries.

Source and use of additional output

An increase in foreigners' purchases of American exports by $110 raises the American GNP and employment. But if we suppose that these exports have an import content of $10, the rise in American GNP is only $100, the difference being spent on foreign goods rather than on U.S.-produced goods and services. Assuming the following levels of product flows before the rise in exports, the source and disposition of output available to the United States "before and after" would be:

	GNP		Imports		Exports		Domestic Expenditure
Before	1000	+	100	=	100	+	1000
After	1100	+	110	=	210	+	1000

In addition, the U.S. national income rises as additional factors of production are employed and paid to produce the exports, and there may be a rise in depreciation charges and excise tax receipts by the government since these are also part of the cost of producing the exports.

Money

Because it is money that is spent to buy goods and services, there must be, when a greater United States GNP is produced and sold, either an increase in the quantity of money or an increase in the number of times that the existing money is turned over in the purchase of final American goods and services (the income velocity of money). These changes involve the mechanism of international payment.

To simplify the analysis, suppose that the $110 of American exports are bought by an Englishman and that the American exporter's bank (the New York bank) and the British importer's bank (the London bank) are correspondents to each other. In the description in Chapter 9, we saw that the process of payment gave additional dollars to the American exporter, took sterling from the English importer, and either added sterling to the New York bank's deposits in London or subtracted dollars from the London bank's deposits in New York. Because importers and exporters are more than likely to make and accept payment through their bank accounts, the transaction can be viewed as a series of entries on the books of banks. Depending upon whether the draft or cable calls for payment in dollars or sterling, the New York bank's balance sheet will change in one of the following ways:

NEW YORK BANK

Assets	Liabilities	
	Demand deposits:	
	American exporters'	+ $110
	London bank's	− $110

or

NEW YORK BANK

Assets		Liabilities	
Deposits in		Demand deposits:	
London bank	+ $110	American exporters'	+ $110

In the first balance sheet, the New York bank pays the American exporter by increasing his bank account, which is a liability of the bank to the exporter because he can demand his money from the bank; the bank offsets this new liability by reducing its liabilities to the London bank. In the second balance sheet, the new liability of the New York bank to the American exporter is offset by an increase in the New York bank's assets abroad, i.e., deposits in the London bank.[1]

The American importer who buys the $10 of foreign goods which are used in the production of U.S. exports suffers a fall in his demand deposits as he pays for the imports. If we assume that these imports come from England and that the British exporter who sells them also uses the London bank, the London bank's deposits in New York rise by $10 or the New York bank's deposits in London fall by $10; these partially reverse the previous shifts in banks' deposits with each other. The combined export and import transactions then have the following effects:

NEW YORK BANK

Assets	Liabilities	
	Demand deposits:	
	American exporters'	+ $110
	American importers'	− $ 10
	London bank's	− $100

or

---

[1] During the early postwar period, American banks kept their balances in foreign banks small because of unstable political conditions, because of fear that restrictions on their right to use them might be imposed, and because their value in terms of dollars might be changed. In addition, American banks had few foreign-currency drafts to collect because of the reluctance of U.S. exporters to draw drafts in foreign currency, stemming from the same reasons which deterred banks from owning foreign currency, from their inexperience with foreign currencies, and from the high demand for U.S. goods which permitted U.S. producers to dictate the terms of sale. This reluctance was encouraged by regulations in some foreign countries for the control of international payments which required dollar payment for trade with the United States.

NEW YORK BANK

Assets		*Liabilities*	
Deposits in		Demand deposits:	
London bank	+ $100	American exporters'	+ $110
		American importers'	− $ 10

In the second of these balance sheets we see that the quantity of money in the United States (demand deposits plus coin and currency) has risen by $100. In the first balance sheet, the quantity of money is unchanged, but the American-owned portion increases while the foreign-owned part falls. If we suppose that the London bank had previously held this money idle, or if we suppose that this expenditure reflects a desire by foreigners to hold smaller cash balances in the United States, we can readily see that the purchase of additional American goods involves a rise in the income velocity of money (the rate at which money is spent on final goods and services).

In summary, the direct impact of a rise in American exports is an increase in the United States GNP and employment levels joined with an increase in the money supply or in its velocity. By virtue of the import content of American exports, U.S. imports rise; the increase in American imports tends to ease the balance-of-payments deficits of other nations which resulted from an increase in their purchases from the United States. Finally, U.S. national income rises as additional factors of production are employed in the production of the additional U.S. exports; the consequences of this change in national income are considered next.

INDUCED CONSUMPTION AND IMPORT EXPENDITURES

Rising output and employment in the United States carry with them higher national income. Some of the additional income may be spent on consumer goods and services. The import content of these additional consumption expenditures may vary from zero to 100 per cent, with the latter, for example, applying to expenditures by American tourists abroad. The percentage relationship between the portion of a given rise (or fall) in national income spent on American-produced consumer goods and services and the rise (or fall) in national income is called the marginal propensity to consume domestically produced goods. The percentage relationship between the rise in imports of goods and services and the rise in income is called the marginal propensity to import. The ratio of the remainder of the rise in national income to the rise in income itself we shall call the marginal propensity to save. These *marginal* propensities relate *changes* in expenditure or saving to *changes* in income. They should be distinguished from *average* propensities which show the proportion of *total* income which is saved or is spent for home-produced goods or imports.

For simplicity of exposition, suppose that there are no depreciation costs or excise taxes; therefore (see p. 187) GNP and national income are the same. Suppose that citizens of the United States spend 50 per cent of any increase in income on domestically produced consumer goods and services and 25 per cent on foreign-produced goods and services. With an initial rise in American GNP and national income of $100 as a result of the direct impact of a rise in exports, consumption expenditures on U.S. output will rise by $50 and imports by $25 with the remainder of the additional income being saved. The additional U.S. imports further ease the balance-of-payments position of foreign nations.

The additional expenditure of $50 on American goods implies and requires an increase in American production (GNP) by $50 to meet the consumer demand. This is in addition to the $100 increase in United States GNP caused directly by the rise in American exports. The additional $50 of consumer goods production in the United States leads to another rise in U.S. national income of $50 as factors of production are hired and paid to produce the additional goods. If the recipients of this $50 spend it in the proportions assumed above, consumer expenditures on American goods rise again by $25 and imports by $12.50 more, with the remainder being saved.

Another rise in United States GNP occurs consequent to the additional $25 of demand for American-produced consumer goods, and this additional rise in GNP further increases national income which, in turn, further increases consumption expenditures for American-produced goods and for imports, etc. The changes become smaller and smaller, however. Since spending on U.S.-produced goods creates the income and induces the output, the fact that only part of any increase in income is spent on American goods means that any given increase in U.S. output and income causes a smaller subsequent increase in output and income. The ratio between the ultimate rise in GNP (or national income) and the increase in exports is the foreign trade multiplier. An appendix to this chapter shows the multiplier process in greater detail.

In sum, we see that because of the rise in expenditures on American-produced consumer goods consequent to a rise in American exports, the United States GNP, national income, and employment levels rise by more than the amount which can be attributed solely to the increase in exports. We also see that American imports rise beyond the level required by the import content of exports; this additional increase in U.S. imports further eases the balance-of-payments pressure on foreign nations resulting from the initial increase in American exports. Because consumption of home-produced goods and imports is higher, the figure for domestic expenditure in the "After" line on page 190 must be increased, and the GNP and import figures on the left must also be raised.

The ultimate rise in United States GNP is limited by the fact that part of every increase in income is spent abroad rather than on American-produced goods and by the fact that some of the income is not spent on goods and services at all, i.e., it is saved according to our earlier definition. If the marginal propensity to consume American-produced goods were 60 per cent instead of 50 per cent as above, the initial increase in consumption of U.S.-produced goods would have been $60 instead of $50, and the consequent rise in United States GNP and national income would have been $60 instead of $50. Each successive increase in consumption of American-produced goods would also have been higher, and thus the ultimate rise in American GNP and national income would have been larger.

The extent to which imports rise is affected by the size of the marginal propensity to import; the greater the marginal propensity to import, the greater the increase in imports for any given rise in income. But the marginal propensities to consume home goods and to save play a role too. Additional expenditures on American-produced consumer goods indirectly increase imports by causing greater GNP and national income which in turn lead to additional imports; additional savings neither directly increase imports nor increase income which indirectly raises imports. Hence the greater the marginal propensity to consume domestically produced goods *and* the smaller the marginal propensity to save, the greater the ultimate increase in imports.

A number of forces appear to affect the sizes of the marginal propensities, including the comparative wealth or poverty of the nation, expectations about prices, the liquid assets of potential consumers, and a host of other factors. One of the factors affecting the marginal propensity to import is whether or not the importation can conveniently be deferred. Imports of essential commodities are not likely to vary as much with income as imports of luxury products. As between two nations which spend the same proportion of their total incomes on imports, the one which relies chiefly on foreign sources for its foodstuffs is likely to have a lower marginal propensity to import.

Thailand, for example, whose imports for over a century have consisted almost wholly of manufactured goods, appears to have a high marginal propensity to import. Thailand has had a merchandise export surplus in all but a few years since 1850 despite wide fluctuations in exports. The reason for the surplus is found in a quick and large response of imports to changes in exports which probably stems from the nature of Thai imports. "The broad subsistence base of the economy enables the bulk of the population to reduce purchases of imported goods when income falls without as painful a reduction in the standard of living as would occur in a country such as Britain."[2] The imports consist largely of goods which

---

[2] James C. Ingram, *Economic Change in Thailand since 1850* (Stanford, Calif.: Stanford University Press, 1955), p. 206.

the Thai people can dispense with when income falls; they are not essential to the basic minimum standard of living of the people. "The bulk of the people have no set consumption patterns as far as most imported goods are concerned. Instead, their surplus money income is spent more or less capriciously, and the stores carry a wide range of novelties with which to tempt the buyer."[3] The response of imports to changes in exports is quick because the rice harvest which occurs at the end of the calendar year is the source of exports for the next year. This allows the Thai import firms to set their orders from abroad to fit the expected volume of exports and income next year. In Cuba, importers adjust their orders to forecasts of the size of the Cuban sugar crop and to international market prospects.

INDUCED INVESTMENT AND IMPORT EXPENDITURES

The multiplier process which expands United States GNP, income, employment, and imports may be assisted by an increase in investment spending, depending upon how close the nation is to full employment and on the state of business expectations. If there is extensive unemployment and idle capacity, current increases in the demand for exports and for consumer goods produced in the United States can be met through greater use of existing productive capacity. But with increased profitability of industry and with the approach to full employment of capacity, some increase in investment expenditures will tend to take place to meet future expected demand. An important form of expanded investment spending will be the increase in inventories required as the total demand for goods and services rises and as the pipe lines of supply are filled.

Product and income flows

Higher investment expenditures have the same effects as the rise in exports which indirectly set them off. The construction of new plant capacity or the accumulation of inventories increases total output (GNP) and raises national income as additional resources are employed to produce them. The higher national income in turn induces greater consumption expenditures on domestic goods and greater imports of foreign products; the higher consumption of domestic goods further raises GNP and so on as before. The investment spending itself may have an import content which causes higher imports directly as the result of the increase in investment expenditures. It was estimated, for example, that during the postwar period every 100-peso increase in Mexican investment expenditures caused a 42-peso increase in Mexico's imports of capital goods.[4] In sum, GNP,

---

[3] *Ibid.,* p. 130.
[4] Combined Mexican Working Party, *The Economic Development of Mexico* (Baltimore: Johns Hopkins Press, 1953), pp. 164–166.

income, and employment rise by an even greater multiple of the rise in exports if induced investment expenditures occur, and an additional rise in imports will also take place. Countries which must rely on foreign sources for capital goods tend to have high marginal propensities to import because investment spending is usually more volatile than consumption spending. This goes back to the generalization that the size of the propensity to import is determined significantly by the ability to defer imports. Investment spending is more easily postponed than consumption spending, and when income drops, the decline in profits will induce a radical fall in investment expenditures and thus in imports of capital goods; this must be qualified for the fact that spending by the government on investment-type projects does not respond to the usual incentives.

The extent to which private investment spending does change when income changes is determined by a multiplicity of factors from government attitudes toward business to the time period over which businessmen believe the demand for goods will be sustained. There is no precise relationship between the sums people are willing to save out of an increase in their income and the extent to which investment spending actually rises. Businessmen do not expand their inventories just because people deposit more money in the banks from which they can borrow short-term capital. The existence of a larger pool of money with which people would like to buy securities does not alone induce businessmen to issue securities to finance plant expansion. Nor do the savings of the people out of income necessarily limit the level of investment spending; banks may have unused lending capacity which permits businessmen to borrow to expand their inventories, plant capacity, or to build houses.

Money

In a previous section we noted that a rise in GNP was conditioned upon an increase in the quantity of money or in its income velocity. We return to the matter of money to determine its significance with regard to investment spending.

Suppose that the payment for American exports is made through a reduction of foreign commercial banks' deposits in American commercial banks. Suppose further that, perhaps because their dollar deposits are below normal working requirements, foreign banks sell some of their U.S. short-term securities in the American market for dollars in order to replenish their balances. Thus the amount of money they are willing to lend in the United States on short term is reduced. The rate of interest will tend to rise, and this will tend to restrain U.S. investment spending since the interest rate is one of the costs of borrowed funds. It may even restrain consumption because the higher rate of interest makes saving more attractive.

The withdrawal of foreign capital to pay for American exports would reduce the supply of loanable funds by the amount of the rise in American exports. Since no more can be borrowed than is loaned, this suggests that investment spending in the United States would have to fall by the amount of American exports. If it did, there would be no increase in American GNP, employment, or income because the higher demand for U.S. goods and services resulting from larger exports would be exactly offset by a fall in the demand for U.S. goods and services through an equivalent decline in American investment spending. But this is unlikely. Persons holding cash pay a penalty for the liquidity and security which their cash provides. The penalty is the interest income which they fail to obtain because they fail to invest their cash in securities. When the interest rate rises, that penalty increases, and we may expect some increase in the willingness of persons to buy securities, i.e., a decrease in the supply of loanable funds in the United States attributable to the withdrawal of foreign capital may be partly offset by a shift from cash to securities induced by the change in the interest rate. If so, investment spending need not fall as much as exports rise and a net increase in GNP, employment, and income will occur.

On the other hand, an assist to the expansion of investment spending occurs if foreign central banks sell gold to the United States to obtain the dollars with which to pay for the additional American exports. Under present law, this gold must be sold to the U.S. Treasury. As can be seen in the balance sheets on page 198, the Treasury pays for it (1a) by reducing its deposit at the Federal Reserve Bank of New York, and (1b) the foreign central bank accepts payment through an increase in its deposit at the Federal Reserve Bank of New York. To replenish its deposit, the Treasury issues gold certificates to the Federal Reserve Bank of New York; the latter adds (2a) the gold certificates to its assets and (2b) increases the deposit of the Treasury.

Though this is not the precise order of events, the foreign central banks, now having additional dollar deposits in the Federal Reserve Bank, sell them to foreign importers having to make payments to the United States. In the process of clearing for payment the drafts and cables giving claim to these dollars, the deposits are transferred from the Federal Reserve Bank through the American commercial bank to U.S. exporters. Thus (3a) the American exporters receive additional deposits in American commercial banks; (3b and 3c) the American commercial banks are compensated for their increased liabilities to the American exporters through an increase in their deposits (an asset) at the Federal Reserve Bank of New York; and the Federal Reserve Bank is compensated for the increase in its liabilities to the American commercial banks through (3d) a reduction in its liabilities to (deposits of) foreign banks.

FEDERAL RESERVE BANK OF NEW YORK

Assets		Liabilities		
		Demand deposits:		
		1a Treasury	−	$100
		1b Foreign central bank	+	100
2a Gold certificates	+ $100	2b Treasury	+	100
		3c U.S. commercial bank	+	100
		3d Foreign central bank	−	100

AMERICAN COMMERCIAL BANK

Assets		Liabilities	
3b Deposits at Federal Reserve Bank of New York	+ $100	Demand deposits: 3a American exporters	+ $100

The critical point for investment expenditures in this series of events is the increase in American commercial bank deposits at the Federal Reserve Bank. These deposits are the commercial bank's reserves; U.S. commercial banks are required to keep a sum equivalent to a certain percentage of demand deposit liabilities, such as those to the American exporter, in a reserve account at the Federal Reserve Bank. With higher reserves, the American commercial bank may carry more deposits; to increase its deposit liabilities, the American commercial bank may make loans to persons, paying them the borrowed sums by increasing the borrowers' demand deposits. Within the banker's restrictions of security and liquidity, the greater interest earnings that the bank can make by lending more funds constitutes the incentive for undertaking additional loans. Because the reserve requirement is less than 100 per cent, the American banking system as a whole can increase its total deposit liabilities (and thus the total of loans) by more than the increase in its reserves.

The significance of this is that, under the circumstances outlined, the supply of loanable funds may increase as an indirect result of an expansion of exports. The greater supply of loanable funds will, by inducing a reduction in the rate of interest or at least by restraining a rise in the rate of interest, assist the expansion of investment expenditures discussed at the start of this section. This result does not actually require the sale of foreign gold to the United States. The effects on American commercial banks are the same if the foreign central banks, instead of selling gold, are willing to reduce their deposits at the Federal Reserve Bank of New York in payment for U.S. goods; the foreign central bank's deposits are reduced and those of the American commercial banks are increased in the process of payment.

These conclusions apply as well to almost every banking system in the world. But in many instances the effect on bank reserves of an expansion of exports is immediate and does not require a movement of gold. When foreign commercial banks obtain additional dollar deposits in the United States as the result of exports to America, they may sell, or sometimes are required to sell, the dollars to their central banks which pay for them by increasing the reserve account of the foreign commercial banks. This then provides the means of expanding the supply of loanable funds within the foreign countries.

A FALL IN EXPORTS

To determine the effect on the United States of a decline in its exports, the previous analysis need only be reversed. The direct impact is a decline in American GNP, employment, and national income along with a fall in imports equal to the import content of the exports no longer sold abroad. A series of induced declines in consumption and American GNP, employment, and national income follow the initial fall in U.S. national income; investment spending drops with the accompanying fall in profits, further depressing GNP, national income, and consumption. Imports fall in accord with the import content of the consumption and investment expenditures that no longer take place. Just as a rise in exports causes a multiple rise in GNP, employment, and national income, so a fall in exports causes a multiple contraction of them. Undesirable as the contraction may be, it does relieve the balance-of-payments deficit caused by the fall in exports by reducing American imports.

ILLUSTRATIONS

United States

In recent years, American exports of goods and services[5] have constituted about 5 per cent of the GNP. From this one should not conclude that variations in exports are unimportant to the general level of business activity in the United States. The American automobile industry is generally regarded as one of the key industries in the level of American business activity. Granting this, exports of goods and services in 1955 of $19.7 billion substantially exceeded consumer purchases of automobiles and parts of $16.8 billion. In 1953–1954 the U.S. economy suffered a slight recession of activity which was reversed in the fourth quarter of 1954. Between the third and fourth quarters of 1954, the United States GNP, seasonally adjusted, rose by an annual rate of $8.3 billion. Somewhat over 16 per cent of the rise was attributable to an increase in the seasonably adjusted annual rate of exports of goods and services. The rise in exports gave more impetus to the upswing than personal consumption expenditures on durable goods, the total of new construction, and each of the other components of domestic expenditures except for the change in inventories.[6]

---

[5] Excluding military goods and services under grant aid programs.
[6] *Survey of Current Business,* February, 1956, p. 12, and June, 1956, p. 21.

Comparing total exports with American GNP also hides the dependence of particular industries on foreign markets, which can be readily seen from Table 3.

Table 3. U.S. Exports as a Percentage of U.S. Production, Selected Products, 1955

Agricultural:

Dry whole milk and cream	44.1%
Dry nonfat milk	37.8
Cheese, excluding cottage and full skim	10.9
Butter	14.2
Lard including rendered pork fat	21.0
Tallow and grease, inedible	44.7
Soybeans	19.2
Flaxseed	59.3
Cottonseed	42.5
Barley	11.8
Grain sorghums	22.1
Rice	25.7
Wheat	27.7
Beans, dry ripe	10.7
Peas, dry ripe	41.1
Raisins, dried and evaporated	23.2
Prunes, dried and evaporated	22.2
Apricots	10.4
Prunes and plums, fresh	16.9
Cattle hides	20.4
Calf and kip skins	28.8
Leaf tobacco	23.0
Raw cotton	25.3
Hops	28.1

Nonagricultural:

Sardines, including pilchards and herring	39.1
Denims	10.2
Turpentine	18.8
Rosin	35.7
Woodpulp, special alpha and dissolving grades	19.7
Newsprint	14.2
Thin fine paper	10.3
Anthracite coal	12.0
Bituminous coal	10.9
Lubricating oil	24.5
Paraffin wax	20.7

Petroleum coke	15.8%
Tinplate and terneplate	14.9
Sulfur	27.4
Copper, total	13.6
Internal combustion engines, except auto and aircraft*	12.3†
Machine tools*	12.3
Construction and mining equipment, graders*	34.0
Oilfield machinery, tools and equipment*	14.2†
Textile machinery*	27.0†
Sewing machines and parts*	22.5†
Paper industries machinery*	16.1†
Pumps and compressors*	10.0†
Typewriters and parts*	13.5†
Calculating and accounting machines and cash registers*	12.6†
Printing machinery and equipment*	16.8†
Agricultural machinery and implements†	13.0
Tractors, tracklaying type*	41.0
Tractors, contractors wheel type*	29.5
Tractors, other wheel type, except garden*	15.1
Motor trucks and coaches	15.8
Complete civilian aircraft*	34.2
Locomotives*	16.2†
Penicillin	33.6
DDT	42.6
Copper sulphate	47.9
Carbon black	25.1
Phosphate rock	17.2
Pens, mechanical pencils, and pen points*	15.2†

* Based on values rather than physical quantities.
† 1954.

SOURCE: U.S. Department of Commerce, "Exports in Relation to U.S. Production," *Statistical Reports,* (August, 1956).

From the foregoing analysis we see that foreign markets are important to the levels of employment and output of the United States. This is the more so for many other countries which have more extensive foreign economic relations than the United States, as shown in Table 4.

New Zealand

A study of New Zealand's general economic activity from 1840 to 1914 gives evidence on the importance of fluctuations in exports to an economy largely dependent on foreign trade.[7] During that period there

[7] C. G. F. Simkin, *The Instability of a Dependent Economy* (London: Oxford, 1951), p. 192.

Table 4. Exports of Goods and Services as a Percentage of Gross National Product, Selected Countries, 1954

Australia	18%	Ireland	33%
Austria	23	Italy	12
Belgium	34	Japan	12
Burma	15	Korea	4
Canada	22	Netherlands	45
Ceylon	54	New Zealand	25
Denmark	29	Norway	35
Dominican Republic	28	Panama	49
Finland	22	Portugal	18
France	15	Philippines	13
Western Germany	18	Sweden	27
Greece	13	Turkey	5
Guatemala	18	United Kingdom	22
Honduras	22		

SOURCES: International Monetary Fund, *Balance of Payments Yearbook*, Vols. 6 and 7; *International Financial Statistics*, July, 1956; Economic Commission for Europe, *Economic Survey of Europe in 1955* (Geneva: United Nations, 1956). *Note:* the definition of GNP is not the same for all of the above countries nor are the items included in exports of goods and services necessarily the same.

were some twenty upswings and downswings in New Zealand's general economic activity. Of these, eleven were attributable chiefly to changes in the level of exports from New Zealand.

In one of the clearest cases of the influence of changes in New Zealand's exports on her internal economic activity and the balance-of-payments adjustment process, data reveal that for twelve years (1896–1907) "New Zealand experienced rising prosperity, unmarred by a general recession. . . . The main factor was undoubtedly the expansion of exports from £8,400,000 to £19,800,000. . . . All available indexes of economic conditions reflect the great improvement in New Zealand's position. . . . Imports nearly trebled, both in real and monetary value, as import prices remained fairly constant. The marriage rate and current public revenue per head both rose by one-half, and the immigration rate rose from .13 to 1.42 per cent. Bankruptcies fell from .7 to .4 per thousand, and unemployment from 10 to 3.9 per cent."[8]

Canada

Because exports of goods and services constituted about 22 per cent of Canada's GNP during the last half of the 1920's, any shift in exports meant an important shift in Canada's GNP. The data given in Table 5 are consistent with our previous analysis.

[8] *Ibid.*, pp. 182, 194.

The increased production of consumer goods indicated in the table is consistent with the idea that a rise in exports of goods and services induces an increase in consumption expenditures. The previous discussion regarding investment expenditures finds support in the expansion of construction and of production of producers' goods. Increased exports of newsprint and of nonferrous metals to the United States during this period apparently led directly to an increase in investment expenditures in those industries in Canada; newsprint production increased about 85 per cent and newsprint production *capacity* rose about 80 per cent. Investment in the pulp and paper and in nonferrous metals production led to investment in complementary fields such as explosives, electric power, electrical equipment, and chemicals, among others.[9]

Table 5. Changes in Canadian Economic Activity, 1924-1929

Exports of goods and services	+ 24%
Gross National Product	+ 35
Employment	+ 27
Industrial production	+ 55
Manufactured consumers'-goods production	+ 34
Producers'-goods production	+ 64
Residential construction	+ 41
Nonresidential construction	+ 142
Imports of goods and services	+ 78

SOURCE: Vernon W. Malach, "External Determinants of the Canadian Upswing, 1921–1929," *Canadian Journal of Economics and Political Science,* XVII (February, 1951), 51, 54.

Data are not available on the import content of exports or on precisely how the changes in consumption in Canada affected her imports. But in 1929 one-third of Canada's imports consisted of producers' goods, reflecting the fact that Canada did not have a well-developed capital-goods industry. The rise of investment expenditures required the importation of capital goods.

The late 1920's boom in Canada was not attributable solely to the expansion of exports. Technological developments and the banking system played both complementary and independent roles in the expansion of domestic production and exports.[10]

[9] Vernon W. Malach, "Internal Determinants of the Canadian Upswing," *Canadian Journal of Economic and Political Science,* XVI (May, 1950), 197; also pp. 61 f. of his article cited in Table 5.

[10] For a thorough discussion of this period in Canada's history and its relevance to the aforementioned ideas see Edward Marcus, *Canada and the International Business Cycle, 1929–1939* (New York: Bookman Associates, 1954), and also Vernon W. Malach, *International Business Cycles and Canada's Balance of Payments, 1921–1933* (Toronto, Ont.: University of Toronto Press, 1954.)

Ratio of Changes in Imports and Exports

Additional evidence of the pervasiveness and effectiveness of the forces we have been discussing in reducing balance-of-payments pressures is provided in Table 6. Each percentage shows the ratio between changes in imports induced directly and indirectly by changes in exports, based on data for the 1920's and 1930's. In all but five countries, the economic relationships within each nation were such that any change in exports would lead to a change in imports half as large or more.

Table 6. Ratio Between Changes in Imports and Exports

New Zealand	1.00	India	.65
Australia	.98	Chile	.57
Finland	.98	Germany	.57
Yugoslavia	.98	Switzerland	.56
Denmark	.88	Argentina	.55
Czechoslovakia	.82	United Kingdom	.50
China	.81	Ireland	.47
Netherlands	.77	Norway	.46
Indonesia	.76	Japan	.34
Sweden	.71	France	.28
Canada	.68	U.S.	.24
Hungary	.67		

SOURCE: J. J. Polak, *An International Economic System* (Chicago: University of Chicago, 1953, copyright 1953 by the University of Chicago.) Summary Table.

CHANGES IN IMPORTS

The foregoing analysis has emphasized the important role of changes in exports in determining the levels of GNP, national income, and employment. Imports have varying roles to play.

A rise in a nation's imports as a consequence of an increase in its national income, output, and employment merely restrains the rise in its general economic activity. Because some of the additional income is spent on foreign goods rather than on home-produced goods, additional employment and output at home cannot be as great as it would be if the income were spent entirely on home goods.

A rise in a nation's imports, not as a consequence of higher income but because of a change in prices, tastes, or other forces, tends to depress its national income, employment, and output. Thus if Americans buy more French wine and less California wine, the level of income and employment in the American wine industry declines, and this sets off a multiplier fall in consumption and investment expenditures in the United States which further depresses GNP, employment, and national income.

Conversely, when the imports consist of "bottleneck" goods, the imports tend to increase economic activity in the importing nation. In some nations, particularly the less developed ones, an investment project may wait upon the import of a particular type of equipment. Imports of these bottleneck goods can hardly be considered depressing or restraining of income and employment since, when they occur, they permit much larger flows of investment spending within the importing nation. Many of the goods imported into Europe during the early postwar period of reconstruction were undoubtedly of this variety. Recognition of the bottleneck phenomenon (at least a latent bottleneck) was seen in the U.K. Labour government urging workers in the early postwar years to greater efficiency and hard work in the production of exports. These exports were required to pay for British raw material imports necessary for the fabrication of manufactured goods; without the imported raw materials, the British Labour government warned, factories would close and unemployment would result.

INTERACTIONS OF NATIONAL INCOMES

The imports of one nation, obviously, are the exports of other nations. Since the imports of each nation vary with its national income and output, and since the exports of each nation determine in part its output, income, and employment, it should be clear that international exchange ties together the incomes, output, and employment levels of all nations.

Suppose that there is a decline in American GNP, employment, and national income caused by a fall in government spending, consumption expenditures, or investment spending. That is, assume that American exports are constant—for the moment at least. The fall in economic activity in the United States will depress American imports, and therefore it will depress foreign nations' exports. The fall in foreign nations' exports will, assuming that nothing else happens, force down the output and employment levels in those foreign nations, and consequently, their imports from each other and from the United States will also decline. The consequent fall in American exports further depresses the already declining level of American economic activity. It was once said that when the United States sneezes, the rest of the world gets pneumonia. The pneumonia may take one or both of two forms: the fall in GNP and employment just described, or, as suggested in the previous chapter, a serious balance-of-payments problem if the foreign nations do not have adequate reserves with which to cover any balance-of-payments deficits which they may sustain as a result of the fall in American imports. Whether or not a nation can give other countries trouble depends largely on its size. In 1953 the United States was the largest single supplying nation to 22 other countries. These included all of the major nations of the Western Hemisphere, as well as France, Western Germany, Iceland, Italy, Spain, and Yugoslavia, in Western Europe; and in the Far East, Japan, the Philippines, and Indonesia.

Thirteen other countries, which included practically every other major country in Western Europe and in Asia, found her as their second, third, or fourth largest supplier. The United States, in 1953, was the major single export market for 17 nations, including the Western Hemisphere nations, as well as Japan, Iceland, Philippines, Switzerland, and Turkey. For 14 other nations she ranked from second to fourth as their most important market. A Liechtenstein could not give any nation a cold, but the United States can; see the trade map of the world at the end of Chapter 1.

The principles of interaction are the same when we suppose that foreigners' buy more American goods and fewer of their own, i.e., that they substitute U.S. products for their own because of a shift in prices, tastes, or other forces not related to a change in foreigners' incomes. The higher level of American exports induces an expansion of American GNP, employment, national income, which results in a *rise in American imports*. On the other hand, the lower purchases by foreigners of their own products depresses their nations' GNP, employment, and income, which in turn *reduces foreigners' imports* from the United States. Notice the interaction of incomes through trade. (1) The fall in foreigners' imports from the United States induced by a fall in foreigners' GNP tends to reduce the level of American exports below the new level obtained consequent to the switch in foreign purchases which started the process moving; this in turn restrains the rise in American GNP and imports. (2) The rise in American imports tends to restrain the fall in foreign GNP because the volume of foreign exports rises.

PRICE CHANGES

An important part of the process of removing balance-of-payment difficulties and an important problem in its own right is the change which takes place in prices as a consequence of shifts in international trade.

Causes of general price changes

Up to this point we have supposed that prices remain unchanged, but this is patently unrealistic. A rise in American exports induces higher GNP, employment, income, and *spending*. If the physical volume of output increases as fast as the flow of spending, prices need not rise since the supply increases as fast as the demand. This is quite possible when extensive unemployment exists. But full employment places a limit to the expansibility of the supply of goods and services, apart from productivity growth or an increase in the supply of factors. Any increase in total spending when high employment prevails is almost certain to raise the general level of prices. Even before full employment is reached, bottlenecks will occur as output rises; as demand presses against supply at these bottleneck points, prices begin to rise. As full employment is approached, businessmen will find it more difficult to obtain labor; instead of opening their gates to unemployed workers, they will have to bid workers away from alternative employments by offering more favorable wages. The same is true of raw materials. With costs rising but demand rising too, businessmen will find that charging higher prices is an easy alternative to cutting costs and that buyers do not resist the higher prices by cutting their orders. Labor unions, eying increased profits and goaded by a rising cost of living, demand higher wages which, in a period of ebullient demand, businessmen can pass on through higher prices without cutting sales.

Conversely, when spending drops, prices fall. The prices of some products, such as agricultural goods, are exceedingly flexible so that a fall in demand is immediately met with a drop in price. Other products, such as manufactured goods whose prices are shifted by businessmen with changes in demand, may undergo a sluggish drop in prices; in these cases, part of the effect of a decline in spending is absorbed by a drop in production rather than a decline in prices.

Substitution: simplified case

In order to determine the significance of price changes to balance-of-payments problems, suppose that American exports of goods rise as a result of a shift in purchases by foreigners from their own goods to American goods, putting pressure on foreign nations' international reserves. As the previous analysis has shown, output, spending, and employment rise in the United States, and this will be accompanied by a rise in the American price level. Conversely, the drop in spending and output abroad will be accompanied by a fall in prices abroad.

As a first approximation, suppose that the United States and the rest of the world produce different products. Suppose that they are not perfect substitutes for each other, i.e., a rise in the price of one does not induce consumers to shift their purchases *entirely* to the other.

Suppose they are, however, substitutes for one another, though somewhat imperfect ones, such as tea and coffee. As prices rise in the United States and fall abroad, consumers in all countries will substitute non-American products for American products. That is, Americans will buy more foreign goods, and foreigners will buy fewer American goods. Thus the physical volume of American imports rises and the physical volume of American exports declines. Since the initial problem was that American exports had risen and that this imposed international reserve losses on the rest of the world, it would seem that the price changes have tended to rectify the initial imbalance in the balance of payments. But this conclusion rests on certain assumptions about the responsiveness of the quantities demanded to price changes, i.e., on elasticities of demand. When the price of American goods rises, foreigners may reduce the physical quantity of their purchases so little that the value of American exports actually increases. Similarly, when the price of foreign goods drops, Americans may buy so little extra of them that the total value of American imports declines. The greater the substitutability of the products, the greater the shifts in physical volumes of purchases; therefore, the cessation of the reserve movement is, at this level of abstraction, contingent upon sufficient substitutability of American and foreign goods in consumer budgets. Because the prices of American goods rise and the prices of foreign goods fall in international trade, the terms of trade of foreign nations worsen, which, taken by itself, lowers the real income of the foreign nations.

Substitution: complex case

A more comprehensive explanation of the role of price changes in adjusting the balance of payments is obtained if we suppose that the products of each nation are divided into three groups: export products, import-competing products, and domestic goods. The export products of one nation are in competition with and substitute for the import-competing products of other nations. Domestic goods are sheltered in varying degrees from competition with foreign products by transportation difficulties; houses are too bulky to transport; milk is too perishable, and haircuts and maid services are difficult to import and export.

When inflation occurs in the United States, the availability of substitutes in foreign nations restrains the increase in prices of American export goods and import-competing products. But no such restraint exists for American domestic goods; their prices consequently rise relative to the price of American export and import-competing products. As a result, two types of substitution will occur: one in consumption and the other in production. Because of the increased profitability of domestic goods production, factors will shift out of the production of import-competing goods and out of the production of export products toward the production of domestic goods and services. Consequently U.S. exports decline, and U.S. imports rise to take the place of units of import-competing goods no longer produced in the United States. At the same time, American consumers shift their purchases from the sheltered domestic goods, whose prices are rising relatively, to the products which the United States produces for export and to imports. This also tends to increase American imports and reduce American exports.

Converse shifts take place in the rest of the world, which is undergoing deflationary pressure because of an increase in its imports at the expense of spending on home-produced goods. The prices of the rest of the world's domestic goods fall sharply because they are not in competition with American produced goods and services. But the level of prices of the rest of the world's exports and import-competing products tends to be sustained because they compete with American goods. As a consequence, foreigners shift their purchases toward domestic goods and away from export products and imports. Simultaneously, factors of production in the rest of the world shift from domestic goods production into export and import-competing goods production. Together these shifts increase the rest of the world's exports to the United States and reduce its imports from the United States. Therefore they tend to remove the balance-of-payments deficit we assumed at the start. Whether or not the rest of the world's terms of trade worsen in the process depends upon the nature of the substitutions. The ratio of the prices of exports of the rest of the world to its import prices will rise, i.e., its terms of trade will improve, if (1) when *resources* shift out of domestic goods, they move primarily to import-competing rather than export goods production, for then the supply of the former increases relative to the latter, and (2) when *demand* shifts to domestic goods, the shift is primarily from imports and import-competing products rather than from export products, for then the demand for the latter is sustained relative to the former.

In sum, price and income changes combine to remove balance-of-payments deficits. A rise in a nation's exports leads to a rise in its GNP, employment, and income which increase its imports; it also leads to price inflation which tends to reduce the value of its exports and increase the value of its imports, given sufficient substitutability in production and/or consumption. A rise in a nation's imports which causes a fall in spending on its home-produced goods depresses its GNP, employment, and income, and tends to reduce its imports; it also leads to price deflation inducing an increase in the value of its exports and a fall in the value of its imports, given sufficient substitutability in production and consumption.

Once we introduce significant flexibility in prices, we are obliged to modify our earlier analysis of the relation between changes in exports and employment. The reason why a decline in spending results in unemployment is that businessmen, in the face of lower demand for their products, either do not lower their prices or, having lowered their prices, cannot remain in production because they cannot reduce their costs of production. If prices and costs are flexible, an excess supply of any raw material or service such as that of labor would cause the price and costs to fall until the excess supply was absorbed.

To the extent that a fall in demand for a nation's exports is met by a decline in the price of the exports and in their costs of production, employment in those export industries need not decline. This does not mean, however, that income changes no longer tend to remove a balance-of-payments deficit caused by a fall in exports. The drop in the price of the exports means that the terms of trade of the exporting nation worsen. The nation can, for a given physical volume of exports, buy fewer foreign goods. Thus the real national income of the nation has fallen, and this will induce a drop in consumption, investment, and imports as before.

C. CHANGES IN THE CAPITAL ACCOUNT

The principles developed in conjunction with the current account need only slight modification to show how changes in capital movements affect internal activity and prices. Suppose that foreigners decide to invest more funds in American bonds or stocks. If we assume that there was no movement of international reserves prior to the capital shift, the movement of capital causes an outflow of reserves from the capital exporting country, i.e., to provide dollars to foreigners who wish to buy American securities, the foreign monetary authorities must sell gold or give up dollar balances in New York.

The increase in the supply of loanable funds consequent to foreigners offering more dollars for securities depresses the American interest rate. This fall will be accelerated by an increase in American commercial banks' reserves, permitting greater lending by them; their reserves increase as a result of foreign banks selling gold or transferring balances held in the Federal Reserve Bank of New York to American commercial banks.

The lower rate of interest in the United States increases investment spending, and it may increase consumer spending because saving becomes less profitable. The rise in spending raises American GNP, employment, and national income, and sets off a multiplier rise in U.S. economic activity. It also tends to cause price inflation. Just as in the instance of an initial rise in American exports, these changes induce a fall in U.S. exports and a rise in U.S. imports.

In the rest of the world, converse shifts occur. The reduction in the supply of loanable funds abroad as capital is shifted to America induces a rise in the rate of interest. In addition, when foreign commercial banks buy dollars from their central banks to satisfy their customers' needs, the commercial banks pay for them by a reduction of their reserves at the central banks; this tends to further restrict the supply of loanable funds and increase the interest rate abroad. The higher rate of interest reduces investment spending in the rest of the world, and it may reduce consumer spending because saving becomes more attractive. As a consequence, GNP, employment, national income, and prices fall in the rest of the world. These changes in turn induce an increase in exports and a fall in imports by the rest of the world in its trade with the United States.

We observe that the process of adjustment involves a rise in U.S. imports and a fall in U.S. exports. America gives up fewer goods to the rest of the world and it takes more goods from the rest of the world; this is the way in which the capital is transferred in the form of real goods and services, and, without these shifts, the United States would have received nothing but money.

Summarizing, we see that changes in the current and the capital accounts induce changes in output, employment, income, and price levels in the process of adjusting the balance of payments to an initial disturbance. These changes, while desirable in that they relieve a balance-of-payments deficit, have certain unwanted effects. A fall in exports, a rise in imports at the expense of spending on home-produced goods, and a rise in capital exports impose deflationary pressure which may lead to unemployment and to price deflation, but deflation benefits only those with fixed incomes. Converse changes lead to price inflation if a nation is at or close to full employment. Rising prices tend to reduce the real income of those on fixed salaries or pensions. General inflation encourages strikes as workers demand higher wages, and it leads to political strife as group is set against group in the struggle to maintain real income. The effectiveness of the price mechanism in allocating resources to the most desirable uses may be impaired; few commodities are subject to downward price pressure and thus the pressure to move resources to other employments may be reduced. Prices of land and of inventories usually rise most, and large profits are obtained by holding these items; investment is misdirected since some saving is diverted from financing permanent additions to capital equipment. Even the flow of personal saving may be damaged because the real rate of interest becomes negative—money loaned today buys fewer goods and services when it is repaid than when it is first loaned. These undesirable effects of internal economic instability have caused national governments to take measures preventing balance-of-payments disturbances from being adjusted through internal changes.

APPENDIX: THE FOREIGN TRADE MULTIPLIER

The following tables present three models of the response of U.S. income, consumption, imports, and saving to a change in U.S. exports. In the first model we assume no change in saving, in the second we allow for changes in saving. In both we assume that exports rise to a level which is sustained. We disregard the effect of the increase in U.S. exports and the effect of the induced rise in U.S. imports on the rest of the world's income, both of which would normally change the level of U.S. exports and thus of U.S. income. In the third model, these interactions are considered.

In all three models, the following assumptions are made: no import content of exports; no changes in government spending or investment expenditures; no depreciation or business excise taxes, i.e., national income equals GNP; periods of time are arbitrarily selected so that the income earned in one period cannot be disposed of until the next period, and flows of spending and income exist prior to the initial change in U.S. exports such that there is no saving out of income and that U.S. exports of $100 plus consumption of U.S.-produced consumer goods of $900 create a U.S. national income (GNP) of $1,000. (Expenditures on imports and saving, if there were any, would be excluded from the calculation of national income because they do not induce U.S. production and therefore do not create U.S. national income.)

Table 7. Foreign Trade Multiplier: No Saving

1	2	3	4	5	6	7
						Changes in
			Consumption of		*National*	*National*
Period	*Imports*	*Saving*	*U.S. Goods*	*Exports*	*Income*	*Income*
0	$100	0	$900	$100	$1,000	
1	100	0	900	200	1,100	+ $100
2	150	0	950	200	1,150	+ 50
3	175	0	975	200	1,175	+ 25
4	187.5	0	987.5	200	1,187.5	+ 12.5
5	193.75	0	993.75	200	1,193.75	+ 6.25
.						
.						
n	$200	0	$1,000	$200	$1,200	

In the first model we assume that the U.S. marginal propensity to import is 50 per cent and that the U.S. marginal propensity to consume American-produced goods is 50 per cent; a change in U.S. income does not change U.S. saving. From Period 0 to Period 1, U.S. exports rise from $100 to $200 (column 5) which immediately increases U.S. national income from $1,000 in Period 0 to $1,100 in Period 1 (column 6), causing a change in national income between the two periods of $100 (column 7). The additional income obtained in Period 1 is disposed of in Period 2: the increase in imports from $100 in Period 1 to $150 in Period 2 (column 2) is determined by multiplying the rise in income of $100 by the marginal propensity to import of 50 per cent. The increase in consumption of U.S.-produced goods from $900 in Period 1 to $950 in Period 2 (column 4) is determined by multiplying the rise in national income of $100 by the marginal propensity to consume American-produced goods of 50 per cent. The national income in Period 2 of $1,150 is determined by adding the U.S. exports of $200 in Period 2 and the consumption of U.S.-produced goods of $950. The increase of $50 in national income in Period 2 over Period 1 is disposed of in Period 3, and its allocation between imports and U.S.-produced consumer goods is made as before, namely, the marginal propensity to import of 50 per cent times $50 additional income giving $25 of additional imports and the marginal propensity to consume U.S.-produced goods of 50 per cent times $50 for a rise of $25 in consumption of

U.S.-produced goods. For each successive period, national income is determined by adding columns 4 and 5, and the changes in columns 2 and 4 are determined by applying the appropriate propensities to the changes in income of the previous period shown in column 7.

Final "equilibrium" is shown in Period *n*. The change in the level of the U.S. national income between Period 0 and Period *n* may be obtained by multiplying the initial change in exports times the multiplier determined by the following formula:

$$\text{Multiplier} = \frac{1}{m + s}$$

where "m" stands for the marginal propensity to import and "s" for the marginal propensity to save, which is assumed to be zero in this instance. Substituting the marginal propensities we have assumed, we get

$$\frac{1}{.50 + 0} = 2$$

and 2 times $100, or the multiplier times the initial change in U.S. exports, is $200. The changes between Period 0 and Period *n* of imports and of consumption of U.S.-produced goods may be obtained by multiplying the change in income determined from the above formula by the appropriate marginal propensities. We observe that in Period 1 there was an export surplus of $100; in Period *n* this surplus has been removed. The reason is that, in this model, we assumed that savings would not increase.

A marginal propensity to save of 20 per cent is introduced in the second model (Table 8), and the marginal propensity to import has been cut to 30 per cent. The method of calculating the entries is the same in every respect as in the first model. United States national income rises by the same amount in both models because the rise in U.S. exports is the same and because the marginal propensity to consume U.S.-produced goods is the same. That is, the forces raising American GNP are the same, and therefore the rise in national income is the same. The U.S. export surplus is not removed, however, in the second model; ultimately it rests at $40. The introduction of the marginal propensity to save means that some part of every increase in income neither buys imports directly nor increases consumption of U.S.-produced goods in the next period. A rise in consumption increases national income in the subsequent period and therefore indirectly raises imports so long as the marginal propensity to import is positive. We could remove the U.S. export surplus if we assumed that investment spending rose in each period by an amount equal to the savings of each period, because the savings would then create additional income through expenditures for buildings, machines, and inventories and would, like additional consumption expenditures, indirectly increase imports.

Table 8. Foreign Trade Multiplier with Saving

1	2	3	4	5	6	7
						Changes in
			Consumption of		National	National
Period	Imports	Saving	Home Goods	Exports	Income	Income
0	$100	$0	$900	$100	$1,000	
1	100	0	900	200	1,100	+ $100
2	130	20	950	200	1,150	+ 50
3	145	30	975	200	1,175	+ 25
4	152.5	35	987.5	200	1,187.5	+ 12.5
5	156.25	37.5	993.75	200	1,193.75	+ 6.25
.						
.						
.						
n	$160	$40	$1,000	$200	$1,200	

In the third model (Table 9), the same propensities are assumed as for the second model. In addition, we assume that the rest of the world has precisely the same propensities as the United States; it therefore follows that equivalent changes in income in the United States and in the rest of the world have the same effects on the imports, savings, and consumption of home-produced goods of each area. We further assume that the initial increase in U.S. exports occurs at the expense of spending by foreigners on their own home-produced goods; therefore the rise in U.S. exports of $100 between Period 0 and Period 1 reduces national income in the rest of the world by $100 while increasing the U.S. national income by the same amount.

The fall in the rest of the world's national income between Period 0 and Period 1 induces foreigners to cut their imports from the United States by $30: the marginal propensity to import of the rest of the world of 30 per cent times the fall in the rest of the world's national income of $100. Therefore, instead of U.S. exports remaining at $200 in Period 2 as in the previous models, they now recede to $170. Because the rest of the world's propensities are assumed to be the same as those of the United States, the change in national income abroad is the same as in the United States, though in the opposite direction. Therefore the changes in the rest of the world's imports from the United States and of U.S. imports from the rest of the world are the same, though in opposite directions. Consequently the extent to which U.S. exports fall in each period after Period 1 is the same as the extent to which U.S. imports rise in each period.

The method of calculating the entries for all but the export column is the same as in the previous models. The change in the level of U.S.

national income between Period 0 and Period n is obtained by multiplying the initial change of U.S. exports (from Period 0 to Period 1) by the multiplier determined according to the following formula in which the subscript "u" stands for the United States and "r" for the rest of the world:

$$\text{Multiplier} = \frac{1}{m_u + s_u + m_r \left(\dfrac{s_u}{s_r} \right)}$$

The changes from Period 0 to Period n in imports, savings, and consumption of U.S.-produced goods are determined as in the previous models. United States national income does not increase as much in this model as in the previous one; the reason lies in the contraction of foreign income which forces a fall in U.S. exports after they initially increase. The U.S. export surplus, however, is smaller in this model ($25) than in the previous one ($40). The fall in foreign income restrains the total rise in U.S. exports,

Table 9. Foreign Trade Multiplier: Interaction of Incomes

1	2	3	4	5	6	7
Period	Imports	Saving	Consumption of Home Goods	Exports	National Income	Changes in National Income
0	$100	$0	$900	$100	$1,000	
1	100	0	900	200	1,100	+ $100
2	130	20	950	170	1,120	+ 20
3	136	24	960	164	1,124	+ 4
4	137.2	24.8	962	162.8	1,124.8	+ .8
.						
.						
.						
.						
n	$137.5	$25	$962.5	$162.5	$1,125	

and, even though U.S. income is lower because of the restraint on U.S. exports, U.S. imports do not fall proportionately. Just as imports rise less when exports rise because savings intervene, so imports fall less when exports fall because part of the burden of the fall in income is absorbed by a reduction of savings rather than of imports or consumption of home-produced goods which indirectly cause demand for imports.

SELECTED READINGS

Adler, John H., Eugene R. Schlesinger, and Evelyn van Westerborg. *The Pattern of United States Import Trade since 1923*. New York: Federal Reserve

Bank of New York, 1952. An analysis of the determinants of the level of U.S. imports, including a discussion of the difficulties in making accurate statistical estimates of elasticities of demand for imports.

Chang, T. C. *Cyclical Movements in the Balance of Payments.* Cambridge: Cambridge University Press, 1951. Estimates import propensities and price elasticities for many countries and discusses, in Chapter 2, the determinants of average and marginal import propensities.

Economic Commission for Europe. *Economic Survey of Europe in 1954.* Geneva: United Nations, 1955. Chapters 1 and 4 discuss why the U.S. recession of 1953–1954 did not have adverse employment and balance-of-payments effects abroad.

Economic Stability in the Postwar World. Geneva: League of Nations, 1945. Chapter 6 explains the international spread of booms and depressions.

"Gold Inflows and Foreign Spending, and Their Effect on Member Bank Reserves," *Bank Reserves: Some Major Factors Affecting Them.* New York: Federal Reserve Bank of New York, March, 1951. A brief explanation with some historical discussion.

Lovasy, G., and H. K. Zassenhaus. "Short-Run Fluctuations in U.S. Imports of Raw Materials, 1928-39 and 1947-52," *International Monetary Fund Staff Papers,* III (October, 1953), 270–289. Especially useful in connection with the effect of inventory changes on U.S. imports.

Machlup, Fritz. *International Trade and the National Income Multiplier.* New York: Blakiston, 1943. The standard treatise on the foreign trade multiplier. Chapter 10, titled "Apologies and Confessions," is recommended for those who fret over exact formulas for incomplete theories.

Meade, James. *The Balance of Payments.* London: Oxford, 1951. Chapters 3 through 7, 15, and 18 provide a comprehensive theoretical discussion of destabilizing forces and the process of adjustment.

Polak, J. J. *An International Economic System.* Chicago: University of Chicago Press, 1953. Contains estimates of multipliers, marginal import propensities, and price elasticities for numerous nations and a summary of the theory.

Tsiang, S. C. "Balance of Payments and Domestic Flow of Income and Expenditures," *International Monetary Fund Staff Papers,* I (September, 1951), 254–288. A comprehensive discussion of the effect of international payments on domestic income, including an extensive exposition of the relation between capital movements of various types and domestic economic activity.

12 Monetary and Fiscal Policies

The previous chapters centered attention on the problem of internal instability caused by variations in international economic relations and that of balance-of-payments deficits or losses of international reserves. In the remainder of Part III, we consider policies that governments may employ to alleviate these difficulties.

A. ELEMENTS OF ADJUSTMENT AND STABILIZATION POLICIES

Three separate, though sometimes related, problems face the open economy: balance-of-payments deficits, general unemployment, and general inflation.

BALANCE-OF-PAYMENTS DEFICITS

Supposing that there are no unilateral transfers and no capital movements apart from international reserves, a balance-of-payments deficit would consist of a deficit on current account and would imply an excess of domestic expenditure over GNP. The basic equation might show the following magnitudes:

GNP		Imports		Exports		Domestic Expenditure
$1,000	+	$200	=	$100	+	$1,100

By moving exports to the left side and GNP to the right side, we pinpoint the problem:

Imports		Exports		Domestic Expenditure		GNP
$200	—	$100	=	$1,100	—	$1,000

The nation is spending more (domestic expenditure) than it is producing (GNP); or, if we suppose that there are no depreciation charges or excise taxes so that GNP and national income are the same, the nation is spending more than its income. It is living beyond its means.

The excess of domestic expenditure over GNP implies that the demand for goods and services which is not satisfied out of the nation's own production is satisfied through imports of goods and services. Or, to put a slightly different light on the problem, domestic expenditure is so great relative to GNP that an insufficient part of the GNP is exported and too much is used at home.

Removal of the gap between imports and exports, and thus the cessation of the reserve losses, implies removal of the gap between domestic expenditure and GNP. The methods by which both gaps are closed involve changes in income, spending, output, and prices.

Monetary policy

By raising the rate of interest and reducing the supply of loanable funds, the government may cause a reduction of investment spending and of consumption expenditure (an increase in saving), i.e., a reduction in domestic expenditure. The fall in domestic expenditure reduces the demand for imports to the extent of the import content of the domestic expenditure. It also releases home-produced goods and services from domestic use and makes them available for export, or it releases resources from the production of goods for the home market to the production of different goods for the foreign market.

The decline in domestic spending will induce some fall in prices which may assist the process of balance-of-payments adjustment. Export products become more attractive to foreigners because of lower prices. Domestic substitutes for import products become more attractive to residents because of their lower prices. Whether or not these price changes induce a favorable movement of the current account depends upon the elasticities of demand. If the foreign demand for the nation's exports is inelastic, the decline in price will lead to a smaller total foreign expenditure on the exports; the physical volume of exports will not rise by enough to offset the unfavorable effect on the value of exports resulting from the drop in their price. An elastic demand, on the other hand, means a more than proportionate increase in the physical volume of purchases as prices fall so that foreigners' total expenditures for the exports rise. Even if the foreign demand for exports is inelastic, the balance of payments will improve if the value of imports falls even more than the fall in the value of exports. Thus the elasticity of demand for imports with respect to changes in prices is equally as important as that of foreigners for exports in determining the success or failure of price changes.

While the reduction of domestic expenditure would in itself tend to reduce GNP and employment, an improvement in the current account tends to offset these results; the demand for imports is shifted to home-produced goods and the level of exports increases. But this presumes sufficient mobility of resources so that the transfer of employment can be readily made. If it cannot, a reduction of domestic expenditure is self-defeating, for the GNP falls as fast as domestic expenditure and consequently the gap between exports and imports cannot be closed.

Fiscal policy

The process of improving the balance of payments is not significantly different if the government reduces its own expenditures or raises taxes so as to reduce the expenditures of citizens. In either event, domestic expenditure declines, setting off the responses just indicated.

Exchange-rate policy

Quite different in the point of initial impact is a policy of exchange-rate variation. The British government may decide to change the exchange rate from $4 per £1 to $2 per £1. Immediately, British goods become less expensive to Americans since each pound costs half as many dollars, and American goods become more expensive to Englishmen because each dollar costs twice as many pounds. By changing the prices of exports and imports, the shift of the exchange rate raises the physical volume of Britain's exports and reduces the physical volume of her imports. Whether or not the balance-of-payments deficit is reduced depends upon the elasticities of demand, for the value of trade depends upon both prices and physical volumes.

Reduction of the deficit also depends upon changes in the GNP and domestic expenditure. A rise in exports and a substitution of home goods for imports as a result of price changes increases the real GNP, though only if unemployment exists. When full employment prevails, it is impossible to increase total output, apart from productivity growth.

If unemployment prevails, the rise in real GNP increases real national income which in turn may lead to a rise in domestic expenditure as residents have more income to spend. Success depends upon real GNP (national income) rising more than real domestic expenditure.

If full employment does prevail, the entire burden of adjustment must be borne by a reduction in domestic expenditure. However, the growth of productivity provides some escape from an absolute reduction in the home use of goods and services. The additional output attributable to higher productivity can be directed to foreign markets and can be used to replace imports through the incentives provided by the change in the exchange rate.

Direct controls

Finally, the government may limit the value of imports through controls such as those which specify that only a certain amount of goods may be imported over a given period. This is not a sufficient condition for the improvement of the current account, however. The income no longer spent on imports may be diverted to the purchase of home-produced goods. Resources which produce exports are absorbed into production for the home market, assisted by the fact that, as spending on home output increases, prices rise, making exports less attractive to foreigners. Unless the diversion of demand from imports to home goods is accompanied by a rise in saving, domestic expenditure (which includes the expenditure on both home goods and imports) is unchanged; if GNP cannot be increased, no improvement in the balance of payments results.

UNEMPLOYMENT

Suppose that a nation has general unemployment caused by a fall in GNP attributable to either a fall in foreigners' expenditures (exports), a fall in domestic expenditure, or a shift in the composition of domestic expenditure such that more is spent on foreign goods and less on home-produced goods. By means of the policy instruments discussed above, the government may attempt to remove the unemployment. A fall in the interest rate (monetary policy) may induce a rise in investment spending and in consumption with the result that domestic expenditure increases. A rise in government purchases or a fall in taxes which permits citizens to spend more (fiscal policy) has the same effect. A change in the exchange rate can be engineered so as to make exports more attractive to foreigners and foreign goods less attractive to residents than domestically produced goods; a rise in GNP results. Finally, a reduction of imports through direct controls will divert demand to home goods.

INFLATION

Suppose that a nation has a general price inflation caused by a rise in foreigners' expenditures (exports), a rise in domestic expenditure, or shift in the composition of domestic expenditure such that more is spent on home goods and less on foreign goods. The appropriate policy techniques are those which reduce spending, reducing the demand for goods and services, i.e., the converse of those used to prevent unemployment.

B. MONETARY POLICY

The importance of money to the problems discussed above is readily perceived when it is remembered that it is money that is spent to buy goods and services. A variation in the quantity of money or in its rate of turnover to buy final goods and services implies a variation in the total spending.

We saw in Chapter 11 that imports reduce the money supply while exports increase it. Therefore a balance-of-payments deficit covered by a loss of reserves implies a reduction in the quantity of home-owned money.

A balance-of-payments deficit also implies an excess of domestic expenditure over GNP. But such an excess cannot long persist if the quantity of money is falling, unless velocity rises, for the means of spending declines. Therefore the persistence of a deficit depends upon new money being created just as fast as the balance-of-payments deficit wipes it out, or upon a compensating rise in the velocity of money.

Standard methods of reducing the money supply and spending are for the central bank to (1) raise reserve requirements so that each dollar of reserves supports fewer dollars of demand deposits, thereby forcing a contraction of banks' loans and demand deposits; (2) raise the cost of borrowing reserves from the monetary authorities, which induces banks to raise interest charges to their borrowers and warns the banking community that the monetary authorities desire credit restraint; and (3) sell securities from its own portfolio to commercial banks, which pay for them by reducing their deposits (reserves) at the central bank, and/or to the public, which pays for them by reducing its demand deposits at commercial banks; sales to the public lead to a fall in bank reserves as the public's funds are transferred from commercial banks to the central bank. When an increase in the money supply is desired, the ground may be laid through opposite actions on the part of the central bank, which are designed to increase bank reserves.

THE BANK OF ENGLAND IN THE NINETEENTH CENTURY

During the seventy-five years before World War I, England, standing highest among the trading nations, pioneered in the use of monetary policy to prevent serious balance-of-payments difficulties. The major instrument was the bank rate, i.e., the rate at which the Bank of England, Britain's central bank, would lend money.

The operations were as follows: If England were losing gold to foreign nations, the Bank of England would raise the bank rate. The higher bank rate would cause the general level of interest rates in Britain to rise, which induced capital imports and reduced capital exports. Also, the higher interest rates reduced borrowing for speculative buying and for investment spending, especially for inventories, with a resultant decline in domestic expenditure and prices, which tended to raise exports and reduce imports. The improvement of the current and the capital accounts prevented and sometimes even reversed the outflow of gold.

The intermediaries through which the mechanism worked were the British commercial banks and the London discount market. The latter had the function of financing both foreign and domestic trade; it consisted primarily of bill dealers and discount houses. A merchant selling goods at home or abroad would draw a bill of exchange (draft) on the purchaser of the goods or the purchaser's agent. If this were a time draft, it would be sold at a discount from its face value in the discount market. By selling the draft, the merchant obtained his funds immediately; the purchaser of the commodities received credit until the maturity of the draft. The difference between the amount provided to the seller of the goods by the discount market and the amount paid at maturity by the purchaser of the goods constituted the interest income for the discount market operators. As the years passed, the discount market became a gigantic revolving fund with money moving from bill to bill as old bills matured and new ones were discounted. Bill dealers and the discount houses provided part of the funds from their own resources, but they supplemented them by borrowing without a definite repayment date from the commercial banks.

The Bank of England held control over the operations in this money market. An outflow of gold reduced the reserves of British commercial banks, and if the reserve ratio fell below the conventional minimum they felt compelled to reduce their demand deposits and/or increase their reserves. This they did by calling in the loans they made to the discount houses and bill dealers.

But the discount houses and bill dealers did not have the funds which they had borrowed from the commercial banks, because the borrowed money had been invested in the bills of exchange which they had discounted. To obtain the money with which to repay the borrowed funds, the discount houses borrowed from the Bank of England.[1] But they could do this only at a high cost; the Bank of England, observing the loss of gold, would raise the bank rate. The discount market was able to obtain the needed funds, but, faced with higher borrowing costs, it raised the rates of interest it charged on discounting bills, and thus the general level of interest rates in Britain rose.

Short-term capital in search of more attractive income moved to London, and short-term capital which was about to be withdrawn remained in London. Foreign merchants who normally borrowed money to finance their purchases or sales in London turned elsewhere for the needed funds, reducing British short-term capital exports. And because London was also a major source of long-term loans to foreigners, a higher rate of interest deterred foreigners from borrowing in London. Thus movements of capital substituted for movements of gold.

The Bank of England's policy protected the London money market and the British economy from the extreme vicissitudes connected with gold outflows. By lending funds to the discount market when they were needed, the Bank of England relieved the extreme pressure on the market and a monetary panic was averted, though some burden was imposed by raising the bank rate. The full deflationary pressures of gold outflows were avoided.

---

[1] If the money market was too liquid to force the discount houses to borrow from the Bank of England, the latter often sold British consols, government bonds, to the public in order to mop up the excess liquidity and force borrowing from the bank.

In the three-quarters of a century before World War I, the Bank of England changed its bank rate over four hundred times. But in the later portion of that period, other devices were utilized which protected England's thin gold reserves without penalizing the money market and the economy through a higher bank rate. On numerous occasions the Bank was able to attract foreign gold coins to its coffers by raising the pound price it paid for them. Similarly, by raising the price at which gold bars were sold, the Bank deterred the export of gold from England. Under the law the Bank was obligated to exchange gold sovereigns (a British gold coin) for Bank of England notes at a fixed price; but in order to discourage the export of sovereigns, the Bank would select the *minimum* legal weight coins for sale to exporters when sovereigns were demanded. Sometimes the Bank would make interest-free loans for short periods on the promise that the loans would be repaid in gold.

By developing these gold devices as a substitute for the bank-rate mechanism and by developing the bank-rate mechanism before that (all of which protected Britain from the inflationary or deflationary influences of gold flows), the Bank of England moved a good distance from the principles of the Bank Act of 1844. The theory of the latter was that the note issue of the Bank should be tied precisely to fluctuations in the gold holdings of the Bank and that the variations in the quantity of notes would be sufficient to produce the necessary price and income adjustments to increase exports and reduce imports so as to recover lost gold.

STERILIZATION OF INTERNATIONAL RESERVE MOVEMENTS

Central Bank operations

Before World War I, the Bank of England was one of only a very few central banks in the world. But as knowledge of the importance of money grew and as the conviction developed that the management of money was the key to controlling business fluctuations, central banks were established throughout Europe and in several other countries, including the United States. Partly by accident and partly by design, these institutions began to weaken the link between international payments and the domestic money supply.

After World War I, the need abroad for American goods and services for reconstruction and for the satisfaction of postponed demands was intense. To pay for the needed commodities, foreign governments shipped gold to the United States—a step which, without interference, would have increased demand deposits and bank reserves in the United States. But the effect of the gold inflow was neutralized. American commercial banks used some of the gold to repay their borrowings from the Federal Reserve Banks so that reserves which would have resulted from gold inflows merely substituted for the borrowed reserves, leaving the over-all reserve position relatively unchanged. In addition, the Federal Reserve System sold securities which absorbed more reserves of commercial banks and counteracted the normal effect of gold flows on bank reserves.

The purpose in the Federal Reserve's action was to hold down inflation in the belief that the inflow of gold was a temporary consequence of disorganized conditions abroad. Many countries had untied their currencies from gold during the war and expected to return to the gold standard later; this would necessitate their buying back the gold to form part of the legal base of their currency. Had the gold inflow been permitted to cause inflation in the United States, the new gold would have been made a constituent part of the U.S. credit system; when the gold later flowed out to meet the monetary needs of foreign nations, there would have been a contraction of credit in the United States with a concomitant depression of internal economic activity.

America was not alone in offsetting the effects of reserve movements. A study of central bank accounts of 26 countries between 1922 and 1938 shows that in 60 per cent of the cases central banks' assets shifted in such a way to tend to neutralize the effects of movements of international reserves on domestic credit conditions. In 1937 and 1938, a number of countries lost international reserves, but there were none that did not offset the deflationary monetary consequences.

Stabilization funds

The 1930's were years of fear. The weight of the world-wide depression and the cataclysmic political changes crumbled confidence in currencies and in the future. National and private finances were in difficulty. With the need to expand exports to sustain employment and in the face of losses of international reserves, countries loosened their currencies from gold. The United States increased the value of an ounce of gold from $20.67 to $35, thereby depreciating the value of the dollar. Britain allowed the value of the pound (in terms of gold and the dollar) to fluctuate with supply and demand. Other countries did the same or imposed direct controls on trade and payments.

In view of the political fright of the time, of the frequent and nearly universal changes of exchange rates, and of the imposition of controls designed to limit the freedom to make international payments, it is not difficult to see why the 1930's were also years of "hot money," i.e., of speculative and flight capital movements.

Though not originally set up for this purpose, several nations created stabilization funds which had the incidental effect of ameliorating the internal monetary effects of hot-money flows. Chief among these is the Exchange Equalisation Account created in 1932 by Great Britain.

An inflow of foreign capital, like a rise in exports, tends to increase demand deposits and bank reserves; the Exchange Equalisation Account worked primarily to counteract bank-reserve changes, thus reducing the multiple change in demand deposits which may follow a change in bank reserves since the reserves held were usually a small fraction of the deposits they supported.

As capital flowed in, the Account, rather than commercial banks, would buy the foreign exchange which was offered for sterling. The foreign capitalist was credited with an increased demand deposit at some British commercial bank; the funds of the Account at the Bank of England were reduced; and the reserves of the commercial bank which was host to the foreign capitalist's deposit were *temporarily* increased. The Account's pound balance at the Bank of England was replenished in a manner designed to wipe out the last-mentioned increase in bank reserves. Short-term securities were sold by the Account in the discount market at attractive prices; to obtain the funds to pay for them, the purchasers borrowed money from the commercial banks. The borrowed money was transferred to the Account's balance at the Bank of England, reducing the reserves of the commercial banks which made the loans to the discount houses. The demand deposits and the loans of the commercial banks rose, but the level of bank reserves was unchanged. Meantime, the foreign exchange obtained by the Account was sold to foreign countries for gold, which was held by the Account.

In the event of a capital outflow, the procedure was reversed. The Account would accept pounds from persons wishing to export capital, giving foreign exchange or gold in return. The purchase of the foreign exchange or gold from the Account depressed deposits and bank reserves. But the Account used the pounds it obtained to purchase securities in the London money market; the result was a rise in bank reserves to their level prior to the export of capital.

The United States created a similar agency called the Exchange Stabilization Fund. It was given $2 billion from the "profit" obtained on gold holdings of the government when the price of gold was raised from $20.67 to $35 per ounce. Having gold, the American Fund was in a good position to satisfy the demand for gold or for foreign exchange (the gold could be sold abroad for foreign currencies) in the event of a capital outflow. But a capital inflow—a demand for dollars—found the Fund useless in the insulation of bank reserves. To obtain the dollars to satisfy the demand, the Fund would have to sell some of its gold to the Federal Reserve Bank of New York. The deposit received by the Fund at the Federal Reserve Bank would be transferred to the commercial bank at which the capital importer kept his money, and this would raise bank reserves.

The British Exchange Equalisation Account was more fortunate than the American Fund. The British Account was equipped with securities to be sold to obtain pounds to meet a capital flow to London, which is what occurred first. The U.S. Fund was filled with gold to face the threat of a capital outflow, which was the opposite of what happened.

Treasury gold sterilization

Between 1931 and 1939, there was a net flow of gold to the United States of approximately $10 billion. This unprecedented avalanche reflected the repatriation of American long-term and short-term investments abroad and an inflow of foreign capital, motivated largely by economic and political uncertainty. The capital inflow created a need for dollars which could be obtained only through the sale of gold to the United States because it was not accompanied by a U.S. current account deficit. Between 1934 and 1936, the amount of gold acquired was $4.2 billion, and American commercial bank reserves rose by $4 billion—or to twice their initial level.

In the depths of the U.S. depression, the enhanced liquidity of the economy resulting from the capital inflow caused little concern to the monetary authorities. But late in 1936, a fear of inflation, stimulated by a boom psychology and the hyperliquidity of the banking system, gripped officialdom. Thereafter the gold acquired was sterilized in so far as its effects on bank reserves were concerned until early in 1938, when the inflation psychosis disintegrated in the face of a deepening depression.

The process of gold sterilization by the Treasury involved it in the sale of securities. When the Treasury bought gold it paid for it by reducing its account at the Federal Reserve Bank of New York; the funds transferred to the seller of the gold were then disbursed in a manner which increased commercial bank reserves and demand deposits. Usually the Treasury replenished its deposits by issuing gold certificates to the Federal Reserve Bank, but during the sterilization period, the Treasury obtained the funds to replenish its deposits by selling securities to the public and the banks. Payment for the securities, whether bought by the public or the banks, was effectuated by reducing the reserves of commercial banks, thus offsetting the rise in reserves caused by a gold inflow. There was an additional decline in demand deposits if the public did the purchasing. The effectiveness of this procedure is indicated by the fact that commercial bank reserves rose by less than one-sixth of the increase in U.S. gold stock during the sterilization period compared to an increase in reserves equal that of the gold inflows during the presterilization period.

POSTWAR MONETARY POLICY

Inflationary pressures

During World War II much of the cost of the war was financed through the issuance of public debt and the creation of money. Interest rates were held low in order to permit borrowing for war expenditures as cheaply as possible. The money supply responded passively to the needs of production. In Britain, for example, the money supply rose by 150 per cent. The debt of the U.K. government was three times its prewar size and twice the size of the GNP compared to about 1½ times the GNP before the war.

In countries occupied by the Germans, much the same events took place. In Belgium, for example, the "sophisticated looting" by Germany created a money supply four times its prewar level. Belgium was forced to export extensively to Germany; the Belgian central bank created the francs with which the Belgian exporters were paid and received a credit in Berlin. The costs of occupation by German troops were also financed by the creation of new money.

In still other countries, the rise of exports to belligerents added to the money supply as did continued budget deficits financed by sales of securities to central banks. For example, short-term capital in the United States owned by Latin America, which reflected the rise in exports to the United States, rose substantially; demand deposits rose as commercial banks bought drafts from exporters and received deposits in the United States, and bank reserves rose as the dollars were sold by the commercial banks to Latin American central banks. Budget deficits increased the money supply. The central bank would pay for securities purchased from the government by increasing the government's deposit at the central bank; when these newly obtained funds were paid out to citizens by the government, the public's demand deposits rose, as did the reserves of banks in which the checks were deposited.

Price and rationing controls and other measures tended to contain the basic inflationary forces during the war. But in containing inflation a situation of latent inflation was created. At the end of the war, the amounts of money and other liquid assets, such as government securities held by the public and the banks, were abnormally high relative to the general price level and to the volume of transactions as measured by the GNP. In Britain a third of the money supply was redundant; in Norway the ratio of the money supply to the GNP was four times higher than before the war. The large-scale issuance of government securities during the war loaded the economy with highly liquid assets which, along with excessive money supplies, encouraged spending since the public felt that, when pinched for cash, it could fall back on its wartime savings.

The excessive liquidity after the war plus the needs of reconstruction meant a virtually insatiable demand for anything—home or foreign produced. Inflationary pressure absorbed goods for home use which otherwise might have been exported, and enhanced the demand for imports, worsening international reserve positions. What was required was the removal of the excess liquidity and the stopping of further increases in the money supply. Unless the excess liquidity was removed, restrictive monetary policy would be frustrated by the ability of the public to spend more than its current income by drawing on its own assets.

Governmental policies

With only a few exceptions, until the Korean War adequate restraint through monetary policy was lacking. Many nations wished to avoid a general rise in interest rates which a strict monetary policy would induce. Cheap money (low interest rates) was a long-standing policy. During the depression, interest rates were held down to facilitate economic recovery. During the war, they were restrained through the creation of money to finance the war effort. After World War II cheap money was continued out of fear of a postwar recession, out of a concern over the cost of servicing the public debt (which had grown precipitously), and in the belief that the reconstruction of worn-out and bombed-out facilities required lower interest rates. Antipathy toward the rentier class and dissatisfaction with the apparently unselective character of high interest rates in holding down all types of investment added to the case for cheap money.

In Britain, for example, the rate of interest on short-term government securities was held at ½ per cent until late in 1951 by Bank of England purchases, which held up their price. Because their price was fixed, the short-term government securities owned by the commercial banking system became as good as money. The demand for credit by the private sector of the economy could safely be satisfied by the banks as long as they had sufficient short-term securities to exchange for reserves at the Bank of England in case excessive lending (demand-deposit creation) jeopardized their reserve positions. The Bank's rate of 2 per cent was of little consequence; if the discount houses wished to borrow money, they could do so easily from the highly liquid commercial banks, and the latter could lend cheaply.

One of the major instruments of credit control in Britain was qualitative or selective. Under a gentleman's agreement, the Bank of England gave instructions to the commercial banks regarding the priorities they should give to various types of requests for loans. The Capital Issues Committee passed upon borrowing outside the banks for capital expenditures. Under this qualitative control, borrowing for nonessential use was limited, and borrowing to finance priority activities like export production was encouraged.

In France, banks were directed to refuse credit for nonessential purposes. A gentlemen's agreement between the banks and the central bank provided that the banks would not unload their government securities; had they done so, the central bank would have had to buy them in order to support their price (hold down the interest rate on them) and, in doing so, would add to commercial bank reserves. Later, the support price was lowered, giving rise to higher interest rates, while the bank rate was also increased. But none of these measures was pushed hard enough to control the inflation of prices in France. During 1946–1948, there was a 600 per cent rise in bank credit to the private sector, the money supply doubled, and prices rose to 4½ times their previous level. A major inflationary force was the persistent budget deficit of the French government which required central-bank financing; the government's spending of the newly created money added to the economy's liquidity faster than the aforementioned monetary restraints could control it. An effective monetary policy is quite difficult to operate unless the government budget is under control.

Effective anti-inflationary monetary policy usually implies a rise in interest rates on government securities. The decline in the supply of loanable funds which accompanies monetary restraint reduces the funds available for buying all types of securities including those issued by the government for deficit financing. If the government is unwilling to pay higher rates of interest and if it is able to persuade, cajole, or force the central bank to its point of view, the central bank cannot tighten money and may have to support the prices of government securities through its purchases. For example, the Swedish central bank increased its holdings of government securities between 1946 and 1948 to the point that it acquired 20 per cent of the government debt in the process of supporting the prices of government securities.

Currency reform provided another method of controlling the money supply. Soon after the liberation of Belgium, for example, the money supply was reduced from 164 billion francs to 57 billion, thus cutting out much of the latent inflation. The technique was to block from use part of the currency and bank deposits. Some of the money was blocked temporarily, while the remainder of the blocked money became a forced loan to the government which was later repaid out of revenue from a capital levy. In Germany, Reichsmarks were exchanged for new Deutsche marks at the rate of 10 for 1, as were bank deposits. A portion of the remaining bank deposits were blocked and then later simply canceled. Numerous other European countries did much the same; some did it several times. In some instances the purpose was less to combat inflation than to determine who had money and other assets in order to lessen the chances of evading later capital levies or to catch wartime black marketeers and other illegal operators.

Traditional monetary policy, especially the use of the bank rate and higher interest rates, was re-employed at the start of the Korean War by a large number of countries when the previous systems of inflation control had fallen into disrepute and when new inflationary pressure threatened. While inflation was not completely thwarted, the international-reserve position of these countries was improved as a result of stricter monetary measures. "Raw material countries that applied restraining monetary policies in 1950 and 1951 were able to retain a considerable part of the reserves they accumulated during the boom. Industrial countries with effective monetary policies were able to build up reserves during the period of the Korean boom and retain these reserves after the boom had terminated. The industrial countries that lost reserves in 1950 and 1951 and then took effective monetary measures showed large gains in their [international] monetary reserves early in 1952."[2]

SOME PROBLEMS OF MONETARY POLICY

Anti-inflationary policies

A major question concerning monetary policy is whether or not higher interest rates are an effective restraint on spending. Some argue that the interest rate is such a small part of the cost of doing business that higher interest rates have little effect on investment and therefore little effect on spending and borrowing. While such a view may be valid for low ranges of interest rates on short-term loans, it overlooks the fact that in some countries banks make long-term and medium-term loans on which the total interest payment is an important part of the cost of business. Further, tightening the short-term rate on bank loans tends to increase the interest rate on long-term securities since the two markets for loans are not entirely separated. In addition, higher interest rates and greater confidence in the currency may induce greater savings which substitute for inflationary sources of finance for investment.

Others minimize the effectiveness of higher interest rates on the ground that borrowers' expectations of continually rising prices will offset higher interest charges as far as profit expectations are concerned; thus there is little incentive to reduce borrowing. But the expectations of borrowers are affected by their confidence in the ability of the government or central bank to pursue a tight monetary policy; if the monetary authorities give the appearance of dealing strongly with inflation, then expectations of inflation do not persist. Finally, monetary policy to combat inflation does not work solely through the effect of higher rates of interest on spending. It also involves credit rationing; the supply of loanable funds is reduced, and loans to some credit-worthy borrowers are denied.

Monetary policy suffers in that it may sometimes set off reactions which defeat the purpose. A higher rate of interest increases the cost of holding money idle. Therefore persons and institutions may economize on their cash balances, i.e., increase the rate at which they turn them over in the purchase of goods and services. Whether this happens depends on a host of factors, not the least of which are the expectations held regarding future prices.

In addition, in a number of underdeveloped countries exports constitute the most important determinant of the course of prices and internal activity; domestic investment, upon which monetary policy works, is rela-

---

[2] E. M. Bernstein, "Accomplishments of Monetary Policy," *The Revival of Monetary Policy* (Washington: International Monetary Fund, 1953), p. 15.

tively insignificant. Hence the field of play for monetary policy is automatically limited.

Antidepression policies

The use of monetary policy to combat a recession of business activity is subject to a severe shortcoming: banks cannot lend unless there are borrowers. If business is poor and expectations are unfavorable, businessmen are unlikely to borrow. Since banks cannot lend money to just anyone who passes the front door, easy money and excess liquidity do not necessarily call forth borrowers whose requests for loans cause the creation of money which accompanies economic expansion.

But monetary policy is still useful in a depressed economic situation. By adding to the reserve base of the banking system or by making reserves easy to obtain, the monetary authorities make it less likely that contractionist forces in the economy are accentuated by a bank-induced reduction of loans. Also, low rates of interest may induce capital exports which indirectly buoy economic activity. Of course, as indicated before, capital exports are, by themselves, deflationary because they reduce the supply of loanable funds, raise interest rates, and reduce investment. But if the capital-exporting country is highly liquid, i.e., has much idle cash, the deflationary impact of capital exports is negligible because the supply of loanable funds will be easily replenished from hoards. When any of the borrowed money is spent for the lending country's exports, the rise in exports sets off a multiplier rise in GNP and employment.

Specific devices

Among the specific devices available to monetary authorities, selective credit controls are of limited use in restraining nonessential lending because, unlike a rise in interest rates, they do not affect the demand for all types of credit. A firm, desiring to borrow money for a nonessential expenditure and knowing that its request will be denied, will ask for a loan for some permissible purpose which it normally finances out of its own cash. The borrowed money will be used for the permitted expenditure while the firm's own resources are used for the nonessential one. The loan makes the nonessential expenditure possible.

Currency reforms have their shortcomings too. Administrative difficulties result from the multiplicity of types of demand deposits connected with reform of the currency. Austria had three reforms which overlapped with regard to the types of deposits affected. By the time the third reform came along depositors found it difficult to determine what they fully, only partially, or no longer owned. Besides the administrative problem, the use of currency reforms suffers in that it works by affecting liquidity. What is needed is a reduction of spending. Moreover, if there is an expectation that additional currency reforms will follow, the individual has an incentive to spend assets which the last currency reform left him. A further effect is a loss of international reserves as citizens attempt to get their assets beyond the reach of the government; this seems to have been the case in postwar Germany where a currency reform was widely expected, probably because similar action had been taken after World War I.

Exchange stabilization funds and gold sterilization are not necessarily effective in offsetting completely the internal consequences of changes in international payments. Their only certain effect is on bank reserves; the demand deposits created and wiped out through the inward and outward flow of capital may be unaffected. Consider the instance of a flow of capital to Britain, which adds to bank reserves and demand deposits. The sale of securities by the Exchange Equalisation Account absorbs the added bank reserves no matter whether the securities are bought by banks or the public. As for the newly created demand deposits, if the foreign owner simply holds them idle, there is no monetary effect since his right to spend the new pounds lies unused. The system works perfectly if the foreigner happens to buy the securities issued by the Account; the demand deposit of the foreigner disappears as money is transferred to the Account's deposit at the Bank of England, and the rates of interest are unaffected since the foreigner's additional demand for securities is just met by an increase in the supply of them from the Account. But if the commercial banks or the discount houses buy the new securities (the latter with borrowed funds) issued by the Account while the foreigner puts his money in the stock market, for example, damage may be done. Stock prices rise, a boom psychology is created, and inflationary pressure may appear. The same points apply to the American gold-sterilization procedure. The increase in demand deposits caused by the gold inflow is wiped out only to the extent that the securities issued by the Treasury are bought by the public.

Finally, the use of increases in the interest rate to induce the return of international reserves, such as described in connection with the Bank of England during the nineteenth century, is not always effective. It used to be said that a 7 per cent rate would bring gold from the moon. But the moon must have confidence in the currency it is urged to buy. During the monetary collapse of 1931, several nations used the traditional bank-rate device to little avail. Germany, for example, put her rate up to 15 per cent. When a loss of international reserves is caused by capital flights, a rise in the bank rate must be sufficient to overcome the fear that motivates the outflow if it is to reverse the loss. But if the cause of the flight is an expectation of devaluation of the currency, then a few more percentage points of interest that may be earned can hardly reverse an outflow induced by fears of a capital loss of, say, 10 to 30 per cent. (The same reasoning explains why the bank rate is ineffective against politically induced capital flight.) Of course, an exceedingly high bank rate, such as the 30 per cent suggested by one popular German economist in the early 1930's, might turn the tide; yet the psychology of panics is such that stiff action even far short of 30 per cent may heighten fears, being interpreted as an official confirmation that severe trouble lies ahead.

C. FISCAL POLICY

The conscious variation of government expenditures and taxes to combat internal economic instability became important during and after the 1930's. Fiscal policy was used to alleviate unemployment partly because of the unsatisfactory results obtained from monetary policy and partly because expanded government expenditures fitted the growing belief in a larger role for governments. During and after World War II, some nations placed heavy reliance on fiscal policy to combat inflation both because of a reluctance to use monetary policy for reasons indicated earlier and because high taxation, especially of the well-to-do, conformed with the social objectives of many governments.

SOME EXAMPLES

Disinflation through budgets

An anti-inflationary fiscal policy was used by Britain at times in the post-World War II period when her international reserves were under pressure. In 1946 and 1947, the financial accounts of both local and central British governments showed an over-all deficit of £1 billion and £600 million, respectively, compared to a GNP of about £10 billion. A new Chancellor of the Exchequer, Sir Stafford Cripps, then started a policy of "disinflation," i.e., removal of inflationary pressure without causing deflation. Among other things, he turned the previous years' deficits into a surplus of £88 million; the British government ceased to add to demand. In terms of the source and use of British resources the results were these in constant prices:

	GNP		Imports		Exports		Domestic Expenditure
1947	10,299	+	3,043	=	1,575	+	11,767
1948	10,722	+	2,979	=	1,983	+	11,718

Virtually all of the increase in GNP between 1947 and 1948 was used to expand exports; imports were not only prevented from rising but were actually cut, through direct controls. The composition of domestic expenditure was changed; total consumption fell, government purchases of current goods and services dropped, and the resources thereby freed were used for capital formation. These favorable changes cannot be attributed solely to fiscal policy since Sir Stafford used other devices, such as improving direct controls over investment. However, without the improved fiscal situation, the rearrangement in the use of British resources undoubtedly would not have been as large or as effective or perhaps even possible.

Excise taxes

Since excise taxes often bear most heavily on the poor and middle class who, by virtue of their numbers, do most of the spending, variations in excise taxes can be an effective means of controlling domestic expenditure. In addition, they have a selective feature which increases their usefulness. For example, in 1949, twice as many British autos were sold in the home market as the government desired. In the next budget, the purchase tax on domestic sales of autos was doubled in order to reduce domestic sales and thereby release autos for export. Later, a different objective was served by reducing the purchase tax on textiles. The British textile industry suffered because of a loss of export markets induced by growing self-sufficiency abroad while the economy as a whole enjoyed full employment. To aid the industry through a reduction of (say) personal income taxes probably would have been of doubtful help; too little of the increment in the disposable income of citizens would have been devoted to buying the products of Lancashire, while increased consumer spending elsewhere would have added to inflationary pressures in the otherwise fully employed British economy.

Export taxes and subsidies

Export duties and subsidies provide a means for protecting an economy from internal instability that would be caused by variations in exports, and they can have important effects on international reserves.

When foreign demand for a nation's exports is rising, the imposition of an export tax will divert to the government some of the extra income which would otherwise go into private hands. Conversely, when foreign demand declines, the reduction of export taxes lessens the fall in private income and thus tends to sustain internal income and economic activity.

Some of the underdeveloped raw-material-producing countries rely on export duties as a major source of government revenue. And since the proceeds vary automatically with exports, export duties are potential automatic stabilizers of internal activity. The stabilizing effect is greater with an ad valorem tax than with a specific tax because the proceeds vary with the price as well as the volume. Even more effective is a sliding-scale tax, such as Malaya applied to rubber, which takes an increasing proportion of the value of the exports as their prices rise.

When the government can restrain its own spending during an export boom, the case for export taxes is strong. By restricting a rise in private incomes, export taxes also hold down imports, and international reserves therefore accumulate. When the boom collapses, a reduction of export taxes sustains income and therefore sustains imports. A balance-of-payments deficit may result from lower exports while imports are sustained, but this may be comfortably covered by paying out the extra international reserves which were accumulated during the previous boom. Such a procedure makes it less likely that primary producers, which suffer wide variations in their exports, will undergo the twin problems of internal instability and international payments crises. But the accumulation of reserves requires a country to save some of its income (foreign exchange) during a boom; some countries are too poor to afford the luxury of stability obtained in this way.

The outbreak of the Korean War brought fabulous export earnings to many primary-producing countries as a result of feverish purchasing, partly by governments for rearmament and stockpiling and partly by private business in anticipation of future price increases. From the first half of 1950 through the first half of 1951, foreign-exchange earnings by all primary-producing nations rose by over 50 per cent.

A number of governments imposed additional taxes on exports to siphon off the increased income. But the boom came and went so quickly (prices collapsed in 1951) and the governments were so slow to act, that the taxes diverted only a small portion of the flood of earnings into government coffers. Malayan export duties seized only 8 per cent of the increments in rubber and tin export earnings during the boom, and Indonesia taxed away sums equivalent only to 14 per cent of the increase in total export earnings.

There are several variations on the export-tax scheme. The government may, for example, monopolize the sale of the exportable product. A fixed or at least relatively inflexible price is paid to domestic producers, no matter what the price in the world market may be. During the years in which the world price exceeds the price paid to the domestic producer, the state monopoly obtains revenue which, when the price in the world market falls below the domestic price, it pays back to the export producers. Some of the outstanding examples of export monopolies are the Rice Bureau in Thailand, the State Agricultural Marketing Board in Burma, the cocoa boards in Nigeria and the Gold Coast, and the multiproduct Argentine Trade Promotion Institute. In Thailand and Burma, the boards succeeded in almost completely insulating the domestic economies from the inflationary impact of the Korean raw-material boom.

Still another variation on the export-tax procedure is illustrated by New Zealand's policy during the Korean boom. One-third of the proceeds of the wool crop was blocked in special accounts under the wool growers' names. They could not be used by the growers until released by the government. Such a procedure is more palatable to export producers (who are often the dominant political interest) than an export tax because income is not lost forever. But the anti-inflationary effect is limited since growers can expect to receive the funds when times get difficult; with this cushion they have less incentive to restrain their spending now. A similar means of making export taxes politically acceptable is to use part of the proceeds for the general development of the taxed industry, for example, in research work by the government as was done in Norway during the Korean boom.

Export subsidies may be used both to increase domestic economic activity by expanding export income and to increase foreign-currency earnings for balance-of-payments reasons by reducing the price charged foreigners and by inducing an expansion of export production. The balance-of-payments purpose is served only if the foreign demand for exports is elastic. Only then will a decline in the price charged foreigners lead to increased foreign expenditures on exports.

However, freedom of action regarding export subsidies is limited. Some nations, such as the United States, impose countervailing duties on imported goods whose production is subsidized abroad. In some cases, the subsidizing nation is subjected to diplomatic or other pressure, by countries whose exports or domestic industries suffer additional competition, to stop its subsidization of exports. Often, possibly to cover up the policy, subsidies do not take the form of a direct contribution by the government to the exporting firms or producers. Rather, schemes are used such as the remission of social security or income taxes on a firm in proportion to the ratio of its exports to its total output. In some cases, the government provides raw materials to the exporter at lower prices than must be paid in the market place. Government-operated insurance for exports against risks of nonpayment has been used as a subtle means of subsidizing exports; the insurance is not always provided on sound insurance principles.

PROBLEMS OF FISCAL POLICY

General difficulties

Certain political and social features of a nation may limit the use of fiscal policy to provide internal economic stability or to halt a loss of international reserves. During a business recession, some may oppose the encroachment of the government on private enterprise which is implied in a rise of government spending. On this count, it may be desirable to stress tax reduction so as to avoid any unfavorable effects on the volume of private investment through the creation of distrust by private business. Obviously, in combating inflation, higher taxes meet resistance among the voting population.

There are, in addition, delays in changing taxation and spending. Very often a change in tax rates or government expenditures requires time-consuming legislative action; in addition, it takes time to prepare programs for legislative action and to carry them out after funds are appropriated. Monetary policy, when run by the central bank, can be altered almost overnight; in this regard, it is superior to fiscal policy since the key to stabilizing internal activity and, in some cases, preventing a movement of reserves is to stop incipient inflation or deflation before the change becomes cumulative.

In varying degrees, flexibility in fiscal policy is obtained through automatic features of public finance. For example, if the tax system is progressive among income classes, the rising incomes which accompany inflation push citizens into higher income-tax brackets, thereby raising tax revenue without legislative action. This will have an immediate effect if taxes are withheld from salaries and wages each pay period instead of being paid at the end of the year. The same reasoning holds for a decline in economic activity, since a progressive tax schedule means that taxes will fall faster than incomes. Automatic features are also found in government expenditures: for example, unemployment compensation varies inversely with changes in employment. Differences among countries in the degree of automaticity are great. In underdeveloped countries, the cost of collection and the political role of the well-to-do class have militated against significant use of the progressive income tax.

Specific fiscal instruments

Higher personal-income tax payments do not reduce domestic expenditure by the amount of the revenue collected, and therefore their effectiveness in preventing inflation is not equal to the revenue. Since a portion of the income taken away from the taxpayer by the government would have been saved by him instead of spent, domestic expenditure falls by less than the cut in the taxpayer's spendable income.

Added to this shortcoming is the disincentive effect of income taxation. If the government takes a larger proportion of a person's marginal income, the taxpayer may reduce his effort.[3] For example, the short fall of British coal production in the early postwar period was accentuated by absenteeism attributed to this effect.

Earlier we observed that an excess of imports over exports could be removed either by expanding GNP or by reducing domestic expenditure. The favorable effect on international reserves of a decline in domestic expenditure after a rise in personal income taxes may be more than (or less than) completely offset by the unfavorable effect on incentives and thus on GNP. The net result depends upon the marginal spending-saving relationship and the reaction of incentives.

Similar adverse effects on production can result from a rise in taxes on corporate earnings. Such a tax reduces the incentive for investment and reduces the funds available for disbursement as dividends and for invest-

---

[3] This need not always be the case. Higher tax rates may induce the taxpayer to work harder to obtain the same, or nearly the same, real income as before the tax increase.

ment in capital goods, thereby reducing domestic expenditure through a fall in both consumption (by dividend recipients) and investment. But a reduction in capital formation reduces the ability of the nation to expand production through greater output per man at a time when more output (GNP) is needed to rectify a loss of reserves.

To the extent that the attraction of venture capital and high rates of capital formation depend upon the earnings of corporations, increased corporate tax rates slow the long-run economic progress of a nation. The same may be said of higher taxes on personal income which reduce saving and thus reduce capital formation. With the decline in the growth of output per man caused by slower capital formation, a nation may find it increasingly difficult to sell its exports (without reducing real wages) in the face of competition from countries in which productivity is growing faster. This effect was a factor in Belgium's decision in 1954 to encourage capital formation by a subsidy of one-third of the interest cost of borrowing and by a partial tax exemption of profits used for productive investments.

The adverse effects on capital formation of higher taxes may be offset if the tax receipts are spent by the government for capital formation instead of for current services such as health and defense. The problem, then, is whether the government or private business is the better entrepreneur. As indicated on page 211, under inflationary conditions, private investment may not be allocated to the appropriate ends, but government funds may not be either. Governments have not only misallocated funds for capital formation, but have also yielded to the pressure to use the tax receipts for current services which provide immediate benefit to the voters instead. A startling case of government misallocation was the proposal of the British Labour government—amidst severe balance-of-payments difficulties in 1947 —to electrify a railroad for the purpose of saving coal since that industry was short of manpower. Calculations indicated, however, that the scheme involved 12,000 man-years of labor over 4 years to save the labor of less than 400 men in the coal mines per year.

Major difficulties in the use of excise taxes for anti-inflationary purposes arise from matters of equity in income distribution and from the response of wages to prices. Stabilization is only one of the objectives of the state; heavy taxation of spending by the poor and middle-income groups conflicts with the expressed desire of some governments to redistribute income from the rich to the poor. Furthermore, the cost-of-living index may rise as higher excise taxes raise prices. In many countries, labor-union wage demands are very sensitive to variations in this index; hence the anti-inflationary effect of excise taxes can be wiped out by an increase in money wages and thus in workers' consumption.

The effectiveness of export taxes in providing internal stability depends largely on what happens to the magnitude and composition of government expenditures when changes in export-tax revenue occur. That there is heavy pressure to increase expenditures or reduce taxes when revenues increase is a well-recognized phenomenon. If the government simultaneously absorbs some of the increase in exporters' incomes during a boom in raw-material sales and increases its own purchases of domestically produced goods, the effect of increased exports would still be felt at home because the government does the spending in place of the private sector of the economy. The resulting increase of imports will restrain the accumulation of reserves. The same holds true if the government were to reduce other taxes because the increased private spendable incomes would be used for home-produced goods. If the government does spend the increased revenue on imports rather than on domestically produced goods, the growth of reserves is restricted and the possibility of stabilizing the level of imports in the next recession is reduced. But there may be an advantage in not waiting for the next recession in exports to spend the accumulated foreign exchange. After the collapse of the Korean primary-commodity boom, the import prices of manufactured commodities continued to rise; at the start of the boom, industrial prices were somewhat sluggish in rising so that early expenditures might have been justified in the interest of obtaining maximum real goods and services with the increment of foreign-exchange earnings.

D.   COMMON PROBLEMS OF MONETARY AND FISCAL POLICIES

In addition to the specific difficulties of the various monetary and fiscal instruments outlined above, there remain certain problems of prime importance which are common to both monetary and fiscal policies.

UNEMPLOYMENT AND DEFLATIONARY PRESSURES

Germany, during 1930–1932, provides an example of both the effectiveness of and the problems in using monetary and fiscal policies to prevent a loss of international reserves.

The contraction of economic activity in Germany consequent to the world-wide depression brought a fall in revenues and a budget deficit; the new Bruening government attempted to balance the budget by cutting incomes of civil servants, by reducing unemployment benefits, and by increasing taxation. In addition, Bruening forced a reduction of prices and wages, which was possible even prior to Hitler, for they were controlled by the state or by organizations largely under the direction of the state. The bank rate was raised. This deflationary policy, along with other devices and with the fall in raw material import prices connected with the depression, eased a desperate balance-of-payments situation created by a capital flight and a cessation of long-term capital imports. The surplus in the balance of merchandise trade rose from 36 million Reichsmarks to 2.8 billion between 1929 and 1931. But the cost of the policy was a rise in unemployment from 2 to 6 million.

An opposite policy might have held up employment and preserved political stability. While Germany's deflationary fiscal policy helped to ease the international reserve position, it hurt internal economic activity. Any nation which is simultaneously losing reserves and suffering a depression faces a conflict in the use of monetary and fiscal policies since the appropriate action to protect reserves harms the internal economy and vice versa.

Even at high levels of employment, the application of stricter monetary policy may create unemployment because of immobilities, as after Britain tightened money in 1951 and 1952: "The moderate disinflation in the United Kingdom led to little redistribution of labor toward export industries, but rather to arrangements for temporary lay-offs and short-time working. This immobility, associated with continuing shortages of specialized materials and of suitable capacity, hampered the expansion of export industries."[4]

AN EXTERNALLY INDUCED FALL IN EXPORTS

Suppose that a nation's export earnings drop in consequence of a decline in foreign economic activity. The decline in employment and GNP attributable to the drop in exports will be accompanied by a loss of reserves. If the fall in exports is allowed to set off a multiple contraction of output and employment with a concomitant fall in prices, the loss of reserves may be stopped. But if the government sustains the level of employment through monetary or fiscal policies, the general levels of incomes, output, and prices remain approximately at their levels prior to the decline in exports. Unchanged incomes and prices keep the demand for imports high with the result that, with exports down, the balance of payments remains in deficit. But the supply of international reserves may not be sufficient to cover the continuing deficit. The balance of payments becomes the Achilles heel of domestic full-employment policies; either the full-employment policies must be given up or some other means of adjusting the balance of payments must be found.

Disregarding any loss of reserves, full employment may be extremely difficult to obtain through domestic monetary or fiscal policy when the cause of the unemployment is a drop in exports. Government internal policy may be successful in preventing a decline of home consumption and investment (and employment therein) caused by the drop in incomes earned by factors in the export industries. But the export industries may continue to suffer unemployment despite the government's internal actions.

If the goods not now exported can be sold at home, monetary or fiscal policy may ease the unemployment in the export industries. But, to take an extreme case, Brazilians are unlikely to drink much more coffee despite easier credit or a rise of government expenditures. The same holds true for a nation suffering unemployment in an industry which normally exports capital goods. Government inflationary policy can be of little help in buoying home sales of normally exported capital goods, because the demand for capital goods (investment) is only partly related to existing

---

[4] International Monetary Fund, *Annual Report* (Washington: 1953), p. 14.

levels of income. Sales of capital goods depend also upon expectations and innovation.

If domestic demand will not replace the foreigners' demand for exportable goods, the unemployed men in the export industries might be moved to useful work in strictly domestic industries. But this requires a degree of mobility which, in modern societies, seems lacking in the short run. The export workers may not have the prerequisite skills for their new jobs. There may not be sufficient surplus equipment in the domestic industries with which the unemployed export workers can work. Labor unions in the domestic industries may not admit the export workers. The export industries may be highly concentrated geographically while the domestic industries are spread across the countryside. If so, the export workers may not wish to move to the domestic industries; auto workers in England went on strike in 1956 in support of 6,000 union members who did not want to be moved out of the industry, preferring to take a wage cut in order to permit their continued employment.

Even if all these factors are favorable, one objection remains when the shift in foreign demand is temporary. If the workers do move to the domestic industries, they may not return to their old places in the export industries when foreign demand picks up. If they do not return, the degree of international specialization is reduced and a long-run fall in the world's real income results. Again, monetary and fiscal policies fall short of serving all objectives.

SELECTED READINGS

B. MONETARY POLICY

Bank for International Settlements. *Annual Report.* Basel, Switzerland. The post-World War II issues provide current records of monetary policy and analyses of monetary conditions, mostly in Europe.

Beach, W. Edwards. *British International Gold Movements and Banking Policy, 1881–1913.* Cambridge, Mass.: Harvard University Press, 1935. A comprehensive study having special relevance to the manner in which bankrate changes affected the balance of payments.

Bloomfield, Arthur I. *Capital Imports and the American Balance of Payments, 1934–39.* Chicago: University of Chicago Press, 1950. See Chapter 8 for a comprehensive discussion of the U.S. gold sterilization program in the 1930's. Chapter 6 considers the operations of the U.S. Exchange Stabilization Fund.

Brown, A. J. *The Great Inflation, 1939–1951.* New York: Oxford, 1955. An analysis of the experience of some fifty nations under world-wide full employment in an attempt to test monetary theory against the facts.

Gurley, John. "Excess Liquidity and Monetary Reforms," *American Economic Review,* XLIII (March, 1953), 76–100. A concise discussion of many postwar monetary reforms with an extensive bibliography.

Hawtrey, R. G. *The Art of Central Banking.* London: Longmans, 1932. Chapter 4 provides a discussion of the British money market and bank-rate policies in the nineteenth century.

Midland Bank Review. London. One issue each year reviews monetary and fiscal policy in Britain.

Monthly Review of Credit and Business Conditions. Federal Reserve Bank of New York. Several issues each year are devoted to monetary policies abroad.

Nurkse, Ragnar. *International Currency Experience.* Geneva: League of Nations, 1944. See chapter 4 on neutralization of reserve movements during the period between the two world wars. Chapter 6 discusses exchange stabilization funds.

Patel, I. G. "Monetary Policy in Postwar Years," *International Monetary Fund Staff Papers,* III (April, 1953), 69–131. A survey of different monetary techniques and their postwar use by six countries.

Polak, J. J., and Wm. H. White. "The Effect of Income Expansion on the Quantity of Money," *International Monetary Fund Staff Papers,* IV (August, 1955), 398–433. This article considers, among other matters, the response of income velocity to a reduction in the money supply attributable to a balance-of-payments deficit.

Sayers, R. S. *Bank of England Operations, 1890–1914.* London: King, 1936. Chapter 4 provides a discussion of the devices used by the Bank of England to avoid changing the bank rate when reserves were under pressure. This is reprinted in *Papers in English Monetary History,* T. S. Ashton and R. S. Sayers, eds. Oxford: Clarendon Press, 1953.

————. *Modern Banking.* London: Oxford, 1947. Chapters 6 through 8 provide summary discussion of bank-rate policy, of the gold standard, and of the Exchange Equalisation Account.

Sen, S. N. *Central Banking in Underdeveloped Money Markets.* Calcutta: Bookland, Ltd., 1952. An excellent source on the special problems of monetary policy in underdeveloped nations.

Southard, Frank A. *Foreign Exchange Practice and Policy.* New York: McGraw-Hill, 1940. A summary discussion of stabilization funds is provided in pp. 174–184.

"The Treasury-Central Bank Relationship in Foreign Countries," Board of Governors, Federal Reserve System, Washington. Reprint of Appendix I to *General Credit Control, Debt Management and Economic Mobilization* (materials prepared for the Joint Committee on the Economic Report by the Committee Staff, 82d Cong. 1st Sess. 1951). A review of postwar monetary policies abroad is included.

Waight, Leonard. *The History and Mechanism of the Exchange Equalisation Account.* Cambridge: Cambridge University Press, 1939. A comprehensive study.

C. FISCAL POLICY

Economic Stability in the Postwar World. Geneva: League of Nations, 1945. Section II discusses a wide range of antidepression measures, including fiscal policy, and their difficulties. Chapter 17 considers the international implications of the national antidepression measures, and Chapter 18 gives special attention to the techniques which might be used by primary-producing nations.

Ilersic, A. R. *Government Finance and Fiscal Policy in Post-War Britain.* London: Staples, 1955. A commentary on and history of British postwar fiscal and monetary policies.

Millikan, Max, ed. *Income Stabilization for a Developing Democracy.* New Haven, Conn.: Yale University Press, 1953. This volume presents a clear and fairly comprehensive discussion of fiscal policy, though not directly related to international economic affairs.

Reubens, Edwin P. "Commodity Trade, Export Taxes, and Economic Development," *Political Science Quarterly,* LXXI (March, 1956), 42–70. A description and analysis of the use of export taxes by underdeveloped countries during the Korean War.

Soloway, Arnold. "Economic Aspects of the British Purchase Tax," *Journal of Finance,* IX (May, 1954), 188–208. A brief discussion, in part directly relevant to balance-of-payments problems.

D. COMMON PROBLEMS OF MONETARY AND FISCAL POLICIES

Marcus, Edward. "Countercyclical Weapons for the Open Economy," *Journal of Political Economy,* LXII (December, 1954), 479–493. A general survey of the effectiveness of various policies, including monetary and fiscal policy, in combating instabilities in both the balance of payments and the domestic economy.

Meade, James. *The Balance of Payments.* London: Oxford, 1951. Part III outlines the theory of monetary and fiscal policies related to international economic affairs; Chapter 10 considers conflicts between internal and external objectives, giving attention to actions of other countries.

Meyer, F. V., and W. A. Lewis. "The Effects of an Overseas Slump on the British Economy," *The Manchester School of Economic and Social Studies,* XVII (September, 1949), 233–265. Special attention is given in pp. 245–252 to the problem of absorbing unemployed resources formerly working in export industries.

Nurkse, Ragnar. "The Relation between Home Investment and External Balance in the Light of British Experience, 1945–55," *Review of Economics and Statistics,* XXXVIII (May, 1956), 121–154. In addition to discussing the relationship between investment and the trade balance, this article considers the merits of using variations in investment spending as a means of stabilizing the balance of payments. In the latter regard, see also ECONOMIC COMMISSION FOR EUROPE. *Economic Survey of Europe in 1955.* Geneva: United Nations, 1956.

13 Exchange-Rate Policies: I

The problems of internal economic instability and a loss of international reserves can be met through changes in the rate of exchange among currencies. Exchange-rate adjustments may substitute for undesirable internal adjustments of prices and incomes or for movements of international reserves in balancing international payments. The need for exchange-rate adjustments depends on the extent to which adjustments are permitted in the internal activity of the nation, on the level and flow of international reserves, and on the type of exchange-rate system in use.

A. EXCHANGE-RATE SYSTEMS

STABLE EXCHANGE RATES

Exchange rates which fluctuate within rather narrow limits are called stable exchange rates. The gold standard and pegged-rate systems provide stable rates.

Pegged rates

A government, in order to restrain fluctuations in the price of foreign currency (the exchange rate), may buy and sell foreign exchange at prices straddling a legally established par value.

The par value states a precise relation between a nation's currency and foreign currencies. Imagine, for example, that some Latin American government establishes a par value of 100 pesos per U.S. dollar with the intent of pegging the rate. The government, or an agent such as the central bank, will then stand ready to sell claims on dollars to any person demanding to buy them with pesos at a price of, say, 101 pesos per dollar. No one would pay more than 101 pesos per dollar since dollars can be obtained from the authorities at that price. Similarly, the government would buy all dollars offered to it at, say, 99 pesos per dollar. No holder of dollars needs to accept less than 99 pesos, since the government automatically provides an unlimited market for them at that price. When private individuals or banks are trading foreign exchange between 99 and 101 pesos per dollar, there is no demand for the authorities to buy or sell dollars. But when the rate of exchange at which individuals and banks trade foreign exchange reaches either limit, the authorities will buy or sell dollars to hold the rate of exchange within the predetermined range. Some spread is necessary between the central bank's buying and selling rates in order to cover costs of operation, but these costs are negligible. The chief determinant of the spread is the degree of exchange-rate variation considered desirable.

Within the authorities' buying and selling rates, the exchange rate at any moment of time depends upon the demand for and supply of dollars. Or, since a demand for dollars means a supply of pesos, it depends upon the supply and demand for pesos. Thus, within the two prices, the exchange rate is determined by supply and demand as is the price of any commodity.

The government or the central bank can always create pesos to satisfy the dollar demand for them and to maintain the dollar buying rate (99 pesos per dollar). But it cannot create a supply of dollars to hold the rate at its dollar selling point. If the demand for dollars becomes so great as to press their price to 101 pesos, and if the authorities plan to defend the exchange rate, they must supply dollars at 101 pesos per dollar without limit. This presupposes a supply of dollars held by the authorities in U.S. banks, central or commercial, short-term investments which may be sold for dollars, and/or a supply of gold which may be sold to the U.S. Treasury for dollars.

If the government wishes to change the exchange rate, it simply changes its par value. For example, if the above government wished to devalue its currency, it might announce a par value of 200 pesos and stand ready to buy dollars at 198 pesos and to sell dollars at 202 pesos. No one need accept less than 198 pesos per dollar for his holdings of dollars and no one would pay more than 202 pesos for a dollar. As a result, the exchange rate would be at one of or within these two points.

Gold standard rates

Prior to 1931, Americans could buy a bank draft giving a claim to British pounds at a price between $4.88 and $4.84 per pound. The limitation of the exchange-rate movements to this range resulted not from buying and selling of foreign exchange by the governments as above, but from the convertibility of the two currencies into gold at a fixed price.

Under the law, a British gold sovereign (a pound sterling) contained 113.0016 grains of pure gold and the American gold dollar contained 23.22 grains; paper currency and other coins could be exchanged directly or indirectly at the Bank of England and the U.S. Treasury for gold at these rates, i.e., an ounce of gold could be purchased or sold at the U.S.

Treasury for approximately $20.67 and at the Bank of England for approximately 3 pounds, 17 shillings, and 10 pence.

Because of the foregoing legislation, the pound contained approximately 4.86 times as much gold as the U.S. dollar; hence the mint par of exchange between the two currencies was $4.86 per £1, i.e., it took $4.86 to buy as much gold from the U.S. Treasury as a pound would obtain from the Bank of England. The limits to exchange-rate fluctuations were roughly $4.88 and $4.84. These gold points, as they were called, were determined by adding and subtracting, respectively, two cents from the mint par of exchange. The two cents approximately equaled the cost of shipping gold between the two countries.[1]

With a mint par of exchange of $4.86, Americans normally would not have to pay more than $4.88 for a £1 when buying drafts or cables. A £1 debt could always be paid by buying $4.86 worth of gold from the U.S. Treasury, shipping the gold to London at a cost of 2¢, and exchanging the gold for £1 at the Bank of England at a total cost of $4.88. Clearly, no one would pay *more* than $4.88 for a draft or cable—the U.S. gold export point—to meet a £1 debt. But private traders rarely shipped gold; rather, as the price of drafts and cables rose to the gold export point because of a higher demand for sterling, banks and bullion dealers would ship gold to London. They would add the sterling proceeds to their accounts in banks in London, and sell drafts and cables giving claim to that sterling to persons desiring to make payments to Britain.

Conversely, Americans holding sterling bills of exchange need not sell them for less than $4.84 per £1, the U.S. gold import point. Any claim of £1 was equivalent to gold worth $4.86 because £1 of gold imported into the United States could be sold by American banks to the U.S. Treasury for $4.86. Subtracting the 2¢ shipping costs, any pound was ultimately worth $4.84; competition among foreign-exchange buyers kept the price of a £1 draft or cable at $4.84 or above.[2]

If the government wished to change the price of foreign currency by an amount greater than that permitted by the gold points, it could change the gold content of its currency, i.e., change the price at which it would freely exchange gold and its own currency. Because the authorities would buy or sell gold at the new price, the exchange rate could not lie

---

[1] This cost included freight, insurance, packing, an assay charge to determine the fineness of the gold upon its sale, interest on the money which was tied up in the gold while it was being shipped, commissions for the firms or banks actually performing the purchase and sale of the gold, and perhaps a minting charge by the monetary authorities in the country receiving the gold.

[2] The gold points did not always restrain fluctuations of exchange rates. Just before World War I, for example, Europeans moved out of dollars and into their own currency at such intensity and speed that the price of foreign exchange in New York rose materially above the gold export point. Gold could not be exported quickly enough nor in sufficient volume so that an alternative source of foreign exchange did not exist, contrary to the situation described above.

outside of the gold points surrounding the new mint par. However, changes in the metallic content of currencies tied to gold during the era of the gold standard, chiefly the years from 1870 to 1914, were not frequent; for example, the sterling price of gold was constant between 1821 and 1914.

The fact that the government can set the par value does not mean that it may set the rate without regard to market forces. Under both pegged and gold rates, a rise in the price of foreign exchange is checked only because the authorities make gold available for export or supply the market with foreign exchange. With a strong demand for foreign currencies, the rate of exchange cannot be defended indefinitely, because the government's international reserves eventually will be exhausted. A new rate must be set which reflects the conditions of supply and demand more closely and does not drain gold or foreign-exchange reserves.

The pressure may be relieved without changing the par value if the automatic forces of adjustment discussed in Chapter 11 increase the supply and reduce the demand for gold or foreign exchange for foreign payments, but the consequences of allowing the automatic forces to work must be considered. In 1925, Britain set her exchange rate at a level which, in conjunction with her internal prices, costs, and incomes, made U.K. exports expensive to foreigners. The difficulty Britain had in selling exports created unemployment and led to the famous General Strike of 1926.

FLUCTUATING EXCHANGE RATES

Take away the authorities' buying and selling rates or the fixed tie of the currency to gold, and the exchange rate will fluctuate more widely than under stable exchange rates. The exchange rate adjusts to equate the supply and demand for foreign exchange. Because changes in international receipts and expenditures are not likely to occur simultaneously or in equal size, fairly wide and frequent changes in the exchange rate must be expected.

If the government does not intervene *at all* in the foreign-exchange market to stabilize the exchange rate, it is called a *freely fluctuating* exchange rate. But the government may intervene to regularize fluctuating rates without creating a stable rate, in which case there is a *flexible* exchange rate. The authorities buy foreign exchange when they think its price is too low and sell it when its price is too high. Such intervention is at the government's own volition and not at predetermined exchange rates such as at the limits of a pegged rate.

No matter whether the exchange rate system involves stable or fluctuating rates, market forces maintain the same exchange rate in all foreign-exchange markets in different countries, unless there are government restraints on the freedom of international payment. This follows from the general principle that a standardized commodity tends to have the same price in all markets. The process by which this happens is called exchange arbitrage. Imagine, for example, that the rate of exchange is $4.86 to £1 in New York and is $4.85 to £1 in London. New York banks, finding sterling cheaper in London, would buy it in Britain rather than in New York. The reduced demand for sterling in New York and the increased demand for it in London would bring the two exchange rates together.

The mechanism by which arbitrage works includes the cooperation in London of the correspondent bank of the New York bank. Given the exchange rates mentioned above, the New York banker *sells* sterling in New York at $4.86, and simultaneously his correspondent *purchases* sterling for $4.85 in London. The purchase of sterling in London provides the New York banker with the sterling he sells in New York; the sale of dollars in London is covered by the dollars which the New York banker obtains when he sells sterling in New York. Considering the transactions as a whole, the New York banker makes a profit of 1¢ per pound because he sells sterling at a higher dollar price than his correspondent paid for it.

Exchange arbitrage not only equates exchange rates between currencies in two different markets but also prevents disparate cross rates from arising among several markets. Assume the following direct exchange rates:

$$\$4.87 = £1$$
$$Fr.100 = £1$$
$$Fr.100 = \$4.84$$

The direct rate between the franc and the dollar of $4.84 per 100 francs differs from the indirect rate (cross rate) between the two currencies, which is obtained by valuing the two currencies through their rates with the pound. That is, since $4.87 equals one pound and since 100 francs equal one pound, the indirect rate is $4.87 per 100 francs as compared to a direct rate of $4.84 per 100 francs. Given these exchange rates, an American banker would buy 100 francs for *$4.84,* use the 100 francs to buy one pound, and use the pound to buy *$4.87,* making a 3¢ profit. In doing this, the banker will, though not purposely, bring together the direct rate and the cross rate between the franc and the dollar. The initial purchase of francs with dollars will raise the dollar price of francs above $4.84; the final sale of pounds for dollars will, by increasing the supply of pounds relative to dollars, reduce the dollar price of a pound from $4.87. When the two meet in between, say at $4.85½, and assuming the franc-pound rate unchanged,[3] the direct rate and the cross rate are the same.

---

[3] The franc-pound rate will change, however, as the francs bought with dollars are sold for sterling. This raises the franc price of sterling while, as mentioned above, the dollar price of pounds declines. Thus the cross rate moves toward $4.84 on two counts: (1) because the dollar value of the pound falls, and (2) because the franc price of the pound rises.

Since the arbitrage works under either stable or fluctuating rate systems, it has little bearing on the decision as to which system to use. The major factor in that decision is their differing impacts on the flow of reserves and on internal economic activity.

B. EXCHANGE RATES, RESERVES, AND INTERNAL ECONOMIC ACTIVITY

CONSEQUENCES OF EXCHANGE-RATE ADJUSTMENTS: PRICE EFFECTS

Suppose that Britain shifts the exchange rate from one peg to another, say from $4 per £1 to $2 per £1; the immediate impact is that British goods become cheaper to Americans in terms of dollars. This same exchange-rate change may be noted as a shift from £¼ to £½ per dollar; American goods therefore become more expensive to Englishmen in terms of pounds.

In Britain the sterling prices of exports and import-competing goods rise as follows: The sterling price of imports from the United States rises; this induces an increase in the demand for import-competing products produced in Britain and causes a rise in their prices in sterling. At the same time, because the dollar price of British exports has fallen, Americans increase their demand for British goods, which causes their sterling price to rise. The reason why, after devaluation, that the dollar price can be lower than before devaluation while the sterling price is higher is that each dollar is equivalent to more sterling.

Devaluation of the pound has therefore raised the prices of British exports and import-competing products relative to those of British domestic goods, namely, those which are not in competition with American products by reason of transportation costs. In consequence, factors of production will shift out of domestic-goods production and into export *and* import-competing production. Simultaneously, consumers will substitute domestic goods for the higher-priced imports *and* exports. Given sufficient substitutability in production and consumption, the value of exports rises and the value of imports declines.

The conditions for success or failure in improving the current account (increasing exports and/or reducing imports of goods and services) are found, at least approximately, in the elasticities of demand in terms of price changes for British exports and imports. If the American demand for British exports is elastic, the decline in their dollar prices increases the total number of dollars spent on British exports by Americans. But if it is inelastic, the number declines. The relevance of inelasticity of American demand was recognized by a member of the British Labour Party who urged that the price charged Americans for exports of Scotch be raised, saying that "Even if our sales [the number of fifths] did go down slightly

. . . what harm? We should get more dollars in total and have more whiskey for ourselves."[4]

As long as the British demand for American goods is less than perfectly inelastic, i.e., the physical volume of imports responds at least somewhat to price changes, the higher sterling price of American goods will induce a drop in the physical quantity of imports. As long as the dollar price of British imports does not rise, any reduction in the physical quantity of British imports results by definition in a fall in British dollar expenditures for imports. It is not impossible that the dollar price will fall; the reduced British demand for American goods will produce that result unless the U.S. export producers can readily find alternative markets for their goods or unless they are unable to reduce the costs of production, in which case the volume of U.S. production falls without a drop in price.

The degree of elasticity of the American import demand *plus* that of Britain determines, when only price changes are considered, the effect of the devaluation. Thus, a fall in dollar earnings by Britain stemming from an inelastic American demand could be more than offset by a fall in dollar expenditures by Britain even if the British demand were inelastic also.

The extent of the fall in the physical volume of British imports in response to the rise in their sterling price (the elasticity of British import demand) will be greater (1) the more willing that consumers are to substitute domestic goods for import-type products and (2) the more willing that factors of production are to shift from domestic goods to import-competing production which will replace units of the imported product. The same conclusions apply to the United States, though the direction of substitution in both production and consumption must be reversed.

The extent of the rise in the volume of British exports in response to the rise in their sterling price (the elasticity of British export supply) is affected in a similar manner, though the relevant substitution in this case is between export products and domestic goods.

The ultimate levels of both the dollar and sterling prices depend upon the interaction of British and American demands and supplies. For example, if the American demand for British exports is quite elastic, any reduction in the dollar price will induce an extensive increase in the quantity demanded. But if the British export supply is rather inelastic so that higher sterling prices induce very little increase in the export supply, the initial reduction in the dollar price of British exports will be in large measure reversed. This is because the greater American demand at the lower dollar price goes unsatisfied as a consequence of the failure of British export supply to rise greatly.

The impact of these changes on the British terms of trade is uncertain. The dollar prices of her exports and imports may fall; the effect on the terms of trade depends upon which falls further. If the dollar price of

---

[4] *Journal of Commerce*, November 13, 1953, p. 9.

exports falls more than the dollar price of imports, each physical unit of the products which Britain exports will pay for fewer physical units of import products. But if British factors shift mainly into import-competing production rather than export production, and if British demand shifts mainly away from import-type products rather than away from export products, the price of exports will tend to be sustained while the price of import products will fall. Few additional units of the export product will be produced in England, and few of them will be released for export by a reduction of British domestic demand for them; hence the export supply will increase little. At the same time, the demand for import-type products will fall greatly, and the supply of import-competing products will rise greatly, with the result that the demand for imports falls precipitously.

We may generalize that the terms of trade of countries which are negligible suppliers and demanders of products traded in world markets will remain unchanged in consequence of devaluation. As they produce more export products, the additional supply leaves little or no imprint upon the foreign currency price of their exports; and, as they demand less, the foreign suppliers hardly feel the retrenchment of demand.

DEVALUATION AND UNEMPLOYMENT

The full consequences of devaluation are not found solely in the effects resulting from price changes, as the application of earlier reasoning will show. The improvement in the current account, supposing that unemployment exists prior to devaluation, implies an increase in British real GNP and real national income, subject to an adverse shift in the terms of trade. This is so because the volume of British export production rises while devaluation induces Englishmen to shift their purchases from imports to home-produced goods. The foreign-trade multiplier process described in Chapter 11 is set off, tending to reverse the price-induced improvement in the current account. Rising British output and real national income increase the Englishmen's demand for imports and also raise their demand for their own export products. Therefore the current account does not change as much as the elasticities of demand would indicate; allowance must be made for the marginal propensities to import and to purchase a nation's own export products. Only so long as domestic expenditure rises less than the GNP does the current account improve. Though the effects through changes in income and output restrain an improvement in the balance of payments, the changes in income and output may constitute the chief merit of the devaluation when unemployment exists, as we see next.

Externally induced unemployment

Suppose that exports fall as a result of a decline in business activity abroad. The results are a balance-of-payments deficit and a fall in employment in the export industries. If the decline in income and employment in the export industries is allowed to cause a multiple fall in income and output through induced declines in consumption and investment, and if a fall in prices ensues, the balance-of-payments deficit may be removed.

But suppose that the government is unwilling to allow employment to fall and therefore undertakes expansive monetary and fiscal policies. By sustaining the level of employment and prices, the full-employment policy of the government tends to maintain the level of imports; therefore the balance-of-payments deficit persists, and some other measure, such as devaluation, becomes necessary to rectify it.

Whether devaluation will succeed in removing the deficit is subject to question. If the initial fall in exports reflects a serious depression abroad, elasticities of demand for imports are likely to be low. For example, when devaluation by one nation leads to a reduction in the import prices of another nation which also has unemployment, the volume of imports of the latter may not rise greatly if at all. Factors of production in the import-competing industries of the latter nation cannot find alternative employments because the general level of employment is low; they may prefer to accept reductions in their rewards in order to permit a reduction of costs so as to allow continued production and sales despite the lower price of imports.

Apart from the need to remove the balance-of-payments deficit, devaluation may be required as a constituent part of the government's full-employment policy. It was argued at the end of the previous chapter that it may not be possible, despite expansionary monetary and fiscal policies, to absorb in the home market those resources which were previously employed in the export industries. In fact, it may not be desirable to shift those unemployed resources to domestic production lest the advantages of international trade be permanently lost through an unwillingness of the factors to redeploy to export production when foreign markets improve. Thus devaluation may become necessary to sustain production and employment in export industries as well as to prevent a loss of reserves when governments desire to maintain full employment in the face of a fall in exports. Such devaluation may be regarded as a means of defending the economy from the misfortunes of others. But devaluation has an offensive aspect also.

Internally induced unemployment and the equilibrium exchange rate

When a nation's unemployment stems from a decline in internal spending (domestic expenditure), devaluation is of questionable merit. An improvement in the current account consequent to devaluation will raise the general level of employment through the foreign-trade multiplier process. However, an improvement in the current account of one nation implies, by definition, a worsening of the current account of others and a tendency for their employment levels to decline. A nation which devalues in an attempt to solve unemployment originating within its own economy is exporting its unemployment; it beggars its neighbors.

By setting the exchange rate at the equilibrium level, a nation avoids beggaring its neighbors. This is a rate which, over a period of time sufficient to allow the long-run forces affecting the allocation of resources to work themselves out, does not lead to (1) a net movement of international reserves, or (2) internal unemployment, or (3) the imposition of direct controls on trade and payments by the government.

An exchange rate that must be defended by a movement of reserves is considered unacceptable, because some nation would be required to deflate internal prices and employment to stop a loss of its reserves. A rate which can be defended only through a low level of imports caused by low output, income, and employment is considered undesirable because the unemployment and low production are undesirable. And a rate which requires the assistance of direct controls to limit expenditures to receipts is not considered an equilibrium one, because it does not equate supply and demand for foreign exchange.[5]

The selection of the equilibrium rate is difficult. Evidence that a particular rate which is set today is a disequilibrium rate may not appear for some time after the fact. For example, a nation with steady reserves today at a newly set rate may eventually lose or gain reserves because it takes time for resources to respond and adjust to the new rate. Or, with a given exchange rate, a loss of reserves may result from temporary factors which will right themselves soon, in which case the existing rate is at equilibrium. But it may not be obvious that the difficulty is temporary. For instance, the boom in raw-material prices during the early part of the Korean War put pressure on the reserves of some nations. Had the war spread, raw material prices would have remained high, but, as it was, the pressure soon eased as prices began to topple.

In the 1930's, when an unprecedented wave of exchange rate depreciations took place because of balance-of-payments difficulties, the favorable domestic effects of the beggar-thy-neighbor devaluations that took place were probably largely defeated. Counterdevaluation by other nations tended to leave exchange rates unchanged, while a contraction of incomes and prices in the nations which did not devalue reduced demand for the devaluing country's exports. Nonetheless, those countries which did not

---

[5] Each of these qualities of the equilibrium rate is chosen because of the ethical judgment that free market determination of the exchange rate is desirable and that unemployment is undesirable. As Professor P. T. Ellsworth asserts ". . . our concept of what is desirable has modified our concept of what is normal; it is now generally agreed that we must take a broader view of equilibrium." *The International Economy* (New York: Macmillan, 1950), p. 607.

devalue until late in the 1930's suffered. France, which did not devalue until 1936, underwent a 46 per cent fall in her exports between 1929 and 1935 while world trade fell only 18 per cent.

While the early devaluers in the 1930's probably gained little employment via the beggar-thy-neighbor route, they did use the freedom from the threat of a loss of reserves which devaluation provided to employ expansionary monetary and fiscal policies at home. The evidence is clear that in those countries which did not devalue their currencies until 1935 and 1936 (the gold bloc, consisting of Belgium, France, Holland, and Switzerland) industrial production recovered less fast than in those nations that had devalued earlier. Even the devaluation of the U.S. dollar in 1933 and 1934 finds some justification in the freedom which it gave the United States to pursue a cheap-money policy. (It could not be justified on the basis of preventing a serious decline of international reserves, as many contemporary devaluations could, because the U.S. gold stock was so large.) An embargo on the export of gold from the United States, which initiated the depreciation of the dollar because the tie to gold was cut, stopped the gold exports which had been frustrating attempts by the monetary authority to increase bank reserves.

The evidence further suggests that trade among those nations which devalued early in the 1930's grew more than that of countries which devalued later. The probable explanation for this lies in the expansion of imports consequent to internal economic expansion resulting from inflationary monetary and fiscal policies in the devaluing nations. This in turn may explain why some countries which had devalued early in the 1930's were desirous that the members of the gold bloc, which had not devalued, realign their currencies. That is, some of the early devaluers were actually not desirous of maintaining the competitive advantages in foreign trade which their devaluations had provided them, perhaps in hopes that the gold bloc would be able to inflate internal activity and increase their imports from the early devaluers.

Because any devaluation amidst unemployment, by improving the current account, may have a beggar-thy-neighbor effect, the problem arises of how to prevent such results without also preventing purely defensive devaluation. One suggestion is that a nation should first obtain full employment through domestic policy; only then, if a loss of reserves occurs, should it devalue. While this approach removes the danger of beggar-thy-neighbor devaluations, such timing may sometimes be impossible. If internal monetary expansion through government action raises doubts about the ability of the nation to maintain a given exchange rate or if the nation's international reserves are very low, speculative capital movements in anticipation of devaluation may denude it of reserves before enough time has elapsed to determine whether an exchange-rate adjustment is actually necessary.

DEVALUATION AND FULL EMPLOYMENT

In the years since World War II the world has, by and large, been blessed with high levels of employment and output; at the same time many countries, especially those of Western Europe, were cursed with balance-of-payments difficulties stemming from the structural shifts induced by the war, from internal inflationary conditions, and from the needs of reconstruction. Many nations which had not been smashed by the war suffered price inflation, and the stifled wartime demands for goods burgeoned over their borders with the advent of peace.

In 1949, starting with the devaluation of the pound sterling from $4.03 to $2.80, nations accounting for two-thirds of the world's trade reduced the value of their currencies in terms of the American dollar. These were not the only devaluations of the postwar period; many countries, particularly in Latin America, have undertaken successive adjustments of their exchange rates, but the 1949 round of devaluations was the most important.

In the view of the International Monetary Fund, the structural changes and postwar inflations

made readjustments of exchange rates inevitable. The uncertain question was not whether such adjustments would take place, but when. As long as there were serious shortages throughout the world, the inflated prices of Europe and other regions did not prevent their exports to Western Hemisphere countries from expanding with the growth of world trade. . . . But as long as capacity to produce for export had not fully recovered, devaluation might be expected to generate additional [export] demands that in many countries could be satisfied only at the expense of already severely rationed domestic markets. During 1948 and 1949, however, this situation changed gradually. Production, particularly in Europe, had expanded greatly, but growth in dollar exports [i.e., to the United States, Canada, and certain other Western Hemisphere nations] was slackening or had halted. The expansion of world trade began to slow down.[6]

The timing of devaluation was also affected by several short-run factors. British reserves fell from slightly less than $2 billion in March, 1949, (which was considered the basic minimum for safety) to about $1.4 billion in September. This was partly the product of a recession of American economic activity; though chief blame cannot be placed on this factor, because the fall in British reserves far exceeded the decline in the relevant purchases of the United States. Speculation against sterling developed as traders and others became increasingly convinced that a devaluation would be forthcoming. British importers hastened their purchases and payments abroad in the expectation that delay would find them having to pay more

---

[6] *Annual Report* (Washington, 1950), pp. 3–4.

Table 10. Official Alterations in Exchange Rates 1939-1950

Countries	National currency units	U.S. DOLLAR MIDDLE RATE				PERCENTAGE CHANGE	
		Aug. 24, 1939	Dec. 31, 1945	Sept. 15, 1949	March 31, 1950	Sept. 15, 1949 to March 1950	Aug. 24, 1939 to March 1950
Austria	Schilling	5.34(1)	10.00	10.00	21.36(2)	— 53.2	— 75.0
Belgium	Franc	29.58	43.83	43.83	50.195	— 12.7	— 41.1
Bulgaria	Leva	83.90	287.36(3)	287.36(3)	287.36(3)	—	— 70.8
Czechoslovakia	Koruna	29.235	50.00	50.00	50.00	—	— 41.5
Denmark	Krone	4.795*	4.80	4.80	6.90¾	— 30.5	— 30.6
Finland	Markka	48.40	135.70	160.00	230.00	— 30.4	— 79.0
France	Franc	37.755	119.10	272.49½(4)	349.60	— 22.1	— 89.2
Germany	Reichs Mark/Deutsche Mark	2.493	10.00	3.33(5)	4.20	— 20.7	— 40.6
Greece	Drachma	117.60	500.00	10,010.00(6)	15,000.00(6)	— 33.3	— 99.2
Hungary	Pengo/Forints	5.20	104,000.00	11.74	11.74	—	— 55.7
Iceland	Króna	5.7683*	6.4889	6.4889	16.32(7)	— 60.2	— 64.7
Ireland	Pound	0.2126	0.2481	0.2481	0.3571	— 30.5	— 40.5
Italy	Lira	19.00	100.00	575.00	624.79	— 8.0	— 97.0
Netherlands	Florin	1.86	2.65	2.653	3.80	— 30.2	— 51.1
Norway	Krone	4.27	4.96½	4.96½	7.14¼	— 30.5	— 40.2
Poland	Zloty	5.325		400.00(8)	400.00(8)	—	— 98.7
Portugal	Escudo	23.36	24.815	25.025	28.77½	— 13.0	— 18.8
Roumania	Lei	143.59	3,635.00(9)	151.50(10)	151.50(10)	—	— 5.2
Spain	Peseta	9.05	11.085	11.085(11)	11.085(12)	—	— 18.4
Sweden	Krona	4.15*	4.19	3.59½(13)	5.17½	— 30.5	— 19.8
Switzerland	Franc	4.435	4.30	4.30	4.29½	+ 0.1	+ 3.3
Turkey	Lira	1.267	1.305(14)	2.8126	2.8126	—	— 55.0
United Kingdom	Pound	0.2126	0.2481	0.2481	0.3571	— 30.5	— 40.5
U.S.S.R.	Rouble	5.30	5.30	5.30	4.00	+ 32.5	+ 32.5
Yugoslavia	Dinar	44.05	50.00	50.00	50.00	—	— 11.9
Canada	Dollar	1.0047	1.1025	1.0025(13)	1.1025	— 9.1	— 8.9
South Africa	Pound	0.2279(15)	0.2488	0.2488	0.3581	— 36.4	— 36.5
Australia	Pound	0.2822(15)	0.3108	0.3109	0.4474	— 30.5	— 36.9
New Zealand	Pound	0.2814(15)	0.3125	0.2500	0.3599	— 30.5	— 21.8
Argentina(16)	Peso	4.325	4.0675	4.8075	9.02	— 46.7	— 52.1
Brazil*	Cruzeiro	16.50	16.50	18.72	18.72	—	— 11.9
Japan	Yen	3.67(15)	15.00(17)	360.00	360.00	—	— 99.0

* Official selling rate.
(1) January, 1938.
(2) Effective rate: 40% at basic rate (14.40) and 60% at premium rate (26.00).
(3) Official rate plus premium of 250%.
(4) Mean rate between basic and free official rate.
(5) Export-import rate.
(6) With Exchange Certificates.
(7) The new rate after the second change in the par value of the krone on March 20, 1950.
(8) With premium surcharge of Zl. 300 in practically all financial transfers abroad.
(9) Including the supplementary premiums.
(10) The new lei was introduced on August 15, 1947 and was equal to 20,000 old lei.
(11) In addition a sliding scale of rates, ranging from Pts 12.59 to Pts 21.90 for specified export goods and from Pts 13.14 to Pts 27.375 for specified import goods, has been applied since December 3, 1948.
(12) In addition a sliding scale of rates, ranging from Pts 13.14 to Pts 28.47 for specified export goods and from Pts 15.76 to Pts 39.401 for specified import goods, has been applied since October, 1949.
(13) Revaluation in July, 1946.
(14) Official rate, excluding premium.
(15) Buying rate on New York.
(16) Free-market selling rate.
(17) This military rate was first established at 15 yen per U.S. dollar in August, 1945, raised to 50 yen on March 12, 1947 and to 270 yen on July 5, 1948, at which level it remained until the present official rate was established on April 25, 1949.

SOURCE: Bank for International Settlements, *Twentieth Annual Report* (Basel: June, 1950), p. 154.

sterling for the dollars they required; and foreigners, anticipating a lower price for sterling, slowed their purchases from and payments to Britain. When Britain finally took the plunge, many other nations followed; they had been reluctant to do so before for fear of worsening their terms of trade with Britain, and they had little choice after, since the British devaluation would have given England a competitive advantage in trade.

The effectiveness of devaluation in closing a balance-of-payments deficit tended to be restricted by the economic environment of the postwar period. For many nations improvement had to come on the export side; little adjustment could be expected or was considered desirable in imports. Imports were already cut to the barest minimum by administrative controls prohibiting imports above a certain total value. Permitted imports were often those of an essential nature, and therefore their volumes could not be expected to vary greatly with price changes.

In the absence of appropriate internal monetary and fiscal policies, the existence of full employment also acts as a deterrent to improvement in the current account. To return to the theoretical setting, the discussion of the price effects of devaluation suggested that devaluation worked by inducing a shift of demand toward domestic goods and a shift of resources out of the production of domestic goods. With no unemployed resources which can be drawn into the production of domestic goods, the result is a rise in their price; this restrains the substitutions mentioned above and the improvement in the current account is thwarted.

The general level of money prices may rise after devaluation, canceling the price advantage which is initially gained over foreign products through devaluation. Any improvement in the current account will increase the money supply; and, under conditions of full employment, rising quantities of money are virtually certain to lead to higher prices. To avoid inflation, money must be wiped out just as fast as the current-account improvement creates new money. If money spending on home-produced goods remains unchanged while money spending by foreigners on exports increases, price inflation is certain to result, for full employment limits the extent to which the supply of goods and services can be increased.

Inflationary forces may be bolstered by the cost-price spiral. When devaluation induces a rise in the price of imports and import-competing goods, workers may demand a pay increase to compensate for the loss in real income stemming from higher prices. Even in the depressed 1930's, German labor unions, recalling the inflation and exchange-rate depreciation of the mark after World War I, made it clear to the German government that devaluation of the mark would be followed by equivalent wage demands. If wages are raised in consequence of higher import prices, the general level of costs rises, removing some of the price advantage obtained by devaluation. After the British devaluation of 1949, the Labour government pressed organized labor for a standstill of wages to which they agreed, with some reservations; the index of weekly wages rose only from 109 in 1949 to 111 in 1950.

The fact that someone must suffer when devaluation takes place under conditions of full employment is a matter of simple arithmetic. Because full employment prevails, it is difficult to expand the real GNP; to obtain an improvement in the current account, real domestic expenditure must fall, i.e., the total amount of goods and services used at home for any purpose whatsoever must drop. If every resident of the devaluing nation successfully demands that his real income remain unchanged and if each resident spends the same proportion of his real income as before, the devaluation will have failed. For devaluation to succeed, the nation as a whole must spend less, i.e., save more.

Restrictive monetary and fiscal policies must be undertaken in order to insure that the money supply does not rise, that domestic spending on home-produced goods falls, and that home use of goods and services declines. In the absence of positive government action on the internal economy, devaluation is very likely to fail when full employment prevails. The failure to undertake appropriate action explains in part the repetition of devaluation by a number of the underdeveloped, primary-producing countries during the postwar period.

It may be cogently argued that devaluation should not be undertaken until internal inflationary pressures are wiped out, for, when they are removed, the devaluation may be unnecessary. Professor Harrod remarks, with respect to the 1949 devaluation,

. . . this devaluation occurred at a time when inflation was still proceeding in most of the countries concerned. The correct policy was first to eliminate the inflation and then, that done, to see what kind of deficit remained. No one knows what the deficits would have been had the various countries been able to cultivate their export markets assiduously and to deliver promptly; internal inflationary pressures were making this impossible. . . . It was a trifle absurd to stimulate new export demands by offering goods at lower prices when one could not even deliver the goods that were demanded at the old prices.[7]

Of course, a country can undergo a balance-of-payments deficit without simultaneously suffering actual price inflation; it may be that the balance-of-payments deficit extinguishes money just as fast as internal sources create it. In that event, the combined forces of monetary and fiscal policies of a restrictive nature plus devaluation have much to recommend them. The devaluation will act as a pull on resources into export and import-competing production while the restrictive monetary and fiscal policies push resources, through deflationary pressure, out of the domestic-goods industries; transitory unemployment is less likely than when just monetary and fiscal pressure is used.

In the old days, devaluation was considered to be financial debauchery,

[7] Roy Harrod, *The Dollar* (New York: Harcourt, Brace, 1954), pp. 125 f.

an immoral act involving the scaling down of debts owed to foreigners. Not the least of the advantages to Britain of her devaluation of 1949 was the reduction in the dollar value of certain of her short-term liabilities to foreigners. Today, devaluation does not suffer that opprobrium; yet governments are generally reluctant to undertake this step, partly because of economic consequences such as inflation and changes in the terms of trade, and also because, in some countries, the exchange rate stands as a symbol of national strength and financial solidity. For the government in power, devaluation is a politically dangerous act; devaluation is a blunt advertisement of weakness, and the shock of the act may have important political repercussions.

INFLATION

If a nation suffers inflation, whether stemming from internal or external forces, it may be relieved by internal anti-inflationary policy or by exchange-rate appreciation.

If inflation results from an expansion of exports, internal deflationary monetary and fiscal measures are objectionable in that they thwart the automatic rise in incomes and prices that tends to reverse the inflow of international reserves. Failure to stop the inflow of reserves increases the balance-of-payments difficulties of the reserve-losing nations. On the other hand, if the inflation results from an increase in internal spending, internal deflationary government policy restrains a concomitant increase in imports which would create inflationary pressures abroad (by increasing foreign countries' exports) and stops an incipient loss of reserves of the country threatened by inflation.

Exchange-rate appreciation to combat inflation has been rarely used, though it was urged by one international organization during the inflationary period of the Korean War.[8] The success of appreciation in combating inflation does not depend upon the fall in the local currency prices of imports and exports of the appreciating country; rather, success depends upon its effect on the total flow of spending within the appreciating country. For example, leaving aside exports, if the demand for imports is inelastic, appreciation tends to enhance inflationary pressure rather than reduce it. The decline in the prices paid for imports by citizens of the appreciating nation reduces the total amount spent on imports and releases income to be spent on home goods, with consequent inflationary pressure.

Appreciation works by reducing exports and/or increasing imports measured in local currency. These changes suggest another condition of success, namely, that the appreciating country have sufficient international reserves on hand to pay for a balance-of-payments deficit should one develop; the 10 per cent appreciation of the Canadian dollar in 1946 for anti-inflationary purposes very soon failed on this ground.

[8] Economic Commission for Europe, *Economic Survey of Europe in 1950* (Geneva: United Nations, 1951), pp. 157–164.

If currency appreciation has the purpose of removing inflation caused by internal spending, the appreciating nation, by worsening its current account and improving that of other nations, exports its inflation. This is analogous to a policy of devaluing to export unemployment, and both policies hurt one's neighbors. On the other hand, if inflation is caused by a rise in exports and the accompanying inflow of reserves, appreciation worsens the current account and reverses the flow of reserves, thereby helping the appreciating country's neighbors. By and large, nations do not perform this latter service for their neighbors, preferring to absorb the inflow of reserves and to offset its inflationary effects through domestic monetary and fiscal policies; in this way, reserves are set aside "for rainy days."

In each of the foregoing cases, exchange-rate adjustments are substitutes for internal adjustments. A loss of reserves may be stopped by devaluation *or* by deflationary monetary and fiscal policies. Unemployment may be eased by devaluation *or* through internal inflationary monetary and fiscal policies. Inflation may be alleviated through appreciation *or* by domestic deflationary policies. The choice between internal adjustments and exchange-rate adjustments, though a nation may do a little bit of both to solve its problem, depends upon their effectiveness, upon the importance of the additional problems which they may create, and possibly upon their effects on other countries.

If a nation chooses exchange-rate adjustments, it still has to choose between more or less frequent changes, provided under fluctuating or stable-rate systems, as discussed in the next chapter.

APPENDIX: DIAGRAMMATIC ANALYSIS OF DEVALUATION

The effects of exchange-rate changes on prices, physical volumes, and values of exports and imports may be explained graphically as follows. It is assumed that, despite other changes, the import-demand and export-supply schedules of a nation remain fixed in terms of prices *stated in its own currency*. By this assumption, we exclude from consideration the effects on imports and exports of certain consequences of devaluation; for example, a rise in consumption and investment expenditures and/or a cost-price spiral which may accompany an initial improvement in the balance of payments would change a nation's demand and supply schedules, stated in terms of its own currency, in such a way as to restrain an increase in exports or a decrease in imports. In the accompanying graphs, we shall assume that the exchange-rate change is a devaluation of the pound sterling from $4 per £1 to $2 per £1 and that the United States and Britain are the only nations in the world.

BRITISH EXPORTS

Figure 8(a) shows the American import-demand schedule (D) for British bicycles; it indicates the various quantities of British bicycles that Americans will buy at various *dollar* prices. By assumption, this schedule is fixed. It may be converted through the exchange rate into an American import-demand schedule for bicycles at various *sterling* prices. The schedule in terms of sterling prices will vary with the exchange rate as follows: If

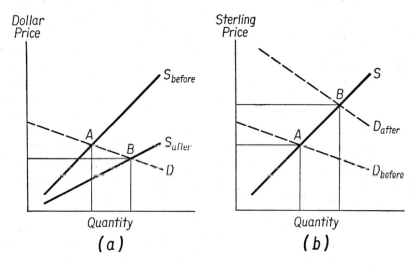

(a)   **(b)**

Fig. 8   U.S. Import Demand for and U.K. Export Supply of Bicycles

Americans are willing to pay as much as $40 for each of 1,000 bicycles and if the exchange rate is $4 — £1, they are in effect willing to pay £10 for each of the 1,000 bicycles. However, if the exchange rate is $2 = £1, Americans are in effect willing to pay £20 for each of the 1,000 bicycles because, at $2 = £1, £20 is the same as $40, which is all that Americans are willing to pay for each of 1,000 bicycles. Thus devaluation from $4 to $2 per pound doubles the number of pounds that Americans are willing to pay for any given quantity of British exports. This is shown in Figure 8(b); the American import-demand schedule marked "D before" shows the American demand in terms of sterling prices before devaluation when the exchange rate is $4 per £1. The schedule marked "D after" shows this same demand after devaluation when the exchange rate is $2 per £1; the latter schedule is exactly twice as high as the former, measured vertically, at each possible quantity of bicycles.[9]

Continuing, Figure 8(b) shows the British export supply (S) of

---

[9] For any given height on the vertical axes of both the left and right graphs, the dollar price is four times the sterling price.

bicycles; it indicates the various quantities of bicycles that Englishmen will offer for export at various *sterling* prices. By assumption, this schedule is fixed. It may be converted through the exchange rate into an export-supply schedule of British bicycles at various *dollar* prices. The schedule in terms of dollar prices will vary with the exchange rate as follows: If English exporters required £10 per bicycle to induce them to offer 1,000 bicycles for export and if the exchange rate is $4 per £1, American importers must pay $40 for each of the 1,000 bicycles. But if the exchange rate is $2 per £1, they need pay only $20 per bicycle because, at $2 per £1, $20 is the same as £10, which is all that is required by the British exporters to supply the bicycles. Thus devaluation from $4 to $2 per £1 cuts in half the number of dollars which American importers must pay for *any* given quantity of British bicycles. This is shown in Figure 8(a). The British export-supply schedule marked "S before" shows the British supply in terms of dollar prices before devaluation; the schedule marked "S after" shows the British supply in terms of dollar prices after devaluation and is precisely half as high as "S before," measured vertically, at each possible quantity of bicycles.

In both graphs we observe that the equilibrium prices shift from A to B upon devaluation of the pound. The fall in the dollar price of British bicycles is attributable to the shift to the right (or a downward shift) of the British export-supply schedule in terms of dollar prices. The rise in the sterling price is attributable to the shift to the right (or an upward shift) of the American import-demand schedule in terms of sterling prices. Each of these shifts reflects the other. The rise in the quantity of British bicycle exports from the level indicated by A to that indicated by B in Figure 8(b) is the same as the rise in U.S. imports indicated by A and B in Figure 8(a), as it must be since U.S. imports are British exports in a two-country world.

Elastic U.S. import demand

The demand for a product is said to be elastic when, with a small decline in its price, total expenditures (price times quantity) rise and when, for a small rise in its price, total expenditures fall. The demand is inelastic when converse movements in total expenditures occur with price changes. In Figure 8(a) we observe that the rectangle which has B at its northeast (upper right hand) corner is larger than the rectangle having A at its northeast corner. Since the total size of each rectangle equals price times quantity, i.e., total expenditure, it follows that devaluation leads to a rise in the total dollar value of British bicycle exports and that the American import demand is elastic within the relevant price range.

Inelastic U.S. import demand

In Figure 9 we consider the effects of devaluation on American imports of Scotch whiskey. The diagrammatic technique is the same as

that described above. The difference between Figure 9 and Figure 8 lies
in the shape of the American import-demand schedule. We observe that
the fall in the dollar price from A to B causes a decline in the total dollar
value of British Scotch whiskey exports since the rectangle which has B
at its northeast corner is smaller than the rectangle which has A at the
northeast corner. Thus devaluation reduces total dollar earnings by Britain,
and the American import demand for Scotch is inelastic.

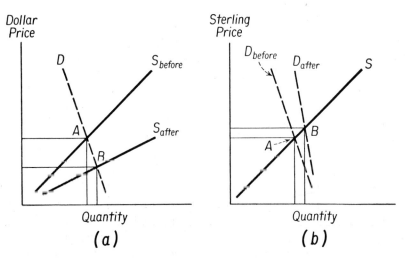

Fig. 9 U.S. Import Demand for and U.K. Export Supply of Scotch

In Figures 8(b) and 9(b) relating to bicycles and Scotch, we note
that the total sterling value of British exports increases. The sterling value
of British exports rises because of both a rise in the sterling price of
exports and a rise in the physical volume of exports; in each instance, the
higher sterling price is required to induce the greater supply.

BRITISH IMPORTS

Figure 10(b) shows the British import demand schedule (D) for
American beef at various *sterling* prices. By assumption, this schedule is
fixed. It may be converted through the exchange rate into a British import
demand schedule for beef at various dollar prices. This schedule will vary
with the exchange rate as follows: If Englishmen are willing to pay as
much as £25 for each of 1,000 sides of beef, and if the exchange rate is
$4 per £1, they are in effect willing to pay $100 for each side of beef.
But if the exchange rate is $2 per £1, they are in effect willing to pay
only $50 for each side of beef. Thus devaluation cuts in half the number
of dollars which Englishmen will pay for any given quantity of beef imports.
This is shown in Figure 10(a) where "D after" is exactly half as high as
"D before," measured vertically, for each possible quantity.

Figure 10(a) also shows the U.S. export-supply schedule of beef (S) at various dollar prices; by assumption this is fixed. Upon devaluation, each dollar costs twice as many pounds, i.e., a shift from $4 to $2 per £1 is the same as from $1 = £¼ to $1 = £½. Therefore the cost to Englishmen in pounds of any given amount of dollars doubles, and since the supply schedule showing the quantities of beef which will be offered to England at various dollar prices does not change, the cost to Englishmen in pounds of all possible quantities of beef also doubles. This is shown in Figure 10(b); "S after" is twice as high as "S before."

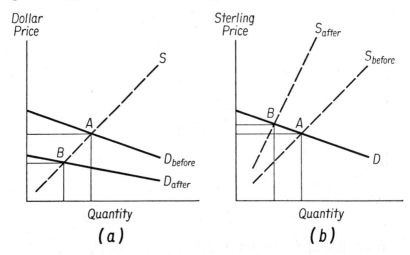

Fig. 10   U.K. Demand for and U.S. Export Supply of Beef

In both graphs of Figure 10, the equilibrium prices shift from A to B. The fall in the dollar price of British imports of beef is attributable to a shift to the left (or a downward shift) of the British import demand schedule in terms of dollars. The rise in the sterling price of beef is attributable to a shift to the left (or an upward shift) of the U.S. export supply of beef to England in terms of sterling prices. The extent of the fall in the dollar price and the rise in the sterling price are interrelated as before.

Elastic U.K. import demand

By comparing the rectangles formed at each equilibrium price in Figure 10(b), we observe that the total sterling expenditure on British imports of beef falls with the devaluation of the pound, i.e., the British import demand for beef is elastic between the prices A and B. The same comparison in Figure 10(a) shows that total dollar expenditures on imports of beef also fall.

Inelastic U.K. import demand

In Figure 11 we consider the effect of devaluation on tobacco imports into England. The diagrammatic technique is exactly the same as before. In Figure 11(b) we observe that the total sterling expenditure on tobacco rises as the sterling price moves from A to B; this is contrary to the previous case, i.e., the case of an elastic U.K. import demand. In Figure 11(a) we see that the total dollar expenditure falls as in Figure 10.

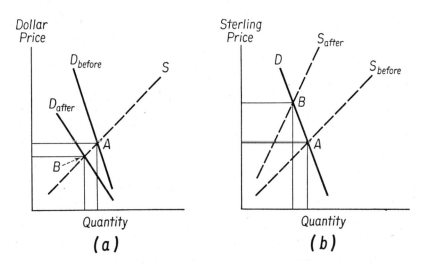

(a)   (b)

Fig. 11   U.K. Import Demand for and U.S. Export Supply of Tobacco

VARYING U.S. IMPORT DEMAND AND U.K. EXPORT SUPPLY ELASTICITIES

Elastic U.S. import demand

We have observed above that the sterling value of British bicycle and Scotch exports rise. This is always true save in the exceptional case that the United States would buy no greater physical quantity of British exports upon devaluation (a perfectly inelastic or vertical U.S. import demand); in that event there would be no additional demand for British exports to drive up their sterling price, nor any greater physical quantity of purchases to increase the total value of British exports in sterling.

Let us concentrate on the effect of devaluation on the total dollar value of British exports, giving consideration to the significance of different export-supply elasticities. The supply schedule of one product is more elastic (less inelastic) than the supply schedule of another product if, for a small and equivalent percentage change in their prices, the quantity supplied of the former changes by a greater percentage than the latter.

Figure 12 duplicates the U.S. import demand for bicycles which appeared in Figure 8. We determined that the schedule is elastic and that devaluation with respect to bicycles would increase Britain's dollar receipts. On Figure 12 we have imposed two alternative British export-supply schedules which might exist before devaluation; both of them intersect the predevaluation price of A. The dotted schedule is relatively inelastic as compared to the solid schedule in the price range around A; i.e., the quantity supplied is more responsive to price changes in the area around A along the solid schedule than along the dotted schedule.

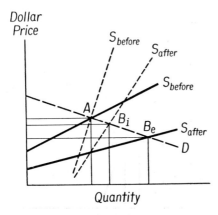

Fig. 12   U.S. Import Demand for Bicycles and Varying U.K. Export Supply Elasticities

With the more elastic British export-supply schedule, the dollar price drops to B_e; with the more inelastic schedule, the dollar price drops only to B_i. In both instances, the total dollar value of British exports rises above the value at A, but it rises to a higher level at B_e than at B_i. Therefore if Britain devalues in face of an elastic American import demand, the more elastic the British export supply the greater the rise in Britain's dollar earnings.

Inelastic U.S. import demand

Figure 13 duplicates the American demand schedule for Scotch whiskey which was used in Figure 9. We determined that the schedule is inelastic and that devaluation with respect to Scotch would reduce Britain's dollar earnings. As above, we superimpose two different supply schedules of British exports, the dotted schedule reflecting a more inelastic supply schedule than the solid one in the price range around A. We observe that the total dollar value of British Scotch exports is larger when the price falls to B_i (less elastic or more inelastic supply) than when it falls to B_e. In both instances, the total dollar value of British Scotch exports declines from A, but the decline is smaller when the British export-supply schedule is inelastic. Therefore if Britain devalues with an inelastic American import demand, the less elastic the British export supply the smaller the fall in Britain's dollar earnings.

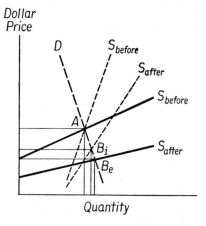

Fig. 13 U.S. Import Demand for Scotch and Varying U.K. Export Supply Elasticities

---

VARYING U.K. IMPORT-DEMAND AND U.S. EXPORT-SUPPLY ELASTICITIES

Elastic U.K. import demand

Figure 14 duplicates the U.K. import demand for beef which appeared in Figure 10. We determined above that this schedule is elastic and that devaluation would reduce Britain's total dollar expenditures. We have superimposed two different U.S. export-supply schedules, both of which intersect the predevaluation price of A; the short-dotted schedule is less elastic than the long-dotted schedule. The total dollar value of British beef imports is smaller at B_e than at B_i. We therefore conclude that, given an elastic British import demand, Britain's dollar expenditures fall more the less inelastic the American export supply.

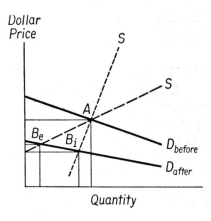

Fig. 14 U.K. Import Demand for Beef and Varying U.S. Export Supply Elasticities

Inelastic U.K. import demand

Figure 15 duplicates the U.K. import demand schedule for tobacco which appeared in Figure 11. We determined above that the schedule is inelastic, and that devaluation would reduce Britain's total dollar expenditures on tobacco. We have superimposed two different U.S. export-supply schedules; the short-dotted one is less elastic than the long-dotted one. Comparison shows that the total dollar value of British tobacco imports is less when the price drops to B_i (less elastic supply schedule) than to B_e. Therefore, given an inelastic U.K. import-demand schedule, Britain's dollar expenditures fall more the less elastic the American export supply.

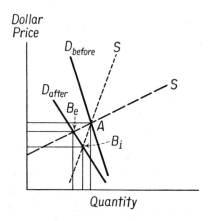

Fig. 15 U.K. Import Demand for Tobacco and Varying U.S. Export Supply Elasticities

In summary, suppose that Britain devalues to remove a dollar deficit. If the U.S. import demand is elastic, the U.S. dollar expenditures rise more the more elastic the British export supply; if the U.S. import demand is inelastic, U.S. dollar expenditures fall less the less elastic the British export supply. If the U.K. import demand is elastic, British dollar expenditures fall more the more elastic the U.S. export supply; if the U.K. import demand is inelastic, British dollar expenditures fall more the more inelastic the U.S. export supply.

AGGREGATION OF DEMAND AND SUPPLY

If at each exchange rate we aggregate all the receipts and all the payments forthcoming, we obtain the supply (receipts) and demand (payments) for foreign currency at the various exchange rates. For example, when we add the total British dollar earnings which would be forthcoming through Scotch whiskey exports when the rate is $2 = £1, the total British dollar earnings from bicycle exports at the same rate, and the other dollar receipts from other transactions such as capital movements, we obtain the total supply of dollars to England when the rate is $2 = £1. We may obtain the demand for dollars at $2 = £1 by adding the total British demand for dollars for the purchase of tobacco at that rate, the total British demand for dollars for the purchase of beef at that rate, and all other demands for dollars.

Normally, the quantities of foreign currency demanded and supplied vary with the exchange rate. The various quantities may be plotted to give demand and supply schedules for foreign currency. In one sense, the demand and supply of foreign currency are always equal; the balance of payments always balances, for total debits must equal total credits. If we exclude from the demand and supply schedules international reserve movements and those capital and unilateral transfers which take place for the purpose of substituting for reserve movements, then supply and demand do not automatically equal one another at any given exchange rate; the intersection of these demand and supply schedules would then provide an equilibrium rate of exchange in the sense that demand and supply are equated without the government providing or absorbing supply with the purpose of equating supply and demand. If we assume that the government controls international payments and receipts and that the supply and demand are artificially determined at each exchange rate, the intersection of the governmentally determined supply and demand schedules would provide a controlled equilibrium rate. If we assume that the government adjusts its monetary and fiscal policies to equate the demand and supply for foreign currency, then the supply and demand schedules are also interfered with by the government, though the type of intervention is quite different.

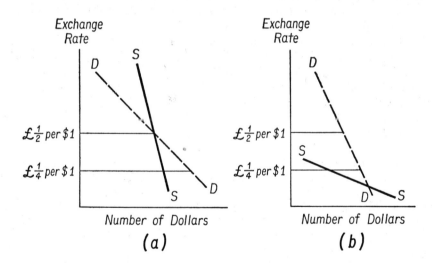

Fig. 16 The Foreign Exchange Market and the Efficacy of Devaluation

Excluding movements of reserves and substitutes for reserve movements from demand and supply, consider in Figure 16 the British exchange-rate adjustments which might be required to remove a deficit. While the supply schedule of dollars to Britain is normally such that devaluation of the pound leads to an increase in the number of dollars supplied, it is possible, as in the case of Scotch, that devaluation of the pound will reduce the supply of dollars. In that event, the supply schedule takes the unusual shape of rising to the left. If the intersection of such a supply schedule and the demand schedule for dollars is such as that shown in Figure 16(a), devaluation may nonetheless be used to remove the dollar deficit. Thus, at $4 = £1 (£¼ = $1), the supply of dollars falls short of the demand; the $4 rate can be maintained only through a movement of reserves. A change in the rate to $2 = £1 (£½ = $1) would remove the deficit. If the exchange rate were free to fluctuate and there were no reserve movements, it would automatically move to $2 = £1 because the demand for dollars exceeds the supply at $4 = £1.

But if the supply schedule intersects the demand schedule as shown in Figure 16(b), appreciation rather than devaluation is required to remove the deficit at $4 = £1 (£¼ = $1). If the exchange rate were free to fluctuate, it would *not* move toward the equilibrium rate (where supply and demand intersect) but in the opposite direction.

SELECTED READINGS

Alexander, Sidney S. "Effects of a Devaluation on a Trade Balance," *International Monetary Fund Staff Papers,* II (April, 1952), 263–278. A theoretical analysis of devaluation in terms of its effects on aggregate income, output, and spending. For an assessment, see Fritz Machlup, "Relative Prices and Aggregate Spending in the Analysis of Devaluation," *American Economic Review,* XLV (June, 1955), 255–278.

Ellsworth, Paul T. "Exchange Rates and Exchange Stability," *Review of Economics and Statistics,* XXXII (February, 1950), 1–12. A diagrammatic analysis of the effects of exchange-rate changes in terms of price elasticities.

Gardner, W. R., and S. C. Tsiang. "Competitive Depreciation," *International Monetary Fund Staff Papers,* II (November, 1953), 399–406. A discussion of some difficulties in defining and determining the existence of competitive exchange-rate depreciation.

Gilbert, Milton. *Currency Depreciation and Monetary Policy.* Philadelphia: University of Pennsylvania Press, 1939. An analysis of exchange-rate depreciation by Australia, Britain, and the United States in the early 1930's.

Gutt, Camille. "Policies to Make Devaluation Effective," *Money, Trade, and Economic Growth.* New York: Macmillan, 1951, pp. 94–101. Emphasizes the need for internal monetary and fiscal restraint in the event of devaluation.

Haberler, Gottfried. "The Market for Foreign Exchange and the Stability of the Balance of Payments," *Kyklos,* III (1949), 193–218. A theoretical analysis of the effect of exchange-rate changes in terms of supply and demand elasticities.

Harris, Seymour E. *Exchange Depreciation.* Cambridge, Mass.: Harvard University Press, 1936. Parts III and IV discuss the effects of British and American devaluation in the 1930's.

Harrod, Roy F. *The Pound Sterling.* Essays in International Finance, No. 13. Princeton, N.J.: International Finance Section, Princeton University, February, 1952. In addition to providing a broad survey of the pound in the 1930's and Britain's economic problems in the postwar period, this essay contains a heavy attack on the British devaluation of 1949.

Hawtrey, R. G. *Towards the Rescue of Sterling.* London: Longmans, 1954. A general survey of Britain's postwar balance-of-payments difficulties including, in Chapter 2, an extended criticism of the 1949 devaluation.

Hinshaw, Randall. "Currency Appreciation as an Anti-Inflationary Device," *Quarterly Journal of Economics,* LXV (November, 1951), 447–462. Responses to this article appear in the February, 1952, issue of the same journal.

Machlup, Fritz. "The Theory of Foreign Exchanges," *Readings in the Theory of International Trade,* Howard Ellis and Lloyd Metzler, eds. New York: Blakiston, 1949. A comprehensive discussion of the foreign-exchange market through supply and demand schedules with applications relevant to this and the succeeding chapter.

Meade, James. *The Balance of Payments.* London: Oxford, 1951. Chapter 18 presents the theory of devaluation.

Nurkse, Ragnar. "Conditions of International Monetary Equilibrium," *Readings in the Theory of International Trade,* Howard Ellis and Lloyd Metzler, eds. New York: Blakiston, 1949. An exposition of the equilibrium rate of exchange.

———. *International Currency Experience.* Geneva: League of Nations, 1944. Chapter 5 discusses exchange-rate variations between the two world wars; the section on the 1930's is particularly useful in connection with this chapter.

Polak, J. J., and T. C. Chang. "Effect of Exchange Depreciation on a Country's Export Price Level," *International Monetary Fund Staff Papers,* I (February, 1950), 49–70. An empirical analysis of the comparative effectiveness of depreciation under low and high employment conditions.

14 Exchange-Rate Policies: II

If governments decide that some reliance shall be placed upon exchange-rate adjustments in order to rectify internal economic instability or balance-of-payments deficits, there remains a choice between adjustments which are more or less frequent. The present chapter considers the relative merits of each; it then discusses the extent of cooperation among nations in changing exchange rates and the rules to which nations have agreed in order to restrict undesired exchange-rate changes.

C. STABLE VERSUS FLUCTUATING EXCHANGE RATES

ADVANTAGES OF FLUCTUATING RATES

The major advantage of fluctuating exchange rates is that they give the maximum possible protection from external events to both internal activity and international reserves. Suppose there is a depression abroad which induces a decline in a nation's exports.

With a fixed exchange rate, disregarding changes within the pegs or gold points, a fall in exports causes a loss of reserves, deflation, and unemployment. But with a fluctuating exchange rate, the reduced supply of foreign exchange which accompanies a fall in exports causes an immediate depreciation of the exchange rate. Exporters' incomes are sustained as the commodities they sell abroad have a higher value in their own currency. Domestic producers' incomes are sustained as the higher cost of imported goods induces citizens to switch their purchases to home-produced goods. The rise in exports and contraction of imports stops a loss of reserves. In fact, the government's international reserves are unaffected by the drop in exports, unless the government sells some of its foreign-exchange holdings to restrain the depreciation of its currency. The advantage of a fluctuating rate is that the government is not obliged to defend the exchange rate, as it is under a stable system. Thus a nation

272

may follow internal monetary and fiscal policies to maintain full employment and price stability without regard to the state of its reserves and independently of the level of prices, incomes, and employment in other countries.

Fluctuating rates, however, do not entirely protect a nation from its own excesses. Under a fixed rate, the inflationary or deflationary effects of changes in internal spending are restrained by changes in the balance of payments. Thus, the rise in exports and the fall in imports resulting from internal deflation limit the deflation; opposite movements tend to check internal inflation. A fluctuating rate, however, does prevent the effects of changes in internal spending from spreading abroad, since exports and imports are equilibrated by changes in the exchange rate.

Some of the advantages of fluctuating rates may be obtained under an "adjustable peg" system. That is, if the government were to change a stable rate in response to serious variations in the balance of payments, a greater degree of protection for the internal economy from external changes and a greater degree of protection for international reserves could be provided than if there were no exchange-rate changes at all. The government might, for example, change the rate in all but temporary difficulties, "temporary" meaning seasonal or short-term cyclical variations. An objection to this system is that the government may set the wrong exchange rate —wrong in the sense that it would induce international receipts and expenditures such that there would be a net long-term movement of international reserves or such that neighbors would be beggared. Proponents of fluctuating rates argue (or imply) that over the long pull a freely fluctuating rate can never produce these results.

Another objection to the adjustable-peg approach is that, since exchange-rate depreciation is often politically difficult, governments may wait too long to make the appropriate changes if they can do so at all. Still another objection arises out of capital movements, as discussed below.

ARGUMENTS AGAINST FLUCTUATING RATES

The arguments against fluctuating rates and in favor of stable rates stem from the large variations in the exchange rate which may be expected in the absence of gold points or of pegs; these variations add to business risks, affect the allocation of resources, and have a significant impact on capital movements. It is possible, however, to offset some of these disadvantages.

Risks

Exchange-rate variations impose a risk upon international trade and long-term capital movements which tends to discourage international transactions, thereby reducing the degree of international specialization and the extent of factor movements. The essence of the problem is the incalculability of final results. For example, if a British exporter ships goods to the United States and *requires payment in dollars,* he runs the risk that the dollars he eventually obtains will exchange for fewer pounds than necessary to cover his costs. Of course, he also accepts the happier chance that the dollars may be worth much more than enough pounds to cover his costs. Since the exporter is not in business to gamble, international trade under fluctuating rates provides less attractive business opportunities and the volume of international transactions declines accordingly. If the British exporter were to require payment in pounds, the effects on international trade would be the same because the risk would be shifted to the American importer, who would also be loath to gamble on erratic fluctuations in the price he pays for imports. Capital investors or borrowers undergo the same risks in determining what the cost (or value) of their interest and amortization payments will be, thereby reducing the international flow of capital.

Against this view, however, it may be contended that, over the long run, the risks of international traders are reduced by allowing the exchange rate to fluctuate. Internally induced inflation, by raising imports and reducing exports, causes a depreciation of the rate. The inflation raises exporters' costs of production but the depreciation preserves the exporters' profit margins. A loss of foreign markets does not hurt exporters' profits as much under fluctuating rates as under stable rates, because the reduced supply of foreign exchange induces a depreciation of the exchange rate. Profit margins are also stabilized in the face of internal deflation or external inflation. These points can also be made in support of an *easily* adjustable pegged-rate system.

Regarding risks in capital movements, mere fluctuations around some norm would hardly deter international investment. The danger comes in some permanent shift in the rate. But even this may be of little concern as long as the external and internal values of the currency move similarly. Thus an American lender may lose dollars if the dollar appreciates between the time he made the loan and the time he repatriates his funds. But if the purchasing power of the dollar over goods (its real value) increases because of a simultaneous deflation in the United States, he may have lost nothing of real value through the exchange rate change. (Simultaneous appreciation and deflation do not cancel exactly unless the prices of items which the creditor purchases change in the same degree that the exchange rate changes.) It is not unlikely that the exchange rate will adjust with general price-level movements, because deflation, for example, will expand exports and contract imports which, under a fluctuating rate, will cause an appreciation of the currency. But the price level and the exchange rate may not move proportionately. If there is a change in the level of employment or in the flow of international investment, neither may affect the price level significantly, depending on the existing level of employment, but both may radically change the demand and supply of foreign exchange, thus changing the exchange rate.

Unnecessary shifts of resources

Variations in the exchange rate lead to shifts of resources within a nation as the export and import-competing industries are alternately more and then less profitable. To the extent that such exchange-rate variations are temporary and to the extent that resources do move in response to them, a useless reallocation of resources results. The reallocation is useless in the sense that it is reversed when the temporary balance-of-payments difficulty disappears and the exchange rate returns to its former level. If there are frequent reallocations, both time and resources are wasted. This, however, is clearly a matter of degree, for, under stable rates, a change in international trade may lead to waste by causing unemployment.

Capital movements

Undesirable short-term capital movements may be induced under fluctuating exchange rates, increasing the instability of the exchange rate. However, as we shall see, short-term capital movements that make balance-of-payments problems more difficult may also occur under stable rates. The effect of capital movements in both instances depends upon anticipations.

Under stable exchange rates, when there is no expectation that the par value or gold content will be changed, short-term capital movements perform the useful function of providing funds which cover a deficit in the balance of payments; time is then allowed to make the fundamental shifts in the allocation of resources required to remove a deficit. They also provide means of financing a temporary deficit which, because it will soon be righted, does not require a reallocation of resources.

Assume that the United States, while on the gold standard, has a deficit in her balance of payments. A shortage of, say, sterling forces the exchange rate to depreciate to the U.S. gold export point. With a mint par of $4.86, as the rate approaches $4.88 per pound, it becomes increasingly profitable for persons or banks holding sterling to sell it for dollars, since each pound is worth more dollars. Such sales increase the supply of sterling (a short-term capital import) and cover the balance-of-payments deficit. Except in extreme cases, the price of sterling cannot exceed $4.88 so there is no profit in continuing to hold sterling once the rate has reached the gold export point.

As the rate approaches the gold export point, exporters may draw sterling drafts on British importers a bit sooner than otherwise in order to take advantage of the more favorable price of sterling. Persons who must make payments in sterling, on the other hand, may postpone their purchases of pounds in the hope that the price of sterling will decline. These responses ease the shortage of sterling.

If gold leaves the United States to cover the deficit and if this reduces the supply of loanable funds in the United States, the rise in the rate of interest[1] may attract capital from abroad or reduce an outflow of capital along the lines discussed in connection with the Bank of England during the nineteenth century (pages 221–223). The net inward shift of capital eases the shortage of sterling. For example, a finance bill might be drawn to move capital from low to high interest-rate markets. Thus an American bank would arrange to draw a time draft on some London bank. The draft would be accepted by the London bank and discounted in the London money market at the low rate of interest prevailing there. The sterling proceeds would be added to the deposits of the New York bank in London; the New York bank would then sell the pounds to Americans wishing to make payments in sterling. The dollars received by the American bank from purchasers of sterling would be loaned in the New York money market at the higher rate of interest prevailing there. The difference between the rate of interest received in New York and that paid in London, less the cost of the transaction, constitutes the New York bank's profit. The inflow of sterling is a short-term capital import into the United States and eases the balance of payments. The incentive to move capital in this manner is increased as the exchange rate moves to the gold export point. The New York bank cannot lose money when it later repays the borrowed funds, because sterling cannot become more expensive than the rate of $4.88 per pound which prevailed when the borrowed sterling was sold in New York.

The foregoing movement of short-term capital is stabilizing because it provides funds to cover the deficit, reducing the need for gold flows, and because it restrains the depreciation of the dollar by increasing the supply of sterling.

But such stabilizing movements do not occur if persons expect the exchange rate to change, as may be the case under an adjustable-peg system. A short-term capital *outflow* occurs if the government is *expected* to devalue the currency to adjust a balance-of-payments deficit. For example, persons will obtain as many foreign-currency assets as possible in advance of the expected devaluation. If the currency is devalued, they

---

[1] The rate of interest may not rise if the demand for funds declines as quickly as the supply. This may be the case if the U.S. deficit is caused by a drop of exports or an increase in imports at the expense of spending on U.S.-produced goods because American business activity (and therefore the demand for loans) would decline. But if the cause of the deficit is an outflow of capital, the demand for loanable funds is less likely to drop; therefore a rise in the interest rate will occur. Of course, the interest rate may be forcibly increased by monetary policy, e.g., the Bank of England and the bank rate.

obtain more units of their own currency on sale of their foreign assets than they paid for the assets before the devaluation. In addition, leads and lags in payments and receipts add pressure to the balance of payments. Importers speed up their purchases and payments to avoid paying the expected higher price for foreign exchange; exporters delay their shipments and sales of foreign-exchange earnings in the hope of obtaining more units of their own currency for the foreign exchange they earn. Such short-term capital movements increase the loss of international reserves and therefore increase the likelihood of devaluation. They are destabilizing.

Fluctuating rates may induce capital movements which either stabilize or destabilize the exchange rate, depending upon the correctness of speculators' anticipations. Imagine that, with an exchange rate of $3 per pound, Englishmen shift their demand from Austins to Cadillacs. Besides creating something of a traffic problem, the additional demand for dollars to buy the cars and additional gas to run them causes a depreciation of sterling. Assume that the pound will eventually level off at a *long-run* equilibrium rate of $2.50; this depreciation, by increasing British exports and reducing British imports of other products, provides foreign exchange to pay for greater Cadillac imports. But it takes time for resources and demands to shift in response to price changes. Before exports can increase and before British importers can adjust their expenditure patterns to the higher cost of dollars, the supply of dollars may not be sufficient to hold the rate at $2.50 because of the added demand for dollars to buy cars. Hence the value of the pound is likely to *fall below* $2.50 until British resources and demand can shift.

If speculators correctly anticipate that the exchange rate will eventually come to rest at $2.50 per pound, they will act in a stabilizing manner. When sterling depreciates below $2.50, speculators buy the cheap pounds in the expectation that they can make money by holding them until the value of sterling rises to $2.50. The added demand for pounds when their price falls below $2.50 tends to prevent an unnecessary depreciation of sterling. The increased demand for pounds means an increased supply of dollars which constitutes a short-term capital import into Britain. It covers the balance-of-payments deficit during the period in which British resources are shifting into export industries and in which British demand is shifting away from other imports, allowing more Cadillacs and other goods to be imported than otherwise would be the case.

But if speculators do not correctly anticipate the future exchange rate of $2.50 per pound, destabilization is the result. It is possible that the speculators may interpret the depreciation of the pound as evidence that it will depreciate further. Rather than buy sterling, as above, speculators buy dollars as the pound falls below $2.50, causing a capital outflow from Britain. The speculative demand for dollars causes a further depreciation of sterling, perhaps by more than would occur in the absence of any speculation and certainly by more than is necessary to induce the appropriate long-run reallocation of resources and demand in Britain.

Fluctuating rates may also misfire if speculators underestimate the extent to which sterling will eventually depreciate. Thus if speculators buy pounds at $2.75 (expecting it eventually to stabilize at $2.90, for example, instead of at $2.50), the exchange rate may not depreciate enough to induce the necessary reallocation of resources and demand which will sustain the rate of $2.50. Exports will not rise enough and imports will not drop enough, and the exchange rate of $2.75 can be sustained only by a continual inflow of capital in demand for sterling. When the speculators discover their mistake, the cessation of the capital inflow will force a radical depreciation of sterling, especially because the speculators demand dollars to withdraw their capital. As sterling depreciates from $2.75, the speculators receive fewer dollars for their pounds than they paid for them and therefore absorb losses for their errors of judgment.

On the assumption that speculation is not a strong enough force to affect independently the long-run level of an exchange rate, speculators perform a useful service as long as they buy cheap and sell dear, i.e., as long as they correctly anticipate the future exchange rate. By buying cheap they restrain an unnecessary fall in the value of a currency, and by selling dear they restrain an unnecessary rise in its value. This is precisely the previous characterization of stabilizing speculation. A "bad" speculator is one who loses money. One may be tempted to argue that because "bad" speculators lose money they cannot bother the exchange rates for very long, since their capital funds would eventually be wiped out. However, there may be a never-ending supply of suckers to take the place of fallen speculators; this is clearly the case at the professional gaming table, because the "house" usually wins in the long run.

Some of the disadvantages of fluctuating rates may be mitigated through the forward exchange market and through the stabilization funds of governments.

FORWARD RATES

In the forward market, claims on foreign exchange are traded for *future delivery*. (The spot market covers sales and purchases for immediate delivery.) An exporter, expecting to receive a claim on foreign currency in ninety days, will arrange, at a price agreed upon *now,* to deliver the exchange to a buyer in the future. If the value of the foreign exchange should be lower in ninety days than it is now, the exporter is not affected, because he receives the agreed price when he delivers the exchange ninety days hence. Similarly, an importer, knowing that he must make certain payments in foreign currency in the future, will contract to buy the required exchange in the future at a price determined now.

Banks enter into forward contracts with traders, though often in a way which tends to minimize their exchange-rate risks. A bank may attempt to match its forward sales to importers with its forward purchases from exporters so that, on the day of delivery, foreign exchange is put in its hands equivalent to the amount it has promised to deliver. If the bank does not match its sales and purchases, it may find itself with foreign exchange whose current value in the spot market has changed from the price the bank agreed to pay for it—possibly in the direction of a loss. Or the bank may not have enough forward exchange coming in to meet its forward-sale contracts; in this case it must buy exchange in the spot market to fulfill its commitments and, in doing so, may take a loss if the spot price is higher than the negotiated forward price. If the bank's sales and purchases are not equal, it is in an "uncovered position."

Speculators also enter into forward contracts, but they purposely take an uncovered position in hope of gain. If a speculator believes that foreign exchange ninety days hence will be cheaper than the present forward rate for foreign exchange, he will contract to supply exchange in ninety days. When the delivery date arrives, he buys spot foreign exchange to fulfill his deal and, if the spot rate is lower than the forward rate he agreed to, the speculator makes a profit. If he expects foreign exchange to be more expensive, he will *buy* forward exchange.

The forward rate, though determined by the supply and demand for forward exchange, is not independent of the spot rate. When the balance of expectations is that foreign exchange will become more expensive in the future, the demand for forward exchange will rise as importers and speculators buy forward exchange at prices below the expected future spot rate. If, as a result of the higher demand, the price of forward exchange rises above the current spot rate, banks have an incentive to sell forward exchange to those demanding it and to buy spot foreign exchange to hold until delivery is required. By buying the spot exchange to hold against its forward sales, the bank is in a covered position and therefore stands no exchange risk. The additional supply of forward exchange reduces the price of forward exchange, while the additional demand for spot exchange raises the price of spot exchange; these transactions tend to bring the two rates together.

There is a mutual interaction between the forward and the spot rates stemming from the fact that they may differ, in normal times, by no more than an amount equal to the difference between interest rates in the money markets of the countries whose currencies are involved. When a bank sells forward exchange and simultaneously covers itself by buying spot exchange, it loses interest at home because the local currency which it could have loaned is spent to buy spot foreign exchange. But the bank gains interest abroad if these foreign funds are invested in short-term securities in the foreign-money market. If the interest gained abroad exceeds the interest lost at home, the bank will charge (under the force of competition) a lower price for forward exchange than spot exchange by an amount equivalent to the gain in interest. If the forward rate were not lower by that amount, additional profits could be made by banks by buying spot and selling forward; but in attempting to make such profits, the banks raise the price of spot as more is demanded and lower the price of forward exchange as its supply is increased.

Both the forward rate and the spot rate will vary under a fluctuating rate system because the forward rate changes with anticipations, because the spot rate moves under the force of the supply and demand for foreign exchange, and because the two rates are intimately related. The implication of these movements is that, although a forward contract removes the exchange rate risk from the particular transaction which it covers, it does not stabilize exchange rates—forward or spot. Thus succeeding transactions may be made at spot rates or be covered by forward buying or selling of exchange at rates which may be more or less favorable to the international trader. Hence, the profitability of producing goods for export still varies with exchange-rate fluctuations. Uncertainty over the future course of exchange rates may deter the expansion of international trade, unless one assumes that some businessmen enter the field because it does provide some opportunity to gamble. The fact that not all traders do enter into forward contracts suggests that the utility of gambling is high for some traders, though some may be deterred from making forward contracts by the costs involved.

STABILIZATION FUNDS

Stabilization funds, such as the English Exchange Equalisation Account, have been used to minimize the above shortcomings of fluctuating (spot and forward) exchange rates by damping their fluctuations without disturbing the tendency toward a long-run equilibrium exchange rate. Having a supply of foreign exchange, the fund may support the price of its currency against undesired depreciation by selling some of its foreign-exchange holdings for its own national currency. Conversely, the fund may stop an unnecessary appreciation of its currency by buying foreign exchange with its own currency. This procedure is similar to the pegged-exchange-rate system except that fixed pegs do not exist.

The undesirable exchange-rate movements which these agencies may combat often include those resulting from seasonal variations in the balance of payments, from speculative capital movements, and from the different timing of day-to-day receipts and expenditures.

Seasonal and daily exchange-rate variations are not necessary to the maintenance of long-run stability of international reserves, i.e., they are not required as a means of reallocating resources in a nation to rectify persistent balance-of-payments deficits or surpluses. Therefore there is little objection to offsetting them to reduce risks to traders.

But the case for stopping fluctuations induced by speculative capital movements is not so clear. Earlier discussion indicated that speculators may correctly anticipate the specific future exchange rate which induces the appropriate readjustment of exports and imports. Thus an equalization fund may unwittingly combat an appropriate exchange-rate adjustment by offsetting speculative purchases or sales of foreign exchange. However, speculators may also be wrong, and the problem for the operators of a stabilization fund is to know which is the case. In an uncertain world, this is not easy to determine.

Finally, a stabilization fund cannot provide long-run stability (any more than can a pegged-rate system) in the face of a persistent demand for foreign exchange. It cannot resist *forever* an appropriate depreciation of its currency because it will eventually run out of foreign exchange to supply the market. The fund may, however, *hold* the currency at an inappropriately depreciated rate by offering an unlimited supply of home currency for foreign exchange. This means that it is possible for a fund to undertake a beggar-thy-neighbor policy of exporting unemployment under a flexible exchange-rate system just as could occur under stable rates.

D. INTERNATIONAL FINANCIAL COOPERATION

GOLD STANDARD

Prior to World War I, most of the major trading nations were on the gold standard, and many others fixed their exchange rates in terms of others which were on gold. Balance-of-payments equilibrium was the result of an intricate meshing of moving parts. A large measure of price, cost, and income flexibility was made possible by a relative lack of labor-union wage fixing and government interference in the market place. The automatic forces of adjustment were not greatly hindered. Fixed exchange rates were the general rule, though exchange depreciation was a frequent occurrence in the raw-material producing countries when they faced extreme balance-of-payments difficulties. The flexibility of prices and costs made extensive unemployment a less likely result of automatic adjustments under stable exchange rates. The problem of internal deflation was further relieved by the secular boom of the nineteenth century, connected with rising population and the industrial revolution, which permitted a reallocation of resources through faster growth of the most buoyant industries rather than through unemployment in the unfavored industries.

In the forty years before World War I, Britain stood at the center of the adjustment system. The British bank-rate policy attracted and repelled short-term capital in a manner which stabilized gold reserves in the face of temporary balance-of-payments disequilibriums. In addition, because London was the major money market of the world, the increased liquidity and low interest rates which accompanied a flow of gold into Britain would induce foreign borrowing on long-term accounts which would reverse or stop an inflow of gold.

London cleared most of the world's transactions. Drafts all over the world were drawn in sterling and paid in sterling, and many foreign banks kept some of their reserves invested in the London money market. Since sterling was the chief currency in world trade and payments, it was essential that the supply of sterling made available to the rest of the world remain relatively stable. In part this was obtained by Britain's free trade policy since changes in British imports, as they were required to produce balance-of-payments equilibrium, were not prevented by artificial obstacles. In addition, emigration and domestic and foreign investment played an important role. When British lending abroad increased, so also did her exports as the borrowed pounds were utilized to buy British goods. The increased capital expenditures in the borrowing countries expanded their economic activity, and this was accompanied by a movement of people out of Britain. Emigration from Britain reduced her population growth and contracted British domestic investment, particularly in home construction. When her investment abroad dropped off, emigration and capital exports from Britain declined. The relative rise in Britain's population increased home investment and raised the general level of British economic activity; as a result, her imports of foodstuffs and raw materials rose, maintaining the supply of sterling provided other nations, which otherwise would have fallen as foreign lending declined. Thus imports and lending abroad, tied together through investment and flow of people, alternated to provide continuing supplies of sterling to foreign nations.[2]

INTER-WAR PERIOD

In a world in which nations accepted the consequences of automatic adjustment and acceded to the dictates of the Bank of England, there was little room or need for formal international financial cooperation. But such a world did not last, for, as we saw in Chapter 12, central banks began to offset on a large scale the effects of the flows of international reserves after World War I. The postwar inflations during 1920–1925 prevented a ready return to prewar exchange relations.

There was some cooperation during the 1920's in stabilizing exchange rates, such as the reduction of rediscount rates of the Federal Reserve Banks in 1924 and 1927 to relieve pressure on European currencies by reducing the flow of gold to the United States. Several international conferences on exchange-rate stabilization were held (e.g., Brussels in 1920 and Genoa in 1922), though the United States did not participate.

---

[2] Brinley Thomas, *Migration and Economic Growth* (Cambridge: Cambridge University Press, 1954), pp. 233, 177–178.

But the early 1930's saw an almost calculated unwillingness to co-operate. After the pound and the dollar were set free to fluctuate,[3] the London Monetary and Economic Conference was held in 1933 to discuss numerous questions relating to international economic relations, particularly exchange-rate stability. A draft resolution (which was prepared for the acceptance of the Conference) called for a temporary truce in exchange-rate adjustments; but it was summarily rejected by President Roosevelt, who seemed to regard stable exchange rates as being among the "old fetishes of so-called international bankers."[4] The United States was not ready to stabilize exchange rates, because she was in the midst of efforts to raise internal prices which Roosevelt felt would be compromised by stable exchange rates.

Also suggestive of the atmosphere at the time is the fact that the Exchange Stabilization Fund, the American counterpart of the British Exchange Equalisation Account, was established not only to iron out undue fluctuations in the dollar, but probably also to prevent a British-contrived depreciation of the pound.

In the absence of cooperation, the depressed 1930's strained the balance-of-payments adjustment mechanism under fixed exchange rates until it fractured beyond repair. In the 1930's virtually every currency was depreciated at one time or another. In some instances the exchange rate was depreciated to a new, stable level, while in other instances the exchange rate was allowed to fluctuate. Competitive devaluations occurred as nations depreciated to reduce their unemployment and to ease their reserve losses resulting from their own internal efforts to get out of a depression, and from depreciation by other countries. Competitive exchange depreciation led to the risks and uncertainties which plague international trade and capital movements when exchange rates change frequently. No one country gained greatly from the round of devaluations. Since depreciation is a relative matter, it is impossible for *all* currencies to be depreciated relative to one another. Therefore the general pattern of exchange rates that appeared in 1936 after the depreciations from 1929 rates showed only a few currencies actually depreciated.

The only concerted effort at international exchange-rate cooperation was made under the 1936 Tripartite Monetary Agreement when the franc was about to be devalued. Britain, the United States, and France feared another round of competitive depreciation such as had been started by the depreciation of the pound in 1931. Though the Agreement provided no

---

[3] Starting in 1931 for the pound and remaining so until 1939, and from March, 1933, through January, 1934, for the dollar.

[4] Franklin D. Roosevelt, *The Public Papers and Addresses*, Vol. II (New York: Random House, 1938), 265. "The sound internal economic system of a Nation is a greater factor in its well-being than the price of its currency in changing terms of the currencies of other Nations." Pages 264–265.

technique of stopping this, it did include a vague declaration of the need to avoid unnecessary exchange-rate fluctuations, and it provided a mechanism for very short-term stabilization.

Prior to the Agreement, neither the British nor American funds operated in each other's currencies because the American fund, if it bought sterling, ran a risk of loss since the pound was not convertible into gold at a fixed price. Therefore both funds, with minor exceptions, operated to stabilize their currencies in terms of currencies convertible into gold, i.e., the franc. But when the franc went off gold, this alternative mechanism was no longer available. The virtue of the Agreement was that it made it possible for the funds to operate in terms of each other's currencies with safety through a twenty-four-hour period. Each nation stated the daily price at which it was willing to sell gold for its currency; this price would remain fixed for at least twenty-four hours so that the funds could buy and hold each other's currencies during that period without fear of loss. Nothing prevented a nation from changing the daily price at which it would buy gold, and therefore exchange-rate depreciation was still possible. In fact, the franc did depreciate after the Agreement. Nonetheless, the Agreement did provide for cooperation on exchange-rate matters at the technical level. The stabilization funds and the Agreement were the historical precursors of the postwar International Monetary Fund.

INTERNATIONAL MONETARY FUND

The International Monetary Fund Agreement was signed in 1944 by 44 nations, largely to relieve the world of the international financial difficulties observed during the 1930's. It began operation in 1947.

Its main purposes are to (1) promote international monetary cooperation by providing machinery for consultation among nations, (2) promote exchange-rate stability and eliminate competitive exchange depreciation, (3) assist in the removal of direct controls on foreign exchange, and (4) provide a "secondary reserve" of foreign exchange from which members could borrow to meet *temporary* balance-of-payments deficits, so as to reduce the need for exchange-rate and/or internal economic adjustments. This reserve, contributed by the members, consists of gold and their own currencies.

The effectiveness of the Fund in obtaining these objectives depended upon the correctness of the assumptions as to the postwar world in which it was to operate. The assumptions for which the techniques of the Fund were appropriate were that, after a short transitional period from war to peace, a world-wide system of multilateral trade and payments would be restored and that, during the transitional period, governments would be moving as rapidly as possible away from the use of controls to the free-market determination of costs and prices. That is, the postwar world in which the Fund was to operate was to be one in which trade relations and international payments were determined largely by actions of private individuals and not by governments.

Contrary to expectations, governments have been very reluctant to give up their direct control over international transactions. They have retained exchange restrictions, despite the efforts of the Fund to get them removed. This has made the consultation of members with the Fund important, especially in coordinating short-run policies and use of direct controls. The U.S. administration has ascribed a highly important role to the consultations within the Fund:

In the interim [until exchange restrictions are removed], the Fund has an important role as an international consultative body and as a forum for dealing with important questions relating to foreign exchange. In the long-run this may prove to be the Fund's greatest contribution to the solution of the international economic problems of our times.[5]

Apart from the consultation provided by the Fund and its efforts to get nations to relax their exchange restrictions, its most important activities were to be in maintaining stable exchange-rate systems. It was supposed to achieve this through its members agreeing to maintain stated par values for their currencies and through the Fund's own provision of additional reserves to members on a temporary basis.

Exchange-rate cooperation

Members of the Fund agree to maintain stable exchange rates by freely buying and selling their currency within a 1 per cent spread on each side of the agreed par value. These par values may be changed only under specified conditions. In order to prevent competitive devaluation, members are required to consult with the Fund regarding any proposed change in their par values. Members are permitted, however, to alter their par values without approval of the Fund by as much as 10 per cent of the par value they maintained when the Fund started operations. But no member is supposed to propose any change unless necessary to correct a "fundamental disequilibrium." Devaluation by more than 10 per cent is permitted to ease a persistent or chronic balance-of-payments disequilibrium, or when "necessary to protect a member from unemployment of a chronic or persistent character, arising from pressure on its balance of payments."[6] But the Fund

---

[5] National Advisory Council on International Monetary and Financial Problems, *Second Special Report* to the President and the Congress on the operations and policies of the International Monetary Fund and the International Bank for Reconstruction and Development, May, 1950, p. 24.

[6] *Report of the Executive Directors and Summary Proceedings,* September 27 to October 3, 1947 (Washington: International Monetary Fund, 1946), pp. 105–106. The U.S. National Advisory Council stated in 1950 that "In the view of the Council retention of exchange restrictions on current account transactions or quantitative import controls by a member of the Fund should be considered as *prima facie* evidence of fundamental disequilibrium." Such a situation called *not* for borrowing

may *not* object to a change in the par value to correct a fundamental disequilibrium which is caused by the "domestic social or political policies"
of the member. If a member devalues without the permission of the Fund,
it may be denied the privilege of borrowing from the Fund.

As is evident from the earlier analysis of this chapter, exchange-rate
adjustments are of concern to other countries besides the one taking action.
International consultation in exchange-rate matters is useful, at least to
restrain retaliation by those who do not understand the necessity for another
country's depreciation. "Yet the Fund has not succeeded in the important
objective of making exchange rate changes a matter of international de-
liberation and judgment."[7] In September, 1949, when virtually every
principal currency was devalued with respect to the U.S. dollar in response
to the depreciation of the pound from $4.03 to $2.80, the Fund had a week
end to consider the proposal of Britain. The British Chancellor of the
Exchequer, in announcing the devaluation, said that it "had to do with
matters that were entirely our own concern and upon which there was no
question of consulting others, even our best friends." The meager consultation irritated some nations, and the French Minister of Finance called the
new par a "trade-war rate."

Selection of initial par values

Efforts of the Fund to coordinate exchange-rate policy began prior to
the Fund's opening its doors to borrowers in 1947. It attempted to avoid
the difficulties of the post-World War I period in which freely fluctuating
rates prevailed for several years followed by a stabilization at hit-or-miss
par values. Members were required to establish par values of their currencies in consultation with the Fund. The Fund could reject rates which could
not be maintained without a drain on the country's reserves or which would
require more than temporary borrowing from the Fund.

The Fund rejected none of the par values proposed by the members,
stating that "The major significance of the present step is not in the particular rates of exchange which are announced, but in the fact that the
participating nations have now fully established a regime wherein they are
pledged to promote exchange stability. . . ."

Considering the radical changes which had occurred in prices and
costs among countries and the differential impact of the war on nations'
money incomes and productive facilities, some critics were surprised at the
Fund's action. But the Fund, while admitting that the accepted rates created
substantial disparities between the price and cost levels of a number of
members, argued that such disparities were not so important because of

---

from the Fund but for measures which would eliminate the disequilibrium and
permit the removal of the controls first. (See *Second Special Report, op. cit.,* p. 22.)

[7] R. F. Mikesell, *Foreign Exchange in the Postwar World* (New York:
Twentieth Century Fund, 1954), p. 24.

the abnormal times. It argued that depreciation of the exchange rates would not expand exports because their volume was limited mainly by difficulties of production. Furthermore, depreciation might aggravate internal tendencies toward inflation. Finally, the growth of productivity and the recovery of production from the disruption of war was expected to bring cost structures into line with those of other countries.[8]

These arguments have not gone uncriticized.[9] The assertion that supply considerations limited exports fails to note that the direction of exports can be changed by devaluation without increasing their supply. The core of the international financial problem of the postwar period was the insufficiency of foreign countries' dollar earnings from the United States to finance needed and desired purchases from this country. The excessively high value placed on some currencies relative to the dollar (their overvaluation) deterred exports to the United States. Exports to other countries were not similarly deterred, since nondollar currencies tended not to be overvalued in terms of each other but only in terms of the dollar, and since general inflationary conditions within each country tended to maintain the demand for the goods of others. In these circumstances, depreciation of exchange rates against the dollar might have been an appropriate means of diverting exports to the United States. In addition, such depreciation, unless it caused internal inflation (which could be stopped through internal measures), would assist in reallocating resources toward export and import-competing industries to solve the long-run balance-of-payments problem which most of Europe faced.

The problem of selecting appropriate exchange rates is perplexing, especially after a long period such as during World War II, in which existing exchange rates have not been significant determinants of the distribution and volume of trade. One method of selecting them is to use the "purchasing power parity" technique, which had considerable acceptance among economists in the 1920's. The purchasing-power par is an exchange rate which preserves some predetermined relationship between the real value of trading nations' goods and services by compensating for relative changes in their general price levels. For example, if the exchange rate were $4 per £1 in one year and the U.S. price level had risen from an index number of 100 to 200 by the next year while the British price level had remained unchanged, the purchasing-power par would be $8 to £1. While the dollar price of American products had risen 100 per cent, at a new exchange-rate par of $8 per £1, British importers could buy 100 per cent more dollars ($8 instead of $4) for a pound so that their purchases from the United States would not be deterred by the U.S. inflation. Similarly, the relative rise in the U.S. price level would make British goods more attractive to

---

[8] *Annual Report* (Washington: International Monetary Fund, 1947), pp. 70–71.
[9] R. F. Mikesell, "The International Monetary Fund," *International Conciliation* (November, 1949), pp. 848, 854.

Americans, thereby increasing U.S. imports; but the 100 per cent rise in the price of a pound would offset that attractiveness and therefore restrain U.S. imports.[10]

If the objective in setting an exchange rate is to determine a rate which will cause no persistent movement of international reserves, the purchasing-power parity calculation will not necessarily provide the appropriate one. Relative prices are not the only determinants of the volume of exports and imports and are therefore not the only forces affecting the need for movements of international reserves. Nor are exports and imports the only determinants of the flow of international reserves.

If a nation suffers inflation relative to the rest of the world but is simultaneously importing significantly more long-term capital than it was in the base period, the purchasing-power par overstates the necessary degree of depreciation. Foreign exchange obtained through capital imports finances part of the nation's imports, and therefore exports need not be expanded nor imports contracted as much as an exchange-rate adjustment dictated by the purchasing-power par would suggest. Also, if a nation had extensive unemployment in the base period but has full employment at present, the current purchasing-power par may understate the necessary degree of depreciation. The additional real income accompanying the rise in employment expands the demand for imports, and the extent of depreciation may have to be greater in order to expand exports by enough to finance the additional imports.

Finally, the use of an index of prices covers up changes in relative prices within a nation which may be significant in determining the appropriate exchange rate. A calculation of the purchasing-power par may show that the existing exchange rate is suitable because no change in the general level of prices has occurred in either country. But the stability of the price index in one country may have resulted from offsetting (as far as the index is concerned) changes in prices within that nation. If the prices have fallen on commodities for which good substitutes may be obtained abroad, imports of substitutes will decline substantially. If the prices have risen on commodities for which only poor substitutes are available abroad, imports of these poor substitutes will rise little. The total level of imports will have fallen, international reserves will be flowing in, and the exchange rate should be appreciated rather than left unchanged as indicated by the purchasing par.

---

[10] The general formula for determining the purchasing-power par is: base-period price of foreign exchange times the ratio of the price-level indexes of the two countries involved. The price indexes have the same base period, equal to 100, as the base-period price of foreign exchange, and the numerator of the ratio of the price indexes must be the price index of the country in whose currency the price

of foreign exchange is measured. Purchasing-power par = exchange rate $\times \left\{ \dfrac{\text{prices}}{\text{prices}} \right\}$

Had the purchasing-power par for the pound in terms of the dollar been established in 1946 by the Fund, a pound would have cost between 16 per cent and 36 per cent more dollars than it did in 1946, i.e., the pound would have been appreciated from its then current value. In view of the later balance-of-payments difficulties which Britain suffered, such appreciation would probably have been inappropriate.

Fluctuating rates

The success of the members of the Fund in maintaining stable exchange rates has not been complete. Some of the more important members (Canada, Italy, and France, for example) have permitted their exchange rates to fluctuate. The Fund's position on such aberrations from stability has not been rigid. While asserting firmly the advantages of stable rates, the Fund has admitted that "there may be occasional and exceptional cases where a country concludes that it cannot maintain *any* par value for a limited period of time, or where it is exceedingly reluctant to take the risks of a decision respecting a par value, particularly when important uncertainties are considered to exist." In such circumstances "if the Fund finds that the arguments of the member are persuasive it may say so, although it cannot give its approval to the action" of instituting fluctuating rates.[11] Members were warned that the use of fluctuating rates should be only temporary and that it was essential for the member to remain in close consultation with the Fund.

The Fund did not specify the special circumstances which it would consider persuasive. In the instances of Peru and Canada, which turned to fluctuating rates in 1949 and 1950—actions which the Fund did not disapprove—the official reason each country gave was the difficulty in selecting a par value which could be defended, i.e., which would not have to be changed very soon. Some persons inferred that the general level of the rate under free conditions would point toward a defensible par value. The Fund appears to attack such an approach, saying,

Those who advocate allowing rates to find their "natural" level, permitting market forces to determine a rate of exchange that will be stabilized, seek to provide a simple solution for a very complex problem. There is no such thing as a "natural" level for the rate of exchange of a currency. The proper rate will, in each case, depend upon the economic, financial and monetary policies followed by the country concerned and by other countries with whom it has important economic relationships. If the economy of a country is to adapt itself to a given exchange rate, there must be time for the producers, sellers and buyers of goods and services to respond to the new set of price and cost relationships to which the rate gives rise. This means that the short-run changes in the exchange rate are either no test or a very poor test of basic economic

[11] *Annual Report* (Washington: International Monetary Fund, 1951), pp. 38–39.

inter-relationships. It also means that whether a given exchange rate is at the "correct" level can be determined only after there has been time to observe the course of the balance of payments in response to that rate. Moreover, past experience with fluctuating rates of exchange has proved that movements in the rate are significantly affected by large speculative transfers of capital.[12]

While the advantages of stable exchange rates may still hold for the postwar world in which the Fund has operated, it cannot be denied that the circumstances in which the stable par-value system was expected to operate did not arise in the postwar period. Instead of unemployment as in the 1930's, there was inflation. Instead of willingness to devalue as in the 1930's, governments found such action repugnant. High and unequal rates of inflation among countries made exchange-rate adjustments necessary if balance-of-payments stability was to be achieved. The choice of making adjustments through 10 to 30 per cent leaps under adjustable pegs, as are possible under the Fund, or through the creeping depreciation of fluctuating rates rests on the arguments concerning stable versus fluctuating rates. In part, the answer depends on whether or not one believes an exchange rate can be properly managed by government. This decision in turn is affected by the question of whether it is politically more difficult to devalue a stable currency than to let it adjust through a free market mechanism. But the final decision does not rest solely on these considerations. Some of the problems attached to stable exchange rates can be alleviated if an adequate volume of international reserves is held by all countries. In order to make more effective use of the existing supply of international reserves, members contributed to the Fund gold, dollars, and their own currencies as a "secondary reserve" available to all.

Secondary reserves

Each member was to be permitted to borrow in one year (by selling its own currency to the Fund) an amount of foreign currency totaling no more than 25 per cent of its contribution. The loan was to be used to meet *temporary* deficits in its balance of payments to make devaluation or internal deflation unnecessary. This borrowing was not to be permitted automatically, but the presumption of most members was that they could borrow fairly readily. However, the Fund has found it necessary to limit more severely the borrowing "rights" of members. The type of balance-of-payments disequilibrium which most countries faced after World War II was not the temporary, cyclical variety which was seen as a justifiable occasion for borrowing from the Fund. There were no depressions, no beggar-thy-neighbor devaluations. The postwar disequilibrium has been chiefly the "fundamental" type resulting from structural and monetary causes. Because the Fund is an international institution, its resources must

---

[12] *Ibid.*, p. 38.

constitute a revolving fund available to all at any time.[13] If the Fund's lending was not repaid repeatedly, its useful resources would disappear. (In place of currencies needed by members, the Fund would hold only those currencies of countries in persistent deficit, whose currencies would therefore not be needed by others because they would not be in short supply.) The provisions of the Fund require a member to repurchase its own currency when its international reserves reach a certain level. A persistent balance-of-payments deficit might prevent the reserves from reaching the repayment level. To prevent an exhaustion of the Fund's useful resources, the executive directors (under strong insistence from the U.S. government) adopted a policy of restricted lending. Its loans have been much less than members in payments deficits wished.

Many members considered that the restrictive policy was actually reducing the volume of reserves available because the Fund sat on the gold and dollars they had contributed. The Fund argued, however, that members should first ease their restrictions on exchange payments and remove internal inflationary pressure. In an effort to use its resources to meet some of their complaints and to achieve its objectives, the Fund announced policies of (1) giving each member the overwhelming benefit of the doubt in making loans equal to the gold and dollars it contributed, (2) making further loans conditional on increased anti-inflationary measures in the borrowing nation and on the relaxation of its controls on trade, (3) making short-term loans for periods not exceeding 18 months, and (4) reducing the interest cost for borrowing for periods of less than one year while increasing that for periods in excess of two years in order to induce quicker repayment and to increase the revolving nature of the Fund's resources. Since these measures did not increase the Fund's lending or accelerate repayments satisfactorily, it adopted a policy of extending six-month stand-by credits in advance of a need for foreign exchange on the condition that, if used, the borrowing member should take measures to enable it to repay the borrowed funds. Members are obliged to repay within three to five years. Thus the Fund moved from the viewpoint that members might borrow for indeterminate periods when in temporary difficulties to a policy of lending under time limitations and on condition of remedial action in a world of persistent difficulties. In this way the Fund has hoped to unfreeze its assets without jeopardizing the revolving nature of the resources.

---

[13] The world-wide inflation of prices and the 50 per cent increase in the money value of world trade since the inception of the Fund has reduced the real value of the Fund's resources. This in turn limits the extent to which it may cover balance-of-payments deficits. One study estimates that a U.S. recession of equal intensity as that of 1937–1938 would reduce the supply of dollars made available to the rest of the world by $10 billion. United Nations, *Measures for International Economic Stability* (New York: Columbia University Press, 1951), pp. 33–34. The total gold and dollar holdings of the Fund are currently about $3.5 billion. Because the United States has not suffered a severe recession, this limitation on the Fund's assistance has not been important.

SELECTED READINGS

C. STABLE VERSUS FLUCTUATING EXCHANGE RATES

Einzig, Paul. *The Theory of Forward Exchange.* London: Macmillan, 1937. A comprehensive study and analysis.

Meade, James. *The Balance of Payments.* London: Oxford, 1951. Chapter 17 provides an excellent discussion of the relation between speculation and fluctuating exchange rates.

Nurkse, Ragnar. *International Currency Experience.* Geneva: League of Nations, 1944. A major theme of this study is an indictment of fluctuating exchange rates; see particularly pp. 210–211.

Southard, Frank A. *Foreign Exchange Practice and Policy.* New York: McGraw-Hill, 1940. Pages 96–105 provide a brief discussion of forward exchange.

The following present cases for flexible or fluctuating rates:

Friedman, Milton. "The Case for Flexible Exchange Rates," *Essays in Positive Economics.* Chicago: University of Chicago Press, 1953. Specific consideration of the arguments given by Nurkse, among others.

Graham, Frank D. "Fundamentals of International Monetary Policy," *Postwar Monetary Standards.* New York: Monetary Standards Inquiry, 1944, pp. 51–81.

Whittlesey, C. R. *International Monetary Issues.* New York: McGraw-Hill, 1937, Chapters 4 and 7.

On stabilization funds, see selected readings for Chapter 12.

D. INTERNATIONAL FINANCIAL COOPERATION

Behrman, J. N. "Alternative Lending Policies for the International Monetary Fund," *Review of Economics and Statistics,* XXXVI (August, 1954), 338–342. A brief review of the various lending policies adopted by and open to the Fund.

Brown, W. A. *The Gold Standard Reinterpreted, 1914–1934,* 2 vols. New York: National Bureau of Economic Research, 1940. Chapters 7 and 8 describe the post-World War I environment in which the gold standard operated, involving a redistribution of economic and financial power from London to New York, and Chapter 13 analyzes predepression efforts to cooperate once the gold standard was re-established.

Halm, George N. *International Monetary Cooperation.* Chapel Hill: University of North Carolina Press, 1945. A brief discussion of the conditions of the interwar period which led to the creation of the International Monetary Fund and of the alternative plans for international financial organization.

Metzler, Lloyd. "Exchange Rates and the International Monetary Fund," *International Monetary Policies.* Washington: Board of Governors, Federal Reserve System, 1947, pp. 1–45. Contrasts the determination of exchange rates after the two World Wars and includes criticisms of the purchasing-power-parity theory.

Mikesell, Raymond F. *United States Economic Policy and International Relations.* New York: McGraw-Hill, 1952. Chapters 5 and 9–10 concern financial cooperation between the two world wars and in the postwar period, respectively.

Williams, John H. *Postwar Monetary Plans.* New York: Knopf, 1947. Parts I and II include essays on various plans for international financial cooperation after World War II.

15 Direct Controls: Unilateral

If a nation is losing international reserves and the government prefers not to devalue the currency or deflate internal prices and economic activity through monetary and fiscal policies, it must regulate its international transactions directly. The demand for foreign exchange may be restricted and its supply rationed. Direct controls, devaluation, and deflationary monetary and fiscal policies all involve some government action. The difference between direct controls and the other techniques lies in the kind of government intervention in private decisions. Under direct controls, an international trader must consider whether a proposed international transaction is profitable and whether or not the government will permit it. Under devaluation or deflation, he need only consider its profitability.

There are several different means of directly controlling trade and payments. Each has some advantages over the others and each has distinct advantages and disadvantages compared with devaluation and deflation.

A. NATURE OF DIRECT CONTROLS

Perhaps the most extreme form of intervention is state trading. The government displaces private enterprise in exporting and importing. Government agencies buy the produce of private domestic businessmen, paying them local currency and selling the goods abroad for foreign exchange. Similarly, government agencies buy goods from foreigners for resale domestically. Though not its chief purpose in every instance, state trading does provide an effective means of controlling foreign-exchange expenditures. In 1949 approximately one-half of Britain's imports were obtained through government agencies; in the exchange crisis of that year, government purchases from abroad were cut back in order to conserve exchange.

Without actually exporting and importing, the governments may determine the volume of trade in a particular product by requiring that a certain percentage of the output of a product be exported. Britain, during

294

part of the postwar period, prohibited domestic sales of decorated pottery and required that 80 per cent of the autos produced be exported. In some instances, these requirements are enforced by direct regulation of the exportable products. In others, an inducement to export is provided by allocating raw materials to an industry or a firm according to its export performance.

Among other controls that have been used is the allocation of manpower to export and import-competing industries, though this has proved politically difficult. The relative wage rates of different occupations may be set by the government in order to attract labor to essential industries, and the government may attempt to control the general level of wage rates in order to restrain increases in the cost of production which would make exports more difficult to sell abroad and in order to restrain total labor income so as to restrict domestic expenditure.

The most important of the various direct controls are those over receipts and expenditures of foreign exchange by private individuals and firms. Recipients of foreign exchange are required to sell it to the government or its authorized agents, often commercial banks. The government determines the amount of foreign exchange that may be spent and directs its uses through either quantitative or cost restrictions. Quantitative restrictions place numerical limits on the amounts which may be spent or bought abroad; cost restrictions have the same effects through charging different prices for foreign exchange used for different transactions.

QUANTITATIVE RESTRICTIONS

When the government substitutes its judgment for that of a free market in determining the volume and composition of international payments, it must arrive at answers to questions which the free market settles automatically. What goods and services shall be imported? How much shall be spent on each type? For what purposes shall capital be exported? How much capital? Who shall be permitted to perform these transactions? From what countries shall goods and services be imported? To what countries shall capital be permitted to flow?

In some nations the answers to these questions begin with the preparation of a foreign-exchange budget, which is drawn up every six or twelve months. Estimates of future foreign-exchange receipts are made, and the distribution of that exchange among alternative uses is determined by agencies of the government, often in consultation with interested private groups or individuals. Specific allocations may be made to the various types of goods imported, to interest and dividend payments, shipping fees, royalty payments, investment abroad, repayment of debts to foreigners, gifts, and so on. On the other hand, some nations merely allocate the exchange on an *ad hoc* basis. All allocation systems tend to give the highest priority to those expenditures considered most essential.

To insure that foreign exchange is used for the precise purposes selected by the government, individual transactions must be controlled. Controls on foreign-exchange expenditures take the form of import quotas, import licenses, and/or exchange licenses. A quota sets a limit to the total amount (volume or value) of a product which may be imported. An import license gives the holder permission to import a given volume or value of a product. An exchange license gives permission to buy a certain amount of foreign exchange from an authorized bank. Very often the grant of an import license carries with it the right to buy foreign exchange. Exchange licensing is broader in scope than import licensing because invisible payments as well as merchandise imports are controlled. But exchange licensing may not prevent a serious balance-of-payments deficit from arising if imports are not also licensed; importers may buy on credit, piling up foreign-exchange debts which cannot be paid.

A quota may be a global quota, not specifying the amounts of imports to come from individual countries, or it may be an allocated quota which sets the amount each nation may supply. Quota restrictions will not work satisfactorily unless licenses are used to divide total permitted imports among firms. In the absence of such licenses, firms rush to import before the quota is filled. Inequity may result. The biggest firm usually has better international contacts and can complete import transactions more quickly than smaller firms, thus squeezing them out. Also, goods ordered while the quota is open may arrive at the dock after it is filled, causing losses. Thus heavy imports tend to occur in the early part of the period for which the quota applies, permitting no imports toward the end of the quota period. Because of such wide variations in the supply, the price of the imported product fluctuates unnecessarily.

These difficulties may be met by licensing individual importers to bring in certain amounts of a product in a given period. There are numerous criteria for determining how the licenses shall be distributed among importing firms. Frequently, the distribution of licenses is made on the basis of the relative imports of the firms in some previous period. If one company imported 50 per cent of the total imports of a product in the base period, it would receive 50 per cent of the quota for current imports. Those firms fortunate enough to be importing larger than normal amounts during the base period are favored by the base-period approach. The amount of the license sometimes depends upon the firm's capital, the price and quality of its previous imports into the country, the amount of taxes it has paid, the number of employees, and a host of other more or less arbitrary criteria. In some nations part of the quota may be set aside to allow the issuance of licenses to newly organized importing firms which otherwise would not be able to import at all. To reduce the ill will resulting from government allocation of licenses, the government may work with the trade association concerned with the particular product for which licenses are to be allocated. On occasion, the government may avoid ill will at home by giving licenses to foreign exporters rather than to local importers.

In place of planned distribution of import licenses, the authorities may grant them on a first-come, first-served basis; this technique may lead to severe complaints, depending on who gets there first. Another technique is for the government to grant licenses on an *ad hoc* basis; this involves a maximum degree of discretion for the authorities, which may lead to unfairness and to graft, depending upon the wisdom and the honesty of the bureaucrats.

Because the currencies of some nations are not readily available, their exports are treated differently under control systems from the exports of other nations. Some products may be imported under licenses which are given freely for imports from certain countries but not from others. Imports from certain countries may be permitted to enter without licenses.

COST RESTRICTIONS: MULTIPLE EXCHANGE RATES

Instead of rationing foreign exchange through quantitative restrictions, some governments have restrained the demand for foreign exchange, in total and for particular transactions, by setting various prices for foreign exchange. In place of a single exchange rate, a nation has several rates which apply to different types of payments according to their alleged essentiality. Latin American countries have made extensive use of this technique, as have some Middle Eastern nations. Paraguay, at the end of 1955, had fourteen different rates at which foreign exchange could be bought for making payments for goods and services. The most depreciated rate, 75 guaranies per dollar, applied to luxury imports; the lowest price, 21 guaranies per dollar, applied to certain government payments abroad.

This multiplicity of exchange rates extends to international receipts. Recipients of foreign exchange in Uruguay, at the end of 1955, could sell it at thirteen different rates of exchange, the particular rate being dictated by the type of transaction involved. The rates varied from 1.59 pesos per dollar to 3.64 pesos per dollar; the higher peso prices were paid for dollars arising out of transactions which the government wished or was obliged to encourage.

The number of exchange rates in a multiple rate system is sometimes increased by mixing rates. Exporters, for example, may be required to sell part of their exchange at one official rate and the remainder at another, sometimes a fluctuating one. The same may apply for purchases of exchange for payments abroad. The percentages which are sold or bought at each rate vary among commodities and by types of transactions so that fine discrimination among various receipts and payments is possible even though the government may have established only a very few official rates.

Multiple rates and quantitative restrictions

A multiple exchange-rate system must be supported by import licenses. Without some mechanism to channel payments and receipts to the appropriate rate of exchange selected by the government, private individuals and firms would naturally purchase foreign exchange at the lowest price (most appreciated rate) while they would sell foreign exchange at the highest price (most depreciated rate). Hence exporters are obliged, with some exceptions, to surrender foreign exchange to the government or its authorized agents, and importers and other persons intending to make payments abroad must obtain licenses for their transactions to insure that the appropriate rate is applied. As long as the government *freely* issues licenses for transactions at the appropriate rates, the rates, not the licenses, restrict the demand for foreign exchange. Such rates are called pure cost restrictions.

Sometimes under a multiple rate system, the entire burden of import restriction is placed on the quantitative restrictions, and the multiple rates merely ease their administration. For example, a high price for exchange used to import luxuries reduces the demand for them and therefore reduces the number of times that the authorities must say "No" to requests for exchange licenses to buy luxuries. Where the control system uses both cost and quantitative restrictions, it is called a composite system.

Fluctuating multiple rates

Several techniques are available to obtain in a multiple rate system some of the advantages of a fluctuating exchange rate. Holders of exchange arising from certain types of transactions may not be obligated to surrender it to the government; if the government permits others to buy this exchange for certain uses, a type of "free market" is created. Unless the government enters into the purchase or sale of exchange in this market to stabilize its value, the rate fluctuates with changes in private demand and supply. This rate is not really a *free* rate because the exchange traded in the market arises from, and is used for, only specified transactions. Receipts and payments for invisible items are frequently assigned to this fluctuating market because the government finds it difficult to enforce surrender requirements for nonmerchandise foreign-exchange receipts since they do not cross customs. The fluctuating rate is then little more than a legalized black-market rate; in some Latin American countries the black-market rate was simply recognized by the government and thereby became the so-called free market rate.

Even though the government does require the surrender of all exchange, a fluctuating rate may be created through the exchange-certificate system. Recipients of exchange who surrender it to the government receive exchange certificates in return. These certificates may be sold by them at free market prices to others who may obtain the equivalent foreign exchange from the government for use for specified purposes. A variant is for the government to take surrendered exchange at fixed rates and to auction all or a part of it to buyers at prices determined by their bids.

B. DIRECT CONTROLS VERSUS DEVALUATION AND DEFLATION

Direct controls to adjust the balance of payments are considered desirable when neither devaluation nor deflation would be successful or when other goals besides the removal of balance-of-payments difficulties are sought.

CAPITAL FLIGHTS

The major purpose for the imposition of direct controls on international payments in the early 1930's was to prevent flights of capital. In the last half of 1931, after the international financial crises of that year described in Chapter 10, twelve nations imposed controls to stem capital withdrawals. Deflation or devaluation is of questionable help in meeting them. It takes time for the economy to respond to the incentives and penalties imposed by devaluation or deflation; merchandise exports and imports do not change rapidly enough to prevent the loss of reserves caused by a flight of capital. Furthermore, if the flight is transitory, devaluation or deflation would induce unnecessary shifts of resources. To the extent that capital movements are induced by political unrest or by unwarranted fears of devaluation, they are economically useless, and the case for their control is strong.

Direct control of capital flows

Among the various types of quantitative restrictions, exchange licensing is a means of stopping capital movements. Under multiple exchange-rate systems, rather than prohibit undesirable capital transactions, governments may channel them through a free market for exchange. As long as the government makes no attempt to stabilize the free rate by purchases and sales of its own holdings of exchange, it need not suffer a loss of its reserves because of capital export. Furthermore, most other payments are made at fixed official rates so that trade is not greatly affected by exchange-rate fluctuations in the free market.

However, as one expert put it, "Many persons otherwise law-abiding feel no moral compunction about breaking or evading currency laws or cooperating with others who do so."[1] Direct controls on international

---

[1] Raymond Mikesell, *Foreign Exchange in the Postwar World* (New York: Twentieth Century Fund, 1954), p. 190. The extent of the postwar flight of capital is unknown. However, one estimate puts the flight from Western Europe until 1953 at an amount in excess of the total U.S. government aid to Europe during the same period (Michael Hoffman, *New York Times,* July 25, 1953).

payments do not provide absolute protection against unwanted capital movements.

Capital movements under direct controls

The mechanics of capital movements under direct controls are as follows. The leads and lags in payments and receipts which were discussed in conjunction with the adjustable-peg system of exchange rates are short-term capital movements of the speculative variety. Though speculative purchases or sales of foreign exchange may be prohibited, if devaluation is expected exporters will not cash their drafts so rapidly and importers will speed up their payments. As the discussion of international payments techniques in Chapter 9 suggested, much international trade is financed with short-term commercial credit. Under exchange-control laws, exporters are usually required to surrender the proceeds of their exports to the government within three to six months. If the government required exporters to surrender their exchange immediately after exportation, the credit aspect of international trade would be adversely affected. The time which must be provided for surrendering exchange affords the exporter an opportunity to adjust his surrender date with regard to his expectations of exchange-rate adjustments. Such actions do not involve violations of exchange-control laws, but they are severely disruptive of international reserve positions.

Improper invoicing of merchandise transactions provides a means of exporting capital. An importer, with the aid of someone abroad (often the foreign exporter of the imported goods), presents to his government a padded invoice showing how much exchange he claims he needs to make payment. If the authorities are fooled, the importer receives more exchange than is actually necessary to make payment for the imported goods, and the surplus is deposited in some foreign bank account, usually under a pseudonym to protect the importer from detection by the authorities. Exporters export capital by underinvoicing their merchandise exports, so that less foreign exchange need be surrendered to the authorities than is actually received by the exporter. To control these evasions, customs authorities check the invoice, export license, or import license against the goods to determine if the stated value differs from prices in world markets; therefore evasions through trade in standardized commodities having organized world markets are more easily detected than through other products.

Another technique of exporting capital is to smuggle domestic bank notes out of the country to be sold at a discount. In January, 1952, sterling notes could be bought for $2.37 while the official exchange rate was $2.80. The demand for such notes comes in part from tourists expecting to travel in the country from which the notes have been smuggled. To prevent a loss of foreign-exchange earnings resulting from the failure of tourists to buy local currency through official channels with their own currency, restrictions are imposed on the quantity of a nation's own bank notes which may be imported. Sometimes bank notes are remitted to the issuing country through the mails as gifts; to detect such inflows, censorship of the mails is required. The British are supposed to have an electronic spotting device which catches a large proportion of the mailed notes, which are then confiscated.

Local black markets provide a similar means of obtaining illegal exchange. Tourists, servicemen, and others import their own country's bank notes, travelers' checks, or write personal bank checks for sale to local citizens, who thereby gain claim to foreign currency. The government does not obtain the exchange, and its international reserves suffer accordingly.

An alternative form of capital flight is the purchase of gold. In many countries, private international gold transactions are outlawed, but because gold is the supreme hedge against inflation or currency depreciation, restrictions on the import of gold are extensively evaded in order to obtain it for private hoarding. Black markets in which premium prices are paid for gold have cropped out in many countries, and these premium markets have attracted gold from gold-producing countries including the Soviet Union. Dealers in illegal gold often must pay dollars for it. To obtain these dollars, the dealers must evade exchange regulations or must buy dollars which have evaded the regulations, since the government will not knowingly provide dollars for this purpose. Therefore the importing nation's reserves suffer through a loss of dollars to pay for the gold, which in turn goes into private hoards rather than into the international reserves of the country.

INCONVERTIBLE CURRENCIES

Another circumstance in which devaluation and deflation may be ineffective for a particular nation is when the currencies in which it trades are inconvertible.

Suppose that a nation is in over-all balance-of-payments equilibrium, and that this equilibrium is compounded of a surplus of sterling matched by a deficit of dollars. Normally, the nation would exchange her excess sterling with Britain for dollars with which to pay the dollar deficit. But suppose that Britain has a severe dollar deficit of her own. In that event, Britain may not freely convert sterling into dollars on behalf of foreigners, because she needs the dollars herself. Unless some action is taken, the nation will simply accumulate unwanted sterling while paying out gold and dollar reserves to cover its dollar deficit.

Devaluation or deflation would remove the dollar deficit by expanding exports and contracting imports with the United States. But it would also increase the sterling surplus, i.e., the accumulation of unwanted foreign currency.

One way out of this dilemma is for the nation to devalue its currency with respect to the dollar and appreciate its currency with respect to the pound, for that would tend to remove the dollar deficit while inducing greater imports from and fewer exports to Britain. If this is done, the cross rate is broken. In 1949, Peru found herself in this situation and broke the cross rate as follows. The official exchange rate between the dollar and the pound was $4.03. In Peru, the authorities allowed sterling to sell in a free market for approximately 56 sols while the dollar was quoted in the free market at about 18 sols; thus, in terms of sols, the pound was worth only about $3.00, i.e., the pound had a lower price in terms of sols than the dollar as compared to the official rate of exchange between the United States and Britain. Other nations, such as France, Italy, Greece, and Lebanon have done much the same in the postwar period.[2]

The major objection to broken cross rates is that they may lead to a theft of dollars. The most important examples of this are found in the use of "cheap sterling" during the postwar period. This type of sterling is not freely convertible into dollars. Under British regulations, Americans are supposed to buy sterling with dollars at the official exchange rate, but they may obtain it more cheaply as follows. An American foreign-exchange dealer arranges for an agent abroad, frequently in Holland, to acquire inconvertible sterling; this sterling is probably earned through exports from the agent's country to Britain. An American wool importer "buys"[3] the sterling from the foreign-exchange dealer, and the dealer deposits dollars in the New York account of his agent abroad. The number of dollars paid for the inconvertible sterling tends to be less than the official exchange rate between the dollar and the pound. For example, inconvertible sterling could be bought for about $2.40 in January, 1952, when the official rate was $2.80 per pound. The foreign agent is willing to accept fewer dollars for the sterling than the official rate because he cannot convert it, under British regulations, into dollars. And the foreign agent is pleased to get the dollars because he can sell them in his own country's black market or use them to buy goods from the United States which otherwise cannot be obtained in sufficient quantities because of his own country's import controls. The foreign agent orders wool from Australia and pays, legally, the inconvertible sterling to the Australian exporter. When the wool arrives at the port of the foreign agent's country, it is transshipped to the United States for the American importer. Commodity arbitrage replaces the exchange arbitrage

---

[2] Another way of discriminating among currencies was used by Argentina. On the occasion of the British devaluation of 1949, Argentina did not change the classifications among her multiple rates of those commodities which she predominately exported to Britain. Hence, because of the depreciation of the pound, the Argentine peso was appreciated with respect to those commodities. At the same time, Argentina depreciated the rates for those commodities predominately exported to the United States or moved the commodities to more depreciated rates. The cross rate was maintained equal to the official rate between the dollar and the pound for each commodity, but the distribution of Argentina's commodity exports was disparate enough to produce the same discrimination as provided by broken cross rates.

[3] Americans are not allowed to own, according to British regulations, this inconvertible sterling, so the foreign agent holds the sterling on behalf of the American.

which would occur in the absence of government control because the cross rate is broken. (The wool is first sent to the agent's country in order to maintain legal appearances; sometimes the goods may be shipped directly to the United States, but this usually involves falsification of shipping documents, for otherwise the Australian authorities would not approve the transaction.) The results are these: the American importer profits by paying fewer dollars for the pounds to finance the transaction; the country of the agent has dollars it otherwise would not have; Australia loses dollars it otherwise might have obtained by shipping the wool directly to the United States. One estimate suggests that 25 per cent of American private imports of wool, rubber, jute, cocoa, tin, and other products from the sterling area (a grouping of countries which use sterling for their international reserves) have been financed in this way at times during the postwar period.

The same loss of dollars results from the Peruvian cross-rate situation if Americans buy sols for dollars, use the sols to buy sterling, and use the sterling to buy goods from Britain which could have been sold directly to the United States instead of being transshiped through Peru. The only difference between this and the above cheap-sterling deal is that the Peruvian rate situation resulted from overt Peruvian government policy, whereas the exchange rate for the cheap sterling did not. However, when such cheap-sterling transactions do occur, it frequently is with the tacit approval of the authorities in the agent's country. In any case, the commodity arbitrage resulting from broken cross rates or cheap sterling must be included among the devices for evading exchange control regulations.

The fundamental reason for the commodity arbitrage and the theft of dollars does not lie in policies of the country breaking the cross rate or in the country of the agent who facilitates the cheap-sterling deal. Rather, the inconvertibility of the pound into the dollar makes such transactions profitable, and this inconvertibility could be removed if England were to devalue or deflate so as to earn more dollars.

ELASTICITIES

If the foreign demand for an exportable product is inelastic, devaluation or deflation actually hinders balance-of-payments adjustment with respect to that product. That is, the lower price charged foreigners as a result of devaluation or deflation brings smaller rather than larger foreign-exchange earnings. This would not itself render devaluation or deflation ineffective if foreign-exchange expenditures on imports fell even more. But few nations will devalue or deflate if it will bring them less foreign exchange, since that would oblige them to forego even more imports, which they consider valuable.

Quantitative restrictions avoid such a loss of foreign exchange by affecting only the expenditure side of the balance of payments. Multiple exchange rates avoid it through devaluation only with respect to those commodities for which the foreign demand is elastic, leaving unchanged or appreciating the currency on those items for which the foreign demand is inelastic.

Argentina appears to have used her multiple rate system in a manner designed to allow for elasticity considerations. During the round of devaluations in 1949, she devalued the peso by the same percentage as most other countries did on those products in which she competed with other devaluing nations for dollar sales (e.g., wool, hides, some dairy products, quebracho extract). Competition made the demand for these Argentine products elastic. Argentina did not, however, devalue the peso with respect to products for which the foreign demand was inelastic. Germany faced a hard-pressed balance of payments in the middle 1930's caused by rising employment which brought greater import demand and by lower exports attributable to foreign import controls and depressed economic conditions abroad; she instituted a complex multiple rate system under which she subsidized the exports of products facing elastic demand.

Inelasticity renders devaluation ineffective in other respects. If export supplies are perfectly inelastic, devaluation will not increase supplies for export. And if the demand for imports is perfectly inelastic, devaluation will not reduce the quantity of imports, even though their prices have risen in terms of the local currency of the devaluing country. (The demand for foreign exchange to pay debt-service charges and to repay debts denoted in foreign currency is perfectly inelastic because a fixed amount of foreign currency must be paid no matter what the exchange rate.)

Probably the highest incidence of inelasticity of demand and supply is found among primary products. The demand for foodstuffs is closely related to physiological requirements. The demand for raw materials is derived from the demand for the products which use them; the demand for raw materials is inelastic if the raw-material component constitutes a small proportion of the total cost of production of the final product. When it is only a small proportion any change in the price of a raw material causes a very small change in the price of the final product—insufficient to alter significantly the demand for the final product and therefore the demand for raw materials which go into it.

On the supply side also, inelasticity often rules for primary products, at least in the short run. The lengthy growing period for some agricultural products reduces the responsiveness of supply to upward price movements. A cacao tree does not bear until about five years after planting; approximately the same holds true for coffee. Also, supply may not fall with a decline in price because a firm minimizes its losses by continuing production for short periods as long as a *part* of the fixed costs and all of the variable costs are covered by the price obtained in the market place. For some agricultural products and for some minerals, the fixed costs of production are so great a part of the total cost that a decline in price has little impact on output in the short-run period.

If these conditions held for primary products in general, it might be argued that the underdeveloped nations would be justified in using direct controls in preference to devaluation or deflation. But there are enough exceptions to the foregoing to indicate that each nation's policies must be considered separately. The demand for beef (important in the exports of Argentina, Uruguay, and Brazil) is quite elastic because of the extensive number of substitutes such as fish, eggs, and other types of meat available. The fact that wool constitutes a significant proportion of the total cost of the final product in which it is used makes the demand for wool more elastic than the demand for cotton. The existence of substitutes for linseed oil such as tung or palm oil makes the demand for linseed oil fairly elastic. On the supply side, the production of corn, wheat, and wool, for example, can be increased significantly in twelve to twenty-four months, while mineral production can be increased somewhat by drawing on additional workers to labor in less efficient mines.

For all nations the short-run import demand and export supply may be inelastic because it takes time to adjust consumption and production patterns to price changes. But in the long run, the elasticity of demand *for imports* of a product is greater than the elasticity of demand for the product because of alternative sources of supply. A decline in the price of an imported product as a result of foreign devaluation or deflation not only increases the volume of imports by expanding consumption, but it also knocks out domestic production of substitutes so that imports increase further. In addition, within the devaluing or deflating country, the rise in the local currency price of the exported products not only increases production but also reduces domestic consumption of the exported products, thereby making even more goods available for export. The existence of alternative sources of supply also tends to increase the elasticity of demand for the export products of any particular nation. An exporting nation may, through devaluation or deflation, take from its competitors some of their markets, a possibility which tends to make the demand for its products elastic; however, this may be of little advantage if the competitors retaliate by similarly depreciating or deflating.

The devaluations of 1949 would have provided a basis for careful analysis of the impact of devaluation on the balance of payments had not the Korean War nine months later so drastically changed all demand and supply conditions. Nonetheless, prior to Korea, one estimate indicates that the devaluations caused a 5 per cent increase in the value of certain European countries' exports to the United States and a 10 per cent increase in the dollar value of their exports to other Western Hemisphere markets.[4] A study of manufactured exports found that, compared with those countries that devalued little or not at all, nations which devalued significantly

---

[4] J. J. Polak, "Contribution of the September 1949 Devaluations to the Solution of Europe's Dollar Problem," *International Monetary Fund Staff Papers*, II (September, 1951), 1–32.

increased their shares of the world market between 10 and 15 percentage points.[5]

Because demand elasticities may be low in the short run, a fall of imports and a rise in exports through devaluation or deflation may not occur quickly enough to stop a loss of reserves within the available time. Furthermore, the difficulties of knowing in advance the elasticities of demand and supply argue for the use of quantitative restrictions instead of devaluation or deflation when precise, immediate results are required. When a nation's international reserves are low, it must reduce its foreign expenditures by a specific amount within a very short time. Quantitative restrictions afford a means of reducing such spending by specific amounts, whereas devaluation and deflation do not, because, with the elasticities imperfectly known, the precise degree of devaluation or deflation which is required to rectify the balance of payments is difficult to determine. Quantitative restrictions are not entirely satisfactory substitutes, however, because their impact on foreign-exchange payments may not be felt for several months. Imports ordered prior to the tightening of such restrictions continue to arrive after the government takes action, while imports which have already arrived must still be paid for if bought on credit.

TERMS OF TRADE

The terms of trade of those nations which are important buyers and sellers of products in the international economy vary with the volumes of their trade. Brazil, for example, may well consider the effects of various coffee-export volumes on her terms of trade; contrarily, Venezuela, which exports an infinitesimal portion of the world's supply of coffee, cannot expect to affect significantly the world's price of coffee by varying her coffee exports. A number of underdeveloped nations are important producers of primary products and are vitally affected by changes in the terms of trade. The dependence of Britain's standard of living on imported goods makes her especially vulnerable to adverse movements in the terms of trade, some of which occur because of changes in the volume of her trade.

Devaluation and deflation worsen the terms of trade as compared with direct controls. Quantitative restrictions stop a loss of reserves by reducing imports. Devaluation and deflation expand exports as well as reduce imports. To the extent that exports increase through devaluation or deflation, imports need not fall as much as they would under quantitative restrictions to close a given balance-of-payments deficit. Hence devaluation or deflation causes greater exports and *permits* greater imports than would be the case under quantitative controls. If the devaluing or deflating nation is a significant seller in world markets of the goods which it exports, the

---

[5] Economic Commission for Europe, *Economic Survey of Europe in 1950* (Geneva: United Nations, 1951), p. 106.

extra supply of its export products on world markets will depress the prices, measured in foreign currency, which foreigners pay for them. And if a nation is also a significant buyer in world markets of the products it imports, the extra demand for imports under devaluation or deflation, compared with the demand under direct controls, will keep the foreign currency prices paid for imported products higher than they would be under quantitative controls. Because export prices are lower and import prices are higher under devaluation or deflation than under direct controls, each physical unit of exports buys fewer physical units of imports, i.e., the terms of trade are less favorable.[6]

As argued in Chapter 3, at some point it ceases to be profitable for a nation to expand its trade, because exports are sold at lower and lower prices while imports are bought at higher and higher prices. But a worsening of the terms of trade does not itself indicate that an expansion of trade is undesirable. This depends upon what use might be made of the resources put into the production of those goods which are exported to pay for imports. Trade should be restricted only if the domestic resources required to produce substitutes for imports are fewer than those required to produce the exports with which to pay for the imports. Currently it appears that, given the estimated costs of producing agricultural goods and export products in Britain and the probable degree to which her terms of trade would worsen as her trade expands, it would be wise for Britain to restrict her agricultural imports somewhat; she could use the resources freed from the production of goods which must be exported to pay for agricultural imports to produce agricultural products more cheaply at home. This is a startling conclusion when it is remembered that Britain's high real income long rested upon extreme specialization and the exchange of manufactures for foodstuffs and raw materials.

DISTRIBUTION OF THE BURDEN OF ADJUSTMENT

Devaluation and deflation do not permit the government to select who shall bear the burden of balance-of-payments adjustment. Devaluation raises the prices of all imports without regard to their essentiality or to the income status of their consumers. Also, the foreign currency prices of those exports having relatively inelastic export supplies do not fall much, because little increase in output occurs upon devaluation; hence the local currency prices of such exports rise considerably, greatly enhancing the earnings of resources producing such exports without these resources contributing much to the improvement of the balance of payments by increasing

---

[6] The terms of trade may improve upon devaluation or deflation, depending upon supply and demand elasticities, but this does not contradict the above statement because direct controls on imports would improve the terms even more. For a full discussion of the effect of devaluation on the terms of trade see James Meade, *The Balance of Payments* (London: Oxford, 1951), Chapter 18; for a qualification to this footnote, also see pp. 310–311.

exports, i.e., windfall profits accrue to owners of export-producing firms. Deflation leads to unemployment, which is generally objectionable and which hits the various sectors of the economy unevenly.

Direct controls are used to avoid these problems. Import licenses are usually given relatively freely for those commodities which the government considers essential to the health and welfare of the nation. Imports of luxuries, some of which are consumed by the well-to-do, are usually restricted severely. Multiple exchange-rate systems give the most appreciated import rate of exchange to essential items, while luxury imports are subjected to depreciated rates. Windfall profits which would accrue under devaluation to exporters of goods in inelastic supply may be avoided by depreciating the currency only with respect to those products which have sufficiently elastic export supplies. In a number of Latin American countries the less important exports, which are struggling to obtain or maintain markets abroad, are given especially favorable export rates while the traditional exports which are already entrenched in foreign markets are subjected to less favorable rates.

Measures to gain equity and to balance payments sometimes support each other. The restraint of the incomes of some exporters reduces the likelihood of inflation which would tend to frustrate an improvement in the balance of payments. Similarly, favorable treatment of essential imports reduces the chance of a wage-price spiral resulting from a rise of prices of products important to the workers' real income.

The political difficulty of undertaking a general devaluation (see p. 259) may be eased through use of multiple exchange rates. Given any set of multiple rates, the average exchange rate for all imports and exports may be depreciated by reclassifying commodities to more depreciated rates. Instead of exchange rates changing, the commodity classification shifts, and the fact of devaluation is less apparent to the population. To the extent that this is true, necessary exchange-rate adjustments are made more quickly and a balance-of-payments deficit is less likely to become cumulative than under a single exchange rate.

Several conflicts develop in the use of direct controls. Just as windfall profits may accrue to exporters under devaluation, so may they accrue to others under quantitative restrictions. The enforced restriction of the supply of imports raises their prices in the importing country's home market without simultaneously raising the price paid to foreign suppliers by importing firms. The greater margin between the importers' buying and selling prices leads to "quota profits" for the import firms fortunate enough to obtain import licenses.[7] Internal price control can restrict these profits, but without an effective rationing system the advantage then goes to the

---

[7] A diagrammatic exposition of the economics of quota profits is provided by Paul T. Ellsworth, *The International Economy* (New York: Macmillan, 1950), pp. 647–651.

lucky consumer who obtains some of the restricted imports. Multiple exchange rates can be used to avoid quota profits by imposing very depreciated import rates on those products whose importation is severely restricted by quantitative controls. In such an instance, the importing firm must pay a higher price for its purchases abroad. The desirability of using multiple rates or some similar device to tax away the quota profits is increased by the possibility that, if foreign suppliers of an imported product are not competitive, they may raise the price charged importers to the level prevailing within the restricting nation, thereby obtaining the quota profits for themselves. In this event, the restricting nation undergoes a worsening of its terms of trade.

The existence of extremely favorable import exchange rates designed to keep the cost of essential imports low is often an irresistible attraction to the authorities classifying commodities among the various import rates. In Colombia, about 90 per cent of the imports in 1950 came in at the most appreciated rate, with the result that the multiple exchange-rate system did little to ease Colombia's balance-of-payments problem on the import side. The fact that government imports are often transacted at the most favorable rate similarly has adverse effects on the balance of payments. One Latin American government outfitted its army with imported shoes because it was so cheap to import them at the government import rate even though domestic production capacity was available.

The unfavorable export rates imposed on some sales of exchange also have had adverse balance-of-payments consequences. In Chile, the foreign-owned copper companies used to exchange dollars for pesos to be used to meet their local expenses at a rate of 19.37 pesos per dollar, while other dollars exchanged at 110 pesos or more. One of the effects was that the copper companies imported explosives for their mining operations rather than purchase the Chilean-produced explosives which were relatively expensive to the copper companies because of the unfavorable exchange rate.

Although the windfall profits that might accrue to exporters through devaluation do not induce them to expand production significantly out of existing capacity, unfavorable export rates may restrain an expansion of capacity. The profit incentive for investment is reduced and earnings which could be invested in the industry are removed; by restraining an expansion of investment, the long-run expansion of these exports is retarded.

An important over-all influence of direct controls is to dull incentives. A life with few luxuries gives little encouragement to people who wish to enjoy the fruits of their labors or their risk-bearing. The successful harnessing of individual efforts and initiative requires inequality of rewards; direct controls, to the extent that they do have a bias toward the essentials of life, reduce the real value of rewards paid to the most successful, the most energetic, or the most lucky. An Englishman, opposed to his government's internal controls, wryly commented that the industrial success of Britain was due in part to enterprise, foresight, and self-reliance:

> There was no waiting for a Government to initiate action. Shakespeare was not frustrated by a Paper Controller; Captain Cook was not thwarted by an overseas travel permit; and Henry VIII certainly wasn't worried about his week-end ration. Would Raleigh, do you think, have thrown his cloak into the puddle if he had expended his clothing coupons?[8]

NATIONAL PLANNING

Considering the power which direct controls give to the government over the composition and extent of a nation's imports and exports, the link between controls on the internal economy and controls on international trade is clear. External events must not be allowed to interfere with internal plans. Should the government wish to raise the prices (and incomes) received by a specific group by restricting production or supply, the effort would go for nought if imports could freely compete with the restricted domestic production. Domestic price controls and rationing would be thwarted by imports at higher world prices. Any controlled allocation of domestic resources requires the control of imports supplementing them. Thus trade controls to assist internal planning are required, because plans for specific commodities must not be upset by imports of the same commodities.

Since socialism holds as a prime goal the maintenance of high levels of employment, measures to achieve them may unbalance international payments. If the planners are unwilling to devalue the currency (some of the staunchest opponents of the British devaluation in 1949 were socialists), only controls can prevent the loss of reserves. Furthermore, a member of the New Zealand treasury has contended that controls are needed to obtain full employment:

> It is commonplace that the maintenance of a level of employment so high that hardly anyone is ever out of work, requires that there should always be a number of unfilled vacancies. . . . The only way to insure that . . . people [who lose their jobs] will be able to find a job immediately is to have excessive demand for labour in a wide variety of trades, all over the country.
> There can be an excessive demand for labour only if there is an excessive demand for the product of labour. . . .
> . . . . Full employment requires that there be unsatisfied demand for local production. This unsatisfied demand will tend to turn, at least in part to imports. If it is wholly satisfied by expenditures on imported goods, then there remain no excess demand to maintain full employment internally. It therefore seems that Governments must insure that some part at least of the demand

---

[8] Leslie Gamage, "The Export Drive," *The Industrial Future of Great Britain* (London: Europa Publications, 1948), p. 128.

for imports is kept unsatisfied and so turned back to maintain excessive demand for local products.

The practical consequence is that if a Government wants to maintain full employment it must continually apply import controls. . . .[9]

The author goes on to point out that his statement is not that an economy with full employment must inevitably use controls on imports because it is inevitably faced with a loss of reserves. He argues, rather, that import controls are a necessary condition of full employment. But this is not valid. The excess demand which the quoted author is afraid will escape to the rest of the world can be turned back to domestic goods through the depreciation of the exchange rate. In fact, the persistent inflation which will probably accompany the maintenance of excess demand will require frequent devaluations to avoid a loss of reserves. Furthermore, the excessive demand may always be created through domestic monetary and fiscal policies; no matter how much demand is lost to the rest of the world, a sufficiently spendthrift government can create more at home.

If a nation is willing to settle for something less than overfull employment (more job opportunities than workers), both high levels of employment *and general price-level stability* can be obtained through domestic monetary and fiscal policies without the use of controls on imports. Should balance-of-payments difficulties arise, exchange-rate adjustments can solve them in the long run if demands and supplies are elastic; if international reserves are sufficient at the start of difficulties, there is no need to worry about the short run. Of course, every time the exchange rate is changed, the flow of income and spending will also change as exports and imports adjust, and this will tend to upset internal stability. But this may be prevented by appropriate changes in internal monetary and fiscal policies. If every nation were to maintain full employment and price stability through internal policy and promptly adjust its exchange rate to shifts in its balance of payments, controls on international payments would be unnecessary, with the possible exception of controls to stop capital flights.[10] It is only when the objectives of planning include the control of specific commodities and the allocation of specific resources (detailed planning) that direct controls become a necessary adjunct to internal planning.

USE FOR REVENUE AND PROTECTION

So far, the discussion of direct controls has been couched largely in terms of their need or use in balance-of-payments problems. While their

---

[9] G. J. Schmitt, "Economic Stability and the Balance of Payments," *Economic Stability in New Zealand*, ed. by R. S. Parker (Wellington, N.Z.: New Zealand Institution for Public Administration, 1953), pp. 98–99.

[10] For further exposition of this view, see James Meade, *The Balance of Payments* (London: Oxford, 1951), chapter 11.

application has been most frequently aimed at balancing payments since World War II, certain additional objectives have been served through the use of direct controls. Furthermore, controls may be retained for these purposes after they are no longer necessary for balance-of-payments reasons.

Revenue

Multiple exchange rates may produce revenue for the government, whereas devaluation, deflation, and quantitative restrictions do not. The government need only set its exchange rates so that, on the average, it buys foreign currencies at a lower price in terms of its own currency than it sells them for. In particular, the unfavorable rates which have been applied to purchases of local currency by foreign-owned companies, such as those in Chile and Venezuela, are largely tax devices. Virtually all the nations using multiple rates do obtain revenue from them. Before World War II, Paraguay got as much as 40 per cent of her federal revenue from a multiple rate system, though a frequent current figure for most nations is between 5 and 15 per cent.

Because the cost of collecting internal taxes is great in underdeveloped countries, partly because of evasion, the most efficient tax is one that is collected at the border. Also, internal taxes in such nations, especially those on the well-to-do, are politically difficult to impose, and the export interests oppose export taxes. One solution is, as internal inflation occurs, to devalue the currency with respect to imports (especially those consumed by the rich) and some of the minor exports, while devaluing the rate on major exports little or not at all. The internal inflation and the unfavorable export rate combine to cut the profits of the producers in the major export industry; some of the burden of the revenue from the multiple rate system is borne by them, while import consumers, who must pay higher prices for foreign exchange, also bear part of it.

Protection

Protection of particular domestic interests from import competition is not possible through deflation or devaluation. But by providing few licenses for the importation of a product or by imposing a very depreciated import rate in a multiple rate system, particular domestic producers can be protected. In fact, quantitative restrictions provide better protection than a tariff or multiple rates because the quantity, or at least the value, of imports is restricted to a specific amount, whereas this is not so under tariffs because any foreign producer can jump a tariff wall if he lowers his costs of production enough. France and some other countries, in the early 1930's, introduced quotas as a temporary expedient to protect domestic agricultural producers from the effects of radically falling agricultural prices; tariffs would have soon been hurdled as foreign prices and costs fell. Later France used her quotas to obtain expanded foreign markets for her goods; those nations which agreed to permit more French goods into their markets received a greater quota than they otherwise would have. During part of the 1930's France also used her quotas for balance-of-payments reasons.

Multiple rates provide a means of benefiting particular exports in the same way so that they may be used to protect certain domestic interests. Argentina provides an example of a nation that has stimulated its economic development through differential export rates. After the British devaluation of 1949, Argentina reclassified a number of her commodities and changed several exchange rates. The resulting commodity classifications showed that "worked-up" products received more favorable export rates than did their raw-material components. Thus, quebracho logs received a less favorable rate for export than quebracho extract; tobacco received a less favorable rate than cigarettes, etc.

C. THE GENERAL CASE AGAINST DIRECT CONTROLS

The case against direct controls is the same as the case against tariffs; they misallocate *world* resources, thereby reducing *world* income and output. Direct controls, like any restriction on trade, break the equality of relative prices among countries necessary to maximize *world* output and necessary to insure that no consumer can be made better off without some other consumer being made worse off. Within the nation imposing controls on imports, prices of commodities of the imported type are higher relative to the prices of exportable goods than they are in other countries. And where commodities are differently treated according to "essentiality," the prices of luxuries are higher relative to essentials in the importing country than they are in other countries.

The reduction of world income and output under direct controls is accompanied by a reduction in world trade as compared to other measures of adjustment. Direct controls on imports close a deficit in the balance of payments by reducing imports by the amount of the deficit. Devaluation and deflation do not restrict imports as much, because exports rise to cover part of the deficit. Direct controls on imports therefore leave a smaller volume of world trade than other measures do and they permit a smaller degree of international specialization.

Additional costs are involved in the use of direct controls through the red tape accompanying them. The difficulties of dealing with governments are well known; they are especially great in those countries where the art of government is relatively underdeveloped. In a number of countries, high-level business executives are obliged to spend their time in the offices of import-licensing authorities, hoping their importance will help their requests for licenses. Needless to say, the time and effort of these executives would be better spent making production decisions.

The fact that the availability of exchange or import licenses may be quickly changed by the scratch of a bureaucrat's pen creates uncertainty for international traders. If the choice is between fixed exchange rates and direct controls on the one hand and fluctuating rates on the other hand, this uncertainty and the costs to traders of the red tape must be weighed against the risks and costs imposed on international traders through fluctuating rates.

Unfairness, dishonesty, and the subversion of democratic processes may also result from direct controls. The power to determine the exchange rate applicable to a particular transaction or to determine whether or not exchange shall be made available for a particular transaction has been used by governments to obtain the "cooperation" of private individuals and firms in political matters. Bureaucrats making such decisions are in the position to receive money under the table for making a decision favorable to particular persons. They are also in a position which permits them to punish the political opponents of the government in power. In a number of countries such behavior on the part of governments is an accepted part of the governmental process.

Even if graft and political power were not meant to be the results of direct controls, inequities would still arise. The ability of a firm to import is no longer dependent upon its efficiency or upon its performance in the market place, but on the decisions of the authorities.

SELECTED READINGS

Alexander, Sidney S. "Devaluation versus Import Restriction as an Instrument for Improving the Foreign Trade Balance," *International Monetary Fund Staff Papers*, I (April, 1951), 319–396. A theoretical analysis.

Bernstein, E. M. "Some Economic Aspects of Multiple Exchange Rates," *International Monetary Fund Staff Papers*, I (September, 1950), 224–237. A theoretical analysis of the effects of multiple-exchange rates.

Bloomfield, Arthur I. *Speculative and Flight Movements of Capital in Postwar International Finance*. Princeton, N.J.: Princeton University Press, 1954. Includes an explanation of techniques by which exchange controls are avoided and an analysis of possible solutions to the problem of hot money.

Chalmers, Henry. *World Trade Policies*. Berkeley: University of California Press, 1953. A collection of contemporary surveys over the period 1920–1953 with regard to all facets of trade and exchange policy including direct controls.

Ellis, Howard S. *Exchange Control in Central Europe*. Cambridge, Mass.: Harvard University Press, 1941. A discussion of the nature and purposes of exchange control in the 1930's with case studies of its use in Austria, Hungary, and Germany.

Gordon, Margaret S. *Barriers to World Trade.* New York: Macmillan, 1941. A comprehensive discussion of the reasons for, the nature of, and the effects of direct controls during the 1930's.

Haight, Frank A. *A History of French Commercial Policies.* New York: Macmillan, 1941. Book III considers French direct controls in the 1930's.

Heuser, H. *Control of International Trade.* New York: Blakiston, 1939. A discussion of the causes, methods, and results of direct controls, mostly of import and exchange licenses and quotas, during the 1930's.

International Monetary Fund. *Annual Report on Exchange Restrictions.* Washington. Each report provides a description of the exchange control systems of numerous countries.

Marris, R. L. "The Purchasing Power of British Exports," *Economica,* XIII (February, 1955), 13–28. A statistical estimate of the response of British terms of trade to various volumes of British trade. For a criticism by D. J. Morgan and F. W. Paish and a rejoinder, see the same journal, November, 1955, and February, 1956.

Mattera, Albert. "Foreign Exchange Budgets in Latin America," *International Monetary Fund Staff Papers,* IV (February, 1955), 288–309. The nature, functions, preparation, implementation, and problems of foreign-exchange budgets.

Mikesell, Raymond F. *Foreign Exchange in the Postwar World.* New York: Twentieth Century Fund, 1954. A comprehensive discussion and description.

Orcutt, Guy. "Measurement of Price Elasticities in International Trade," *Review of Economics and Statistics,* XXXII (May, 1950), 117–132. A criticism of statistical estimates of import demand elasticities which are relatively low. See also Fritz Machlup, "Elasticity Pessimism in International Trade," *Economia Internazionale,* III (February, 1950), 118–141.

Reddaway, W. B. "Governmental Intervention and Influence in Foreign Trade," *Banking and Foreign Trade.* London: Europa Publications, 1952, pp. 80–96. Especially valuable in its discussion of the difficulties involved in successful, efficient, and fair internal intervention for balance-of-payments reasons.

Schlesinger, Eugene R. *Multiple Exchange Rates and Economic Development.* Princeton, N.J.: Princeton University Press, 1952. A theoretical analysis with some description.

Sherwood, Joyce. "Revenue Features of Multiple Exchange Rate Systems: Some Case Studies," *International Monetary Fund Staff Papers,* V (February, 1956), 74–107. A description plus a comparison with other methods of raising revenue.

Triffin, Robert. "Exchange Control and Equilibrium," *Foreign Economic Policy for the United States,* Seymour Harris, ed. Cambridge, Mass.: Harvard University Press, 1948, chapter 23. A comparison of direct controls with devaluation and deflation.

United States Tariff Commission. *Foreign-Trade and Exchange Controls in Germany.* Washington: Government Printing Office, 1942. A detailed description of Germany's direct controls in the 1930's.

Viner, Jacob. *International Trade and Economic Development.* Glencoe, Ill.: Free Press, 1952. Chapter 5 examines the relation between internal planning and trade controls.

Woodley, W. J. R. "The Use of Special Exchange Rates for Transactions with Foreign Companies," *International Monetary Fund Staff Papers,* III (October, 1953), 254–269. A discussion of multiple exchange rate systems as they apply to foreign-owned companies.

16 Direct Controls: Intergovernmental

Intergovernmental agreements regarding international payments were used extensively during the 1930's and after World War II as a means of expanding trade among the participants and/or of regulating its flow. With few exceptions, these arrangements have involved discrimination against countries not party to them, and their use has resulted in the loss of some of the advantages of multilateralism. To minimize this loss, nations have associated themselves in various regional payments systems, such as the sterling area and the European Payments Union, in the postwar period. On an even wider scale, countries have joined in international agreements to restrain the use of direct controls on international trade and to obtain nondiscrimination and multilateralism.

A. CONVERTIBILITY, DISCRIMINATION, AND MULTILATERALISM

Balance-of-payments difficulties which give rise to inconvertible currencies for certain types of transactions lead to discrimination and the restriction of multilateralism. To understand why this is true and then to comprehend its significance, we must first explain our terms.

SOME DEFINITIONS

Complete convertibility of currencies exists when any person may without restriction exchange his own country's currency or a foreign currency which he holds for any other currency. A currency is convertible for *residents* of the nation issuing the currency if they can freely exchange it for other currencies. The exchange controls discussed in the previous chapter remove this freedom. Controls on imports such as quotas or import licenses have the same effect, because they deny the right to enter into

317

transactions which would give rise to the need to exchange local currency for foreign currency.

A currency is convertible for *nonresidents* of the nation issuing the currency if foreigners can freely exchange their receipts of that currency for another foreign currency. The pound sterling would be convertible for nonresidents if Britain were to allow Peruvians, for example, to sell sterling for dollars without restriction.

Discrimination in international trade exists when a nation artificially restricts payments to or trade with one country more than it does with another. A country which imposes higher duties on imports from one nation than on imports from another discriminates among its sources of supply. So does a nation which more freely gives import or exchange licenses for purchases from one country than from another. The greater the difference in the treatment of foreign countries, the greater the degree of discrimination.

Multilateralism exists when a country uses its excess earnings with one nation to pay its deficit with another nation. The more offsetting of deficits against surpluses, the greater the degree of multilateralism. Bilateralism exists when a nation balances its receipts and payments with *each* country separately rather than with the world as a whole. Given complete freedom to choose among foreign markets or foreign sources of supply, importers buy in the cheapest foreign market while exporters sell in the dearest foreign market. Because their decisions to import and to export are made independently of one another, there is no reason to believe that payments among nations would normally balance bilaterally.

RESULTS OF NONRESIDENT INCONVERTIBILITY

The previous chapter discussed the implications of restricting resident convertibility, i.e., of imposing exchange and trade controls which limit payments by residents to foreigners. What are the results of restricting nonresident convertibility?

Suppose that Britain has a balance-of-payments deficit and, in particular, a severe shortage of dollar earnings relative to the demand for dollars. When England imposes direct controls to remove its deficit, it will probably suspend or limit nonresident convertibility of the pound as well. Suppose that Peru normally has a surplus of sterling which she uses to pay a dollar deficit by converting the sterling into dollars. Given Britain's balance-of-payments difficulties, if Peruvians get British banks to exchange the sterling for dollars, England would have even fewer dollars. Or, if Peruvians transferred the sterling to American banks in exchange for dollars, then American banks could sell the sterling to American importers who would then pay for British goods with sterling instead of dollars. Either way, Britain loses dollars, and she will be strongly motivated to limit such conversions.

When England restricts nonresident convertibility of sterling, she imposes policies of discrimination and bilateralism on Peru. Unable to convert her sterling earnings to pay her dollar deficit, Peru must control payments which require dollars in order to balance bilaterally her dollar receipts and dollar expenditures, but she need not reduce her sterling payments. Thus, nonresident *in*convertibility of a currency widely used to settle international debts leads to discrimination and bilateralism.

The critical role of nonresident inconvertibility can be seen by supposing that Peru has a balance-of-payments deficit while the pound and the dollar are convertible. Peru could impose direct controls on her imports without regard to their source because it would not matter whether Peru attained equilibrium with a sterling surplus and a dollar deficit or vice versa, just so long as she obtains over-all balance-of-payments equilibrium. Peru need not undertake policies of discrimination and bilateralism for balance-of-payments reasons, though she might discriminate in favor of one of the countries for other reasons.

B. THE CASES FOR AND AGAINST DISCRIMINATION

THE CASE FOR NONDISCRIMINATION

The argument for nondiscrimination, and hence for multilateralism and for convertibility, is the argument for free trade. When discrimination prevails, direct controls and import duties must exist. Taking a cosmopolitan point of view, we see that these controls and duties prevent the equalization of relative prices and alternative costs which maximizes world output and which insures that no consumer can be made better off without hurting some other consumer.

Taking a nationalistic point of view, we see that the discriminatory application of trade controls hurts the nation imposing them if it cannot affect its terms of trade. As long as import restrictions give no artificial inducement to importers to buy in one foreign market instead of another, importers tend to buy in the cheapest foreign market. Discrimination prevents them from buying in the cheapest foreign market when the price is measured in foreign currencies. Hence the foreign exchange earned by a nation's exports is not used to buy as many physical units of foreign goods as would otherwise be possible, and the nation's gain from trade is accordingly reduced.[1]

---

[1] But where a nation's terms of trade with different countries respond differently to equivalent restriction of imports from each of them, discrimination serves the national interest, as shown in Chapter 3. In these circumstances, to improve its economic position, the restricting nation should reduce its imports more from that nation with which the terms of trade improve more, always giving consideration, however, to the cost of replacing the foreign goods from domestic production.

THE CASE FOR DISCRIMINATION

A case for discrimination can be made when nations have balance-of-payments difficulties stemming from their trade relations with one or with a small number of countries. Suppose that the United States has a recession which causes it to reduce its imports from all other countries. Imagine that Monaco's exports fall by $100. If Monaco has decided to remove her balance-of-payments deficit through direct controls, she may cut her imports discriminatorily by reducing them from the United States *alone* by $100 without restricting trade with other nations. Or Monaco might restrict her imports nondiscriminatorily from *all* countries by a *total* of $100; this would put her in over-all balance-of-payments equilibrium; and, if all countries maintain nonresident convertibility, Monaco's surpluses with other nations would provide the funds with which to cover the dollar deficit she continues to sustain because she has cut her imports from the United States by less than $100.

If every country adversely affected by the American recession cuts its imports *only* from the United States, the volume of world trade falls less than if they apply their controls in a nondiscriminatory pattern. If Monaco restricts her imports from all nations by a total of $100, the other countries (except the United States) go into even greater balance-of-payments deficits. If they, like Monaco, follow a nondiscriminatory policy, they will cut their imports from all countries including Monaco. In that event, Monaco's initial import reduction of $100 is insufficient to balance her accounts, and she will be forced to cut her imports from all countries again. And this will induce another import reduction by the other countries, because their exports to Monaco fall further. If this seesawing goes on long enough, the deficits with the United States eventually disappear, because each time a nation cuts its imports from all countries it also cuts its imports from the United States. But, in the process of attaining dollar equilibrium, trade declines among the nations suffering a fall in their exports to the United States. Such a decline can be avoided if each country initially reduces its imports from the United States by precisely the amount of the fall in its exports to the United States. Dollar balance and over-all balance would be immediately restored by directing import restrictions solely against imports of American products.

The shortcoming of this argument for discrimination is that it dwells upon the volume of international trade without regard to its composition or pattern. If the rest of the world restricts imports only from the United States, trade among the countries of the rest of the world will increase as people turn to other markets when their purchases from the United States are forcibly restricted. If they buy goods from each other which might have been sold in the United States, or if they buy goods produced by resources which otherwise would produce different goods for export to the United States, the balance-of-payments of each country with the United States is worsened. Therefore another round of import cuts from the United States is required. This would be of little concern if American goods were less desired by the citizens of the restricting nations than the additional goods they buy from each other. However, the American goods may be more greatly desired. Furthermore, had the other nations imposed cuts against each other's products (nondiscrimination), exporters who therefore lost markets might divert some of their exports to the United States. The additional dollar earnings might permit people of the rest of the world to import goods from the United States which would be more useful to them than the goods they fail to import from each other because of reciprocal import reductions under nondiscrimination.

The arguments, pro and con, are not different in principle when the discrimination would result from the mutual relaxation of existing restrictions. Suppose, for example, that two countries are using direct controls to restrict imports from each other and from the United States for balance-of-payments reasons, but that the United States imposes no controls because it has no balance-of-payments difficulties. If the two nations reciprocally relax controls on imports from each other, the volume of trade between them expands, and their payments remain in equilibrium so that reserve losses do not occur. The United States is discriminated against because controls against its exports are not relaxed. America cannot participate in the mutual relaxation of restrictions, because it has none to relax, and it therefore has no way of assuring countries who might otherwise relax their controls on imports from the United States that American imports would simultaneously rise to prevent a loss of their reserves. Although the growth of trade between the relaxing countries serves a useful purpose by itself, resources in each country may be diverted from the production of goods for the American market to the production of goods for each other; in that event, the growth of trade between the liberalizing countries would require a reduction of trade with the United States, including a reduction of imports from America which might be more greatly desired than the goods they would buy from each other.

C. BILATERAL PAYMENTS AGREEMENTS

In the 1930's, international trade and payments were depressed by low levels of economic activity and by balance-of-payments difficulties. To surmount these troubles, nations turned to bilateral financial arrangements. After World War II, because of balance-of-payments difficulties, several hundred bilateral payments agreements were established to finance international transactions.

REPATRIATION OF BLOCKED FUNDS

One of the chief purposes of such agreements in the 1930's was the repatriation of blocked funds. As a means of protecting their reserves from capital flight, many nations prohibited the payment of foreigners' claims upon them. In some instances, blocked claims arose because the debtor nation permitted imports without controls but restricted payments for imports; import controls should have been imposed to prevent imports for which sufficient foreign exchange was not available.

Persons whose funds were frozen abroad pressured their governments into agreements with the blocking nations to obtain their release. In the early 1930's, between 10 and 30 per cent of a debtor nation's export earnings from a particular creditor nation were often allocated by the debtor to the liquidation of claims owed to that creditor; on occasion, as much as 75 or 80 per cent was so allocated. Since the use of these export earnings was limited to payments to the country from which they were obtained, there was a tendency toward bilateralism and discrimination.

THE CREATION OF TRADE

The 1930's

A different type of agreement served in the 1930's to permit trade where it otherwise might not have occurred. Plagued by a shortage of international reserves, many nations entered into arrangements that provided a means of expanding trade while avoiding reserve losses. In each of the participating countries, importers would pay for their imports by depositing their own currency in a special account with the central bank or some other official institution in their own country. Exporters in each nation received payment for their sales from the account in their own country. Hence Austrians who exported to Switzerland could receive no more schillings in total than Austrians importing from Switzerland paid into the account. When imports fell short of exports, the exporters simply had to wait until importers made more funds available.

In the early 1930's, transactions carried on in this manner were generally not subject to exchange control, so the effect was probably to sustain some trade which otherwise would have collapsed in the face of low levels of economic activity and exchange controls. In 1939, there were about 170 agreements of this and the previous type among about 40 nations.

Germany used her bilateral agreements with Southeast Europe in the 1930's for sinister purposes. She established a close economic dependence with the Balkan nations because they were a source of raw materials and foodstuffs which was not likely to be cut off in the event of war. And the Balkan nations in turn accepted the arrangements to obtain a ready market for goods in surplus because of the depression. Germany stimulated imports of primary products from these countries through her import control system, and the exchange rate established in the agreements tended to make Balkan exports to Germany very profitable. The result was that Germany ran an import surplus which was "paid" for by an accumulation of marks in the special accounts; this accumulation amounted to a forced loan by particular Balkan nations to Germany. Some of the agreements involved stipulations that the Balkan nation expand industries which would serve German needs. The heavy German purchases of Balkan commodities tended to divert their exports from other markets, and, on occasion, Germany bought goods from them only to sell the goods in other countries for foreign exchange which Germany required. The effect was to incarcerate the Balkans in the German economic sphere. The Balkan countries were not entirely defenseless; on some occasions, Balkan governments would restrict exports to Germany to a given percentage of imports from Germany in order to avoid the accumulation of balances. On other occasions, however, they would buy useless and unneeded products—several carloads of aspirin in one case—to use up the accumulated marks.

Post-World War II period

In the early post-World War II period, dollars and gold were extremely valuable because they could be used to buy desperately needed American goods; nations with low gold and dollar reserves were extremely reluctant to permit imports from countries other than the United States if they required dollar payment in settlement. At the same time, some countries which had adequate reserves (Switzerland and some of the Latin American nations) feared a loss of export markets as other nations imposed direct controls to avoid a loss of reserves. In 1947, there were in operation approximately two hundred bilateral-payments agreements designed to avoid these results; approximately four hundred were in use in 1954. Although the procedural details of these agreements have varied widely, payments and receipts of each participant are recorded either immediately or ultimately in special accounts in central banks.

Supporting these payments agreements are trade-quota agreements which have the purpose of balancing payments and receipts. Trade-quota agreements provide lists of commodities which the state trading agencies of the particular countries agree to exchange and/or lists of commodities for which the partners will grant import and export licenses. However, businessmen will not necessarily find it profitable to import the permitted goods in the projected amounts. To allow for possible differences between receipts and payments without requiring a movement of gold and dollars, payments agreements have often included provisions for a "swing credit." Each partner agrees to sell its currency for the other partner's currency up to a certain limit in order to provide funds to pay for an import surplus; beyond that limit, gold or dollars must be used. Thus a deficit country buys its partner's currency with which to meet the deficit by crediting the account held in the deficit country's central bank by the surplus country's central bank; when the account reached a certain level, gold or dollars would be paid for any additional deficits. The swing-credit device has been an improvement over the 1930's financial agreements which obliged exporters in one country to wait for payment until importers in that same nation had provided sufficient funds.

While the postwar trade-quota and payments agreements undoubtedly permitted much trade that otherwise would not have occurred, their operation has not been satisfactory. Trade has almost never reached its projected levels under the trade-quota agreements. Only occasionally could this be explained by the failure of one of the nations to issue the necessary import licenses; most frequently the explanation lay in inflation in one of the countries which restrained its exports.

In addition, rather than the swing credits being used first by one partner and then by the other to finance alternating deficits in payments, net payments have tended to run one way, leading to the persistent accumulation of excess balances by one country with another. In some instances the persistent creditor nation merely increased the swing credit (and therefore its holdings of the debtor's currency) in order to sustain its exports in the future, knowing that otherwise the debtor would restrict its imports to avoid dollar or gold payments; this was done at the cost of internal inflationary pressure within the creditor nation.

In other instances, special devices were used to remove the excess balances which involved the implicit devaluation of the debtor's currency. "Switch" transactions occurred in which the creditor nation would import goods from the debtor for resale in another country, thereby using some of the excess balance. Because of the high prices of the debtor's goods, they often could be sold in third countries only at a loss. But if the debtor's goods were sold in other countries for dollars, the goods then bought with dollars could be sold for a premium in the creditor country or elsewhere because the importation of dollar goods was severely restricted. This premium tended to offset the loss on the sale of the debtor's goods. Even though all the transactions were carried out at official exchange rates, switch transactions involved an implicit devaluation of the debtor's currency because the debtor's goods were initially sold at a loss in third markets.

Another device for removing excess balances has been a free market in the creditor country for the currency of the debtor. Since variations in the free market exchange rate would equate the supply and demand for the debtor's currency, accumulation of excess balances ceased. Unfortunately, both switch and free market transactions may impose a loss of dollars on the debtor if its goods are sold in the United States either through switch transactions or through commodity arbitrage resulting from the discount on its currency in the creditor country. But at the same time, they tend to move the world resource allocation out of the pattern imposed by bilateralism and discrimination.

D. POSTWAR CURRENCY AREAS

The growth of bilateralism in the postwar world has been restrained and reversed through regional convertibility of currencies and regional multilateralism. Three major currency areas have existed during the postwar period: the dollar area, the sterling area, and the European Payments Union.

The dollar area consists of the United States, Canada, the Central American nations, and some of the northern South American countries. These countries generally have exported only for dollars. Because they have commodities which have been considered extremely useful or because their markets have been largely in the United States, they have been able to demand dollars for sales to countries outside the dollar area. While some of these countries impose quantitative restrictions and multiple exchange rates, they generally have not discriminated among sources of supply. Because most of their sales have been for dollars and because the dollars they earn are acceptable in payment for imports from any country in the world, discrimination by dollar-area countries has been unnecessary.

Within the sterling area and among members of the European Payments Union, nondiscrimination and nonresident convertibility have generally prevailed. Members of both regional payments systems discriminate against transactions requiring payments to the dollar area, and conversions of their currencies into the dollar are restricted.

More generally, the trading world has been divided into hard and soft currency areas during the postwar period. In the former categories fall the countries whose currencies could not be obtained in sufficient quantities to meet the demand, e.g., the United States dollar. In the latter are the currencies which have been abnormally easy to acquire through international trade. Soft-currency countries have been obliged to discriminate against hard-currency countries in order to balance their hard-currency accounts.

STERLING AREA

The sterling area consists of the British Commonwealth countries minus Canada plus several Middle Eastern countries, Burma, and Iceland. The area became an official entity in 1939 when Britain first imposed exchange controls. Prior to that time, its "membership" changed and its boundaries were difficult to define.

Development of the area

Before World War I, the system of international payments made the whole world the sterling area. The British pound was the major currency for settling international transactions among countries, and many countries kept their international reserves in London in the form of sterling. After the financial crises of 1931, the sterling area shrank. The pound was set free to fluctuate vis-a-vis gold and the dollar. Many countries, especially those having important trade and financial relations with London, stabilized their exchange rates in terms of the pound and continued to hold their international reserves in London. Stable rates on London protected these countries' exports and imports, which were predominantly with Britain and other Commonwealth countries, from undue exchange-rate fluctuations, and stabilized the service costs on their debts to London. Sterling was the most liquid form in which these countries could hold their reserves, for the predominant portion of their payments was to Britain.

With the advent of World War II, most of the non-Commonwealth countries dropped their "membership" in the sterling area for fear the pound would be an unhealthy currency to hold. Among the remaining countries, then called officially the sterling area, the pound sterling was freely transferable for making international payments; but the pound could not be so freely transferred out of the area for settling international transactions. Members of the sterling area agreed to sell their dollar and other hard-currency earnings to the Bank of England for sterling; when they needed hard currency to settle deficits with the United States, they obtained dollars from the "dollar pool" in exchange for sterling. The purpose of the dollar pool was to mobilize the hard-currency earnings of the sterling-area countries to finance international transactions with the rest of the world during the war.

Postwar operation

This wartime structure persisted after the close of World War II. Without formal organization and with a minimum of high-level and technical contacts, the politically independent countries of the Commonwealth and the nonself-governing territories of Britain were melded into a limited multilateral trade and payments system involving discrimination against the dollar. Within the area, sterling balances, with the exception of certain amounts accumulated during the war, may be transferred freely to settle debts. Direct controls are imposed on trade and payments; for example, an Australian does not have the right to buy as many British goods or British pounds as he wishes. However, there is little or no discrimination in trade and payments. Because the British pound can be used to settle Australia's payments to any member of the area, there is no reason for Australia to restrict its imports from, say, India any more than it restricts from Britain.

Thus the sterling area during the postwar period has provided a widespread multilateral system of international trade in which the sterling earnings of a country within the area can be used to pay its debts to any other country within the area.

Connected with the sterling area through agreements with Britain are the transferable-account countries. These include all countries in the world except those in the dollar and sterling areas. Sterling earned by such countries is freely transferable to other transferable-account nations and to the sterling area in so far as British regulations are concerned; this broadens even further the system of multilateral trade based on Britain. However, these countries also impose direct controls on purchases of sterling. No formal dollar-pooling arrangements exist for them.

The sterling area has not had a sufficient supply of dollars. In order to reduce the demand for dollars from the dollar pool, members impose discriminatory restrictions on transactions requiring payment in dollars. Members usually follow the lead of Britain in determining the stringency of the controls.

Dollar pooling in the sterling area has been justified as a means of economizing dollar and gold reserves. It is argued that if each member were to maintain its own gold and dollar reserves, the total amount individually held would have to be greater than the amount held under the pooling system. This is the case so long as not all members need additional dollars simultaneously. The dollars which, in the absence of pooling, would be held by a nation(s) not needing additional dollars at the moment are automatically made available through pooling to others. However, while the dollar-pool mechanism has released dollars from reserves to be spent on goods, the fact remains that numerous reserve crises have occurred and that on a number of occasions some of the members have cut their contributions to the pool just when others have needed them most.

The pooling system involves some questions of fairness in the distribution of the burden of contributing and of the benefit of withdrawing much-desired dollars from the pool. The nonself-governing territories (the British colonies) as a group have been net contributors while the politically independent members have been net drawers. The different patterns of dollar use seem to have resulted from differing degrees of British control over the imports of the two groups. On those occasions when the independent members of the area have been transitory contributors, such as during the early part of the Korean War, their contributions were in some instances made rather reluctantly.

In theory, as a means of saving dollars, members are not to buy goods from the dollar area which can be obtained within the sterling area. But, even when supplemented by some formal agreements and conferences among the finance ministers, this rule has not been sufficient to stem extensive use of dollars by the independent members. Dollar pooling tends to reduce the responsibility of each member for the state of its dollar accounts; if one member spends too much, the burden is borne by others.

Discussions of the fairness of the distribution of the dollar burden among members of the sterling area are complicated by the virtual impossibility of knowing the precise contribution or subtraction of any member from the dollar pool. Australian wool which is sent to Britain may actually earn dollars if the British use it in textiles to be sold in the dollar market; similarly, British exports to members may indirectly save dollars if the member's restrictions on imports from the United States depend upon the availability of British goods.

The balance of gains and losses by Britain from the operation of the area is also difficult to compute. It does gain invisible earnings by providing banking and other services; those would be smaller but for the extensive convertibility of sterling within the area. She also gains because citizens of the sterling area are forced, through governmental restrictions on dollar imports, to buy British goods when dollar goods are generally preferred. But there have been losses too. Britain restricts domestic investment for unessential purposes; at the same time, there has been little limitation on capital exports from London to the rest of the area. The use of British sterling to build luxury apartments and milk bars in the dominions has not been pleasant for the austerity-plagued Englishman. Capital exports from Britain have approximately equaled U.S. government aid to England. Britain is probably obliged to allow such extensive capital exports because the availability of loanable funds from Britain maintains the membership of some countries in the area. Yet there is no clear loss to Britain because some of the capital is used to develop facilities within the area which reduce the members' need for dollar imports. On balance, Britain and most of the members apparently feel that they have a net gain from the area's operations, but many desire relaxation of discrimination against the dollar and a more rapid movement toward over-all currency convertibility.

EUROPEAN PAYMENTS UNION

Origin

The bilateral payments agreements among European countries after World War II encouraged trade which otherwise would not have taken place. But the agreements did not solve the basic problems of payments. The credits provided under some of the agreements were exhausted when one of the bilateral partners ran a persistent deficit. Creditors became reluctant to extend further credit and debtors were reluctant to pay gold and dollars for further imports after the credit was exhausted; when this happened it threatened any further expansion of trade. In some instances, trade declined as debtors attempted to balance their bilateral accounts by restricting imports. These results were, in part, unnecessary because some of the debtors were also creditors, i.e., a nation would be in deficit with one country but in surplus with another. If these deficits could be offset against the surpluses, trade could expand once again. But since the bilateral balances of countries were not freely transferable to other countries, this offsetting could not take place.

Several compensation devices were established in Europe to clear away some of the accumulated debts. For example, if A owed B, B owed C, and C owed A, it was possible to pay the debts among them in the amount of the smallest bilateral debt through a round-robin payment with each country receiving as much as it paid. This "circuit clearing" was limited, however, by the fact that several countries tended to be creditors or debtors with all of their payments partners. No circuit through them was possible, because, unlike the A-B-C example above, all were not simultaneously creditors and debtors. Furthermore, when circuits were possible, if the debt between A and B was the smallest of the three debts, the circuit left uncleared debts between B and C and between C and A. If C could have used its remaining credit with B to pay its remaining debt to A, additional bilateral debts could be cleared; however, such a transfer would result in B owing A instead of C. Depending upon the size of the swing credit in the bilateral payments agreement between A and B, this transfer might lead to a gold or dollar payment from B to A and therefore B might not permit the transfer. Or A might not wish to hold B's currency if it were weak.

The failure of these compensation schemes to clear sufficient debts forced persistent discrimination among European nations. Because payments were still essentially bilateral, a nation would grant licenses more freely for imports from countries with which it had a surplus than for imports from countries with which it tended to have a deficit. To reduce the discrimination and to rid Europe of as many bilateral debts as possible, seventeen nations of Western Europe organized the European Payments Union in mid-1950.

Operation

At the end of every month, each member of the Union reports its bilateral position with each other member to a central clearing agent. The agent determines the *net* position of each country with respect to *all* the other members. This procedure automatically offsets all of a nation's bilateral deficits against all of its bilateral surpluses, leaving its net position. The net position of each country is then financed partly through credit and partly through dollar transfers. A net creditor receives part of its surplus in dollars from the EPU agent and extends credit to EPU for the remainder; the EPU agent collects dollars or gold for part of the deficits of the net debtors and extends credit to them for the remainder.

In addition to clearing more debts and thereby permitting more trade, the EPU reduced discrimination in Western European trade. Because a member no longer had to concern itself with its position vis-a-vis each individual nation but only with its position with the Union as a whole, it need not distinguish among other European countries in its import-licensing policies. Since the EPU allows a nation to use its surplus earnings with one member to pay its deficit with another, the EPU, like the sterling area, provides a multilateral system of international trade among its members.

The extent of discrimination within Europe has been reduced and the volume of intra-European trade increased by reciprocal relaxation of quantitative restrictions among members. From time to time, Western European countries have agreed to free a certain percentage of their imports from each other (except those bought by the government) from quantitative controls. While this action increased intra-European trade it also increased the relative degree of discrimination against dollar imports.

The net result of EPU has been an increase in the convertibility of Western European currencies into each other (since, in effect, a credit with one country could be used to pay a debt with another) and into the dollar (through the partial settlement of net positions in dollars). The politically dependent territories of the Western European countries are included within EPU, and Britain is a member of the EPU on behalf of all countries in the sterling area. Thus the area of multilateral, non-discriminatory trade and payments comprises both Western Europe and the British Commonwealth.

Conflicts of operations and policies

The reciprocal relaxation of quantitative restrictions did not move forward smoothly because, on occasion, nations had to reimpose restrictions in the face of severe balance-of-payments difficulties vis-a-vis other Union members. The monthly meetings of the EPU afforded members an opportunity to embarrass debtor nations into deflationary internal policies and to induce creditors to relax their quantitative restrictions and to ease their monetary restraint. EPU pressure was beneficial in the case of Germany but it has had little effect on the United Kingdom and France.

The least liberalization of quantitative controls was obtained on agricultural imports. Desire to protect domestic agriculture for internal political and social reasons kept the liberalization percentage for agricultural products consistently below that for all other western European imports.

In addition, low-tariff countries were reluctant to relax their quantitative restrictions when other countries protected both their balance of payments and their domestic industries through high tariffs. The relaxation of quantitative restrictions by some countries did not increase their imports much because of their high tariffs. This conflict was drawn tighter by the differing degrees of liberalization among countries, resulting partly from disparate payments positions in the Union. In those countries that liberalized extensively, domestic industries complained of the additional import competition while export industries complained that European markets were closed to them because of inadequate liberalization in other countries.

The proportion of dollars and of credit used in settling net positions was a source of conflict among the members, especially as certain countries became extreme and persistent creditors or debtors. Creditors generally urged a higher ratio of dollars to credit; debtors threatened that such a change would force them to restrict their imports in order to reduce dollar losses.

In spite of the large disequilibrium of some countries in the EPU with other members, the Union has been criticized for balancing intra-European trade too closely and maintaining discrimination against the dollar. American approval of the Union was based on the assumption that the formation of the EPU would ease Europe into convertibility with the dollar and would eventually permit *world-wide* nondiscriminatory trade and multilateral payments. But, in fact, the Union tended to encourage balance-of-payments equilibrium by each member with EPU members as a group. The natural tendency for some nations to be in surplus with other European nations and deficit with the dollar area (or vice versa) was restricted. For example, in 1951, when Belgium was a strong creditor to other EPU members, she eased her restrictions on imports from EPU countries in order to reduce her EPU surplus and simultaneously increased her restrictions on dollar imports in order to induce greater imports from EPU countries.

The argument that EPU would advance the cause of convertibility into the dollar was that, by creating a wide market with free competition, EPU would increase the efficiency of Western European producers. This would cause a reallocation of resources and a reduction of costs which would facilitate over-all balance-of-payments adjustment, including that with the dollar area. There is no general evidence—either way—of the effect of EPU on productivity within Europe.[2] Individual cases of growing efficiency are available, but it is difficult to say whether or not they were the result of the EPU mechanism. And there are instances of industries which have expanded under the cover of discrimination against U.S. exports and which probably will not be able to stand a stiff blast of competition from the United States in the event that discrimination against dollar goods is removed. Industries which may be sustained only in a discriminatory market may have a vested interest in preventing eventual convertibility with the dollar and the reduction of nondiscrimination against U.S. exports.

---

[2] Professor Haberler says "At any rate the optimistic expectations of the proponents and defenders of EPU that EPU would greatly increase competition, eliminate high-cost producers, and thereby tend to increase the 'viability' of the whole area have hardly been fulfilled, because quota reduction has largely been confined to noncompetitive items." "Reflections on the Future of the Bretton Woods System," *American Economic Review*, XLIII (May, 1953), 93 n,

PROBLEMS OF CONVERTIBILITY

The key currency in a return to world-wide multilateralism and non-discrimination is the pound sterling, because it, along with the dollar, is widely used to settle international transactions. When sterling is made freely convertible into dollars, at least for nonresidents, discrimination by many nations between transactions requiring sterling payment and those requiring dollar payment can cease.

One of the obstacles to making sterling convertible into the dollar for current account payments is the possibility that other nations would, once sterling is convertible, tighten their restrictions against British exports to gain sterling which could be converted into dollars. That is, convertibility, rather than ease direct controls on trade and payments, might increase the use of direct controls. Even in the absence of increased controls on imports from the sterling area, foreigners might reduce their purchases of the high-priced British goods as restrictions on purchases from the United States were eased. Unless foreign governments would not consciously tighten restrictions on British goods and unless British exports were competitive with American goods, Britain runs the risk of a severe loss of gold and dollars. In this event, British reserve losses could be stopped only by tightening British import restrictions (1) on *nondollar* imports, thereby reducing the number of pounds foreigners would have to convert into dollars, or (2) on *dollar* goods, thus saving dollars to give to foreigners for sterling.

If convertibility led to either of these results, it would hardly improve the allocation of world resources. In addition, it might be extremely difficult politically for the British government to tighten controls on British dollar imports so that foreigners could have more dollars to buy goods from the United States. Against this critical view, it has been argued that convertibility of the pound would put additional pressure on British exporters because they would have to be competitive with American exporters to retain their foreign markets. The increased efficiency of British exporters would enhance Britain's dollar-earning power and would generally improve her balance of payments.

An additional factor making it difficult for Britain to undertake non-resident convertibility is the possibility that speculative pressure would develop on British reserves. Once convertibility is established, some countries might convert their current earnings of sterling into dollars in the expectation that Britain would lose so many dollars that she would have to restrict convertibility again and thus end their opportunity to gain dollars.

The above limitations call attention to the adequacy of Britain's international reserves. The British view has been that it should not attempt convertibility unless reserves are at a level of $5 billion to $6 billion, a figure far in excess, relative to the volume of trade and payments, of the amount held during the nineteenth century and much more than her current reserves. Prior to World War I, smaller reserves were sufficient because sterling was an international currency and seldom exchanged for gold in large volumes. When Britain was in a deficit position, others built up sterling balances, thereby providing short-term capital to cover the deficit. Now, a deficit in Britain's international accounts drains her reserves. In addition, the growth of trade, in both real and money terms, has required greater reserves.

It has been frequently proposed that the International Monetary Fund and/or the U.S. government provide a stabilization credit of dollars to nations undertaking convertibility to help them meet the added demand for dollars which might arise. The mere availability of such credit might itself prevent some of the dollar drain by giving confidence to the holders of newly convertible currency that they need not fear a quick end to their opportunity to convert into dollars. If speculative fears were the only force which would cost a country dollars, the credit might never be used because of the confidence engendered.

But a more fundamental requirement is that each country attain, without added import restrictions, a balance-of-payments position which reflects increased competitive strength and a currency nearly as hard as the dollar. Otherwise, resident and nonresident demands for dollars will exhaust reserves and end convertibility. While the U.S. government has officially urged a more rapid advance to convertibility, it has also emphasized the necessity of establishing appropriate prerequisites, for a short-lived convertibility would be worse than a further postponement because of the damage done to future efforts.

It is difficult to decide whether Europe should have proceeded earlier to make its currencies convertible and how fast it should now proceed. Professor Mikesell, commenting on the period before EPU when bilateral payments agreements were extensively used, has written the following in this regard:

It is interesting to speculate what might have happened if this payments network had not developed and nations had organized their postwar trade on a convertible basis. The low levels of [international reserves] and the demand for dollar goods would undoubtedly have kept trade between non-dollar countries at a substantially lower level. Competition for markets would probably have forced countries to depreciate and unless internal deflationary steps had been taken, hyper-inflation might have occurred in a number of countries. *But the pattern of production and trade would probably have adjusted itself far more rapidly to a system of non-discriminatory trade and currency convertibility* than it has in the nine years since V-E day [June 1945]. However, the social and economic costs of this adjustment would undoubtedly have been more than the non-dollar countries of the world were willing to pay and it would be difficult to prove that they were wrong in adopting the course they did.[3]

---

[3] R. F. Mikesell, *The Emerging Pattern of International Payments.* Essays in International Finance, No. 18 (Princeton, N.J.: International Finance Section, Princeton University, April, 1954), pp. 6–7. Italics supplied.

E. INTERNATIONAL COOPERATION

Most of the Free World nations have agreed to certain limitations on their right to impose quantitative or exchange restrictions and multiple exchange rates, or to employ discriminatory practices by virtue of their acceptance of the General Agreement on Tariffs and Trade (GATT), established in 1947, and their membership in the International Monetary Fund (IMF).

PRINCIPLES AND EXCEPTIONS

Members of the IMF agree that, except with its approval, (1) they shall impose no restrictions on making payments for current international transactions; (2) they shall not engage in multiple exchange-rate practices or discriminatory currency arrangements; and that (3) foreign-owned balances of their currencies arising from current international transactions shall be convertible into other currencies (Article VII). Parties to GATT agree that they shall not discriminate and shall impose no restrictions on imports other than duties and taxes, thereby excluding the use of multiple exchange rates, quotas, and import licenses (Article XI). The formal division of authority between the two institutions is that the IMF controls restrictions on payments while the GATT covers the use of trade restrictions.

Both organizations permit certain exceptions to these rules of conduct. The Fund's articles of agreement permit members to maintain restrictions on payments during the "postwar transition" to peacetime relations. Members were allowed a period of recuperation and adjustment before they were obliged to remove controls on payments. The period ended in 1952; since then members are supposed to consult with the Fund regarding the retention of any controls. If the Fund concludes that a member should abandon some or all of its controls or loosen them, it may say so. If the member does not follow the Fund's suggestion, the Fund may deny it the privilege of borrowing. However, in these matters the Fund is obliged to give the member the benefit of any reasonable doubt (Article XIV).

The Fund agreement expressly allows discrimination in a "scarce currency" situation. If the demand for a particular currency from the Fund threatens the ability of the Fund to supply the currency to borrowers, the Fund may formally declare that currency scarce. Members are then permitted to restrict exchange operations in that particular currency, thereby allowing discriminatory controls on payments (Article VII). The scarce-currency clause was written with an eye to the U.S. depression of the 1930's, which had thrown world trade into a serious downswing. In a future U.S. recession, the Fund might not be able to provide sufficient dollars to settle deficits with the United States. Countries would be unwilling to deflate their internal economies in the advent of a balance-of-payments deficit induced by a U.S. depression; devaluation of their currencies, when the deficit arises from cyclical difficulties, would be restricted by the Fund as outlined in the previous chapter. Therefore the imposition of controls must be permitted; the clause permits nations to balance their receipts and expenditures of the scarce currency through discriminatory direct controls. The fact that Fund approval in the form of a declaration of scarcity would be required might make the process and timing of discrimination more orderly. One justification for the clause lies in the case for discrimination suggested in section B, page 320; the volume of trade will not fall as much as if nondiscriminatory controls are imposed. The disadvantages of discrimination discussed above would be less significant if the depression (and thus the need for discrimination) is temporary.

The general obligation of Fund members to refrain from imposing restrictions on payments extends only to current transactions; control over capital movements is permitted. The Fund may even request a member to impose controls on capital movements in order to prevent that member from using resources borrowed from the Fund to finance a large or sustained outflow of capital (Article VI). Members are supposed not to exercise controls on capital in a manner which restricts current account payments; however, some supervision of current transactions is necessary to prevent evasion of capital controls through, for example, under- and over-invoicing (see page 300).

Among a number of exceptions to the general GATT rule against the use of direct controls by members, there are several relating specifically to balance-of-payments circumstances. Members are allowed to impose import restrictions to stop a serious drain on their international reserves or to build up excessively low reserves (Article XII). These restrictions may be discriminatory if the nation imposing them is concurrently permitted to discriminate by the International Monetary Fund under the transitional period or scarce-currency clauses (Article XIV).

A series of balance-of-payments exceptions apply to underdeveloped countries; their nature differs little from the foregoing. The underdeveloped countries asked for and received special consideration in the imposition of controls on the grounds that rapidly growing economies have a chronic tendency to run balance-of-payments deficits and that foreign exchange must be reserved for the more essential uses such as capital-goods imports.

Members of the GATT are obliged to consult with the organization regarding their controls. Any member whose trade is adversely affected by another nation's restrictions may challenge the other country before the GATT. If a member is found to offend the rules or another member, it may be requested to withdraw the offensive restriction. If it does not, those countries whose trade is adversely affected by the restrictions are permitted to withdraw certain tariff or other concessions previously given to the offending nation.

USE OF EXCEPTIONS

During the postwar period, the foregoing exceptions (save for the scarce-currency clause) have been the general rule. All but a few countries in both organizations have persistently imposed discriminatory direct controls on international trade. The latent demand for imports, particularly for dollar goods, has been so great that the removal of all controls would have caused rapid losses of international reserves or rapid exchange-rate depreciation. Except for the reciprocal relaxation of quantitative restrictions in Western Europe, there was little reduction in the use or in the restrictiveness of direct controls until 1953. Then, a general improvement in most countries' international reserve and balance-of-payments situations occurred. Least progress has been made in removing or simplifying multiple exchange-rate systems, particularly in Latin America.

Some of the direct controls are used for protectionist or revenue reasons. But most of them serve to restrain the demand for imports, particularly of dollar goods, for balance-of-payments reasons. The necessary condition for their relaxation, therefore, is an improvement in the balance of payments of the restricting nations. If the restrictions are to be dismantled entirely, the international reserves of such nations must rise to a level which allows them to cover temporary deficits through a loss of reserves. The International Monetary Fund, in its annual reports and in its consultations with members using restrictions, has emphasized the need for anti-inflationary monetary and fiscal policies to remove the pressure on payments. In addition, the Fund urged the devaluation of the pound sterling prior to the British action in 1949. The Fund has generally taken the position that the source of the balance-of-payments difficulties lies within the deficit countries; on occasion, it has cautioned the United States and other surplus nations that they should relax their tariff and other barriers to imports.

The Fund concluded in 1954 that the reserve and balance-of-payments positions of many countries would permit relaxation of restrictions; it suggested that the controls retained were excessive. It proposed that in some countries restrictions should be relaxed as reserves were built up.[4] In its consultations with members, the Fund found that they were aware of the undesirable effects of the restrictions on their own economies.[5] Members recognized the internal inflationary impact of restrictions on

---

[4] International Monetary Fund, *Annual Report, 1954* (Washington: 1954), pp. 78–79.

[5] International Monetary Fund, *Fourth Annual Report on Exchange Restrictions* (Washington: 1953), p. 4. This report gives the fullest account of the Fund's first consultations; reports on subsequent consultations have been meager.

imports. They were also conscious of the fact that, by trading in soft-currency markets rather than in the hard-currency countries against which they discriminate, they pay more for their imports. Brazil's coffee exports brought her less than half as many imports when she traded with soft-currency countries. Restricting countries also acknowledged that their controls provided (undesirable) protection for domestic industries.

At the same time, members have advanced many reasons for retaining direct controls and for avoiding exchange-rate adjustments and tighter monetary and fiscal policies. The reasons are generally those discussed in Chapter 15, section B, on the deficiencies of devaluation or deflation. In addition, countries which were in a position to dismantle control systems delayed doing so for fear that a later deterioration of their balance of payments would require the re-establishment of the controls. The fear of future balance-of-payments difficulties was founded most often on expectations of future U.S. recessions and on the instability of the prices of primary products which provide foreign-exchange earnings to many countries.

SUCCESS OF COOPERATION

The attempt to provide for a cooperative removal of controls through the Fund may be judged a failure by some; the transitional period after World War II has passed, and controls are still imposed for reasons largely unrelated to wartime damage and difficulties. Yet the Fund's consultations have provided an opportunity for examining the basic difficulties which underlie the use of restrictions. They have helped member countries to discover ways of overcoming these difficulties and may have discouraged the introduction of contemplated restrictions.

In view of the persistent balance-of-payments difficulties, it is understandable that the GATT procedures have had no more success in causing the removal of controls than have those of the Fund. Yet, as with the Fund, some usefulness can be claimed for the consultations among GATT members in providing a mild stimulant in inducing members to relax quantitative restrictions. In particular, Belgium, Holland, and Germany appear to have relaxed their restrictions under pressure from the United States and others through the GATT.

The role of GATT, in part, has been to police controls imposed for balance-of-payments purposes to see that they were not actually used for protectionist reasons. There is little else that can be done when an imbalance of payments is not adjusted through devaluation or deflationary measures. To reduce the protective effects of balance-of-payments controls, members of the GATT have been urged to warn domestic producers of the temporary nature of the controls, to restrict investment in import-competing fields, to vary the amounts of individual commodities which may be imported in order to heighten the uncertainty of profitable domestic production, and to permit token imports of foreign goods which would act as a reminder to domestic producers of the cheapness of foreign products and of the future availability of foreign goods.

Because international institutions have a membership of sovereign nations, force cannot be used to obtain acceptable behavior. Penalties, such as withholding borrowing privileges as in the Fund, or permitting retaliation as under the GATT, must be weak lest members decide that it is best to withdraw from the organization. Suasion can be of only limited success, because those to be persuaded have to consider domestic criteria for judging their actions as well as international rules of behavior. Yet attempts to persuade through institutions such as the IMF and GATT can bring some progress. Governments are multi-unit organizations; within each government there is often at least one department which would like to have its government follow the international rules of behavior, sometimes for foreign (political) policy reasons. Such departments can use the pressure of international opinion and the prestige of the international organization which lightly chastises their government as support against other departments in the formulation of their government's policies.

How far international institutions may go in obtaining acceptable behavior on the part of their members depends partly on how many members are behaving badly; the number and weight of the violations determine in part how strong the agreement is and thus determine the prestige of the institution itself. The strength of the agreement relies partly on the concept of sovereignty held by members; there is a thin line between the preservation of sovereignty and the submission to rules of international organizations. Governments have moved toward the articulation of principles of international behavior but do not consider the principles to be rules which are enforceable by an international authority. In the renegotiations of the GATT in 1955, members rejected a proposal that each nation obtain formal approval from others for the imposition of new balance-of-payments restrictions or the maintenance of existing ones beyond a certain date. Governments wished to retain "their right to determine when it was necessary to impose restrictions to protect their external financial position and when it was safe to eliminate such restrictions." But they were willing "to accept an obligation to adhere to certain criteria governing the use of restrictions and to take whatever consequences might follow if they failed to live up to their obligations."[6] The international agreements on direct controls are still primarily subjected to the test of consistency with the national interest.

---

[6] Report to the Secretary of State by the Chairman of the United States Delegation to the Ninth Session of the Contracting Parties to the General Agreement on Tariffs and Trade held at Geneva, Switzerland (mimeo.), October 28, 1954–March 7, 1955, p. 15.

SELECTED READINGS

A. AND B. CONVERTIBILITY, DISCRIMINATION, AND MULTILATERALISM; CASES FOR AND AGAINST DISCRIMINATION

Hirschman, A. O. "Types of Convertibility," *Review of Economics and Statistics,* XXXIII (February, 1951), 60–62.

Meade, James. *The Balance of Payments.* London: Oxford, 1951. Chapters 28–31. A description of techniques and an extensive theoretical treatment.

C. BILATERAL PAYMENTS AGREEMENTS

Andersen, P. Nyboe. *Bilateral Exchange Clearing Policy.* London: Oxford, 1946. A general theoretical discussion and description of bilateral clearing and payments agreements in the 1930's.

Basch, Antonin. *The Danube Basin and the German Economic Sphere.* New York: Columbia University Press, 1943. Chapters 10–16 are concerned primarily with Germany's trade drive in southeastern Europe during the 1930's.

Gordon, Margaret S. *Barriers to World Trade.* New York: Macmillan, 1941. Chapters 6, 7, 12, and 13 provide useful discussions of clearing and payments agreements in the 1930's.

de Looper, Johan H. C. "Current Usage of Payments Agreements and Trade Agreements," *International Monetary Fund Staff Papers,* IV (August, 1955), 339–397. A comprehensive description including the main features, purposes, difficulties, and effects.

Trued, M., and R. F. Mikesell. *Postwar Bilateral Payments Agreements.* Princeton, N.J.: International Finance Section, Princeton University, 1955. A description and analysis of their success or failure, along with a case study of Western Germany's agreements.

D. POSTWAR CURRENCY AREAS

Bell, P. W. *The Sterling Area in the Postwar World.* London: Oxford, 1956. A systematic survey of the area's financial mechanism and cohesion during 1946–1952.

Boyer, Frederic, and J. P. Salle. "The Liberalization of Intra-European Trade in the Framework of the OEEC," *International Monetary Fund Staff Papers,* IV (February, 1955), 179–216. A comprehensive statistical presentation and a discussion of some of the difficulties met in liberalizing European trade.

Day, A. C. L. *The Future of Sterling.* London: Oxford, 1954. This brief book provides an historical introduction to the sterling area, a discussion of its advantages at various stages, and the problems which it faces.

European Payments Union. *Annual Report.* Paris: Organization for European Economic Cooperation. A description of the economic situation of each of its members and of the operations and problems of the EPU.

Haberler, Gottfried. *Currency Convertibility.* Washington: American Enterprise Association, 1954. A vigorous plea for convertibility including a discussion of the real and alleged conditions necessary for a successful attempt to make currencies convertible.

Mikesell, Raymond F. *Foreign Exchange in the Postwar World.* New York: Twentieth Century Fund, 1954. Chapter 6 concerns the principles and the operations of regional clearing mechanisms including the EPU.

Polk, Judd. *Sterling.* New York: Harper, 1956. A survey of the British and sterling area international economic problems; primarily concerned with the postwar period.

Thorp, Willard L. *Trade, Aid, or What?* Baltimore: Johns Hopkins Press, 1954. Chapter 7 provides a survey of the extent of, problems of, and means to convertibility.

Wright, K. M. "Dollar Pooling in the Sterling Area," *American Economic Review,* XLIV (September, 1954), 558–576. This and Eliot Zupnick. "The Sterling Area's Central Pooling System Re-examined," *Quarterly Journal of Economics,* LXIX (February, 1955), 71–84, provide useful commentaries on dollar pooling in the sterling area.

E. INTERNATIONAL COOPERATION

Mikesell, Raymond F. *Foreign Exchange in the Postwar World.* New York: Twentieth Century Fund, 1954. Chapter 20 outlines a suggested code of fair foreign exchange practices among nations, and Chapter 22 considers desirable roles for the IMF and the GATT.

Vernon, Raymond. *America's Foreign Trade Policy and the GATT,* Essays in International Finance, No. 21. Princeton, N.J.: International Finance Section, Princeton University, October, 1954. A favorable assessment of the role of GATT.

SUMMARY OF PART III: Choosing a Policy

The open economy is faced with two major problems: internal economic instability caused by changes in its international economic relations, and balance-of-payments deficits. A change in the volume of exports induces multiple changes in GNP, national income, and employment, and leads to price changes through induced changes in consumption and investment expenditures accompanied by changes in the money supply or income velocity of money. Similar results attend a shift of expenditures between imports and home-produced goods and services and a change in the flow of capital. Balance-of-payments deficits, as seen in a loss of international reserves or the use of borrowed or gift funds to take the place of movements of reserves, stem from structural shifts and from changes in internal economic activity and prices, including various movements of capital (long, short, speculative, and/or flight). The forces creating internal economic change are those which provide an automatic tendency for the relief of balance-of-payments deficits.

Both problems may be met through monetary and fiscal policies, exchange-rate adjustment, and/or direct controls. The selection of a particular policy or set of policies depends upon which of the various policies will obtain the desired goals and what additional effects each policy may have.

A nation undergoing inflation may ease its internal difficulties by restricting credit, raising taxes, reducing government expenditures, appreciating its currency, and/or relaxing controls on imports to allow more goods into the country. If the internal inflation has induced a balance-of-payments deficit which cannot be continued, the inflation itself can be handled by the same internal policies, but the deficit must be met with opposite external policies, namely, the depreciation of the currency or the imposition of stricter direct controls.

Unemployment may be reduced by easing credit, lowering taxes, raising government spending, depreciating the currency, and/or restricting imports through direct controls to turn the demand for imports toward home-produced goods. If the unemployment is caused by a fall in exports or a rise in imports which puts the balance of payments in deficit, the deficit may also be removed by the same external measures, but the internal measures must be the opposite (credit should be tightened, taxes raised, and government spending reduced) so as to reduce import demand and raise exports.

These variations indicate that any given policy may worsen one problem while tending to solve another. A nation with unemployment and a deficit might reject monetary policy in favor of exchange-rate depreciation, whereas a nation with inflation and a deficit might not.

TECHNICAL DEFICIENCIES

But even though a particular policy may serve both objectives or may serve to obtain a single goal where only one is paramount, it may be rejected for technical reasons:

1. Monetary and fiscal policies and exchange-rate adjustments influence the balance of payments partly by changing relative prices; if foreign-export demands and home-import demands are inelastic, these policies may increase rather than help remove balance-of-payments deficits.

2. Devaluation may fail to improve the balance of payments when followed by an inflation, as tends to happen under full employment in the absence of monetary or fiscal restraint, or when wage or other income demands are particularly sensitive to import prices. On the other hand, the improvement in the balance of payments after devaluation may be thwarted, when unemployment exists, by the rise in imports which results from a rise in internal economic activity.

3. Monetary and fiscal policies and exchange-rate changes may not produce changes in the balance of payments quickly or precisely enough to reverse a critical loss of reserves.

4. A higher bank rate may frighten short-term capital out of the country rather than draw it in; the same holds when there is an expectation of devaluation occurring, whether under stable or fluctuating exchange rates.

5. Taxation may adversely affect incentives, both to work and to form capital, with unfavorable effects on output and thus on the balance of payments; this applies to the taxation of export industries through multiple exchange rates as well as to general taxation.

6. Spending and borrowing may be unresponsive to interest rate or credit changes; this casts doubt on monetary policy as a means of obtaining either internal economic stability or removing balance-of-payments deficits.

7. Fiscal policy may be difficult to shift quickly because of legislative or planning inflexibilities.

8. Monetary and fiscal policies, unless they lead to capital exports or take the form of export subsidies and the reduction of export taxes, may not prevent unemployment of resources in export industries consequent to a fall in foreign business activity.

9. The use of export subsidies may be limited by foreign governmental pressure, including the application of countervailing duties.

10. Direct controls are subject to evasion, and wide swings in international reserves occur under direct controls because of administrative lags and because of shifting leads and lags in payments and receipts.

11. Bilateral payments agreements and trade-quota agreements have not brought forth their projected volumes of trade and have created problems of uncleared balances between partner countries.

12. Direct controls may dull incentives to work and to risk capital.

ADDITIONAL EFFECTS

Besides the technical efficiency of any given policy, certain broad issues are involved in choosing among the alternative techniques of obtaining internal stability and removing balance-of-payments deficits:

1. All the techniques except direct controls may induce an adverse shift in the terms of trade which may reduce the total gain from trade for a particular country. However, direct controls may restrict the volume of trade so much that a nation may find itself wasting its resources, particularly when it discriminates. That is, as between foreign countries, or as between foreign countries on the one hand and the home country on the other, the nation fails to buy in the cheapest market and sell in the dearest market, measured in terms of real resources. Aside from any benefits that direct controls may bring to a particular country, direct controls misallocate world resources, just as tariffs do.

2. The distribution within a nation of the burden of balance-of-payments adjustment may be more "appropriate" under one technique than under another. For example, deflationary monetary and fiscal policies may add to existing unemployment or create it, depending upon the mobility of resources and the rigidity of product prices and factor rewards; devaluation changes the distribution of real income. The distribution among countries of the burden of obtaining internal stability and/or removing balance-of-payments deficits may be "unfair" if nations employ beggar-thy-neighbor policies.

3. Governments have numerous aims such as equity, defense, etc., which cannot always be shoved aside to permit the budget to be used to obtain internal stability or remove balance-of-payments deficits. Changes in taxation and interest rates affect the distribution of income, and monetary policy affects the cost of servicing the national debt.

4. The use of fluctuating rates may lead to uncertainty for traders and investors, which lowers the volume of world trade, the degree of international specialization, and the flow of capital among countries. Unnecessary movements of short-term capital between countries may also result. Direct controls, however, involve uncertainty and red tape which may burden world trade and investment. Moreover, direct controls involve specific governmental intervention in private decisions, with possible adverse consequences to freedom in political affairs.

These points show that no policy is necessarily perfect. There are too many objectives to be served and too many special interests to be satisfied to make the selection of any policy an easy task. The problem of weighing objectives against objections is a formidable one. Virtually no nation uses one of the available techniques to the complete exclusion of others, but differences are found among countries in the degree to which they rely on one technique as compared to the others. The relative emphasis placed on the alternative techniques by any given nation varies from time to time. As internal or external conditions change, the efficiency of the various policies changes. The severity of the problems to be solved may change, or the objectives of policy may shift with changes in problems and with changes of the party in power.

As a general principle, the international organizations oppose the use of direct controls. Member nations have agreed to minimize their use and have restricted the right to use other devices, such as exchange-rate depreciation, in particular cases. However, exceptions within the agreements on which these organizations are founded and the extensive use of direct controls in the past decade raise doubts that the general principles in the agreements actually reflect the state of member governments' opinions.

PART IV UNITED STATES POLICIES ON AID, TRADE, AND INVESTMENT

17 International Objectives and Transitional Policies

Especially since World War II, the formation of foreign economic policies among nations has strongly reflected a melding of economic and political objectives. Prior to World War II, diplomacy and economic bargaining were frequently separated and were not overtly directed toward a common concept of national interest. Their integration now seems permanent. Foreign economic programs are repeatedly urged on Congress with an eye as much on the general foreign-policy consequences as on the economic effects, and foreign aid has been recognized, in the words of President Eisenhower, as an "integral part of the fabric of our international relations."

The unification of economics with politics in the realm of foreign policies has not been complete. Shifting assumptions about the nature of the politico-economic world and quick changes in real conditions have brought forth a multiplicity of programs with varying economic and political purposes. The pattern of policies seems more like a patchwork quilt than a bolt of cloth showing a consistent or repeated design. This result is in the nature of things, where the only constant is change.

After World War II, the major problems facing the U.S. government in the formation of foreign economic policies have concerned the extension of foreign aid for relief, recovery, and rearmament; assistance to developing areas; and the use of commercial policies to obtain both the long-run objective of an expansion of world trade and the immediate objective of reducing trade with the Sino-Soviet bloc. Each of these problems has its roots in either the interwar experience, or the disruption of the war, or postwar political conflicts. The economic predominance of the United States in the world is well known; American policies have been and are of singular importance to the rest of the world and, of course, to Americans as citizens.

A. U.S. INTERNATIONAL ECONOMIC OBJECTIVES

Those responsible for planning the postwar foreign economic policies of the United States considered that two important lessons were to be learned from the period preceding World War II: (1) that divergent economic policies were an important source of friction between nations and were a basic factor contributing to internal economic instability, and that nations had not fully comprehended the importance of international cooperation in the solution of their common problems; and (2) that cooperative solutions had been precluded largely because nations were preoccupied with problems of domestic instability.

The problems of post-World War I adjustment and the Great Depression led to continued increases, during the 1920's and 1930's, in tariff rates and to the imposition of import quotas. To protect domestic agriculture and industry, nations found numerous ways to prevent the failure of producers whose expansion was encouraged by wartime isolation. Protection was desired also as a means of maintaining industrial and agricultural production essential for national defense. High tariff rates and short-term commercial agreements were used for bargaining purposes. During the Depression, nations attempted to relieve domestic unemployment by reducing import competition. As a consequence of growing protectionism, most-favored-nation pledges were circumvented; discrimination increased, especially by British Empire countries against the outside world.

U.S. officials argued that, after World War II, domestic economic fluctuations could be controlled and that the successful cooperation during wartime could be carried over into peacetime. They therefore set out to reduce international friction through intergovernmental cooperation and to increase the prosperity of all nations through the expansion of trade. These objectives were to be gained through a multilateral, nondiscriminatory system of trade and payments operating under some agreed-upon rules administered by intergovernmental agencies.

Plans for multilateral, nondiscriminatory trade and payments included (a) the reduction of tariff barriers; (b) the elimination of all other barriers to trade and payments, such as quotas, exchange controls, licenses, and payments agreements; (c) the implementation of the unconditional most-favored-nation principle in trade and payments; (d) the maintenance of stable exchange rates; and (e) the development of economically backward areas.

Members of the United Nations proposed the establishment of several permanent international economic organizations to help implement this program. The three organizations upon which almost all economic cooperation among the United Nations was to be built were the International Monetary Fund (IMF), the International Bank for Reconstruction and

Development (IBRD), and the International Trade Organization (ITO). They were to form a triad—a three-legged stool—relating to exchange-rate policy, foreign lending, and commercial policies. Without one, the governments agreed, the other two would be inadequate and would probably fail to gain their objectives. Each was aimed mostly at the long-run period which was to follow after the transition from war to peacetime economic activity. The operations of the Fund have been discussed in Chapters 14 and 16, and those of the Bank will be examined in Chapter 22; the failure of the ITO to be ratified and its substitution by another organization are discussed in Chapter 23.

In addition to these key organizations, the United Nations Economic and Social Council was established to help coordinate several specialized international agencies in the fields of economics and social welfare: the Food and Agriculture Organization, the World Health Organization, the International Labor Organization, the International Civil Aviation Organization, and others.

The establishment of long-run intergovernmental agencies presupposed that the member nations would be economically and politically healthy and stable. It was generally recognized that participation in the organizations could be successful only if the groundwork for economic stability had been laid through relief and reconstruction programs after the war; nations concerned almost wholly with survival can give little attention to problems of international cooperation. The other members of the United Nations were in dire straits during and immediately following the war; they needed food, clothing, housing, industrial plant and equipment, etc. Their economic systems were disorganized. In order to encourage a relaxation of controls and induce wholehearted participation in the above organizations, the United States took the official position that a primary objective of the transition period should be the removal of these pressing needs.

B. PLANS FOR THE TRANSITIONAL PERIOD

The experiences after World War I had taught the United States something of what to expect as the aftermath of World War II. During 1919 and 1920, the immediate problems abroad were relief and reconstruction; the problems were met only partly with American gifts and loans. But one of the impediments to international harmony during the interwar period was the existence of the war debts. The debts owed to the U.S. government by its allies after World War I amounted to $10 billion. The debtors considered that the funds had been used in a joint effort and therefore should be canceled or scaled down drastically. The U.S. government refused to cancel them, on the ground that the debts should be a matter of honor and good credit standing; President Coolidge reportedly asserted that "They hired the money, didn't they?" Through repeated negotiations the debts were funded into long-term obligations, but the Depression caused the debtors to default; only Finland paid off her debt.

To avoid the frictions arising from war debts after World War II, the U.S. government extended military items and other goods to its allies during the war under the lend-lease program. During 1939–1942, France and Britain had used much of their gold and dollar reserves to buy food and other materials from the United States. Britain had been forced to take a loan from the U.S. Reconstruction Finance Corporation for $425 million in order to assure payment of some early contracts with U.S. suppliers. The United States adopted the lend-lease program also to relieve her allies of the burden of financing imports of U.S. goods and services.

The U.S. government considered that it was in its own political and military interest to supply lend-lease items. They were looked upon as the U.S. contribution to mutual defense, especially necessary once the United States entered the war and until her forces could be placed in the field. The total volume of such aid was $49 billion, with the United States receiving some $8 billion in reverse lend-lease from her allies. Though the amount of aid seems large, it equaled only 15 cents of every dollar of U.S. military expenditures in World War II.

One of the first orders of business in the postwar period was to settle the lend-lease accounts and thus to remove the anxiety over repayment. The U.S. government accepted some $1.3 billion in notes from its allies, to be repaid over periods from twenty-five to thirty years, beginning in 1950. These notes covered goods still possessed by the Allies and useful in reconstruction; the rest of the lend-lease items were considered as consumed in the war effort, and for these no repayment was required.

A more pressing problem was the relief of distress in the occupied and liberated areas. The U.S. government expected that it would take from three to five years to remove the distress and reconstruct Europe to the point where it could stand on its own feet. During this period it recognized that financial assistance would have to come largely from the United States. Relief aid would probably not be required for more than two years; *most* of the reconstruction would have to be done by the European nations themselves.

Relief aid was extended primarily under the Government and Relief in Occupied Areas (GARIOA) program and through the United Nations Relief and Rehabilitation Administration (UNRRA); aid was sent mainly to the liberated and occupied areas. The U.S. military establishment provided relief goods under GARIOA to these areas to stabilize and protect the rear, i.e., as an essential part of battle operations. After hostilities ceased, it extended relief to prevent the spread of disease and unrest. Other programs for relief were continued, after GARIOA and UNRRA ceased operations, under the U.S. Foreign Relief Program, the International Refugee Organization, and the International Children's Emergency Fund.

Reconstruction assistance was provided through the Philippine Rehabilitation Program, the sale on credit of surplus war materials, the expansion of Export-Import Bank lending, a large-scale loan to Britain, and some reconstruction loans by the International Bank. This assistance took up where relief stopped; it helped to rebuild communication and transportation facilities and industrial plants, to replace destroyed or stolen equipment, and to restore productive capacity. In contrast to the financing of relief assistance by grants, almost all the reconstruction programs were financed by loans, on the ground that they contributed to the ability of the borrower to repay. Also, in contrast to the fact that most of the relief grants went to former enemy countries, most of the reconstruction loans were directed to the wartime allies of the United States—a fact which later caused some dissatisfaction among aid recipients because the ex-enemy countries actually fared better.

Table 11. U.S. Government Grants and Credits for Relief and Reconstruction

	(In millions of dollars)	
Relief Programs		
Government and Relief in Occupied Areas (GARIOA) *	$5,634	
United Nations Relief and Rehabilitation Administration (UNRRA)	2,671	
Foreign Relief Program (Post-UNRRA)	299	
International Refugee Organization (IRO)	243	
International Children's Emergency Fund (ICEF)	97	
Interim Aid Program	556	
Total relief aid		$ 9,500
Reconstruction Programs		
Philippine Rehabilitation Program	627	
Lend-lease settlements	1,383	
Surplus property credits	1,336	
Export-Import Bank loans	1,612	
British loan	3,750	
International Bank loans of U.S. dollars	548	
GARIOA credits	268	
Total reconstruction aid		$ 9,524
Grand total		$19,024

* Operations prior to June 1950, before Korean war.

SOURCE: Department of Commerce, *Foreign Aid, 1941–1951,* Supplement to the *Survey of Current Business,* Washington, 1952.

These two sets of programs for relief and reconstruction led to grants and credits by the U.S. government of over $19 billion, as shown in Table 11. They were supposed to carry the United Nations safely through the transition period from war to a peacetime position from which they could more readily pursue the long-run international economic objectives set forth above.

C. BREAKDOWN OF WORLD-WIDE COOPERATION: UNRRA

UNRRA was seen as the first step toward lasting peace. It was to be a means of removing distress and of proving the workability of international cooperation. Few doubted that relief aid should be extended; several doubted that it should be done through an international organization in which the United States supplied most of the funds but had only one vote. But the U.S. executive branch argued that it was the "least cost" way of paying for a concomitant expense of war, since other countries would contribute funds and since the administration of the aid would not rest wholly upon the United States. Congress approved UNRRA largely on the ground that this experiment in "international democracy" (one nation, one vote) should be given a trial, for if UNRRA could not operate successfully then no agency for international cooperation could.

UNRRA was a success in its major objective of easing the suffering of people overrun by the Axis forces. In the words of Herbert Lehman, its first director, it "saved millions of people in Europe and Asia from starvation, fatal disorder, and black despair." But UNRRA was unable to complete the task. The job was more difficult than envisaged at first and much greater than the $3.6 billion of funds at UNRRA's disposal.

UNRRA also ran into political problems. It had to operate through existing governments; it did not have an organization which could disburse aid directly to the people. Many governments were not fully in control of the domestic political situation, and they used the aid to bolster their political power. This action was extensive in the countries of Eastern Europe which had been occupied and liberated and then came under the shadow of the Kremlin. Most of UNRRA's aid went to these countries because of a policy determination to give aid only to countries having insufficient foreign exchange reserves. This decision led to some dissatisfaction in the U.S. Congress, however, for these areas became oriented sooner or later toward the Soviet orbit.

Conflicts arose directly with Russian representatives in UNRRA. Russian officials insisted on sending large tractors and heavy farm machinery to Eastern European countries, which would be used on collectivized farms, despite the United States desire to see private property maintained throughout the area. Another conflict arose over the treatment of refugees. The Russian government wished them to be forcibly repatriated, but the U.S. government successfully persuaded UNRRA not to return any person to his homeland against his will. This principle of voluntary repatriation—employed again to captives in Korea after the truce in 1953—meant that Russians who could get into Western Europe would not have to go back and that any Russian surrendering in battle would not have to face his Russian superiors later.

Another source of dissatisfaction was that the U.S. government did not feel that the people of the recipient nations were fully informed of the humanitarian purposes of the aid nor of the United States role in the relief program. The United States was not the beneficiary of political and economic goodwill of the recipients as she desired to be. Several factors entered into the failure of this goodwill to materialize. One was that many of the recipient governments did not feel that they had any obligation to identify the aid with the donors, because they had led their people in resisting the occupying forces and had been promised prompt relief assistance if they did so. They considered the aid as payment for their part in liberation rather than as charity which required "appreciation." A second factor was that the Eastern European countries were so closely watched by Russia that it was practically impossible for them to express their appreciation, even if they felt it. The facts that many of the recipients seemed to be going toward communism and that many governments were not publicizing the aid caused much criticism, partly by those who wanted the United States to benefit from goodwill and partly from circles inside the United States which wanted to see the internationalist approach to economic relations rejected in future policy.

These political differences were matched by disagreements as to what countries should be given aid and how much each member nation should donate to UNRRA. The United States provided over two-thirds of the goods supplied through UNRRA but could not control their use. Other members wanted nations politically or economically close to them to be made eligible or to receive more aid. These administrative and political disagreements brought an end to UNRRA in 1946 despite the continued need for relief aid to Europe.

The decision of the U.S. government to continue to send relief to Western European countries, excluding those deep in the shadow of Russia, reflected its determination henceforth to select the recipients unilaterally. The extension of this and succeeding aid under bilateral arrangements resulted from the failure of the East and the West to cooperate and from the inappropriateness of the principles of "international democracy" for an organization unequally financed by its members.

D. THE KEY TO THE "TRANSITION": THE BRITISH LOAN

Britain had been a key country in international trade and payments before World War II, and especially before World War I. She provided an international currency to those countries clearing payments through London.

Her own trade was important to a large area of the world, and she had made large foreign investments. Before World War II, Great Britain had imported one-fifth of all the exports of all other countries and had been the principal customer of the United States and a good many other countries. These imports were paid for by goods or out of income from foreign investments and other invisibles such as insurance and merchant shipping. Pursuit of the war caused a large drain on her gold and foreign-exchange reserves, caused her to sell much of her foreign investments, to pile up foreign debts (sterling balances), to suffer heavy damage to the shipping fleet, and to withdraw from some export markets. At the end of the war, her exports were down to about a third of the 1939 level, and credit was desperately needed to provide goods to reconstruct her economy, especially her export capacity.

It was thought that, if Britain's economy could be reconstructed and her currency made convertible, the U.S. and British economies would provide a sound foundation upon which to build the system of multilateral trade and payments which was to be guided by the new organizations for international economic cooperation. The objective of the loan to Britain in 1946 was to remove the pressure on her balance of payments and thus to permit her to relax restrictions and join in creating a multilateral system of nondiscriminatory trade and payments.

THE ANGLO-AMERICAN FINANCIAL AGREEMENT

Provisions

A British delegation, headed by Lord Keynes, arrived in Washington late in 1945 to ask for a gift of $6 billion or, failing that, an interest-free loan. Despite the extensive justifications brought by the British delegation and the fact that the American officials were fully convinced of Britain's need, the amount of $3.75 billion was decided upon. The decision was the result of the administration's second-guessing the reaction of a Congress which was reluctant to add to the volume of foreign aid already extended.

The loan was to be used over a period of five years to ease Britain's dollar deficit. But to the U.S. government the loan was not the most important part of the Agreement. It saw the agreement more significantly as "an understanding on over-all commercial policy . . . a joint advance by two of the world's largest economic units on the general problems of world trade."[1]

This "joint advance" related to the return of Britain to the sort of world economy which existed prior to World War I: one in which tariffs were to be reduced, quotas cut to a minimum, trade carried out on a "business basis" rather than as a phase of political policy, reduction of

---

[1] Speech by Secretary of State Byrnes before the Foreign Policy Association on February 11, 1946; see *New York Times,* February 12, 1946.

cartelization and of export restrictions, return to convertibility, and the removal of discrimination. In ratifying the Agreement, Britain accepted the principles of multilateralism and nondiscrimination by agreeing to the tenets of the ITO and by undertaking the obligation to join the Fund and the Bank.

Britain was to move rapidly toward freer trade and payments by introducing sterling convertibility during mid-1947. The U.S. government wanted to accelerate the removal of discrimination caused by the inconvertibility of sterling. But not having many dollars because of her low volume of exports, Britain could not permit holders of sterling to exchange it freely for dollars. Under the financial agreement, Britain was to permit, within one year, all those countries receiving sterling from current (as distinct from capital) transactions to exchange it for any currency desired, including the dollar.

The major reservation concerning convertibility was that the blocked sterling balances, aggregating about $14 billion equivalent, were not to be released with the funds made available under the line of credit. The balances consisted of sterling given by the British government to members of the commonwealth during the war in exchange for vitally needed goods and services. These sterling balances were intended to be used after the war, but because of her balance-of-payments difficulties, Britain could not permit their use. According to the Agreement, Britain was to seek a scaling-down of the balances by agreement with the holders and then their funding into long-term debt.

These provisions on trade and convertibility supposedly would make Britain an ally of the United States in a movement away from economic nationalism of the prewar period toward "the traditional liberal American dream of a freer world of trade," as Secretary of State Byrnes put it.

Attitudes toward the Agreement

This sweeping claim was an attempt to gain American support for the Agreement. It was disliked on both sides of the Atlantic. The Administration, Congress, and the American people did not wish to extend the loan, nor did Britain wish to receive it, at least not in the form agreed upon. Both sides felt they had no choice; Americans feared that otherwise Britain would turn to socialism completely and the British feared that without the loan they would lose their position within the Empire.

British opponents of the Agreement disliked the loan's being mixed with other financial and commercial arrangements and argued that the country had been forced to accept a "very hard bargain indeed." None of the opponents were able to come forth with an alternative plan, however. Many of them were persons who believed in national planning as a solution to Britain's problems and who argued for a more "independent" British policy which would involve continued control over trade and exchanges and closer ties to the commonwealth. They argued against being forced to adopt the American view, which in turn, they felt, reflected a desire of the United States to secure more markets for herself abroad by getting discrimination removed.

The "British trading community held the agreements to be harsh, unjust, and commercially unwise, and a wider public resented 'the dollar dictation'" implied in the tying of the loan to long-run agreements.[2] These sentiments arose from the desire to maintain and extend the discriminatory system of preferential tariffs existing throughout the Empire. Opponents also argued that the credit would probably not be sufficient in amount and that "reasonable elasticity of action" in maintaining direct controls on international trade was not permitted, especially in the requirement of an early return to convertibility.

In regard to convertibility, Lord Keynes argued that it was to the interest of the United Kingdom, as the Agreement required, to remove restrictions on currently earned sterling. If sterling were not to be convertible, the danger was that others in the commonwealth would pull out of the "dollar pool" (see page 326) and make payments arrangements with the United States and other countries independently of the United Kingdom. These countries would want Britain to repay her debts to them, Lord Keynes said, and any effort on her part to restrict convertibility of current earnings of sterling and thus to pile up more balances would be met with strong opposition. And, finally, the way for England to become an international banker once more was to begin again to permit checks to be drawn upon her and cashed for other currencies. The alternative, he argued, would be to build up an economic bloc, excluding Canada and consisting mostly of countries to which the United Kingdom was already in debt; sterling-area members would be asked to lend money to her in the form of further blocked balances which they could not afford and/or to buy goods from Britain which she was then unable to supply. This result was wanted by neither the British government nor the U.S. government.

The opposition to the loan generated during the British parliamentary debates did not ease its passage through Congress in mid-1946. Some congressmen argued that the policy of the Labour government was not to permit a relaxation of controls over trade and exchanges and that the progressive nationalization of industry would make a return to principles of private trade more difficult. When it appeared that passage of the loan was doubtful, Speaker of the House Rayburn asserted that, despite doubts about the economic and financial terms of the Agreement, without it Britain would be pushed further along the road to socialism through economic restrictions and bilateralism, and possibly even into the arms of Russia; the United States owed it to the world and to herself to help

---

[2] See *The Times*, London, December 18, 1945.

reconstruct one of the major trading countries. His speech has been credited with swinging a sufficient number of votes to assure the passage of the Agreement through Congress. Thus, in the eyes of many, the loan was more than an economic measure; it was also a political technique of binding to the West another strong ally in an effort to shore up its defenses against a recently more aggressive Russia.

FAILURE TO REVIVE BRITAIN

The Agreement was unsuccessful in achieving an early restoration of a world economy operating under the principles of multilateral, nondiscriminatory trade and payments, as evidenced by the almost immediate failure of convertibility in mid-1947 and by the continued need for direct controls. But the size of the loan was not the cause of the failure. Rather, the problems carried over from before the war, the policies adopted after the war, and changing economic conditions combined to make the dollar deficit of Britain larger than expected.

Structural problem

A long-run problem of Britain's trade and production, which she has not yet completely met, has been a structural maladjustment to changed conditions of world production and trade. Britain's exports before World War II consisted mostly of the staple trades and coal, but even in the prewar period they were declining in volume and value. She has also faced problems arising from industrialization abroad: a decline in demand for her textiles and a reduced availability of foreign raw materials for her industries. Full British recovery required (and to some extent still requires) an adaptation to the shift in demand toward new types of consumer goods and machinery necessary for industrial development abroad. This adaptation in turn required a mobility and flexibility which has been thwarted by policies of both labor unions and the government, although technical skills have been available. What has been lacking is competition sufficient to induce the introduction of new technology or a shift of resources to meet new consumer demands. Competition has been inadequate because the government has condoned a regime of industrial self-government under which business seeks security in dividing foreign markets and protecting and dividing the home market. The weakness of Britain's industry in foreign competition has been evidenced by her use of protection of the home market.

After World War II, she had the choice of reducing her reliance on imports through an improvement in the competitive position of import-competing industries, of expanding her exports by making them more competitive, or of imposing extra sacrifices in real income through the restriction of imports. But the choice was complicated because Britain's reliance on imports was so great that, if she relaxed restrictions *before* expanding exports sufficiently, a large gap in her balance of payments would result.

Internal policies to expand exports

It was necessary to increase substantially the industrial output per man, to increase the level of expenditure on capital equipment, to make certain that this increase was within an appropriate structural pattern of production, and to avoid inflation. These conditions were not easily pursued simultaneously by the same methods. Thus an increase in capital investment might easily lead to inflation; efforts to increase the productivity of labor through incentive wage increases might also lead to inflation. The problem of inflation was further complicated by the large backlog of consumer demand financed by wartime savings and by the expansion of social services by the British government aimed at equalizing real incomes.

Not a great deal could be expected in the realm of labor productivity within two or three years, but the British economy did increase its output per capita about 1½ to 2 per cent a year during the immediate postwar years. Capital investment after the war did not rise greatly until 1947, when it hit a level of over 20 per cent of national income for three years. Significantly, much of the increase was directed toward industrial re-equipment rather than to the more politically popular construction of new housing and clearance of slums. The rate of growth of output per man was not out of line with what was accomplished in other countries; it was in fact better than most. But of greater importance was the question of what items were produced. In this, Britain's record was also fair; she shifted production to the metal-using and engineering industries to offset a drop in demand for exports of coal, textiles, and agricultural products. But these shifts were not adequate and their small gains were more than offset by the combined forces of overfull employment and continued inflationary pressure bolstered by extensive subsidy and welfare programs. The result was a "dollar shortage" in international payments which was incompletely covered by the loan.

External results

The results of the British effort, as shown in her balance of payments during 1946 and 1947, were not encouraging. During 1946, the deficit was only £344 million rather than £750 million estimated during the negotiations in Washington for the loan. Hopes were raised that it would be no larger in 1947, declining thereafter. But the 1947 deficit rose precipitously to £545 million, with the dollar deficit even larger (only partly offset by surpluses elsewhere). The dollar credit was virtually gone by September, 1947, and was completely exhausted early in 1948.

What were the major forces which caused this drain? They stemmed from inflationary pressure, adverse terms of trade, and abortive sterling convertibility. Each of these operated on both sides of the balance of payments to cause an increase in the deficit during 1947. On the import side, the continued pressure of postwar demand for consumption and investment and a 19 per cent rise in import prices from the end of 1946 to the end of 1947 combined to raise imports to a value £100 million more than anticipated in 1947. On the export side, the continued inflated level of domestic demand which drained exportables into the internal market and an inability to resurrect the primary industries (especially due to the coal shortage), plus an unrealistic exchange rate, combined to dampen the rise of exports; by the end of 1947, they had reached a level only 118 per cent of prewar compared with the goal of 140 per cent which was necessary to balance payments.

The precise impact of the postwar inflation in the United Kingdom on its international payments is not measurable, and experts still disagree as to whether or not it was the predominant factor. Prices were prevented from rising rapidly chiefly by the imposition of internal price controls and rationing. The suppressed demand was then prevented from increasing the balance-of-payments deficit through additional import controls and export subsidies. The demand for goods was still there; it was just not satisfied. The demand was increased by the government's policy of maintaining full employment. The strong demand for import and export goods could have been removed by permitting the pound to depreciate far enough to limit imports without controls and to encourage exports without directing them. But, given policies of overfull employment and expanded social services, and given the strong internal demand for imported food and raw materials and for exportable goods, any devaluation would have had to be supported by direct controls.

Controls could not, however, remedy the adverse movement in the terms of trade which afflicted the United Kingdom during the postwar years. Estimates of the volume of exports which would be needed to balance international payments (with the aid of the American credit) were officially set at 175 per cent of the prewar level on an assumption of constant terms of trade. If adjustments were made for the deterioration in the terms of trade for Britain, the 1946 and 1947 exports would have had to rise to about 200 per cent of prewar. Part of the adverse movement in the terms of trade resulted from the inflation in the United States, which has been estimated to have cut the real value of the loan by 25 per cent. Had it not been for the deterioration in her terms of trade, Britain would have obtained substantial balance in her payments by 1948. Instead of achieving solvency at this time, she faced what seemed to be a continuing problem of "dollar shortage."

Part of her insolvency resulted from the abortive attempt in 1947 to achieve sterling convertibility, as stipulated by the financial agreement.

There was an increase in world demand for American goods during 1947, which, along with the rise in U.S. prices after the removal of price controls, accelerated the drain on Europe's reserves. In addition, Britain's foreign commitments for support of her armed forces abroad and support of other governments' military efforts (such as Greece) often required payment in gold or dollars or drained her export capacity by diverting goods from possible sales in the dollar area.

These demands were enough to run rapidly through her reserves, but in addition the dollar account of the rest of the sterling area worsened during 1947, dropping from a surplus of $64 million to a deficit of $759 million. The drain was accelerated by anticipatory buying for fear that dollars would become scarce within the area because of extensive conversion of sterling into dollars. Also, other countries which exported to Britain began to restrict imports from her in an effort to gain sterling balances to convert into dollars. Britain and the sterling area therefore became a source of dollars for many nonmember countries, notably for Belgium and Argentina, in the amount of some $400 million as a result of sterling convertibility during July and August, 1947.

The drain of sterling forced the U.S. government to agree that convertibility should be suspended. Britain was permitted further to discriminate against dollar goods, despite her prior agreement not to do so. The requirement of early convertibility of sterling, while probably politically necessary, given the attitude in the United States, and while not the whole cause for the crisis in 1947, certainly contributed to it and made Britain extremely cautious in making any future attempt at convertibility.

Britain's early postwar difficulties continued to plague any efforts to return to convertibility. A further reason for the continued drain on U.K. international reserves has been the withdrawal of some of the sterling balances held over from wartime purchases. These withdrawals meant that Britain exported in return for sterling balances rather than for imports. The U.S. government had foreseen that the loan might be dissipated through paying off these balances in dollars and required that they be reduced and funded. Britain accomplished little toward reducing their amount and obtained agreement only on a schedule of releases over a period of ten years or more.

Despite the fact that these releases were a factor in the loss of reserves and the continuation of aid to Britain after 1947, neither the United States nor Britain was willing to press for cancellation of the balances. The British government considered that, since a readjustment of the burden of war financing could not be imposed on all the allied nations, it should not be imposed only on countries of the commonwealth. It also saw the debts as ones of "honor" which should not be repudiated, and the damage which either repudiation or long-delayed repayment would do to London as a financial center would be considerable. The U.S. administration, on its part, recognized that the countries holding the blocked balances needed assistance in expanding imports and would turn to the United States for aid if the British forced a reduction of the balances or prevented their use. In order to assist the holders of these balances in accelerating their economic progress, the agreements on release of the balances were much more favorable to the holders (e.g., Egypt and India) than to Britain as compared to other war-debt settlements.

At the end of 1947, the outlook for Britain was dark. The loan was all but gone, and the sterling area was piling up dollar deficits rapidly. Further restrictions on imports were in the offing unless new sources of aid were forthcoming. Most of Western Europe was in a similar predicament. The winter of 1946 had been harsh and had slowed reconstruction; and a drought in 1947 cut harvests, requiring greater imports. Economic conditions in France, Italy, and Austria were deteriorating rapidly, while Germany continued to receive sizable aid under the GARIOA program. An Interim Aid Program providing over $500 million was passed by Congress in special session to prevent France, Italy, and Austria from losing the last of their reserves of gold and dollars and so to permit needed imports of fuel and foodstuffs.

The hope of attaining the U.S. international economic objectives seemed indefinitely deferred.

SELECTED READINGS

A., B., AND C. TRANSITIONAL PROGRAMS AND THEIR SETTING

Behrman, J. N. "Political Factors in U.S. International Financial Cooperation, 1945–1950," *American Political Science Review*, XLVII (June, 1953), 431–549. The discussion of UNRRA is of particular relevance.

Brown, W. A. and R. Opie. *American Foreign Assistance*. Washington: Brookings, 1953. An extensive study of all U.S. aid programs from lend-lease through the Mutual Security Program in 1952. It has detailed coverage but little analysis.

Department of Commerce. *Foreign Aid, 1941–1951*. Washington, 1952. The official statistics on aid programs over the first decade with a basic description of their purposes and operations.

Gardner, Richard N. *Sterling-Dollar Diplomacy*. Oxford: Clarendon Press, 1956. A thorough examination of Anglo-American collaboration in the reconstruction of multilateral trade and payments through the British loan and the major international economic organizations; the period covered is that of World War II to about 1950.

International Finance Section. *Survey of United States International Finance*. Princeton, N.J.: Princeton University Press. Annual surveys, covering the years 1949–1953, which present the purposes of aid, the issues considered by Congress, and the administration of the programs.

Myrdal, Gunnar. *An International Economy*. New York: Harper, 1956. Several chapters relate to the problems giving rise to foreign aid, to the reception given aid programs abroad, and to the success of aid.

Penrose, E. F. *Planning the Peace*. Princeton, N.J.: Princeton University Press, 1953. A description of the problems facing U.S. officials during the last months of the war, the negotiations with allies on postwar problems, the problems to be solved through aid, and the changing economic and political setting. Chapters 8 and 9 cover the problems surrounding relief aid.

White, T. F. *Fire in the Ashes*. New York: Sloan, 1953. A description of the problems of Europe in midcentury, the reactions of Europeans to American policies on aid, and the attempts of European countries to meet the problems of reconstruction and recovery.

D. THE BRITISH LOAN

Amery, L. S. *The Washington Loan Agreements*. London: Macdonald, 1946. British criticism of the Agreement and the program of international cooperation to which it was supposed to lead.

Crosland, C. A. R. *Britain's Economic Problem*. London: J. Cape, 1953. A review and analysis of the problems facing Britain after the war and into the 1950's.

Harris, Seymour (ed.). *The New Economics*. New York: Knopf, 1947. Chapter 28 reprints Lord Keynes' speech before the House of Lords in defense of the Agreement.

Kahn, A. E. *Great Britain in the World Economy*. New York: Columbia University Press, 1946. An analysis of the economic developments in Britain prior to World War II, the impact of the war, and their influence on her postwar adjustments.

18 European Recovery Program

Since the early frustration of efforts to gain the long-run international economic program of the United States, the foreign economic policies of the U.S. government have been altered with the changing economic and political conditions. It was evident by the end of 1946 that the Soviet Union had no intention of carrying out many of its wartime agreements to cooperate in postwar economic and political policies. A formal parting of the ways came at the Moscow Conference in the spring of 1947, when the failure to agree on unification of Germany was finally confirmed. But the East-West conflict had already been heightened by the outbreak of civil war in Greece, supported by supplies from Communist-oriented Yugoslavia and Albania. During 1947–1950, the U.S. government extended economic aid to meet the threat of a possible loss of Europe to Russia by default—i.e., through internal disorder and subversion—and military aid to Greece and Turkey to prevent their loss through aggression.

When Britain, who had been helping to stabilize conditions in Greece, notified the U.S. government that she could no longer finance the security of that nation, President Truman responded with the "Truman Doctrine" of "containment of Communism." The doctrine was implemented in part by the extension of aid to the Greek and Turkish governments; this aid was highly successful in winning the Greek war against Communist guerillas and in strengthening the Turkish border against the pressure put on it by Russian demands for territory and for a role in the administration of the Dardanelles.

To prevent the deterioration of the European economy which allegedly would make it easy for Communist groups to take over those nations, the European Recovery Program (Marshall Plan) was projected. It was to be the capstone to the relief and reconstruction assistance previously provided by the U.S. government. Secretary of State Marshall invited all European nations including Russia to accept aid and join in regional efforts to help themselves and to help each other to recover fully from the war's ravages.

The plan was aimed at placing Western Europe once again in a position to stand on its own feet and not to tremble from economic and political insecurity. The program was unprecedented and, in the words of Winston Churchill, was "the most unsordid act in history."

A. PURPOSES OF THE PROGRAM

Since reconstruction of Europe was not accomplished by 1947, even with some $10 billion of U.S. aid, the attainment of the international economic program of the United States waited upon additional measures. The administration asserted in March, 1947, that the financial resources available to foreign countries "will not, by reason either of their amount or of the nature of the developing needs abroad, prove adequate for the accomplishing of the purposes for which foreign financial assistance has been provided."[1] In May, 1947, Under Secretary of State Acheson declared that "further emergency financing" would be needed and that it should be concentrated "in areas where it will be most effective in building world political and economic stability, in promoting human freedom and democratic institutions, in fostering liberal trading policies, and in strengthening the authority of the United Nations."[2] These several purposes were to be pursued through the recovery of the European economy.

In his June, 1947 invitation to European countries to cooperate in a large-scale effort for recovery aided by the U.S. government, Secretary of State Marshall disclaimed that U.S. policy was directed against any country or doctrine; rather, he asserted, it was directed against "hunger, poverty, desperation, and chaos." Yet the overriding objective of the proposal was political, because the removal of these ills was intended to prevent the further spread of communism in Europe and, if possible, repel its recent advances into Poland, Hungary, and Czechoslovakia. The underlying thesis was that communism spread where economic chaos (poverty, disease, and unrest) or low living standards existed. The major means to be used to prevent the spread of communism was to be the raising of living standards in Europe. Of course, economic recovery and equilibrium in international payments were desired as ends in themselves, apart from their effect on the political balance of power, especially since they would remove the conditions making aid necessary. And since trade between Western Europe and the Soviet bloc would accelerate recovery, the United States was willing for Russia and her satellites to share in the aid and in economic recovery, especially if Russia ceased her pressure on Western Europe. As evidence of this attitude, the Economic Cooperation Act of 1948 authorizing ERP aid stated that the plan for European recovery was "open to all such nations

---

[1] *House Document No. 265,* 80th Cong., 1st Sess., p. 25.

[2] "The Requirements of Reconstruction," Department of State *Bulletin,* May 18, 1947, p. 993.

which cooperate in such plan." If Russia would join, it would have allegedly been evidence of a cooperative attitude, lessening the fear of Communist subversion. But, since Russia did not join, the recovery of Europe became the means of preventing the spread of communism.

The broad attack on economic and political instability was to be through a strong productive effort leading to an expansion of trade, elimination of barriers to trade, financial stability (both internal and external), and regional economic cooperation in the attainment of these objectives. The attainment of economic prosperity and political stability was supposed to permit foreign nations to obtain "genuine independence," to erect "free institutions," and to provide "individual liberty" to their citizens. These would be bolstered by the creation of healthy and expanding economies which would be possible only through the relaxation of domestic controls and a return to the free-market determination of the use of resources.

Schematically, the objectives of ERP of political stability and economic viability and the broad means of accomplishing them were, according to the legislation, as follows:

Ultimate Goals: I. Prevention of the Spread of Communism
    II. Independence of Further Extraordinary Aid

These were to be gained by the creation, in Congress' words, of:

    A. Individual liberty
    B. Free institutions
    C. Genuine independence

which in turn were to be facilitated by the related but also independent objectives of:

    1. Creation of healthy and growing economies through—
        a. intensified production efforts
        b. sound currencies, budgets, and finances
    2. Establishment of stable international economic relationships through—
        a. elimination of trade barriers
        b. "equitable" exchange rates
        c. regional economic cooperation

These objectives, in turn, were to be attained through the extension of direct aid by the U.S. government and the supervisory authority which accompanied it and through concerted efforts of self-help and mutual assistance by the ERP recipients, looking toward the eventual economic unification of Europe.

There was little official discussion of the fact that some of the objectives or demands on the program might be in conflict. It is not clear that multilateralism is compatible with European economic unification or with rapid economic recovery. Underlying the entire aid program was an assumption whose validity economists and political scientists are still arguing: that economic recovery and stability is a prerequisite to political stability and that economic and/or political stability is a necessary condition of preventing the spread of communism.

The sixteen nations which accepted participation in ERP were encouraged to help themselves and each other through the establishment of an Organization for European Economic Cooperation (OEEC). It helped to guide and coordinate national programs of recovery and to facilitate the liberalization of trade. They also formed a succession of mechanisms to multilateralize intra-European payments, discussed in Chapter 16. The domestic measures employed to expand production and gain financial stability were left more or less to the participating nations; no direct control was asked by the U.S. government.

B. DETERMINATION OF AMOUNT AND TYPE OF AID

Since the overriding purpose of ERP was political, the first decision which had to be made was what amount of aid was necessary to gain political stability. This problem was approached through the view that political unrest stemmed largely from the low standards of living compared to prewar. The administration decided that an initial aim of the aid program should be to raise living standards to the 1938 per capita level; thus, despite its assertion that the "time for relief had passed," the aid it proposed consisted largely of "relief and rehabilitation" goods. Any national income above the 1938 per capita level was supposed to go into investment for improving plant and equipment to sustain that level of consumption after aid was cut off and later to raise living standards.

After a year and a half of operation, Economic Cooperation Administration (ECA) Administrator Hoffman reported that this general plan had been carried out. Aid for projects over and above that necessary to reach the 1938 consumption level went to help in the recovery of all types of production and in the expansion of world trade. The total volume of aid was determined, therefore, with reference to this basic consumption objective plus that of making Europe able to sustain and later raise the level of consumption while achieving balance in its international payments through a liberalized trading system.

DETERMINATION OF AMOUNT OF AID

Given the above criteria, the precise determination of the amount of aid was a product of three actions: estimation by Europe of its needs, calculation by the U.S. government of Europe's needs and of U.S. resources, and reduction of these estimates by Congress.

Europe's production was still well below prewar levels. Larger populations made the agricultural problem more acute; increased production of meat depended on imports of foodstuffs to enable the diversion of land to grazing, while increased production of bread grains depended on imports of fertilizer and agricultural machinery. Resurrection of industrial production was made difficult by the fact that per capita production of fuel and power in 1946–1947 was only 60 per cent of prewar, with coal and steel production being 80 per cent and 66 per cent respectively.

These shortages required the drawing down of international reserves. Restriction of imports had already been tightened to the point of excluding fuels, food, and raw materials vital to the continuation of existing levels of production. By mid-1947 the virtual exhaustion of reserves of some countries threatened to prolong the economic and political insecurity and even to reduce living standards.

European participants in the ERP met in 1947 to estimate their requirements for the years 1948 through 1952. By and large, the goals for production in specific fields were those of prewar levels or higher in order to match population growth or to make up for losses in a competing field; for example, the decline in coal production in some countries was to be offset by expansion in oil refining.

The program of recovery projected by the ERP participants required imports of foodstuffs during 1947–1948 in volumes higher than prewar. Import programs of other materials and equipment were aimed at restoring production capacity to prewar or above. The projected balance-of-payments deficits for the four-year program were estimated at $22.4 billion—not all of which was expected to be met by direct aid, however. Some was expected to be financed through private foreign capital flows and some through the International Bank, but neither met these expectations.

Once the needs of Europe were determined, the next step was to calculate the availability of goods in the United States. This phase was carried out much more thoroughly than for any previous or subsequent aid program. In no earlier instance had any concerted effort been made to determine America's ability to extend aid. To marshal the facts on the necessity of aid and the ability of the United States to extend it, the President ordered three separate committees to make studies and recommendations: on the nation's resources to determine the ability to supply the items needed by Europe, on the probable impact of the aid on the domestic economy, and on the needs of Europe and the limits of the ability of America to supply them.[3]

Each of the reports indicated that some items desired by Europe were in "short supply" in the United States and that some inflationary pressure could be expected. A close husbanding of resources was called for, but each committee approved a volume of aid between $6 and $8 billion for the first

---

[3] A penetrating editorial in *The Economist,* October 11, 1947, pp. 585–586, pointed out the "futility" of minutely examining the need of Europe for aid, since the need was apparent and fully documented in the requests from Europe, but also the "necessity" of such an examination in order to convince Congress and other U.S. officials.

year. The administration finally decided on a volume of aid of about $18 billion over the four-year period, with $6.8 billion extended in the first fifteen-month period, ending June 30, 1949. Aid during the remaining three years was expected to decline to $5 billion, $4 billion, and $3 billion respectively.

The problems of determining the amount needed and available for aid were pointed up more sharply when Congress began consideration of the program. Its examiners reportedly found many inconsistencies and contradictions in the figures and were on the whole displeased with the presentation and justification of detailed amounts, asserting that administration witnesses were completely unable to substantiate their proposals. The administration used broad selling techniques of predicting "dire consequences" from nonaction, avowing "great expectations" from proper action, and claiming that this new aid program was an "inevitable next step" to protect past aid.[4] Despite such assertions, Congress repeatedly authorized amounts less than requested by the administration, and the sums actually appropriated were lower than the amount authorized. The reductions were not all made on sound "economic" judgment of the requirements and availabilities; rather, many were made for domestic political reasons, and much emphasis was placed on the probable increase in the U.S. government debt.[5] Over the entire program, about $12 billion were appropriated.

GRANTS VERSUS LOANS

One of the more important problems concerning the amount and type of aid was the question of whether loans or grants should be extended. The controversy had important implications for the over-all foreign economic policies of the United States in that loans would relieve the long-run burden of internal debt on the U.S. government but would later require a U.S. import surplus to allow repayment; also loans would increase Europe's debt burden and make it more difficult to balance its future payments because

---

[4] In expressing such sentiments, the administration fell into its former error of arguing that *each new* program was the capstone necessary to secure U.S. international economic objectives. Such tactics may have been thought necessary to persuade Congress, but they became dangerous for the passage of ERP, as one critic argued at the time: "we cannot afford the luxury we indulged in when we were awakening support for UNRRA, the Reciprocal Trade Agreement renewal, the British Loan, and the International Bank and Monetary Fund, namely of pretending that the step under consideration was the unique and final measure needed to discharge our responsibilities toward Europe." (Stacy May, "Measuring the Marshall Plan," *Foreign Affairs*, April, 1948, p. 458.) For discussions of these techniques in selling Congress, see Bolles, B., "Foreign Policy in the Making: The E.R.P.," *American Perspective*, June, 1948, pp. 77–110; and Neumann, W. L., "How to Merchandise Foreign Policy," *American Perspective,* September, 1949, pp. 183–193, and October, 1949, pp. 235–250.

[5] This argument that the aid would increase the government debt, since the budget was unbalanced, was urged more strongly against aid than against other expenditures. Yet no one expenditure is the cause of deficit spending.

of the fixed debt charges and would reduce the future levels of consumption in the borrowing countries during the period of repayment.

The administration determined that *some* loans would be extended under the program, but it was only under congressional pressure that the State Department testified in 1948 that some 20 to 40 per cent of the aid might be extended as loans. These were to be restricted to financing imports of capital equipment and of raw materials to be used in connection with capital formation. Congress specifically set aside $1 billion for loans; it did not want to leave discretion to the administration for fear it would extend all of the funds as grants. Congress justified its action not only on the ground that something ought to be returned for the aid but also because much of the assistance consisted of capital goods which would enable Europe to repay.

The administration decided that Congress wanted the entire $1 billion loaned regardless of whether the potential borrowers were strong enough to meet debt payments in the future. It decided that Congress would object if countries readily accepted gifts but not loans; it thus required recipients to accept loans in a predetermined ratio to the grants they received. The loans were made as general lines of credit available for purchases to be agreed upon later rather than, as had been the original justification, the loans being made *only* after a project was found which would directly increase the borrower's ability to repay.

In subsequent requests for funds, the administration argued that Europe's fixed-debt charges were all that should be imposed for the post-ERP period, even with the low interest rate and long-period maturity. ECA concluded that any further large charge upon Europe's future dollar earnings would be a deterrent to the long-run objectives of ERP. But extensive argument was required to convince Congress that there was no possibility of a "good loan" to Europe until Europe had recovered completely. In fact, Congress was not convinced and provided $150 million during the second year to be used only for loans, but in the third year the administration's advice was taken and nothing was reserved for loans. Over the whole operation of ERP, only 10 per cent of the aid was extended as loans. Aid to each country as loans and grants is shown in Table 12 on page 370.

C. ECA AID OPERATIONS

Despite the fact that the orientation of ERP changed after the start of the Korean War in 1950 from economic recovery to military rearmament of Europe, the types of commodities supplied did not change much during 1951—the last year of ECA's official operation. As explained earlier, the first year's program was largely relief in nature, with over 50 per cent of the commodities being food, feed, and fertilizer; fuel accounted for about 22 per cent, with the rest consisting of raw materials, semifinished products, and equipment. As the program progressed, greater emphasis was placed on industrial recovery; the proportion of food, feed, and fertilizer declined to less than 30 per cent in 1951 while that of raw materials and semifinished products rose to over 33 per cent and the percentage of machinery and vehicles rose from under 4 to over 18 per cent.

Table 12. Aid Provided by ECA to ERP Participants, April 3, 1948 through December 31, 1951
(in millions of dollars)

Countries	Grants	Credits	Total	Net Aid after Clearing Operations*
France	$2,074	$194	$2,268	$2,570
United Kingdom	2,407	353	2,760	2,290
German Federal Republic	1,289	4	1,293	1,190
Netherlands-Indonesia	798	151	949	1,140
Italy	1,069	75	1,144	1,060
Greece	507	1	508	830
Austria	574	0	574	800
Norway	186	35	221	400
Denmark	229	31	260	290
Turkey	56	74	129	210
Ireland	18	128	146	150
Belgium-Luxembourg	498	54	552	90
Portugal	10	29	39	50
Sweden	90	20	111	30
Iceland	18	4	22	20
Trieste	32	0	32	15
EPU	238	0	238	—
Unclassified areas	143	0	143	—
Totals	$10,237	$1,153	$11,391	

* Some ERP nations were extended grants conditioned upon their extending aid to other ERP recipients to finance the balance-of-payments deficits of the latter with the former. The amounts of these credits extended (received) have been subtracted from (added to) the total of aid from ECA to obtain an estimate of the *net* aid each country received.

SOURCE: G. Patterson, and J. N. Behrman, *Survey of United States International Finance, 1951* (Princeton, N.J.: Princeton University Press, 1952), Appendix Table I, p. 301.

The dramatic impact of the aid is better revealed by the shiploads of wheat for the undernourished, of oil to homes and factories, of machines to industry, of tractors and combines to reap the growing harvest, of enough cotton to keep more than 150,000 workers employed and working an entire year, and of tobacco and other items to ease the tension of austerity and provide some diversity in consumption, giving the labor force an incentive to increase productivity.

One of the major problems in determining the items and the quantities which should be supplied was whether the United States had enough of those required by Europe. Another was whether Europe should be required to buy commodities in the United States. Congressional winds blew in different directions on these questions as the commodities concerned became scarce or plentiful in the United States. For example, restrictions were put on the shipment of agricultural machinery from the United States while U.S. farmers needed the same equipment; and minimum requirements were put on the proportion of wheat that had to go out as flour while U.S. millers were unemployed, despite the additional cost to ECA, but were lifted when millers became more prosperous and wheat became more plentiful. Also, as required by law, most requests for agricultural goods of the types declared surplus in the United States were met from U.S. stocks. Further, the legislative requirement that 50 per cent of the shipments from the United States had to be in U.S. cargo vessels was complied with despite the increased cost and the adverse effect on shipping earnings of ERP nations.

These requirements to purchase U.S. goods and services were intensified by the general presumption that aid funds would be spent in the United States. This administrative restraint was relaxed upon occasion, however, when the price to be paid in the United States was excessively higher than in other countries. Over the four years (1948–1951), the United States was the origin of about 60 per cent of the industrial commodities and about 78 per cent of the agricultural commodities purchased with aid funds. The administration and Congress had led Latin American countries to believe that they would indirectly gain from the ERP through the expenditure of some 40 per cent of the funds in that area; but they were a poor third to Canada. Much of the purchasing outside the United States was of minerals and petroleum from sources in which American direct investments were prominent.

The later claims, by Latin Americans especially, that Western Hemisphere countries benefited little from purchases of their exports with aid funds are substantiated by the figures. Latin Americans were especially disappointed by the fact that the proportion of agricultural commodities supplied by the United States rose rapidly (from 61 per cent to 93 per cent of aid so used) as its own domestic supply increased, although most of the commodities were available in Latin America.

One of the important aspects of ERP operations was the sharing of technical and managerial skills. This activity did not require large funds, because no goods were involved, but it did require large numbers of personnel. American technicians were sent to Europe to observe and teach, while European foremen and technicians came to the United States to observe, learn, and report to groups back home. United States firms, labor unions, and professional groups played host to a variety of European "productivity teams" seeking American know-how. The result was a widespread increase in productivity not only of the several thousand individuals who made the trip to America but also of those whom they in turn instructed. This technological spurt was not the only benefit from this activity. It was also an effective propaganda tool. It gave Europeans a chance to find out for themselves what it was that made Americans and their economy tick, and it increased the interest in European recovery of those Americans sent abroad by ECA. Some reports of European teams showed that the United States had gained enthusiastic disciples for a different brand of capitalism than existed in most countries of Europe.

Instead of the Marxist picture of capitalist exploitation of the worker, British labor-union officials reported that "American unions' attitude to company profits is typical of their acceptance of a capitalist economy. However high, profits, at least in competitive industry, are not regarded as immoral or a social evil; indeed they give proof of solvency and assured employment . . . the main concern of unions is to obtain a fair share of them." Many commented on the spirit of "cooperation between management and labor," on the "sense of camaraderie based on mutual respect," and on the genuine interest of employers in their workers. On a broader scale, some Norwegian labor-union leaders reported that "A visit to the U.S. gives one greater confidence in the ability of democracy to solve its problems. . . . The country is still . . . moving forward both culturally, socially, and economically." And a British gray-iron foundry team observed that "If members of the team had learned nothing else from their travels in America and Britain, they would have learned one valuable thing, namely, the remarkable amount of good will which exists between people in the Western Hemisphere."

These statements were read and heard attentively because they did not come from Americans and were written in the same reports which displayed aspects of the American way of life which the teams did not approve, such as the pace of activity. The general conclusion of all visiting teams was that the essentials of American success were importable without requiring a change in the basic way of life of the importing country.

D.   SUCCESSES AND FAILURES OF ERP

The European Recovery Program was supposed to last four years— to mid-1952. In fact, it ended unofficially in mid-1950 with the outbreak of the Korean War. The wording on ECA's emblem was thereafter changed from "For European Recovery" to "Strength for the Free World." This shift was reflected in the use of ECA to determine and supply the economic needs of European rearmament and of its machinery to supply military aid allotted by the Department of Defense during 1950.

The period from April 3, 1948 to mid-1950 is, then, an appropriate one for judging the effects of ERP; the goals of aid changed after that time. There was considerable evidence that if ERP had been allowed to continue to mid-1952 (without the interruption of the Korean War) it would have seen greater success. But, as of mid-1950, it had failed to secure its goals in some areas though it surpassed its four-year goals in others within only two years. The areas to be examined here are: political stability, physical salvage, financial stability, structural adjustment of production, and economic unification.

POLITICAL STABILITY

The overriding objective of ERP was that of political stability, which meant the prevention of the spread of communism and the weakening of its strength in Western Europe. Political stability was also to be reflected in the release of governmental controls and the increase of individual freedom.

If the evidence adduced by ECA is taken as proof—that of the decline in the number of Communist members in parliaments and in labor unions —communism had been halted in Europe. But the internal threat had by no means been eliminated, for it continued in France and Italy, having a strong hold on labor unions and being a disturbing force in their parliaments.

ECA planners had based their attack on communism on the belief that the benefits of aid and recovery would "trickle down" to the workers and provide them an incentive to reject Communist propaganda. But the recovery of European production did not bring great relief from the misery of the workers, many of whom remained in slums while the well-to-do began again to ride in big cars and to give fancy dinners and parties. While it could be claimed that ERP aid had prevented workers from being wholly unemployed and had raised their real income, this was scant comfort to people whose clothes were shabby and who lived in smelly, unhealthy settlements. It gained no love for the United States by proving that the aid prevented death and starvation, because the employment and incomes America provided were under the same "capitalistic" conditions as had been detested prior to the war and which the Communist-led laborers were taught to believe was contrary to their interests.[6]

ECA was caught in a dilemma in its efforts to achieve economic recovery and satisfaction of the masses simultaneously in so short a time. There is an inherent conflict in trying to expand production and exports rapidly while at the same time increasing social services and raising wages.

---

[6] See T. H. White, *Fire in the Ashes* (New York: Sloane, 1953), especially p. 69.

By the summer of 1950, ECA officials had prepared a new attack on the problems of income distribution and on productivity of labor and wages. The object was to "Americanize" European capitalism and win the workers to democracy, but the plan was only partially implemented and rearmament took precedence. The failure to obtain a wider distribution of benefits among people left some apathetic to the "new Europe." It was partly because of this apathy that many congressmen later charged Europeans with not having the "will to defend" their country against Russia.

As to the other aspect of political stability—that of moving toward freer enterprise and the removal of controls—there was a significant relaxation of some governmental controls. But Europe was still hampered by many restrictive practices of both government and private enterprise. A free market economy was far from being established, and technological advance was still slow.

Despite these failures, Western Europe was genuinely independent of foreign intervention, and the governments accorded a large degree of individual liberty to citizens. ERP was a "holding action." It prevented Europe from falling into chaos and helped prepare those countries to make the long-run decisions as to their place and responsibility in international affairs.

PHYSICAL SALVAGE

The "holding operation" was achieved almost wholly through placing Europe once again in command of a functioning economic system. Its *physical* salvage was complete. By mid-1950, ECA had reported that the recovery which many thought could be achieved only in four years had been reached in two and with total aid expenditures of less than half the original amount requested.

The over-all industrial output of the ERP countries rose about 28 per cent from the inception of the program to mid-1950. This was exemplified by a higher output of motor vehicles than ever achieved in Western Europe, by a postwar peak in steel production, by the virtual cessation of coal imports consequent to the expansion of domestic supplies, by an increased electric-power capacity of 12 per cent over 1948, and by a textile output of 25 per cent over the 1948 average. Agricultural production was up 9 per cent over prewar averages but was still below the prewar level on a per capita basis as a result of a 10 per cent increase in population since the war; the most bountiful harvest since the war was reaped in 1950 as a result of good weather, better supplies of fertilizer, and more adequate stocks of farm equipment. High agricultural and industrial production carried with it a reduction in unemployment and higher output per worker. This rise in general productivity was accompanied by longer hours of employment, repair and reconstruction of transportation, increased supplies of fuel to consumers, and a steadier and more adequate flow of raw materials and of food for consumption.

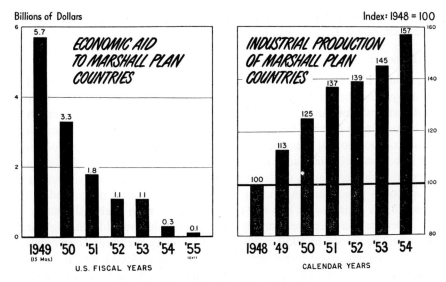

Fig. 17   Marshall Plan Result in Europe

SOURCE: International Cooperation Administration

The above improvements were reflected also in an expansion of intra-European trade and trade with the Western Hemisphere. An impeding factor in the restoration of trade was the need to channel industrial output into reconstruction at home, but ECA reported that during late 1949 and early 1950 these bottlenecks were largely broken. These results, along with the favorable effects of devaluations in September, 1949, brought the level of international trade of the ERP countries in late 1949 to 17 per cent above the 1948 level, and intra-European trade exceeded the prewar volume for the first time since the war. The balance-of-payments deficit with the United States was reduced continuously from late 1949 to mid-1950, at which time Western European exports reached a new high in volume of 121 per cent of prewar. These advances permitted economic assistance to Europe to decline greatly after 1950. It appeared that the fundamental economic objective of ERP—"the re-establishment of the ability of European countries to support themselves without outside assistance"—was practically achieved or at least within sight. In fact, the industrial growth of Europe continued after the cessation of aid.

It must be recognized that this physical recovery was not accomplished wholly by ERP aid. Aid received by Europe yearly was only about 5 per cent of the GNP of the recipients. But the aid did provide equipment, fuels, materials, etc., necessary to putting entire plants into operation. It was therefore a key factor in providing critically short items so that domestic economies could expand production. This remarkable record of achievement in physical recovery was not accompanied, however, by a similar record in the attainment of other goals set forth by Congress in the 1948 and subsequent ERP legislation.

FINANCIAL STABILITY

Only incomplete success could be claimed with regard to financial stability. The program did encourage a return of confidence in currencies and a renewal of business contacts through the restoration of production. This confidence induced farmers who had previously hoarded or consumed their products to sell them in town markets, increasing the supply of food for urban consumption and thus stabilizing prices. Food prices were an especially thorny source of discomfort in the French economy. During a four-month period in the latter half of 1947, retail food prices had risen over 50 per cent; wages had not bought so little even during the war.

Despite the increased supply of goods made available through aid, there still remained in 1950 significant inflationary pressures (accentuated in some countries by unbalanced governmental budgets) which warped economic decisions and kept pressure on international balances. Complete financial stability or convertibility of currencies was not attained. Some stability was achieved through stringent monetary policies (such as credit restrictions) and wage and price controls. By these measures, the inflation was reduced to the "creeping" stage in some countries and was halted in others. It was accelerated again by the rearmament drive in late 1950. Experience under ERP gave evidence that the solution to the problem of inflation is not to be found in aid but depends more on the domestic policies of governments.

STRUCTURAL ADJUSTMENTS

The same frustration of ECA's goals was evidenced in the absence of appropriate structural adjustments. Adjustments were needed to help meet both the problems of international imbalance and of domestic financial instability. These problems in turn required a rechanneling of resources to meet new foreign trade demands, to improve selling techniques so as to compete better abroad, and to revise income payments so as to increase incentives and thereby productivity; i.e., real income should reflect productivity rather than be determined, as through consumer subsidies, without regard to output.

A study by the U.N. Economic Commission for Europe in 1953 concluded that the major shifts in the sources of Western European imports had been precisely the opposite of those required to gain equilibrium in its dollar balance and that the use of labor and capital had been turned toward narrow national objectives; little advantage had been taken of specialization among European countries.[7] The heavy inflow of ERP aid should have

---

[7] *Economic Survey of Europe Since the War* (Geneva: United Nations, 1953), Chapters 6 and 8 especially.

given Europe a chance to make structural adjustments, but the director of the Economic Commission for Europe sadly reported in another study that "American aid was used by the receiving countries to raise their national production while consolidating still further the autarchic structure of West-European industry."[8]

Nor is there any evidence that ECA used *its* influence in the program to build facilities appropriate to the "integrated" European economy for which it was supposedly striving. ECA placed greater emphasis on a *rapid* expansion of production and employment, which could best be done, it thought, through the existing structure of production; whether that system was prepared to function in the new world community as conceived in the U.S. international economic objectives or in the prewar world of economic nationalism was another question. A congressional staff study called attention to the fact that little progress was being made toward integration in the following terms:

There is reason to believe that basic factors which were making the industrial and commercial structure of Europe obsolete before the war persist, and must be either counteracted or compensated if Europe is to perform the military and political role which United States foreign policy contemplates. In particular it appears unlikely that Europe can ever regain its place as the workshop and banker for Asia, Africa, and Latin America.[9]

Specifically, the projects undertaken to restore the iron and steel industry retarded the attainment of the integration objective. The evidence in this industry and in others (such as textiles, power, oil refining, and chemicals) was that prewar plants were rebuilt regardless of the changed pattern of world demand and trade. Instead of becoming a pattern of complementarity in industry and agriculture along lines of comparative advantage, Europe's prewar patterns tending toward self-sufficiency were rebuilt.

Congress has continued to argue, and the Economic Commission for Europe has agreed, that a major solution to these problems would be the economic integration of Europe, meaning the removal of export and other subsidies and of restrictions on production and trade, the reduction of tariffs and taxes, and the closing of uneconomic plants.

ECONOMIC UNIFICATION

Congress has repeatedly emphasized its interest in the "political federation" and "economic unification" of Europe. Unification of Western Europe into an integrated economic unit would create one mass market allegedly providing the benefits of internal and external economies of large-scale production. Such integration also would require substantial coordination of

---

[8] Gunnar Myrdal, *An International Economy* (New York: Harper, 1956), p. 62.
[9] "An Analysis of the ECA Program," *Congressional Record,* June 16, 1950, p. 8708.

monetary and fiscal policies to minimize balance-of-payments difficulties. Furthermore, the removal of conflicting wage and investment policies would be necessary to obtain the best allocation of resources. European countries have been unwilling to eliminate their nationalistic policies regarding the use of land, labor, and capital. Only Belgium, the Netherlands, and Luxembourg have made some progress in forming a customs union (Benelux) during the past decade.

To reduce the bilateralism which characterized Europe's trade and payments, the OEEC members did agree on a progressive liberalization of restrictions. Even so, the expansion of trade was not large in volume, and the significance of the increase was blurred by the postwar shifts in demand, prices, and production. Also, the removal of restrictions *within* Europe increased discrimination against outsiders, especially the United States, because restrictions on trade with non-European countries were not relaxed significantly. The integration of Europe into a fully multilateral system of trade and payments was far from accomplished. A congressional staff study concluded in 1950 that the failure was attributable to internal policies of participants:

> In many respects the multiplicity of import quotas and exchange restrictions which characterize the European economy today should be regarded as symptoms of a disease rather than as a disease itself. As long as countries are consuming more than they produce, spending more than their revenue, and maintaining uneconomical industries in order to keep workmen from losing their jobs, they are forced to impose restrictions on the movement of goods and services.[10]

The most successful move to widespread integration was through the European Payments Union, discussed in Chapter 16, but a major problem has remained of extending convertibility beyond the Union. The key position of the dollar in the success of European convertibility and economic integration and in establishing a world-wide system of multilateral trade and payments has caused some observers to propose a plan for liberalizing trade and payments within the Atlantic community, including the United States and Canada. Despite the support received for the proposal in Europe, neither the United States nor Canada has shown any great interest in a grouping which might require them to extend still more credit or aid to cover their surplus accounts with Europe.

Given the limited scope of the liberalization of trade to countries within Europe and the limited convertibility, the move to integration has resulted in a system which is based upon discrimination. Unless the system can eventually be broadened to remove the intra-European preferences or to include the whole Free World, the U.S. emphasis on European integration seems to have been contrary to her own international economic

---

[10] *Ibid.,* p. 8709.

objectives of a multilateral system of nondiscriminatory trade and payments.

Various proposals have been made to make Europe one economic and/or political unit, either step by step, taking one industry or area at a time, or by sweeping transfers of authority to a supranational agency. The step-by-step approach was begun through the European Coal and Steel Community (Schuman Plan); it opened the markets in coal, iron, and steel of each European member nation to all other members and placed their industries under a supranational authority. One purpose of the Plan, which received wide U.S. governmental support, was to make difficult, if not impossible, any war between Germany and France. It was also aimed at improving the efficiency of production and assuring member nations of access on equal terms to products and raw materials. A common market in coal and steel was sought through a gradual removal of duties, subsidies, and restrictive devices as well as removal of discriminatory practices among buyers, producers, and consumers. Free movement of coal and steel workers among the six nations was also allowed. The external duties of members on coal and steel and their products are set within limits determined by the High Authority of the Coal and Steel Community. The High Authority also has power to borrow funds, coordinate investment programs, impose fines, and otherwise regulate the industry.

This move toward integration has been successful enough to encourage the High Authority to take advantage of a clause in the agreement of the Community urging it to seek additional measures for economic and political integration and to sponsor conferences looking to that end. Additional efforts were made for European integration in connection with the military rearmament of Europe, but agreement on a European Defense Community which was negotiated with proferred American support failed of ratification. However, it must be noted that none of these steps toward unification came as a *direct* result of the U.S. foreign-aid programs, though the experience in cooperating through OEEC has been an important factor in paving the way to collaboration in other areas.

SELECTED READINGS

No comprehensive study of the European Recovery Program has yet been made; however, some fairly intensive analyses and some extensive description will be found in the general readings listed at the end of Chapter 17. The following selections relate to the need for recovery aid, the operation of ERP, and the process of recovery during and after ERP.

Bok, D. C. *The First Three Years of the Schuman Plan.* Princeton Studies in International Finance, No. 5, Princeton University, 1955. A review of the plan in operation, the effects of competition, and economic achievements.

Diebold, W. J., Jr. *Trade and Payments in Western Europe.* New York: Council on Foreign Relations and Harper, 1952. An examination of the problems and success of economic integration of Europe's trade and payments through efforts at liberalizing controls and at making currencies convertible.

Economic Commission for Europe. *Economic Survey of Europe Since the War.* Geneva: United Nations, 1953. This comprehensive survey of the success of Europe's recovery efforts from 1946 through 1952 also analyzes the impact of American aid; Chapter 6, 7, and 12 review and analyze the inadequacy of structural readjustment, the conditions necessary for restoration of external equilibrium, and the problems of economic integration. This study is complemented and continued by the ECE's annual *Economic Survey of Europe* and by its quarterly *Bulletin*.

Economic Cooperation Administration. *Report to Congress.* The semiannual reports of ECA to Congress provide a contemporary review of the operations under ERP and of the problems which ECA considered most important.

Ellis, H. S. *The Economics of Freedom.* New York: Council on Foreign Relations and Harper, 1952. An examination by several contributors of the many facets of European recovery, including the ERP. This volume is the nearest to a comprehensive evaluation of ERP that exists.

European Coal and Steel Community. *Newsletter.* The ECSC publishes a periodical information sheet on its activities and problems and progress of European integration.

Gehrels, F., and B. J. Johnston. "The Economic Gains of European Integration," *Journal of Political Economy,* LXII (August, 1955), 275–292. An analysis of the benefits to Europe of closer economic cooperation in the form of a customs union or federation.

Haberler, G. "The European Recovery Program," *American Economic Review,* XXXVIII (September, 1948), 495–525. An examination of the problems facing Europe in early 1948 and the prospects of the success of aid.

Harris, S. E. *Foreign Economic Policy for the United States.* Cambridge, Mass.: Harvard University Press, 1948. Part IV is a preview of the problems and prospects of European recovery as seen by various writers, and Chapters 24 and 25 are analyses of the "dollar shortage."

————. *The European Recovery Program.* Cambridge, Mass.: Harvard University Press, 1948. A scanning view of the problems leading to the ERP and of the obstacles to success of aid.

Hazlitt, Henry. *Will Dollars Save the World?* New York: The Foundation for Economic Education, Inc., 1947. A critique of the technique of aid in obtaining the objectives sought; the conclusion is that dollars of themselves cannot save other nations, and the reasons are provocative.

Hoover, C. B. "Foreign Aid and Communism," *Journal of Political Economy,* LIX (February, 1951), 1–13. An analysis of the extent to which the subsiding of Communist pressure in European countries could be attributed to foreign aid.

Organization for European Economic Cooperation. *Interim Report on the Recovery Program.* Paris, 1948; and *European Recovery Programme, Second Report of the OEEC,* Paris, February, 1950. Reports on the projected balance-of-payments deficits by Europe, the proposed uses of aid, and the results of a year and a half of aid. The OEEC now issues annual reports on the economic conditions in Europe.

Williams, J. H. "Europe after 1952: The Long-Term Recovery Problem," *Foreign Affairs,* XXVII (April, 1949), 426–448. An examination of Europe's prospects for recovery at the end of ERP made at the end of one year of aid. Subsequent analyses of the success of ERP are "The Marshall Plan Halfway," *Foreign Affairs,* XXVIII (April, 1950), 463–476, and "End of the Marshall Plan," *Foreign Affairs,* XXX (July, 1952), 593–611.

19 Aid for Military Security

Instead of disarming after World War II, Russia increased her military strength. In 1948, she stood mobilized around her western borders. Her divisions were deployed so that they might cut across the north German plains into the Low Countries and France and through the slender waist of West Germany. The threat was of an almost overnight march which would result in the seizure of an industrial grouping in Western Europe more than double the capacity of Russia and would leave America without a continental bastion.

Western Europe could have provided only token defense. Defense forces in Germany were for occupation rather than fighting, and their lines of communication were parallel and so close to the front that they could have been scissored within forty-eight hours. Reserve strength behind this crust of protection consisted of the demobilized armies of Britain, France, and the United States (a full month away). Air defense was almost nonexistent. Russian fighting strength was more than three times that of the West. "All the Russians need to get to the Channel," observed one American military statesman at the time, "is shoes."[1]

Something was stopping the Russians; *or* they did not want Western Europe. United States policy could not accept the latter view. The sole counterweight to Russian might was the temporary monopoly of the atomic bomb held by the United States, deliverable by its Strategic Air Command from several localities around the rim of Sovietland. But Russia was busy building her own atomic weapons; success was announced in 1949 with the explosion of the first Soviet nuclear bomb. Western strategists then estimated that by 1953 the Russians would be in a position to retaliate atomically and would be able to launch a destructive if not successful offensive.

Between 1949 and 1953, the West poured billions of dollars, hundreds of thousands of men, and untold man-hours of midnight oil burning into

---

[1] Quoted in T. H. White, *Fire in the Ashes* (New York: Sloan, 1953), p. 295.

redressing the power balance in Europe. By the end of 1953, this balance had shifted from the East to the West—based largely on the West's air power, though divisional strength had increased also. The strength of these divisions was being improved continuously. Over 5 million tons of American military supplies, over 500 planes, and almost 100 warships had been sent to Europe by the end of 1953, making every continental army a composite of American equipment and European soldiers. The Western front was protected, if not secured, by the North Atlantic coalition and U.S. military aid, backed by U.S. atomic bombs.

Since 1953, greater emphasis has been placed on building military forces in other areas. Regional defense arrangements have been set up in both the Far East and the Middle East supplementing the pact already existing among the Americas. The military strength of these areas is still inadequate. They cannot support the forces they have without U.S. aid or without an excessive drain on their own production. Even the forces they have are inadequate protection in the event of war. Yet, over the world, the U.S. government succeeded by 1955–1956 in inducing a braver military posture confronting Communist aggression. It believed that, because of this success, Russia had relaxed her aggressive pressures in mid 1956, as shown by the facts that no *new* aggression had been started since the Korean War in 1950 and that Russia had shifted her tactics vis-a-vis the West to emphasize economic competition.

A. PURPOSES AND MAGNITUDE OF ASSISTANCE

Geopoliticians call the Eurasian land mass extending from the western borders of Russia into Siberia, Manchuria, and China "the Heartland." It has often been claimed that "who rules the Heartland rules the World." An opposing thesis has been that the formation of a Rimland around the Heartland would enable others to contain the outward expansion of the rulers of the Heartland. Whether or not the U.S. government subscribes to either thesis, its policies on military assistance have been oriented toward the formation of a rim around the Sino-Soviet bloc strong enough to repel its advances. This Free World area—extending from Britain and Western Europe, around the Mediterranean, across South Asia, and around the Pacific up to Korea and Alaska—supposedly provides ample bases for military operations. And, coupled with the economic strength of the United States, Canada, and Latin America, it would provide a preponderance of power as compared to the Soviet bloc.

American military aid to encircle the Heartland has been justified in the interest of peace and justice. President Eisenhower has stated that "the sole objective" of the Mutual Security Program (including all military and economic aid) is the attainment of "peace and justice" and that the United States has no other interest to advance. The assistance is supposed "to

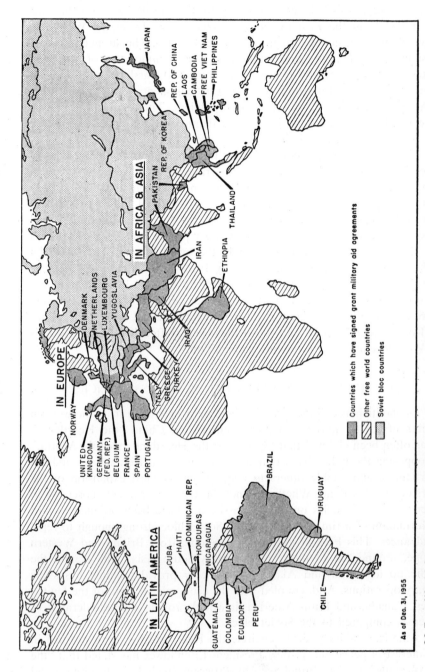

38 Free World Countries Have Entered into Agreements for Grant Military Aid under the Mutual Security Program

SOURCE: International Cooperation Administration

As of Dec. 31, 1955

Countries which have signed grant military aid agreements

Other free world countries

Soviet bloc countries

IN EUROPE
NORWAY
UNITED KINGDOM
GERMANY (FED. REP.)
BELGIUM
FRANCE
SPAIN
PORTUGAL
DENMARK
NETHERLANDS
LUXEMBOURG
YUGOSLAVIA
ITALY
GREECE
TURKEY

IN AFRICA & ASIA
PAKISTAN
REP. OF CHINA
REP. OF KOREA
JAPAN
LAOS
CAMBODIA
FREE VIET NAM
PHILIPPINES
THAILAND
IRAN
IRAQ
ETHIOPIA

IN LATIN AMERICA
CUBA
HAITI
DOMINICAN REP.
HONDURAS
NICARAGUA
GUATEMALA
COLOMBIA
ECUADOR
PERU
BRAZIL
URUGUAY
CHILE

further the cause of freedom and independence and to develop the military strength necessary to protect and defend it."[2] The U.S. government has made repeated assertions that aid would not be used to erect American-style democracies abroad. Rather, the objective has been to build up "independent" and "strong" governments so that nations allied with the United States would be stable enough to choose the form of government they themselves want. Presumably this would permit an "independent" government to choose a form of communism or totalitarianism if it wanted to, so long as it was done without assistance from or revolution inspired by the Sino-Soviet bloc—witness U.S. support of both Yugoslavia and Spain.

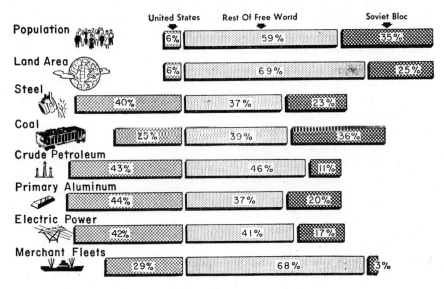

Fig. 18   Combined Strength of the Free World Is Vital To Peace
SOURCE: International Cooperation Administration

Assistance to increase military strength was given primarily to Europe under the Mutual Defense Assistance Program (MDAP) beginning in 1949. MDAP has been continued under the broader Mutual Security Program. In 1953, after Europe was considered secure, military funds were shifted to the Far East and more recently to the Middle East and South Asia. Latin America has only a small role to play in the Rimland thesis because it is considered safe from aggression; it has been accorded only token amounts of military assistance compared to the other areas.

The assistance has been given on both a country-by-country basis and on a regional basis. The U.S. government has attempted to obtain regional defense arrangements with the key areas surrounding Sovietland, but it

---

[2] Message to Congress on the Mutual Security Program, March 19, 1956.

has failed to complete the ring. It has filled in with bilateral arrangements. Countries having agreements with the United States almost encircle the Sino-Soviet bloc.

Before 1953, almost 90 per cent of military aid went to Europe, and Europe also received most of the nonmilitary assistance. Since then, the ratio has shifted so that nations of the Near and Far East (including South Asia) are receiving over half the military assistance and about 80 per cent of the nonmilitary aid. Despite the emphasis on military buildup in the Far East after the Korean War, military aid to that area has not reached the total extended to Europe; between 1950 and 1955, average appropriations of funds for Europe were $3 billion a year and average expenditures less than $2 billion. Nations of Asia and the Far East have received an average of $500 million annually, while those in the Middle East have averaged $400 million and Latin American countries only about $30 million annually.

The military assistance has consisted mostly of military equipment and supplies but some items have also been given for the direct support of defense forces, such as food and clothing for soldiers and petroleum for vehicles and fuel. Over the first six to seven years of operation of MDAP (1949--1955) the U.S. government shipped over $13 billion of aid, including 40,000 tanks and combat vehicles, 1,200 naval vessels of all kinds, 44,000 artillery pieces, 7,000 aircraft (half of which were jets), 2 million small arms and machine guns, and billions of rounds of ammunition, plus various electronic and other equipment for communication and detection, besides several billion dollars of defense-support items.

The U.S. government has approved the aid on the ground that it would yield a faster and larger return in terms of U.S. national security than could be obtained by increasing the budget of the U.S. Armed Forces by the same amount. The U.S. government would not bear the full cost, and the total cost of the same defense built abroad, rather than in the United States, was less. The average annual cost of maintaining an American soldier has been estimated by the Department of Defense at about $6,000; the average cost to the United States of maintaining a foreign soldier was estimated at about $750—a ratio of 8 to 1. Based on the cost of maintaining forces and defense expenditures equal to those in NATO Europe, the Defense Department estimated that for the United States to obtain the same facilities and number of soldiers at American pay scales would have cost not the $2 billion in aid sent yearly from 1950 through 1954 but an additional $25 billion yearly. The aid program also provided a means of utilizing obsolescent equipment held by the U.S. Armed Forces. The cost of the aid was also argued to be small in comparison with war, which it was hoped would be avoided as a result of the aid. The annual cost of all military aid was far less than the average cost of one month of war during

World War II, which had been about $7 billion a month for forty-five months of war.

Initially, the military objective of the aid was to expand the power of Western Europe and other nations friendly to the United States until a "parity of power" was reached with the Soviet bloc. This parity was calculated on a "year of maximum danger," which was supposed to be 1953, at which time the Soviet build-up, backed by atomic bombs, would constitute a maximum threat to Europe. Because of the rapid development of thermonuclear weapons and the shift in emphasis to air power, parity was never reached in ground forces. But by 1956, a stalemate seemed to have developed which permitted a shift of the European aid program to a stand-by basis and greater emphasis on the military build-up around the rest of the Rimland.

B. ECONOMIC SUPPORT FOR REARMAMENT

In addition to aid in the form of military supplies, the U.S. government has felt it necessary to support the defense effort of other nations with economic aid and with additional dollars provided through contracts placed abroad for aid goods.

DEFENSE-SUPPORT AID

During the shift from emphasis on European economic recovery to military rearmament in 1951 and 1952, the U.S. government sent significant amounts of raw materials and manufactured items to support mobilization in Europe. The justification was that increased rearmament expenditures added to the pressures on balances of payments by increasing the demand for exportable goods and for imports; imported materials were needed for mobilization, and the rise in over-all demand increased the demand for imports indirectly through inflation. Britain, especially, faced a cut in living standards as domestic goods and imports were shifted into military uses and production. Such a reduction was not considered desirable in view of the previous efforts to raise living standards through the European Recovery Program. The nations of Europe could, of course, have freed resources for their military expansion by reducing private domestic demand (consumption and investment) through heavier taxes and higher interest rates. They did increase taxation and did sustain temporary cuts in consumption later made up through continued economic growth. But the U.S. government considered that their unassisted efforts would not be sufficient for U.S. and Free World security.

To alleviate these economic pressures, most European nations called for less military aid and greater economic aid for defense support. The more the military aid, the greater the drain on the (private) domestic economy in order to supply men to use it and matériel to complement it. The U.S. Congress was, however, never wholly sold on the idea of large economic aid for military security, because it seemed too much like recovery assistance which it had supposedly terminated. Many congressmen also feared that Europeans would not put enough of their resources into military production if economic goods were given them rather than military items. Thus Congress was, until 1956, much more eager to extend military assistance than defense-support aid; it also felt that it could justify such aid much more readily to the American people.

The administration replied that the distinction between recovery aid and defense support was not so much in the goods (which were mostly of the same type as sent under ERP) but in the purpose; the purpose was now to make possible the expansion of defense efforts for mutual security. Without defense-support aid, the "heart and soul" of the military program would be cut out, the administration argued; defense support was "the most important single item" in the development of European security. Congress provided funds reluctantly and in decreasing amounts; in 1956, no more of such assistance was given to European countries save Spain and Yugoslavia until the oil crisis in Europe resulting from the blocking of the Suez; in December, the U.S. government inaugurated a program of oil supply to aid members of the OEEC. But the Near and Far East required increasing amounts of non-military aid.

With the increased emphasis on the military build-up in Asia, most of the defense-support aid has been sent during the past few years to that area. Such assistance has in fact constituted the largest single type of aid to Asia. The items sent have included raw cotton, fertilizer, petroleum, coal, machinery and vehicles, clothing, and agricultural items to build a stronger economic base for military strength.

A military establishment subtracts from consumer goods available to the people. The U.S. Government has desired that some of its allies have larger military establishments than they can readily bear in the face of domestic political and economic pressure. Defense-support aid has permitted the financing of such establishments at a cost to the United States far less than the same military protection in terms of U.S. forces. An example is provided by South Korea. It supports the same number of divisions as the United States out of a population of 22 million with per capita GNP of $80 a year. But the cost of maintaining these twenty divisions is comparatively small, so that U.S. aid of some $300 million can provide a substantial part of the cost of Korean forces plus the cost of some power plants, of reconstructing some railroads, and of some consumption goods to help halt inflation resulting from military expenditures.

Almost two-thirds of all defense-support aid to the non-European areas has been in the form of commodities purchased in the United States (agricultural surpluses where feasible) and sold in the recipient country for counterpart funds (local currencies). These funds are in turn used to support military forces, to build transportation and communication facilities, housing, industry, etc., necessary to increase the strength of the nation and to accelerate its economic progress. Congress has recently been much more willing to send defense-support aid to these areas than it has been to send it to Europe; it agreed with the administration that U.S. allies "cannot be strong and stable if an unbearable defense burden makes it impossible to meet the reasonable aspirations of their peoples for progress."

The assumption underlying the objective of economic development to gain military strength has been that if these nations "succeed in reasonable development, it is likely they will remain as part of the Free World and be strong enough to resist the subversive efforts of Communism."[3] Examination of this proposition is left to Chapters 21 and 22.

OFFSHORE PROCUREMENT

Another technique aimed at increasing the productive capacity of allied nations, especially in military items, has been that of procurement of U.S. aid goods in foreign countries. Rather than shipping goods abroad from stocks held by its Armed Forces or placing orders in the United States, the U.S. government has contracted to pay dollars for aid goods produced either in the recipient country itself or by another allied nation. From September, 1951, when the procedure was adopted, to December, 1955, contracts amounting to $2.8 billion were let; all were in Europe except $100 million in the Far East. (This does not include purchases by the U.S. Military Establishment for support of its forces abroad, which is a larger figure.)

The major purposes of this technique have been more diffuse than cost saving, though many of the contracts have resulted in a reduction of aid costs. A major objective has been to provide additional dollars to meet Europe's balance-of-payments deficits. Several other advantages are claimed for offshore procurement. It is alleged to be a builder of morale, since the allied nations feel that they are responsible for their own progress and security when they produce much of their own military equipment. Also, it is supposed to initiate a broad production base, "triggering" production abroad of desired goods. Some military production abroad is desirable to shorten supply lines and to prevent the "distortion" of the U.S. economy which would result from production of all military aid goods in the United States.

The encouragement of foreign production through U.S. procurement abroad was also supposed to permit the placing of orders in such a way as to discourage cartels, to reduce pockets of unemployment, and to encourage democratic labor unions. United States officials have at times

---

[3] *The Mutual Security Program, Fiscal Year 1957,* a summary presentation by the Departments of State, Defense, and the International Cooperation Administration, April, 1956, pp. 49, 50.

refused to give contracts to companies having Communist-dominated labor unions; they have sometimes refused contracts to firms participating in cartels, and they have placed orders with firms where unemployment was threatening to create disorder. Such actions are supposed to have improved productivity and enhanced the role of private enterprise and individual initiative. But these criteria for placing contracts have engendered some ill will in Europe and have run counter to principles of free enterprise. The lowest bidder has not always been awarded the contract, even when the bid was solicited. Contracts to other than the lowest bidder have been awarded upon the bases given above and whether or not the firm would require a future contract from the United States to continue in production or the recipient government would take over the orders.

C.   SUPPORT TO REGIONAL MILITARY STRENGTH

United States military aid is only part of the rearmament of the Free World. The success of aid is measureable partly by the efforts others have made to increase their military strength. Broadly, the U.S. government claims that its allies "are bringing into being" more than 200 divisions, over 2,000 naval vessels, and about 300 air squadrons that the United States is helping to equip and support. This force is about ten times the number of U.S. divisions, about the same number of air squadrons, and about the same number of U.S. active naval vessels. However, the phrase "are bringing into being" is without timetable and gives no indication of the actual strength of these programmed forces. The decisions as to how fast to reach full strength in each country can be affected only indirectly by U.S. officials and U.S. aid.

NATO SUPPORT

The primary objective of U.S. military aid to Europe has been the build-up of military strength among the members of the North Atlantic Treaty Organization. NATO was established in 1949 to provide a basis for cooperation among the Western European nations, the United States, and Canada; later Greece and Turkey joined. Under decisions taken through NATO and with the support of U.S. aid, military budgets of NATO members have more than doubled since 1949. European NATO members have put up 85 per cent of the total cost of their military build-up, with the United States providing the remaining 15 per cent. NATO Europe has also supplied 90 per cent of NATO's integrated ground forces, 75 per cent of the combined air forces, and a substantial part of naval strength. The administration has claimed that military aid has helped Europe to raise the 12 divisions of ground forces existing in 1949 to between 90 and 100 in 1955 with varying strength; the 400 aircraft were increased to more than 6,000; a few hundred naval vessels were multiplied manyfold. In addition, a vast complex of airfields, naval bases, radar systems, arsenals, fuel storage tanks, pipe lines, and telecommunications have been built up. Of the total costs of over $2 billion (half of which was for airfields), the U.S. government paid only about 38 per cent. Europe has supposedly assumed a stronger military posture.

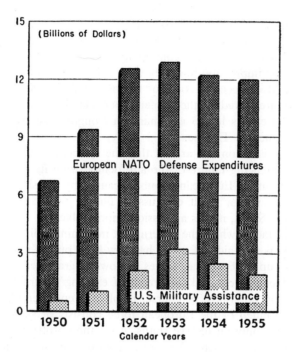

Fig. 19 European NATO Countries Financed the Bulk of Their Military Efforts
SOURCE: International Cooperation Administration

But critics of military aid argue that much of the growth of NATO strength is "on paper"; the divisions vary from some with practically no men or matériel to only a few with full strength. The *New York Herald Tribune* reported authoritatively on May 25, 1956, that the total number of divisions available to NATO was between 45 and 49; an additional 20 divisions were supported by NATO members but were not available for NATO operations. About 2.4 million men were in the armies of NATO Europe; the remainder of the 7 million total were in the navy and air force; half of the total were U.S. troops. An additional 48 divisions were supposed to be available within thirty days after a mobilization call, but they were considered doubtful. The United States itself had 23 active divisions, of which 6 are available to NATO; Canada had 2 in the country with one third available to NATO. The air power was represented by 139 European air squadrons available to NATO; the United States had an additional 34 squadrons and Canada 12. Within NATO Europe, 126 airfields had been built for NATO use. The preponderant strength lay, it seemed, with the air force. Critics of military aid argued that, instead of a joint effort to protect Europe, NATO's strength rested on the U.S. divisions in Europe and U.S. air power.

Many congressmen have felt that Europeans did not have the "will to fight," as they had contributed so little to the Korean War effort; these congressmen were additionally disappointed by the unwillingness of Europe to form a European defense community. Some NATO members gave congressmen the impression that they were doing the United States a favor by rearming. More recently some of the principal NATO members have indicated a desire to reduce their defense budgets. The growing neutralism of these countries has led to a demand in Congress for a reappraisal of military assistance to Europe.

The administration has argued that the difficulties arising in NATO, rather than evidencing failure of the aid, demonstrate its success. That is, the relaxation among European members caused by Russia's turning from snarls to smiles was a result of Russia's finding that Europe's strength, buttressed by U.S. aid, makes aggression unprofitable.

A second factor which the government maintains indicates the success of military aid is that aid to Europe has now been put on a stand-by basis. No new build-up of European forces is now programmed—only the improvement of equipment and fulfillment of existing programs. The fulfillment of existing programs, of course, involves a considerable increase of strength, since much of the European force consists of skeleton divisions and/or divisions only on reserve status. Also, the obsolescence of existing weapons will oblige the United States to continue assistance if she wishes to maintain Europe's strength. For example, a new missile and advanced weapons program, costing initially over $500 million, has been proposed for 1957.

The administration has continued since 1951 to claim that any sizable reduction in the military aid requested would indicate to Europe that the United States was no longer counting so heavily on European rearmament and would tend to encourage Europeans to cut back on their efforts. (It did not have to make such a claim in 1950, for Congress readily approved both an initial request of over $1 billion and, after the outbreak of the Korean War, passed a supplemental request of $4 billion for military aid to Europe; in neither case did it seriously question the purpose or magnitude of the aid.) Since 1950, and despite the protestations of the administration, Congress has cut the President's requests for military aid on each occasion, sometimes as much as 25 per cent; the cuts were never as deep, however, as they were in the economic aid programs until 1956. In 1956, Congress decided to wait to see what turn events would take in Europe since some nations indicated intentions to cut back on military expenditures; Congress then detoured some of the military aid intended for Europe to the other Rimland countries. The events in the Near East and Eastern Europe in late 1956 gave rise to a reconsideration during 1957 of the role of NATO and of the desirability of continuing the same types of military aid as in the past.

SUPPORT TO ASIA

The experience with aid to strengthen Asiatic nations is even shorter than the European experience. Emphasis on the Far East did not arise until Europe's basic needs were met and until the aftermath of the Korean War. After the loss of China in 1949, and until 1953, the de-emphasis of the Far East was not wholly a matter of strategic preference for Europe. The Communist aggression in Korea had been a strong impetus to military aid to the area. But in most cases, the military aid that the Far Eastern nations could utilize was limited by their lack of proper institutions and personnel to make effective use of large sums or to raise large armies, though Nationalist China received considerable aid to defend itself on Formosa. Many nations were also unwilling to tie themselves politically and/or militarily to the United States.

The Indochina conflict heightened in some South Asian and Far Eastern countries the fear of Communist China and Russia, and it accelerated the drive of the United States to increase military and political strength in the area so as to prevent the spread of communism. Despite U.S. efforts during 1952 to organize the area into a regionally cooperating unit, it failed to materialize. But a beginning was made in 1954 through the formation of the South–East Asia Treaty Organization including Pakistan, the Philippines, and Thailand plus the United States, Australia, New Zealand, France, and the United Kingdom. The area defended by the members of SEATO includes Indochina also—i.e., Cambodia, Laos, and Free Viet-Nam. Formosa, Japan, and South Korea have bilateral treaties with the United States providing for mutual defense in the event of attack. The United States is also tied trilaterally to Australia and New Zealand in the ANZUS pact.

The importance of the Asiatic area to the United States is heightened by the fact that it supplies 32 per cent of U.S. consumption of chromite, 37 per cent of manganese ore, 69 per cent of tin, and 22 per cent of U.S. consumption of tungsten. It also supplies rubber and oil to the Free World. And the large population allegedly provides a valuable source of soldiers, depending on the nature of future wars.

Aid has been spread over nine different countries on a country-by-country basis. The bulk of the aid has been sent to Fomosa and South Korea, but the rearmament of Japan calls for increasing amounts. The Philippines, Thailand, free Viet Nam, Laos, Cambodia, and Pakistan have also received military aid. And all but Japan have received defense-support assistance. The total of military and defense-support aid requested for the area in 1956–1957 was nearly $2 billion, an amount equal to that sent Europe at the height of its build-up.

Most of the defense-support aid in the past has gone to Formosa to relieve the burden of military efforts on the civilian population and thereby increase the stability of the government and to improve the effectiveness of the armed forces; it consisted largely of fertilizer, raw cotton, and machinery. During the last couple of years, increasing attention has been paid to the economic foundation of the other Free World nations of Asia.

The shift of emphasis in programs for Asia from military build-up to economic strength draws on lessons that were learned in aiding Europe. It was considered that European repulsion of communism required first a sound economic foundation; then, after the nations were given "something to fight for," their military rearmament was considered timely and effective. The approach to Asia has been the reverse: military armament was emphasized first, despite the arguments of the nations concerned that economic problems were more pressing and were more important even from a military viewpoint. The insistence of the U.S. government on extending military aid made several of the Asiatic governments feel that the United States was interested in their nations more as cannon fodder than as friends in need.

The views of the recipient governments may have been important in the recent congressional emphasis on economic assistance, but several critics in and out of Congress have argued that the probability of "brushfire" wars has greatly diminished with the shift in Russian tactics to Russia's own brand of "trade and aid" in competition with the United States. The basic security of all the nations of the Free World would then depend upon the United States, for the ultimate source of strength is America's power to retaliate with nuclear bombs. If this view is accepted, the need for conventional weapons, for military aid, and for defense support would be greatly diminished if not eliminated.

Some fundamental questioning has been given to the necessity of nations such as South Korea maintaining 20 or 21 divisions in a standing army. Rather than continue to support such large forces abroad, which may be ineffective or impotent in time of nuclear war and which seriously drain the economic production of the less advanced nations, some congressmen would emphasize economic aid, but still as a means of providing strength against the threat of communism.

SUPPORT TO THE MIDDLE EAST AND AFRICA

The strategic importance of the Near East lies in its being a primary producer of critical materials, particularly oil, and in its geographic position. It stretches across lines of communication between the West, South

Asia, and the Far East, and it is the bridge between Asia and Africa. Africa also is a source of critical materials for the West.

Within this area, military equipment was first sent only to Greece, Turkey, and Iran, which were under the immediate threat of Soviet expansion. The program to Greece and Turkey began in 1947 after Russia put pressure on the Turkish border and after Britain announced that she could no longer help the Greek government quell the uprising of Communist guerillas in Greece. The Greek-Turkish program was considered highly successful in that the pressure from Russia was relieved and the guerillas were eliminated; it was also comparatively inexpensive. The small expense was due partly to the fact that the cost of maintenance and supply of a Greek or Turkish soldier was exceedingly small compared with the same for a European or American soldier. The Turkish soldier received about 21 cents per month as pay, one uniform for two year's service, and one pair of shoes each six months, and he slept in unheated barracks or tents.

In 1953, Congress authorized aid to the Arab states, Israel, Libya, Ethiopia, and Pakistan. Pakistan was included to encourage her to associate in an area-wide defense organization which the United States hoped would shape up in the Middle East. Funds were also authorized for use through any regional defense organization which might be created; none materialized. Only Ethiopia was extended military assistance during 1953 besides Greece, Turkey, and Iran. No military aid was actually given Israel or the Arab states. Aid was offered Pakistan, but criticism immediately arose from India that the United States was arming a potential aggressor against India. The dispute between India and Pakistan over Kashmir was critical, and boundary disputes were pressing enough to cause armed clashes. The U.S. government then offered similar aid to India, but she refused it, not desiring to tie herself with a Western military alliance.

Aid was later extended to Pakistan despite objections from India, and Israel was extended some military aid despite outcries from the Arab states, who later turned to Russia and Czechoslovakia for arms. The disputes between Israel and the Arab states have made it difficult to obtain a regional defense organization and to plan any long-range program of defense against communism. Disputes among Middle Eastern nations are too explosive. The U.S. government, despite the sale of arms to Egypt by the Soviet bloc, refused in 1956 to give any further aid to Israel and has given none to any country bordering on her. Political tensions were heightened by the touchy problem of resettlement of refugees who fled Palestine during the 1948 war between the Arabs and Jews. The United States hoped to obtain a solution through a regional program of economic and political stability and growth, but cooperation was not forthcoming. The outbreak of war once again between Israel and Egypt and the interference by France and Britain have brought to a head the problem of attaining a settlement in the area.

The inability to obtain a regional defense organization in the Middle East has been a signal disappointment to U.S. officials, for it constitutes the major gap in U.S. military alliances. A substitute arrangement has been developed out of a treaty known as the Baghdad Pact signed by Turkey, Iraq, Pakistan, and Iran plus the United Kingdom. The U.S. government has supported the treaty both morally and materially by giving its blessing, extending aid individually to each of the Middle Eastern members, establishing liaison with the secretariat, and becoming a member of the Pact's economic committee. The largest amount of aid to the Pact members consists, however, of nonmilitary items. Defense support is given in the form of food, clothing, and fuel for the use of armed forces mostly in the countries of Greece, Turkey, and Iran.

As in the support of strength in the Far East, the complications of underlying economic and political conditions has given rise to a reassessment of the desirability of military as compared with economic aid programs as means of gaining U.S. foreign-policy objectives.

SUPPORT OF THE RIO PACT

In 1947, the U.S. government entered a collective security agreement with the nations of Latin America under which all would come to the defense of a member nation attacked by another member of the treaty or by any outside nation. Military assistance to Latin American countries has the major objective of enabling troops in the area to defend it against attack from the outside and thus relieve the burden on U.S. forces. Aid has been given in line with a resolution of Pact members to orient military preparations toward common defense of the hemisphere rather than toward individual national efforts.

The United States has given only small amounts of military end items to its southern neighbors, but it does not consider them any the less desirable. They contain strategic materials and defend important sea lanes and lines of communication. But they are not so nearly under the threat of Communist aggression. The threat is more from internal subversion which is not treated by military preparedness, as we shall discuss in succeeding chapters.

In sum, the United States decided that it could not use economic aid alone to obtain its ultimate foreign-policy goals but that the areas which wish to remain free of Soviet domination had to be protected militarily. Once their internal and external positions became consolidated, they could turn to the long-run business of economic and political growth along lines of their own choosing but which the United States hopes and assumes will be toward the Western values of economic and political democracy.

Russia, in her turn, has not stood still. Her development of nuclear weapons and rapid technological advance in jet engines and other armaments have not permitted the United States to rest. Military assistance may have strengthened U.S. allies, but it certainly has not brought a continuing preponderance of military power to the West.

Fundamental questions remain of whether protection of the rest of the Free World is obtained best with or without military aid, with or without economic aid, or with a combination of military and economic aid. A reappraisal of all aid programs has followed a re-emphasis of the importance of adequate economic growth to provide underlying strength and stability prerequisite to the "will to fight." To meet the changing tactics of Russia, the administration has asked for more flexibility in directing aid funds to economic or military purposes and in selecting recipient nations within the Near and Far Eastern areas. It has also requested authorization by Congress to make commitments to extend aid over a ten-year period to any country needing continuing support and assurances of such support in order to program its requirements. Congress, unable to bind a succeeding Congress, has stated only that it is committed morally to continue aid so long as a threat of Communist expansion remains.

SELECTED READINGS

There is practically no literature devoted solely to the military-assistance programs. Most of the material in this chapter has been taken from the administration's testimony on the Mutual Security Program before the Senate Foreign Relations Committee, the House Foreign Affairs Committee, and the two committees on appropriations in Congress; the semiannual reports of the agencies administering the aid programs have also been used.

Nonofficial discussion of these programs has been either descriptive or coupled with other aid programs in an analysis of broad foreign policy problems. Descriptive readings are cited after Chapters 17 and 18; see particularly W. A. Brown and R. Opie, *American Foreign Assistance*, Chapters 8, 11, and 15 and the whole of Part 5. Analytical readings are noted at the end of Chapter 20. Contemporary analytical description may be found in the Princeton University, International Finance Section, annual *Survey of United States International Finance*, particularly volumes covering 1950 through 1953.

The single most informative public source on NATO is a review of its formation, operation, and accomplishments by NATO's Secretary General (Lord Ismay) under the title *NATO: the First Five Years, 1949–1954.*

20 Issues and Problems of Foreign Aid

Since the end of World War II the U.S. Government has extended over $50 billion of economic and military aid for a variety of purposes and with varying success. The uniqueness of the programs in international economic relations, their magnitude, and their broad purposes caught the public's attention and focused discussion on them to the partial eclipse of other foreign economic policies. In fact, the aid programs did become the means of entangling the United States in alliances and of causing her to become concerned with the details of the internal and foreign affairs of other nations to a degree she had never before experienced. Both the administration and Congress have asserted that foreign aid has become a part of the fabric of U.S. foreign policy, though neither is particularly wedded to a given type of aid program.

The types of aid programs have ranged from outright grants of unrestricted dollars to strengthen governments' budgets and their balances of payments, to loans which were tied to purchases of specific goods in the United States. Their nature has ranged from the purest of relief aid to military assistance, i.e., from aid aimed at merely mitigating suffering of humanity anywhere to aid intended to strengthen certain nations against a common enemy. And they have ranged in size from several million dollars a year to several billion.

The issues and problems surrounding the successful use of foreign aid in the pursuit of international economic and political objectives relate primarily to the determination of (a) the purposes for which aid should be given, (b) how much aid should be extended and to which countries, (c) what types of aid should be provided, and (d) the restrictions or controls to be imposed by the donor. These are the specific aspects of aid programs which we will examine in this chapter.

Aid may be placed in a broad perspective by regarding it as an attempt to make the best use of available goods and services in pursuit of a given foreign policy. The decision to extend aid should be made after assessing several alternatives. The first decision is between seeking the purposes of aid programs or pursuing other objectives; for example, the improvement and expansion of the U.S. road system and its own economic development *or* the security of the Free World. If the security of the Free World is chosen, a second set of alternatives arises, of whether aid to build up divisions abroad is better than a missile program to improve the fire power of U.S. forces. If the aid program is still chosen, a third set of alternatives relates to the financing of the aid: should it be through increased taxation or inflation, thus reducing the choices available to American taxpayers, or should it be through dropping out some other items of government expenditures, leaving a freer choice to U.S. income earners?

Each side of the three sets of alternatives has its proponents. Some assert that the United States should look after her own welfare and strength first, and that this in turn will provide the greatest strength for the Free World. Others favor aid programs merely because they effect a redistribution of incomes over the world, which they consider to be in the interest of peace and harmony. But if redistribution is the objective, the tax systems of donor and recipient countries must be examined to make certain that funds are not being taken from poorer classes in the United States and winding up in the pockets of the richer groups abroad.

There should be no presumption one way or another on the above alternatives relating to any given aid program at a particular time. Each set of circumstances should be examined anew. But we are not without some guideposts, for the technique of aid has been developed *within* nations over the past few decades through the use of central government grants-in-aid to lower governmental units. Many of the problems surrounding foreign aid are similar to those relating to federal grants-in-aid within nations: e.g., interference, control, contributions of the recipients, relative levels of taxation, types of aid, specific purposes of aid, criteria of amount, selection of governmental units to receive aid, etc. The extension of aid into the area of foreign relations should be accompanied by the recognition that it should not automatically take priority over other techniques, nor that it should be placed at the bottom of the government's budget. Its use should be carefully examined in the light of its effectiveness as compared to other means of accomplishing similar objectives.

The lack of adequate presentation of aid in the above light has caused the administration to feel that it must "sell" Congress on the idea of aid each year. It has therefore employed tactics of persuasion which included excessive claims for what aid would accomplish and which has consequently led to later disappointment in the eyes of Congress and the public. Part of the difficulty in presenting aid programs in a favorable light has been that it is practically impossible to measure the success of a given aid program. The objectives and results are colored by political considerations which makes measurement in precise economic terms unreal or irrelevant.

While the economic growth of a recipient country can be measured during and after the period of aid, it is not possible to ascribe any given portion of that growth to the aid, nor is it possible to determine what would have been the growth without the aid. It is also not possible to ascribe any given movement toward a relaxation of trade barriers or toward currency convertibility to aid programs, because a host of domestic factors are involved.

One of the main concerns of those in Congress responsible for extending aid has been the U.S. capacity to bear the burden of aid. Once again, this concern would not have been so pointedly directed at aid programs if the assistance were considered in the light of all the resources available to the United States (and her friends) to pursue given objectives. With reasonable factor mobility within the United States, the only limits to the amount of aid which can be borne by the economy arise from the limits to taxation or inflation which the government considers that the people will bear. This decision cannot be made for aid separately from other items in the government budget, because other items may be reduced to make way for aid. But the nature of the problem is not an economic one of "productive capacity" nearly so much as a political one of "how much taxation or inflation will the public stand and for what purposes?" It is partly because of the political nature of the decision to extend aid that Congress has insisted on identifying it strongly at times with military objectives and at other times with humanitarian relief, depending on its members' belief in whether or not their constituents will support their positions.

A. PURPOSES OF AID PROGRAMS

The broad objectives of almost all aid programs have been to prevent other nations from falling under totalitarian systems and to permit and encourage others to pursue the U.S. international economic objective of an expansion of world trade and investment through a system of multilateral, nondiscriminatory trade and payments. The U.S. government has sought, through the aid programs, to obtain the cooperation of others in preventing the spread of communism and in advancing the Free World toward freer trade. Aid has essentially been employed as a tool in the ideological, political, economic, and military competition between the United States and Russia. But there have been two other avowed purposes which must be examined: the granting of aid to express the fundamental humanitarianism of the American people and the use of aid to purchase goodwill abroad. The latter, as we shall see, borders on the main objective of obtaining cooperation.

TO EXPRESS HUMANITARIANISM

The objective of helping other nations, whether or not they would eventually be able or willing to return the favor, has been at the bottom of a variety of relief programs involving extensive aid. The U.S. government has assisted World War II refugees in resettlement within and outside Europe; it has helped homeless children all over the world; it has loaned or given food to famine- and flood-stricken areas in faraway lands; it has assisted refugees from Palestine and salved the war-torn areas of Korea and Indochina; and it has even offered food to areas behind the Iron Curtain when starvation seemed imminent. It is highly likely that requests for such aid will be received in the future and that the United States will feel compelled, as a reflection of the moral content of her foreign policy,[1] to offer relief aid again, whether or not it is requested.

Some congressmen have questioned the right or duty of the government to extend humanitarian assistance or even to have charitable feelings for foreigners. The logical extension of this view would be to question

---

[1] Secretary of State Dulles, in a speech in April 11, 1955, emphasized the moral responsibilities which he believed underlay the actions of the U.S. government:

"There are some who believe that moral considerations ought not to influence the foreign policy of a nation, that moral considerations are all right for the individual but not for the collective unity. Corporate bodies, it is argued, should be directed only by material considerations.

. . . . .

"It is, indeed, generally the case that those who represent government operate only for the immediate and direct self-interest of the nation they represent. That is why suspicion generally attaches to governmental grants. It is assumed that governments do not give away their taxpayers' money unless they see some specific *quid pro quo*.

"The Government of the United States has, I like to believe, a rather unique tradition in this respect. Our nation was founded as an experiment in human liberty. Our institutions reflect the belief of our founders that all men were endowed by their Creator with inalienable rights and had duties prescribed by moral law. They believed that human institutions ought primarily to help men develop their God-given possibilities and that our nation, by its conduct and example, could help men everywhere to find the way to a better and more abundant life.

. . . . .

"We exert in every part of the world an influence—an influence which we try, as far as is humanly possible, to make an influence for justice and not an influence for self-aggrandizement.

"No doubt we have made mistakes. But broadly speaking, our nation has played a role which I believe history will judge to have been honorable. It is a role which we could not have played unless those who exercised the power of government had believed that they were justified in putting moral considerations above material considerations." (State Department *Press Release*, No. 203, pp. 6, 7.)

whether the aid goods would be better used abroad or at home. Are there not many areas in the United States which could benefit from substantial programs of assistance? George Kennan, in his published lectures on *The Realities of American Foreign Policy,* has argued at length that one of the prerequisites for successful American leadership in the world is the setting in order of its own house: the removal of slum areas, the improvement of education and health, and the reduction of juvenile delinquency, to say the least.

What is the reason that relief aid is sent abroad rather than used at home? Is the humanitarian urge stronger toward strangers? This is not usually thought to be the case. Is it that Congress would not appropriate funds to reduce suffering, ignorance, and poverty at home and that *some* charity, even if directed abroad, is better than none? The decision of the U.S. government on aid has not generally been couched in terms of the relative advantages of foreign or domestic charity. Rather, the decision has involved, as far as American taxpayers are concerned, not so much an examination of alternative government expenditures as of the reduction of the U.S. tax burden, which is already heavy on the lower-income groups. Thus, while aid has expressed humanitarian feelings, it has not been compared to domestic charitable expenditures in order to determine how much aid should be given.

It is possible, of course, that charity does not require any *particular* amount of assistance to one's fellow men. Even if charity is accepted as a technique of international policy, does it require that one group or nation support another at any specific level of well-being compared to its own? Does it require merely that another nation be set upon its feet in such a way that it can thenceforward support itself? If so, are there any requirements as to the ways in which people of the recipient nation are enabled to support themselves—that is, as to the equality of opportunity, social equality, and political equality, without which progress may be seriously impeded? These questions involve not only problems of administration but also certain ethical judgments which are difficult to make and to implement. As Aristotle wrote in the *Nicomachean Ethics,* "to give away money is an easy matter, but to decide to whom to give it, and how large a sum, and when, and for what purposes, and how, is neither in every man's power, nor an easy matter. Hence it is that such excellence is rare and praiseworthy and noble."

TO PURCHASE GOODWILL

One objective repeatedly sought from early aid programs was that of gaining goodwill from the recipient governments. One American diplomat and foreign policy strategist has stated that "it would reflect not only great ignorance and superficiality but also a certain impropriety on our part to expect assistance granted by this government to other governments, in the deliberate promulgation of our own foreign policy, to be regarded as an act of charity, deserving of a spirit of grateful and sentimental obligation on the part of others."[2] And it is a psychological phenomenon that people do bite the hand that feeds them; a story is told of Henry Clay that a friend warned him that a certain person was campaigning bitterly against him and in favor of Clay's opponent. Clay remarked, "I can't understand that, I don't recall ever doing him a favor." The same characteristic exists among nations and, when coupled with national pride, makes it highly unrealistic to expect gratitude. Gratitude is also unlikely to arise when the donor is considered by the recipients as a "rich uncle" who could have provided more and who is placing obstacles (such as tariffs) in the path of the recipients' improving their own position independently. The extension of charity is hardly a sound basis on which to build continuing international relations. Each nation wishes to have self-respect and to feel that it can take care of itself. A positive dislike arises if the donor *expects* gratitude, and many recipients have felt that the United States attempts to take too much credit for her aid by identifying herself with every dollar donated, through labels, symbols, and announcements and by claiming that local improvements were a direct result of aid. Gratitude is a feeling best expressed when given freely.

Additional factors prevented a free expression of gratitude by some aid recipients toward the United States. Any expression of goodwill by some countries receiving UNRRA aid was prevented by their later coming under Communist domination. Those receiving assistance from the U.S. Military Establishment during and after the war knew that it was necessary to carry out U.S. military and political policy, and in any case, assistance was a part of the occupation policy. Aid to Korea was officially stated to be a means of making that country a "bastion of democracy in the Far East." Refugees obtaining assistance saw as many obstacles placed before their resettlement as were removed, sometimes by the same governments extending the aid. Finally, recipients of military aid have considered that they were "selling manpower" which the United States wanted.

Even if aid were not aimed at implementing other aspects of the broad foreign policy of the United States, most recipients cannot believe that there is no motive other than charity. Of course, the motives are usually mixed, tending to reduce the gratitude of the recipient; the words of Dean Grueber, spoken from the pulpit of the Berlin Cathedral, are significant: "Verily, when the members of the church help each other, it is like the miracle of the loaves and the fishes. . . . But when a charitable project [in this instance a fully publicized U.S. gift of food to East Germans after the 1953 revolt] is undertaken without the true spirit of love, the blessing turns into a curse . . . we absolutely refuse to cooperate with those

---

[2] George F. Kennan, "Foreign Aid in the Framework of National Policy," *Proceedings,* Academy of Political Science, XXIII (January, 1950), 454.

persons or powers who use works of charity to disguise their political and propaganda warfare."

Let us suppose, however, that one nation *could* purchase the gratitude of another. In what way would the purchaser want it to be expressed?—in pious phrases, laurel wreaths, and monuments? or in domestic and foreign policies which benefit the donor? If it is the latter, there are numerous examples of the failure of feelings of gratitude to become active in policy changes, or even in implementation of treaties based partly on feelings of gratitude. For example, after the Revolutionary War the treaty of the newly independent American states with France under which they were to come to the aid of France was partly an expression of gratitude for her assistance. But Americans did not support France during the Napoleonic Wars against England and others on the continent. The arguments used to prevent the entry of America into that war were to the effect that gratitude was an insufficient reason to act contrary to the national interest. Again, the gratitude of the Italian people for large-scale aid has not been strong enough for them to overthrow the threat of communism completely, and Yugoslavia's gratitude did not prevent her from moving toward a reconciliation with Russia. Nor has aid aggregating $2 billion to Greece since the war been sufficient to induce her not to cause disturbances among NATO countries over Cyprus; when U.S. officials have mentioned to Greek officials that greater cooperation should be forthcoming, the reply has been "but you are not giving us much aid now!" Finally, aid to Britain and France was not a sufficient basis for their agreement with the United States on the treatment of the Suez problem in 1956. These observations indicate that the search for goodwill is closely tied to the attempt to obtain cooperation abroad in the pursuit of given policies.

Another problem in purchasing goodwill or cooperation through aid is that of how long the recipient should show gratitude. If the aid is a one-shot program, such as the wheat loan to India in 1950 or the Philippine Rehabilitation Program, would the gratitude carry over more than a short time or cease when the aid ceases? And how much aid should be extended to turn gratitude into favorable action toward the donor over a longer period of time? The very Congress which is disturbed by the absence of a return in long-run goodwill cannot itself bind a succeeding Congress to irrevocable policies. Also, the history of U.S. relations with some countries has been that more ill will was generated by the impending cessation of aid than was gained by its extension.

The contradictions between the fundamental purposes of extending aid to gain general foreign-policy goals and the stated ones of goodwill and humanitarianism have not only placed the U.S. government in difficult positions vis-a-vis the recipient governments but have also placed the aid programs themselves in jeopardy. For example, Congress and the people are led to expect a greater harmony between donor and recipient, and when it does not arise, such as in the aid to India, disappointment ensues. Future programs are then looked upon skeptically because too much has been expected.

TO OBTAIN COOPERATION

The U.S. government has always been concerned with what the United States would receive in return for its aid. Although most of the programs have been justified on the ground that cooperation of one sort or another would be received in return for American generosity, some of the programs have stipulated that the recipients should repay loans in critical materials desired by the United States or make available to the United States certain commodities on terms at least as favorable as those given to any other country.

The broader fields of cooperation sought by the U.S. government through aid relate to the foreign economic policies of recipients and their military rearmament. Each of these areas involves the selection of recipients in such a way that the maximum amount of cooperation is obtained from the aid funds. As we have already seen in Chapters 17 and 18, efforts to obtain cooperation in the economic objectives of currency convertibility and multilateral trade through the British Loan and ERP fell short of success. Efforts to gain cooperation in rearmament have been more or less successful depending on the country considered and on the extent to which it was not cooperating prior to the aid. The selection of recipients therefore is important to success in obtaining the purposes of aid.

If a nation already "friendly and cooperative" is selected to receive aid, the funds might be quite successful in shoring up inadequate defenses. However, it might be more important to assist a nation not so clearly in the friendly category in order to swing it into such a grouping. The question is raised of whether "neutral" countries should be aided. If more aid is given them than those taking sides in the conflict, it seems to make "neutralism" profitable. On the other hand, not to aid neutrals would seem to guarantee their loss to the enemy eventually. The absence of a clear criterion as to the countries which should be strengthened has left the recipient countries uncertain what they should do to become eligible for aid. Some nations have been led to think that they should flirt even more with communism or drum up an internal or external communist threat in order to obtain more financial attention from the United States. The story has been circulated that an official of one of the South Asian countries requested France to send it some Communists so that it might receive aid from the United States.

Specifically, the questions are whether aid should be given in larger amounts to those already in the U.S. camp, such as Canada and Mexico? or to those which are fairly firmly in the friendly class but are having internal problems of economic and political instability which are dangerously increased by a sudden disaster, such as Italy and Western Germany? Should the major emphasis be placed on those nations under the shadow of the enemy, such as South Korea and Indochina? or upon those which have defected or might defect from the enemy, such as Yugoslavia or Eastern Germany?

A broad distinction can be made between a policy of "rewarding" a country already pursuing objectives desired by the United States and one of "inducing" others to do the same. Various problems arise in either category. As was pointed out in the previous chapter, the cooperative assumption of defense burdens in Europe has led some nations to cut back on their efforts. Some recipient governments have taken the attitude that if they waited long enough and did not assume a given responsibility the U.S. government would do so. Thus the extension of assistance to those able to remedy their own problems has tended to induce laziness on the part of some. An administration official has stated that the government has been "unduly worried" over the loss of countries which have tried to play the neutrality game a "little cagey," but that the United States *could* "establish the principle, and make it stick . . . that we help most those who help themselves." Secretary of State Dulles has asserted that the United States has tried to avoid the bribery technique because "when we work out this program of aid we try to do it not necessarily upon a basis of rewarding certain countries who do what we want to have them do. . . . We do it on the basis of trying to help situations which in turn we think help us."[3]

The points emphasized in this statement are readily demonstrated in the experience with Egypt in 1956. A major objective of Western policy has been to prevent the infiltration of Russia into the Middle East; concessions were made to Egypt on the evacuation of British soldiers and on military and aid matters. But Premier Nasser saw fit to attempt to play Russia and the United States off against each other for assistance in the building of the Aswan Dam. While there may be some advantage to potential recipients in causing donor governments to compete in the extension of aid, the attitude built up is hardly that of cooperation between the donor and recipient government.

Any effort to induce nations within the Iron Curtain to defect from Russia through the offer of later assistance runs also into immediate snags. First, the defection must be successful so that actions taken by the U.S. government cannot be considered as interference. Second, the defecting nation must continue its separation from Russia, else the aid will have been wasted from the U.S. viewpoint and might even be used against Americans in a future war. The experience with Yugoslavia has been frustrating in this regard.

These observations indicate that the assistance extended by the United

---

[3] *Mutual Security Act of 1955,* Hearings before the Committee on Foreign Affairs, House of Representatives, 84th Cong., 1st Sess., May-June, 1955, pp. 20, 42.

States is supposed to have a reciprocal aspect. For this reason the omnibus program covering all aid has been called the *Mutual* Security Program. Recipients are supposed, in their turn, to support the economic and security objectives of the United States. The desire for mutuality has affected the selection of recipient nations, the volume of aid to each recipient, and the control mechanisms employed by the U.S. government to insure a maximum of cooperation. Much of the power to induce cooperation was lost, however, as soon as the United States embarked upon a given program. Prior to the inception of the program, persuasion could be used to gain acceptance of certain cooperative actions by the recipient. But as soon as the funds were transferred or the program begun, the bargaining power shifted to the recipients. They knew that the United States could not afford to renege on a program once started, and they seldom took seriously the threats of Congress or the administration to terminate aid prematurely. Instead, many found that they could proceed with domestic programs out of line with the policies (e.g., relaxation of direct controls or acceleration of rearmament) which would provide the cooperation desired by the United States and that the U.S. government would pick up the check anyway.

There are no rules of thumb or even broad principles by which to determine what countries to aid for the purpose of maximizing cooperation or what policies they should be asked to adopt to provide the desired cooperation. Choosing the recipient nations and the specific cooperative policies desired could lead to criticism from other nations involved. For example, Latin American countries have criticized the U.S. decision to give more aid to Europe and other areas; India criticized the decision to give military aid to Pakistan because the arms might be used against her; the Arab states criticized both military and economic aid to Israel; Russia criticized aid to Europe and the proffer of aid to areas behind the Iron Curtain; some European nations criticized the aid programs to the totalitarian countries of Yugoslavia and Spain; certain colonial areas seeking national independence have criticized the extension of aid to metropolitan countries because it increases the latters' power over the colonies; finally, the U.S. government has been attacked for placing too much emphasis on military cooperation and not enough on economic growth.

The emphasis on military build-up in non-European areas has not been resoundingly successful. The U.S. government insisted that they join in defense alliances, but when that insistence backfired, it asserted that it was interested only in strong, independent governments and economies— even if they were neutral. The hope, of course, was that such governments would become dedicated to the cause of freedom and would attempt to protect their own independence and that of others in time of attack. Some congressmen have wished, however, to tie aid to a modification of neutrality positions; the administration has argued that aid was needed while nations "make up their minds."

The de-emphasis of military alliances has resulted partly from the conclusion that insistence on cooperation in a military effort has not brought the desired cooperation and partly from the increased economic competition of Soviet Russia. The wooing of the "uncommitted" nations through emphasis on their independence is justified by the administration and Congress in that once the neutral nations gain their independence and achieve a sound economy they will become ideologically associated with the Western democracies. Russia, of course, hopes to keep the same nations stirred against the West or at least dissociated from the West long enough to entice them into her orbit.

The experience in not gaining goodwill indicates that aid alone will not gain "neutral friends." But the U.S. government is faced with a dilemma: it has no assurance that it will gain from its aid, but it considers it almost certain that it will lose by not extending aid.

B.   CRITERIA OF AMOUNT OF AID

Once the purposes of aid are selected and the recipients decided upon, decisions have to be made as to how much aid will be extended, in what form, and what controls are necessary to make the aid effective. When the aid program is bilateral—as with the Government and Relief in Occupied Areas Program, the Post-UNRRA (or Foreign Relief) Program, Interim Aid, the European Recovery Program, the Mutual Defense Assistance Program, the Indian Loan, the Yugoslav Emergency Food Assistance, the special programs of aid to Korea, the Arab states, Israel, and the surplus-food aid programs—the two questions of how much the recipient is to get and how much the donor should give are the same problem. But when the aid program is multilateral in character—as with UNRRA, the International Refugee Organization, International Children's Emergency Fund, United Nations Relief and Works Agency for Palestine Refugees in the Near East, and the United Nations Korean Reconstruction Agency—an additional set of problems arises as to how much each nation should contribute.

Regardless of the type of aid program, the criteria used to determine how much any nation should receive relate to its need or ability to use the aid effectively. This calculation has usually been made through an examination of the nation's balance of payments and the factors creating deficits, i.e., the level and structure of internal economic activity which affect its import requirements and its ability to export. The criteria regarding the appropriate contribution of one nation to the sharing of a common burden of assistance or rearmament involve not the balance of payments so much as some principle of equality of sacrifice among members.

BALANCE-OF-PAYMENTS AND RELATED CRITERIA

Since the objective of aid is to provide the recipient with more goods and services than would be available without it, and since the postwar problems of many other nations have involved an effort to live beyond their domestic means, the balance of payments has been the means of indicating the need for the extent of aid. Pressure on balances of payments after World War II was reflected first in a loss of international reserves; it seemed most appropriate therefore to take the level of reserves as an approximate indication of the amount of aid needed. Western European countries were deemed to have sufficient reserves to care for their immediate relief needs and were thus excluded from UNRRA aid; however, when the reserves of Italy and France began a rapid decline in 1947, their fall was considered justification for a special Interim Aid Program.

The inadequacy of the level of reserves as a criterion of the need for aid becomes evident when one examines what the level of reserves should be before aid is considered necessary. Should it be below some predetermined level, such as in a prior representative period? Should it be falling rapidly or "dangerously"? Should a rising level of reserves preclude aid? And what level of reserves should be restored before aid is discontinued?

There is, of course, no necessarily appropriate relationship between a previous period's reserves and the currently desirable level. Even when the two amounts are made comparable through use of price indexes to allow for changes in the real value of reserves, the factors in the balance of payments which provide or require the reserves may have changed greatly and/or the balance of payments itself may be more (or less) stable than before, requiring less (or more) reserves to perform the same functions. Rather, the level of reserves and its movement up or down are determined by a host of factors which themselves must be examined. What is important is not the level of reserves or even its movement but the forces behind that level or movement.

The level of reserves is merely a symptom, and measuring the disease by the symptoms does not always give an indication of the seriousness or pervasiveness of the causes. Emphasis on reserve positions was one factor which tended to limit early aid to *ad hoc* programs and led to an underestimation of the magnitude of the underlying maladjustments. Though the reserve position may provide an indication of the need for aid, it cannot be used to determine the precise *amount* of aid, for the determination of the level of reserves to be restored must rely on other criteria, such as the level of GNP and domestic expenditure.

Economic aid under the ERP had the objective of raising consumption to 1938 levels and then of increasing capital formation to levels which could sustain and later improve living standards. The rates of spending (domestic expenditure) implied by plans of European governments exceeded their nations' available resources (GNP) so that a balance-of-payments deficit was necessary. In effect, European governments were encouraged to plan a deficit which would be covered by aid. Aid was purposely given to allow nations to live beyond their own means.

The reconstruction plans requiring investment to rebuild destroyed plant and equipment, along with the continuing large overseas commitments, led to budget deficits. These deficits, coupled with large wartime savings which swelled postwar demand, resulted in inflation. Confidence in the currency of some countries tended to be destroyed. This lack of confidence (especially evident in France) in turn tended to deter trade and commerce (both between rural and urban centers and among individual enterprises), thus slowing economic recovery. It also reduced the incentive of factors to move from less to more efficient employments and thereby restrained a rise in the real GNP.

The inflation was a drag on the productivity of workers also in that they often received wages which they could not spend for goods they desired, either because of their inadequate supply (especially when controls forced exports or restricted imports) or because of rationing. Despite the slow rise in productivity, workers pressed for higher wages to improve their living conditions. This pressure was difficult for unstable governments to oppose. Thus wages tended to rise faster than productivity; domestic expenditure tended to rise over GNP, and costs rose; both results made it difficult to export (especially to the United States) even after controls were imposed to force a reduction of domestic consumption of exportables.

In addition, European nations were already committed to social-welfare programs, to policies of overfull employment, and to redistributive taxation. These commitments were politically based in that they were considered necessary to keep public support behind the governments. These commitments added to the flow of domestic spending, further widening the gap between domestic expenditures and GNP to be covered by aid.

The continued unwillingness or political inability of European governments to cope with the problems of inflation and structural adjustment to a new pattern of trade and production, and the acceptance by the United States of the European policies underlying the inflation were the bases for continued aid in the postwar world and significantly affected its amount. Until the proper adjustments were facilitated by a revision of domestic policies and until financial, monetary, and fiscal stability could be obtained, pressure on the balance of payments would continue. Given the existing political conditions and social unrest, external financing was "necessary." But it was necessary only in the sense that the U.S. government did not wish to risk a decline of the economic or political strength of Europe. It therefore approved of Europe's spending more than it produced, largely for political reasons. Otherwise, the dollar shortage would not have existed; its continuation depended upon unilateral grants from the United States. Without that aid, Europe would have been forced to draw down its reserves and then cut its imports to the level of its ability to earn foreign currencies. The resulting restrictions on trade and payments would have moved Europe still further from the world-wide system of multilateral, nondiscriminatory trade and payments desired by the United States, and Europe would have been less strong economically and politically than she is today.

SHARING A COMMON BURDEN

The multilateral extension of aid has certain advantages claimed for it over bilateral programs. Even when there is only one donor country, the multilateral determination of how the aid is to be distributed among a group of countries tends to reduce friction between the donor and recipients; the latter feel more dignity in the partnership and feel less sensitive about handouts. One of the major advantages of the operation of the Organization for European Economic Cooperation (OEEC) in helping to determine the distribution of aid to participants in the ERP was that the United States was able to shift criticism from itself to OEEC. Also, knowledge of the claims of others permitted officials of ERP participants to point to the claims of others as legitimately affecting its own national share of total ERP aid. Even with encouragement from the United States, however, the OEEC admitted defeat after two years of trying to find a formula for the division of aid among its members; it merely accepted the previous percentage shares. Even so, for these same reasons, the United States insisted on the OEEC determining the distribution of oil given in late 1956 to European nations cut off from Middle East supplies by the Suez blockage.

Additional advantages are supposed to arise from multilateral administration when several nations are contributing and also receiving aid. These advantages stem from the fact that the fear of interference or imperialism because of unilateral aid would be reduced, that the responsibility for success or failure would be spread, and that the burden of assistance would be spread over several economies proportionate to their ability to bear it. The first two advantages become disadvantages when the donor nation is interested in obtaining goodwill for itself or in controlling the use of aid so as to maximize the cooperation of the recipient. It is these considerations which have caused the U.S. government to provide most of its aid bilaterally.

Two major types of assistance programs participated in by the United States have involved a sharing of costs. The first relates to programs under the United Nations, such as UNRRA, UNKRA, and other organizations; the second concerns the financing of mutual defense against Russia. The principles involved in the determination of the amount of aid contributed are only slightly different.

Under both the UN programs and the financing of NATO expenditures, the basic principle developed was that of equality of burden among contributors. UNRRA attempted to implement this principle by the application of a fixed percentage to each nation's national income to determine its annual contribution. This proportional assessment meant that the nations with the largest incomes contributed most, but not progressively more than others.

The U.S. government has concluded that such a principle does not necessarily get from others the largest contributions of which they are capable; in application it has meant that the United States has paid over half the costs of UN programs. Since 1946, the U.S. government has attempted to set as its maximum contribution to any multilateral program an aggregate of 50 per cent of the budget. It has then set its contribution at levels which it hoped would induce others to contribute adequate amounts. Thus, under the UN program for Palestine refugees and that for reconstruction of Korea, the United States offered certain amounts contingent upon others matching them. These efforts were not always successful, for when others failed to contribute, the United States still felt compelled to see the programs through.

There is some economic justification for the matching formula when all nations are standing on their own feet, when there is a political reason for getting other nations to share responsibility, or when the United States has given others aid enabling them to contribute to multilateral programs.

In the case of the UN programs, the principle of equality of burden gave way in practice to a more pragmatic formula of matching contributions. It met a similar fate under the cost-sharing exercises of NATO members. In an effort to determine whether the cost of the build-up of NATO defenses in terms of the resources contributed by each was being shared appropriately, the NATO Council attempted to determine what would be "fair shares." In 1951 it concluded that the burden should be shared "equally," but it was unable at any time to determine the way in which equality should be measured or attained. The result was that, once again, the U.S. government determined its contribution unilaterally (though after joint consultations with the other NATO members) and attempted to induce others to increase theirs. Others were reluctant to increase their contributions since they felt no obligation such as might arise under a donor-recipient relationship. They considered that they were contributing resources to a program of mutual security under which they had certain rights and had accepted certain responsibilities for the common defense.

The U.S. Congress has been continually dissatisfied with the contributions of European countries compared to what it thought was their "fair share." Congress had early insisted that an equality of burdens should be sought in the financing of the common defense and that "equality" meant equal per capita expenditures in each country. Congress saw higher per capita expenditures in the U.S. defense budget than in those of European countries and asserted that Europe was not doing enough. But several problems of measurement arise. The question has been raised of whether the entire military expenditures of the nations concerned be taken into account—overseas forces or just NATO troops—particularly when some

NATO members are quelling revolutions in which members would not care to be involved, even indirectly. Also, should account be taken of the fact that the cost of maintaining equal forces with the United States was considerably lower?—for the pay to soldiers and their cost of maintenance was lower than in the United States and varied widely even within Europe.

Another difficult problem arose from the argument over whether a larger proportion of per capita incomes would be required from Americans to equal the burden of the Europeans. "Equality" was defined by some as contributions based on "progressive taxation." "Progressive contributions" could be applied not only among nations but also among the people of different member nations. An examination of existing tax structures would be required to determine whether they were equally progressive in each country. And agreement would have to be reached as to precisely what progression would bring "equality of burdens." The widely varying progression of income taxes among nations indicates that agreement on this point would be difficult to obtain. A related problem is that tax enforcement in each country is different. For example, France has argued that it cannot obtain more funds for defense expenditures, but it has also been shown that her taxes are not as progressive as others and that they are insufficiently enforced.

Given these problems, the U.S. government has not allowed its contribution to NATO defense to be determined by the members of the organization, even on a percentage basis. It has also held the power of determination of aid in its hands for the purpose of accelerating certain actions by the NATO European members. For example, to encourage the formation of a European Defense Community (EDC) with integrated military forces, Congress set aside aid under the 1953 Mutual Defense Assistance legislation to be contributed only to an EDC or similar organization. When this did not bring the desired organization into being, it stated in the 1954 legislation that no aid should be given to any country opposed to EDC or a similar organization. After EDC was killed by the failure of France to ratify the treaty, the Western European Union was formed to bring German forces into NATO and provide a central organization to watch over the size of national forces and armaments.

Despite these problems and the failure of OEEC to find any formula for dividing European Recovery Program aid, several officials and private critics have continued to urge an expansion of multilateral administration of aid. The U.S. Ambassador to the UN, Henry C. Lodge, Jr., has argued that multilateral aid would prevent the playing off of Russia against the United States by aid recipients, and others have stressed the cooperative aspects of international organization. But the U.S. government has so far remained adamant against any but small amounts of aid through multilateral agencies as compared to its total grants. A compromise proposal has been suggested by the Canadian Foreign Minister that a "foreign aid clearing house" be established within the UN to receive information as to the nature and extent of each nation's assistance programs. In this way, the propaganda technique of making large claims followed by few concrete accomplishments would be reduced. Also, since each country would know what the others were doing and planning, duplication would be eliminated and any effort to use aid as "peaceful penetration" into less powerful countries would be readily detected. This compromise would leave the determination of the volume of aid to the donor country, but some of the advantages of multilateral consultation and coordination would be obtained.

C. TYPES OF AID

The major problems surrounding the types of aid chosen have arisen over the extension of grants versus loans and of economic aid versus military items; a collateral problem is that of whether to purchase aid goods at home or abroad.

GRANTS VERSUS LOANS

A decision was made with reference to the early postwar aid programs to extend relief assistance (food, clothing, fuel) as outright grants and reconstruction aid (materials and capital equipment) in the form of loans. The basis for the decision was that relief goods would only increase consumption whereas capital goods and materials would raise industrial and agricultural productivity and thus provide a means of repayment.

This distinction is spurious, however. So far as the question of the type of aid is concerned, it matters little whether production is increased by the addition of a machine or provision of raw materials or by the maintenance of a worker through provision of consumer goods. In fact, where labor is a large factor in production, the maintenance of the labor force through foreign aid (e.g., food surpluses) would support expansion of production and therefore of ability to repay the aid.

Further, it is by no means certain that the capital goods and materials provided will be used to make it possible for a country to repay foreign borrowing without a reduction of its real domestic expenditure. The repayment of borrowing requires that the level of exports be expanded over that of imports or that imports be reduced—i.e., that GNP be raised relative to domestic expenditures. This surplus will arise automatically through movements in the balance of payments and will induce resources to move into exportable or import-competing items. The export surplus required during repayments will be attained without a reduction in the home use of goods and services (domestic expenditure) if the proceeds of the loan are used productively—i.e., to increase the GNP. However, any export surplus means that the nation does not use at home as much as it produces.

The decision as to extension of grants or loans turns then on the extent to which the donor country wishes the recipient's domestic expenditures to be reduced relative to GNP.

This decision itself may depend on political factors. If consumption and investment can be cut and if resources are mobile, there is no economic reason why the borrowing country could not repay loans. *But,* if the goal of the aid program was the attainment of a *given* level of consumption and reconstruction of facilities to *sustain* it, then grants would be more appropriate than loans because the objective is to sustain high levels of consumption and investment. Any aid above the amount required for the desired consumption and investment levels could be extended as loans. Under this approach, grants would have been the more appropriate type during the early part of ERP, and loans would have been extended, if at all, only when, at the end of the program, the economy was shown strong enough to carry loans. This conclusion was reached by Congress after a year's operation of ERP, after which time it cut drastically the proportion of loans to grants.

One of the aims of aid programs was, however, to gain conditions which would make the extension of further aid unnecessary. This result could be attained only with appropriate adjustments in domestic monetary policies and production structures. It is possible to argue that if all the aid had been extended as loans, which must be repaid, it would have been used more cautiously by recipients. They would probably have requested smaller amounts and/or made more effective use of the funds to hasten the day of independence from aid and increase their ability to repay. Whether or not such loan aid would have satisfied the humanitarian urges of the American people or given rise to whatever gratitude would be induced by grant aid is another question. Also, it is not absolutely certain that efforts by the recipient governments to reduce future reliance on loans would have been more in line with the goal of a multilateral world trading system than was their use of the grant aid.

Another problem in the selection of grants versus loans is whether repayment of aid should be required in order to "get something in return." The possibility of getting a return for the aid was frequently in the minds of congressmen. But repayment may conflict with other goals of the aid program, for it would require an export surplus and would thus burden future balances of payments of debtors. In order not to burden balances of payments and yet get something in return, some congressmen argued that at least some ERP aid should be "repaid" in strategic raw materials for the U.S. stockpile, which was depleted. The decision to impose such a requirement should be made in the light of the effect on future dollar-earning capacity of the debtor and thus on the goal of recovery. That is, the requirement to repay in materials would probably take these goods out of the regular market in which dollars were earned, reducing current earnings after the aid program was over so that a burden would be imposed on the balance of payments in any event.

A final factor in the decision to extend grants or loans is the presumed greater control which rests with the donor of grants. If loans are made and interest charged and if, in addition, certain conditions are imposed on the borrowers—as under the British Loan—the conditions appear as usury. Grants would supposedly permit imposition of conditions on the use of the funds because the recipient is not required to repay them. It is precisely for this reason that some potential recipients have requested loans rather than grants. India, for example, requested a loan even in the instance of emergency food aid in 1950; the U.S. administration urged Congress to extend a grant on the ground that it was for humanitarian relief and would not increase India's ability to repay. But Congress decided upon a loan and in addition expected India to show her appreciation by a more conciliatory attitude toward Western policies; it was disappointed.

As to the ability of the donor to impose conditions on the use of a grant or loan, it must be noted that, in either case, the balance of power shifts to the recipient as soon as the negotiations are over. In the case of a loan, the lending nation is placed on the defensive in order to prevent a default of the loan. Even in the case of a grant, once the donor nation has entered into a program of assistance, it is restrained from withdrawing aid by two pressures. First, if aid is cut off to punish noncompliance, the original objectives are definitely lost; it may be deemed best to attempt to make "bad" money good by spending more. Second, a withdrawal of assistance, unjustified in the eyes of potential recipients, would reduce their willingness to enter assistance agreements.

ECONOMIC VERSUS MILITARY AID

The decision as to whether to emphasize economic assistance or military aid became crucial in the eyes of the U.S. government during the shift from programs of economic recovery for Europe to rearmament in 1950. And the question of emphasis is still not decided. During the period 1950–1953, Congress was vehement in its denunciation of any aid based on a calculation of balance-of-payments deficits abroad, for it considered that such aid would not contribute much to the military strength of the recipients. It carried over this conviction into aid to Southeast Asia during 1953–1956. But during the years 1955–1956, there occurred a considerable shift in the emphasis toward economic aid for the same purpose of mutual security. What then may be said about the distinctions between military and economic aid?

The major distinction between the two types of aid turns on what each requires the recipient economy to do. If, for example, European nations were agreed on what particular levels of rearmament they would achieve, it would matter little whether the aid provided by the United States to reach these levels were in the form of economic goods or military items. Military items could consist of tanks or planes; *or* the items could consist of food and maintenance for troops. Or, raw materials and capital goods could be sent to permit production of either of the above set of items in the foreign country. Or consumer goods could be sent, permitting foreign resources to shift out of consumer goods production and into that of raw materials, capital goods, military maintenance, or tanks and planes. The effect of aid would be the same regardless of the form it took. But the indifference as to military or economic goods does not extend to specific aid goods. It is important to select as aid those goods (whether economic or military) in which the recipient does not have a comparative advantage.

These conclusions rest, of course, on the assumption that there is mobility in the recipient economy which would permit the movement of resources required. If, as in the case of many countries in the Near and Far East, there is little economic mobility, largely because of a lack of diversified output, then the decision as to military versus economic aid is different. In such a situation, the nation does not have a comparative advantage in military items nor can it expand its exports enough to import them. If the objective of the United States is to build up military strength in such countries, aid must be sent in the form of military equipment *and* economic goods. The goal is to create forces larger than the countries themselves could sustain; in two nations of the East, military expenditures consisting of 50 per cent of each country's GNP would be required to maintain the forces now supported with U.S. aid. It is for this reason that emphasis was shifted in 1956 to building up an economic base which could support such large forces.

More difficult problems in the decision as to economic versus military aid arise when both military rearmament and economic growth are sought but in different degrees by the donor and recipients. The impact of military aid on economic growth is twofold: it provides additional goods permitting domestic resources to be diverted to economic growth, but it also requires the manning of divisions and the production of complementary items of war by the recipient country if the military aid is to be made effective. The latter problem raises that of the absorptive capacity of the recipient nation: how much aid can it match with domestic resources without inflation and undue pressure on its levels of consumption and investment?

By and large, European recipients of aid have argued that they required more economic than military assistance to permit them to maintain levels of economic activity necessary to support their own military expenditures and make effective use of the aid. But, since 1950, Congress has been doubtful that European governments would divert their own resources to military expenditures if given economic assistance. It has not been convinced that European nations would seek agreed-upon force goals unless compelled to do so. Congress has attempted to force their decision by providing military equipment, which would require the diversion of European resources into military lines in order to put the aid to use. But, to the extent that France, say, was producing some of the items received as aid, it could still limit its rearmament effort. If it did not want to assume the rearmament burden asked by the United States because of domestic or balance-of-payments pressures, it could move its factors out of the production of items similar to aid goods and use them in economic growth.

The same problem of absorptive capacity arises also with economic aid, depending on its nature. There is, of course, little limit to the amount of purely consumption goods that a country could absorb if given freely. But if the aid is given in the form of materials or capital goods, the ability to match these factors with its own capital, land, and labor is limited. As with military assistance, inflationary pressure may accompany the attempt to use too many aid goods of this sort.

The U.S. government faced this latter problem in the use of offshore procurement. It argued that it could not extend as much assistance in the form of purchases in the recipient country of aid goods as it might have liked because of the threat of inflation in the recipient country. The government decided in favor of contracting abroad for the production of goods to be given away on the grounds that it would encourage the production of military items abroad so as to lessen Europe's dependence on overseas supplies—and for other reasons presented in Chapter 19. The basic factors in the decision to use offshore procurement have been those of the strategic location of military production, the least cost of aid, the European balance-of-payments position, and the future recovery of export markets by Europe.

Offshore procurement has benefited the recipients' balances of payments through building up dollar balances. The following entries tracing procurement through the balance of payments demonstrate their effect on reserves:

Offshore Procurement Entries in the U.S. Balance of Payments

Credits		Debits	
1a Short-term capital import	$1,000	1b Imports of OSP goods	$1,000
2a Export of OSP goods	1,000	2b Unilateral transfer	1,000
3a Export of goods & services	1,000	3b Short-term capital export	1,000

In the first entry, the foreign producer is paid for goods delivered to the U.S. government; foreign balances held in the United States rise, constituting a short-term capital import by the United States. The OSP goods are then (2a and 2b) donated to a foreign recipient. The dollars held by OSP producers may be used to purchase goods in other countries, but unless they are held as reserves they will eventually be used by foreigners for U.S. exports of goods and services (3a) leading to a short-term capital export by the United States (3b) as dollar balances are drawn down. OSP dollars have then returned to the United States and provided added goods to foreign recipients.

Since the dollars are eventually returned to the United States as demand for some U.S. exports, it should matter little to U.S. producers whether the contracts for aid goods are let abroad or at home. During the years of prosperity since 1950, little complaint over offshore procurement has been heard from American business in general, but some particular industries having small backlogs of orders have objected to orders being placed abroad. For example, an attempt by the administration to place orders for locomotives in India to be given as aid to Europe was met by strong opposition from U.S. interests and from Congress, despite the fact that their production in India would have provided evidence of progress to her people and thus added strength to the Free World.

There was some dissatisfaction over the method of placing contracts— not according to low bid but according to a host of broad politico-economic considerations. Holland has urged that the orders be placed so as to give a stimulus to unemployed industries, whereas Belgium, having little unemployment, has argued that orders should be let not only on the basis of cost but on a long-term basis so as not to result in adverse effects from the shift of orders among nations. Most countries have complained at one time or another about the attempts to use the procedure to relieve unemployment, obtain strategic objectives, fight Communist labor unions, etc. These varied objectives indicate that, like the aid under ERP, offshore procurement has not been used primarily to make Europe viable without aid or to move Europe toward a system of multilateral trade and payments through an expansion of industries in which it has a comparative advantage.

D.   CONDITIONS ON AID

In order to insure that aid would be used effectively for the objectives desired, Congress imposed a variety of conditions on its use and requested certain guarantees from the recipients. The guarantees usually related to measures which were aimed at increasing goodwill for the United States, spreading its institutions of freedom, and increasing the efforts of the recipients.

Countries of Eastern Europe and South Asia which received aid (such as Poland, India, and Yugoslavia) were requested to guarantee freedom of speech, free elections, freedom of press, full publicity of the aid, and that aid would be distributed without regard to political affiliation and in such a way that the "masses" would get an equitable share. These guarantees were not deemed necessary of recipients whose friendship to the United States was unquestioned. And it was deemed inadvisable to attempt to impose them on the countries which were neither moving toward communism nor already strongly related to the United States, for fear of pushing them into a position where the governments could be attacked for becoming subject to American interference. The imposition of these conditions made several nations feel that the United States was trying to make others over in its own democratic image and to obtain too much publicity for its generosity.

Another set of requirements was imposed in the 1951 Mutual Security Program legislation to encourage recipients to increase their efforts toward rearmament. The law required that each nation, before it could become eligible for aid aimed at furthering the military effort, sign an agreement stating that it would join in keeping the peace, help in eliminating international tensions, fulfill military treaty obligations to which the United States was a party, and develop to the full its defense capacities. Several countries refused to sign the agreements; some never received the projected aid, and aid to some others was delayed pending a satisfactory solution, which usually meant assurance by the United States that there would be no encroachment on the other nation's sovereignty. Despite the intent of Congress that recipients should alter their policies and thus show more eagerness to rearm and to defend the West against Russia, it was evident that insistence on the U.S. interpretation of what constituted "full contribution to defense" and a "reduction of international tensions" would mean that the agreements would not be signed, that aid would not be extended, and that the purposes sought by the program would go unfulfilled. The U.S. administration therefore found it necessary to water down the eligibility requirements in order to induce others to accept the aid.

Additional efforts were made through the aid programs to encourage recipients to adopt institutions of American capitalism by preventing the socialization of European industry and by encouraging private enterprise and free labor unions. The principle of free competition was, however, contradicted by requirements that purchases of some goods with aid funds be made in the United States rather than let other nations compete for the business.

A final set of conditions attached to the programs related to the use of the aid in the foreign countries in gaining recovery or rearmament. These conditions were implemented through the control over counterpart funds and through advice and supervision by the U.S. aid missions abroad— those sent by the Economic Cooperation Administration (later, Mutual Security Agency, then Foreign Operations Administration, and lately International Cooperation Administration) responsible for economic aid and the Military Assistance Advisory Group (MAAG) sent to advise on military programs.

SOCIALIZATION AND NATIONAL PLANNING

In the debate on the British loan and ERP aid, some congressmen expressed fear that aid to Britain and other countries would be used to socialize industry. They argued that aid should be withheld from any country nationalizing its industry on the ground that the United States should not "fight Communism with Socialism" and that socialization and state trading created foreign monopolies with which American industries would have to compete.

In reply, the administration asserted that ECA's terms of reference were to gain the greatest recovery for all ERP participants, even though this purpose might be hindered by nationalization and the aid might support socialist governments abroad (e.g., the British Labour government might have gone out of power sooner if internal conditions had been permitted to deteriorate further). The U.S. government, officials argued, could not require a change in others' policies of socialization. Such a requirement on the use of aid would be "undesirable and ineffective interference"; it would be just the sort of action which would bolster (Communist) elements in European countries which were against the acceptance of U.S. aid. ECA officials asserted also that U.S. policy was not to *bargain* for removal of trade controls, state trading, and discrimination but to gain economic conditions abroad conducive to their removal.

Moreover, some observers have argued that the foreign aid to Europe could not have been effectively used without national planning and that the requirements by the U.S. government that projected balance-of-payments deficits be spelled out depended on close national programming. Also, the careful guidance of recovery programs and the close supervision required to prove that the aid was effectively employed and to justify further aid implied national planning to a degree which would make congressmen blanch if such things were requested of them for the U.S. economy.

The administration took the general position that no conditions should be imposed on aid other than those necessary to make the aid effective. This position meant, in ECA's view, that internal policies of the recipients would be exempt from control by the United States. It wished to avoid any taint of interference which might be considered an infringement of sovereignty and which would give fodder to Communist propaganda charges of "imperialism." Senator Taft, an outspoken opponent of most of the administration's foreign economic program and a foe of socialization and planning, agreed with this position when he stated:

If we go into these countries we open ourselves to charges of interference and imperialism. If we impose conditions which turn out to be unpopular with the people, we nullify to a large extent such credit which we might otherwise obtain.

It seems to me that the only conditions which can safely be enforced are conditions as to the particular type of goods which can be exported from the United States, and a limitation of any commitment to one year.[4]

Against the administration's position it must be noted that any government is made up of persons with diverse views. What might be considered

---

[4] *New York Times,* November 11, 1947.

an infringement of sovereignty by one group might be welcomed as necessary and desirable by others as a means of inducing the government to do things which they feel it should do but which it cannot because of domestic political pressures. Thus the aid might be used to support elements in the foreign government who already agree with U.S. objectives but need some assistance in the form of pressure from the U.S. government to put their policies into effect. Members of foreign governments faced strong pressures from within their own country to distort the aid programs; conditions placed on the use of aid by the U.S. government would prevent such a distortion. Officials favorably disposed to the U.S. position could argue that, however painful the measures employed, they were necessary for the continuation of U.S. aid.

ENCOURAGEMENT TO PRIVATE ENTERPRISE

Several congressmen expressed concern that workers and consumers were not sharing adequately in the benefits of increased production in Europe. Citizens might therefore not be sufficiently willing to defend their country against attack. But Congress was opposed to benefits being extended to workers through the "social reform" measures widely employed in Europe. These were seen by many congressmen as diverting capital and other goods from the rearmament effort. ECA officials replied that these measures had only a slightly retarding effect on Europe's military efforts. As was stated in Chapter 18, the distribution of benefits was an unresolved problem of ERP aid. ECA officials testified that they were planning to obtain a wider dispersion of benefits by pressing for changes in legislation and in business practices in recipient countries. But progress in this area was not sufficient to please Congress. An amendment was passed in 1951 aimed at encouraging free enterprise abroad. Vigorous protests were made by the minority who felt, like Senator Taft, that it was "a most outrageous interference with the affairs of other nations."

The ostensible objective of encouraging free enterprise abroad was that it would increase production and productivity of workers. The provision required the Mutual Security Act to be so administered as

(1) to eliminate the barriers to, and provide the incentives for, a steadily increased participation of free private enterprise in developing the resources of foreign countries consistent with the policies of this act, (2) to the extent that it is feasible and does not interfere with the achievement of the purposes set forth in this Act, to discourage the cartel and monopolistic practices prevailing in certain countries receiving aid under this Act which result in restricting production and increasing prices, and to encourage where suitable competition and productivity, and (3) to encourage where suitable the development and strengthening of the free labor union movements as the collective bargaining agencies of labor within such countries.[5]

---

[5] *Mutual Security Act of 1951* (P. L. 165) § 516.

By the end of 1952, the administration reported that it was well along the way to setting up programs to lend funds to private companies for the purpose of financing research, education, and demonstration in new and existing production and managerial techniques. A European Productivity Agency was established to disseminate technical knowledge. But in December, 1952, an evaluation mission concluded that, though the objective of raising productivity and distributing benefits more evenly was well taken, the amendment was unwise. It required U.S. officials to undertake the direction of policies and practices in the recipient countries which they had "neither the wisdom, the experience, nor the resources to carry out"; in fact, the provisions had proved "unworkable."[6] The new administration and Congress deleted the enforcing clauses of the provision but left the sentiment by declaring in the 1953 act that it was "the policy of the United States . . . to encourage the efforts of other free countries" to expand the area of free enterprise, to discourage monopoly, and to support the development of free labor unions.

TIED PURCHASING

Given the propensity of congressmen to accede to the requests of constituents, it is amazing that the foreign aid programs were affected as little as they were by pleas of special interests. Over the past decade of aid, Congress has been asked for hundreds of favors in channeling aid purchases to specific groups; over one hundred requests were made during the early discussions of ERP. Yet Congress has employed the aid programs to protect or subsidize only two major interests: shipping and agriculture.

There was little difficulty in making a decision not to direct aid purchases to any given area in the United States during the early years of aid, because until 1949, most producers had ample backlogs of orders. ERP legislation did, however, include some requirements that given percentages of wheat shipments be in the form of flour to assist in the employment of American millers. Some requirements were included to prevent purchases of items in scarce supply in the United States, such as farm machinery.

Given the large volume of shipments overseas under ERP aid programs (and U.S. lending), Congress considered it appropriate to require that 50 per cent of shipments under grants and loans should be made in U.S.-flag vessels. The yearly additional costs of shipping imposed by this requirement were estimated at about $8 million. But despite requests from officials administering the aid programs to remove this stipulation, Congress has continued it.

The shipping requirement has, no doubt, increased the costs of administration and has been a thorn in the side of foreign shippers who would have liked to earn the dollars. But the aggregate amount of aid diverted has been small, and it would hardly make a dent in the balance-of-payments

---

[6] *Foreign Commerce Weekly,* December 22, 1952, pp. 18–19.

problems of Europe as a whole; even so, for some countries, such as Holland and Norway, who stood to benefit the most from the shipping trade, the loss was significant.

The decision as to whether or not to introduce a shipping subsidy into aid programs must be made in light of the entire program of shipping subsidies and preferences, which have been justified as means of supporting a national-defense industry. The shipping requirement was readily removed with regard to shipments of agricultural surpluses, however, when Congress realized that it would reduce the volume of surplus disposals.

Disposal of U.S. agricultural surpluses has been authorized by Congress through several humanitarian programs of emergency relief aid. And congressmen have considered that the continuing aid programs provide a means of reducing stocks of surplus commodities. But the administration has argued that, though such stocks would be used whenever feasible, it would be inappropriate to *require* that aid recipients take surplus items. Many recipients produce similar commodities or do not include them in their diets. In some countries surpluses of similar commodities existed. These surpluses posed a dual problem for U.S. disposal of its own stocks. First, the foreign country would look askance at any action of the United States which cut into the former's normal world markets. Second, offers of foreign countries to sell their agricultural surpluses to the United States instead of accepting aid were usually turned down. Thus Burma requested that the United States purchase its rice surplus so as to raise prices and prevent economic disturbances which might lead to communism. When the U.S. government refused to "monetize" Burma's surplus, Burma turned to barter with Russia—an action which displeased the United States and which caused the United States later to help Burma market its rice.

Once again, the decision as to the proper use of aid programs as means of subsidizing U.S. agriculture (more precisely, reducing the burden of surpluses on the government) depends on the entire program of support to agriculture and the role of agriculture in international trade; these problems are discussed in Chapter 24.

COUNTERPART FUNDS

In almost all of its aid programs, the United States has required that each participant deposit in a special account the local currency "counterpart" of the dollar cost of economic aid goods it received on a grant basis. Of these deposits, 5 per cent or more was set aside for use by the United States, and the remaining sums were for use by the recipient country for purposes agreed upon by both that country and the U.S. aid missions.

Two illusions arose from the existence of the counterpart funds. One, held by importers of recipient countries, was that they personally did not get any benefit from the aid because they had to pay local currency for the goods they imported from the United States. Each importer did pay for U.S. goods and thus gained nothing directly but they did gain indirectly since the nation as a whole obtained free goods, because the imports would not have been possible at all had the United States not extended the grants to governments. The other illusion was one on the part of some recipient governments and U.S. officials. They asserted that the counterpart funds gave "the Marshall Plan dollar" power to "do double duty, and benefit the European twice over."[7] ECA representatives argued that the jointly controlled funds, when retained in the account, contributed to financial stability and, when released to promote production, increased economic stability.

Because of this alleged potency of the funds, some in Congress wanted the U.S. government to retain complete control over the use of the funds. But the administration argued that such ownership would give U.S. missions the "power of financial life or death over these countries" and that the "enormous magnitude" of the funds in some of the countries would give the controller of them so much power that it would be unwise for the United States to have sole control. Such statements were an exaggeration of the influence of counterpart funds, but they show the importance attached to them by the administration. ECA Administrator Hoffman asserted, in fact, that during the program and after his retirement as ECA Administrator the funds had given ECA power to exercise a great constructive influence on the financial conditions of the ERP countries.

This view that counterpart funds were a potent influence over the recipient economy does not stand up under close scrutiny. The local currency proceeds resulting from the sale of aid goods did *reflect* an important reduction in inflationary pressures, since money was taken out of private channels. But this potential effect *could* be and was offset by other budgetary and monetary policies, e.g., budgetary deficits financed in inflationary ways.

To avoid nullification of the deflationary effect of counterpart deposits, an integrated policy was required which recognized that counterpart funds were merely the financial reflection of goods already imported. Because the imported goods were already used, the counterpart funds did not add any real resources to the economy. That is, once the aid dollars were spent and the imports "sold" for local currency, the only addition to real production was the imports themselves and the new production they permitted. The local currency proceeds held by the government were no more and no less powerful in raising production than new money printed for government use. The expenditure of counterpart funds, whatever their use, is by itself inflationary. The combined acts of accumulation and then expenditure of counterpart funds are together neutral in their price-level effects. To combat inflation, the counterpart funds should be hoarded.

U.S. policy was, according to the above analysis, only partly appro-

---

[7] ECA, *Information* (pamphlet 4776), July 1, 1950, pp. 7–8.

priate. Use of only one-fourth of total deposits during the ECA's program for debt retirement and the immobilization of a similar portion appear to have been the most important means of restricting inflationary policies of recipient governments. But even this effect was small, because yearly counterpart *deposits* were as low as ½ per cent of national income in some countries and ranged no higher than 10 per cent in others. Total deposits averaged less than 3 per cent of national income for Europe as a whole, and less than half was used for anti-inflationary purposes. If this power was all that was afforded by the counterpart funds over domestic financial and budgetary policies and practices of recipient governments, they hardly determined "financial life or death."

Despite the fact that the counterpart funds did not themselves provide a strong influence over the recipient economy, the fact that they were jointly owned did give the U.S. missions an opportunity for continued consultation and advice on a multitude of economic matters ranging from budgets to investment programs and the balance of payments. The joint ownership provided the explicit recognition that the U.S. government had a legitimate interest in the fiscal and monetary affairs of the recipient. It is important that the channels of consultation be informal and constantly open so that suggestions may be made without their seeming to be formal interference.

The necessity of making joint decisions as to the use of counterpart funds also provided U.S. officials with extensive information as to the operations of the recipient government and the economic activity of the country. Officials knew first-hand what the day-to-day conditions in the economy were and did not have to accept an end-of-the-year assessment made by the officials of the recipient government. They were enabled to make their aid programming more realistic and their advice more relevant, even if the advice was not always followed or was avoided through budgetary dodges.

ADVICE AND SUPERVISION

United States officials have had some effective power in their "advisory" and "supervisory" roles in the aid missions abroad. They have helped plan recovery and rearmament programs and, before approving aid to a given country, have recommended changes in recipients' requests. The limitation on such advice and supervision has arisen from the inability of U.S. officials to insist on preferred policies or needed reforms.

The U.S. administration did not attempt (save in a few instances) to counteract or interfere with established political and economic policies of European countries, and its control over part of the recipients imports did not provide sufficient influence. It is of little advantage to supervise the use of one portion of foreign exchange while the rest is unsupervised. ERP recipients, if they found that the U.S. missions would not approve imports of certain materials or equipment for financing with aid funds, would merely look into their programs for items that would be approved and import the others with currently earned dollars. Similarly, with reference to counterpart funds, recipients could accept the determination of their use suggested by U.S. officials and yet easily circumvent the intended use of resources. The recipients could shift their own funds, which they might have spent for those purposes approved by the U.S. officials, into projects unapproved by them while using the counterpart funds for the approved projects. Because of the difficulty of supervisory control, some observers have contended that all supervision should be dropped and aid provided in the form of unrestricted dollars, the use of which could be determined as the recipient government saw fit. An advantage of this method is that it would reduce friction between the donor and recipient governments.

Policies of noninterference were adopted even though they seriously hampered the success of ERP in some respects. Although the purpose of aid was to permit a higher living standard in Europe than could be obtained out of its own production, it also in effect supported domestic policies of overfull employment, enlarged social services, expanded investment, and subsidized consumption. These, in turn, increased the need for aid and lengthened the recovery process.

At a time when the United States government was attempting to foster stability of economies and governments abroad, it was not ready to say to ERP recipients: "You must first stop the inflation and reduce your investment programs and cut your social services to a level for which you can pay, then we will see if you need help in reconstruction." Such an attitude, the administration thought, would have resulted in Europe closing many trade (and perhaps diplomatic) doors to the United States and in cries, especially from Communist quarters, of "dictation and intervention."

The U.S. government did not stress the reform of domestic policies as *prerequisite* to assistance or as a necessary accompaniment of aid to make the programs successful.[8] Little or no pressure was brought to bear to change the production structure to shift away from the autarchic and nationalistic lines which existed prior to the war or to reduce the restrictive practices of cartels within Europe. Rather, the most rapid physical recovery was desired; this was generally obtainable by restoring former production facilities without regard to whether the projects were in line with comparative advantage and would make recipients self-supporting in world trade.

Given the general antipathy of the European governments toward freeing trade and payments, it is no small wonder that the multiple goals of ERP were not attained. It is difficult to see how a multilateral nondiscriminatory trade and payments system (requiring free markets) can be gained *through* controls and discriminations; with controls, the pricing system is

---

[8] Professor R. G. Hawtrey has asserted that the British devaluation in 1949 was significantly a result of American opinion that the pound was overvalued and that British costs were too high; this "American opinion," he added, "could not be ignored at a time when Great Britain was dependent on Marshall Aid." (*Cross Purposes in Wage Policy* [London: Longmans, Green, 1955], p. 67.)

prevented from allocating resources according to comparative advantage.

To have established conditions necessary to the attainment and maintenance of the U.S. international economic program, aid recipients would have had to stop current inflation by mopping up excess liquidity arising from wartime savings and preventing the expansion of the money supply; they would have had to adjust foreign exchange rates, and return to determination of economic activity essentially through free markets. European governments accepted these objectives *in principle,* but they (and ECA in its early years) were much more concerned with the need for increased output of goods and services regardless of whether orthodox principles of fiscal and monetary policies were implemented. The U.S. government settled for all it considered feasible—an expression of intent by the recipients plus whatever impact its day-to-day consultations would have.

Since the aid recipients did raise their standards of living and increase national output somewhat, they did use the aid to some advantage, but it is not clear that they used it to "buy time" in which to make the structural adjustments that would have been required to sustain themselves in a multilateral, nondiscriminatory system of trade and payments.

SELECTED READINGS

In addition to the sources at the end of Chapters 17, 18, and 19, the following were found valuable:

Balogh, Thomas. *Dollar Crisis.* London: Blackwell, 1949. An analysis of the postwar "dollar shortage" which argues that the remedy for continued pressure on European balances of payments is a redistribution of wealth from the richer countries (namely the United States) to the poorer.

Committee for Economic Development. *Economic Aspects of North Atlantic Security,* New York, May, 1951. A pamphlet discussing the reasons for European rearmament, Europe's contribution, burden-sharing, and U.S. aid.

Cottrell, A. "Drama of the 'Counterpart Funds': Potent Phase of ECA Operations," *Foreign Commerce Weekly,* November 15, 1948, pp. 6 ff. An example of the extravagant claims of the administration for the power of counterpart funds in guiding and controlling the activities of the recipients of aid.

Malenbaum, W. "Grants and Loans in U.S. Foreign Assistance," *World Politics,* VI (April, 1954), 338–357. A critique of grants versus loans, of multilateral versus bilateral aid, and of the need for foreign aid.

McLeod, A. N. "Local Currency Proceeds of an Import Surplus," *International Monetary Fund Staff Papers* I (February, 1950), 114–122. A critique of the additional resources supposedly provided through the counterpart technique. The conclusion drawn is that they may be effective in reducing inflationary pressure if the governmental budget is coordinated with the use of the funds.

Meade, J. E. "Some Economic Problems of Atlantic Union Rearmament," *Lloyd's Bank Review,* October, 1951, pp. 35–51. An examination of the problems of the amount of rearmament effort, of burden-sharing, of location of productive activity, and of institutional cooperation.

Schelling, T. C., "American Foreign Assistance," *World Politics,* VII (July, 1955), 606–626. A review article of W. A. Brown and R. Opie. *American Foreign Assistance,* Washington: Brookings, 1953. The reviewer concentrates on several of the more difficult problems of extending aid bilaterally and multilaterally, such as burden-sharing, control over aid, conditions on aid, etc.

————. *International Cost-Sharing Arrangements.* Essays in International Finance, No. 24, Princeton University, International Finance Section, September, 1955. An analysis of the treatment of the problem of burden-sharing under the various aid and cooperative assistance programs since World War II; the conclusion is that certain precedents have been set for future policies even though the decisions taken previously have not been implemented.

21 Problems of Economic Development

One of the most significant facts of the postwar period has been the determination of the economically backward countries of the world to find their "place in the sun." The growth of nationalism, accelerated by World War II, created a greater demand for progress; the growing contacts with the wealth and power of the industrialized nations demonstrated to the underdeveloped nations that progress could be won.

The developing nations have seen that Russia has taken a place as a "great power" through her phenomenal economic growth within three decades. Both the American standard of living and the power of Russia are seen as a result of industrialization. Most backward areas tend to indentify wealth and power with the smoking chimneys of Pittsburgh, Gary, Kiev, and Krivoi Rog.

By contrast, the backward areas display low living standards, little industry, and little economic growth. Almost two-thirds the world's population lives on an average annual per capita income of about $100, compared with five to ten times that in Europe and about fifteen times that in the United States. Of course, not all the people have so low an income, and the annual averages range from about $50 to around $300 per capita in the underdeveloped countries. An underdeveloped country can be characterized also by low average food consumption per capita (an average of 2,000 calories of food a day—less than half the U.S. calorie intake and barely enough to sustain life), a high death rate (most have a life expectancy of thirty years compared with sixty years in the advanced countries), widespread illiteracy, a low ratio of savings and investment to national income, and low productivity per worker. By comparison, the annual value of production in the United States and Western Europe is about five times as great as that of all the underdeveloped areas of the world combined.

The underdeveloped countries lie in a broad belt extending across the face of the earth from South and Central America, north and east through Africa, the Middle East, Southeastern Europe, South Asia, and the Far East. Not all countries have the same potential for growth, since resource endowment varies widely. Nor is this endowment the only important limit, for Indonesia is well endowed but has not progressed, while India is poorly endowed but has been successful in efforts to raise per capita income somewhat.

All these nations have the common desire to increase their wealth and power. Their major objectives are higher living standards, greater economic stability, political independence, and international prestige. The rising tide of nationalism in these areas is almost an overriding factor and must be kept paramount in the minds of Western policy-makers. These countries have advantages which were not available to other nations during the early period of industrialization and development: they can draw upon a stock of technological knowledge abroad which need only be imported, adapted, and applied (not created), and the advanced countries are willing to give various encouragements to their economic growth.

The more developed countries of the West view the problems of economic development abroad from four angles: economic, military, political, and humanitarian. Despite the difficulty of tracing the impact of humanitarianism through congressional action or of analyzing its importance in the formation of U.S. foreign economic policy, its significance must not be discounted. Not only is it a strong aspect of the public support in America for aiding others but it is also, from the viewpoint of the developing countries, one of America's strongest assets, for it exports the American belief in the desirability of progress and in the dignity of man.

From the political viewpoint, the West is interested in reducing the threat to peace which it thinks results from economic instability or poverty. Some people argue that those who are dissatisfied with their economic lot are likely to attempt internal revolution, or to look overseas with envy and be easily led by an ambitious ruler into external aggression.

From a military viewpoint, the West desires that the poor countries be strong enough to help defend themselves against attack. It also is anxious for these areas to develop supplies of raw materials which are needed by the West for its mobilization base.

From an economic viewpoint, the Western nations want the poorer countries to become richer, though the ways and methods are not yet agreed upon by the developed nations. There is little agreement as to just what constitutes desirable development and as to how the obstacles may be removed most effectively. Specifically, what does the U.S. government mean when it says it seeks "economic development" for others? and what problems must be solved by the developing countries? After an examination of these questions in this chapter, the succeeding one analyzes the problems of assistance to foreign development.

A. UNITED STATES AIMS

The broad economic objective sought by the U.S. government for developing nations is a decrease in the number of people living at subsistence (or minimum) levels of consumption. But there is no proof that such an increase in living standards will meet the political and military objectives of U.S. foreign policy. Rather, there is increasing evidence that the process of economic growth itself may encourage radical movements toward communism or fascism. They develop from the disappointment of rising expectations and from the disturbances to normal social and cultural relations. Torn from family ties and unemployed as the structure of production shifts, workers may readily seek a radical outlet for their energies. Russia has been able to capitalize on the "revolution of rising expectations," and the West feels that it must prove that the aspirations of the developing areas can be met best through democratic measures.

There is little doubt that the distress of backward areas could be relieved; sanitation and health could be improved; consumption of food, clothing, and shelter could rise; and the masses could be made more satisfied in material things. But the removal of hunger and destitution may induce revolt, because people do not revolt until they see a chance of change. The mere fact of economic growth will not necessarily cause nations to become more friendly toward capitalism and democracy, especially of the American variety. The developing countries currently show little desire for the institutions of private property, free enterprise, freedom of contract, and individual initiative which are supposed to characterize the American system; and their interpretation of what constitutes democracy is different from that of the West. If they adopted "democracy," it would not necessarily follow that they would become friendly toward the United States. In sum, *economic development does not necessarily make nice people* nor is it possible to "buy friends" with aid. It is not, therefore, certain that economic development abroad will raise the strength of the United States, because the developing countries might not side with the West. Many of these nations have shown a positive desire *not* to take sides in the East-West conflict at all.

Even if the developing countries do side with the Free World, the type of development desired by the backward country may not be that which the United States deems desirable. For example, the U.S. government is highly interested in the expansion of international trade, particularly in critical materials. But the developing countries see such projects as making them more dependent on foreign markets and delaying their industrialization. They would, apparently, prefer to industrialize in areas in which the U.S. economy is proficient. America's exports would be reduced and her supplies of raw materials curtailed or cut off. The expansion of trade, even if it occurred, is likely to involve a shift in U.S. resources at some cost and discomfort to the nation, depending on the pattern of development and

the commercial policies adopted by both the United States and the developing countries.

The success of economic development in one country may make its
loss to the enemy more likely, either through a *coup d'etat* or open warfare.
The country becomes a more succulent plum to pick. ECA Administrator
Hoffman reported in 1950 that the outbreak of the Korean War was accelerated by the success of the ECA missions in developing South Korea.

The point in raising these questions is not to argue that economic
development is undesirable but to suggest that it conflicts with some interests
in the United States. The conditions under which economic development
abroad will serve some of the purposes sought by the U.S. government
include the expansion of private enterprise abroad, the improvement of
agriculture prior to industrial expansion, including the expansion of raw-
materials production needed by the U.S. economy, and the expansion of
international trade and investment under policies of nondiscrimination.

EXTENSION OF PRIVATE ENTERPRISE

The U.S. government, especially Congress, has insisted that the developmental assistance be employed in such a way as to give the maximum stimulus to private enterprise. Emphasis was placed not only on
nondiscriminatory treatment of U.S. private investors abroad but also on
policies abroad which would encourage the expansion of private industrial
enterprise.

The justification for this approach is the belief that economic growth
is more sufficient and satisfactory when tied to individual incentives and
goals. If the objective of progress is to satisfy the individual's desires in the
most efficient way possible, not only must the individual be permitted to
express those desires in a free market but also the means of production
must be in private hands which are eager to satisfy those desires. Government allocation of production overwhelms the desires of individuals as
reflected in the market place, and it creates problems of economic organization and production which are not always resolved in the most technically
efficient manner. The view of the U.S. government has been that only
through a free enterprise system can the individual drives to progress be
tied to the production process, and only through a free market can the
multitude of economic decisions be taken without running into bottlenecks
of poor coordination and into bureaucratic restrictions. Support for this
view has been found in the surveys of progress in developing countries
made by the International Bank for Reconstruction and Development:
"The experience of the Bank has made very clear that in most countries
the pace of economic growth depends in large measure upon the degree of
private initiative and the extent of private investment."[1]

---

[1] Statement by Robert L. Garner, vice-president of the IBRD at the tenth annual
meeting of the board of governors of the Bank, September 15, 1955.

ECE Director Gunnar Myrdal has written that "Without the fixed idea that

Recipients of aid, however, are wary of private enterprise. They have had experience with "exploitation" and "one-sided" development under both foreign and domestic private enterprise. Most of the foreign governments take the view that private enterprise can not be expected to do the job wanted. Domestically, the experience has been that there is no middle class of entrepreneurs capable of directing economic activity; the "enterprising spirit" is rarely found in underdeveloped countries.[2] Most of the people are too ignorant, too poor, and too fixed in traditional patterns of behavior to exercise much independence of action. Governments have felt that the individual has defaulted and that they must direct economic programs. And even the U.S. administration has insisted that the countries receiving aid set up a rather thorough-going plan for development—a request contrary in principle to its desire for noninterference.

The aims of U.S. policy in regard to the ownership and direction of enterprise may be quite unattainable. Continued insistence by the U.S. government on the extension of private enterprise abroad may cause it to become dissatisfied with otherwise adequate progress abroad. Some progress toward free-enterprise may also come without U.S. pressure. It has been the experience in India that the absence of a crude insistence by the West on a private-enterprise philosophy has let that nation find out for itself the advantages of a growing reliance on the private sector.

INDUSTRIALIZATION VERSUS AGRICULTURAL DEVELOPMENT

The U.S. government, in its official statements and publications, has been careful to avoid using the word "industrialization" in referring to the process of economic growth abroad. This reflects its belief that most of the backward countries first require a rise in agricultural productivity. The argument is that, before men and materials can be moved into industrial

---

credit is business, that profitability is important, and that there is a market where economic demand and supply for capital meet, international finance spills over into the indeterminate ocean of power politics, where the crackpots and demagogues swim with great pleasure. The real danger is, of course, that with the disappearance of the capital market in the oldfashioned sense of the word, really worthwhile investment projects stand to lose their chance of being financed, or else they are modified by political reasons; in many cases they may then lose much of their economic character as self-liquidating investments." (*An International Economy* [New York: Harper, 1956], pp. 112–113.)

[2] This phenomenon has been explained with reference to Southeast Asia as follows: "The age-long influence of the West . . . failed, with only few exceptions, to instill its economic activity and enterprise into the minds and habits of these peoples. The Western apparatus of finance, commerce, and production remained an alien, undigested and indigestible element in Southeast Asia. It had created institutions, means of production and communication and a stability far beyond the achievements of the past, but it had hardly awakened a new economic initiative or industry. . . . The social solidarity, the public spirit, and the economic energy that were necessary for a vigorous resurgence were lacking." (H. J. Van Mook, "The Needs of Underdeveloped Areas," in J. B. Condliffe, ed., *International Cooperation for World Economic Development* [Berkeley: University of California, 1950], p. 20.)

production, there must be enough food to support the new urban population.

Many developing countries sought, in the first flush of development programming after World War II, to give priority to industry; some still seek to do so. Early applicants for loans and grant aid frequently declared, "We want a steel mill." Many countries have noticed that the prosperity of the more wealthy nations is coupled with a high proportion of industry and that their own economies were highly dependent upon the level of operations in the industrial countries.[3]

As the developing countries have met the problems of programming and executing plans, they have repeatedly come face to face with bottlenecks of agricultural production (both food and raw materials). Many have become less emphatic that industry is immediately desirable. For example, the Colombo Plan for economic development of several British Commonwealth countries includes agricultural projects costing one-third of the total, with mining and industry taking only 10 per cent and the rest going to development of various basic services. India has emphasized agricultural over industrial development. Russia and China (and for a while Argentina) have pursued the reverse policy.

It is not difficult to reconcile, at least in the early stages of growth, the desire of the U.S. administration for emphasis on agricultural development with the desire of backward countries for industrial growth. Developing nations need to export primary materials to obtain capital goods most cheaply; the United States and other nations need these materials for their economic expansion and military effort.

TRADE POLICY

The drive for industrialization and diversification of economic activity leads to a desire for protection. These developing countries observe that the recent rapid rise of Russia and the growth of the United States occurred largely behind barriers to international trade. Whether or not these barriers were *needed,* and whether or not they may have reduced the wealth of each nation using them as compared with what could have been under freer trade, the fact was that protection was employed. The developing areas argue that they must be afforded the same opportunity to employ restrictive

---

[3] A representative of an underdeveloped country (Mr. George Hakim, Legation of Lebanon, Washington, D.C.) has written that "The underdeveloped countries believe that in the long run no appreciable rise in the national income can be achieved without a substantial development of manufacturing industries. In fact, in some of the densely populated countries of Asia and the Middle East, which have considerable underemployment in agriculture, industrialization is the only method of achieving a significant increase in national production by utilizing the surplus labor that can be withdrawn from agriculture without reduction in output. It is also the only way of finding employment for a growing population in countries where the possibility of extending cultivation to new land is extremely limited." (*The Progress of Underdeveloped Areas* [Chicago: University of Chicago Press, 1952], p. 264; see, in reply, *ibid.,* pp. 192–195.)

measures to facilitate their internal growth; they have, in fact, done so, using either the free enterprise and/or socialist techniques. The U.S. government, on the other hand, argues that what is required is a lowering of barriers and the establishment of nondiscriminatory, multilateral trade.

There is a strong probability that the interests of the developing country and the United States are identical in the field of trade policy during the early phases of growth. Professors Buchanan and Ellis stress the desirability of linking economic development into a strong international economy, giving three basic reasons: (a) the traditional techniques of production and trade are more readily broken by the contacts among nations and traders which international trade provides by the introduction of an "aggressive class of entreprenuers" along with direct investment, and by the reduction

U.S. EXPORTS IN 1955 PER INHABITANT OF THE COUNTRY

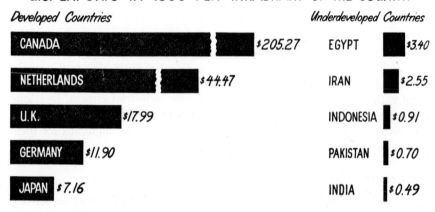

Fig. 20 The More Developed Countries Are Better U.S. Customers
SOURCE: International Cooperation Administration

of social and other barriers to higher productivity accompanying trade and investment; (b) the imports of capital goods necessary for continued progress are obtainable only through foreign trade, and (c) foreign private-capital investment will be encouraged if international trade is flourishing. Thus an expanding world economy provides an environment in which the interests of the United States and the developing countries can be made to coincide. In addition, the adjustments required during rapid growth can be made more easily.[4] Once industrialization has been attained, the market for exports of previously industrialized countries will be larger as a result of higher incomes in the developing nations. But the adjustments in traded items and in the direction of trade will require shifts of resources as a result

---

[4] *Approaches to Economic Development* (New York: Twentieth Century Fund, 1955), pp. 431–433.

of competition from protected industries in developing countries and will lead to conflicts of interest both within and among nations.

One important problem facing developing countries is the instability of prices of key exports, from which they obtain most of their export earnings. They have insisted that some form of intergovernmental agreement is necessary to stabilize prices and thus income from these exports, but the U.S. government has so far refused to cooperate in this fashion, for reasons discussed in Chapter 24.

A further conflict may arise if the United States does not extend capital or lower its own tariffs. If other countries are to gain capital goods from the United States they must be able to borrow from or export to her. Although there are few barriers on raw materials imports, some tariffs and quotas have been imposed on such goods—the more competitive they are with U.S. production the more stringent the restrictions.

From the above characteristics of the economic development abroad desired by the U.S. government, it is evident that American purposes and policies may conflict with the objectives or techniques of the developing countries themselves. Even if the objectives sought by each were not in conflict—or even if the conflicts could be resolved—there are a host of problems facing the developing countries which impede the process of development.

B. PROBLEMS OF THE DEVELOPING COUNTRY

The elements of economic development are the same, in general, as those which economists have been talking about for several centuries: capital formation, labor productivity, and improvement of technology. The development of the wealthier countries proceeds along principles enunciated by Smith, Ricardo, Mill, *et al.* But the problems of backward areas are more varied, encompassing a host of noneconomic obstacles; the solutions are different, if not in kind at least in significant degree, and the changes required are more extensive.

First among the required changes is one in attitude. The people, especially the political and economic leaders, must become receptive to new ideas and new ways of doing things. Leaders in Saudi Arabia rejected assistance from the United States in 1954 for fear that social changes would occur, upsetting their power. Where they have been receptive to change, progress has been more rapid; for example, India shows much more willingness to adopt new approaches than do Thailand and Indochina. People who work only to live as their grandfathers did are not susceptible to economic development. New social, economic, and political institutions are required to encourage enterprise, and adaptations must be made to the new distribution of power resulting from growth. Increased mobility will be necessary to hasten technological change; to attain it, shifts in occupational distribution will be required as well as in the age distribution and size of the population. Changes will occur in production and consumption and in the volume and composition of international trade. In order to channel the desired changes in production and consumption into desired areas, the methods and magnitudes of capital formation will have to be altered and expanded.

These changes can be accomplished either through the free market or through government direction. Either approach may give priority to more immediate satisfaction of consumer demands as incomes rise or capital accumulates. The former may result in a rate of growth in productive capacity so slow as to be hardly perceptible, but the latter defers consumption and thus does not meet the people's desire for prompt alleviation of their misery. Which is more desirable "progress" will depend on whether the immediate aim is to increase the welfare of the populace immediately but slightly, or to enhance the position of certain groups who are able to direct and increase capital accumulation for a higher rate of long-run growth.

The developing countries have found it difficult to decide between the two approaches. Although they have talked in terms of the first approach (stating that technical advance and other aid must reach the majority of the people who are the producers of national wealth and that any resulting increase in wealth must be shared by the majority of the people, or else the programs of development will fail), some development programs have leaned toward assisting those who are already landowners and capital holders in increasing their control over the economy. Which of these approaches is more necessary or desirable cannot be firmly decided apart from a study of the specific problems faced in each country. A general examination of some of the conditions in the developing countries will be a partial guide to understanding their attitudes. Of primary importance in the process of growth are the problems of relieving population pressure, improving public administration, accelerating capital formation, and altering social mores and religious traditions.

POPULATION PRESSURES

In some developing economies, such as nineteenth century America and twentieth century Canada, an expansion of population probably has been an impetus to economic growth. But where the size of population is already pressing against national production, further growth is more a detriment than a benefit; the problem is to prevent such a continued rise. Demographers are in general agreement that the most effective check to an excessive rate of growth of population in the long-run is the material advance of a nation. Once the adults of procreating age see the possibility of increasing the standard of living of their families by restricting births, they will do so. As long as it is not understood that a reduction in births will raise these standards, there is little incentive or effort to restrain the growth of families; the checks to population are then the Malthusian ones of war, famine, and disease. These checks will work automatically to keep the population within the bounds of the production of the economy. If they are removed, population tends to grow rapidly, giving rise to serious problems of feeding and care of the newly expanded numbers.

However, removing the checks of disease and famine is a way to increase labor productivity. Where a large part of the population suffers from yaws, malaria, or trachoma, etc., labor is ineffective and sporadic. Further, the high death rate means an early death age; labor is therefore extremely costly in the long run, because there is a relatively long period in which the person is dependent on society before he enters the labor force and a relatively short period in which he contributes to his own and others' support.

Improved health measures, sanitation, and medical care are necessary for the revitalization of the populations of developing areas, but they involve an extension of life also among the aged who are unlikely to produce enough to support themselves. The dilemma then is that of having to raise the chances of a longer and healthier life and at the same time risk an increase in population higher than or equal to the rise in productivity. A long-run solution lies in ways of raising productivity relatively faster than the rate of population increase, as was done by Western Europe in the nineteenth century. In nations where population pressure is strong, governmental policy is usually behind efforts to increase capital formation, i.e., to provide the economic break-through out of the Malthusian trap. Some of the population pressure may be relieved even in the short run, if the government encourages birth control. Experiments in Haiti and India along this line seem to be making some headway, partly because they have been sold to the people as a precondition of economic development.

CAPITAL FORMATION

It has been said of the developing countries that the basic reason for their being poor is their poverty. The truth of this is seen nowhere better than in the realm of capital accumulation. These countries have very little capital investment, and the incentives which must exist for both the saving and investing functions are lacking.

On the side of the supply of capital funds, there is little ability to save, since the level of real income is low. The low level of real income is a result partly of low productivity, which in turn results from a lack of capital. On the side of the demand for investment funds, the incentive to invest may be low because of the smallness of the market. That is, with small real incomes, buying power is low, and demand for products in large quantity is lacking. Yet, again, the low real income is partly due to low productivity resulting from a lack of capital.

The major problem of capital formation is how to generate it domestically without leading to inflation. When the redirection of resources to capital formation is done by government financing through a budget deficit, the possibility of inflation exists. Many countries have employed this as a means of popping out of the Malthusian trap, but unhappy results have arisen on other counts.

When the government creates new money to finance development projects it purchases goods and services which would otherwise be devoted to private use; the populace must then accept an involutary reduction in its standard of living—that is, forced saving. Because of wage-rate rigidities, the new money is distributed more in favor of profit receivers than wage earners. But large profits do not always lead to an equal amount of saving on the part of the profit receivers, and that part invested does not necessarily go into the best projects for investment. The record shows that the prospect of further inflation leads to construction of houses and buildings and accumulation of inventories, both of which rise in value with the inflation. But these types of investment are not those which best contribute to a higher level of production and a rise in living standards.

Investment is most appropriate in the export industries, so as to earn foreign exchange to pay for expanded imports, and in goods for low-income consumers in order to relieve poverty and absorb some inflationary pressures. Yet these fields are penalized by the inflation through rising costs and relatively stable prices. The inflation also discourages saving by middle-income groups, who see the value of their funds declining; it thus inhibits the accumulation of private capital necessary to economic growth. It has an adverse effect on the value of existing savings also, much of which leaves the country in capital flight in order to preserve its real value. This flight accentuates the problem of balancing international payments, which is already made difficult by the tendency to import more than is exported as a result of the inflation.

The import of capital goods is hampered by the inflation because individuals have more money to spend for "luxury" imports. In order to curb imports of "nonessential" goods, the government either must devalue (which then makes the imports of capital goods more expensive, unless they are given a special rate under a multiple rate system) or impose import or exchange restrictions; the smaller amount of foreign exchange earned is thus retained for capital goods imports. The above effects can be avoided if the government adopts a policy of gradual inflation, using the funds to reduce underemployment in agriculture, especially. For lack of alternative job opportunities, much labor is literally wasted on the land. More people are settled on the land than are needed to work it efficiently. These unneeded workers can be released from agriculture for urban activities without a decline in output. The effects of *gradual* inflation on capital formation, however, are not very great. But it takes a strong government to administer an inflation to prevent it from becoming not so gradual. A government strong enough to handle such a situation would probably also be strong enough to tax and encourage development without inflation.

Relief from the problems of inflation can be gained to the extent that private saving and long-run investment are encouraged. The wide disparity in distribution of incomes in many developing countries makes it possible for some few individuals to accumulate vast fortunes out of which they can save for investment. But their pattern of income use has shown high expenditures on luxuries and investment of savings in more stable and prosperous countries abroad. One of the first objectives, therefore, is to inhibit the export of domestically accumulated funds. Once this is done, a mechanism for channeling it into investment is needed. Most low-income countries lack an efficient credit system or a functioning capital market. The creation of such mechanisms and the mobilization of savings may take a considerable period of time, but it is necessary in order to direct funds into agricultural development and into small-scale enterprises. In addition, an active government-bond market must be established to absorb saving and thus restrain inflation. In this latter effort, the most important step is to place the public finances on a sound basis, especially through revision of the tax system. Where incomes are highly unequal, a progressive income tax is a good revenue earner. Yet it is difficult in some countries to employ income taxation at all, whether progressive or not. General sales taxes or excise taxes are valuable revenue earners and do not dampen production during inflation, but they are a burden on low-income groups. Land taxes could provide much revenue and would rest on the rich, but they are difficult to legislate or apply.

Another means of financing the capital invesment is through borrowing abroad. But the types of investment needed to provide the social capital, e.g., roads, sanitation, education, communication, are not ones which induce private foreign lending, because they do not directly lead to an ability to repay through increased exports and some are not profitable. Foreign borrowing may indirectly increase the nation's ability to repay, however, through over-all economic growth while not yielding a profit in the particular project for which the funds were borrowed.

The amount of foreign borrowing need not be restricted to the import needs of an investment project. If only import needs are financed from abroad and the remainder of the cost is met by domestic inflation, the net effect on development may be adverse, for the inflation may worsen the balance of payments and make it more difficult to obtain needed imports or to sell exportables. There is no reason why all the money required to finance a given investment should not come from abroad—save for the later pressure on the balance of payments from debt service. If funds borrowed abroad are used for local materials and labor instead of imports of capital goods, then the foreign exchange is available to buy other imports. If the foreign funds are used to buy "grubstake" items of food and clothing for workers or raw materials for the project, which are normally produced at home, domestic resources are released to be applied to the development in other ways.

Some limits on foreign borrowing do exist (a) in the political unwillingness of the developing country to become dependent for its progress on a foreign power and (b) in the difficulty of releasing domestic resources to be combined with foreign capital.

There are no simple solutions to the problem of capital formation. It is clear that private savings and investment, government spending, and some foreign capital will be needed to provide economic growth in developing countries. The successful use of each depends heavily on the quality of public administration.

PUBLIC ADMINISTRATION

In general, the public administration of backward areas is not of the best quality. Civil servants are frequently ill trained and underpaid; they often rely for their livelihood on payments for their "influence" and on their ability to "squeeze" others. Many are part of a bureaucracy filled with friends, relatives, or supporters of successful office-holders. Such officials are so driven by their desire for prestige and fear of losing their jobs that they spend large amounts of time currying political favor instead of working effectively. In fact, many are afraid to make on-the-spot inspections of field offices or projects for fear of losing their jobs while away.

Such an atmosphere breeds development programs which include projects designed to bring prestige to the personnel in government. Public works projects are planned to provide personal monuments rather than public services. The location of projects is often decided so that they are carried out in the home districts of particular officials (or in areas requested by their supporters) despite the fact that economic considerations would dictate their being placed elsewhere. (It must be recognized that, when a people want international prestige, they do not always seek it through greater production. Display may have a higher priority. Such was the case when Russia reportedly gained more benefit propaganda-wise by constructing buildings and paving streets in the capital of Afghanistan than the United States did by financing a dam needed for irrigation of desert lands in that country.)

These problems reflect the underlying difficulty of obtaining professional administration in nonspecialized societies of backward areas where loyalties are primarily to family, caste, or community rather than to the nation or the populace. In some countries, the feudal landholding interests hold a veto over development programs. Such familial groups are seldom in sympathy with land tenure reform or with projects aimed at raising productivity; they see the aspirations of the general public as a threat to their economic security and political power.

Given the facts that most governments are dominated by small, landholding groups and that the government has been seen almost wholly in the role of tax collector, staffed by corrupt officials and rapacious soldiers, one can hardly blame the masses for distrusting suggestions of reform made by the government. It is not easy to accept the government as suddenly interested in the general welfare and administered by public-spirited and well-trained officials. The government may be the only agency capable of carrying out certain projects and reforms, but it may not be capable of carrying out the responsibilities effectively.

It was largely for these reasons that Bolivia was provided a shadow cabinet in 1952 through the UN Technical Assistance Board to help formulate and carry out her development program. This cabinet was made up of experts from a number of foreign countries; it had the prestige attached to experts and was obviously impartial both with reference to domestic pressure groups and foreign interests. It therefore obtained the respect of the people and avoided any inference of imperialism from a foreign power. The experiment has worked well and shows the importance of having unbiased advice from an international agency.[5]

In the main, those giving advice or assistance to underdeveloped countries are faced with the problem of dealing with a domestic public administration which may be either incompetent or unable to carry out its part of the functions necessary to development. Its inability is sometimes a result of obstacles stemming from the social mores, customs, and religious beliefs and traditions of the people.

MORES, CUSTOMS, AND TRADITIONS

Many cautions have been enunciated concerning the problems which accompany the export of ideas and production techniques from one economic and cultural system to another. Foreign technical experts have been sent to aid underdeveloped countries and cautioned to avoid changes that might conflict with religious beliefs or practices. They have been warned not to assume that the material values so highly held in some Western nations are primary in the lives of other peoples. And they have been told not to try to apply the techniques and practices developed in the complex market economies of the West to the large number of almost nonmonetary economic activities of underdeveloped countries. All these cautions have been necessary; they reflect problems which would have arisen in the seventeenth through the nineteenth century if the then more developed countries in Western Europe had tried to acclerate the economic growth of their neighbors.

Many peoples in the developing areas are actually afraid of change. There seems to be a sort of natural conservatism. The social scientists

---

[5] Efforts at extending "unbiased" advice have not always been so well received. The mission of the International Bank in Turkey at the latter's request was asked to leave after a dispute over the Turkish government's inflationary policies. (See *New York Times*, March 21, 1954.)

have not as yet fully analyzed this phenomenon, but its causes are extremely important. As one U.S. government official emphasized: "If it is conservatism because change would impinge on deeply held beliefs or status-determining relationships, that is one thing; if it is conservatism because change involves risk, that is another."[6] Both causes of conservatism may be dealt with successfully, but with different methods. The former requires considerable experimentation, demonstration, and education; the latter may be met by a reduction of the circumstances causing risk, the development of an attitude of willingness to assume risks, and/or the joint assumption of the risk by the government and the persons likely to be affected.

Another element which impedes change is the widespread existence of discrimination based on sex, race, religion, occupation, class, etc. Discrimination is persistent in almost every society; yet it reduces the very mobility (both geographical and occupational) that is requisite to economic growth. Discrimination based on class and position has prevented many of the more intelligent people from assisting in the development of manual skills. Even a citizen of the developing country, trained as an engineer or soils expert abroad, upon his return most frequently demands a "black-coat" job—meaning one in which he sits at a desk most of the day and does not sully his appearance or demean his position by working outdoors. An example is provided by an experience of Albert Schweitzer—Nobel prize winner, philosopher, composer, musician, theologian, missionary, doctor, architect, engineer, and carpenter: While helping to build a small jungle hospital in the midst of Africa, Schweitzer saw a fairly young and well-dressed individual standing by, watching the proceedings. Schweitzer was carrying some heavy boards to the building site and he requested the bystander to lend a hand. The reply was, "Oh, I couldn't do that; I am an intellectual." Schweitzer's calm retort was: "You are lucky, I have been trying for thirty years to become one." Prestige for the trained person is supposedly gained by delegating work to others—not in actually performing the job for which he was trained.

What is lacking in many countries is a corps of technicians trained as foremen, supervisors, etc., who are willing to get their hands dirty to get the project going. This does not mean that a major problem is solved merely by a larger number of people receiving technical and professional education; in some countries, such as India, a large number of unemployed, highly educated young people await the opening of suitable professional jobs. The jobs available are mostly technical—not the kind which the young men and women were educated for; hence they float about, becoming dissatisfied with the rate of progress of their country because it does not open up "professional" positions. They are therefore quite susceptible to left-wing entreaties.

Another factor which impedes the development of complex market

---

[6] B. F. Hoselitz (ed.), *The Progress of Underdeveloped Areas, op. cit.,* p. 210.

economies in the backward areas is the attitude toward business ethics and the law. There is, in most areas, little understanding of the importance of honesty in building the institutions of an exchange economy. Professor Condliffe has reported on the early efforts of Japan to industrialize, saying that while the Japanese correctly understood that "industry rested upon credit . . . they did not realize that fundamentally credit rests upon good faith and individual and collective honesty . . . the moral basis of the western civilization."[7] The slow recognition of this fact is one reason why the structure of Japanese industry and commerce remains built on the family and is highly monopolistic.

The problem of morality is reflected also in the desire of the reactionary groups to maintain the existing economic and social order so as to protect their own position despite the damping effect on over-all growth and the creativeness of others. Rather than lead the way to effective and stabilizing changes, these reactionary groups are powerful enough to require government authorities to compromise their reforms or make none at all, leaving the situation one of endemic revolt. They do not seem to realize the dangers which they and their country face from failure to deal effectively with the basic social and economic ills; continuation of such suffering has sometimes been a factor in revolution.

The power of reactionary groups in backward areas poses an acute problem for the United States, which would like to support the middle-of-the-road governments abroad so as to avoid totalitarian regimes. But the more moderate regimes seek a compromise solution; they delay reforms and request assistance from the U.S. government. Yet, without some considerable reforms, the assistance may be of little or no use.

The reforms in the organization and conduct of business, in government, and in social relations necessary to successful development involve new institutions for health and education, more efficient public administration, political leadership more representative of the will of the people, changes in land tenure, extension of rural credit, assistance to farmers, modernization of business procedures, mechanisms for capital formation, and changes in the usual size of families. The reforms are certain to be resisted, not only because they would change normal habits and traditions, or violate religious beliefs, but also because of the changes in privileges and power involved.

The way in which these reactions affect U.S. policy has been succinctly stated by Eugene Staley as follows:

All this poses a delimma for any outside nation that, like the United States, has a political, economic, and humanitarian interest in promoting the sort of development of underdeveloped areas which will be successful in the broadest sense. If we concentrate on a narrow range of direct production problems to help these countries raise their economic efficiency, without doing

---

[7] *Ibid.,* quoted on p. 212.

anything to stimulate "reform," our efforts may be wasted, or worse. On the other hand, if the United States does show an interest in internal reforms it runs against the principle of noninterference in the domestic affairs of sovereign nations. Furthermore, on practical grounds we have to be careful lest espousal by a foreign government of internal reforms should boomerang by antagonizing not only the conservatives but also supersensitive nationalists. Our support might in some circumstances defeat the very reforms we should like to aid. There is much to be said for the principle that it is better for people to manage their own affairs, even when they manage them badly.

The dilemma may be put another way. If we assist "reactionary" governments to suppress popular discontent, while privileged social groups prevent changes in land customs, business methods, educational systems, and the rest, a political explosion may result which will give the Communists just the kind of opportunity they are most adept at exploiting. If, on the other hand, we declare ourselves in favor of "revolution" against outmoded regimes and actively encourage dissident elements, the old ruling group may be repudiated before any democratically minded group is strong enough to take over. The power vacuum thus created would provide opportunities for a well-organized Communist minority to seize power.

These are some of the headaches that come with world power and world responsibility. Robert C. North has put the matter very well:

"If the West gives aid, it will be feared for its imperialism; if it withholds aid, it will be denounced for its indifference. If it establishes garrisons, it will be attacked as expansionist; if it keeps its troops at home, it will be written off as impotent and unable to keep its commitments. If it expresses no political preference (or relies solely on military might), it will be accused of siding with reaction and the status quo; if it supports progressive forces, it will be condemned for intervention.

"In other words, we are damned if we do and damned if we don't."[8]

SELECTED READINGS

Most of these sources cover subjects examined in both this and the succeeding chapter.

Bernstein, E. M., and I. G. Patel. "Inflation in Relation to Economic Development," *International Monetary Fund Staff Papers.* II (November, 1952), 363–398. This is a survey of the problems of governmental financing of investment; it is complemented by a study of India's program, "Economic Development with Stability," in the February, 1954 issue, pp. 313–386.

Buchanan, N. B., and H. S. Ellis. *Approaches to Economic Development.* New York: The Twentieth Century Fund, 1955. This volume analyzes the problems of capital accumulation, the importance of social, cultural and demographic factors in development, and reviews the economic progress of selected countries. Half of the volume is devoted to contemporary

---

[8] Eugene Staley, *The Future of Underdeveloped Countries* (New York: Council on Foreign Relations, 1953), pp. 357–358,

policies and practices of developing nations and the problems of foreign assistance.

Condliffe, J. B., and P. H. Odegard (eds.). *International Cooperation for World Economic Development*. Berkeley: University of California Press, 1950. This document records the addresses of a host of participants at a conference during March, 1950, on the subject of economic development. The variety of topics covered makes it valuable reading.

Economic Development and Cultural Change. A journal devoted entirely to the problems of development, published by the University of Chicago Research Center on Economic Development and Cultural Change.

Elliott, W. Y., et al. *The Political Economy of American Foreign Policy*. New York: Holt, 1955. The report of a study group which examined the concepts, strategy and limits of American foreign economic policy; Chapters 4, 5, and 9 are concerned with problems of economic development.

Hoselitz, B. F. (ed.). *The Progress of Underdeveloped Areas*. Chicago: Chicago University Press, 1952. This also is a compilation of papers delivered before a conference of experts on economic, social, political, and cultural problems of growth; participants included officials from the U.S. and foreign governments as well as non-official personnel.

Lewis, W. A. *Theory of Economic Growth*. Homewood, Ill.: Irwin, 1955. A text presentation of the various theories, approaches, and aspects of economic growth.

Myrdal, Gunnar. *An International Economy*. New York: Harper, 1956. Chapters 12 and 13 present penetrating analyses of the entire sweep of internal and external problems facing the developing nations.

Nurkse, Ragnar. *Problems of Capital Formation in Underdeveloped Countries*. New York: Oxford, 1952. This is a revision of a series of lectures given in Brazil on the relation of the size of the market, population, and the standard of living to saving and investment, on the sources of capital, commercial policy and capital formation, and on the theory and practice of international capital movements.

Staley, Eugene. *The Future of Underdeveloped Countries*. New York: Council on Foreign Relations, 1953. This is an extensive study of the desirability of economic development as seen by the advanced and underdeveloped countries, of the Communist measures for development, and of the democratic paths to economic growth.

United Nations, Department of Economic Affairs. *Land Reform: Defects in Agrarian Structure as Obstacles to Economic Development*. New York, 1951. An analysis of an important problem in development which is not treated in this chapter.

————, Department of Economic and Social Affairs. *Processes and Problems of Industrialization in Underdeveloped Countries*. New York, 1955. A summary of the problems, stressing that industrialization is closely linked to growth in social, political, and other aspects of life.

————. *Measures for the Economic Development of Under-Developed Countries*. New York, May, 1951. A set of recommendations by experts on means to accelerate development, including a presentation of the problems.

Viner, Jacob. *International Trade and Economic Development*. Glencoe, Ill.: The Free Press, 1952. A revision of lectures given in Brazil; while it is mainly devoted to the principles of trade and economic policy, it contains some chapters on the planning road to growth and on the major criteria and principles of economic development.

Williamson, H. F., and J. A. Buttrick (eds.). *Economic Development*. New York: Prentice-Hall, 1954. This volume is intended as a basic text in the principles and patterns of economic development; it reviews the major factors in economic growth and presents case studies of Japan, India, and Mexico.

22 Private Foreign Investment and Aid for Economic Development

During the nineteenth century and up until the last decade, the foreign financing of economic development came primarily from private sources. Capital flowed out of Europe, especially England, to all corners of the world to assist in the process of raising incomes. This flow all but dried up during the period between the world wars.

After World War I, the U.S. government took a position of removing itself from international lending and leaving in private hands the responsibility for the flow of U.S. capital. The government did attempt to encourage lending to European countries for reconstruction, particularly to Germany, but it took no stand on investment in the less advanced countries save to attempt at various times to protect the interests of U.S. investors whose debtors had defaulted.

The number of defaults increased during the Great Depression, and many American firms and investors lost their funds. Although, on the whole, the payment of interest and return of principal by debtors showed a fairly good rate of return to total U.S. foreign investment during the interwar period, the experience of the defaults and of the Mexican expropriation of oil properties loomed large in the minds of American investors. American expectations as to private capital outflows after World War II were not optimistic.

Yet a considerable volume of foreign capital could be absorbed by countries looking for means of rapid advancement after World War II. With the flow of capital was expected to go a sizable amount of technical know-how, which had historically accompanied private investment. But investment fell short of even the pessimistic expectations as to American capital outflows. Requests from abroad for American private and public capital went unmet, and developing countries considered that their pro-

449

grams were being hampered by the lack of adequate financing and by the lack of technical know-how.

In his inaugural address in 1949, President Truman asserted as his fourth point that "we must embark on a bold new program for making the benefits of our scientific advances and industrial progress available for the improvement and growth of underdeveloped areas." Emphasis was placed on the provision by the United States of technical assistance in contrast to capital assistance. Congress approved the Point Four Program in 1950 by extending technical assistance grants to certain backward areas. It also contributed funds to an expanded program of technical assistance through the United Nations. The International Bank for Reconstruction and Development and the Export-Import Bank expanded their lending to such areas, and increased attention was paid to the encouragement of private foreign investment.

Among the reasons for the new spurt in aid to underdeveloped countries was not only the humanitarian wish of the American people to help others to help themselves in rapid material advance but also the belief that such an advance would encourage them to reject "false doctrines" and to become associated with the United States in the pursuit of economic and political democracy.[1] More specific and direct benefits were thought to accrue from the hoped-for increase in U.S. foreign trade, from an increase in production of mineral and raw materials desired by the United States, from an increase in U.S. economic stability, from a strengthening of the United Nations, and from the helping hand which economic development over the world would give to European recovery. As we saw in the foregoing chapter, it is not certain that these results will flow from the encouragement of economic development.

After 1952, the administration played down the idea that aid was justified mainly by the Communist threats. Congress began to question whether economic development would dampen the appeal of communism. Some were concerned that the disruptive effects of development would cause a sort of ferment (arising from land reform and the process of industrialization) and create sufficient "anarchy and confusion" to permit an expansion of communism. But administration officials replied that, while it was not certain that mere development would make the recipients of aid more sympathetic to Western nations or Western ideals, if the recipients

---

[1] The administration position in 1952 was that the peoples of the underdeveloped countries were becoming increasingly discontented and that unless "we provide technical and economic assistance, and do it promptly, to help these people begin to improve their conditions, there is serious danger that they will fall into the trap of the shrewd and ruthless Communist machine which is cynically promising quick cures for age-old ills. This could be just as grave a blow to our security as if they fell to Communism through armed attack." ("Mutual Security Act of 1952," U.S. Senate, *Hearings,* Committee on Foreign Relations, 82d Cong., March–April, 1952, p. 7.)

were anxious to safeguard their independence and work out their future independently of outside interference, the aid would help eliminate the conditions which breed dissatisfaction.

A. ROLE OF PRIVATE INVESTMENT

Although the U.S. government recognized toward the end of World War II that private U.S. capital would be timid about going abroad, it adopted a policy of encouraging its outflow in line with the reliance placed on private trade and finance.[2]

RELIANCE ON PRIVATE FOREIGN INVESTMENT

Early in the planning of its postwar foreign economic policy, the U.S. government estimated that annual capital outflows would be about $2 billion after the initial readjustment in economic and political affairs and that most of this would go to developing countries. The Export-Import Bank and the International Bank for Reconstruction and Development were to provide investment funds in the meantime and thus set the stage for a return to private lending.

But for only one year (1950) during the decade 1946–1955 did the volume of *net* private long-term lending reach a level of $1 billion. The annual average has been around $800 million, of which by far the largest portion has been direct investment. Portfolio investments have declined in importance. They reached a peak of ∴ver $460 million (net) in 1950, but declined to a net inflow during 1953 and have risen only slightly since then. This small portfolio investment reflects the general fear of Americans of foreign government securities and of companies controlled by foreigners; direct investments provide continued control by the investor. Since World War II one-fourth of all direct investment has been in petroleum abroad. This concentration has been a reflection of the strong postwar demand for oil and of the unique position that the oil companies held in the various countries of Latin America and in the Middle East; these countries provided considerable economic freedom and political stability for them. Events in late 1956 may have signaled a withdrawal of this favorable reception. Manufacturing enterprises are second, and mining and smelting projects rank third. Other classes trail far down the list. By area, the Latin American countries have received most of the investment, taking about one-third of the total since the war. The largest single recipient has been

---

[2] Discussion of the role of private investment in a chapter on aid for economic development does not mean that investment in the more advanced areas is unimportant. However, these countries are already set up to receive and use foreign capital effectively, and it is only a minor supplement to their other means of progress while it is (or should be) a major source of developmental financing for backward areas.

Canada, which has a vast amount of undeveloped resources and which holds a favored position because of her close economic and political ties to the United States; she has received between a fourth and a half of the net direct investments each year.

These figures, and the enterprises and areas to which the investments were directed, indicate that the volume and distribution of private foreign investment fell far below what potential investors were considered able to absorb.

OBSTACLES TO THE EXPORT OF PRIVATE CAPITAL

In examining the obstacles which prevented the expansion of private foreign lending, the reader will recall the world-wide economic and political conditions reviewed in the previous chapters. These conditions displayed widespread uncertainties and instabilities. The importance of these instabilities is pointed up by the fact that private investments are usually directed to particular pursuits and areas for the *profit* (or interest return) expected to be gained. Wherever economic or political instability exists, the risks of loss are greater. Therefore, the continuance of widespread economic and political instability in areas desiring the capital imports has been a major obstacle to an international flow of funds.

Had the American economy been less fully employed, and had the domestic alternatives been less attractive, capital might still have flowed abroad. But the fact was that the American economy, despite dire wartime predictions of unemployment and depression, has been expanding. The returns on capital investment in the United States were often larger than those which were anticipated from foreign investment; however, industry by industry (save for public utilities) profits were greater abroad than in the United States during the years 1950 and 1951.

The political instability and continued inflation abroad gave rise to a variety of policies by potential borrowers which in turn restricted the volume of private capital outflow from the United States. In order to conserve foreign exchange for essential uses, nations placed extensive restrictions on the transfer of earnings from foreign investments in their countries. These restrictions made many investors reluctant to export their funds for fear of not being able to repatriate the capital or earnings. In addition, the difficulties faced by borrowers in their balances of payments made the possibility of depreciation of the foreign currency seem strong, so that a prospective investor was faced with a potential loss merely through a change in the exchange rate.

Restrictions were also imposed by borrowing nations on the operations of enterprises. Price controls, rationing, wage controls, discriminatory taxes on the foreign firm, and restrictions on the hiring of foreign technicians and managers tended to reduce the profit potentialities. Also, the pressure in some countries for nationalization of minerals and raw material resources turned what might have been profitable opportunities for foreign investment into highly risky operations. The nationalization experiences in Iran, Guatemala, Bolivia, and Egypt made the U.S. investor even more reluctant. Though cases of expropriation and nationalization have been few compared to the amount of foreign investment outstanding, they loom large in the eyes of investors.

OFFICIAL ENCOURAGEMENT OF PRIVATE INVESTMENT

Because of the low volume of private lending and the resultant demands for government loans, Congress in 1950 felt that steps should be taken to improve the "climate" abroad for private investment. Congressmen and administration officials agreed that a more favorable climate could be obtained if the borrowers were willing to provide it. To this end, agreements with borrowing nations have been sought covering treatment of U.S. investors abroad, convertibility of earnings on capital, and taxation.

Investment treaties

As a means of replacing the nineteenth century influence which the investor's government could wield to assure "favorable treatment" of the investor with an agreed "code" of action, the U.S. government has negotiated "investment treaties." These are an expansion of the old "friendship, commerce, and navigation" treaties between the signatory countries which provided the reciprocal terms of treatment of each other's nationals. The postwar treaties are designed to assure potential investors that they will be given nondiscriminatory treatment, prompt and adequate compensation in the event of expropriation, and a reasonable opportunity to manage their property and to withdraw their earnings and capital.

The U.S. officials in charge of the program have gained little ground. They can offer few inducements to the foreign country to sign such guarantees because the conditions which would induce capital movements to the United States already exist in the American economy. There was no reciprocal offer to give the foreign country, especially since the treaties can not guarantee that private investment would follow. Only about a dozen such treaties have been signed since 1945.

Some governments (notably India, Turkey, Israel, and some in Latin America) have taken unilateral action to induce private capital to enter, such as more lenient taxes, assurances of transfer of earnings, rapid amortization or depreciation allowances, assurances of freedom to bring in managers and technicians, and removal of restrictions as to percentage of participation of domestic capital in any enterprise.

A willingness to take such actions is prerequisite to the success of the investment treaty technique and in a sense makes the treaty itself unnecessary. If the agreements were merely formal, they would not be sufficient. Their effect will depend greatly on the willingness and eagerness of the foreign government to implement the agreed code if problems of expropriation, compensation, equality of treatment, etc., arise. The willingness of the borrowing countries to carry out the code provisions depends on whether they see the code as clearly in their national interest. If they do, the treaty does at least set up broad criteria under which negotiations can be carried out concerning any dispute.

Before they can consider the investment codes as being in their national interest, however, borrowing nations feel that they must have assurances that foreign investors will observe the nation's social and economic patterns of conduct, that its citizens will be trained as technicians, and that reinvestment policies will be tempered by long-range considerations of the welfare of the developing country and not just short-run profit. Many U.S. investors have accepted the philosophy that reasonable profits are more likely to insure private ownership and operation in the long run than a policy of exorbitant profits which invites criticism and gives rise to dissatisfaction abroad. The central, unresolved problem of the investment codes is that of providing adequate protection to the private investor without encroaching on the right of the foreign government to use the nation's resources, including foreign exchange, as it sees fit. This right has been exercised through expropriation and exchange restrictions.

Investment guaranties

In order to reduce some of the uncertainty of foreign investment arising from direct controls and expropriation, the U.S. government extends guaranties to private lenders against inconvertibility of foreign funds arising from investment abroad and against war risks and inadequate compensation in the event of nationalization. Convertibility guaranties were first provided by the ECA for Europe under the 1948 ERP legislation but later through the Export-Import Bank to other Free World countries. In 1950, despite the fact that less than 10 per cent of the guaranty authority had been used, Congress decided that a larger coverage and wider scope of the guaranty would make it more attractive. Thus compensation was permitted under the guaranty for any losses from expropriation or confiscation by action of the government abroad. Guaranties are extended only to investment in "productive enterprises."[3] Although U.S. investors have been

---

[3] This phrase was inserted to mean that guarantees would not be extended on projects which would duplicate productive facilities already in the United States. To make certain that this was not done and, thereby, that investments would not be in products made with "cheap foreign labor" to be exported to the United States, an amendment was inserted in the Act denying a guaranty to investments which would result "in uneconomic and unsound duplication and expansion of production and productive facilities already existing in the United States and other countries." This amendment was agreed to without debate; Congress apparently accorded with Under Secretary of State Webb's testimony that "Competition should be avoided wherever it is in the common interest to do so." (See Gardner Patterson and Jack N. Behrman, *Survey of United States International Finance, 1950,* [Princeton, N. J.; Princeton University Press, 1951], p 111 and note.)

taking increased advantage of the privilege, they have not relied on it extensively.

Several groups, inside and outside of the government, have requested abolition of the guaranty privilege on the ground that it encourages the foreign country to permit the very abuses guaranteed against; i.e., inconvertibility, expropriation, and confiscation. In order to encourage the foreign country to remove these obstacles, they argue, the guaranties must be removed.

To prevent the borrowing country's government from relying on the guaranties to improve the climate for private investment, a requirement was written into the law that the country to which the investment was to go must sign an investment treaty with the U.S. government, including provisions at least granting nondiscrimination to U.S. investors, compensation for expropriation or any impairment of the value of the investment through government competition, and conversion into dollars and transfer of an "appropriate share" of the earnings or any compensation (for expropriation, etc.), taking into account the "essential needs" of the recipient country for foreign exchange.

Others have claimed that a salutary effect has arisen out of the fact that some potential investors had been encouraged, because of the existence of the guaranties, to look into possible foreign projects more closely and had then found them profitable even without the guaranty. Still others have argued that the guaranties, to be really significant, must cover risks of exchange rate depreciation, revolution, and insurrection.

The government has increased the guaranty authority to $500 million, and $125 million of guaranties have been issued. Though their use has increased, there are difficult problems which must be solved, including that of the additional skepticism induced in the mind of investors by the fact that a guaranty is deemed necessary. Also, the cost of a guaranty is not small, running to as much as 5 per cent; information may have to be given to the Export-Import Bank which a firm would rather not divulge. The retention and later use of the foreign funds coming into the possession of the EIB may give rise to financial conflicts with foreign governments. And problems of definition of what is a war risk, what is expropriation, etc., have not been solved.

Tax conventions

Many potential U.S. investors have insisted since the war that one of the major deterrents to private foreign investment is the double taxation of earnings—that is, taxation by the foreign government when earned and by the U.S. government when brought home. There is no general agreement, however, among tax experts, the Treasury, economists, and financial advisers as to the precise impact of such taxes on investment decisions.

Regardless of the importance of the problem, pressure from private interests has caused the State Department to negotiate conventions covering the double taxation of income and the taxation of estates and inheritance. Negotiating problems have centered on the question of which country would lose revenue. The developing countries argue that taxes should be paid only to the government in which the income was earned, but the U.S. government has been reluctant to agree to such a principle not only for reasons of a loss of revenue but also because of competitive advantages which might accrue to enterprises located abroad. In addition, many governments employ a complex system of taxes which are not on income but have a similar impact instead of the more generally accepted forms of income taxes; these practices make it difficult to obtain agreement on the treatment of business taxes.

The U.S. government has provided some tax encouragement through permitting taxes on foreign income as offsets against U.S. taxes. Also, a reduction of corporate income taxes by 14 percentage points has been proposed in Congress. Where the foreign tax is lower than the U.S. tax, a major result would be to subsidize existing firms, and the government would lose revenue. Where the foreign rate is as high as the U.S. rate and the firm thus pays no taxes to the United States because of the offset privilege, a reduction of the U.S. rate would provide no inducement unless the foreign country also could be persuaded to reduce its rate.

B. ROLE OF GOVERNMENT LENDING

To supplement the small flow of private investment, the U.S. government expanded the operations of the Export-Import Bank immediately after World War II and joined the International Bank for Reconstruction and Development. Prior to 1948, both of these institutions were heavily oriented toward lending for purposes of reconstruction and therefore mostly to European countries. After that date, they emphasized loans to developing countries. The policy of both the IBRD and the Export-Import Bank has been to encourage the export of private capital.

EXPORT-IMPORT BANK POLICY

Prior to World War II, the major lending policy of the EIB was that of providing short- and medium-term loans to finance the sale abroad of U.S. commodities, mostly wheat and cotton. With the growing demand for funds for development projects after World War II, the EIB began to use a larger part of its $3.5 billion to help finance specific projects. The pressure of U.S. mobilization after 1950 required greater imports of strategic materials, and in 1951 the EIB was authorized to lend up to $4.5 billion partly to help finance production of raw materials and minerals and partly to accelerate general development abroad. Its authority has since been increased to $5 billion.

The dominance of developmental lending persisted from 1949 until

1953. Most of the loans tended to complement the government's aid programs; they were for such projects as roads, irrigation, water supply, railroad electrification, production of cement for home use and of strategic materials for export to the United States. In 1953, the administration reoriented EIB operations more toward short-term lending to finance U.S. commercial exports. The increasing competition in third markets between European exporters and American enterprises led to requests from some private interests for more export financing. During 1953, EIB lending for development projects dropped to less than 10 per cent of its previous annual volumes, and financing of exports on shorter-term credit rose sharply.

In view of the objections, particularly by Latin American nations, that the developing countries were not obtaining a proportionate share of aid from the U.S. government compared with other countries, assurances were given in early 1954 that the EIB would return to its former policy of considering all applications for the financing of "economically sound" development projects abroad.

Export-Import Bank policy has been to scrutinize carefully the applications to make certain that each project was a "sound business" proposition and that the financed exports of equipment, materials, and services would contribute directly to the expansion of productive capacity of the importing country and to an improvement in its balance of payments. The EIB has not found any large number of suitable applications for loans to finance development projects; its lending has varied between $100 million and $300 million per year, while its disbursements under development loans have averaged about $200 million per year. It has a record of repayment which would make any commercial bank envious.

One bothersome question has recurred, however: whether or not the EIB's lending has in some instances been dictated by political policy. The EIB officials have asserted that the Bank has made no loans which the State Department found "undesirable" on political grounds but that the State Department could not and had not tried to force the EIB to make loans which were economically "unsound." The EIB has, they said, investigated a loan to determine its economic justification after the State Department represented that a loan would be politically desirable.

One objection to the policy of the EIB—though not raised by Congress —has been its practice of tying the proceeds of most of its loans to purchases in the United States. Most of the applications have been in connection with orders for U.S. goods, and no substantial problems have arisen. But the practice of tying the loans has sometimes meant that the borrowers could not buy in the cheapest market.

INTERNATIONAL BANK OPERATIONS

In 1944 the United States joined with 43 other nations in signing articles of agreement for the International Bank for Reconstruction and

Development; the Bank now has 56 members and a subscribed capital of $9 billion. It was organized for three major purposes: to aid in the immediate reconstruction of war-torn areas, to aid in the development of backward areas, and to facilitate the flow of private capital. It was given three different powers to pursue these ends: it can lend funds out of the subscriptions paid in by the member nations; it can borrow in private capital markets and relend the funds; and, in order directly to encourage private lending, it can guarantee payment of interest and repayment of the principal of private investment and participate with private investment in financing a project.

The importance of the first means has been limited by the fact that only 2 per cent of the subscriptions to the Bank was paid in gold or dollars and was thus free to be used by the Bank for lending. An additional 18 per cent of the subscriptions was paid in the currency of the member but could be loaned by the Bank only with that member's permission. In practice, the Bank has had to rely mostly on borrowing in the capital markets of the United States, Switzerland, the Netherlands, and a few other countries and on the lending of funds from the subscriptions of a few governments who put no restrictions on the use of their 18 per cent contributions. Most governments have not released the latter for they would receive for exports bought with the borrowed currency, no imports in return. If they are to permit capital exports, they would apparently rather direct them themselves, as Britain and France have done in limiting most of their outflow to their colonies or associated nations.

The Bank loaned $500 million to European members for reconstruction purposes during 1947. But, after the inception of ERP, it turned its attention almost wholly to aiding the development of backward areas, authorizing an average of $200 million a year for development purposes. Since 1948, the Bank has made loans of over $2 billion, about two-thirds of which has gone to underdeveloped nations, with the rest going to development projects in Europe. The underdeveloped areas have considered this amount inadequate, especially since the Bank was established with an expressed purpose of assisting in development.

The loans by the Bank have been made almost wholly out of funds contributed to or borrowed by it. It has not guaranteed any loans of members obtained in private capital markets, despite the fact that it was early thought that such operations would be of primary significance among those of the Bank. Only a few applications for such guaranties have been received by the Bank, and they were considered unsuitable. United States officials have urged the Bank to do more to expand the volume of private lending, but potential borrowers have argued that both the United States and the Bank seemed to think that much more reliance could be placed on private investment than is feasible. In fact, they have argued, capital from international agencies is more satisfactory to them than private investment; private capital can not be accepted for the projects deemed most important by the developing countries, because private investment still arouses fears of "exploitation" and "interference" and because private investment is usually more costly to the borrower than government funds. The position of many of the underdeveloped countries has led them to urge an expansion of the resources of and lending by the Bank.

The potential borrowers have also argued that the Bank should not restrict its lending to specific projects approved by it but that it should provide funds for broad programs of development. The objection against the project loan has been that the process of development requires more foreign exchange than the import content of specific projects. The project leads to an expansion of production, investment, and consumption which in turn increase imports and require additional exchange. But even the financing of all foreign-exchange needs is insufficient in the eyes of some critics. They argue that the Bank should lend also to help meet the internal (local currency) costs of the programs in addition to the over-all foreign-exchange costs. These costs can not be met readily from internal sources, they argue.

During the early 1950's, the Bank did adopt lending policies which permitted program loans and funds to meet local-currency costs, but it has continued to lend almost wholly on a project basis and for direct foreign-exchange costs. It argues in reply to its critics that the major reason for the small amount of lending is not that the Bank's resources were so small but that the applications have been so poorly supported. This is reflected in the facts that almost every country has been aiming at too rapid development of industry, that projects have not been integrated, and that the over-all programs have not been well conceived. To assist members in making better applications, the Bank has sent survey missions to prospective borrowers to help them develop appropriate programs and then to present their applications to the Bank.

Bank officials, supported by U.S. officials, have stated that the developing areas can do much more for themselves in the way of capital investment than they have been doing. The obstacles which these countries themselves have to remove are, in the eyes of Bank officials, a tradition of political irresponsibility, low standards of education and training, and impatience with the effort, sacrifices, and time required for development. In addition, Bank officials have argued, the developing countries can do much to redirect domestic investment funds—for example, through the proper use of public investment and the mobilization of domestic funds for internal uses by providing incentives for private saving and domestic investment and by preventing capital flight. The governments should do much more toward "programming" their development. This does not mean "blueprinting the economy" and then employing "coercive" controls but means, rather, the formulation of broad and specific development projects and the setting of priorities for those wishing to engage in them.

A further obstacle to large lending by the Bank has been the lack of adequate complementary private equity investment in projects. One of the major obstacles to the encouragement of such private investments has been that any private enterprise wishing to borrow from private sources with a Bank guarantee (or directly from the Bank) had to obtain a guarantee from the government of its country. This requirement has proven to be a large stumbling-block, for governments have proven reluctant, largely for domestic political reasons, to guarantee loans to private enterprise; they have been afraid that charges of favoritism would be leveled against them if they rejected guarantee requests from private citizens. Conversely, private enterprises are reluctant to ask for government guarantees for fear of inviting government interference in management.

To remedy this defect, the International Finance Corporation was approved in 1956 to make equity investments, without a government guarantee, out of funds contributed by member governments. The IFC is attached to the Bank, which will oversee its operations. It has a capital of $100 million, of which $35 million is contributed by the United States; it has the authority to borrow funds by issuing its own securities. Though its total authority is small, it intends to revolve the loans by selling the securities which it originally purchases and thus contribute many times the size of its own capital to the flow of international investment. The IFC is restricted to investment in productive private enterprises. It cannot provide the entire capital for any enterprise and must associate with private investors in an enterprise, but it is not to compete with private capital by financing an enterprise for which sufficient private capital could be obtained on reasonable terms. The IFC, though it invests in equity-type shares, will not be able to assume responsibility for managing an enterprise; nor will it be able to own capital (common or preferred) stock. The securities which the IFC will obtain will, however, probably require some participation in profits and a right, when the security is sold by the IFC, of the purchaser to convert the security into capital stock. Through these operations, the IFC is intended to expand the volume of equity financing, increase the opportunities for sound loans by the Bank itself, and increase the flow of private capital both through participations with the IFC and through the sale of the securities originally purchased by the IFC.

Despite the criticism of the Bank from potential borrowers because of its small volume of lending, the U.S. government has been highly satisfied with its operations. This satisfaction is itself based largely on the fact that the Bank's lending policy is similar to that of American commercial banks—conservative—and may be explained partly by the fact that the voting in the Bank is weighted according to subscription, with the United States holding practically a veto power. The Bank can be considered, from a U.S. foreign economic policy viewpoint, one of the most successful of postwar institutions.

C. GOVERNMENTAL GRANTS

Despite its emphasis on private capital flows, the U.S. government has, since 1950, extended about $2 billion in grants for economic development. The volume is still considered too small by the recipients, many of whom have urged the formation of another intergovernmental agency to disburse funds for development.

BILATERAL ECONOMIC AID

At the same time that the Point Four Program was approved in 1950, the Administration asked that funds be made available for the extension of economic assistance to various countries in Southeast Asia. The conflict between communism and the West was one of open warfare in Indochina at that time and the government feared that, unless something was done to strengthen other nations threatened in the area, the conflict would spread. Once again, the fear was of internal subversion from "poverty-based" or "class-stimulated" communism rather than of the spread of open warfare.

The immediate purposes of aid were to ease the economic pressures, to induce social and land-tenure reforms so as to expand production (especially agricultural and mineral), and thus to gain economic and political stability. In justifying aid to the Middle East, the State Department asserted that the general aim of American foreign policy in that area was to overcome the "anti-Westernism" and "neutralism" growing there and at the same time to bind it to the Western security system so as to gain the advantage of its strategic location and supplies of oil.

Aid to fight communism

The problem of preventing internal subversion by American aid was complicated by the fact that many nations of the area were striving for independence from European dominance. Since the United States was associated in many ways with the European nations, it received some of the hatred directed from these countries toward Europe. A further complication was the fact that Communist elements could readily use the nationalistic drive to foment unrest and direct it against the West.

The saving of these countries from communism was not, of course, wholly a question of gaining political allies or even of increasing the military strength of the West. It was also importantly a question of keeping these areas as sources of raw materials needed by the West.[4] This same set of purposes existed for economic aid to South Asia, the Middle East, and Africa.

The political and military goals were less certain of accomplishment than that of aiding growth. It was by no means evident that the recipient countries would, because of the aid, become political allies of the West; in fact, many of them wished devoutly to take a neutral position between the East and West. Some of the intended recipients rejected the aid (e.g., Burma) because they felt that its acceptance would imply that they were "in the camp of the West." In any event, the idea of building up "Asians to fight Asians" is too simple, because the Asiatic countries friendly to the West are limited in their ability to launch a major military effort. Before any significant military strength can be attained in those countries, extensive economic development must take place.

In the South Asia region, India and Pakistan were beneficiaries of special economic assistance programs. The U.S. administration and Congress considered in 1953 that the political and economic conditions in these countries required a "speed-up," partly for fear that the peoples of these nations would become dissatisfied with a slow rate of economic growth and thus become disenchanted with Western democratic processes. As information concerning the development of Communist China became available, the U.S. government began to feel that the success or failure of India's program would mean the success or failure of democracy in Asia, because other Asian countries saw India as a showcase of Asiatic democracy. Close attention was paid to the "race for development," but India seemed reluctant to accept much outside assistance, particularly from the United States, partly as a matter of national pride and out of a desire to prove that she could "do it herself."

A special program for Iran was also based on the likelihood of that nation being a political and military strongpoint for the West. With the return of the monarchy to power in Iran, the U.S. government found it desirable to extend emergency assistance in order to replenish Iran's depleted treasury—depleted by the shut-down of her oil industry immediately following nationalization.

Aid to the Middle East was also justified in large measure by the necessity of keeping the area calm and supplying oil to the West rather than to Russia. But attempts to help both sides of the Israeli-Arab conflict ran into criticism from each. Israel required large amounts of aid to help sustain her immigration policy, to maintain and raise her living standard,

---

[4] The desire of the U.S. government for such materials was shown explicitly in the provision of the bilateral aid agreements which stated that the recipient would make available, on no less favorable terms than given any other nation, materials in which the United States was deficient. These bilateral agreements also carried a provision under which the recipient agreed to cooperate in the reduction of international trade barriers.

and to maintain her large armed forces. The Arab countries disliked further Jewish immigration, saw no reason why the United States should support much higher living standards in Israel than existed in Arabia, and were offended by U.S. support of Israeli policy. The American aid given to Israel has been several times that given to the Arab states combined; though the U.S. government has attempted in recent years to treat the two sides equally, the Arab states have rejected any idea that they should be given aid, as a group, equal to Israel's. The aid has not satisfied either side nor prevented continued friction and conflict, but so far, the West is still supplied with Arabian oil, though the flow became smaller with the blocking of the Suez and cutting of several pipelines in late 1956.

Aid to Latin American states was justified on the broad basis that internal subversion by Communist-led groups was a serious threat to the area which could be met most effectively by a diversified economic development of the continent. But once again the political content of the aid raised questions of "equitable distribution." The United States was sending much more to the Far East, which was closer to falling into Communist hands, while a friendly, cooperative Latin America was given, as they saw it, barely crumbs from the tables of aid to Europe and the Far East. They have argued that they are as much endangered by Communist subversion as others and that economic progress would quell the threat. So far, the division of aid has remained much the same, with Latin America having to rely mostly on loans for foreign financing of development programs.

Competition with Russia

During 1955 and 1956, Russia apparently decided that economic assistance was not necessarily imperialistic, as she had previously charged of American aid. She began a series of offers of "trade and technical assistance" to countries in South Asia and the Middle East; she was, of course, already extending assistance to her satellites and to Communist China, having provided over $5 billion in long-term loans by 1956. Russia asserted that her offers had advantages over American bilateral aid in that there were no political conditions on the agreements, that the credit terms on purchases of machinery and tools desired by the developing nations were better than on American loans, and that she would take in return commodities which were in burdensome surplus in the developing countries and which the United States would not buy.

Only a few countries have responded, however, partly because Russia has a poor record on delivery of its exports and partly because a troop of Russian technicians appeals little more to the nations trying to maintain independence and political stability than does a corps of American technicians or officials. Even so, some agreements were made between Russia and Afghanistan, Burma, India, Yugoslavia, and Egypt involving credits of over $600 million plus technical aid. These nations have continued to trade with and/or accept aid from the United States, though Burma has placed more emphasis on trade, asserting that it "forms a more solid basis of friendship than acceptance of gifts."[5]

The U.S. government has been urged from several quarters to take up the challenge of "competitive capitalism" versus "competitive communism" by an expansion of aid and trade. But so far it has decided that the increased economic attention by Russia to the developing areas should not be considered dangerous. Rather, it considers imitation the best form of flattery. Instead of trying to "outcompete" Russia and thereby increase the drain on U.S. resources, the U.S. government has decided to continue its operations along the lines already set out. If the recipients got the impression that they could "play off" one country against the other, their demands would become unreasonable and the cooperative attitude sought would turn into a strained relationship.

Economic limitations on aid

The aid to developing areas has consisted mostly of shipments of goods in the form of consumer items, fertilizer, fuel, and raw materials and semifinished products which could be sold quickly by the receiving government. These items have relieved certain hardships and increased production. At the same time, they have provided the government with local currency just when its revenues were low; thus, aid substitutes for increased taxes. These additional receipts have been used to reduce inflation or to provide local funds to support aid-sponsored projects. Aid has also taken the form, in small part, of machinery and equipment for improvement of transportation, power, and other public utilities and for the promotion of agriculture and production of critical and strategic materials.

The volume of aid, running about $250–$350 million a year, and the types of aid have been limited by several factors. In many instances, the recipient country is not capable of using complex and costly machinery. Its people have only the most rudimentary knowledge of machinery; in one instance, an entire shipment of jeeps was ruined because those receiving it lacked technical know-how.

Apart from the necessity in many instances to send the less costly items, a nation's ability to absorb large volumes of capital goods is limited. Capital goods are but one factor of production and must be coupled with others. Though land may be plentiful in some areas, arable land suitable for mechanized cultivation is not always available; in that case, shipments of tractors would be inefficient. In some instances, the small number of skilled people limits the number of machines which can be employed effectively. Finally, in an over-all sense, the receipt of aid

---

[5] Premier U Nu of Burma, quoted in Senate Committee on Foreign Relations, Subcommittee on Technical Assistance Programs, "Soviet Technical Assistance in Non-Communist Asia," *Committee Print,* Washington, 1955, p. 21.

goods requires financing of domestic labor and capital expenditures which may be inflationary, leading to problems we have discussed in the previous chapter. Thus, in the early stages of growth the absorptive capacity of a nation limits the amount of capital assistance which can be effectively used. Once the basic "social capital" has been provided and know-how developed, a larger volume of capital funds can be effectively used.

The United States still has much to learn about the preconditions of effective use of foreign capital and the optimum combination of capital and technical assistance. Despite these problems, many developing nations still consider that lack of capital is the primary bottleneck and have urged creation of a new international source of funds.

SPECIAL UN FUND FOR ECONOMIC DEVELOPMENT

One of the continual complaints of developing areas has been that there are inadequate funds for financing projects which do not directly provide a return sufficient to repay a loan. The lack of financing for these "nonself-liquidating" projects has been the cause of pressure from several groups for the formation in the UN of a new agency (SUNFED) to receive and disburse governmental contributions for grants and low-interest, long-term loans. The underdeveloped countries have grasped readily at the suggestions.

Because most of the funds for the new agency would come from the advanced nations, their attitude was crucial to its creation. The U.S. government would have to supply the majority of funds, and its position has been death-dealing. United States officials at the UN have argued that grants are not an appropriate means of financing development except in special cases, that these special cases could best be met bilaterally, and that the goods and services which are wanted on a grant basis have simply not been available because of the rearmament drive. Canada and other potentially contributing nations argued against the creation of the agency on the grounds that it would be currently too costly and that their own experience was proof that development could take place without grant aid.

Nonofficial critics have asserted that SUNFED is intended to redistribute income and wealth over the world along socialist lines. Their view has been given credence by some rather extreme statements by representatives of underdeveloped countries that the advanced countries "owe" them assistance and that "the only thing which the underdeveloped countries request is a fair treatment, a fair share of the world's income, based on a good understanding of our needs, not from the viewpoint of bare commercialism, but from that of human idealism . . . in line with the ideas of our Father who has created us."[6] Such statements may be for home consump-

---

[6] Sjafruddin Prawiranegara, the Governor for Indonesia, of the International Monetary Fund before the eighth annual meeting of the Board of Governors, *Summary Proceedings*, 1954, p. 61.

tion, but others who hear them are affected. They are not shared by all underdeveloped countries; for example, Prime Minister Nehru has on occasions refused grants on the ground that Indians will appreciate their progress more if they work for it themselves.

Representatives of the underdeveloped countries have replied that they could not pay the debt charges on more loans, that they required outside assistance for development, and that it was unbelievable that additional amounts of goods could not be spared, especially by the United States. If it were true that the United States could not spare more aid, they have argued, it is because the U.S. government has placed excessive emphasis on rearmament and aid to Europe when the most important long-run problem facing the world is that of economic development; any further postponement of the development of backward areas would, in their view, be extremely dangerous to the safety of the West. They emphasize that they can not uphold their share in defense without greater development, that this development requires capital accumulation, which they are unable to do adequately by themselves, that foreign-exchange requirements are more than they can earn, that the IBRD's policies of lending for foreign-exchange costs of project-type loans have been "unsuitable," and that they could do nothing more to induce an inflow of private capital.

Despite their continued arguments that SUNFED is needed, the underdeveloped countries have been compelled to go along with the advanced countries and merely study the proposal for successive years. The study of how to establish the new fund has been somewhat irrelevant, however, for the two sides can not agree as to whether it was desirable to establish it at all. The debate of these issues in a multilateral agency (the UN Economic and Social Council) has provided the developing countries with a sounding board for their grievances; though often for home consumption, the multiplication of grievances is hardly a means of creating harmony. The public forum also provides a means of putting political pressure on the wealthy countries to share more of their wealth. Despite the fact that President Eisenhower has stated that more aid would be given for development as soon as armament expenditures could be decreased, he has also asserted that it will be extended largely bilaterally or to nations cooperating regionally.

Representatives of the underdeveloped countries have argued that they cannot wait until savings accrue from disarmament, for this might be indefinitely far away. They also fear that the adamant position toward an international agency means that the U.S. government wishes to interfere with development programs, and they have already given notice that they would countenance no dictation, even from an international agency, in the use of grants. These conflicting attitudes have resulted in an impasse over the establishment of a multilateral organization to assist in the financing of nonself-liquidating projects.

D. TECHNICAL COOPERATION

Improvement of technical know-how and skills has been regarded as a basic prerequisite to economic development, and the U.S. government has decided that the required improvements will not come rapidly enough without its assistance, despite the fact that it would cost the developing countries little to hire technical experts. The United States sees this cooperation as a low-cost, high-return means of displaying concern for the underprivileged countries.

Technical cooperation has been described by the administration as "a simple, down-to-earth self-help program designed primarily to assist other peoples in increasing the food production, bettering their health conditions, and improving their educational systems" and as a means of helping others to "create opportunities for the urban populations of the underdeveloped countries to make use of their improved education and newly acquired ideas; to introduce land reform in order that the farmer might share in the fruits of new techniques; and in general to make underdeveloped countries realize that development is a long-run problem and that both self-help and the encouragement of the investment of domestic and foreign capital are essential to the fulfillment of the programs."[7]

BILATERAL PROGRAMS

Through 1956, the United States had extended technical aid averaging just over $100 million a year. To make certain that the programs would be *cooperative,* Congress included a requirement that each recipient should pay a "fair share" of the cost of the technical-assistance projects. The calculation of what is a "fair share" is all but impossible, but Congress let it be known that it did not consider that a U.S. contribution greater than 50 per cent of the cost of the project was fair. Actually, the share paid by the recipient countries has varied from zero to 98 per cent. But such a monetary measure of the extent of cooperation is unreal. The contribution of the receiving country may properly reside elsewhere in efforts to make the technical assistance effective. Its resources must be allocated over the entire development program and it may be too restrictive to require that a given amount of domestic resources be used to match U.S. aid in a specific project. On the other hand, a matching requirement may bring forth funds which otherwise would not be made available at all.

Because Congress cannot provide funds more than one year at a time, problems of coordination have arisen. The recipients have found it difficult to plan their demonstration and training projects and/or to obtain funds from their own legislatures because of the absence of long-range programs

---

[7] As reported by W. A. Brown and R. Opie, *American Foreign Assistance* (Washington: Brookings, 1953), p. 397.

of aid. They have not known how much they would receive as technical assistance or how much they would be called upon to contribute themselves. The participants consider that more efficient and coordinated development programs could be formulated if they were assured of financial assistance for several years at a time. In recent years, President Eisenhower and influential private groups have urged a long-term commitment by the United States to programs of technical cooperation and capital assistance.

Technical-assistance projects have been cooperatively administered through a joint agency composed of U.S. officials and officials of the recipient country. Most of these projects aim at improving skills and knowledge in areas of industry, reclamation, labor, transportation, general economic development, social security and social services, mineral resources, fisheries, housing, public administration, geologic surveys, statistics, communications, finance, and weather.

Primary emphasis has been placed on agriculture and forestry and on health and education so as to attack quickly the problems of hunger, disease, and illiteracy. The kind of advice or aid needed to improve education and health conditions was often quite simple. Village schools in Iran had no windows; the supply of frames and glass pleased the elders and made them more amenable to allowing little girls to attend as well as boys. In many villages, the people made no distinction between mosquitoes and flies; a spraying with DDT, and some posters distinguishing the two, reduced malaria from an incidence of 90 per cent to 10 per cent, and incidentally rid the populace of bedbugs. In some villages, the only water supply is the gutter running through the village in which the people bathe, wash clothes and vegetables, from which they draw cooking and drinking water, and which serves as a sewer besides. The authorities were persuaded to require persons at least to take water for household purposes from the top of the flow and water the animals at the other end. The impact of the resulting better health and sanitation on population growth has been given little attention except in India. But, the mere control of malaria in some areas has increased labor efficiency so that food production on the same land has risen 50 per cent.

The nature of many of the projects is such that it is not feasible to extend advice only; commodities are also needed, such as hoes and plows, seeds, simple tools, and some items needed for demonstration. Because many areas were still plowing with wooden shares, cultivating with sticks, and harvesting with the sickle, gifts of iron plowshares, hoes, and scythes have increased production of grains more than tenfold where they have been provided. The provision of as simple a tool as a plow has not been without problems, however. In India, the introduction of the steel plow overthrew long-established community relationships and caused ill feeling. Previously, farmers inherited a contract with a carpenter to keep the wooden plows in repair, and the carpenter's family was included in many of the farmers' festivities; the new plow tended to destroy this tie. Further, the new plow was heavier and required a heavier draft animal which ate more fodder; it was heavier to carry from one cultivation strip to another; and when the blade broke, it required a blacksmith, who was several villages away. As we noted in the preceding chapter, the process of development is complex; it requires changes at all levels of social, economic, and political life, and the people must be willing to bear the adjustments.

In some countries, advice has been more important than goods. It is the experience of many developing countries that the officials in charge of the programs (usually ministers of health, agriculture, public works, etc.) are not of the same political stature (power) as are Finance or Defense Ministers; the prestige added by having a foreign expert, backed by funds from the U.S. government, is influential in getting recommendations on development programs carried through. This factor has also led many foreign governments to obtain experts of widespread reputation in their fields so as to lend weight to the recommendations, instead of those who might have been technically as competent but less well known.

However, a supply of suitable technicians has not been readily forthcoming. Even in the United States there is a shortage of capable technicians through the fields of agriculture, social welfare, public administration, education, and sanitation. (This bottleneck alone prevents the U.S. program from rising much above the $100 million level, unless foreign experts are employed.) It is also difficult to find trained personnel willing to live abroad several years under conditions less pleasant than in the United States. Even among those going abroad, many are unwilling or unable to make the cultural adjustments necessary and are unwilling to "help-teach" and "help-do"; they would rather do the job themselves because it gets done much faster, and they demand American goods and money for the most modern equipment.

Such attitudes have meant that the advice was economically inappropriate for the recipient country. The process of development requires that factors be allocated in the most efficient way, and the use of modern earth-moving machines or combines in a backward area is often highly uneconomical, despite the fact that it might get the job done more quickly. The best technical means are not always the most economical ones. The economical means in an area with unemployed or underemployed labor is to use the capital-saving and labor-intensive techniques. Also, the complementary skills for successful operation of the machines may be lacking, and repair facilities may be absent. In addition the cost in terms of exports to pay for imports of replacement parts or of complementary machines may be excessive, even if the original machine is a gift. Methods must be used which utilize whatever factors are at hand. Development abroad cannot wait on the creation of know-how and capacity to use the more advanced methods of industrialized countries.

Use of *non-American* experts has helped ease the short supply and has sometimes provided more appropriate advice. Not only are non-American experts in greater supply but, when they are from underdeveloped countries, they sometimes have a keener appreciation of the problems and greater patience. By mid-1953 almost a fourth of all the experts placed in the field by the UN were *from* underdeveloped countries. This method has met the objection by recipient governments that they simply did not want a lot of Americans "wandering around" their country; over 4,000 American technicians were abroad in 1956. But only Saudi Arabia actually canceled her technical cooperation agreement for fear that the "meddling" of U.S. technicians would bring unwanted social changes and upset the political balance among groups. The lower salary given the non-American expert has reduced the cost to the recipients as well as their dislike for the conspicuously high living standards enjoyed by American technicians. But even the UN agencies have found it difficult to obtain a sufficient number of Western technicians "sympathetic" to the problems of the area to which they were sent.

MULTILATERAL PROGRAMS

In 1949 the General Assembly of the United Nations approved an expanded program of technical assistance. Fifty-four countries joined in the program, but the U.S. government has made over 50 per cent of the total contributions; if the costs met by recipients are included, it has paid about 25 per cent of the total cost.

The bulk of these funds have been used to hire over 4,000 technicians from more than 70 countries; only small amounts were for commodities—those necessary in teaching, demonstration, and experimentation in pilot projects. Like the Point Four type of projects, they are primarily directed toward improving food production, public health, and education facilities, though some were to improve transportation and communication facilities and public administration.

Many more requests for assistance have come to the UN than it can meet with the funds available. The lack of funds caused many UN members to complain that the expanded program had not expanded rapidly enough; they called for even larger contributions on the ground that the difference in living standards between the richer and the poorer nations was growing greater rather than diminishing and that the richer nations had a moral responsibility to help the poorer. The UN Technical Assistance Board has reported, however, that the limited operations under the program resulted from the facts that (a) many types of projects which would have qualified for aid were not proposed since they would have involved basic reforms in practices which the governments did not want to give up; (b) some recipients were simply not prepared to use the advice requested efficiently, or they expected results almost immediately, or they underestimated the extent of their own responsibilities; and (c) there was a shortage of capital necessary for the application of many of the techniques proposed by the experts.

American contributions have been relatively small, ranging between $12 and $15 million yearly. This has reflected in part a difference of opinion among U.S. officials as to the desirability of channeling assistance through multilateral organizations. In the early stages of development of the technical-assistance program, some congressmen urged that all aid be extended through the UN on the ground that the UN could find more technical personnel and that reliance on the UN would show U.S. confidence in the world organization. Others pressed hard for a purely U.S. program, arguing that it would be more "efficient" because U.S. officials could keep their hands on the reins and potential recipients would not be voting themselves funds. The administration argued that some use of the UN agencies would reduce fears of "intervention" and counter the Communist charges of imperialism. The problem, as the administration saw it, was simply which method—bilateral or multilateral programs—was more effective in raising living standards.

Despite the arguments in favor of multilateral aid, Congress has been reluctant to vote funds for agencies over which the U.S. government did not have control. Congress has provided contributions to the UN under the justification that some problems are better handled on a regional basis than on a bilateral one, that multilateral aid is politically and psychologically more acceptable to some countries, that multilateral programs cut the cost to the United States, and that foreign technicians are sometimes more capable of handling the problems arising abroad than Americans are.

E. PROBLEMS OF AIDING DEVELOPMENT ABROAD

There has been widespread disagreement, both at home and abroad, over the most appropriate means to assist foreign economic development. The disagreements center on whether private or public lending should be emphasized, whether governmental loans or grants should predominate, whether primary reliance should be placed on capital or technical assistance, and whether the aid should be extended bilaterally between the United States and each recipient or channeled through an international organization.

PUBLIC VERSUS PRIVATE FINANCING

The developing countries and the U.S. government disagree on whether the capital funds should come from public or private sources. Part of the antipathy toward private investment in the developing areas stems from their history of colonialism and one-sided development. They cite the record to show that investments went mostly to projects for the supply of foodstuffs and raw materials for export to the industrialized countries.

This action, they argue, helped to intensify the agricultural and raw material production pattern, making those countries "colonial" in economic (if not political) status and delaying their own economic growth. This feeling of nationalism is currently strong in Canada where an important political issue during 1956 was the U.S. investment which, despite its contribution to Canadian growth, created antipathy and was said to make Canada "an appendage of the United States." Developing countries cite the record to show also that *private* investment goes mostly to countries with relatively high income levels where it is less "needed," and they claim that, in any case, its flow has been so erratic that no long-range development plans could be based upon it.

These indictments have some truth in them. Private investment follows an income motive and, understandably, does not give much regard to the social or political needs of the borrowing country. It therefore shies away from areas of instability and avoids low-income regions which are unlikely to provide a domestic market for production—or, if it goes into such areas, it is to produce items for markets in the higher-income countries—thus the apparent "exploitation." It is also true that American private capital flows have tended to expand during prosperity and decline during depression, just at the time when the developing country may need the funds for its growth.

In rebuttal, it must be stressed that private capital has and can perform necessary and desirable functions. Though it does not flow readily into the more basic projects, it will go into the more immediately productive ones and will diversify development—both desirable results. Also, direct private investment carries with it the requisite technical and managerial know-how to make the capital effective. And when native managers and technicians are trained as replacements, a middle class which appreciates the values of private enterprise and individual initiative is built up. Private investment is more likely to provide sustained economic growth than is governmental capital, because it spawns entrepreneurs and stimulates a willingness to accept risk, to experiment, and to reinvest earnings. The business contacts developed are likely to provide continuous and expanding commercial relationships of mutual advantage. Finally, from the standpoint of both the receiving and lending countries, private investment, since it follows profit inducements, does not involve political conflicts, and it provides firm criteria for selecting the areas to receive the capital.

The criticism concerning instability of foreign lending can be met either by using public lending to offset a decline in private flow or by stabilizing the level of economic activity in the lending countries. The U.S. government has declined to guarantee a continuing flow of capital funds over periods of prosperity and depression, but it has gone far toward adopting means of stabilizing the U.S. economy.

The stabilization of the American economy would be an important contribution to sound economic development abroad. Through the salutary effects of bringing steady growth to the U.S. economy, it would make more capital funds available if the correlation of high income and lending continues, and it would increase U.S. imports, making debt service easier. It would also remove one of the most effective psychological weapons in the hands of the Russians, because their arguments that the free enterprise system is outmoded have found acceptance abroad.

Current monetary and fiscal theories suggest that governments can maintain stability and growth through domestic measures. But *if* the propensity to save tends to outrun the propensity to invest, the outlets provided in foreign investment would be a benefit to both the borrower and the lender. There is a general belief in some foreign countries that the United States and other advanced economies are going to be compelled (along the Marxian lines of reasoning) to export capital. If this were so, it would be a happy circumstance: the richer countries needing to export capital to the poorer, who require it for growth. But, there is no such *necessity* on the part of the advanced countries.

The proposal for countercyclical lending by the United States is that the drop in private capital outflows during depression should be offset by government outflows. This would help to maintain U.S. export volumes and provide funds to continue already existing development programs abroad. It has been proposed that a sort of "shelf" of foreign public works be set up for financing development abroad. The opportunities for private foreign investment during subsequent periods of prosperity would be increased by the development of social overhead capital during a depression. Such a program would go a long way to convincing developing countries that they need not fear fluctuations in the U.S. economy and would thus perhaps induce them to embrace freer enterprise and to permit greater dependence on export markets and imports. Adoption of appropriate domestic measures to forestall depression would make the use of countercyclical aid unnecessary; but the existence of such a program would stand as a guarantee of international economic responsibility on the part of the U.S. government.

The proposal is not a panacea, however; it does not solve all the problems of the spread of depression nor those of developmental investment. If the additional investment funds supplied by the U.S. government merely replace those not loaned by private investors, the effect on the balance of payments of a U.S. depression caused by a decline in U.S. internal spending is not offset. The developing countries would still sustain a drop in their receipts of dollars through a fall in U.S. imports and thus would sustain internal deflationary pressure, reducing their domestic investment and retarding development. Finally, the proposal implies that a given volume of foreign investment is the most appropriate annual flow; this seems to deny that variations in the volume might be desired by the borrower depending on the projects ready for financing.

PUBLIC LOANS VERSUS GRANTS

Not only have most developing countries urged that public funds rather than private be used, but many have also urged that grants be given rather than loans. Their argument is that loans involve repayment, interest, and a continued and undesirable tie to the creditor's government and economy. However, grants do not avoid the implication of the dependence of receiving countries. When grants are regarded as charity, they do not give rise to the goodwill sought by the donor. Even when not so regarded, their extension may have to be "justified"—just as loans do—with cross-examinations of the applications and applicants, which deflates their ego. When the recipients of these grants are faced with a continuing stream of experts, advisers, administrators, inspectors, and coordinators who live on a level far above the people they are assisting and who may arrogate to themselves many of the decisions which would normally be considered "internal affairs," they feel the same galling effect as from the economic ties of lending.

The extension of grants may lead to the attaching of conditions on the aid which are not as likely to be imposed with a loan contract; these usually give rise to feelings of encroachment on sovereignty. The recipient countries argue, however, that if conditions will not be imposed, if they are left alone to seek the best use of the funds as they see it, and if they are not repeatedly held to inquisitorial accounts for the funds, these objections to grants would be alleviated. If this hands-off approach is accepted, the ability to meet debt burdens becomes the decisive factor in the choice between grants and loans.

However, the developing countries must realize that the American people and particularly their government are unlikely to approve gifts indefinitely. And if there is a decline in the importance of winning allies among the backward areas, grants will probably play a smaller role. The proposals to share wealth internationally will then give rise to more severe conflicts of national interest, especially since few countries (donors or recipients) have adopted similar wealth-sharing programs domestically.

CAPITAL VERSUS TECHNICAL ASSISTANCE

Disagreement among the potential grantors of assistance and potential recipients arises also as to the appropriate distribution of governmental aid between technical and capital assistance. The U.S. government has agreed that most countries are going to have to move forward at a more rapid rate than the now advanced countries did if their people are going to be satisfied with their progress. This may require some capital assistance, but the biggest bottlenecks are in techniques—the use of simple tools, improved seeds, crop rotation, etc.—rather than lack of combines and other complex machinery. The advanced countries see the road of progress as being long and difficult, with capital aid only a means of making the passage less painful.

A view commonly expressed by the recipient countries is, however, that capital assistance is the "open sesame" to the riches of economic development. They argue that continuation of a multitude of technical studies and economic reports, without capital to carry out their recommendations, is disappointing. If the projects cannot be carried out, assistance creating a technical foundation is in fact wasteful. The developing countries have therefore stressed capital aid to make technical aid effective.[8]

Such a combination of aid and expert know-how was forthcoming during the nineteenth and early twentieth centuries through the export of private capital accompanied by technicians hired by the companies making the investment. With the increasing flow of government capital, technical assistance does not automatically accompany a capital export, the amounts of technical and capital assistance are decided by different organizations. The decisions must be coordinated with each other, with the rate of development desired and with the ability of the recipients to absorb foreign capital effectively. The disagreement is over these latter decisions, with the potential recipients arguing that the rate of progress must be rapid to serve the security interests of the West and with the West replying that so rapid a development as desired cannot be attained because of the paucity of natural resources, the unfavorable climates, the density of populations, and other obstacles, and because of the scarcity of resources available to the West in defending itself. The acrimony developed during UN debates of these problems has caused some persons to observe that the attempts to aid developing countries have brought not harmony but discord. It has been suggested that the only way to achieve harmony is to divorce the problem from national policies and place it under an international organization.

MULTILATERAL VERSUS BILATERAL ASSISTANCE

The fear of interference and the desire to use their concerted bargaining power have led the developing areas to urge that loans and capital and technical assistance be extended mostly through international organizations.

---

[8] This view was expressed as follows by a representative of an aid-receiving country: "The new technology to be applied in increasing production for raising standards of living must embody itself in durable capital goods and other producers' goods to be utilized in the productive process. It is impossible to separate capital from technology. They are basic elements which should be applied jointly in the process of production. Technical aid therefore will be sterile without financial aid with which to secure the material means of production." (George Hakim, "Technical Aid from the Viewpoint of the Aid-receiving Countries," in B. F. Hoselitz [ed.], *The Progress of Underdeveloped Countries* [Chicago: University of Chicago Press, 1952], p. 263.)

Since they would be members of the agencies, they would have a stronger voice, and the experts and the advice would not be oriented toward the interests of any one foreign power.

There are advantages also from the viewpoint of the richer countries. The funds made available for assistance are likely to come from more than one country, taking the burden off any one country (such as the United States); even some of the more affluent developing areas (such as those receiving oil royalties) might be persuaded to contribute the services of experts if not funds. As in the case of the International Bank, any default on loans made by the agency would be shared by all members. And any ill will resulting from the necessity to refuse aid would be spread over all member countries opposing it instead of being concentrated on one. Finally, conditions imposed by international agencies on the use of aid would be more readily accepted by the recipients. However, the record shows that the voices of recipients are raised against attaching conditions even by international agencies such as the International Bank.

This necessity of attaching conditions on the aid is a strong reason for the *bilateral* programs of the U.S. government, but it is a sufficient reason only if multilateral organizations would be *less* stringent in attaching necessary conditions. There is insufficient experience to draw a firm conclusion as to future operations, but evidence up to now does not show them to be lax in this regard. Finally, an individual donor government might find political reasons for not pursuing a breach of contract by a foreign government.

In the long run, regardless of whether the aid is extended bilaterally or multilaterally, several conditions must be imposed to insure that the funds are used most effectively. The lenders must require that there is a workable fiscal system, reasonably effective monetary control, and the absence of political corruption, in order not to dissipate the funds in inflation or misallocation. Realignment of exchange rates and removal of exchange controls and quotas could be attached as prerequisites, especially when their justification has ceased. Both the International Bank and the Monetary Fund have had some slight success in this regard. Such conditions do not necessarily violate "self-determination."

In the immediate future, however, and so long as the pressure of the "cold war" continues, the U.S. government is justified in extending much of the aid bilaterally *if* this technique serves to win friends to the cause of peace. There are several reasons why bilateral aid would seem to be best. First, the unbalanced participation in multilateral organizations of richer and poorer countries, with the latter outnumbering and outvoting the former, makes these agencies reflect the views of the potential recipients; or the predominant contribution of funds by the United States tends to make the agency reflect its views and turn the agency into an international mouthpiece for U.S. policy. Second, membership in international agencies of Communist nations makes the U.S. government uneasy about placing funds at the disposal of organizations which might vote uses for it not in the national interest of the United States.

SELECTED READINGS

Besides the following, see the selections for Chapter 21.

Barlow, E. R., and Ira T. Wender. *Foreign Investment and Taxation.* Englewood Cliffs, N. J.: Prentice-Hall, 1955. An extensive examination of experience of foreign investors, obstacles to foreign investment, and taxation of foreign income.

Committee for Economic Development. *Economic Development Abroad and the Role of American Foreign Investment.* New York: February, 1956. A balanced statement on national policy toward development abroad by the CED Research and Policy Committee.

Export-Import Bank of Washington. *Semi-Annual Report.* Reports to Congress which provide current information on the operations of the EIB.

Higgins, B., and W. Malenbaum. "Financing Economic Development," *International Conciliation,* No. 502. New York: Carnegie Endowment for International Peace, March, 1955. An analysis of the problems of financing development from resources at home and abroad and the possibilities of international public financing.

International Bank for Reconstruction and Development. *The International Bank for Reconstruction and Development, 1946–1953.* Baltimore: The Johns Hopkins Press, 1954. A review by the staff of the Bank of its operations through 1953; this, coupled with the Bank's *Annual Reports,* provide detailed information on loans, marketing of securities, etc.

International Development Advisory Board. *An Economic Program for the Americas.* Washington: September, 1954. A report by a member of the Board on the significance of Latin America to the United States, on her need for capital, and the problems of private investment in Latin America, with recommendations.

International Finance Section. *Survey of United States International Finance.* Princeton, N. J.: Princeton University Press. The surveys covering the years 1950 through 1953 include presentations of the policies of the U.S. government toward technical and capital assistance.

League of Nations. *Conditions of Private Foreign Investment.* Geneva: 1946. An analysis of the conditions necessary to an expansion of private investment which, in retrospect, explains why the flow is so small.

Lewis, Cleona. *The United States and Foreign Investment Problems.* Washington: Brookings, 1948. A review of the experience during the interwar period with recommendations for postwar cooperation which are still worth considering.

Malenbaum, W. "India and China: Development Contrasts," *Journal of Political Economy,* LXIV (February, 1956), 1–24. Materials permitting an examination of the thesis that the objectives of the West are gained or lost depending on the successful competition between India and China in rapid development.

Mead, Margaret. *Cultural Patterns and Technical Change*. Paris: UNESCO, 1954. A study of the impact of technical change on the cultures of various areas and of the differing capacities for change.

National Planning Association. *Technical Cooperation in Latin America*. Washington: 1956. A detailed description of the cooperative programs with some recommendations for the future. See also its series titled *United States Business Performance Abroad* for case studies of how U.S. firms have assisted foreign economic growth.

Randall Commission on Foreign Economic Policy. *Staff Papers*. Washington, February, 1954. Chapter 3 concerns the climate for private foreign investment, the U.S. instruments for encouraging it, and the relation between public and private lending.

Rubin, S. J. *Private Foreign Investment: Legal and Economic Realities*. Baltimore: Johns Hopkins Press, 1956. A unique study of the problems of expropriation and protection of private investment showing obstacles yet to be overcome.

United Nations. *Domestic Financing of Economic Development*. New York: 1951. A detailed description of the measures required to increase the volume of national savings and to improve the quality of investment by directing savings into those forms of investment leading to economic growth, including a review of the problems and practices of selected countries.

————. *International Capital Movements During the Inter-war Period*. New York: 1949. An examination of the nature, volume, and direction of international capital movements, and the return on foreign capital investments during the years 1920–1940.

————. *International Cooperation in a Latin American Development Policy*. New York: 1954. A report by the Economic Commission for Latin America on foreign investment policy, productivity and technical assistance, trade policy and economic development, and measures to reduce the vulnerability of Latin America to external instability.

————. *Methods of Financing Economic Development in Underdeveloped Countries*. New York: 1949. A report on the possible sources, domestic and external, of revenue for financing development programs.

————. *Report on a Special United Nations Fund for Economic Development*. New York: 1953. A report by a committee of experts on a plan for the establishment, operation, management and control of a special fund for grants-in-aid and low-interest, long-term loans to underdeveloped countries.

————. *The Effects of Taxation on Foreign Trade and Investment*. New York: 1950. A study of the effects of taxation as incentives or barriers to international trade and investment and the problems of double taxation.

————. *The International Flow of Private Capital, 1946–1952*. New York: 1954. An examination of the nature and volume of private capital flows with specific reference to investments by the United States, the United Kingdom, Switzerland, France, Belgium, and Canada.

23 Tariffs and Trade Barriers

American imports are subject to regulation through tariffs, quotas, and/or customs procedures. United States exports are indirectly affected by U.S. government regulations over imports, because U.S. imports provide dollars with which foreigners buy American goods. Some American exports are subject to direct controls. Commercial policies are therefore of primary importance in shaping the nation's over-all foreign economic program. Among the commercial policies, tariffs have received the major share of the public's attention, but the growing use of direct controls by the U.S. government and foreign governments and the impact of strategic considerations on U.S. foreign economic policy require greater attention to the non-tariff means of regulation.

A technical division of commercial policies may be drawn between tariff and nontariff measures, but no such distinction is appropriate as to purpose. Both direct and indirect regulations are employed for the same or similar purposes. In order to simplify the presentation, the chapters on commercial policy are divided so as to emphasize problems of (1) tariff policy directed at regulating the volume and impact of trade, (2) trade in agricultural products and raw materials, and (3) trade regulations based mainly on strategic considerations.

A. U.S. POLICY AIMS

HISTORICAL BACKGROUND

The current aims of U.S. commercial policies have grown out of the experiences of the war and postwar periods and the depression of the 1930's. The past three and a half decades have witnessed a strong nationalistic bias in international commerce.

Tariffs after World War I

Reminiscent of American and French actions after previous wars, Europe and the United States increased tariff duties after World War I.

Protection was used to favor "defense" industries such as chemicals, optical glass, steel, etc. And it was also imposed to support war-born industries and agriculture which were facing harsh competition from abroad. A further cause of the world-wide rise of protection was the fact that many of the new nations, created under the peace treaties, required revenue and were uncertain of their economies' productive power or of their competitive positions. The new governments were too confused to carry out effective policies involving cooperation with others and therefore succumbed to internal pressures for protection. Finally, higher tariffs were substituted for other trade restrictions, and the liberalizing effect of most-favored-nation treatment was dampened because the treaties between Allied and Central powers were denounced. The belligerents had relied more on direct controls than on tariffs to channel production and trade during the war. The Allies agreed that such measures were generally undesirable in peacetime and that only tariffs should be employed to regulate trade. As the direct controls were removed, however, they were replaced with higher and more discriminatory tariffs.

Although most countries engaged in tariff bargaining and adhered to the most-favored-nation principle, the movement of duties was steadily upward. One of the means employed was tariff specialization, i.e., the classification of commodities in tariff schedules so as to restrict the reduction under a reciprocity treaty to the other party alone. For example, the rates on bicycles would be classified so as to lower the duty on British-type bicycles while leaving higher duties on heavier bicycles similar to those produced in the United States. The proliferation of product classifications (about 40 per cent of the rates subject to negotiation before World War II have been reclassified) complicated tariff schedules unduly. This action left the schedule essentially discriminatory despite the fact that the most-favored-nation clause was adhered to.

It must also be recognized, however, that tariff specialization may be used to extend a duty reduction which would not be given if it had to be generalized to other nations. Specialized classification permits the reduction of duties on subclasses of a product which are minimally competitive with domestic production while maintaining higher rates on those types more fully competitive. This calms fears of those who might otherwise successfully oppose a reduction of the duty on the entire class of commodities.

By 1927, the world's trade, although expanded, did not increase as rapidly as the world's production. Many nations were concerned that the higher tariffs and other restrictions were smothering useful trade. If all suppliers could be brought to the same table, officials thought, these obstacles to tariff reduction would be lessened. Under the auspices of the League of Nations, the 1927 World Economic Conference was held to consider ways and means of reducing obstacles to trade. After much debate and wrangling, representatives agreed upon a number of proposals for stabilizing duties at lower levels, principally through the treaty technique and through the widest application of the unconditional interpretation of the most-favored-nation clause. Some relaxation of duties followed; 72 tariff treaties were signed during 1928–1929, and the spirit of the most-favored-nation clause seemed to be widely accepted once again. But the continued pressure on agricultural markets, the instability of world prices in many products, the political instability remaining in many areas of the world, and the government competition in raising tariffs for purposes of negotiation—all made it impossible for governments to implement these multilateral agreements subscribed to by official representatives.

The one country which, because of its over-all trade and payments position and its political stability, could have led a world-wide reduction of trade barriers, chose to move the other way. The United States ended the first postwar decade by raising duties on both agricultural and industrial goods to new heights. This action was hardly calculated to ease the pressure on others' balances of payments. It contributed strongly to economic isolation in the 1930's.

Tariffs in the Depression

Although tariffs became a relatively less important means of restricting trade as direct controls grew after 1933, they set the early pattern. The United States led off with the Hawley-Smoot Tariff of 1930, followed quickly by others. Whether or not other countries would have imposed higher duties anyway because of the extensive depression, the American action gave them righteous cause to do so in retaliation. Britain followed almost immediately by passing an emergency tariff in 1931, expanded by the Import Duties Act of 1932. She then joined, in the Ottawa Conference, with Canada and the other Commonwealth countries in erecting higher duties on non-Commonwealth goods. The Ottawa agreements expanded the system of imperial preference which extended lower duties to goods produced within the Empire than to those exported from other countries. The removal of this preferential system has been a primary objective of U.S. policy since World War II.

Nations retaliated against the Hawley-Smoot tariff in various ways. One investigation records that

After thirty-three foreign nations had filed formal and official protests against our new tariff, several among them began to revise their tariff legislation with the evident intent to retaliate against the United States. Spain passed a new tariff law on July 22, 1930. In Italy an intense propaganda against American-made automobiles and other manufactures resulted in a series of substantial increases in forty-one import duties. In Switzerland an intensive and most effective boycott of American products was started as a measure of retaliation against our tariff increase. France adopted a drastic system of customs quotas designed to reserve the domestic market for domestic producers and to redress the country's trade balance. Canada retaliated in kind by raising its tariff to the highest levels in the history of the country and by hitting severely practically all of our more important exports.[1]

The list of countries retaliating could be extended further. A case has been made that the higher U.S. duties were an important contributory factor in the Japanese military aggressions in Manchuria in 1933. Professor Quincy Wright has argued that the new American import barriers dealt a severe blow to the prestige of the dominant party's policies of industrialization and expanded trade to meet Japan's serious economic problems. The Japanese military clique was then able to argue that the Hawley-Smoot Tariff, which increased the duties on most Japanese-manufactured exports to the United States, was evidence that the peaceful policy had failed.[2]

The repercussions of this drive to raise duties included a widespread and open disregard for the most-favored-nation clauses already in existence and the gradual undermining of previously accepted "rules of fair play" in commercial treaty bargaining. Conventions were called among nations during 1931, 1932, and 1933 to obtain at least a truce in the tariff war, but the efforts were unsuccessful. Countries would enter treaty arrangements only for short periods (even three to six months) and then only if duties could be changed upon notice and if the most-favored-nation clause were restricted to a limited list of commodities.

Reciprocal Trade Agreements Program

The only substantive break in the trend to greater protection was attempted by the very country that touched off the widespread tariff increases. In 1934, the U.S. government began its Reciprocal Trade Agreements Program aimed at reducing tariffs throughout the world. The Program's principles reflected the single-minded purpose of Secretary of State Cordell Hull who, despite extensive opposition, was determined to reverse the trend to economic isolation and to move toward international harmony through freer trade.

The opposition was overcome only through the administration selling the Program to Congress as a means of expanding U.S. exports and of helping to get out of the Depression. The Program would not have been accepted had it been seen as one to permit imports which would compete with U.S. enterprise and labor.

The Reciprocal Trade Agreements Act empowered the U.S. administration to change existing tariff rates by 50 per cent, reducing them only under reciprocal negotiations with other countries, through the uncondi-

---

[1] *International Economic Relations* (Minneapolis: University of Minnesota Press, 1934), p. 37.

[2] "Some Political Consideratioins in Formulating an International Economic Policy for the United States," *ibid.*, p. 282. See also Eugene Staley, *World Economy in Transition* (New York: Council on Foreign Relations, 1939), pp. 103–110.

tional most-favored-nation policy adopted in 1923. Part of the justification for delegating authority over duties to the Executive Branch arose from the facts that the Hawley-Smoot Tariff required almost a year in passage through Congress, that the duties were a result of much swapping and log-rolling (I'll vote for your duty if you'll vote for mine), and that the Senate had failed to ratify reciprocity treaties negotiated under previous authority. But an equal justification was that the United States was interested in obtaining lower duties abroad and hoped to use its own duties as bargaining chips. The Program was passed on the assertion that exporters would benefit while import-competing industries were not to be harmed. The congressional intent was not that of benefiting other countries.

Congress extended the authority for the Program twice before World War II. Each time, the administration had the herculean task of proving that the agreements had resulted in lower duties abroad and therefore higher U.S. exports, but that the duties reduced by the United States had not led to increased imports, because Congress saw the latter as a threat to domestic interests. Though duties were lowered, imports actually did not rise greatly because of the techniques used in negotiating agreements. First, tariff specialization restricted duty reductions to only the reciprocal party. Second, bargaining was restricted to the principal supplier of an import in order to increase the bargaining strength of the U.S. negotiators, but since imports from the major supplier were a larger threat to U.S. producers, the U.S. duty reductions were less. Third, many duty reductions merely removed superfluous rates; that is, a duty of 90 per cent was reduced to 50 per cent, which lower rate was still prohibitive. Fourth, quantitative restrictions were imposed on some commodities to offset duty reductions.

Some eighteen reciprocity agreements were signed during the 1930's, mostly with Latin American countries, and an additional eleven were negotiated during the war period. But despite the duty reductions made by the United States, they did not lead to a general reduction of tariffs by others. Rather, many countries imposed direct controls involving discrimination. The U.S. government was insistent that post-World War II policies should be based on principles of nondiscriminatory, multilateral trade and payments, such as underlie the Trade Agreements Program.

Post-World War II aims

The international economic objectives of the U.S. government were to create out of the chaos, poverty, and insecurity of the immediate postwar world the foundations for freer trade and for a world-wide multilateral and nondiscriminatory system of trade and payments which would permit American private enterprise to compete on "equitable" terms with other traders and which would contribute to the welfare of all nations by expanding international trade. As recognition of the Communist menace grew, proposals for freer trade were justified increasingly on the ground that they would serve the security of the United States and the Free World. Lower U.S. tariffs were asserted to be an important means of increasing Free World economic growth and thereby its military strength. The administration also argued that the act of lowering barriers would be seen abroad as evidence of America's continued interest in the welfare of its allies, upon whom she relied in gaining her political objectives and as evidence of her desire to cooperate internationally.

The U.S. international economic objectives were accepted by all nations which received American lend-lease goods in World War II. Each lend-lease agreement carried the statement that after the war the signatory nations would cooperate in measures to expand world trade, to eliminate all forms of discrimination in international commerce, and to reduce tariffs and other trade barriers. Nondiscrimination, elimination of quantitative restrictions, reduction of tariffs and the elimination of preferences were agreed upon as the long-run goals, and they were to be sought through an International Trade Organization. The ITO was to be the third leg of the stool supporting international economic relations, the other two being the Fund and the Bank. The ITO Charter was negotiated in Geneva during 1947 and finally agreed upon by officials at Havana in 1948. Only Liberia ratified it unconditionally; others did so conditional upon U.S. ratification. Congress failed to ratify the Charter, partly because it covered so many aspects of international economic relations that it elicited criticism from every quarter.

The clauses of the Charter relating to commercial policies were incorporated in a General Agreement on Tariffs and Trade at Geneva in 1947 so as to begin tariff negotiations immediately. The GATT went into effect without congressional approval (or disapproval) since the U.S. administration considered it an executive agreement not requiring ratification.

When the ITO was abandoned, the GATT became the vehicle for international cooperation in commercial policy. The GATT provided the mechanism for tariff reductions on a multilateral basis. It also provided and watched over some rules: nondiscrimination (with the exception of preferences and for balance-of-payments reasons), prohibition of quantitative restrictions (with exceptions for balance-of-payments and economic development purposes), simplification of customs procedures, and others.

TARIFF REDUCTION AND NONDISCRIMINATION

The members of GATT agreed to enter into and carry out negotiations aimed at the substantial reduction of tariffs and the elimination of preferences. The procedures are similar to those under the U.S. Trade Agreements Act. Concessions are offered for reciprocal concessions. Any concession made to one country is automatically extended to all members involved in any given negotiation, i.e., most-favored-nation treatment was provided.

The principle of nondiscrimination means that the same customs duties, laws, and regulations concerning imports and exports are to be applied to all other member countries. An exception is permitted in the historic relations within the British Empire and between the United States and Cuba and the Philippines; additional exceptions are permitted when one nation wishes to extend a unilateral preference to facilitate the economic development or reconstruction of another country.

The GATT aims at eliminating preferences but it permits the creation of customs unions. Preferences provide a lower tariff duty to imports from certain countries than from others; under a customs union, each member gives free entry to imports from all other members, and a uniform tariff applies to all outsiders. Thus a customs union is 100 per cent preference. Because a customs union is more discriminatory than a preference system, it would seem likely that it would cause a greater diversion of trade from nations outside the union than would a preference system, as explained in Chapter 3. Thus it would seem to be less desirable from a world-wide view. However, a preference system allows the members to choose the particular commodities on which tariffs are reduced, while a customs union involves the removal of all tariffs on trade within the union. Members of a preference system are therefore afforded an opportunity to reduce the duties on products in which the main burden will be borne by outside nations rather than on those in the system, and they are apt to do so in order to minimize domestic economic and political consequences. Therefore a preference system tends to cause considerable trade diversion but only a little trade creation.

On the other side of the argument, a customs union may result in a higher degree of protection against the outside countries. The bargaining power of the union is greater than that of the individual members. Furthermore, even if no duty is raised, there is great pressure to accept the highest duty for any item employed by any *one* member as the duty of the union because the adjustments required are then less. The higher duties are also more attractive to the union since the members are a step nearer self-sufficiency. The United States and the USSR are good examples of this. It is highly likely that the tariffs of the forty-eight separate states of the United States, were they independent nations, would be much lower vis-a-vis the rest of the world than are the present tariffs of the United States. The same situation has occurred with Soviet Russia; the barriers have been torn down within Russia and between Russia and her satellites, but she has been able thereby to raise the barriers against Europe and the rest of the world to quite high levels under her state trading arrangements.

STATE TRADING

One of the most difficult practices to reconcile with the principle of nondiscrimination is that of state trading. Most of the European nations ended the war with government agencies controlling and carrying out large portions of their trade. Although the U.S. government does not approve of international trade being carried on by governments and hopes that almost all trade will eventually be returned to private channels, it realizes that many of the state trading agencies are likely to remain. The problem has been how to reconcile their activities, which were essentially discriminatory not only economically but often also politically, with the principles of the GATT. The expedient adopted was to insert a provision that all member governments agreed to operate their state trading agencies on a nondiscriminatory basis and along commercial lines. In order not to use these agencies to raise the difference between the import price and the resale price of the goods on the domestic market (pseudo tariffs), each government agreed to negotiate with others the margins of protection they would grant their own industry through the price differentials.

This provision is an effort at completeness; yet it involves a basic contradiction in the Agreement. The general practice of trading monopolies —state or others—is to discriminate among sellers and buyers so as to maximize profits. On purely commercial grounds, it is like asking a government not to do the thing it set the agency up to do—obtain the best bargain. Further, it is practically impossible for a government not to operate such an agency with political ends in view. And finally, it would be very difficult to determine and prove the existence of discrimination, because the operations of the agency are not generally made public. Since the agencies will discriminate in practice, their existence is in contradiction to a fully multilateral system.

QUANTITATIVE RESTRICTIONS

The GATT prohibits the use of quantitative restrictions to regulate the import or export of any product, save in exceptional circumstances. The chief exceptions are import quotas for balance-of-payments purposes, import restrictions on agricultural products which were subject to governmental or intergovernmental regulation, and export restrictions on foodstuffs or other commodities in critical shortage. Quantitative restrictions are permitted also when used to help a foreign country in its development or, by a developing country, to foster growth of its own industry.

Although the U.S. government employs some quantitative restrictions and has acquiesced in their use by others under the GATT, it maintains as a general principle that the only interferences with trade should be tariffs. Tariffs operate through the price mechanism and therefore are not absolutely prohibitive; in a dynamic world, price and cost changes permit goods to jump even a "prohibitive" duty. Contrarily, import quotas cannot be jumped, and the administrative discretion attached to direct controls introduces considerable uncertainty into international commerce through changes in governmental directives. It is difficult, if not impossible, to make direct controls nondiscriminatory, because the privileges of importing must be rationed both in time and among importers and are usually rationed among sources of supply. But the administrative advantages, as well as those discussed in Chapter 15, make continued use of quantitative restrictions probable, and the most that GATT members have been willing to concede is that their application should be as nondiscriminatory as possible and should be a subject of discussion.

INTERNATIONAL RULES

One of the unique features of postwar commercial policies has been the banding together of many nations for simultaneous reciprocal tariff reductions and for the creation of a set of common rules for trade and tariffs. The early postwar desire for international rules and organizations to facilitate trade stemmed from the spirit of international cooperation and from dissatisfaction with prewar economic nationalism.

The bilateral bargaining under the Reciprocal Trade Agreements Act had been largely unsuccessful in removing any devices for protection other than tariffs; quotas and other restrictions mushroomed during the 1930's. No country bargaining with the U.S. government felt that it could give up its quantitative restrictions for tariff concessions unless others were willing to do so at the same time. Simultaneous bargaining or some common rules seemed a way out of this impasse as well as a means of extending the principle of nondiscrimination to nontariff restrictions.

These considerations, plus the desire of the U.S. government to bring together those aspects of international economic relations not covered by the International Fund or Bank, led initially to agreement on the ITO Charter, by accident to the GATT, and by design to the proposal for an Organization for Trade Cooperation (OTC) to become the secretariat for the GATT.

The GATT has led a tenuous life as a result of frequent congressional caveats in the Trade Agreements Act renewals to the effect that the renewal should not be considered either as an approval or disapproval of the GATT. Members of GATT are attempting to place the organization on a more permanent footing through the establishment of an international agency (the OTC) to sponsor multilateral tariff-negotiation conferences, to administer the rules of GATT, to facilitate the adjudication of complaints among countries regarding commercial policy, and to stand as a sort of court (without enforcement power) on those disputes. The U.S. Congress has not yet ratified the OTC and thus withholds its explicit approval of the rules of GATT, despite strong urging by the administration that approval is needed to show the world that the United States stands firmly for freer trade.

From a free trade standpoint, an advantage of an international organization and a set of rules is that the weight of world opinion may be brought against potentially offensive actions. Member governments are aided in fending off domestic pressure for protection; contrarily, protectionists regard this result as an objection to international organization. Also, the existence of a common set of rules, even with the troublesome exceptions, provides a firmer base for settling disputes among countries than was available under the clauses of the prewar bilateral agreements. Under these it was not always easy to develop the information required from foreign sources to settle a trade dispute over alleged violations. Also, a complaint by one country would frequently be met by a countercomplaint by the other, leading to mutual embarrassment. And, because bilateral discussions regarding commercial policies would frequently shade into other diplomatic discussions (on military or political matters), it became difficult to keep the discussion on the technical operation of the agreement. The OTC, by providing facts and a technical forum for the discussion of trade disputes, is supposed to ameliorate these shortcomings of the bilateral approach.

The major complaints against international rules and negotiation come primarily from the protectionists. Many in Congress consider that the establishment of an Organization for Trade Cooperation (OTC) would be a further delegation of congressional powers over commercial policy which some think have already been too far divorced from its care. They fear that, through the OTC, nations would have a permanent sounding board to develop common policies opposing U.S. positions, putting concerted pressure on Congress. In practice, however, the power of the United States has been sufficient—despite its having only one vote—to obtain "permission" from GATT members to employ practices disliked by others.

The extent to which all members have reservations on the GATT and the tariff reductions made under it are reflected in the facts that there is, after ten years, no agreement on a permanent organization and that the tariff reductions are renewed for only a given period of years (usually three) at which time a member may change or remove past concessions. The basic advantage of the GATT, which keeps members from withdrawing, is that, without it, restrictions imposed by one country would most likely be met with similar ones abroad resulting in a round of retaliation and the reduction of world trade as in the 1930's.

B.   TARIFF REDUCTIONS

Members of the GATT have held several conferences to agree on tariff reductions. Through them, U.S. duties have been lowered in return for duty reductions by other members. Opposition to this freeing of trade still exists within the U.S. Congress, however, and efforts have been made to prevent duty reductions and/or to ease their impact on domestic interests.

GATT NEGOTIATIONS

The members of GATT have negotiated a series of reductions in tariffs among themselves on a bilateral basis. In accord with the most-favored-nation clause in the Agreement, these concessions were usually generalized to all the participants, providing nondiscriminatory treatment among themselves. (Members are not obliged to extend most-favored-nation treatment to a newly acceding member. Japan was not extended the concessions which fourteen members had given to others when it joined in 1955.)

In order to obtain the largest concession for any given duty reduction, negotiations were usually held between "principal suppliers"—that is, each nation would seek to bargain with the largest exporter to its market of a given product in order to gain the largest concession in return. In the bargaining, members agreed to accept the binding of a low or free rate as equal to a reduction of a high duty; this was designed to prevent countries with already low rates from being placed in a weak bargaining position.

Multilateral bargaining is supposed to be to the advantage of the United States also because tariff reductions among other nations are encouraged and these benefit U.S. exports through most-favored-nation treatment. Some people contend that U.S. bargaining strength is enhanced because the American negotiators are able to obtain concessions from little suppliers who otherwise would benefit freely from U.S. duty reductions given to chief suppliers under the operation of the most-favored-nation clause in bilateral agreements, i.e., each tariff concession by the United States obtains more reciprocal concessions. It is questionable whether any one nation's bargaining power is increased by this procedure, since it is available to all negotiating countries and therefore does not provide any *relative* advantage.

Throughout the negotiations, duties were reduced on items comprising about one half the volume of the dutiable imports. Some duties were bound against any increase, and some items were bound on the free list. Despite these negotiations, the U.S. tariff still includes many ad valorem rates over 50 per cent and many specific rates which are the equivalent of much more than 100 per cent duty. As a result of duty reductions under the Trade Agreements Act and through the GATT, some people argue that the level of tariffs of the United States is now exceedingly low as compared to that of other countries. For example, the ratio of customs duties collected to total value of U.S. imports dropped from 15.8 per cent in 1937 to 5.1 per cent in 1951; nine countries had lower percentages in 1937 but only seven in 1951. This decline in duties collected as a percentage of total value of imports was partly a result of tariff reductions under GATT and other bilateral negotiations, but it was also partly a result of general inflation of prices of imports and the consequent reduction in the ad valorem equivalent of specific duties.

Regardless of the cause, the ratio of duties collected to total imports is hardly a measure of the protectiveness of a tariff. In 1951, more than a quarter of the U.S. duties were over 30 per cent, and 35 per cent of the items carried rates of over 20 per cent. But the value of the items coming in with duties over 30 per cent was only 5 per cent of total imports, and those coming in under duties between 20 and 30 per cent amounted to only 9 per cent of the total value of imports. This suggests that duties over 20 or 30 per cent are rather restrictive of imports. (Some foreign exporters have calculated that, in general, duties of over 15 per cent practically prohibit entry into the U.S. market.)[3] The higher tariff rates are thus weighted very lightly in the ratio of duties to total imports because so little revenue is collected from them and so few imports occur at the high rates. In fact, if all duties imposed were prohibitive and if all imports coming in were free of duty, the ratio of duties collected to total imports would be zero; the tariff wall would then be said to be nonexistent. What this type of calculation fails to show is the number and value of imports shut out by the higher duties.

Professor Viner summed up the impact of the reduction of U.S. tariffs on imports as of 1954 as follows:

In general, moreover, it has been the duties or portions of duties which have been of little or no consequence as restrictions on imports which we have been willing to reduce in our reciprocal trade negotiations, and there is no convincing evidence either that any important protective duties have been reduced to an extent sufficient to have caused an appreciable lessening of the hold of American industries on the domestic market, or that the proportion of our imports which consists of commodities on which import duties have been reduced since 1934 is greater now than it was before 1934. . . . The duties of our tariff which have survived the trade agreements negotiations probably account for almost all of the restrictive effect on imports of the tariff as it was before 1934, so that further reductions in duty are likely to be much more effective in opening the way to increased imports than were the earlier series of reductions.[4]

EXTENSIONS OF THE TRADE AGREEMENTS ACTS

The Trade Agreements Act has been extended seven times since World War II for periods ranging from one to three years. The uncertainty

---

[3] A study made by the American Chamber of Commerce in London in answer to questions by the U.S. Chamber showed that there were many items carrying duties over 25 per cent which could not be exported to the United States because of the duty (metal-cutting tools, ceramic tiles, toys, games, glass mirrors, china, needles, surgical instruments, chair seats, rag rugs, taxi meters, lace, etc.) and several others carrying 15 to 40 per cent duties could be sold only in luxury lines (wool, decorated china, shoes, etc.). Of greater importance in heavy-industry products than the duty was assurance that it would not be raised, making investment wasteful. (On this last point, see Michael L. Hoffman, "The Future of GATT," *Lloyd's Bank Review*, October, 1954, pp. 7–9.)

[4] Jacob Viner, "The Role of the United States in the World Economy," in Robert Lekachman, ed., *National Policy for Economic Welfare at Home and Abroad* (New York: Garden City, Doubleday, 1955), p. 179.

as to the renewal of tariff-reducing authority has given the impression that the United States is not fully committed to a policy of freer trade. Though nonrenewal would not abrogate existing agreements and would not force an immediate rise in duties, members of the GATT would be put on their guard against possible withdrawal of concessions at the times provided under the Agreement for review and renewal of concessions. These fears are fed by strong opposition in Congress to the reduction of tariffs and the frequent requests on the floor of Congress for tariff increases or the imposition of quotas.

Opposition to the program

The opposition reflects the desire on the part of many in Congress to return the control of tariff and trade policy to the Legislative Branch. They have considered that Congress has delegated too much authority to the administration (Democratic or Republican), which they have regarded as being oriented to free trade and too willing to sell out the interests of American producers in favor of the broad foreign-policy objectives of international cooperation and collective security. It is, of course, precisely for the reason that legislated tariffs have frequently been more protectionist than the administration desired that the power to negotiate tariffs was requested by the administration.

The 1955 renewal removed the previous authority to reduce 1945 duties by 50 per cent. The President was given authority (a) to reduce any rate above 50 per cent ad valorem (or its equivalent) to that figure and (b) to reduce other rates by 15 per cent of their January, 1955, level. Reductions negotiated cannot be made effective save over a three-year period. Thus under (b), only a 5 per cent reduction may be made in any year. The 1955 renewal continues authority to reduce duties, but in those cases where the former authority of a 50 per cent reduction had not yet been significantly used, the reduction power is greatly curtailed.

Part of the congressional opposition to tariff reduction results from the failure to gain concessions which effectively expand U.S. exports. Countries employing quantitative restrictions and exchange controls concede nothing to the United States through their tariff reductions, because these other restrictions artificially restrain demand. Opponents of the Program have used this failure as an argument for abandoning the technique of reciprocal bargaining. Rather than being an argument for the abandonment of the technique, it would seem to support efforts to bargain U.S. tariffs multilaterally against quantitative restrictions abroad. Multilateral negotiation might be more successful, because some nations fear to remove their quantitative restrictions until others do so. But, under the circumstances of Europe during the postwar decade, removal of the direct controls would have necessitated either devaluation or deflation to prevent a drain on reserves; either would have offset the advantage to U.S. exporters from the removal of direct controls, though not necessarily completely.

Protectionists arguments

Apart from these general criticisms of the technique and locus of authority for tariff reduction, there has been a growing opposition to further reductions of individual duties. This has been evidenced by the number and intensity of arguments in favor of continued and greater protection of specific commodities. A variety of protariff arguments have been used by witnesses testifying before congressional committees. The most frequent arguments used since World War II have been for protection against "pauper labor," "unfair competition" (or price equalization), "specific unemployment," and for the purposes of "retaliation," and "national defense."

The argument that cheap (pauper) foreign labor would reduce wages in the United States, cause unemployment, and/or reduce living standards, and cut profits by forcing lower prices has been used by both management and labor interested in a large number of commodities; e.g., knit gloves; fish and fisheries; dairy products; organic chemicals; leather gloves; glass; wood screws; cordage; luggage; pottery; lace and embroidery; clocks; hats and millinery; pins, clips, and fasteners; band instruments; wine; porcelain; cherries; flower bulbs; coal; lead and zinc; textiles; candy; rubber products; and bicycles.

The pauper-labor argument in some respects borders on and overlaps the "unfair competition" argument—if the foreigner's prices are lower, it is unfair and requires an equalization of prices through a tariff—which has been used by many of the same groups, especially agricultural.[5] Some of these groups were also concerned that the unfair competition from abroad would give rise to unemployment in their particular industry because the factors (particularly labor) were not sufficiently mobile and, in any case, should not be called upon to move for the purpose of a broad foreign policy aimed at helping other countries.

Both the above arguments have been coupled indirectly with that of national defense in that the proponents argue that unemployment in any area would damage national income and prosperity and reduce the ability to maintain the mobilization levels demanded by the security effort. The national-defense argument has been voiced by a wide variety of firms claiming that their products were essential to a military effort—e.g., knit gloves; organic chemicals; balances and weights; wool; wood screws; cordage; watches; pins, clips, and fasteners; porcelain; photographic supplies; soft fibers; insulation board; lace and embroidery; hardboard; powder; coal; lead and zinc; tungsten and manganese; fluor spar; and mica.

---

[5] The voices of various agricultural groups were heard on both sides of the tariff question. Those relying heavily on exports (cotton and wheat) argued for expansion of world trade and consequent reduction of import barriers. Those facing stiffer competition from abroad (fruits and vegetables, dairy products) argued for higher protection, either in tariffs or quotas on imports.

The pros and cons of these arguments have been reviewed in previous chapters, but they have been complicated in the postwar period by the difficulty of determining precisely what is a national defense industry, by the extension of foreign aid, and by the growing pressure to reduce or relieve injury to domestic producers competing with imports.

National defense and the watch industry

A feature distinguishing the postwar tariff debates from those prior to World War II has been the attention given to the national defense. The watch industry's plea for protection provides a good example of the complexity of the issue. The argument for protection of the watch industry rested largely on the danger to the United States of being dependent upon Switzerland for timepieces, timing devices, and other precision instruments during a war. Though it was often granted that, during a war, all industries are essential, proponents of greater protection for the watch industry claimed it to be more essential than the rest, or at least most of the rest.

In the public debates, the industry quoted the admission by the British Chancellor of the Exchequer that during World War II "the inadequacy of the clock and watch industry left a very serious gap in what may be termed [Britain's] industrial armor." This inadequacy allegedly resulted from a contrived German flooding of the British market through subsidies on exports. The U.S. watch industry displayed long lists of obviously important military items which it supplied during World War II. The need for the American watch industry was not, however, based only on what it had produced during past wars, but on the "yet-undreamed-of" military items which the industry might be called upon to produce as a result of military research.

Proponents of greater protection for the industry argued that the skills required in the watchmaking industry have no counterpart in modern industry. Specially trained and highly skilled personnel work at ". . . such tolerances on such microscopic work as to defy imagination." This extraordinary dexterity and almost unbelievable accuracy would soon be lost unless the skills were used *continuously*. If the skilled worker leaves his job because of the industry's difficulty, he may be reluctant to return; and if he does return, extensive retraining—up to three years in some cases—is necessary to regain the skill required for efficient operation. Thus, its spokesmen argued, the industry must have a "healthy" peacetime level of production if it is to serve its essential functions during war. The industry was currently unhealthy, they reported, as seen by the fact that between 1951 and 1954 employment in the manufacture of jeweled movements declined from 8,100 to 4,300 workers.

The opponents of higher protection for the watch industry had an answer to each of these points. The essentiality of the industry was doubted on the ground that the widespread growth of precision work throughout modern American industry had relieved the dependency upon the watch industry. Evidence of this was found in the fact that during World War II nine nonwatchmaking companies provided more workers using those skills usually thought of as uniquely connected with the watch industry than did all the watch companies in the United States combined. Even some Indians in North Dakota successfully adapted their handicraft skills to precision work for the Army during World War II. And companies assembling imported watch movements had supplied the skills and equipment for an impressively large number of military items.

The troubles of the industry were sometimes ascribed to its own shortcomings and not to imports. In the view of some, rather than to restrict imports, competition from imports should be permitted in order to stimulate the industry to greater efficiency. This debate poses the question of why the industry is not already adequately motivated to improve its efficiency; the logical answer might be the existence of monopolistic practices, but no one seemed willing to make such a charge against this industry, though it was used against others employing the national-defense argument.

Apart from the question of efficiency, the experts seem to disagree over the essentiality of the industry. A Department of Defense report stated, "While the jeweled watch facilities listed clearly represented excellent and desirable capacity, the needs of the Department of Defense for industrial capacity clearly demonstrate that no special or preferential treatment for the industry is essential." However, the Director of the Office of Defense Mobilization stated that the industry was essential. An Assistant Secretary of Defense testified that no special treatment should be extended to the jeweled watch industry in preference to the remainder of the horological industry, i.e., assemblers of imported watches. The Department of Defense report and these two views conflicted; according to press reports, the Department of Defense said that its report was intended to say what the Assistant Secretary said. These assertions hardly clarified the question.

If the skills in the industry are considered essential there may be other means of "stockpiling" them—such as through a "reserve training" program, or through a process of breaking down skilled operations so that fewer motions have to be learned, or through a mechanization of skills, as is being done now in the watch and optical-instruments industries. If the industry is considered essential there is still the question of whether aid should not be given through direct subsidies. The argument here is that, since national defense is a benefit to all citizens, its cost should be borne by all through the tax system and not just by those buying watches.

The impact of the tariff on U.S. international relations is well illustrated by the watch-industry case again. When the U.S. government acted in 1954 to raise the duty on watches in the interest of national defense, the Swiss, with 50 per cent of their dollar exports consisting of watch movements and parts were outraged; U.S. restrictions were already curtailing Swiss exports of almonds and cheese. Other European countries worried lest this be the forerunner of a similar action on other imports, which it was not, as it happened. Although the United States action did not enhance its position in world-leadership, it is impossible to measure precisely the damage done, if any, to American relations with Switzerland and other countries.

Further complicating the national-defense question is the fact that increased specialization among countries of the Free World, in which Switzerland should be included, will enhance their combined productive power with favorable effects on the ability to produce military items. This is most easily seen in its direct application to the United States; a contraction of U.S. imports will, for balance-of-payments reasons, force a contraction of U.S. exports, some of which come from national defense industries, e.g., automobiles. Protection of national-defense industries from imports jeopardizes the strength to be obtained through world specialization; yet at some point, trade jeopardizes a nation's own defense by creating dependence. It is difficult to determine the degree to which one nation should depend on others and in what items.

Tariff reduction and foreign aid

The phrase "Trade, not Aid" became a popular plea to substitute U.S. imports via tariff reductions for aid dollars. The advantages noted were that some burden would be relieved from the American taxpayer and that the rest of the world would no longer be dependent on American charity, which was somewhat galling to the recipients at times. But opponents of lower tariffs questioned the morality of imposing upon *certain* domestic industries the burden of caring for Europe. That is, they considered that, if U.S. policy was to help Europe, all Americans should bear the burden through the tax system. (This is a variant of the argument used *against* national-defense tariffs which urges that subsidies paid from taxes be given to assist such industries.)

The importing interests, long vocal but of no great strength, were joined during the past decade by a much more powerful group—large-scale manufacturer-exporters of such items as automobiles, tires, paper, radios, machinery—in advancing the cause of trade. They pointed out that not only was aid costly but also the curtailment of imports eventually meant a reduction of exports. The question, as they saw it, was not whether *one* section (the import-competing) should be forced to adjust to an expansion of trade but *which* sector was going to have to adjust. In order to gain long-run balance of international payments and stop foreign aid, either imports had to increase or exports had to fall, or both.[6]

A major question in the immediate future is whether tariff reduction would cause a rise in U.S. imports sufficient to substitute entirely for foreign aid. To stop aid successfully, foreign countries must be able to export more and U.S. industries have to be able to shift out of import-competing lines into domestic goods and exportables. Until foreign countries remove their restrictions, reduce costs, and begin to live within their means, it is not evident that they will be able to supply more goods to the United States.

Finally, aid makes a *net* contribution to the resources of the recipient; it permits an excess of foreigners' imports over what otherwise would be possible. United States tariff reduction would facilitate the shift of foreign resources into the production of goods for the American market which the reduction of aid would require if foreign nations are to maintain their imports. While this would add to U.S. resources, it would subtract from those of its Allies. The question ultimately is which nation should have the resources equivalent to the foreign aid. It is evident that in so far as U.S. foreign policy objectives are concerned, aid and trade are not satisfactory substitutes.

EASING THE TARIFF REDUCTIONS

In order to make certain that the process of tariff reduction does not injure domestic interests, Congress has imposed peril points and inserted an escape clause. The administration has acquiesced in order to remove some of the objections to tariff reduction.

Peril points

In the 1948 Trade Agreements Act extension, Congress required that the United States Tariff Commission shall determine the duty below which a given domestic industry would be imperiled; this determination is called the "peril point." Congress has repeatedly included it in Trade Agreements Acts as a means of curbing overzealous administrative tariff reduction. However, the President is permitted to reduce the tariff rate below the peril point; he must notify Congress when he intends to do so and why.

The administration has protested that the clause is both unnecessary and undesirable. It was unnecessary, officials testified, because the administration accepted the doctrine that "no American industry or agriculture or segment thereof would be seriously injured under the Act."[7] It was

---

[6] The self-interest of protectionist pleas has long been recognized. The motive of importers and exporters is not different in their pleas for freer trade. A small but revealing instance is that of the National Council of American Importers which opposed an increase in duty-free imports by Americans returning from abroad. (See *New York Times,* June 14, 1954.)

[7] "Trade Agreements Extension Act of 1951," *Hearings on H. R. 1612,* U.S. Senate, Committee on Finance, 82d Cong., 1st Sess., February–March, 1951, p. 15.

undesirable because it introduced rigidities into a program which required considerable flexibility for bargaining purposes. The Secretary of State went so far as to quote approvingly a press editorial stating that "the philosophy underlying the 'peril point' amendment, however, is the philosophy of a country cowering in its corner and unwilling to put its great system of free enterprise to the competitive test."[8]

The President has, in a few instances, authorized U.S. negotiators to go below the rates set as the "peril point" by the Tariff Commission. The extent to which the procedure has actually hampered U.S. efforts to reduce tariffs reciprocally is not public information.

Escape clause

The escape clause permits either party to a trade agreement to modify or withdraw a concession which it finds has caused or threatens to cause serious injury to domestic producers. The modification can take the form of a higher duty, the imposition of a quota, or some other measure to prevent or remedy the injury. But the injury must have been caused, at least in part, by the concession. An escape clause was written into the 1943 Mexican reciprocal trade agreement. An Executive order (1947), issued under pressure from Congress, required that the clause be placed in all new agreements, and a similar clause was included in the GATT. In addition, GATT permits nations adversely affected by removal of a concession under an escape-clause action to withdraw their own concessions or modify their duties (or other practices) to compensate for the loss of the benefit; or, the country initially withdrawing its concession can offer a new one. The advantage of having an organization which "extends" these privileges is that it controls the changes and modifications and thus prevents unnecessary and undesirable retaliation.

To obtain relief under U.S. legislation, the injured American party makes application to the Tariff Commission. The Commission then makes a study to determine whether there is injury (or threat of injury) from increased imports as a result of a concession; the Commission publishes its hearings and findings, recommending either no relief or some relief by the President, who must decide what action to take if any. A first test of injury is whether imports of like or directly competing items have increased relative to domestic production or absolutely. Injury may not be found even if imports have increased relatively, e.g., if the imports are not "directly competitive." An important part of the determination of injury is the definition of an "industry"; how many firms compose an industry? The 1955 legislation permitted relief when only a "portion or subdivision" of an industry is injured; and the fact that a firm could shift into other lines or increase production of other of its multi-products is not to be taken into account in the determination of injury or its threat.

---

[8] *Ibid.*, p. 7.

Applications for relief were not numerous before 1951, and relief had been extended only in one or two cases. Congressmen felt that the administration was not carrying out the intent of the clause. In 1951, Congress put the clause for the first time into the Trade Agreements Act; it strengthened the clause by requiring the Tariff Commission to make a formal investigation, whereas before it did so only if there was "good and sufficient reason." In view of complaints by industry representatives that it was very difficult to prove that injury was the result of greater imports, Congress gave new instructions to the Commission as to how to tell whether injury was sustained or threatened as a result of imports arising out of concession. The Commission was ordered to "take into consideration a downward trend in production, employment, prices, profits, or wages in the domestic industry concerned, or a decline in sales, an increase in imports, either actual or relative to domestic production, a higher or growing inventory, or a decline in the proportion of the domestic market supplied by domestic producers."[9] Thus almost any adverse situation in production of a product affected by a concession could be cause for tariff relief. Finally, in order to place a little more pressure on the President to provide relief if the Commission so recommended, Congress required him to report to the appropriate committees of Congress within sixty days if he declined relief, stating his reasons. Soon after these new procedures were enacted, applications jumped in number, investigations multiplied, and recommendations for relief rose.

The President has extended relief in only a few cases: women's fur felt hat bodies, hatters' fur, alsike clover seed, dried figs, bicycles, watches, and linen toweling. The relief so provided is supposed to last only as long as the threat of injury lasts.

The satisfaction abroad with the small number of requests granted has been dulled by the fact that most of the cases took several months before a decision was made, and an adverse decision did not prevent an industry from reapplying. As further evidence that the fears of Europeans were correct, Congress, considering the relief extended under the escape clause as inadequate, changed the procedures in the 1955 legislation to make it still easier for an industry (or segment thereof) to prove injury and thus obtain a recommendation for relief from the Tariff Commission. Under the new procedure, relief was extended to the bicycle industry by a 50 per cent increase in the duty. This action hit British and Austrian exporters, who had expanded production for the American market to earn needed dollars.

Foreign governments expressed fear that any success in exporting to the U.S. economy, as they were encouraged to do under the European Recovery Program and since, would be met by a withdrawal of tariff concessions. Thus their efforts to export would be wasted. The increased

---

[9] P. L. 50, Sec. 7, 82d Cong., 1st Sess.

Table 13. Selected Dutiable Imports and Ratio to U.S. Production, 1951*

Commodity	Imports (in millions of dollars)	Per cent of Pro-duction	Commodity	Imports (in millions of dollars)	Per cent of Pro-duction
Mineral, Metals & Material:			*Apparel:*		
Iron & steel-structural	44.5	10	Wool		
pig iron	49.2	1	apparel	543.8	209
scrap	13.2	½–1	noils	19.5	52
Nonferrous ores &			top	24.4	5
metals & ferro-			Woolens & worsteds	43.4	4
alloys			Rayon & acetate yarn	4.2	½–1
manganese ore	46.7	657	Staple fiber	38.5	26
ferromanganese	20.1	16	Fur felt hats &		
tungsten ore	17.4	76	hat bodies	2.6	3
aluminum	59.3	20	Boots, shoes &		
bauxite	17.9	143	footwear	11.0	½–1
magnesium	1.2	6	Leather gloves	3.0	7
nickel (metal)	81.5	2800			
lead	78.2	27	*Agricultural Products:*		
zinc	66.6	25	Sugar, cane & beet	389.9	76
copper	270.5	39	Tobacco-cigarette leaf	54.9	5
Petroleum & its			cigar filler	20.7	25
products	533.6	10–15	cigar wrapper	5.9	8
Synthetic rubber	5.7	1	Butter	0.03	1/200
Mercury	6.6	438	Potatoes	5.2	1
Lumber			Tomatoes, fresh	13.7	12
softwood	193.2	8	Cotton		
hardwood	35.3	5	long-staple	29.0	36
plywood	8.3	2	short-staple	10.9	½–1
veneers	8.2	12	Cheeses		
			Italian	7.8	25
Manufactures:			Swiss & Gruyère	5.7	12
Earthenware &			Cheddar	3.3	1
chinaware			Roquefort &		
(table and art)	30.2	26	blue-mold	2.8	‡
Glassware (handmade)	4.5	14	Edam & Gouda	1.5	173
Optical instrument			misc.	1.3	3
glass	0.1	17	Fish		
Optical instruments	6.0	12	fresh or frozen	306.6	20
Musical instruments	12.8	7	tuna (in oil)	1.4	1
Watches, movements			other (in oil)	6.3	441
& parts	61.5	95	Grains		
Jewel bearings, watches	4.0	†	barley	19.6	6
Clock & clock			oats	42.2	4
movements	1.4	2	rice	0.1	1/20
Automobiles	26.5	⅓	rye	2.5	8
Motorcycles	3.5	39	wheat	2.1	1/10
Aircraft	9.4	7	Nuts		
Bicycles	5.0	8	almonds	3.5	18
Sewing machines	14.0	9	walnuts	3.5	11
Whiskey	33.8	5	filberts	2.3	92
			pecans	0.3	1
			peanuts	neg.	

* Imports not dutiable and imports of goods not produced in the U.S. are excluded; the items included are a selection of import-competing items coming in under duties.

† Almost no production in the U.S., so ratio would approach infinity.

‡ Roquefort not produced in the U.S. The figure on blue-mold production is not available, but the imports have been held down while domestic production has risen substantially since the war.

SOURCE: Howard S. Piquet, *Aid, Trade, and the Tariff*, New York: Crowell, 1953, Chapter 10.

number of applications under the escape clause (even if relief was not given) was sufficient to give them pause. The State Department tried to calm their fears by asserting that it was the continued policy of the U.S. government to extend relief only in genuine cases of serious injury or threat thereof and not merely to ease the pressure of foreign competition.

While the injury felt by a given firm, industry, or segment thereof may be quite real, a study made by Howard Piquet of the effect of a suspension of *all* duties suggested that it would be minor for the economy as a whole; the required over-all adjustments would be no greater than those involved in technological change. In figures, the value of imports of items which would receive the greatest competition from abroad (that is, with 10 to 90 per cent of domestic consumption being imported) after the suspension of duties would be between 3 to 6 per cent of total U.S. production of manufactures, minerals, and agricultural products.[10] Table 13 shows the extent to which imports "compete with" domestic production of selected items.

While the escape-clause action must be qualified by the broad national interest, the injury to a given firm is still significant. The intent of Congress is that such injury shall not be permitted. If duties are to be reduced, some consideration might best be given those who suffer a loss for a national gain.

Assistance to "injured" industries

One of the most appealing arguments against tariff reduction is that it would dislocate industry and cause a loss of capital and employment during the period of displacement. The displacement may be prevented, as in the peril-point procedure and the escape clause; this is the most satisfactory solution to the import-competing industries because they do not want to be driven out of business, nor do they want subsidies; they just want a chance to compete on a "fair basis"—with a tariff. But if the gains from trade are desired, the displacement may be eased by assisting the movement of factors to new employments.

The displacement may involve long-term unemployment in some areas, with workers going on relief rolls because of lack of adequate mobility. In others, the period of unemployment might be quite short if the capital equipment and workers' skills were readily transferred to other pursuits or if new pursuits could be transferred to their locale.

The impact of increased imports could be relieved either through compensating injured parties for their losses and/or facilitating their readjustment and transfer into new occupations.[11] Where the problem is to

---

[10] See Howard S. Piquet. *Aid, Trade, and the Tariff* (New York: Crowell, 1953), Chapter 6.

[11] Compensation through outright payment to damaged businesses is not usually proposed. Such direct payments would not only tend to retard a movement out of

avoid injury to an industry or segment thereof by accelerating its movement into other lines of production, there are several measures at hand, such as tax relief and "incentive subsidies," which would be extended only if proof were shown that the firm was making every effort to move out.

But an entire community, reliant for its employment on a single industry knocked out by imports, would require aid of a different kind and magnitude. Here an extensive program of community redevelopment to attract new industries would be helpful. Some New England towns have shifted successfully in the face of the movement of textile firms to the South. These communities have made analyses of the area's assets and liabilities, of possible industrial locations; they have raised money for plants, built them, and rented them to new enterprises. The federal government could assist these plans by providing accelerated depreciation allowances to plants moving into depressed areas, extending loans or guarantees to help finance construction, and giving assistance in market analyses and in engineering problems, etc. Export industries which were expanding their production and sales under the increased volume of trade could be encouraged to establish branches in the areas where the import-competing industries were failing.

Finally, where the displacement of individual workers cannot be remedied through either of the above methods of diversifying the firm's production or the employment within the community, more direct means are at hand of encouraging individual mobility or of relieving their unemployment. The existing techniques of unemployment insurance, old-age and survivors' insurance, employment services, and veterans' training could be expanded. Special training and moving allowances could be granted. Where the workers' age and seniority provide additional handicaps to moving, old-age benefits could be accelerated to age 55 or 60, and compensation payments could be extended to make up for losses in paid vacations and other privileges going with seniority. Of course, the longer-run solution in all cases is in the expansion of the economy and the attainment of greater mobility, including movement of resources geographically and product diversification. During a period of continued growth within the

---

the industry but would also run counter to the general concept of free enterprise in the U.S. economy and would set highly undesirable precedents. In its *Report to the President and Congress,* the Randall Commission on Foreign Economic Policy stated that it could not recommend that the government assume any responsibility for adjustments to increased imports, for the effect of tariff changes is but one aspect of the entire problem of human welfare; it stated further that "In a free economy, some displacement of workers and some injury to institutions is unavoidable. It may come about through technological change, alterations in consumer preferences, exhaustion of a mineral resource, new inventions, new taxes, or many other causes. Since it has never been seriously proposed that the burden of all such injury arising in a free economy should be assumed by the Government, the Commission felt that it too was not appropriate to propose such a plan in the tariff area only." (January, 1954, p. 54.)

economy it is much easier to absorb stiffer foreign competition, and it may not be necessary to take any governmental action to relieve such competition.

So far the government has not seen fit to act on the several proposals for increasing mobility in the face of larger imports. This may reflect the belief that the increase in aggregate real income of the nation from greater trade is justification enough for expanded trade; since *any* economic change alters the distribution of total income, the effects of greater imports should not be given *special* consideration. However, experience shows that adequate compensation or relief reduces the opposition to any reform, and since tariff reduction requires legislative approval, it will probably be necessary to find ways to remove the opposition of pressure groups.[12] At present, these groups seek only to slow or stop the reduction of tariff barriers; if they find this impossible, they may accept the change more readily if their interests seem to be taken into account through other measures.

C.   ADMINISTRATIVE RESTRICTIONS ON IMPORTS

Customs administration has become increasingly complex as the ability to commit successful fraud and to evade the laws has increased. While the administrative procedures to enforce the law have grown up, they have provided protection over and above that through the tariffs which they were meant to support. Most nations normally employ customs procedures and other administrative measures to curtail unwanted imports.

CUSTOMS SIMPLIFICATION

Most exporters and importers complain about the restrictiveness of customs procedures. Members of the GATT have agreed that these procedures must be modified if trade is to be expanded. As they stand now, there are an excessive number of complicated documents which must be filled out to get goods through customs. The procedures are often so long-drawn-out that goods deteriorate or become useless while waiting for clearance; for example, cut flowers delivered by air sometimes wither before they get through Customs.

---

[12] Dr. Viner has observed that "According to some historians, the abolition of slavery in the British Empire came a generation sooner than it would have otherwise because the Government gave generous compensation. Similarly, the British temperance movement in the 1870's and 1880's was able to reduce the opposition because the Government reduced the number of liquor licenses by buying up those it regarded as in excess at a fair appraisal of their market value before the new legislation. The lesson I draw from this is that one of the arguments for compensation is not merely the equity of it but also that it makes reform possible by diminishing opposition." (Klaus Knorr and Gardner Patterson, *A Critique of the Randall Commission Report* [Princeton, N.J.: International Finance Section and Center of International Studies, Princeton University, February, 1954], p. 30.)

The determination of the duty and of the valuation on which it is to be imposed may take quite a long time and be subject to change. In many cases a chemical analysis is necessary to determine the elements of a product, sometimes taking several years to complete the job. If a duty is contested, it has to go through customs court, which has a docket list of waiting cases so long as to require over a year (and frequently two, three and four years) for the case to be decided. If the U.S. importer takes the goods in for sale without having received a firm decision, he does not know what his costs will be. And if he accepts the duty first imposed, feeling that he can do a profitable business importing under the given duty, he has no assurance that a higher duty will not be levied on subsequent shipments.

The duty to be imposed is usually chosen so that the highest possible rate is employed. For example, ashtrays could be classified as a "household article" at 15 per cent duty, or as a "smoking requisite" at 30 per cent duty, or as "luxury earthenware" at 50 per cent duty. Items made of several materials usually carry the duty applicable to the material carrying the highest rate regardless of the proportion of materials in the total. For example, a rubber tire of both synthetic and natural rubber will take the duty on whichever is higher. Again, a cotton shirt with an embroidered initial on it takes the much higher rate of "lace and embroidery." The various procedures of valuation have raised the ad valorem duty, as it would have applied to export value, from levels under 100 per cent to well over 1000 per cent in some cases and in the case of one chemical to over 8000 per cent.

Under the procedures *before* 1956, an import was valued according to export or foreign value, whichever was higher. Export value is the usual wholesale value in the foreign market for trade with the United States. Foreign value is the usual wholesale value in the foreign market for home consumption, including domestic taxes of the country of export even though not applied by that country to exports. When foreign value was used, exporters were often subjected to investigations of their cost and invoice procedures which were both annoying and time-consuming, delaying the valuation procedure. In 1956, legislation was passed making export value the basis for valuation of imports, when ascertainable; when not, alternative means are provided. The valuation of selected items (mostly chemicals) is on the higher basis of American selling price.

The change to export value has been estimated to result in a reduction of import valuations by as much as 16 per cent, but on the average only 2½ per cent below foreign value. This difference is a result not only of the removal of foreign taxes but also of the fact that wholesale prices for export are often subject to greater discounts compared with domestic sales because of the larger quantities involved in any one sale. Only 30 per cent of imports subject to ad valorem rates were calculated on foreign value in 1954, but Congress has provided that the new export value basis would not be used if it caused a reduction of import valuations by more than 5 per cent.

Foreign values will still have to be calculated in order to determine whether antidumping duties should be imposed. Under present law, a complaint to the U.S. Treasury that a foreign good is being sold in the U.S. market at less than it is being sold at home will bring a prohibition of further imports and an investigation. Some firms desiring relief from foreign competition have been able to stop imports long enough to regain a significant share of the U.S. market; such was the case with synthetic fibers from Germany, which lost her U.S. market during an antidumping investigation despite the fact that the charge was proved false. The absence of regular calculations of foreign value will delay even more the determination of whether dumping exists.

In addition to regulations concerning the application of duties, customs officials are required to administer various sanitary regulations. These are often imposed in such a way as to make trade unprofitable if not impossible. For example, if an official considers that a shipment of foodstuffs is contaminated, he may hold it for sampling; the whole shipment may deteriorate or become contaminated during the investigation. Regulations on meat shipments have been interpreted so that imports of beef have been prohibited from a country where hoof-and-mouth disease has been found, despite the fact that the disease was in areas far distant from the cattle exported. Other regulations, such as those on packaging to prevent "misleading containers" from being used, have hampered imports by raising costs to producers. Finally, requirements as to marks of origin which state that all imports must show clearly the country of origin make it necessary to process shipments to the American market differently from other production and add considerably to the cost; for example, one customs officer denied entry of an English manufacturer's loose-leaf catalogue because *each* page was not marked "printed in England," though this was on the cover. Some of the obsolete marking requirements were removed in 1953, especially those on knives, scissors, and surgical instruments, which had provided significant supratariff protection on these items.

Efforts have been made through the GATT to bring customs procedures into some semblance of similarity among countries. But, as in the United States, the legislative process to change administration procedures is quite difficult and long-drawn-out. Some easing of requirements was accomplished by an administrative directive to officials, in 1949, from the Secretary of the Treasury, to be more cooperative with importers. Also, the Customs Simplification Act of 1953 streamlined the procedures for settling import valuations; it resulted in a reduction in the number of import transactions on which final liability for duties remained unsettled from a peak of 900,000 in September, 1953, to 630,000 in mid-1956.

The GATT provides that members shall seek to simplify their customs procedures; some specific measures have been suggested, but no formal agreement has yet been attempted. If and when GATT goes into problems of customs valuation and tariff classifications, strong efforts will be required to counter the pressure of domestic groups, customs brokers, lawyers, and officials whose livelihood depends on the continuing complexity of the regulations. Yet progress in this field could eventually be more significant in expanding trade than the tariff reductions so far negotiated.

BUY AMERICAN ACT

Another significant deterrent to increased imports into the United States has been the Buy American regulations. The legislation (passed March, 1933) prohibits federal procurement of foreign materials or commodities manufactured of foreign materials, unless these items are not available in the United States or unless the prices of corresponding domestic goods are "unreasonable." The administrative determination of the difference between foreign prices and "reasonable" domestic prices was that the latter should be more than 25 per cent higher than the former, giving domestic producers supratariff protection of this amount.[13] The Act, however, also permits purchases abroad when domestic procurement is "inconsistent with the public interest"; this permission was apparently the basis for purchases of strategic goods.

The rule has been applied not only to purchases of goods for use in the United States but also for items to be shipped and used abroad and even to the materials (such as wool and cotton) used by private industry in manufacturing items for sale to the U.S. government. It has proven quite costly to the U.S. government. The administration could have obtained foreign goods at lower costs, and domestic bids would undoubtedly have been lower to meet the competition. Savings, which would occur if the provision were removed, have been conservatively estimated at $100 million a year; with another $100 million yearly coming in as tariff revenue from larger imports. With government purchases of materials and equipment running over $30 billion yearly, some significant increase in imports could be expected. Upon the urging of other governments and several U.S. advisory commissions, the President in December, 1954, reduced the "reasonable" differential from 25 per cent to from 6 to 10 per cent. This margin of protection is doubled when the American bidder is located in an area of depressed employment.

As long as these restrictions on foreign buying and the stringent cus-

---

[13] Since the "whole cost," including transportation, assembly, tariff, etc., is the basis for the calculation, the actual differential between foreign cost and domestic price sometimes ran to 60 per cent. The impact of the federal requirement is reinforced by the existence of both state and local government requirements which favor purchases within their jurisdictions. Some building codes also give specific preference to materials of local origin.

toms procedures remain, the U.S. government's plea for greater cooperation in GATT and for relaxation of trade barriers sounds somewhat hollow, regardless of the fact that its own practices are, on the whole, less restrictive than those of most other member nations.

SELECTED READINGS

Ashworth, William. *A Short History of the International Economy, 1850–1950.* London: Longmans, 1952. A brief but accurate review of the commercial and financial policies arising out of postwar nationalism.

Chalmers, Henry. *World Trade Policies.* Berkeley: University of California Press, 1953. A compilation of annual reports on world trade conditions and the problems facing the United States from 1920 to 1953.

Brown, W. A., Jr. *The United States and the Restoration of World Trade.* Washington: Brookings, 1950. An extensive analysis and appraisal of the ITO Charter and the General Agreement on Tariffs and Trade.

Diebold, W. J. *The End of the ITO.* Essays in International Finance, No. 16. October, 1952, Princeton, N. J.: International Finance Section, Princeton University Press. The reasons for the U.S. failure to ratify the ITO Charter are analyzed.

Elliott, G. A. *Tariff Procedures and Trade Barriers.* Toronto: University of Toronto Press, 1955. An extensive analysis with special reference to U.S.-Canadian relations.

GATT. *International Trade, 1954.* Geneva: The Contracting Parties to the General Agreement on Tariffs and Trade, July, 1955. This is the GATT's annual report on the developments in the structure and pattern of international trade, the barriers and controls imposed, and the activities of the members of GATT. Previous reports appeared under the same title, though the first reports had various titles.

Hawkins, Harry C. *Commercial Treaties and Agreements.* New York: Rinehart, 1951. An examination of the content of commercial treaties, of the most-favored-nation clause, tariff specialization, import and export restrictions, and state-trading.

Humphrey, Don D. *American Imports.* New York: Twentieth Century Fund, 1955. An extensive examination of the composition of American imports, injury from tariff reduction, and the desirability of policies to ease the adjustment to increased imports.

International Finance Section. *Survey of United States International Finance.* Princeton, N.J.: Princeton University Press. A series of annual surveys of U.S. foreign economic policies; they were published for the years 1949 through 1953 and contain extensive reviews of U.S. trade and tariff policies and practices.

Joint Economic Committee of the U.S. Congress. *Report on Defense Essentiality and Foreign Economic Policy,* Senate Rpt. No. 2629, 84th Cong. 2d Sess., July 18, 1956. A case study on the watch industry and precision skills as related to tariff protection for national defense.

Knorr, Klaus, and Gardner Patterson (eds.). *A Critique of the Randall Commission Report.* Princeton, N.J.: International Finance Section and Center of International Studies, Princeton University Press, 1954. A report of a conference composed of experts on international affairs which examined the Randall Commission report on Foreign Economic Policy; it includes some incisive criticism of the approach and recommendations of the Commission and the way which the United States is moving in its foreign economic policies.

Kravis, Irving B. "The Trade Agreements Escape Clause," *American Economic Review,* XLIV (June, 1954), 319–338. A critique of the role of the escape clause, its use, and the criteria for determining serious injury under it.

League of Nations. *Commercial Policy in the Inter-War Period; Commercial Policy in the Post-War World.* Geneva: 1942, 1945. These reports of the Economic and Financial Committees of the League review the interwar experience as it bears on postwar policy problems and provide the background for the discussions of international cooperation in commercial policies.

Letiche, J. M. *Reciprocal Trade Agreements in the World Economy.* New York: King's Crown Press, 1948. A study for the Committee on International Economic Policy covering U.S. policy on equality of treatment, the Trade Agreements Act of 1934, the effects of the agreements during the 1930's, and some criticisms of their results.

Public Advisory Board for Mutual Security. *A Trade and Tariff Policy in the National Interest.* Washington: February, 1953. A report prepared for the President under the chairmanship of Daniel W. Bell. It was begun by the Truman and presented to the Eisenhower administration; it was not acted upon, but it provides an excellent analysis of the problems and policies discussed in this chapter.

Randall Commission on Foreign Economic Policy. *Report to the President and Congress.* Washington: Government Printing Office, January, 1954. The recommendations of the Commission appointed by President Eisenhower to reconcile varying viewpoints on U.S. foreign economic policies.

————. *Staff Papers.* Washington: Government Printing Office, February, 1954. The papers prepared by experts serving the Commission, covering the entire gamut of U.S. foreign economic policy; Chapters 6, 7, and 8 provide 200 pages of discussion of topics touched on in this chapter.

Schattschneider, E. E. *Politics, Pressures and the Tariff.* New York: Prentice-Hall, 1935. An excellent study of free enterprise and lobbying before Congress in relation to the Hawley-Smoot Tariff in 1929–1930.

United Nations. *The Quest for Freer Trade.* New York: 1955. This pamphlet examines the impact of nationalism on commercial policies and balance of payments difficulties and reviews the actions taken to remove or reduce the obstacles to freer trade since World War I.

U.S. Tariff Commission. *Operation of the Trade Agreements Program.* Washington: Government Printing Office. A series of yearly reports, beginning in 1949 but extending back to cover the period since 1934; the reports give information on current legislation, on reciprocal trade negotiations, on developments relating to the provisions and administration of the General

Agreement on Tariffs and Trade, on U.S. action under the escape clause, and on changes in tariffs and direct controls of countries with which the United States has trade agreements.

Vernon, Raymond. *America's Foreign Trade Policy and the GATT*. Essays in International Finance, No. 21. Princeton, N.J.: International Finance Section, Princeton University Press, October, 1954. A discussion of GATT's origin, performance and future.

———. "Organizing for World Trade," *International Conciliation,* No. 505. New York: Carnegie Endowment for International Peace, November, 1955. A quick review of the interwar and post-World War II developments which surrounded the creation of GATT, an analysis of GATT's operation, and an examination of the role of an OTC.

24 Agricultural Support and Trade Policies

Agriculture provides the livelihood for over half the world's people. In the poorer areas of the world, over two-thirds of the people are of necessity employed in agriculture; in the United States, only about one-sixth of the working force is engaged in farming. Countries such as the United States, Canada, Australia, and Argentina, which are large agricultural producers are also large exporters of food and other farm products. Exports of wheat, cotton, rice, and tobacco constitute from 20 to 25 per cent of U.S. production of these items. And the United States relies upon foreign producers for many primary products and foodstuffs, such as coffee and cacao, bananas, jute, etc.

Many nations, including the United States, are dependent for large amounts of their income on agricultural production and exports. Changes in agricultural prices and incomes are of primary importance not only to domestic trade but also to international trade policy. Agriculture is subject to wide fluctuations in both prices and incomes. During the two decades 1929–1948, agricultural prices in the United States ranged between index numbers of 50 and 190, while industrial prices ranged between 70 and 150, with the yearly changes in agricultural prices being much greater than those in industrial prices.

Governments of many countries have felt it necessary during the past several decades to protect their agricultural sectors. The disturbances of World War I contributed greatly to these policies. The war brought many regions outside of Europe into large-scale production of basic foodstuffs and primary products; for example, vast areas of the United States, Australia, Argentina, and Canada were put into wheat. High levels of demand continued after the war because Europe could not meet its needs out of its own production. As European agriculture was reconstructed, little attention was paid to the fact that other countries had encroached on Europe's former

509

markets and were unwilling to return to prewar patterns of production and trade. Total production increased after the war because of the continued cultivation of new areas and the use of new techniques developed during the war. Individual farmers did not attempt to increase their incomes by restricting output. Despite the fact that the products generally faced an inelastic market demand, each individual farmer faced an elastic demand and considered it the wisest policy to produce to his utmost.

By 1925, agricultural surpluses were spread over the entire world. Wheat stocks rose from 9 million tons to over 21 million in 1929; stocks of sugar, coffee, rubber, copper, nitrates, and other products swelled. Attempts by national governments to hold the mounting stocks off the markets failed to prevent a decline in prices, which was accelerated by the Depression during the 1930's. National and international techniques of market restriction were intensified, but farm incomes remained low. Protective devices were adopted by the United States throughout the 1920's and 1930's, including tariffs, quotas, and subsidies. But they did not increase the prosperity of the U.S. farmer because U.S. production was already sufficient for the home market and surpluses had to be sold on sagging world markets.

Other countries attempted to keep their agricultural incomes and employment up by imposing import quotas on, and subsidizing production and export of, foodstuffs and primary products. Despite the fact that Holland depended heavily on a large volume of international trade for her national income, she imposed a host of restrictions to help her farmers. The consequent loss of real national income which she suffered reflects the sacrifice a nation may feel compelled to make in order to satisfy one claimant group.

One restriction led to another. Tariffs were raised, but they could do little to prevent the decline in prices resulting from domestic surpluses. Export subsidies were a reply to higher import duties abroad, and the subsidies in turn led to further import quotas and/or countervailing duties —i.e., penalty rates aimed at offsetting the foreign subsidy.

Relief did not come to the agricultural sectors of most countries until the extraordinary demands of World War II removed the surpluses. But as in the preceding postwar period, wartime expansion of capacity and agricultural support policies have increased the world supply of agricultural products beyond what will be absorbed at free market prices. Thus, save for a few years during wartime, the status of agriculture has been one of overproduction.

Since there can be no overproduction in a market sense if prices are permitted to move freely, "surpluses" exist only when prices are not permitted to clear the market. Governments have been reluctant to let the large supply force prices down to the point where farm incomes are so low as to depress not only the agricultural sector but also the industrial sector through loss of farm demand. They have taken measures aimed at increasing farm incomes, but they have not always removed the surpluses which were the cause of lower prices. And they have often employed measures which frequently increased friction among trading nations, including quantitative restrictions, subsidies, and commodity agreements.

The views of U.S. farm groups on such measures have been divergent. Measures which would help the commercial farmer have little effect on the subsistence farmer, and means to support production of import-competing items hinder efforts to support production through the export of other agricultural products. Efforts to remove surpluses of certain items through selling abroad at prices lower than at home, i.e., dumping, are resented by competing exporters overseas. And efforts to keep domestic prices high require the exclusion of imports in order not to spread the support to the entire world. Thus, some measures of farm support make more difficult (if not impossible in some instances) the pursuit of liberal trade policies.

A. U.S. PRICE-SUPPORT PROGRAM

The U.S. government has attempted since the mid-1930's to maintain the level of farm income at a parity with prices which would have to be paid by farmers for nonfarm products.[1] The methods employed were those of buying goods and holding them off the market, of destroying goods, of production controls, and of loans to guarantee minimum prices.

Price support takes the form of purchases by the government or loans with the commodities as collateral. This support is largely on commodities of which the United States is a large exporter: corn, wheat, cotton, rice, peanuts, tobacco. But support is also given to items which would normally have significant import competition (wool, tung nuts, mohair) and some "domestic" products (such as hogs, milk, eggs, chickens, and potatoes). In order to prevent an undue increase in government purchases of items receiving price support, marketing quotas and or acreage allotments have been imposed.

When world prices of any supported items are lower than those in the United States, the higher prices in the U.S. markets attract foreign sellers. If the larger imports are permitted to enter, total supplies in the United States increase, making support of farm prices more difficult and costly for the government (taxpayers). If the government merely continued its support, foreign producers would share in the support program, and the over-all cost to the U.S. taxpayer would be considerable. If foreigners

---

[1] Parity was defined in 1933 in the intent of Congress to ". . . re-establish prices to farmers at a level that will give agricultural commodities a purchasing power with respect to articles that farmers buy, equivalent to the purchasing power of agricultural commodities in the base period . . . August 1909–July 1914." (Agricultural Adjustment Act of 1933.)

are not to share in the supports, their products must be excluded, as at present they are through quotas and other devices.

Furthermore, when world prices are less than U.S. support prices, potential U.S. export producers turn to the domestic market; other countries then increase their exports to non-U.S. markets to take the place of U.S. goods withdrawn from world markets. Total world supplies are increased by the growing production within the United States, induced by the supports, and by the increased production elsewhere. But as the U.S. surpluses held by the government accumulate, pressure to dispose of them through exports becomes greater. Efforts are then made to increase U.S. exports through subsidies or to dispose of the surpluses by other means.

Thus the domestic program of price support drives a wedge between the domestic and world prices. It leads to the use of import quotas and export subsidies which the U.S. government has urged other nations to give up in the attempt to expand trade along multilateral, nondiscriminatory lines. While other countries may be practicing the same sorts of restrictions on agricultural imports and attempting to increase exports, and while they may be wholly sympathetic to U.S. objectives of stabilizing farm incomes, they cannot help but point to the contradiction between principles and practices of the U.S. government. The conflict arises not so much in the objectives of higher and stable incomes for farmers as in the means of implementing them.

B.   IMPORT QUOTAS

The agricultural support prices must be protected by excluding foreign products when they are likely to be imported in significant volume. Since the high domestic prices create an artificial demand, foreign exports are attracted to the U.S. market. To permit other countries to export larger volumes to the United States would reallocate world resources as compared to what would occur without the price supports or under free trade.

IMPOSITION OF QUOTAS

The President is required to impose fees or quotas on imports when he determines that they are entering in amounts which tend to render ineffective or materially interfere with any domestic farm program.[2] He is authorized to impose them to aid any domestic agricultural program irrespective of agreements with other nations. When the U.S. government signed the General Agreement on Tariffs and Trade, it contained a provision permitting import quotas when joined with domestic price-support programs

---

[2] Section 22 of the Agricultural Adjustment Act (1935), The Philippine Trade Act of 1946, The Second Decontrol Act of 1947, The Sugar Act of 1948, and The Defense Production Act of 1950.

employing production or marketing restrictions. But the United States employs price supports on some items which are restricted neither in production nor in marketing. Its international commitment conflicted with its farm support and import quota practices. A "reconciliation" was gained by a waiver of the GATT in 1954; instead of changing procedures, the United States government insisted that its actions be permitted.

United States insistence on this change brought considerable opposition from other members, though they were in general sympathy with U.S. objectives as to her agricultural sector because many of the opposing countries were themselves restricting agricultural imports and supporting domestic production. Even countries like Switzerland and Belgium, greatly dependent on international trade for their national income, cannot remove uneconomic protection of farmers; and Germany, which has been highly successful since 1948 in pursuing freer trade, still maintains strong protection for farmers, despite the fact that other countries would buy more German goods if they could sell more vegetables and dairy products to Germany.

The frictions arising from import quotas are exemplified by those on butter, cheese, and dairy products.[3] These quotas, imposed in 1951, raised immediate complaints from foreign countries (mostly ERP recipients) who relied on the U.S. market. They hit Denmark, Holland, and Italy hardest, just at the time when they were having difficulty earning dollars and just after they had successfully expanded their investment in cheese exports under ECA's advice.

The administration asked for a repeal of these quotas on the grounds that the U.S. interest in dairy products was more in exports than in imports, that they harmed European countries which had been encouraged to export these products to the United States, and that members of the GATT had threatened to retaliate against exports of U.S. apples, tobacco, and other products. The cheese producers replied by asking for even broader restrictions, stating that the dairy industry was essential to national security in that it maintained the "cow population." The evidence showed that less than 5 per cent of U.S. consumption of dairy products came from abroad, that these items were usually noncompetitive with U.S. goods, and that the quota authority had been successfully lobbied for by one small sector of dairy processors—the one making blue cheese. Despite these arguments,

---

[3] Section 104 of the Defense Production Act of 1951 (under the so-called "cheese amendment") required that "no imports of any such commodity or product shall be admitted . . . which the Secretary of Agriculture determines would (a) impair or reduce the domestic production of any such commodity or product below present production levels, or below such higher levels as the Secretary of Agriculture may deem necessary in view of domestic and international conditions, or (b) interfere with the orderly domestic storing and marketing of any such commodity or product, or (c) result in any unnecessary burden of expenditures under any Government price support program." (P. L. 96, 82d Cong.)

the amendment was not dropped until 1953. Even then a wider authority was given the President and the Secretary of Agriculture to impose emergency quotas or embargoes.[4]

REALLOCATION OF RESOURCES

The basic objection to import quotas is that they cause a deviation from the allocation of resources which would exist under free trade. The restriction of imports of goods in which the United States is not self-sufficient means that prices paid are higher than they would otherwise be and that the domestic supply is increased as compared to what would exist with freer trade.

A good example is the sugar quota scheme, under which the U.S. government exercises a cartel-like control over sugar imports. The quota system not only protects domestic producers by guaranteeing them a specified portion of the market but also gives preference to certain territories and to Cuba and the Philippines. Cuba ships about 40 per cent of the entire United States supplies,[5] while mainland producers retain about 28 per cent. Under domestic pressure, Congress allocates a larger share to U.S. producers than would exist under free trade, and nothing has been done to make certain that the growing U.S. demand is allocated to foreign suppliers. Several U.S. government commissions studying foreign economic policy have urged that the allocation of future increases in U.S. demand be made entirely to foreign suppliers and in such a way as to moderate the discriminatory features of the system. But in its 1956 legislation Congress continued the same general quota scheme as before and even gave 55 per cent of the future growth quota to U.S. producers.

Because quotas restrict U.S. agricultural imports, they, along with domestic price supports, tend to increase U.S. production. But the overexpansion of domestic output is restrained in some instances through production and marketing quotas. And the import quotas prevent the overexpansion of foreign production which would occur if foreign exports to the United States were permitted to rise in response to high U.S. support prices. The quotas on imports *and* domestic production therefore

---

[4] The administration has exercised the right to impose quotas on sugar, tobacco and cigars, wheat and wheat products, oats, peanuts, butter and other dairy products, fats and oils, rice, flaxseed, shelled filberts, cotton and cotton waste, cheese, and casein. Imports of butter, flaxseed, linseed oil, nonfat dry milk solids, peanuts, peanut oil, and rice were embargoed. The authority to impose import fees up to 50 per cent ad valorem has been employed sparsely; but in the case of almonds, the higher protection not only turned away imports which had formerly been substantial but provided such an excess of domestic production that export subsidies were employed. These import fees are not subject to tariff negotiation. In addition, tariff quotas, prescribed under the Tariff Act of 1930 (as amended) and permitted under GATT, were applied to milk, cream, butter, some kinds of fish, potatoes, and walnuts; in most instances the tariff doubles for imports in excess of the quotas.

[5] About 60 per cent of the Cuban sugar industry is financed with U.S. capital.

dampen the reallocation of resources which occurs when domestic prices are raised.

In summing up the impact of agricultural protection by industrialized countries and industrial protection by nonindustrial countries, the report by GATT on *International Trade, 1954,* concludes that

While food production in the primary producing areas of the world has barely kept up with the rise in population, mainly as a result of the emphasis placed on industrial production in those areas, a development which was encouraged by agricultural expansion in other parts of the world, a substantial part of the resources of industrial countries is being artificially maintained in agriculture by the insulation of that sector of the economy from normal economic forces. The result of these two tendencies for the world as a whole must inevitably be to retard economic growth.[6]

The report adds that, while there may be some justification for industrial protection by the nonindustrial countries through a greater national production in the future, there is no foreseeable offset to the damage done by continuing restrictions on agricultural production and trade.

C. EXPORT SUBSIDIES AND SURPLUS DISPOSAL

The purchases by the government of commodities under price support have caused the storage of large amounts of wheat, rice, cotton, tobacco, and other products. (The pressure of these surpluses was reduced for several years by large exports under the aid programs. But as agricultural commodities were replaced by capital and military goods in the total aid, the pressure returned.) In order to reduce the volume of stocks it held, the government has authority to subsidize the export of agricultural products and to dispose of surplus commodities both internally and abroad as gifts or at low cost. To finance subsidized sales, the Secretary of Agriculture may draw on 50 per cent of the revenue from import duties. Direct subsidy payments to private exporters averaged about $10 million a year during the first decade of operation (1935–1945), but jumped to about $25 million yearly after World War II.

The use of export subsidies contradicts established U.S. trade policy, which is that governments should not interfere in market prices and that governments are entitled to impose countervailing duties to offset subsidies paid to exporters. Many friendly countries have protested against subsidized exports of U.S. wheat, cotton, rice, dairy products, and other farm items. Yet the U.S. government has attempted to gain international acceptance of its own agricultural export subsidies.

There is some economic justification for use of subsidies in the fact that the high support prices in the United States force U.S. exports off the

---

[6] Geneva, July, 1955, pp. 30–31.

world market; the subsidies merely put them back. The withdrawal of U.S. exports from world markets encourages foreigners to expand their production. But the U.S. subsidy returns the international allocation of resources toward what it would be without a farm support program. In addition, the United States receives some funds for goods which would otherwise merely accumulate, thus reducing the burden on the U.S. tax-payer. However, one can readily see the difficulty, in a dynamic world, of selecting just that subsidy which would preserve a "free trade" share of the world market for U.S. production. The subsidy could give the United States more than its share. The problem of determining the "free trade" allocation is complicated by the fact that the world has not seen since the nineteenth century what a free market situation would be like in agriculture.

Surplus-disposal programs also ran into objections that they disrupt normal markets and increase international friction. The Economic Coopera-tion Administration was required to fill requests from ERP countries for agricultural products which were in surplus in the United States only from U.S. storage or the U.S. market. The Commodity Credit Corporation was empowered to subsidize such exports by selling them below support prices (though it may not do so in the U.S. market).

Under the Mutual Security Act and the Agricultural Trade Develop-ment and Assistance Act, funds were set aside to purchase surplus agricul-tural commodities in the United States for resale to foreign governments for their currencies. These local currencies are similar to counterpart funds. They have been spent to develop markets for American agricultural prod-ucts and to finance foreign expenditures by the U.S. government in connec-tion with other aid programs. When the funds are used by the U.S. govern-ment inside the purchasing country for expenditures which would otherwise have required dollars, the net result is a loss of dollars to the purchasing country. If the funds are used for investment inside the purchasing country, the transaction amounts to a loan of the commodities which generated the local currency. Another use has been to require the purchasing country to lend the local currency to another nation to be used to finance the exports of the country receiving U.S. agricultural products; in this way, trade is expanded. The objectives of these activities are not only to relieve the pressure of surpluses in the United States but also to substitute U.S. sales for purchases that would otherwise be made in the Soviet area (since dollars would not be available for additional purchases in the United States).

Precautions are supposed to be taken to prevent the substitution or displacement of usual sales of U.S. exporters or friendly countries and to make certain that prices are consistent with the maximum world prices for such commodities. Despite the safeguards surrounding the surplus-disposal programs, several governments have complained that the sales have dis-rupted their normal marketings. This result should be expected; not only is the total supply of agricultural products available to foreigners increased but also the purchasing country *can reduce* its usual volume of imports of the item from other countries and shift to other imports.

The techniques of national import quotas and export subsidies have not resolved all of the problems stemming from agricultural instability and from the efforts to make agriculture prosperous. Many nations have considered that these same techniques would be used more effectively and equitably if done cooperatively through intergovernmental agreements.

D. COMMODITY AGREEMENTS

The instability of prices, terms of trade, and national income resulting from changes in demand for and supply of primary products adversely affects almost all countries at some time or another. Intergovernmental commodity agreements have been urged by most nations as a solution to these instabilities. But the U.S. government has stood firm against a *general* acceptance of the technique in any of its forms, though it has joined a few such agreements.

INSTABILITY OF PRICES AND INCOMES

Over the first half of the twentieth century, prices of primary products have varied widely from year to year. While the variation in 25 products averaged about 14 per cent from year to year, average variations in some items were as low as 5 per cent and others as high as 21 per cent. Export earnings showed an even wider average fluctuation of about 23 per cent during the last half of the twentieth century. During the five postwar years, 1946–1951, prices of several important commodities (including cocoa, copper, copra, cotton, jute, lead, rubber, tin, wool, and zinc) sustained *both* price increases of over 50 per cent and price falls of over one-third. The effects of price instability on export earnings and incomes of agricultural producers have been reinforced by changes in the volumes of primary products traded.[7] Variations in the year-to-year export volumes of 18 primary products averaged about 19 per cent during the past fifty years.

These variations in prices and volumes of exports have been accompanied by severe fluctuations in the terms of trade (ratio of import to export prices) among countries producing mostly primary commodities. This instability raises important problems of economic policy. For example, the National Bank of Cuba has estimated that an increase of one dollar in the value of exports has a multiple effect on national income of $2.85;[8] Cuba's national income follows closely the world prices and purchases of sugar, which constitutes over 80 per cent of her exports. This case is admit-

---

[7] See United Nations, *Instability in Export Markets of Underdeveloped Countries,* New York, 1952.

[8] *La Economia Cubana en 1952–1953.*

tedly extreme, but it is indicative of the situation in other countries also; among them are Venezuela with oil, Bolivia with tin, Ceylon with tea and rubber, Egypt and Sudan with cotton, and Denmark with dairy products.

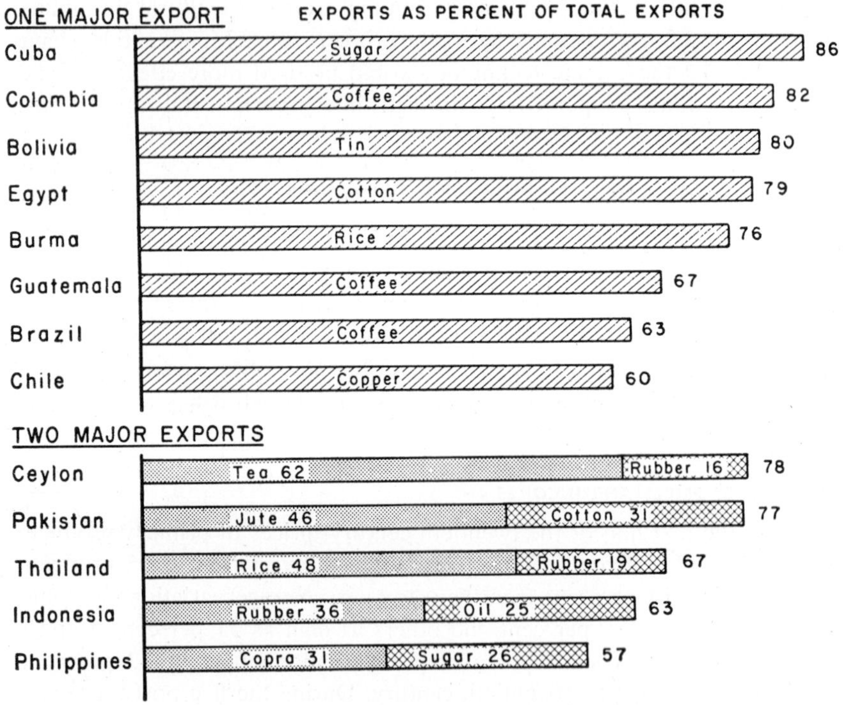

ONE MAJOR EXPORT   EXPORTS AS PERCENT OF TOTAL EXPORTS

Cuba	Sugar — 86
Colombia	Coffee — 82
Bolivia	Tin — 80
Egypt	Cotton — 79
Burma	Rice — 76
Guatemala	Coffee — 67
Brazil	Coffee — 63
Chile	Copper — 60

TWO MAJOR EXPORTS

Ceylon	Tea 62	Rubber 16 — 78
Pakistan	Jute 46	Cotton 31 — 77
Thailand	Rice 48	Rubber 19 — 67
Indonesia	Rubber 36	Oil 25 — 63
Philippines	Copra 31	Sugar 26 — 57

Fig. 21   Unstable Economies Result from Dependence on One or Two Major Exports

SOURCE: International Cooperation Administration

These fluctuations affect the industrialized countries through the impact on their own primary production and through the disturbance to the growth and progress of other countries upon which they rely both economically and politically. Further, the United States is becoming more dependent upon foreign sources of supply for certain primary products. It is to her interest to encourage larger production of strategic items abroad. Increased production requires investment, but capital funds are not moving readily into primary production, partly because of the instability of prices and earnings. Because of the national interests in these problems of instability, many governments have proposed the creation of commodity agreements.

COMMODITY AGREEMENTS BETWEEN THE WARS

As a means of relieving pressure on agricultural and raw-materials markets, governments entered into several commodity-control agreements during the 1920's and 1930's. These agreements were directed at keeping supplies off the market, at maintaining prices high enough to prevent the destruction of inefficient producers, and at dividing the markets so as to reduce competition. The most important agricultural items placed under such controls were wheat, sugar, rubber, coffee, cotton, and tea; other primary products so controlled included petroleum, copper, zinc, lead, tin, potash and nitrates.

The agreements failed to rectify the instabilities or the depressed condition of agriculture, partly because not all of the producers were represented and because the agreement did not include adequate provisions for the reduction of output. Attempts to maintain artificially high prices induced potential producers to enter the market and thereby increased the supply problems. Also, the schemes usually did not permit representation by the major consuming countries. These governments claimed that the operation of the agreements was inequitable because the producers were not content with a "fair" or "equilibrium" price for their commodities but sought to maintain the price far above such levels.

OFFICIAL ATTITUDES

The U.S. government has been under pressure from other countries since the early postwar preparations to support various intergovernmental commodity agreements. They have urged establishment of commodity agreements for each of the most important commodities. About one-third of the total world trade in primary commodities would be involved if the 25 most important items were covered. The proponents argue that agreement on measures to stabilize these commodities, through their favorable impact on incomes, would lend stability to transactions in other commodities and to processing and industrial operations also.[9]

There is substantial agreement among other countries that commodity agreements ought to be set up at least on a test basis to obtain experience with them. The United Nations General Assembly and suborgans of the UN have voted several times to recommend to members the establishment of multilateral arrangements on individual (and groups of) primary products and even some manufactured goods to stabilize prices and encourage economic growth in both consuming and producing countries.

The official attitude of the U.S. government has been that commodity agreements are not generally appropriate for treating problems of instability. Instability should be handled through national action except in unusual and special cases. However, in its early postwar plans, the U.S. government included proposals for intergovernmental commodity agreements to help dispose of surplus stocks of agricultural commodities and raw materials. The Department of Agriculture had proposed agreements on the volume of

---

[9] See United Nations, *Measures for International Economic Stability,* New York, 1951, pp. 17–26. See also, Pan American Union. *Primary Products Surpluses: Measures for Their Disposal* (Washington: September 15, 1954), especially pp. 16–24.

production, prices, and purchasing of temporarily excessive stocks; international agencies would carry out these activities.[10]

The ITO Charter, originally drafted by the U.S. Department of State, provided for only temporary intergovernmental action "when adjustments between production and consumption cannot be effected by normal market forces alone as rapidly as the circumstances require." These agreements were to seek means of expanding consumption and of ameliorating fluctuations in the prices of primary commodities so as to assure a reasonable return to producers. They were to function only so long as required to correct a burdensome surplus of the product which would otherwise lead to widespread unemployment.

The GATT contains no clause concerning the establishment of commodity agreements. When the ITO failed of ratification, support for even temporary commodity agreements was withdrawn by the U.S. government. It remained willing, however, to study the conditions with reference to any given commodity and to enter into consultation concerning more orderly marketing if the circumstances required. Along with other nations, it participated in the International Tin Study Group, a Wool Study Group, the International Cotton Advisory Committee, a Coffee Study Group, and a Rubber Study Group. It has even become a member of agreements covering wheat and sugar. But the U.S. government remains opposed to most of the commodity agreements proposed on the ground that each falls heir to one or more of the serious objections examined below.

EVALUATION OF COMMODITY AGREEMENTS

Most of the proposals for commodity agreements can be classified under one of three major types: commodity-control agreements, surplus-disposal plans, and buffer-stock schemes. These types are not mutually exclusive, and they may be either bilateral or multilateral; they may apply to one commodity or to a group of similar products.

Commodity-control agreements

Experience with the commodity-control agreements for tin, rubber, and sugar prior to World War II showed that their primary objective was to protect profits of producers. They employed quotas on production, export quotas, and the fixing of prices. Each of these measures was aimed at keeping prices (at least of exports) high and at maintaining inefficient producers. These plans resembled official cartels having monopolies over a large sector of the commodity controlled. They had no success in reducing excess capacity, which resulted largely from national protection of uneconomic producers. They were unable to introduce regularity into production, and they tended to maintain the existing distribution of production among nations

---

[10] See its pamphlet *A Post-War Foreign Trade Program for United States Agriculture*, April, 1945, especially pp. 19–22.

rather than to expand the production of low-cost producers while reducing that of inefficient ones.

The U.S. government has argued that price setting and control over production are contradictory to the principles of freer and expanded trade. It has therefore opposed the establishment of agreements employing these techniques. It has not joined the International Tin Agreement, and it withdrew in 1956 from a committee set up to formulate a marketing agreement on coffee; the coffee-producing countries have become disgruntled, asserting that they now bear the full burden of regularizing the market for coffee and must proceed on their own to stabilize prices and encourage purchases (no mention was made of curtailing production or eliminating inefficient producers). But the United States did ratify the International Sugar Agreement in 1954.[11]

Yet, since the U.S. government continues an agricultural price-support program which leads to surpluses at home and uses export subsidies to relieve this surplus, it has been interested in obtaining international sanction for subsidization. Wheat is the most important commodity in surplus and receiving export subsidies. The International Wheat Agreement was signed in 1949 and renewed in 1953 and 1956, to "overcome the serious hardship caused to producers and consumers by burdensome surpluses and critical shortages of wheat" and to "assure supplies of wheat to importing countries and markets for wheat to exporting countries at equitable and stable prices."

The Wheat Agreement does not attempt to control production in any country nor to fix market prices for all wheat traded. But it does provide for export and import controls to assure producers and consumers of minimum sales and purchases according to agreed-upon quotas. It sets minimum prices (depending on grades and location) at which importing countries guarantee to purchase certain amounts, and sets maximum prices at which exporting countries guarantee to sell stated quantities. Since the domestic support price of U.S. wheat is above the maximum under the Agreement, U.S. subsidies to bring export prices within the agreed range

---

[11] The International Sugar Agreement is exceptional. It has little applicability to U.S. trade, for it excludes trade in sugar already covered by special trading arrangements (such as under the U.S. quota system). The Agreement set price limits and quotas for exporting countries. Producers are required to restrict production to an amount equal to the needs of local consumption plus their quota of exports plus the stocks permitted under the Agreement. Importing countries guarantee to purchase a proportion of their needs from member exporters and to restrict their purchases from nonmembers. The Agreement does not come to grips with the basic problem in sugar production—the continued production of much of domestic needs by high-cost, protected producers. Foreign trade has been narrowed through these measures, making free market sugar prices even less stable and causing the income of countries such as Cuba to vary widely. Nothing in the Agreement meets these two problems of domestic protection by importing countries and excess capacity in a few exporting countries. (For a review and analysis of "The International Sugar Agreement of 1953," see the article by Boris C. Swerling in the *American Economic Review,* December, 1954, pp. 837–853.)

are legitimized. The Agreement covers about one-third the world's trade in wheat. So long as the price on the market is within the price limits ($2.00 and $1.50 in the 1956–1958 Agreement) no wheat is traded under its provisions.

The Agreement's objective of stabilizing prices has not been achieved, however. World prices have fluctuated within and outside the limits, largely because most wheat trade is not covered by the Agreement. Furthermore, the United States, for political reasons, has not asked (smaller) importing countries to purchase their quotas when the price has fallen to the minimum level.

Conflicts over equitable prices for wheat have already made it difficult to obtain agreement. Nations have varying anticipations as to wheat prices and do not want a price range in the Agreement which would cause them to buy at too high a price or sell at too low a price. Britain, the largest importer, dropped out of the Agreement in 1953 because she considered that the price range was 5 cents too high; events have proved her right, and she has suffered no ill effects from remaining outside. The 1956 Agreement was snagged for several months because the importing countries considered that the maximum price was too high and because they considered the quotas they were expected to purchase at the minimum prices were too large.

Rather than aid in stability, the Agreement seems to have accentuated instability in both prices and production. The existence of maximum and minimum prices has tended to make the prices in the free market higher (when above the maximum) and lower (when below the minimum) than would be the case without the Agreement.[12] When the free market price is above the Agreement maximum, some wheat is sold under the Agreement at prices lower than the market, leaving the free wheat to sell at a price higher than would be the case if all were sold on the free market. Whether the average of the free price and the Agreement price is greater or less than what would exist without the Agreement is difficult to say, but it seems evident that the Agreement forces wider variations on the prices of non-Agreement transactions.[13]

The Agreement has also failed to induce a reduction of resources going into wheat production; the guarantee of minimum prices has apparently induced member nations to continue large production of wheat, and the high maximum prices have encouraged importing countries to increase their home production. Where there is also a domestic program with export subsidies, as in the United States, inducements under the Agreement to reduce production are weakened. The Agreement, because of the absence

---

[12] See F. H. Golay, "The International Wheat Agreement of 1949," *Quarterly Journal of Economics,* LXIV (August, 1950), 442–463.

[13] Helen C. Farnsworth, "International Wheat Agreement and Problems, 1949–1956," *Quarterly Journal of Economics,* LXX (May, 1956), 233.

of production controls and its tendency to maintain high wheat prices, has probably deferred the shift out of wheat production in the United States and other countries. Britain's refusal to join the 1956 Agreement was based largely on failure of the Agreement to do anything to halt surplus production.

The problem of allocation of resources is central to the determination of the value of commodity control (and other types of commodity) agreements. The intention of the agreements is supposedly to avoid wide disturbances to prices and production while seeking to stabilize the long-run price at the equilibrium level so as not to induce inefficient production. When stabilization measures distort the long-run movement of prices and the adjustment of production to them, they do more harm than good. However, the stabilization of prices within a range and under an administration *willing* to alter its policy with regard to specific commodities so as to adjust to long-run changes can reduce instability without misallocating resources.

One of the obstacles to success of commodity-control agreements in the past has been that they were administered by *exporting* countries who were more interested in keeping prices up and in protecting inefficient producers. One of the now accepted principles of commodity agreements is that importing countries as a whole should have voting power equal to the exporting countries as a whole. Whether or not more equal bargaining power will eliminate the problem of misallocation of resources and expand trade appropriately cannot be stated now for lack of experience. However, the experience under the Wheat Agreement clearly shows the difficulty of obtaining "fair" prices even when importing interests are represented. The refusal of the U.S. government to join a coffee agreement indicates that it considers the principle of equal representation to be inadequate protection of its national interests.

Surplus-adjustment arrangements

Agreements have also been proposed to assist in the disposal of surplus stocks of agricultural and primary products. They differ from commodity-control agreements mainly in that they are supposed to be temporary. The entire gamut of restrictive devices would be necessary: export and import quotas, production controls, price regulations, and reserve stocks. However, cooperative efforts would presumably be made to transfer excess capacity and productive resources into other uses. At the same time, consumers would be assured of "adequate supplies" at "fair" prices, and the "more efficient world producers" would be afforded an opportunity to expand their marketings.

The objection to the restrictive measures required might be less if they would actually relieve surpluses, but their value depends on the surplus being temporary. Despite the fact that there have been temporary *shortages* of some important agricultural and raw-material products, the past decade has seen more world *surpluses* than scarcities of wheat, sugar, cotton, wool, and fats and oils. Since the surpluses tend to be permanent, the problems involved are similar to those which the commodity-control agreement is supposed to solve.

The U.S. government would have great difficulty in adhering to even a temporary agreement which would have involved a cutback in its own "uneconomic practices" of agricultural protection. Congress has repeatedly shown an antipathy to any arrangement which might reduce its control over its agricultural program. As long as groups within nations, including the United States, successfully insist on maintaining parity incomes for producers of sugar, cotton, wool, etc., nations will be unable to agree to plans for expansion of production by the more efficient producers and reduction of their own national production.

Buffer-stock schemes

Buffer-stock schemes have interested a number of economists and officials. The schemes proposed generally involve an international agency financed by contributions from governments which would buy and sell the commodity or commodities to be stabilized. Its purchases would be made when the price fell below a specified level, and it would sell freely when the price rose to a given level. These actions would tend to stabilize prices within a range. But the U.S. government has opposed their creation largely on the grounds of financial and pricing difficulties, and the international economy has had little experience with them, the most recent being under the International Tin Agreement of 1955.

One of the most serious objections to buffer-stock schemes is that large funds would be necessary to finance the purchases and storage. Another problem is that of determining the range of buying and selling prices and the price differentials as to quality and location. Considerable variation in prices among regions at given times is desirable to move goods from areas of plenty to areas of scarcity; variations in time help to induce economizing in times of scarcity and private storage in time of abundance; and price variations among grades and qualities encourage substitution among individual grades in times of relative scarcity or plenty. It would be difficult to keep a policy of moderating the degree of instability from turning into one of stabilizing prices on a more or less fixed basis.

Finally, the policies of buffer-stocks agencies could be completely thwarted by national programs which maintain surpluses through subsidy; the agency would be forced to accumulate stocks indefinitely. Most governments, including that of the United States, have acceded to pressure from domestic interests who want higher than equilibrium market prices. When they obtain these, there is always reason to argue that even higher prices are "just" and "equitable" and are required for the national security or for the large and important sectors of the economy. These pressures lead to higher prices, surpluses, and export subsidies, which it is the objective of a buffer-stock agency to prevent.

A final weakness of buffer stocks is similar to all other "price stability" schemes: they do not necessarily bring income stability to the producers. Stable income can be obtained with prices fluctuating contrary to supply movements; while stable prices with changing supplies may cause income to vary widely.

The U.S. government opposed a broad buffer-stock scheme proposed under the Food and Agriculture Organization during 1947, involving the creation of a World Food Board. The Board was to be empowered to buy, store, and sell a variety of foodstuffs in an effort to gain a more equitable distribution of scarce supplies and dispose with less disturbance any surpluses found on the market. United States officials cited several of the above objections as reasons for their disapproval, but the problem of financing and the fear of international control over the U.S. agricultural program were probably the primary obstacles.

A COMMODITY-RESERVE CURRENCY

Many of the objections to the buffer-stock scheme and individual commodity-control agreements would not apply to a commodity-reserve currency scheme. This proposal involves the establishment of an International Commodity Reserve which would issue its own currency against the presentation of a *fixed bundle* of commodities (or warehouse receipts for items composing it) to the Reserve for currency. The Reserve would be interested only in buying the bundle at, say, $980 and selling at $1,020. (There need not be an international agency if the U.S. government were willing to issue dollars on the same basis—just as it is now willing to issue dollars for specific price-supported commodities; under this proposal it would issue dollars for composite bundles.) The Reserve would accumulate commodity bundles (or warehouse receipts) when the prices of one or more items fell enough to make it profitable for brokers (or governments) to gather the commodities together and sell the bundle to the Reserve for international currency.

When there was a world surplus in, say, cotton and the price of cotton fell, the price of the entire bundle would be pulled down from the "support" level, making it desirable to gather up *all* commodities in it (only the *bundle* could be sold to or bought from the Reserve) and sell it to the Reserve. This would increase the demand for cotton, as well as all other items, and sustain the income of the primary producers.

The Reserve would not, however, fall heir to the criticisms against a buffer-stock scheme that it would be difficult to set the price range to be used, that inefficient producers would be protected, and that national programs of protection could break the Reserve's plan of action. Nor would it be subject to the criticisms against commodity-control agreements that they set prices artificially high and maintain inefficient producers. The fact that *no one price* would be stabilized would mean that *relative* prices of all commodities in the bundle are free to change so as to reallocate resources in response to changes in supply and demand. And the stability of incomes provided by Reserve operations would increase the mobility of resources, because a decline in demand for and production of one commodity would be offset by expansion of another. The operations of the Reserve would tend to stabilize the *incomes* of primary producers as a *whole* without removing desirable price flexibility in each commodity. Producers of any *one* item would not find their income stabilized; just as prices must vary, so must returns on production of any given item if the allocation of factors is to be made more economic.

When there were surpluses of goods, and people generally wished more liquidity, goods would disappear into the Reserve and money would flow out. When money was plentiful, tending toward inflation, goods would flow out of the Reserve and money would disappear. This would occur not only within a nation's monetary system but between nations, tending to coordinate monetary policies and reduce the need for exchange-rate adjustments.

The obstacles to institution of such a system lie, as with the buffer-stock schemes, in determining which items to store, at what over-all price, and in the rather high cost of maintaining storage facilities. Such costs might well be met, however, if the returns in stability and expansion of economic trade were high.

SELECTED READINGS

A., B., AND C., U.S. AGRICULTURAL SUPPORT AND TRADE POLICIES

Committee on International Economic Policy and Carnegie Endowment for International Peace. *Studies in World Trade and Employment.* New York: 1947. Three of the studies on agricultural and trade policies, though written during 1945 and 1946, are still worth reading: "How Much Tariff Protection for Farm Products?" by Murray R. Benedict; "The Stake of the Cotton South in International Trade," by John V. Van Sickle, and "The Dairy Farmer and World Trade," by O. B. Jesness.

Hickman, C. A. *Our Farm Program and Foreign Trade.* New York: Council on Foreign Relations, 1949. A general review of the problems and practices with recommendations.

Humphrey, Don D. *American Imports.* New York: Twentieth Century Fund, 1955. Chapter 12 provides a concise review of the problems and U.S. policies.

International Finance Section. *Survey of United States International Finance.* Princeton, N.J.: Princeton University Press. The Section published an annual survey for the years 1949–1953, including a presentation of the conflicts between agricultural and trade policies.

Johnson, D. Gale. *Trade and Agriculture.* New York: Wiley, 1950. Probably the best single examination of the subject of this chapter, including proposals for both domestic and international action.

Randall Commission on Foreign Economic Policy. *Staff Papers.* Washington: U.S. Government Printing Office, February, 1954. Chapter 4 reviews the problem of agricultural instability and suggests remedies for consideration by Congress.

Ropke, Wilhelm. *International Economic Disintegration.* New York: Macmillan, 1942. Parts IV and V give an excellent account of the impact of policies aimed at making agricultural countries more industrial and industrial countries more self-sufficient in agriculture employed during the 1920's and 1930's.

Subcommittee on Foreign Economic Policy of the Joint Committee (84th Cong.) on the Economic Report. *Hearings on Foreign Economic Policy.* Washington: U.S. Government Printing Office, November, 1955. Pages 345–405 present the testimony of several experts on the problems of trade and agriculture, including representatives of farm interests.

D. INTERGOVERNMENTAL COMMODITY AGREEMENTS

Davis, J. S. *International Commodity Agreements: Hope, Illusion, or Menace?* New York: The Committee on International Economic Policy, January, 1947. An analysis of interwar commodity agreements and their appropriateness for the period after World War II.

Dirks, F. C. "U.S. Exports of Surplus Commodities," *International Monetary Fund Staff Papers,* V (August, 1956), 200–217. A description and analytical discussion of current U.S. agricultural surplus export disposal programs, including the attention given to these programs in multilateral organizations.

Farnsworth, H. C. "International Wheat Agreements and Problems, 1949–1956," *Quarterly Journal of Economics,* LXX (May, 1956), 217–248. An examination of the terms and objectives of the IWA, the lack of fulfillment of the objectives, and a presentation of more appropriate objectives in the light of the world's wheat problems.

Food and Agriculture Organization. *Uses of Agricultural Surpluses to Finance Economic Development in Under-developed Countries: A Pilot Study in India.* Rome: FAO Commodity Policy Studies, No. 6. June, 1955. An examination of the economic problems and political obstacles facing the use of agricultural surpluses in the more developed countries to aid others in more rapid economic development. Evidence in India showed that from 30 to 50 per cent of the cost of development projects was for items in surplus in other countries. A variety of interesting uses of agricultural surpluses are proposed though their total would not solve the agricultural surplus problem.

Graham, B. *World Commodities and World Currency.* New York: McGraw-Hill, 1944. A presentation and defense of a scheme for stabilizing agricultural incomes, domestic price levels, and general economic activity, entitled a Commodity Reserve Currency.

International Labour Office. *Intergovernmental Commodity Control Agreements.* Montreal: International Labour Organization, 1943. An examination of the various interwar agreements with recommendations for the future.

Knorr, Klaus. "Market Instability and United States Policy," *Journal of Political Economy,* LXII (October, 1954), 375–389. An analysis of U.S. interest in agricultural instability and its policies toward intergovernmental agreements.

United Nations, Department of Economic Affairs. *Commodity Trade and Economic Development.* New York: 1953. An examination of the problems of agricultural instability by five experts and their recommendations for the establishment of commodity agreements; the commodity reserve proposal is given some support.

———, Interim Co-ordinating Committee for International Commodity Arrangements. *Review of International Commodity Problems.* New York. An annual review of the world production and prices of primary products and foodstuffs and of intergovernmental action to reduce fluctuations.

25 Strategic Trade Policies

Despite their acceptance of the objective of expanding multilateral international trade, members of the GATT have reserved the right to protect their security interests in time of war or other national emergency through controls over trade. The primary objectives of strategic trade policy are to insure that a sufficient supply of critical materials, both domestic and imported, is on hand for an emergency and to reserve from the enemy the supply of critical commodities. To the former end, the supply of strategic raw materials may be rationed among allied nations and trade may be restricted to sustain domestic productive capacity. And to the latter end, the export of resources and products must be controlled. The U.S. government has sought these objectives through a program of stockpiling materials, international agreements to ration scarce materials, controls over exports, and cooperation with Western nations in restricting exports to Soviet-oriented nations.

A. STOCKPILE PROGRAM

UNITED STATES DEPENDENCE ON FOREIGN MATERIALS

Of almost overriding significance in the formation of its foreign economic policy is the fact that the United States has recently become a net importer of a wide range of metal and mineral products. The President's Materials Policy Commission projected in 1952 that, if the 1950 GNP of the United States were doubled by 1975, there would be a 90 per cent increase in mineral requirements. Most of these metals and minerals would have to be obtained from abroad because U.S. producers were already expanding their operations rapidly and still could not keep up with domestic demand. The United States, prior to World War II, was dependent on overseas suppliers only for tin, nickel, platinum, asbestos, chromite, graphite, manganese, mercury, mica, and tungsten. She was self-sufficient in

530   *Strategic Trade Policies*

a long list of strategic materials prior to World War II. After the war, the latter list shrank to only coal, sulfur, molybdenum, and magnesium. United States dependence on overseas supplies is exemplified by the fact that large portions of her manganese come from India, of chrome from the Philippines, of uranium from the Belgian Congo, of tin and rubber from Indochina, and of columbite and cobalt from Nigeria.

A further indication of the breadth of the change is found in a partial listing of imported strategic minerals held in the U.S. stockpile: aluminum,

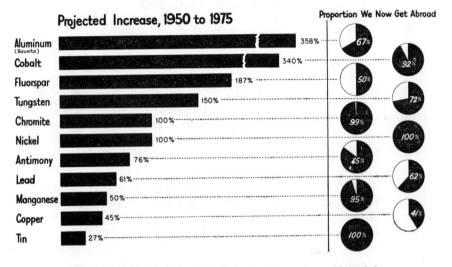

Fig. 22   U.S. Industry Will Require More Raw Materials
SOURCE: International Cooperation Administration

antimony, bauxite, beryl, bismuth, cadmium, cobalt, copper, corundum, industrial diamonds, cyanite, lead, quartz crystals, talc, and zinc. The most striking shifts within this group are those concerning copper, lead, and zinc. Whereas the United States was a net exporter of these items before World War II, she now imports almost 40 per cent of her copper requirements and about a third of her lead and zinc needs despite the fact that domestic production has reached all-time highs in each. These three metals plus steel and aluminum are the most important ones in an industrial economy. One of the most interesting tariff battles has arisen from efforts of the copper, lead, and zinc producers to obtain protection for their industries on the grounds of national defense. The interests of the U.S. government have been found to lie with increased imports of these metals, however, not only because imports are cheaper but also partly because they are a means of encouraging production abroad and of conserving what is left in the United States.

Of further importance for the formation of U.S. foreign economic policy is the fact that 75 per cent of U.S. imports of strategic and critical materials and minerals come from the underdeveloped countries. For some specific items, U.S. dependence on developing countries is much greater.[1] As discussed in Chapter 22, the U.S. government has attempted to expand the production of these and other strategic and critical materials in the developing areas through the extension of loans and grants. It has also offered long-term contracts to encourage their development both at home and abroad.

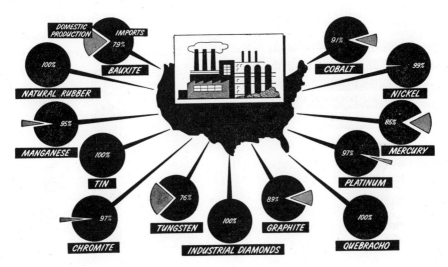

Fig. 23　Strategic Materials from Other Free Nations Are Essential to U.S. Production

SOURCE: International Cooperation Administration

STOCKPILE OPERATIONS

Despite its general dislike of state trading, the U.S. government began, under the Strategic and Critical Materials Stockpiling Act of 1946, to accumulate stocks of minerals and materials in which the United States was deficient. The experience during World War II showed that it was dangerous to rely on foreign sources which could be cut off from the

---

[1] The underdeveloped areas supply 100 per cent of U.S. imports of bauxite, castor oil, chromite, columbite, cordage fibers, corundum, cyanite, mica, palm oil, quebracho, natural rubber, and vanadium. They supply between 90 and 100 per cent of U.S. imports of beryl, coconut oil, industrial diamonds, hyoscine, opium, pyrethrum, quartz crystals, shellac, and tantalite. They supply between 80 and 90 per cent of its imports of cadmium, graphite, manganese ore, and tin ore; 70 to 80 per cent of imports of bismuth and copper. And they provide some 60 to 70 per cent of its import needs of cobalt, lead, sapphires and rubies, tin bars, and zinc ore. (See, *Partners for Progress,* a Report to the President by the International Development Advisory Board, March, 1951, pp. 42–50, 114–117.)

United States during war. So the stockpile is designed "to decrease and prevent wherever possible a dangerous and costly dependence of the United States upon foreign nations . . . in times of national emergency."

The stockpile goals were set as the difference between what was accessible in the United States and neighboring areas—i.e., Canada, Mexico, South America, and a few other areas—and the military and civilian requirements of a five-year war.

The administration made few purchases for the stockpile prior to 1950. These were viewed mainly as a means of helping other nations to reduce their dollar deficits. Large operations were opposed in 1948–1949 by some congressmen who saw them as a possible threat to domestic producers of stockpile items who might be squeezed out by foreign exporters. It was not until the outbreak of the Korean war in 1950 that Congress put pressure on the administration to accelerate purchases.

Over 80 per cent of the purchases for the stockpile have been from foreign sources despite the stipulation by Congress that purchases be made from *domestic* producers under provisions of the Buy American law. For stockpiling purposes, the administration has interpreted the Buy American law rather liberally, leaving domestic producers to supply their normal markets. This policy has been criticized by some congressmen who consider that the Buy American Act has been circumvented and that not enough has been done to encourage production in the Western Hemisphere; they assert that this region could become self-sufficient in strategic and critical materials with the proper encouragement and that it should be given.

PROBLEMS OF STOCKPILING

The question of whether to purchase materials at home or abroad has been a major one in the stockpile program. If purchases are made abroad domestic production is retarded and U.S. resources are "stockpiled" in the ground. To leave them in the ground is currently less expensive, but costs of production would be higher during an emergency, and the possession of the items is not certain unless they are warehoused.

However, the decision to encourage domestic production also raises problems. Marginal producers might be brought into the market at a considerable cost; for example, it has been estimated that the supply of manganese ore of ferro-grade could be raised from the current 10 per cent of domestic requirements to 100 per cent only through increasing the price 100 per cent. Hence the cost of gaining domestic self-sufficiency would be much greater than purchasing the items abroad for stockpiling. Contrarily, it is sometimes argued, if domestic production is expanded, costs may be reduced and the increased demand may encourage technological developments in production methods or may encourage new uses, which in turn will provide more effective or cheaper defense in an emergency. As a consequence the stockpile goals change. Furthermore, if domestic production is allowed to decline for lack of stockpile purchases, the costs and difficulties of starting up closed firms during an emergency may be very great, e.g., mines are subject to cave-ins and flooding. In the decision to encourage domestic production, security considerations should be dominant; cost calculations under market prices and for market uses should be secondary. This does not mean that costs are to be disregarded in making the decision; they provide information on the relative efficiency of alternative methods.

For the reason that security considerations should be predominant, pleas from other countries that the U.S. government should expand stockpile purchases in order to stabilize the world market for specified commodities should be considered only to the degree that stability affects security. Efforts to stabilize prices (either at home or abroad) through a stockpile would involve purchases and sales which would sometimes hinder the strategic purposes of the stockpile. The government has at times sold certain commodities from the stockpile for use in the private sector; for example, copper was sold in 1951 to offset production lost from strikes in the mines. A policy of releasing large quantities in order to even out price changes would not only deplete the stockpile at possibly dangerous times but would also cause rancor among producers who stood to benefit from the current high prices. In this regard, any release of items no longer deemed strategic should probably be done with an eye to its impact on world markets.

The existence of a huge stockpile held by the U.S. government has already caused qualms among several countries. They wonder what would happen if a commodity is declared no longer necessary for the stockpile and is therefore released on the market and what the effect on prices will be when U.S. purchases cease as the stockpile goal on an item is fulfilled. Primary producers are reluctant to sell to a stockpile which may depress future prices, and many have been unwilling to expand production save under long-term contracts (twenty years or more) to avoid price fluctuations. Foreign nations have proposed multilateral stockpile programs. But the U.S. government has steadfastly refused to accept them largely on the grounds that it would bear a disproportionate share of the costs and that the schemes proposed do not meet the problems of instability, discussed in Chapter 24.

The U.S. government has attempted at times to meet problems of supply and price instability by unilateral action. When the administration attempted, in 1950, to stop the rapid rise in prices of primary products, it met stiff opposition from foreign producers. Toward the end of 1950 and early in 1951, the administration took over all importing of natural rubber and of tin metal and tin concentrates, which were sold abroad under near monopoly conditions. It attempted to reduce the prices of these commodities to prevent gouging of buyers and to enable allies to buy at more reasonable cost. It set a buying rate for rubber which was below the market and declared a buyer's strike on tin. Prices of both commodities dropped by about 40 per cent under strong protests from producing areas. Both commodities were returned to private trading in 1952, but free market prices were considerably lower than had been the case during the period of "price gouging" by producers.

Without substantial agreement on means of handling stockpile problems, the U.S. government has not been successful in encouraging other nations to expand production of strategic materials. The U.S. stockpile goals are still several years from fulfillment, partly because heavy purchases in a tight market would have driven prices up unreasonably, as during the Korean War. The goals and composition of the stockpile are dependent upon estimates of the duration of any future emergency. A thirty-day war would require quite different quantities and items from those for a five-year war.

B.   INTERNATIONAL MATERIALS CONFERENCE

The scarcity of supplies during the Korean War and subsequent rearmament drives raised problems not only of price but also of distribution of materials among importing nations. With the threat of widespread war, the U.S. government increased its purchases rapidly. This increase was supplemented by heavy buying from private sectors for inventory in the face of rising prices. The combined forces prevented other nations from gaining materials they needed for both their recovery and rearmament programs and turned the terms of trade against them. They complained bitterly that the United States was "hogging" scarce materials and was following an "inept and uneconomic" procedure in its stockpiling, thus causing an inequitable distribution of supplies. The U.S. government heeded these complaints by cutting back its stockpile purchases and by joining with several of the Western nations in the formation of an International Materials Conference. It was the first multilateral attempt (apart from the Combined Boards in World War II) at a cooperative distribution of scarce supplies.

Twenty-eight nations, accounting for 80 to 90 per cent of the Free World's production and consumption of the items concerned, established the IMC in 1951 to gather and exchange information on the supply and distribution of critical materials.[2] The producing and consuming nations were on an equal footing, and the interests of nonmember governments were given consideration.

IMC members decided that the shortages in copper, zinc, nickel,

---

[2] Seven independent committees were formed to study the situations with reference to copper, zinc, lead, manganese, nickel, cobalt, cotton linters, cotton pulp, sulfur, pulp and paper, wool, tungsten, and molybdenum.

cobalt, tungsten, molybdenum, sulfur, and newsprint made allocations desirable. Distribution plans provided for meeting needs under the following priorities: defense, strategic stockpiling, then essential civilian consumption. Each consuming country was required to demonstrate its needs in the three classifications. Efforts were made to attain a relative equality of sacrifice, which meant that the relatively large U.S. demands sometimes went unsatisfied. It was not difficult to show a defense need. But civilian consumption had to be allocated according to past consumption, despite the recognized inequities which resulted because of changed patterns of demand and requirements. To implement the distribution schemes, import and export quotas were recommended by the committees. Members were free to accept or reject the suggested allocations; nearly all complied.

The U.S. government went a long way to show its desire to cooperate, as evidenced by its decision to permit its production of sulfur (which constituted most of the IMC members' supply) to be allocated through IMC procedures rather than unilaterally even though the resulting allocation was not exactly what it would have desired. By this action, the United States hoped to induce all producers of commodities which she imported to cooperate in distribution plans.

Not all of the producers permitted their entire supplies to be allocated through distribution plans. Chile reserved 20 per cent of her copper to sell outside of the allocation scheme. Brazil rebelled at the allocations of tungsten and at the prices set by the committee; the price limits were dropped in later allocations. Producing countries raised severe objections to price fixing; but they readily agreed to the allocations because it was largely immaterial to them which nations purchased the high-priced supply. Efforts of the tungsten committee to obtain agreement on a long-run scheme to induce producers to expand production and set a price range within which sales were to take place came to nought. The same conflict of interests was reflected in the inability of the group considering wool shortages to agree even on the dimensions of the shortage, much less on an allocation of supplies. These experiences indicate that most nations will cooperate when it is in their national interest to do so but that they will retain strong reservations as to cooperation in programs which might limit their economic advantage.

Congressional opposition to the allocations of the Conference grew strong during 1952, especially since the lack of certain materials was beginning to slow down production in some lines, such as automobiles. Opposing congressmen found a host of reasons for the United States no longer to support the Conference: it had not been approved by Congress at any time; it was a creation of the State Department; it was an international cartel, a "supergovernment" and "socialistic"; it was a "backdoor attempt" to bring part of the ITO into being; and U.S. participation implied that "we were more concerned with equitable allocations and in stabilizing prices than we were in saving the lives of our sons fighting in Korea."[3]

The IMC abandoned its plans to develop long-run commodity agreements for dealing with scarce materials. As the supply situations eased, several of the committees ceased their allocations. In December, 1953, the IMC was disbanded as being no longer necessary. But members recommended its experience and success to future governments who might be faced with similar shortages in times of emergency.

C. EXPORT CONTROLS

Export *duties* are prohibited by the U.S. Constitution, but the government has employed direct controls over exports for a variety of reasons since World War II. The most important single justification has been that of national security, but this reason was the primary one only after 1949. During World War II and immediately after, export controls were authorized to protect the economy from a drain of materials already in short supply, to channel exports into areas which in turn would produce goods needed by the United States (especially critical materials), and to allocate exports so as to hasten recovery in Europe.

After March, 1948, a license was required for *all* shipments to European countries and contiguous territories. This broader restriction was imposed to limit the movement into Eastern Europe of goods which might be useful for military purposes. It was also used in part to help ERP countries in their efforts to keep out "unessential" imports so as to conserve their foreign exchange for recovery purposes.

With the threat of deflation in the United States during late 1949, controls were lifted from a wide range of goods formerly held to be in short supply. After 1949, the emphasis shifted very strongly to control of goods of military significance, and many goods were again added to the control list, particularly those under allocation through the International Materials Conference. A single list was adopted covering strategic items exportable to any country, in an attempt to prevent goods being reshipped from another nation into Eastern Europe.

After the outbreak of the Korean War, exports to North Korea and Communist China were *embargoed*. And controls were placed on a given list of strategic exports, including those in transit through the United States, to Russia and its European satellites. Ships flying the American flag were also prohibited from carrying any strategic goods to these countries, and all tariff concessions which had been extended to Soviet-bloc countries under the Trade Agreements Program were withdrawn.

---

[3] See the Report of the Minerals, Materials, and Fuels Economic Subcommittee of the Committee on Interior and Insular Affairs, *Accessibility of Strategic and Critical Materials to the United States in Time of War and for Our Expanding Economy*, 83d Cong. (Washington: Government Printing Office, 1954), pp. 261–288.

Although not all goods are embargoed to the Soviet bloc, that area has shown little interest in purchasing U.S. exports which the U.S. government considers nonstrategic. The Soviet bloc's practice of economic self-sufficiency has been the most important deterrent to trade, as evidenced by the fact that other countries not imposing controls have found their trade dwindling also. This lack of Russian interest in nonstrategic imports along with the U.S. controls over her exports have cut U.S.-Russian trade to minimum levels. American exports to the Sino–Soviet bloc countries fell from a level of about $400 million in 1947 to less than $5 million in 1951 and to a low of $1 million in 1952, over half of which was tobacco. Since then, exports have risen gradually to around $10 million annually. United States imports from these countries range around $50 million annually; U.S. trade directly with Russia is a small fraction of the total.

The heaviest impact of the U.S. export controls has been on trade with the Sino-Soviet countries, but nations of the Free World have also been affected by U.S. controls. Several problems have beset the administration in establishing and implementing the control system: how to allocate scarce commodities between domestic and foreign civilian purposes, how to set priorities between U.S. and allied military needs, whether to use export controls to bargain for imports of scarce materials produced abroad, how to balance the claims of South America for development against those of Western Europe for recovery and rearmament, and what weight to give to commercial considerations of keeping markets open for U.S. exporters. The controls have not reduced U.S. exports significantly, but they have altered the direction of trade. This redirection has a discriminatory result and is thus contrary to expressed principles of U.S. commercial policy. This provides another example of how economic principles are modified by political considerations.

Although admitting the discriminatory impact of U.S. export controls among Free World nations, a congressional committee examining them took pains to justify their use on the ground that they were "a significant part of the total Western defense program. . . ." As long as the controls were not imposed "predominantly for national interests as opposed to those instituted to promote Western defense objectives" the discrimination was not, it asserted, in opposition to the broad policy aimed at the removal of trade restrictions and at nondiscrimination.[4]

Since the major objective was to implement the Western defense system, the U.S. effort to control trade with Russia and her allies was not complete until other Western countries joined in the same control of exports from their own countries so as to reduce East-West trade to nonstrategic items. The effect of U.S. controls would be avoided if the Soviet bloc could obtain the same or similar items directly from or through other

---

[4] *Senate Report No. 944,* Committee on Interstate and Foreign Commerce, 82d. Cong., 1st Sess., October 12, 1951, p. 9.

countries. Therefore controls over all East-West trade in strategic items were required.

D. EAST-WEST TRADE CONTROLS

During 1947 and 1948, the U.S. administration joined with ERP countries in stressing the necessity and desirability of restoring prewar patterns of East-West trade among European countries. This restoration was considered a prerequisite to the recovery effort of making Europe self-sustaining again. The shift in U.S. policy from cooperation with to containment of Russia and the Soviet bloc's own drive to self-sufficiency combined to cut off the potential expansion of trade. Discussion of the relative advantages and disadvantages of promoting East-West trade has continued since 1948; no definite resolution of views seems in sight though some relaxation of restrictions by both sides has occurred within the last few years.

PROBLEMS AND PATTERNS OF EAST-WEST TRADE

Prior to World War II, the industrial nations of Western Europe relied heavily upon the raw-material products of Eastern Europe, including food, fuel, and timber. Certain countries of the West obtained, and still do, most of their coal, grain, and lumber requirements from the Soviet bloc. Conversely, the Soviet-bloc countries provided markets for fishery products, machinery, and other capital goods of Western Europe. Markets in the East are still of primary importance to a few Western countries; for example, Norway ships about 80 per cent of its exports of herring to the Soviet bloc.

Beginning in 1948, when the U.S. government inaugurated its program of export controls for the purpose of security, many European countries did likewise. The ERP countries and Japan imposed embargoes on arms, ammunition, and other military items and also on much machinery and capital equipment considered strategic. Exports of less strategic items were limited to specific amounts and all trade was kept under surveillance. Japan, which has traditionally traded with mainland China, imposed a near embargo on all trade with that country in 1950. Because it received almost 70 per cent of its coal and coke imports and 53 per cent of its soy-bean imports from China, this loss of trade has been vital in slowing Japan's recovery. The loss of Japan's export market in China for manufactured goods has not yet been made up by trade with Southeast Asia countries or with the United States and Europe.

Not all of the restrictions of East-West trade have originated with the West, however. While Russia has been willing to export some strategic and critical commodities to the West, she has been willing to take in return only items which would be useful in building up her industrial and military potential. Nor has Russia concretely encouraged any *large* volume of trade with the West. She has made concerted efforts to direct the economic activity of her satellites toward Russia, to create a fairly integrated economic unit. Trade of Eastern Europe has been increased greatly with Russia. Industrialization programs for the Soviet satellites have reduced their exports of primary products, which further reduced the opportunity for sales to the West. Until 1956, whenever trade opportunities opened up with the West, Russia was almost certain to ask higher than world prices for her goods, to impose the most stringent of terms, to ask for credit, to promise goods in return which she did not deliver on time or for which she sent substitutes, and to require that exporters assume responsibility for making good on claims for damaged or imperfect goods in shipments which only Russian officials examined. These conditions did much to retard her trade with the non-Soviet world. Under the 1956 Soviet trade offensive, some of these requirements were relaxed. But Russia still uses her trade politically in an effort to show the countries of Western Europe that they must turn to her as a market for items which the United States will not buy.[5]

Communist China has adopted similar practices and has redirected much of her trade toward Russia. China relies heavily on Russia for machinery and finished products and ships raw materials in return. This interdependence is apparently a strain on both countries, politically and economically, because Russia has few manufactures to spare. Individual Western nations have strongly urged a restoration of trade with China.

COOPERATIVE CONTROLS

Western nations came to ready agreement as to the treatment of exports of arms, munitions, and other military items to the Soviet bloc. When the U.S. government introduced a resolution in the United Nations in 1950 requesting that member nations embargo shipments of implements of war, petroleum, and goods used in the production of implements of war to Communist China and North Korea, the resolution passed with only the Communist countries opposing it. A large number of countries were already imposing such controls, and others complied.

It was much more difficult to obtain complete agreement on the non-military items which should be restricted. The voluntary measures which European countries imposed did not always satisfy the U.S. government; shipments slipped through either because of a different interpretation of

---

[5] Russia had been doing the same thing on a smaller scale before; for example, she contracted to purchase the whole crop of Italian almonds after the U.S. government imposed import quotas on them. Russia was given an easy propaganda coup in this instance by the U.S. investigation of Italian production costs so as to find a basis for protection of American almond producers. The investigations were done openly and were a subject of public discussion and irritation in Italy. (See *New York Times,* November 3, 1954.)

what was strategic or through the many ways of evasion, including trans-shipment.[6] In addition, some countries insisted on fulfilling contracts that had been made before controls were imposed, and others permitted exports of strategic items on the ground that their imports from the Soviet bloc were even more important to them.

These explanations did not always satisfy the U.S. Congress; it attempted to require closer compliance by Europe with U.S. control lists. Much of what Europe continued to export to Russia had some strategic value in the eyes of the U.S. government—that is, the goods would contribute directly or indirectly to Russia's industrial growth and thereby to her military potential.

European countries imposed additional controls after the 1950 congressional requirements that economic aid should be cut off to a country if the National Security Council deemed that exports by it to a Soviet-bloc country were harmful to American security. But Western European nations balked at prohibiting certain exports which Eastern Europe insisted upon for certain of its exports to the West. In 1951, Congress attempted, by threatening to cut off aid, to force the cessation of practically all trade of the West with the Soviet bloc; sponsors of the act considered that *all* materials were "war materials" during a time of cold or hot war. The only exception permitted was when the National Security Council deemed a given Western export to be "in the security interest of the United States."

Although President Truman signed the legislation on the ground that he could not quarrel with its purpose, he asserted that its methods were wrong. The problem of trade with the enemy, he said, was "a matter of evaluating, in terms of relative importance, what the free world gets from the Bloc for what it must given in return." He also criticized the fact that the amendment substituted coercion for cooperation, which was an improper way of obtaining common action among nations. Finally, elimination of aid from deserving countries would endanger the defense effort of the West more than it would harm Russia. The National Security Council found that 25 aid-receiving countries were complying with the requirement and that aid to the remaining 36 should be continued "in the interests of United States security" despite their noncompliance. Congressional reaction to this blanket exemption was as vehement as the reaction of the European countries was against the attempted coercion.

---

[6] Any control system sets up its own black market. Evasions appeared in the form of multiple shipments on one license, fraudulent shipments, split shipments, forgeries of licenses, unauthorized transshipments, and diversions in transit. Strategic goods have been traced halfway around the world through numerous hands ultimately into the Soviet bloc. Also, U.S. officials, despite their own tight measures and extensive cooperation by the trading community, have found more than 200 firms and individuals guilty of evading export controls. (For cases in point, see the *Reports to Congress on the Mutual Defense Assistance Control Aid of 1951*, by the Director of the Foreign Operations Administration.)

European officials were afraid that the shift from cooperation to coercion would feed Communist propaganda mills, which charged that the United States was interfering in European affairs. Some anxiously declared that the action reflected a lack of confidence by the U.S. government in the governments friendly to America. Opposition also stemmed from the fact that many European countries were still dependent on Eastern markets to take their exports, which were either excluded from or not readily marketable in the West. In addition, there was widespread sentiment in some countries that trade contacts should be kept open with the East in the hope of providing incentives to some countries to break away from Russia.

A Senate subcommittee studying export controls concluded that two of the most important measures which should be adopted by the United States were (a) to attempt to mobilize public opinion abroad in support of controls by European governments and (b) to find alternative markets for and sources of supply of goods for the West.[7] Unless alternative sources of Western Europe's imports of coal, timber, and grain were found, the U.S. government would have to supply them through aid. These arguments and those used by President Truman supported passage of the Mutual Defense Assistance Control Act of 1951. It provided that economic and military aid be cut off from any nation that exported items to the Soviet bloc of the sort embargoed to that area by the U.S. government; these items to be embargoed or restricted by the United States and her allies were subject to negotiation among themselves.

That feature of the American legislation which permitted the U.S. government to withhold aid from nations violating the embargo was not used (except to interrupt an incipient program with Ceylon), though numerous violations of the controls occurred. In every instance the security interests of the United States, according to the President, would have been adversely affected by using the violations as occasions for withholding aid. In addition, withholding aid would not have brought back the items which had been exported.

In effect, the bludgeon which Congress gave the administration to use was too heavy for the purpose. A more subtle form of prodding, such as pressure from the foreign-aid missions that the *size* (and not *all*) of the aid was dependent on other nations' cooperation, might have been more successful. And as long as it was kept secret, problems of public reaction to America's "dollar diplomacy" would be lessened while the chances of obtaining successful cooperation would be greater in that U.S. bargaining power would be enhanced. The latter seems to follow from the fact that the choice Congress permitted was between no coercion and no aid; a different approach would put the choice to the foreign nation of cooperation or somewhat less aid. The ineffectiveness of U.S. attempts to induce others

[7] See *Senate Report, No. 944, op. cit.,* pp. 10–11.

to tighten controls seems to support the view that the cooperative controls are more important as a symbol of Western unity; as such, it has been argued that *agreement* on the controls is more important than their stringency.

After a thorough review of its control system, the U.S. government agreed with the 15 cooperating European nations during 1954 to relax some of the restrictions on European exports to the Soviet bloc (*not* including China). The embargo list was reduced a third and the quantitative control list by three-fourths. Strict regulations were kept on trade with China as a consequence of her being named an "aggressor" by the United Nations in the Korean conflict. This revision of the control lists moved the United States more toward the European view of expanding trade with the East.[8] In return, European countries agreed to strengthen their controls systems on important items already under control so as to reduce illegal exports.

By mid-1956, under a general fading of the threat of war, additional pressure arose in Europe to relax restrictions. Britain was especially insistent that restrictions on trade with China be placed on the same basis as those on trade with Russia and the satellites; Britain felt that the decline of her trade with China to one-fourth of the prewar level was unnecessary and undesirable. It was reported that the U.S. government had agreed to a reduction of the lists of controlled items and a downgrading of the strategic classifications of others; these reports raised protests from Congress. The precise items involved and the *quid pro quo* that the United States received in each negotiation have remained a matter of secrecy; the negotiations and results have not been publicized on the ground that it would embarrass further negotiations and provide information to the "enemy."

An important problem of policy and strategy is raised by the process of relaxing the cooperative controls over trade with the East: should not the West begin to employ trade as a political weapon, as Russia does,[9] and thus relax its controls only in exchange for economic and political concessions by Russia? Equally important is the question of whether, once the controls are relaxed, the West should leave itself open to the coercion of the monolithic Russian trading organization. Should the West attempt to form, under NATO, a cooperative organization of business, financial, and government interests to act as a clearing house and channel of the

---

[8] The revision was made on the assumption that a "long period of tension" was probable and under pressures to make the controls more practicable, to downgrade some items in order to gain the benefits of trade, increase markets abroad, and substitute for declining aid. (See *Fifth Report to Congress on the Mutual Defense Assistance Act of 1951,* November, 1954, pp. 2–3.)

[9] *The New York Times* (September 18, 1955) reported that Krushchev told a group of U.S. senators visiting in Moscow: "We value trade least for economic reasons and most for political purposes as a means of promoting better relations between our countries."

West's trade with the East? In this way, the West might be able to enforce fulfillment of bargains, reduce monopoly pressure from Russia, and gain a greater advantage to whatever trade was considered desirable. Such a suggestion, of course, reflects the view of many who argue that the only way to trade with a state monopoly is to create an equally powerful monopoly.

An evaluation of the effects of the controls on the strategic position of the West is difficult to make. First, it is difficult to determine precisely the extent to which an item is strategic and, therefore, the extent to which its export would help the Soviet bloc to increase its military potential. Second, it is impossible to know how many shipments slipped through the controls. And third, it is hard to calculate the contribution trade makes to security of the United States and/or her allies. Despite these obstacles, the administration asserted that the rate of Soviet armament and development has been slowed by the export controls of the non-Communist nations and that, on balance, the West has obtained more benefits from the permitted trade than has the East. However, the advantage of "trading with the enemy" or not trading cannot be readily generalized.

E. TRADING WITH THE "ENEMY"

During the nineteenth century and earlier, a nation's commercial policies could be fairly easily divided into those concerning trade with friends and trade with the enemy. In European history, it was not difficult for a nation to distinguish its enemy and to take appropriate measures. Yet the knowledge of who the enemy was likely to be did not elicit measures which stopped all trade. Even during war, many of the trade and financial relations continued as before, because governments did not try to control these transactions and private individuals still found it profitable to continue to lend and to trade. But during the last decade it has become obvious who the enemy of the United States is, and it has become easier to control the major flows of trade and finance. In the belief that the interests of private individuals in pursuing profitable trade might not coincide with the national security interests, governments have taken a closer interest in the direction of trade and capital movements. Many persons have wished that the pre-World War II sale to Japan of steel scrap, which in turn found its way into munitions used against Americans, had been stopped. But since trade is a two-way street, the cutting off of exports to an enemy also eliminates imports from it. There is still widespread disagreement as to the net advantages of trading or not trading with the potential or actual "enemy."

The objective of cutting off trade is to reduce the economic growth and military potential of the enemy. As far as Russia and her allies are concerned, they seem little interested in depending on foreign trade to accelerate their development. Foreign trade is less than 1 per cent of the Soviet bloc's gross national product. The Soviet view is that it must not become dependent upon Western trade, which could be cut off in time of actual war, or which could be used as a political bargaining weapon. It seeks to become invulnerable to such outside pressure. The Soviet bloc can achieve a fairly high degree of self-sufficiency because of its abundant natural resources, and it can shift these resources (as well as capital and manpower) to varied uses through its state controls. Under these latter circumstances, the question arises as to whether the controls imposed by the West do not aid Russia's own effort to become self-sufficient.

What Russia needs most in accelerating her development seems to be those products requiring mechanical and engineering skills, such as machinery, machine tools, electrical equipment, etc. The Soviet bloc has some gaps also in its supply of raw materials, such as copper, natural rubber, and industrial diamonds. (Diamonds were smuggled into the Soviet orbit from Brazil via diplomatic pouch in some instances.) Prohibition of exports of these types of goods has probably slowed the growth of industrialization in the bloc during the past few years. But the net effect of these restrictions cannot be said to be great because they also helped Russia in setting priorities in production. The existence of Western controls during the cold war has helped Russia to find and fill in places where she was most vulnerable to restrictions from abroad. To fill the gaps, she has been encouraged to develop substitutes and to integrate her economy more closely with the economies of her satellites. Out of such developments, new techniques and new skills were born, increasing her industrial growth.

While the controls may not have adversely affected the growth in Russia directly, it is probable that they have done so indirectly through their impact on Communist China. China, being less well developed, requires even more equipment from abroad. Cut off from Western sources, she has had to turn to Russia for industrial products and capital goods. These very products have been vital to Russia's own progress. The trade between the two countries has been a very important factor in their political relations with each other and in their relations vis-a-vis the West. For example, some critics believe that the necessity of China's relying on Russian production was a factor in Russian pressure on China to ease her antagonistic attitude toward Formosa and the Western nations in 1954–1955. Russia reportedly did not want a war at the time, for she was unwilling to supply China and/or fight on two fronts.

While restriction of East-West trade may not hurt Russia greatly, it has handed her a political advantage and injured Western Europe economically. The political advantage has been from two sources. First, a large number of people in Western Europe consider that it is to the advantage of their countries to expand trade with the East both as an economic measure and to maintain contacts with those people in order to win them back to freedom.[10] Whether or not this view is correct, those holding it condemn their governments for restrictions. Second, since the U.S. government has taken the position of "encouraging" restrictions on the part of the Western European governments, Russia has been able to allege an imperialistic content of American foreign policy and to instill in some officials an attitude of distrust toward America as well as foment active resistance to the idea of restriction. The result was to obscure the real merits of restriction of East-West trade and overlay them with problems of political relations. The U.S. government attempted during 1955 and 1956 to stress the restrictive impact of Soviet trade policies and thus shift the blame for low volumes of East-West trade onto Russia.

Even the economic results of severing of East-West trade are uncertain. The loss of trade with the East has been directly harmful to the West. This is not true of the United States; most of her imports from Russia were either luxuries or materials which she found could be obtained relatively easily elsewhere, especially since dollars were in strong demand abroad. But for most of the Western European countries, the loss of imports and markets was acute and indirectly affected the strength of the United States.

But the elimination of imports from the East is not so much a result of the West's export restrictions as it is a result of the fact that most of the materials which the West wants would not be obtained anyway. Despite the fact that a few countries receive important amounts of materials from the Soviet bloc (Norway obtains one-fifth of her bread grains, Sweden one-third of her coal, the United Kingdom one-tenth of its timber; France

---

[10] Winston Churchill spoke for this view in a speech on February 25, 1954:

"There is one agency at any rate which every one can see through which helpful contacts and associations can be developed. The more trade there is through the Iron Curtain and between Great Britain and Soviet Russia and the Satellites the better still will be the chances of our living together in increasing comfort.

"When there is so much prosperity for everybody round the corner and within our reach, it cannot do anything but good to interchange merchandise and services on an increasing scale. The more the two great divisions of the world mingle in the healthy and fertile activities of commerce the greater is the counterpoise to purely military calculations. Other thoughts take up their place in the minds of man.

"Friendly infiltration can do nothing but good. We have no reason to fear it, and if Communist Russia does not fear it that in itself is a good sign. I was therefore, very glad to read of the measure of success which attended the recent visits by British businessmen to Moscow. I do not suggest that at the present time there should be any traffic in military equipment, including certain machine tools such as those capable only or mainly of making weapons and heavy weapons. But a substantial relaxation of the regulations affecting manufactured goods, raw materials, and shipping—which, it must be remembered, were made three or four years ago in circumstances which we can all feel were different from those which prevail—a substantial relaxation would undoubtedly be beneficial in its proper setting, bearing in mind the military and other arguments adduced." (*Fifth Report to Congress on the Mutual Defense Assistance Control Act of 1951,* November, 1954, p. 8.)

receives coal and coke, Netherlands imports timber and cereals, and Italy obtains wheat, coal, and petroleum), most of the materials are absorbed either by the satellite countries themselves or are sent to Russia. The difficult problem facing Western Europe and Japan is a redirection of exports to markets in which dollars can be earned with which to buy imports formerly obtained from the Sino-Soviet bloc.

Since the Western nations are in fact more dependent upon the U.S. economy as a result of the breakdown of East-West trade, it is argued that the U.S. government should take steps to make it easier and more desirable for them to shift their trade to non-Communist nations, including the United States. Japan is a case in point; expansion of her trade is desired by the U.S. government because Japan is an important market for agricultural products. Yet Japan cannot find a ready market for her goods in the United States. She has found it difficult to gain markets also in Southeast Asia because of the inability of particular nations wanting her goods to export things she requires and because of a war-born antipathy to anything Japanese. Nor is it likely that a market exists in China for Japan's manufactures; China has herself become an exporter of textiles and would probably not be willing to increase her trade greatly with Japan. Japan also has found it difficult to enter into European markets, as seen by the reluctance of Britain and others to permit her to join the GATT under which she would obtain the concessions granted others. Japan was permitted to accede only after strong American pressure, showing that the United States was giving some attention to the problem of redirection of trade. But Japan was not given concessions by many other members. It was not easy for Japan to gain concessions from other nations while the United States was unwilling to grant them to her. The U.S. government finally extended concessions on Japanese textiles despite strong domestic opposition; it solved the problem partly by extending concessions to third countries (in northwestern Europe) who gave concessions to Japan; Japan in turn gave tariff concessions to the United States. These activities illustrate how strategic considerations permeate "normal" commercial relations.

In an attempt to compare the noncomparable and cast up a balance of effects on the Free World and the Soviet bloc of the restrictions on East-West trade, a group of experts concluded that

In military and industrial terms, both sides are slightly hurt by the controls and the Soviet Bloc is probably hurt more than the free world. However, the cost of maintaining these controls in the free world must also be measured in other terms as well. The controls clearly strain somewhat the political ties among free-world countries and contribute slightly to balance-of-payments and employment difficulties on our side. Our problem is to ensure that this strain does not, in the end, affect the strength of the free world's military and economic position.[11]

_____
[11] *Staff Papers,* Commission on Foreign Economic Policy, February, 1954, p. 450.

SELECTED READINGS

GENERAL

Jack, D. T. *Studies in Economic Warfare*. London: King, 1940. A careful review of techniques of economic warfare during the Napoleonic Wars, World War I, and the early years of World War II.

Wu, Yuan-Li. *Economic Warfare*. New York: Prentice-Hall, 1952. An extensive review of the economic tactics employed by nations in both offense and defense; it covers topics not included in this chapter, such as economic penetration, preclusive buying, foreign assets control, and the techniques used during World War II.

A. STOCKPILE PROGRAM

International Finance Section. *Survey of United States International Finance*. Princeton, N.J.: Princeton University Press. An annual survey covering the years 1949 through 1953 and including discussion of the U.S. stockpile program and the other topics covered in this chapter.

Office of Defense Mobilization. *Stockpile Report to Congress*. Washington: Government Printing Office. A half-yearly report on the activities and policies affecting the stockpile program.

Paley Report to the President. *Resources for Freedom*. Vol. I, *Foundations for Growth and Security,* vol. II, *The Outlook for Key Commodities,* and vol. V, *Selected Reports to the Commission*. Washington: Government Printing Office, June, 1952. These reports by members of the commission and by experts in the various resource fields have served as the foundation for government policy and recommendations for legislation by Congress. The paper by Horst Mendershausen in vol. V on the economic problems of stockpiling is especially useful.

B. INTERNATIONAL MATERIALS CONFERENCE

Report on Operations of the International Materials Conference, 1951–1952 and 1952–1953. Washington: International Materials Conference, 1953. These are the official records of the activities of the Conference. Analysis of the policies and results is not readily obtainable in the literature.

C. EXPORT CONTROLS

Department of Commerce. *Export Control*. Washington: Government Printing Office. A quarterly report on the administration of export controls.

D. EAST-WEST TRADE

International Cooperation Administration. *Report to Congress on the Mutual Defense Assistance Control Act of 1951*. Washington: Government Printing Office. Half-yearly reports on cooperative controls of the West over the level and direction of East-West trade.

Joint Committee on the Economic Report of the U.S. Congress. "Foreign Economic Policy," *Hearings* before the Subcommittee on Foreign Economic Policy, 84th Cong., 1st Sess., November, 1955, pp. 540–566. A description, analysis, and discussion of cooperative trade controls.

Randall Commission on Foreign Economic Policy. *Staff Papers.* Washington: Government Printing Office, February, 1954. Chapter 9 gives a description of East-West trade and analyzes the effects of the controls.

Index